Publications of the
Carnegie Endowment for International Peace
Division of International Law
Washington

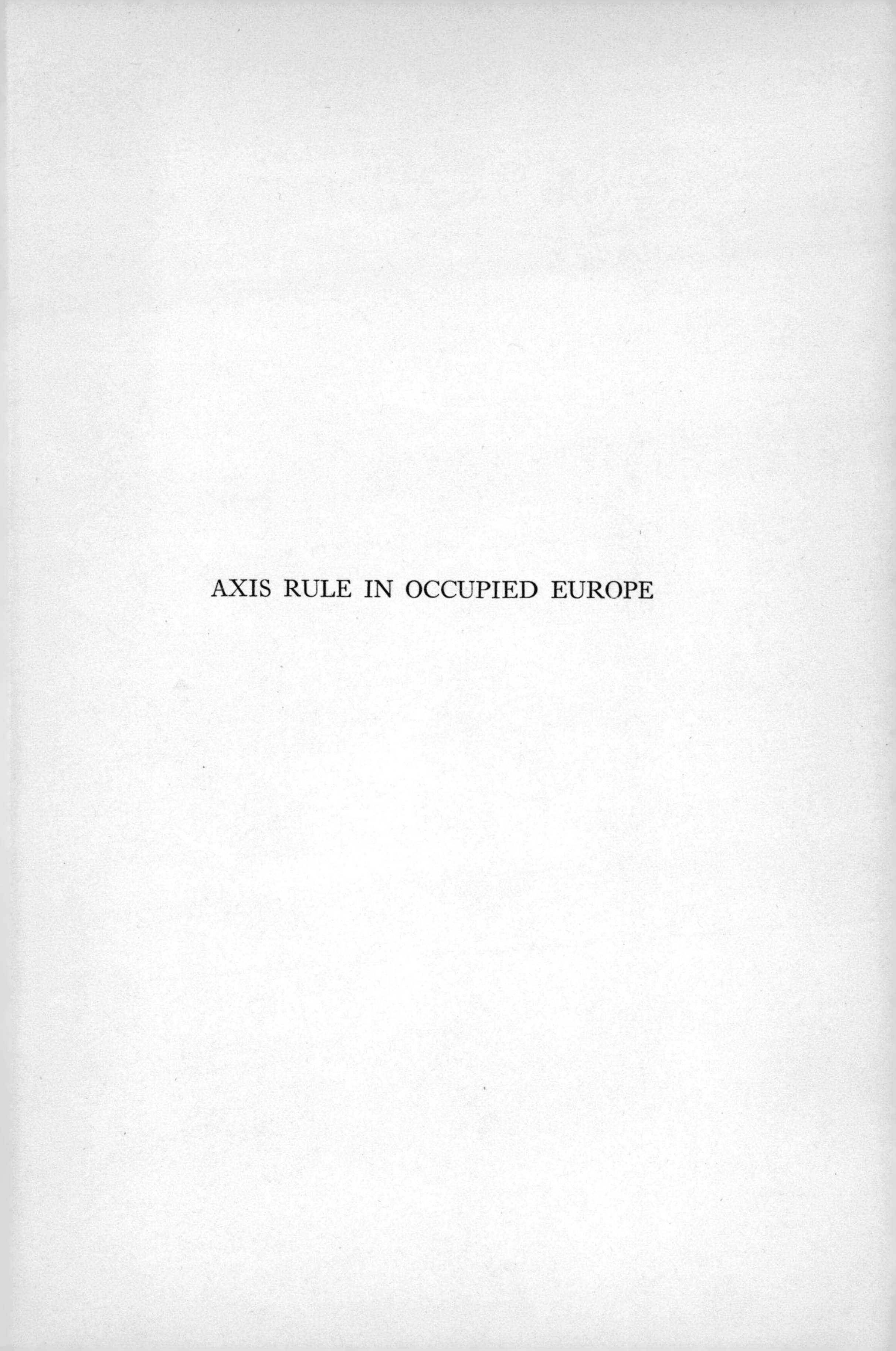

AXIS RULE IN OCCUPIED EUROPE

AXIS RULE IN OCCUPIED EUROPE

Laws of Occupation · Analysis of Government · Proposals for Redress

BY

RAPHAËL LEMKIN

WASHINGTON
CARNEGIE ENDOWMENT FOR INTERNATIONAL PEACE
DIVISION OF INTERNATIONAL LAW
700 JACKSON PLACE, N. W.
1944

PRINTED IN THE UNITED STATES OF AMERICA
AT THE RUMFORD PRESS, CONCORD N. H.

FOREWORD

The major part of this volume comprises the texts of laws and decrees of the Axis Powers, and of their puppet régimes, issued for the government of the areas occupied by their military forces in Europe. Preceding these texts are chapters analyzing the purposes and application of the measures as parts of a general scheme of conquest. Other chapters show the organization of the occupying government set up in each invaded country and the special measures adopted for it.

The law of military occupation does not accord to the armed forces of an invader unlimited power over the inhabitants temporarily under his control. Under this law, as officially interpreted nearly half a century ago by the President of the United States during the war with Spain in 1898, the inhabitants of occupied territory "are entitled to security in their persons and property and in all their private rights and relations," and it is the duty of the commander of the army of occupation "to protect them in their homes, in their employments, and in their personal and religious rights." Further, "the municipal laws of the conquered territory, such as affect private rights of person and property and provide for the punishment of crime, are considered as continuing in force" and are "to be administered by the ordinary tribunals, substantially as they were before the occupation."[1]

The author of the present volume, Dr. Raphaël Lemkin, a noted Polish scholar and attorney, has pointed out the many instances and particulars in which the acts of the Axis Powers fall far below the humane standards previously established, especially those of the laws and customs of war as codified by the Hague Conventions of 1899 and 1907, which sought to diminish the evils of war by placing the inhabitants of occupied territories "under the protection and the rule of the principles of the law of nations, as they result from the usages established among civilized peoples, from the laws of humanity, and the dictates of the public conscience."

The liberators of Nazi-occupied Europe will be faced with stupendous tasks not only of relief and rehabilitation but of restoring family ties and aiding in the repair of the damage done as far as possible. Measures of personal and property reparation must precede the rebuilding of a peaceful world founded upon law and order. The author suggests some modes and agencies of redress. Whether these suggestions or others be adopted, the

[1] General Orders No. 101, July 18, 1898, *Foreign Relations of the United States*, 1898, p. 783. For the similar order to the American Expeditionary Forces when they entered the Rhineland in November, 1918, see General Orders No. 218, November 28, 1918, reproduced by Maj. Gen. Henry T. Allen, U.S.A., *The Rhineland Occupation* (Indianapolis: The Bobbs-Merrill Company, 1927), p. 68. For the expression of appreciation by the German Government of the conduct of the American occupying forces, see the Chancellor's communication to the American commander upon the withdrawal of the troops in January, 1923, *op. cit.*, p. 288.

volume, *Axis Rule in Occupied Europe*, gives in readily accessible form in the English language the basic documents and essential factual information from authentic sources that will be urgently needed when the process starts of untangling the spider web of Axis legislation which has enmeshed the lives and wrecked the fortunes of millions of human beings whose only fault was that they were unable to defend themselves against the modern Juggernaut of total war. It is in this sense that the work is offered as a contribution toward the restoration of peace based upon justice.

GEORGE A. FINCH
Director, Division of International Law

August 18, 1944

PREFACE

The present book grew out of a desire to give an analysis, based upon objective information and evidence, of the rule imposed upon the occupied countries of Europe by the Axis Powers—Germany, Italy, Hungary, Bulgaria, and Rumania. This régime is totalitarian in its method and spirit. Every phase of life, even the most intimate, is covered by a network of laws and regulations which create the instrumentalities of a most complete administrative control and coercion. Therefore these laws of occupation are an extremely valuable source of information regarding such government and its practices. For the outside world they provide undeniable and objective evidence regarding the treatment of the subjugated peoples of Europe by the Axis Powers. The author feels that such evidence is especially necessary for the Anglo-Saxon reader, who, with his innate respect for human rights and human personality, may be inclined to believe that the Axis régime could not possibly be as cruel and ruthless as it has been hitherto described. These laws imposed upon the populations of occupied Europe are very revealing. The occupant has not refrained from formulating as law, dictates which are in fact very grave outrages against humanity and international law, against human rights, morality, and religion. One finds in them, for example, evidence in the form of provisions for confiscations of private property based upon a presumption of future guilt, and for the prohibition of the use of their own language by the population of an occupied country, and such evidence of moral debasement as clauses providing for subsidies to women of subjugated peoples for having illegitimate children by members of the Wehrmacht. The author therefore believed that a collection of occupation laws was essential to supplement an analysis of the Axis régime.

The collection was made by selecting the more representative laws and decrees for each country and for each phase of life. These laws of occupation were promulgated not only by the Axis partners themselves but also by puppet régimes and puppet states, which were established in Norway, Serbia, Croatia, Slovakia, the Protectorate of Bohemia and Moravia, and to a certain extent in Vichy France, as well as by the Secretaries General of the Ministries in Belgium and the Netherlands. The collection forms the third part of the book, while Part I seeks to present a rational synthesis of the techniques of occupation, and Part II analyzes the régime in each occupied country. It has been necessary to adopt such a method of presentation because of the great complexity of the problems involved and also because it was deemed essential to stress local peculiarities in the various countries. Since the German Axis partner is the leader and the main organizer of the system, the first part deals exclusively with German techniques of occupation, whereas the techniques of occupation followed by other Axis partners are dealt with in the framework of the analysis of the régime in the respective countries.

The first part is divided into chapters treating different aspects of government. The chapter on Administration (Chapter I) shows how the Germans have, in violation of international law, incorporated into the Reich large areas of the occupied countries, and how the administration of the incorporated areas differs from the administration of the non-incorporated areas. With their traditional predilection for theories, the Germans have applied the racial theory in effecting these incorporations on the assumption that the incorporated areas are inhabited by Germans, whereas for the non-incorporated areas they have applied the *Lebensraum* theory. The multiple administrative divisions of the occupied countries (Yugoslavia has been divided into ten units, France into five, Poland five, Greece five, and so on) serve the purpose of weakening and crushing the resistance of the captive nations by dividing and enclosing them in separate territorial units, hermetically sealed one from another. The chapter on Police (Chapter II) is an attempt to make clear the especially important rôle and functions of the Gestapo and the S.S. (*Schutzstaffeln*) in Germany and in the occupied countries, and in particular to show that the crimes ascribed to them are not simply a result of the ill-will of individual members but are mainly an essential part of the program of their activities and even of their world outlook. The chapter on Law (Chapter III) presents evidence of the fact that German law imposed upon the occupied countries is bereft of moral content and of respect for human rights. It is not conceived as human justice but it invokes legal techniques simply as a means of administrative coercion. Indeed it appears obvious that the occupant does not respect the limitations imposed by the Hague Convention. He has adopted a unilaterally utilitarian conception of law—law is that which is useful to the German nation; and in this respect the present rulers of Germany are using essentially the same conception of law which was used by Bethmann-Hollweg in 1914, when he declared that necessity knows no law. The organization of the courts (Chapter IV) reminds one vividly of the *Fehme* tribunals of the Middle Ages. The chapter on Property (Chapter V) bears witness to the fact that the occupant has enriched not only the Reich but also individual Germans, and that by permitting only politically desirable persons to possess property, the occupant has converted the institution of property into a powerful political weapon. As for Finance (Chapter VI), it is administered in such a way as to make the occupied countries pay not only the costs of occupation (to an unjustified extent) but also a large part of the costs of the war, thus shifting much of the financial burden from the shoulders of German citizens to those of the people of each occupied country. An elaborate financial system, functioning through instrumentalities of inflated currency and forced borrowing by clearing, helps Germany to seize the economic substance of the occupied lands in such a shrewd way that in some countries there is even created an atmosphere of false business prosperity similar to the hazy state of mind of intoxicated persons. The economy of the subjugated countries has been put in a straitjacket of regulations, controlling its every stage from the production and procurement of raw materials up to their distribution and shipment to Germany and the consumption of finished goods. Mediæval guilds have been revived in the form of compulsory-membership groups controlling trades and occupations. The right to engage in a trade or profession is made subject to the permission of the authorities, the granting of such permission being dependent upon such factors as the citizenship and political reliability of the applicant. As regards Labor generally (Chapter VII), it is clear that conscription and deportations to Germany are squeezing the manpower of occupied Europe, disrupting families, and undermining permanently the health of the workers. The extremely inhuman treatment of Jews (Chapter VIII) serves as a propaganda device for the promotion of the anti-Christian idea of the inequality of human beings and of German racial superiority.

The picture of coordinated German techniques of occupation must lead to the conclusion that the German occupant has embarked upon a gigantic scheme to change, in favor of Germany, the balance of biological forces between it and the captive nations for many years to come. The objective of this scheme is to destroy or to cripple the subjugated peoples in their development so that, even in the case of Germany's military defeat, it will be in a position to deal with other European nations from the vantage point of numerical, physical, and economic superiority. Despite the bombings of Germany, this German superiority will be fully evident after hostilities have ceased and for many years to follow, when, due to the present disastrous state of nourishment and health in the occupied countries, we shall see in such countries a stunted post-war generation, survivors of the ill-fed children of these war years.

The practice of extermination of nations and ethnic groups as carried out by the invaders is called by the author "genocide," a term deriving from the Greek word *genos* (tribe, race) and the Latin *cide* (by way of analogy, see homocide, fratricide) and is treated in a chapter under the same name (Chapter IX). Genocide is effected through a synchronized attack on different aspects of life of the captive peoples: in the political field (by destroying institutions of self-government and imposing a German pattern of administration, and through colonization by Germans); in the social field (by disrupting the social cohesion of the nation involved and killing or removing elements such as the intelligentsia, which provide spiritual leadership—according to Hitler's statement in *Mein Kampf*, "the greatest of spirits can be liquidated if its bearer is beaten to death with a rubber truncheon"); in the cultural field (by prohibiting or destroying cultural institutions and cultural activities; by substituting vocational education for education in the liberal arts, in order to prevent humanistic thinking, which the occupant considers dangerous because it promotes national thinking); in the economic field (by shifting the wealth to Germans and by prohibiting the exercise of trades and occupations by people who do not promote Germanism "without reservations"); in the biological field (by a policy of depopulation and by promoting procreation by Germans in the occupied countries); in the field of physical existence (by introducing a starvation rationing system for non-Germans and by mass killings, mainly of Jews, Poles, Slovenes, and Russians); in the religious field (by interfering with the activities of the Church, which in many countries provides not only spiritual but also national leadership); in the field of morality (by attempts to create an atmosphere of moral debasement through promoting pornographic publications and motion pictures, and the excessive consumption of alcohol).

The other Axis partners—Italy, Hungary, Rumania, and Bulgaria—and the puppet partners Slovakia and Croatia have assimilated their behavior to that of the German master. Montesquieu has said that one must make the choice between liberty and glory. These Axis states (Italy made its choice earlier) have introduced totalitarian systems of government and have engaged in the "glory" of conquest, adopting techniques similar to those of the Germans.

*

The subtitle of this book refers to proposals for redress. The author believes that the grave dislocation of demographic, economic, and cultural values brought about by the occupant should be remedied after the war as much as possible in behalf of the dispossessed and mistreated, and that the considerable numbers of Germans responsible for the great carnage and looting should be punished or reduced to a condition in which they may not again be dangerous to the social order and international peace. As a part of the system needed for that purpose the author proposes an administrative-judicial machinery for the restoration of property to dispossessed persons of occupied countries, namely, one international property restitution agency, national property restitution agencies in each interested country, and property restitution tribunals, both national and international.

Because of the financial situation in the occupied countries and in particular because of the dependence of their actual financial structures upon Berlin and the Reichsmark, it is proposed that the liquidation of the financial consequences of occupation be handled by a specially created international agency for liquidation of occupation finance. Such an agency, with temporary regional interests and scope of activities, should also collaborate, in a broader and more permanent plan for the reconstruction of world finance, with other international financial agencies.

The exploitation by German employers and the German State of millions of workers from the occupied countries calls for reimbursement to the latter of amounts due to them but appropriated by the employer or the German State.

The alarming increase of barbarity with the advent of Hitler led the author to make a proposal to the Fifth International Conference for the Unification of Penal Law (held in Madrid in 1933, in cooperation with the Fifth Committee of the League of Nations) to the effect that an international treaty should be negotiated declaring that attacks upon national, religious, and ethnic groups should be made international crimes, and that perpetrators of such crimes should not only be liable to trial in their own countries but, in the event of escape, could also be tried in the place of refuge, or else extradited to the country where the crime was committed. His proposal not having been adopted at that time, he feels impelled to renew it now after the world has been faced with the tragic experiences of German rule. The negotiation of such a treaty at the present time by all nations of the civilized world, both belligerents and neutrals, would provide not only a more adequate basis of substantive law for the punishment of war criminals but also the necessary procedural machinery for the extradition of such criminals by members of the United Nations and neutrals. Moreover, it would also provide an adequate machinery for the international protection of national and ethnic groups against extermination attempts and oppression in time of peace.

The problem of redress cannot be treated by the author exhaustively at the present moment. The author is aware of the fact that redress should be full and embrace not only additional aspects, both economic and legal, but it should also involve important political and moral considerations based upon the responsibility of the German people treated as an entirety.

Many facts speak for such responsibility. The present destruction of Europe would not be as complete and thorough had the German people not accepted freely its plan, participated voluntarily in its execution, and up to this point profited greatly therefrom. Hitler's *Mein Kampf* has essentially formulated the prolegomenon of destruction and subjugation of other nations. The mere fact that the vast majority of the German people put Hitler into power through free elections is evidence that they freely accepted his program which was secret to nobody.

All important classes and groups of the population have voluntarily assisted Hitler in the scheme of world domination: the military, by training the reserves and working out plans of conquest; the business men, by penetrating and disrupting foreign economies through cartels, patent devices, and clearing agreements; the propagandists, by organizing Germans abroad and preparing fifth columns in countries to be occupied; the scientists, by elaborating doctrines for German hegemony; the educators, by arming spiritually the German youth.

The German techniques of exploitation of the subjugated nations are so numerous, thoughtful, and elaborate, and are so greatly dependent upon personal skill and responsibility, that this complex machinery could not have been successful without devotion to the cause of the persons in control.

The practical ancient Roman had a proverb—*facit cui prodest* (he in whose interest it was, did it). Indeed, all groups of the German nation had their share in the spoils of occupied Europe. The German *Hausfrau* used for her family the food of all occupied countries, Polish geese, Yugoslav pigs, French wine, Danish butter, Greek olives, Norwegian fish; the German industrialist used French and Polish coal, Russian lumber; the German employer in agriculture and industry used for his greater profit imported conscript labor; the German business man bought up foreign interests and properties, taking advantage of the debasement of non-German currencies; the importer benefited through low prices and compulsory credits; and by Hitler's decree of July 28, 1942, the access to women in occupied countries was facilitated for German manhood by fiat of law.

German militarism has been very stubborn. Germany has attacked her neighbors five times since 1864, and in every one of these five wars the methods of occupation and spoliation increased in thoroughness inversely as the ethical level of the aggressors sank lower and lower. Other nations in recent and past times have had cycles of militarism in their history (the Spaniards, Swedes, Danes, French, and many others). However, German militarism is the most virulent because it is based upon a highly developed national and racial emotionalism which by means of modern technology can be released upon the world in a much more efficient and destructive way than any of the pedestrian methods of earlier wars.

The United Nations in the present war are faced with a tremendous task: to destroy this amalgamation of master-race mythology and aggressive technology which makes of the German people a kind of technified myth that stupefies the world. They should plan to replace the aggressive industrial potential by objectively more peaceful patterns of economic life, such as for example, agriculture, and by creating such political and spiritual conditions that the Germans will be impelled to replace their theory of master race by a theory of a master morality, international law, and true peace.

*

The preparation of this volume was begun by the author as early as 1940 in Sweden. It was continued through 1941 and 1942 at Duke University in Durham, North Carolina, and later on was further continued and brought to completion in Washington. A great part of the documents from the author's private collection had previously been submitted to certain Government institutions, from which permission was secured to publish them later on.

In the preparation of this volume the author was fortunate in having the invaluable assistance of individual persons and institutions. First, grateful acknowledgment is due to the Division of International Law of the Carnegie Endowment for International Peace and to Mr. George A. Finch, its Director, for making possible the volume's publication and for providing facilities which made it possible for the author to bring the work to an early completion. Appreciation and gratitude are hereby expressed to the following members of the staff of the Division of International Law: to Mr. Alan T. Hurd for his supervision of the editing of the text; to Miss Ruth E. Stanton for her skilful and thoughtful editing of the manuscript; and to Miss Mary Emily King for her intelligent and considerate aid in the arduous task of transcribing the entire text and in certain phases of reference work. The author is also grateful to the Endowment's Library staff, and in particular to the Librarian, Miss Helen Lawrence Scanlon, and to her assistant, Miss Clara K. Van Nest, for their many courtesies and their assistance in supplying books, documents, and other material.

Especial acknowledgment is due to the Law Library of Congress, and in particular to the late John T. Vance and to Mr. James B. Childs, Dr. Vladimir Gsovski, and Dr. Constantine D. Kojouharoff, for the facilities extended to the author; and to the Library of Duke University for establishing a special documentation center on laws of occupation at the suggestion of the author.

As the present work involved many different countries, problems, and languages, the author was happy to have the assistance and profit by the suggestions of the following persons, to whom he hereby expresses his deep appreciation and gratitude: Professor Bryan Bolich, Professor Robert T. Cole, Mr. Gabriel Dichter, Mrs. Eleanor Lansing Dulles, Dr. Philip K. Edwards, Mrs. Florence J. Harriman, Dr. Ernest Hoor, Dean H. Claude Horack, Mr. Zygmunt Karpinski, Miss Carolyn W. Keen, Mr. Josef Laufer, Mrs. Norman M. Littell, Professor Malcolm McDermott, Dr. Vladimír Palic, and Professor Robert R. Wilson.

The views set forth in this volume are the personal views of the author and are not to be ascribed to any other person or to any institution or agency with which he is or has been connected.

RAPHAËL LEMKIN

Duke University, Durham, North Carolina,
and Washington, D. C., November 15, 1943

CONTENTS

PART II. THE OCCUPIED COUNTRIES

PART III. LAWS OF OCCUPATION

Statutes, Decrees, and Other Documents

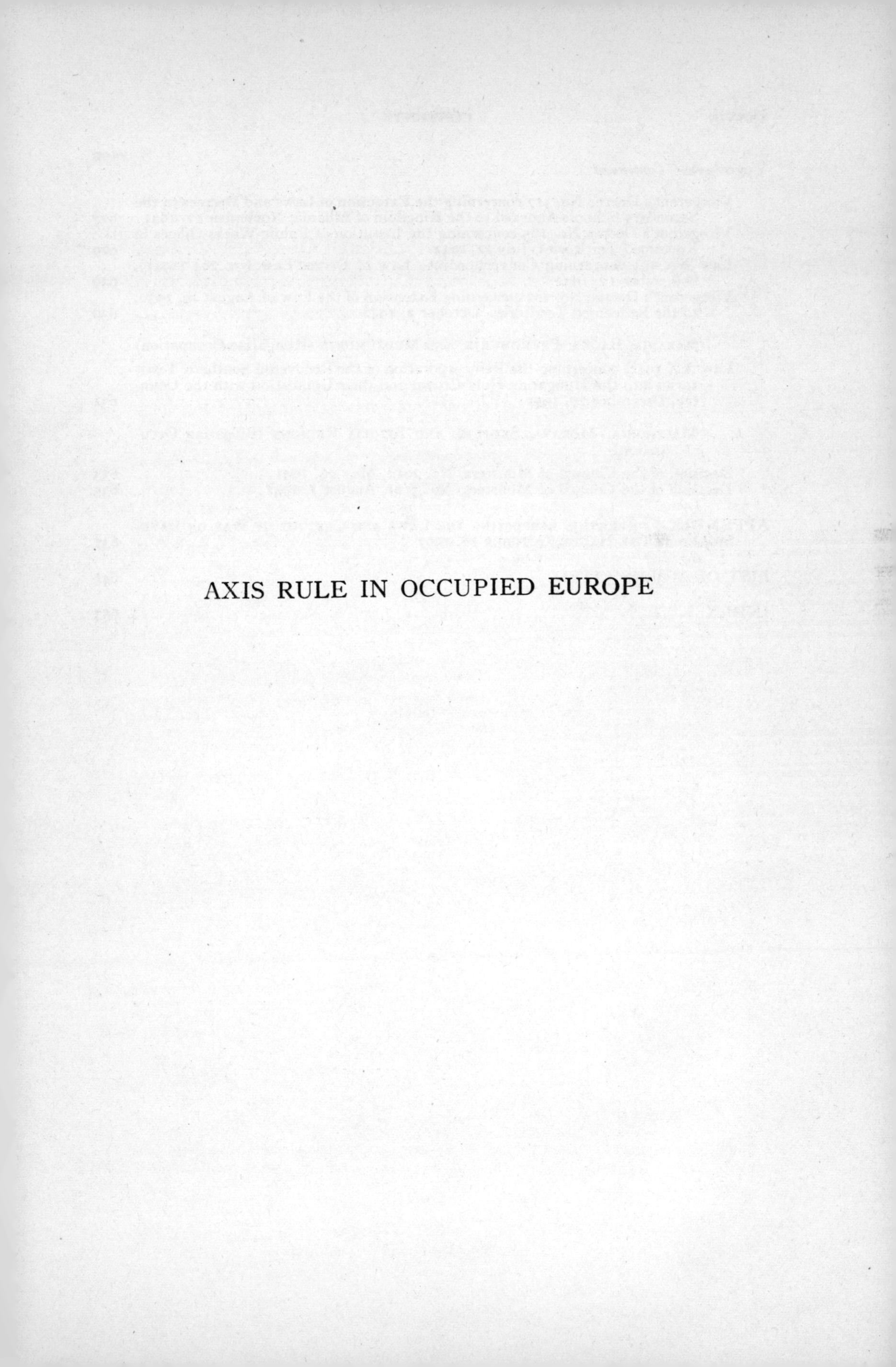

AXIS RULE IN OCCUPIED EUROPE

INTRODUCTION

A PRELIMINARY SURVEY

During the present war and during the period immediately preceding the war the European Axis Powers comprising Germany, Italy, Hungary, Bulgaria, and Rumania have, by means of duress and force, either occupied or occupied and then incorporated into their own territory a large part of Europe. Moreover, by assuming the rôle of supreme arbiters in European territorial problems, Germany and Italy have determined territorial changes in Central and Southeastern Europe. Thus the Axis has occupied or otherwise disposed of the countries indicated in the following paragraphs.[1]

Germany, in the course of the present war, has occupied Poland, Danzig, Denmark, Norway, the Netherlands, Belgium, Luxemburg, France, English Channel Islands, Yugoslavia, Greece, the Baltic States, and parts of Russia, and in several instances has followed the occupation by incorporation of parts of the occupied territory into the Reich. Previously, by bloodless war, Germany had occupied and annexed Austria, and then the Sudeten (belonging theretofore to Czechoslovakia); later it completed the dismemberment of Czechoslovakia by creating the Protectorate of Bohemia and Moravia and the separate state of Slovakia. In March, 1939, Memel Territory was ceded to Germany by Lithuania under pressure and was incorporated into the Reich.

Italy, following the armistice with France of June 24, 1940, occupied the Mentone district; and later on, in the course of the occupation of all France in November, 1942, the Italian occupation was extended to the Rhône valley and to Haute-Savoie. After the downfall of Mussolini in July, 1943, the Italian zone of occupation in France was taken over by Germany. In 1941, after the Greek resistance was crushed by Germany, Italy, which had waged an unsuccessful war against Greece since October, 1940, occupied northwestern parts of Greece, the Ionian Islands, Corfu, and part of Crete. The Albanians were permitted to occupy the provinces of Yanina, Thesprotia, and Prenza. Fluctuations in the military situation led to frequent changes as between the German and Italian occupation forces. Following the downfall of Mussolini, however, all the Italian-held areas were taken over by Germany and Bulgaria. After the invasion of Yugoslavia in 1941, Italy had occupied the province of Ljubljana and Dalmatia, later annexing them, and had occupied Montenegro. Previously, in April, 1939, Italy had occu-

[1] For fuller details, see below, Part I, "Administration," and the respective countries, in Part II.

The rôle of Finland as an occupant being insignificant, the author does not deal with Finnish material in this work.

pied Albania and created a union between the two states. Following the dismemberment of Yugoslavia, Albania, which was under the control of the Italian vicegerent, occupied parts of Yugoslavia, namely, Kossovo, Dibrano, and Struga.

Hungary occupied the following Czechoslovak territories: the southern part of these territories, called by the Hungarians the Highland Regions, was occupied in November, 1938, and March, 1939; and Subcarpathia was occupied in March, 1939. After the dismemberment of Yugoslavia, Hungary occupied the Yugoslav territories of Prekomurje, Medžumurje, and the provinces of Baranja and Bačka in the Voivodina region. In addition, in accordance with the German-Italian arbitration award of August 30, 1940, the northern part of Transylvania, belonging theretofore to Rumania, was occupied by Hungary. All of these territories were subsequently incorporated into Hungary.

Bulgaria has occupied, in the course of the war against Greece, Eastern Macedonia, the Aegean region of Thrace, and the islands of Thasos and Samothrace. Previously, following the treaty with Rumania of September 7, 1940, Bulgaria had occupied Southern Dobruja, which was taken from Bulgaria and given to Rumania by the Treaty of Neuilly in 1919. After the dismemberment of Yugoslavia, Bulgaria occupied Western Macedonia, the Skoplje and Bitolia regions, and part of the Yugoslav province of Morava.

Rumania has occupied, during the war against Russia, Bukovina and Bessarabia, which it had ceded to Russia at the latter's request in June, 1940. In addition, Rumania has occupied the territory between the eastern border of Bessarabia and the lower Bug, with the main city of Odessa, which area is now called Transnistria.

On the territories of the dismembered Czechoslovakia and Yugoslavia there were established two new states—Slovakia, under the protection of Germany, and Croatia, initially under the protection of Italy but actually always under predominant control by Germany. For strategic reasons Germany holds under military occupation certain areas within the boundaries of these puppet states, for example, a western portion of Slovakia and the Zemun area in Croatia.

PART I

GERMAN TECHNIQUES OF OCCUPATION

PART I

GERMAN TECHNIQUES OF OCCUPATION

CHAPTER I

ADMINISTRATION

I. The Administrative Territorial Units

As stated above, Germany has occupied the following countries during the present war: Poland, Danzig, Denmark, Norway, the Netherlands, Belgium, Luxemburg, France, English Channel Islands, Yugoslavia, Greece, the Baltic States, and parts of Russia. Previously, by bloodless war, Germany occupied Austria, on March 9, 1938, the Sudeten, on October 1, 1938, and the remainder of Czechoslovakia, on March 15, 1939. Memel Territory was ceded by Lithuania to Germany by treaty of March 22, 1939.

1. *Incorporated Areas.* Some of these territories occupied before the war and in the course of military operations were expressly incorporated into Germany, those so incorporated being Austria, the Sudeten, Danzig, the Polish provinces—Posen, Upper Silesia, Teshen, Pomerania, Łódź (now Litzmannstadt), Ciechanów, Suwałki, Białystok; the Belgian districts—Eupen, Malmédy, and Moresnet; and the northern Yugoslav provinces of Carniola, Carinthia, and Lower Styria. Memel, also, was incorporated into the Reich. Other territories—Alsace-Lorraine, Luxemburg—were attached to the Reich by including them within the German customs frontier, by making them separate parts of the German districts (*Gaue*), and by introducing into these areas political institutions of the Greater Reich.

2. *Non-incorporated Areas.* The non-incorporated territories include the following territorial units: the central and southern part of Poland, which is administered as the Government General, with headquarters in Cracow; and the territories occupied in the present Russo-German war, which are under the administration of Rosenberg, Reich Minister for the Territories Occupied in the East. The Reich Ministry for these latter areas has created the following subdivisions: (*a*) the Reich Commissariat for Ostland, and (*b*) the Reich Commissariat for the Ukraine. The Reich Commissariat for Ostland consists of four general commissariats, namely, a general commissariat for Estonia (headquarters in Tallinn), for Latvia (headquarters in Riga), for Lithuania (headquarters in Kaunas), and for White Russia (headquarters in Minsk). The General Commissariat for White Russia comprises the eastern Polish territories occupied by Russia in September, 1939, and Russian territories to the northeast of the Polish frontier. The Reich Commissariat for the Ukraine consists of Ukraine proper, the whole of the Polish province of Wolhynia, and the southern part of the Polish province of Polesie.

Besides the above-mentioned territorial divisions, four of the countries occupied in the west—Norway, Denmark, the Netherlands, Belgium (excluding Eupen, Malmédy, and Moresnet)—are administered within their original boundaries.

The non-incorporated German-held part of France was divided into four zones: (1) Northern France and Pas de Calais, under the German commander in Brussels, which we shall call the northern zone; (2) the central western zone delimited in the south and southwest by the German-French armistice agreement; (3) the so-called Vichy zone; (4) the prohibited zone along the coastal line, which has a special régime of military control because of the fortifications built there.

Czechoslovakia, in addition to the loss of the Sudetenland, has undergone the following partition: Bohemia and Moravia were occupied by the German forces and form the so-called Protectorate of Bohemia and Moravia; and the third part of Czechoslovakia was erected as a separate state under the name of Slovakia and was put under the protection of Germany.

In Yugoslavia, Germany established the puppet state of Serbia, as well as Croatia (the latter in collaboration with Italy). The Yugoslav part of Banat, in which a considerable German minority is living, was given a special status and was attached to the puppet state of Serbia. After the downfall of Mussolini, and especially after the signing of the armistice agreement between Italy and the Allies, Germany took over the control of the greater part of Yugoslavia and Albania.

In Greece, Germany occupied Central Macedonia, including Salonika, parts of the Aegean region, and the islands of Lemnos, Mytilene, and Chios. After the armistice agreement between Italy and the Allies, the Germans extended their zone of occupation to the area previously occupied by Italy.

The system of the multiple administrative divisions of the occupied territories is dictated not merely by administrative expediency and the desire for territorial aggrandizement (incorporations); it mainly has for its purpose the weakening of the resistance of the controlled nations by dividing their populations into small groups which are prevented from communication by artificial boundaries.

II. Policies

In regard to local population three different policies have been adopted:

1. *Absorption.* The policy of absorption adopted with respect to the incorporated areas, such as western Poland, Eupen, Malmédy and Moresnet, Luxemburg, and the Yugoslav provinces of Carinthia, Carniola, and Lower Styria, aims at the complete assimilation of a given area with the political, cultural, social, and economic institutions of the Greater Reich. This is effected through the destruction of the national pattern of the area and the

imposition of a German pattern instead. Indoctrination of National Socialism is also employed to a great extent, especially in areas where the German cultural pattern preexisted, as in Austria and the Sudeten.[1]

2. *Forced "Cooperation."* Norway, France, Belgium, the Netherlands,[2] Greece, Czechoslovakia, and to a certain extent also the three Baltic States—Estonia, Latvia, and Lithuania—are being forced into cooperation, which comprises full economic cooperation and in part, as to certain groups, political cooperation as well. Denmark represents a type of forced "cooperation," mainly in the economic field.

3. *Despoliation.* The Government General of Poland, the General Commissariat for White Russia (as part of Ostland), and the administration of the Ukraine and other Russian territories represent a type of despoliation policy. The occupant considers these territories as being the areas of his interests (*Interessengebiete*). Despite some endeavors the occupant has not succeeded in finding in these areas people who would be willing to cooperate in organizing central governments. The main task of the occupying authorities is to draw from such territories raw materials, food, and labor.[3]

III. Types of Administration

The following types of administration are to be distinguished: first, German administration as carried on by German authorities, and, secondly, local administration as exercised by authorities created by the local population under German control.

A. GERMAN ADMINISTRATION

The following three types of German administration are to be considered:

1. *District Administration by "Gauleiters."* This type of administration was introduced into the incorporated areas, which were to be absorbed as a part of the Greater Reich. According to the German pattern of administration, the incorporated areas are divided into administrative districts (*Gaue*), which form at the same time administrative units of the National Socialist Party. The head of the National Socialist Party in the given district (*Gauleiter*) is at the same time governor (*Reichsstatthalter*) of the district. The districts are divided into counties and communities. For special purposes of imposing a German pattern upon these areas, an agent of the Reich

[1] See chapter on "Genocide," below, pp. 83–84.

[2] In the Netherlands the occupant in his first proclamation to the population referred to the community of blood between Germans and Dutchmen. See proclamation of the Reich Commissioner for the Netherlands Territories to the Netherlands population, dated May 25, 1940, below, p. 447.

[3] In the proclamation of the Governor General to the Polish population, of October 26, 1939, it is stated, among other things: "Freed from the compulsion of the adventurous policy of your intellectual governing class, you will, under the strong protection of the Greater German Reich, do your best in the performance of a universal obligation to work." See below, p. 524.

Commissioner for the Strengthening of Germanism is attached to the office of the *Gauleiter*. This system of administration is being carried out in the incorporated Polish territories, in the Sudeten, in Austria, in Luxemburg and Alsace-Lorraine,[4] in Eupen, Malmédy and Moresnet, and in the northern Yugoslav district (Carinthia, Carniola, and Lower Styria).

2. *Administration by Reich Commissioners and Governors*. The non-incorporated areas, which at the time of occupation were not of any important strategic significance, as, for example, Norway, the Netherlands, and central Poland, were handed over for administration to civilian Reich Commissioners.[5] In central Poland (Government General) the civilian head of administration is called the Governor General.

In the same areas there are also military commanders who deal with questions of military security and military operations. A division of jurisdiction is thus created between the Reich Commissioners and military commanders, the Reich Commissioners handling matters which relate to the civil domain and the military commanders those which relate to the military domain.

3. *Administration by Military Commanders*. Countries which at the time of occupation were of pronounced strategic importance, such as Belgium, France (within the borders delimited by the armistice agreement), Yugoslavia, and Greece, were put under the administration of military commanders. The military commanders exercise their authority through field and local military commanders throughout the given country.

The military commanders and the Reich Commissioners in the occupied countries are directly responsible to the Führer and Reich Chancellor himself, which fact shows the importance that Hitler attaches to the problem of administering these countries, and the extent of his responsibility therefor.[6]

B. LOCAL ADMINISTRATION

The occupant has called upon the local population to participate in the administration of the given country for the implementation of the "New Order." The degree of response of the local population to the demands of the occupant, or the lack of such response, is to some degree reflected in the type of central local government which has been created in every one of the subjugated countries.[7]

[4] In Luxemburg, Alsace, and Lorraine there is a special civil administration (*Zivilverwaltung*) headed by a *Gauleiter* and forming a part of the regular *Gau*.

[5] See the decrees of the Führer of April 24, 1940, concerning the exercise of governmental authority in Norway, below, p. 498; May 18, 1940, concerning the exercise of governmental authority in the Netherlands, below, p. 446; and October 12, 1939, concerning the administration of the occupied Polish territories, below, p. 522.

[6] *Ibid.*

[7] However, throughout all the subjugated countries, irrespective of the "degree of collaboration," the elective element in the organization of the local authorities has been abolished. This is especially true as to the administration of municipal and rural communities. Municipalities and rural communities were previously administered by people placed in office through a process of election by the citizens. Thus, the members of municipal and rural communities used to elect members of the city or rural council, and

In countries where there was some degree of response, the following types of local central government are to be distinguished:

1. *Puppet Governments and Puppet States*. In countries where active groups of pro-Nazis, even in minor numbers, were to be found, puppet governments have been created. The puppet government is organized as a cabinet with a prime minister or a president as the head. Its activities are controlled by the occupant. The puppet governments have essentially retained the local authorities (with the exception of agencies whose members are elected by the population) and are using them for the administration of the country. Puppet governments now function in Norway, in the part of Yugoslavia organized by the occupant as Serbia, in Greece, in France (Pétain and Laval) and, with certain special restrictions, in the Protectorate of Bohemia and Moravia.

Puppet states are to be distinguished from puppet governments. A puppet state is an entirely new organism created by the occupant, whereas in a puppet government only the governmental functions are a creation of the occupant, the original state having been in existence before the occupation. Slovakia and Croatia are examples of puppet states. The creation of puppet states or of puppet governments does not give them any special status under international law in the occupied territory. These organizations derive their existence from the will of the occupant and thus ought to be regarded as organs of the occupant. Therefore the puppet governments and puppet states have no greater rights in the occupied territory than the occupant himself. Their actions should be considered as actions of the occupant and hence subject to the limitations of the Hague Regulations. This view, it may be added, is in agreement with the attitude of the Norwegian Supreme Court in Oslo [8] as to the Quisling government, and also of the Yugoslav Government-in-Exile, which has not recognized any transfers of property undertaken in occupied Yugoslavia by the occupant or by the puppet authorities established by the occupant.

2. *Headless or Subcabinet Governments*. In Belgium and the Netherlands a central government, which we shall call "headless government," or "subcabinet government," has been introduced. It consists of the secretaries general of the particular departments of government. Before the occupa-

---

the members of the council in turn elected the mayors and the most important assistants of the mayor. This form of elective self-government grew up in some countries by way of an evolution of democratic institutions (Poland, Norway, France), and in some countries elective local self-government came about as a result of a hard political fight against absolutist régimes. This latter statement is true, generally speaking, of Central Europe after the revolutions of 1848. Municipal and rural self-government were institutions deeply entrenched in the political life of the countries occupied. The occupant, however, abolished the principle of elective self-government and introduced in most of the subjugated countries the German Municipal Code of 1935, which is based upon the principle of leadership (*Führerprinzip*). According to this code, the members of municipal councils, as well as the mayors and their assistants, are appointed by German authorities.

[8] See chapter on "Norway," below, Part II.

tion of Belgium and the Netherlands, the secretary general was the highest public civil servant in a given ministry with the exception of the minister himself. He was second only to the minister. Whereas the minister's tenure of office was subject to political changes, the secretary general, on the other hand, was a permanent part of the civil service and not subject to change to the same extent. Because of their professional skill and sometimes long experience, the secretaries general represent a valuable element in government. The occupant retained them in office and put them in charge of the administration of their ministries. However, the secretaries general do not serve as a cabinet but for the most part act separately, unless they are called upon by the occupant for common action. The occupant controls the activities of the secretaries general by special commissioners.[9, 10] A special kind of headless government has also been introduced in the three Baltic States. Here the heads of the departments are called councillors (in Lithuania) and directors (in Estonia and Latvia), instead of secretaries general. However, the authority and scope of activities of the councillors and directors are less than those of the secretaries general.

3. *Utilization of Services of Minor Authorities.* In countries where no response or collaboration was received the services of only minor authorities and lower officials have been utilized by the occupant. Such a situation has occurred in the Government General of Poland, in the Polish territories included in the General Commissariat for White Russia, and in the Russian territories.

4. *Utilization of Services of All Existing Governmental Authorities.* This situation occurred in Denmark, where the King and practically all authorities continued to function. The German Army in Denmark took charge of the military situation, while control over the Danish Government was exercised by the German Minister in Denmark, whose authority was backed by the Gestapo and the presence of the German Army and military commander. This situation changed after the revolt of August, 1943 (see Denmark).

IV. Usurpation of Sovereignty

Belligerent occupation is essentially temporary. It does not transfer sovereignty over the occupied territory. The occupant holds the territory in trust for the future peace conference to decide upon its ultimate disposi-

[9] The headless governments continue the publication of the official gazettes. The orders and decrees of the secretaries general are promulgated in Belgium in the *Moniteur Belge* and in the Netherlands in the *Staatsblad.*

[10] Because of the excessive zeal "displayed by some of the secretaries general in Belgium in exploiting the country" to the benefit of the occupant, the head of the Belgian Government-in-Exile, in talks over the radio from London, has warned the secretaries general about some of their practices considered by him to be adverse to the national interest. See the magazine *Belgium* (New York), I, No. 11 (1941), p. 36; II, No. 17 (1941), p. 37; also R. Ardenne, *German Exploitation of Belgium* (Washington: The Brookings Institution, 1942), p. 6.

tion.[11] Therefore, the occupant has no right to perform such acts as would indicate that he has usurped sovereignty. However, during the present occupation the German occupant has usurped sovereignty over the occupied areas mainly by the following acts:

(1) By incorporations *flagrante bello* of parts of Poland, Belgium, France, and Yugoslavia, and all of Luxemburg and Danzig.

(2) By using in decrees the word "former" in regard to states whose territory he has occupied. This is especially true as to Poland, with respect to which the occupant uses regularly the expression "property of the citizens of the former Polish State," or "property of the former Polish State," and so on.

(3) By introducing a German pattern of administration in the incorporated areas.

(4) By changing the customs frontiers.

(5) By changing basic laws of the occupied countries and introducing German law and German courts, and by compelling the courts to render justice in the name of the German nation—not in the name of law, as should be the procedure in the occupied area.

Further examples of usurpation of sovereignty are to be seen in the following acts of the occupant:

(*a*) The local German population of the incorporated areas has been granted representation in the Reichstag of Greater Germany. This is granted on the basis of one representative to every 60,000 Germans over twenty years of age living in these areas. The representative must be over twenty-five years of age and is appointed a member of the Reichstag. The act providing for the nomination of representatives in the Reichstag of Greater Germany was promulgated for Eupen, Malmédy, and Moresnet by the decree of February 4, 1941.[12]

(*b*) The Germans living in these incorporated areas became German citizens or German nationals. According to the German Nationality Code, there are two types of nationality. The superior type, called *Bürger*, embraces Germans of German origin who are in every respect loyal to the Nazi régime. Citizenship in this conception confers rights of active participation in the political life of the country, as, for example, representation in the Reichstag, military service, the right to be an official, and so on. The second type of nationality, *Staatsangehörige*, which is merely a conception of legal relationship with the Reich, consists mainly of the right to possess a German passport and all the privileges deriving therefrom. Persons of non-German blood cannot be *Bürger*, but they can be *Staatsangehörige*. In the incorpo-

[11] As to American authorities, see the very clear statement that conquest passes no national title. That is accomplished only by treaty. *De Lima* v. *Bidwell*, 182 U. S. 1, 194; 21 Sup. Ct. 743; 45 L. Ed. 1041 (1902).

See also U. S. War Department, *Basic Field Manual: Rules of Land Warfare*, prepared under the direction of the Judge Advocate General (Washington, 1940), Chap. 10, "Military Occupation and Government of Enemy Territory."

[12] See below, p. 315.

rated areas the Germans have introduced the same division of nationality as in Germany, but they have applied it in a different way. Poles, Jews, Belgians, and Frenchmen cannot become either citizens or nationals. In the incorporated areas nationality of the superior type—that is, citizenship—was granted to persons of German origin, and nationality of the inferior type could be granted to people of German or related blood,[13] such as the Flemings (but not the Walloons). The same principle was adopted in Alsace-Lorraine and Czechoslovakia.[14]

(*c*) Military conscription was introduced in the Polish territories by the decree of the Supreme Commander of the German Armed Forces of April 30, 1940.[15] It was also introduced into Alsace-Lorraine.[16]

The above-mentioned acts regarding citizenship and representation in the Reichstag, as well as military conscription, implied necessarily taking an oath of allegiance to the occupying power, which is contrary to Article 45 of the Annex to Hague Convention IV,[17] and to the prevailing doctrine of international law. Moreover, military conscription in occupied territory is expressly prohibited by Article 52 of the Hague Regulations, which states that the inhabitants of the occupied territory cannot be compelled to take part in operations of war against their country.

[13] As to Eupen, Malmédy, and Moresnet, see decree of May 23, 1940 (below, p. 313), as well as the additional decree on nationality of September 23, 1941 (below, p. 316), which has partially modified the principle of "related blood."

[14] As to Czechoslovakia, see particularly dual citizenship, below, p. 346.

[15] See below, p. 508.

[16] See announcement by the Chief of Police in Strassburg that all males born in the years 1920–1924 must register for military service (*Strassburger Neueste Nachrichten* of September 26, 1942).

[17] For the sake of brevity the annex to this convention, "Regulations respecting the Laws and Customs of War on Land," is hereinafter cited as the Hague Regulations.

CHAPTER II

POLICE

I. German Police in General

1. *History.* German police play a very great part in organizing and maintaining political life in Germany itself and in the occupied countries in particular. They provide the main striking power for National Socialism. The political efficiency of the German police and their faithfulness to Nazism may be explained by their history. It began in the form of the S.S. (*Schutzstaffeln*), or Elite Guard of the National Socialist Party before Hitler took over power. These guards originally gave assistance at party meetings in protecting physically the members of the party against political opponents. On January 6, 1929, Hitler, as Führer of the National Socialist Party, appointed Himmler as Reich Leader of the S.S. After the advent of Hitler to power, the fusion of the S.S. with the police was started. Between March 9, 1933, and April, 1934, the Reich Leader of the S.S. was successively appointed Chief of the State Police in each of the *Länder* [1] outside Prussia (*Reichsführer der S.S. und Chef der deutschen Polizei*). On February 10, 1936,[2] the State Secret Police (Gestapo) was created for Prussia by Göring as Minister-President for Prussia, and Reich Leader of the S.S. Himmler became the Deputy Chief of the Gestapo. The above-mentioned law of February 10, 1936, defines its tasks as follows: "The State Secret Police (*Geheime Staatspolizei*) has the task of investigating and fighting against all movements dangerous to the State in all spheres of State existence, of collecting and exploiting the results of investigations, of reporting to the Government and of keeping other authorities informed on all current issues of importance to them, and providing them with the requisite conclusions." [3] Since then Reich Leader of the S.S. Himmler has acted in a dual capacity as Deputy Chief of the Prussian Gestapo and as commander of the political police of the *Länder* outside Prussia.[4] Later on Himmler by his own orders extended the Gestapo organization (which had existed previously only in Prussia) also to the other *Länder*.[5] Thus Göring started the Gestapo in

[1] By *Länder* is meant the various former states, such as Bavaria, Saxony, Prussia, etc., which were united to form Germany in 1871.

[2] *Reichsgesetzblatt*, 1936, No. 2034.

[3] *Deutsche Allgemeine Zeitung*, June 13, 1942, quoted from "The Nazi Police System in Germany and in Poland," *Polish Fortnightly Review*, No. 69 (London, June 1, 1943), p. 4.

[4] The political police in the *Länder* at that time are to be distinguished from the Gestapo, which existed then only in Prussia.

[5] See reference to these orders of the Reich Leader of the S.S. and Chief of the German Police of April 10 and July 15, 1937, concerning Bavaria and Saxony, and orders of the same of February 15 and March 15, 1938, concerning Anhalt, Baden, Brunswick, Bremen, Hamburg, Hesse, Mecklenburg, the Saar, Oldenburg, Thuringia, and Württemberg. Dr. Karl Schäfer, *Polizeiverwaltungsgesetz* (Berlin, 1939), p. 185.

Prussia and Himmler expanded it throughout all the German Reich and even outside Germany, including the occupied countries.

2. *The S.S. and the Gestapo.* In his capacity as Reich Leader of the S.S., Himmler has created a very intimate connection between the S.S. and the Gestapo. As mentioned above, before the advent of Hitler to power the S.S. consisted of small groups of National Socialist party guards, whose task was to protect the men of the party against physical attacks by political opponents. On the assumption of power by Hitler, the S.S. became the most powerful unit in Germany, in which all the party aristocracy was organized. Himmler endeavored to supplant the idea of the former Prussian Junker caste by the conception of the S.S. organization. Accordingly, special training was established in the S.S. Junker School. The selection of candidates is restricted. The Aryan origin of the candidates is investigated as far back as 1800, and to be accepted for training they must have reached a certain stage in the Hitler-Youth organization and must have the reputation of devout National Socialists.[6]

The S.S. men constitute the reservoir from which the ranks of the German police, especially of the Gestapo, are filled. It may be stated generally that although not every member of the S.S. is a member of the police, every German policeman—and in particular every Gestapo agent—belongs to the S.S.[7]

3. *Differentiation of German Police.* The police are divided into two main groups: (1) *Ordnungspolizei*—Public Order Police; and (2) *Sicherheitspolizei*—Security Police. The *Ordnungspolizei* embrace in the main the uniformed regular police, that is, the *Schutzpolizei* (to be distinguished from the *Schutzstaffeln*), the *Gendarmerie*, and the administrative police, while the *Sicherheitspolizei* comprise the criminal police and the Gestapo. In addition there is a Security Service of the Reich Leader of the S.S., called *Sicherheitsdienst des Reichsführers S.S.*, which acts as an espionage organization for the party and state. In this field it also assists the Security Police (*Sicherheitspolizei*). The Security Service collaborates with all the authorities, who are bound to provide information to it.[8] Its membership is secret and the members do not wear uniforms.

4. *Police and the Law.* Two main problems arise in establishing the relations between the police and the law: (1) Are the police bound to observe the law in their activities; and (2) are acts of the police controlled by administrative courts or by common courts? Both questions are to be answered in the negative. It may be said that little as law is observed by the German state, it is still less observed by the police. The main idea is, on the one hand, to give the police a great striking power, and, on the other hand, not to bind

[6] *Polish Fortnightly Review*, No. 69, pp. 3–4.
[7] See "Government and Politics in Germany," by Karl Loewenstein, in *Governments of Continental Europe*, edited by James T. Shotwell (New York, 1940), p. 489.
[8] See order by the Reich Ministry of the Interior of November 11, 1938, in Karl Schäfer, *op. cit.*, p. 33.

them by procedure in "protecting the interest of the nation." In modern states law plays a rather considerable rôle in police relations because of the inherent necessity of protecting the rights of individuals. But the German police are trained in the idea embodied in the slogan, "You are nothing; the nation is everything." (*Du bist nichts; das Volk ist alles.*)[9] Consequently, provisions of law cannot play any important rôle in their activities. Such views were expressed by leading Gestapo men such as Heydrich, the Gestapo Chief and Deputy Reich Protector of Bohemia and Moravia, killed in 1942.[10]

The police are guided in their activities by principles based not so much on the law[11] as on the doctrines of the Nazi party and the Führer. Regulations of the government and decisions of courts are to be followed only as a secondary source for their guidance. According to the commentators on the German Police Code (*Polizei Verwaltungsgesetz*), Scheer and Bartsch, the hierarchy of sources to be followed by the police as a guide for their activities is:

a) The program of the National Socialist Party and the book of the Führer, *Mein Kampf;*
b) Opinions expressed by the Führer in his speeches and statements;
c) Ordinances of the government;
d) Authors and decisions of courts in the period after Hitler assumed control in Germany.[12]

There follows as a natural consequence of such an attitude the fact that from the decisions of the Gestapo there is no review by administrative courts.[13]

In their further comments on the Police Code, Scheer and Bartsch state significantly: "Even if the Gestapo may have committed an abuse of power, such an act cannot be controlled by administrative courts, nor by other courts."[14]

The specifically privileged position of the Gestapo in relation to law is stressed by the fact that it has judicial autonomy. The law of November 1, 1939,[15] provides special courts (*Gericht der geheimen Staatspolizei*) for the Gestapo. Such courts try Gestapo members and also persons who are guilty of attacks against members of the Gestapo.

[9] Bernhard Scheer and Georg Bartsch, *Das Polizeiverwaltungsgesetz* (Berlin, 1939), p. 11.

[10] In an article by him which appeared in *Deutsches Recht* (1936), he states: "I have from the beginning taken the attitude that it is a matter of complete indifference to me whether any paragraph [of law] is in opposition to our work. For the fulfillment of my task I do fundamentally that for which I can answer to my conscience in my work for the Führer and nation. I am completely indifferent whether others gabble to-day about breaking the law." *Polish Fortnightly Review*, No. 69, p. 2.

[11] "It is of greater importance that the police shall serve, and be close to the life of, the nation, than to follow the letter of the law." Scheer and Bartsch, *op. cit.*, p. 10.

[12] *Ibid.*, p. 12.

[13] See Section 7 of the law concerning the State Secret Police of February 10, 1936 (*Preussische Gesetzsammlung*, 21): "Orders and activities of the State Secret Police are not subject to review by the administrative courts."

It must be noted that administrative courts still function in Germany in certain respects. See R. E. Uhlman and H. G. Rupp, "The German System of Administrative Courts," *Illinois Law Review*, Vol. 31 (1937), pp. 847, 1028.

[14] *Op. cit.*, pp. 30–31.

[15] *Reichsgesetzblatt*, 1939, I, p. 2293.

5. *Recruitment.* Members of the police are appointed first on a temporary basis, with the right of cancellation of the appointment, and later on a permanent basis. In order to be appointed on a permanent basis, quite long probationary periods are required: for officers, five years; for minor members of the Gestapo or criminal police, twelve years.[16] These unusually long probationary periods have for their purpose the inspiring of devotion in the appointed members to the person of the Führer and zeal for his program.

The appointment of any official in Germany is based upon the Reich's confidence in him and the assurance that the official will always endeavor to justify this confidence and will be conscious of his high mission. The Führer and the Reich demand from him real love for the country and readiness to sacrifice everything for it.[17] The relationship of the police to the Führer is not primarily of a legal and administrative character, but is rather of an emotional nature, finding expression in the words, "faithfulness to the Führer till death."

6. *Political Indoctrination.* Members of the police, particularly of the Gestapo, are, practically speaking, the most active fighters for National Socialism. Therefore, they are trained carefully in its doctrines.[18] Such matters as racial theories, geopolitics, history of German ideas of hegemony, eugenics, the Jewish problem, Catholicism as a political problem, Communism, relations with the Anglo-Saxon world, colonial questions, economic and political penetration—to cite only some of them—are basic subjects in the program for indoctrinating the police, especially the Gestapo. This indoctrination is achieved through training, particularly in the S.S. Junker School, as mentioned above, which opens the way to a career in the Gestapo. Also postgraduate work, so to speak, is continuously carried on by means of special courses and publications for the members issued by the Reich Leader of the S.S. and Chief of the German Police,[19] as well as through the publications of the regional chiefs of the police predestined for membership.[20]

II. The Responsibilities of the Police and the S.S. in the Occupied Countries

In the occupied countries the rôle of the police and S.S. is of primary importance. In particular the experience of the Gestapo in foreign countries

[16] See paragraphs 3 and 8 of "Das Deutsche Polizeibeamtengesetz," June 24, 1937, *Reichsgesetzblatt*, I, p. 653, No. 72.

[17] "Deutsches Beamtengesetz," January 26, 1937, *Reichsgesetzblatt*, I, p. 39.

[18] See Heydrich in the *Zeitschrift* of the Akademie für Deutsches Recht (1937, No. 3): "The policeman in the National-Socialist State must be a fighter for the National-Socialist ideas. Purely technical ability is not sufficient. For fighting the enemies of the State there must also be an unconditional comprehension of the National-Socialist movement of ideas and the comprehensive recognition of the fundamental character of his opponent."

[19] *Schriftenreihe des Reichsführers der S.S. und Chefs der deutschen Polizei* and *Mitteilungen des Reichsführers der S.S. und des Chefs der deutschen Polizei.*

[20] *Mitteilungsblatt für die weltanschauliche Schulung.*

before the war enabled that organization to make a special contribution to the German administration in every country later occupied. These pre-war activities of the Gestapo in foreign countries were widespread, reaching into such fields as politics, economics, culture, press, and racial relations. On one hand, the Gestapo gathered information, and on the other hand, it was active in playing different elements in the political life of the foreign countries one against another and in using the weak spots in the social and economic structure of these countries for the benefit of Germany. By spreading Nazi ideology in foreign countries (ideological penetration), the Gestapo paved the way for the creation of fifth columns, which assisted in the military conquest of the respective countries. This was true especially as to Norway. Thus, members of the Gestapo, following in the wake of the military occupation, returned to places which they knew because of their pre-war activities.

1. *Organization.* In every central administration of the occupied countries the police and S.S. have a predominant position in the headquarters of the administration chief. The Chief of Police, who is a ranking S.S. officer, is technically a member of the central administration staff, and is regularly head of the section of public safety. The police and S.S. are represented in headquarters by an officer with the title of Superior S.S. and Police Chief (*Der Höhere S.S. und Polizeiführer*).[21] The Superior S.S. and Police Chief commands not only the units of the S.S. (*Schutzstaffeln*), the Gestapo, and the *Sicherheitsdienst*, but also the German regular police (*Ordnungspolizei*), as well as the police units recruited from among the local population. Because of the special functions he has to fulfill, particularly in such a non-collaborationist country as Poland, the German Superior S.S. and Police Chief in that country was made Deputy of the Governor General of Poland, with the title of Secretary of State for Security Matters (*Staatssekretär für das Sicherheitswesen*). Only with respect to questions of great importance is it necessary for him to obtain the consent of the Reich Commissioner or the Governor General of the given area.[22] The following scheme of organization shows how manifold the police and S.S. functions are:[23]

1. Organization.
2. Combating the movement for independence. National parties, Socialist groups, Communism.
3. The Secret Press.
4. Investigation of foreign contacts.
5. Investigation of Polish centres abroad (in collaboration with the Gestapo headquarters in Berlin).

[21] See Section 1 of decree of the Reich Commissioner for the Occupied Netherlands Territories concerning the organization and establishment of the office of the Reich Commissioner, June 3, 1940, below, p. 450.

[22] Friedrich Wilhelm Adami, "Die Gesetzgebungsarbeit im Generalgouvernement," *Deutsches Recht*, Vol. 16 (1940), p. 608.

[23] *Polish Fortnightly Review*, No. 69, p. 7.

6. Polish press abroad.
7. Industrial defence (counter sabotage).
8. Control of former officers in the Polish Army.
9. Combating enemy espionage.
10. Control of foreigners.
11. Control of railways.
12. Control of Germans from the Reich.

For political reasons the main tasks of the police are carried out, as mentioned above, by the Gestapo and the units of S.S. and the *Sicherheitsdienst.* Of especial importance also in some countries, particularly in Poland, is the so-called *Sonderdienst* (Special Service), which consists entirely of Germans (*Volksdeutsche*). The services of members of the *Sonderdienst* are the more valuable because they know the language of the population and also the local conditions. The *Sonderdienst* is mainly occupied with the collecting of agricultural quotas, the imposition of fines, and the control of prices.

2. *Discretionary Power.* Whereas in Germany the discretionary power of the police is implied in the exemption of the activities of the police from control by administrative courts, in the occupied countries such discretionary power is established also by express provision; thus, an order of the Reich Commissioner of the Netherlands states that "in the fulfillment of his duties the Superior S.S. and Police Chief may deviate from existing regulations."[24] He may even take over the direct administration of entire areas.[25] Under provisions of the same order he "may promulgate rules and regulations, having the force and effect of laws, which are necessary for the fulfillment of his duties." Moreover, "such rules and regulations may contain penal provisions subjecting a defendant to fines of unlimited amount, imprisonment, or jail." Thus, a peculiar situation is created. The population of the occupied country must obey the regulations issued by the police just as if those regulations were laws; but the police themselves are not bound by these rules which they themselves issue.

According to a decree concerning private property in the Government General of Poland, the Superior S.S. and Police Chief may, in certain cases, order sequestrations of property with the object of increasing the striking power of the units of the uniformed police and armed S.S., and in ordering such sequestrations he is not subject to the limitations of the decree concerning sequestration of private property. He has only to notify the fact of sequestration to the Director of the Trustee Administration.[26]

The discretionary power of the police goes so far that they may impose penalties without judicial procedure,[27] or even take over courts martial. Although the courts martial are essentially composed of military men, it is

[24] Order concerning the establishment of administrative courts martial, March 19, 1941, below, p. 475.

[25] *Ibid.* [26] Decree of January 24, 1940, below, p. 534.

[27] See order of August 28, 1940, concerning transactions in real estate in Luxemburg, below, p. 422.

made possible for the police themselves to constitute such courts and to act instead of the military.[28]

The addition of the fact that they have judicial autonomy completes the picture of the discretionary power of the police. Offenses committed against members of the police or committed by the police are tried by "Special Criminal Courts established for members of the S.S. and for members of the police units mobilized for special duty."[29]

3. *Police as Colonizers.* The Superior S.S. and Police Chief in every occupied country is the agent of the Reich Commissariat for the Strengthening of Germanism (*Reichskommissariat für die Festigung deutschen Volkstums*).[30] This commissariat was created in Berlin after the outbreak of the war and was put under the direction of Himmler, Reich Leader of the S.S. and Police Chief. The functions of the commissariat were thus defined: "To bring back from abroad the German element—*Reichs-und Volksdeutsche*—to regulate the position of foreign nationalities, and also to give shape to the new German areas of colonization." In this connection Himmler stated: "Our task is to Germanize the East, not in the old sense of bringing the German language and German laws to the people dwelling in that area, but to ensure that in the East only people of genuinely German, Teutonic blood shall live." [31] This function is carried out by mass deportations of native populations by the police (in such countries as Alsace-Lorraine, Poland, and Slovenia), by providing assistance in the settlement of the German colonists coming into new areas in the occupied countries, and by liquidating owners of business enterprises and putting Germans in their place.

For purposes of colonization the German police have established "Colonization Staffs" (*Ansiedlungsstab*), which carry out all the technical and political work of colonization.

As confiscation of property is a part of the colonization scheme, authority in respect to property seizures has also been granted to the police in certain cases, as stated above in the section relating to discretionary power.

4. *Liquidation of Politically Undesirable Persons and of the Jews.* One of the main functions of the police and S.S. is the liquidation of politically undesirable persons and of the Jews. The Gestapo administers large concentration camps where such persons are being held, and organizes executions. The rounding up of the Jews in all the occupied countries and deporting them to Poland for physical extermination is also one of the main tasks of the

[28] Decree supplementing the decree for the suppression of violence in the Government General, December 2, 1939, *Verordnungsblatt des Generalgouvernements Polen*, 1939, p. 204. See also Adami, *op. cit.*, p. 606.

[29] See order of July 17, 1940, concerning jurisdiction in criminal proceedings in the occupied Netherlands, below, p. 466. See also order for Norway of August 27, 1940, concerning procedure before the German Court, below, p. 501.

[30] See the second order for the enforcement of the decree of the Führer and Reich Chancellor concerning the organization and administration of the Eastern Territories, November 2, 1939, below, p. 507.

[31] *Deutsche Arbeit*, August, 1942. See *Polish Fortnightly Review*, No. 69, p. 6.

Gestapo and S.S. units.[32] The Chief of the Gestapo in Poland, Krüger, who was killed by Polish patriots, organized the liquidation of the ghettos in Polish towns, with the physical annihilation of half a million inhabitants of the Warsaw ghetto. "He also built up the technical apparatus of mass-murder on three main lines: death by gas in special chambers, electrocution, and death in the so-called death trains by the action of quick-lime."[33]

5. *Labor.* The police are mainly responsible for mustering the labor man-power in the occupied countries and deporting it to Germany. They carry out the registration of persons at the Reich Labor Office,[34] and sometimes they round up people for work in the streets, using physical force.

III. Local Police

The extent to which the local police are used by the occupant depends on whether there is in the given occupied country a puppet or a headless government, or whether neither of these two types of government has been established. In the first case, the services of the local police are utilized to a greater extent than in the second. In the Netherlands the maintenance of public peace, safety, and order is entrusted to the Netherlands police, "unless the Reich Commissioner calls on German S.S. or police forces for the enforcement of his orders."[35] In general, the Reich Commissioner appoints and dismisses the Chief Police Commissioners.[36] This is particularly true in countries of a non-collaborationist type like Poland, where, for example, the local Polish police carry out minor functions such as traffic control, protection of buildings, maintenance of patrols and police posts. The Polish criminal investigation police investigate crimes committed by Poles, within the sphere of jurisdiction of the Polish courts. The Polish police have no right to act if one of the parties involved is a German. In such case the Polish police must cede the investigation to the German police.[37]

IV. The S.S. and Police and War Crimes

The foregoing sections show that the S.S. and police are one of the main instrumentalities of the administration of the occupied countries. It should be noted that some higher officials in the administration of the occupied countries, who do not carry out the functions of police, are organizationally connected with the S.S. and are given various titles of the S.S. hierarchy.

[32] See below, chapter on "The Legal Status of the Jews."

[33] *Polish Fortnightly Review*, No. 69, pp. 7–8.

[34] Proclamation concerning entry into the Reich Labor Service, Luxemburg, February 12, 1941, below, p. 437.

[35] Order of the Reich Commissioner concerning the exercise of governmental authority in the Netherlands, May 29, 1940, below, p. 448.

[36] See fourth order of the Reich Commissioner for the Netherlands concerning certain administrative measures, August 20, 1940, below, p. 455.

[37] *Polish Fortnightly Review*, No. 69, p. 8.

Thus, the police and the S.S. are interwoven with the administration of the occupied countries.

The special functions of the S.S. and the police have given them the opportunity to perpetrate the greater part of the war crimes which have occurred during this war. As the United Nations have committed themselves to the prosecution of such crimes,[38] the special structure of the S.S. and police should be an important factor in determining the basis for a new treatment of these crimes.[39]

An analysis of the specific functions of the Gestapo and S.S. and of their program and world outlook leads to the conclusion that in the light of their close connection and combined activities they constitute an association having as its purpose the commission of crimes *in genere*. Such crimes are directed not only against municipal law of the occupied countries, but also against international law and the laws of humanity. Such an association amounts to what is called in Anglo-Saxon law conspiracy, or in continental European law unlawful association. Therefore, mere membership in such groups should be treated as an offense, and all the members of the Gestapo and S.S. should be punished for the sole reason that they are carrying out such functions in the occupied countries. Moreover, if a member of the Gestapo or S.S. has also committed a concrete crime, he should of course be punished for this specific crime.

In connection therewith another issue relating to war crimes arises, namely (aside from the problem of the type of courts having jurisdiction—international *versus* national military tribunals)[40] the problem as to whether or not the plea of superior orders, that is, the plea that the offender acted under orders of his superior, should be taken into consideration as a justifiable defense. An offender invoking this plea asserts in effect that he personally disapproves the act and he would never have committed it had he not been ordered to do so in the particular case. That defense presupposes integrity of character and a respect for law and morality on the side of the offender, who suffers a conflict between his own conscience and the compulsion of service. Such a plea cannot, however, be taken into consideration if the offender is generally and habitually involved in committing

[38] See Declaration on War Crimes, adopted by the Inter-Allied Conference, January 13, 1942, *New York Times*, January 14, 1942, p. 6, col. 1. See also statements of the President of the United States of America and the British Prime Minister on retribution as one of the major war aims, October 25, 1941. Department of State, *Bulletin*, Vol. V, No. 122 (October 25, 1941), p. 317. London *Times*, October 27, 1941, p. 4, col. 7.
See also George A. Finch, "Retribution for War Crimes," *American Journal of International Law*, Vol. 37 (1943), pp. 81–88.

[39] The author does not attempt to treat adequately here the complex problem of war crimes. Only because of the exceptional rôle of the police forces and their specific organizational structure are some of the aspects of this problem dealt with.

[40] See Sheldon Glueck, "By What Tribunal Shall War Offenders Be Tried?" *Harvard Law Review*, Vol. LVI (June, 1943), p. 1059; "Trial and Punishment of the Axis War Criminals," *Free World*, Vol. IV (November, 1942), p. 138; George A. Finch, "Trial of War Criminals Discussed as Military Proceeding," Washington *Evening Star*, August 26, 1943.

similar crimes; if he believes that the commission of such crimes is useful to him and to his group; or if he has voluntarily joined an organization which approves and glorifies such crimes.

Although there is in general a considerable difference of opinion among authorities on international law as to the admissibility of the plea of superior orders,[41] one must say that such a plea could in no case be invoked with sufficient grounds by the S.S. and police. The main reasons seem to be the following:

(1) According to the Hague Regulations, the occupant has the right and the duty to restore and maintain public order and safety in accordance with the laws in force in the country. Under this provision, the police of the occupant should undertake only such acts as are necessary to ensure order and safety in the given area. They cannot engage in activities aiming at the destruction of nations.

(2) The S.S. and the police in the occupied countries are engaged in a program of subjugation, of exploitation, and of destruction of other nations, in which they were trained long before the war, and in which they fanatically believe. The war crimes committed by them are not sporadic incidents of ill-will but are an instrumentality for the carrying out of this program.

(3) Unlike military service, which is based upon compulsory joining of the ranks, service in the police is voluntary and admission to the ranks of the police is based upon competitive examinations.

(4) The relatively long probationary period in the temporary stage of employment in the Gestapo lends itself to the development of the excessively high degree of zeal displayed by its members, which fact emphasizes even more the element of volition in the activities of the individual members of the Gestapo.

(5) The plea of superior orders may rather be made, if at all, by individuals in isolated cases, but not by great masses of offenders acting together, because it is possible for such great numbers to act together also in opposing orders which are contrary to their individual consciences.

(6) The great amount of discretionary power enjoyed by the German police gives to individual members the opportunity to reach their own decisions, for which they naturally must be held individually responsible.

[41] The British *Manual of Military Law* (London, 1914), No. 443; United States War Department, *Basic Field Manual: Rules of Land Warfare* (Washington, 1940), Article 347; Oppenheim, *International Law* (London, 1935), Vol. II, p. 453, are essentially in favor of the plea of superior orders. See a similar view by Ernst J. Cohn, "The Problem of War Crimes To-day," in *Transactions of the Grotius Society*, Vol. 26 (1941), pp. 125, 144. In the main, however, Anglo-Saxon doctrine and practice are opposed to the excusing of war crimes on the plea of superior orders. See George A. Finch, "Superior Orders and War Crimes," *American Journal of International Law*, Vol. 15 (1921), pp. 440, 444; H. Lauterpacht, in his 1940 edition of Oppenheim's *International Law*, Vol. II, p. 454.

For a discussion of this matter, see Georg Schwarzenberger, *International Law and Totalitarian Lawlessness* (London, 1943), pp. 57–81.

CHAPTER III

LAW

I. Introduction of German Law

In occupying every new country, the occupant has made it a practice to declare, in his first proclamation to the population, that local law would remain in force unless contrary to the fact of the occupation. Such a declaration, if made as to any other occupying power than Germany, would imply that there would not be many changes in the law; but when made by the German occupant this statement signifies a program of changing a great body of the laws of a given country. Because the aims of German occupation are not limited to military considerations but are directed toward the integration of the occupied countries into the "New European Order" under German hegemony, it becomes obvious that most of the laws of the occupied countries are incompatible with the aims of the German occupation. Therefore, many important changes in law were introduced by the occupant. These changes in law are not an exceptional phenomenon, as in previous occupations, but a mass phenomenon.[1]

German law has been introduced in the occupied countries in varying degrees. The following gradations may be considered:

1. In the Free City of Danzig, and in Memel, and in the incorporated Belgian districts of Eupen, Malmédy, and Moresnet, practically the entire body of German and Prussian law was introduced. This was possible because these cities were governed before the occupation by a great body of Prussian law; and as to Eupen, Malmédy, and Moresnet, the occupant was eager to document as soon as possible a return to the situation existing before 1918, when these districts belonged to Germany.

2. In Austria and in the Sudeten, it was declared that German laws promulgated after a specified date following the occupation (for Austria, March 13, 1938, and for the Sudeten, October 10, 1938) apply also to these territories, unless a provision to the contrary is made in the given law. Earlier German laws were, after these dates, individually introduced in those countries, such as the Nuremberg Laws;[2] the decree of October, 1936, for the execution of the Four-Year Plan; the law originally promulgated on December 1, 1933, and revised on July 3, 1934, for ensuring the unity of party and state; and the *Reichsstatthalter* Act of January 30, 1935, which defined the

[1] See Raphaël Lemkin, "Law and Lawyers in the European Subjugated Countries," address before the North Carolina Bar Association, *Proceedings of the Forty-fourth Annual Session of the North Carolina Bar Association*, May, 1942 (Durham, N. C.), pp. 107–16.

[2] As to Austria, see decree of May 20, 1938, *Reichsgesetzblatt*, 1938, I, p. 594.

duties and powers of the governors of the provinces of the Reich. Many other examples could be given.

These territories have never belonged to Germany. The legal institutions of Austria had quite a high standing and were based upon traditions of a long evolution of legal culture which had also influenced the legal institutions in other countries. The Sudeten, having been for centuries in this orbit, shared the evolution of the same legal institutions and later on came under the influence of Czechoslovak law when the Sudeten were incorporated into Czechoslovakia after the Versailles Treaty. Therefore, in the beginning the occupant limited himself in these territories to the introduction of law having a special political character and relating to the organization of the state and National Socialism, such as the Nuremberg Laws and a great body of administrative laws connected with the introduction of the *Gau* administration.

3. In western Poland (incorporated into Germany), in Alsace-Lorraine, and in Luxemburg, no provision was published to the effect that laws promulgated in the Reich after the occupation should apply directly to these territories. On the contrary, they had to be individually introduced in each case. However, an extensive volume of law was thus introduced into these areas, such as the German Commercial Code,[3] German extradition law,[4] the German organization of courts,[5] and the German Lawyers' Code of November 1, 1936.[6] The German Criminal Code was made applicable to western Poland by the decree of June 6, 1940,[7] as were a great number of laws of a political and administrative character.

4. In the last group, embracing all the other occupied territories and the Protectorate of Bohemia and Moravia, a great body of German law was introduced pertaining mainly to economy and labor. However, in these countries the law of the "protection of blood and honor" (as limited to Germans only) was also made applicable, and laws pertaining to Nazi indoctrination and the protection of German political institutions, as well as particular German administrative decrees, were introduced.

In the Protectorate of Bohemia and Moravia, the introduction of German law was originally checked by the provisions of the legislative authority of the Protectorate. But later on the Reich Protector made extensive use of the measures giving him the right to change local law.

II. Changes in Local Law

To the extent that German law does not supplant local law in the respective areas the latter law remains in force, but it has undergone many es-

[3] For Poland, see *Reichsgesetzblatt*, 1941, I, p. 319.
[4] For Poland, see *ibid.*, p. 304. [5] For Poland, see *ibid.*, 1940, I, p. 1907.
[6] See *Verordnungsblatt* for Luxemburg, 1941, No. 15, p. 104.
[7] *Reichsgesetzblatt*, 1940, I, p. 844.

sential changes. These changes were introduced under the pressure of the occupant through the puppet and headless governments, and also directly by the German authorities themselves—as was done repeatedly in Poland and in the Protectorate of Bohemia and Moravia.

The fact that the law was sometimes formally altered, not by the occupant directly but by the puppet or headless governments, does not validate the changes. The puppet or headless governments, acting on behalf and under control of the occupant, derive their authority from the occupant. Therefore they cannot have rights superior to those of the occupant, who is limited by Article 43 of the Hague Regulations.

The following are additional examples of changes in local law beside those quoted elsewhere in this work:

The Dutch law on citizenship was altered. According to Dutch law as it existed prior to the occupation, a Dutchman serving in a foreign army lost his citizenship. But as the Germans were eager to see the Dutchmen form an anti-Bolshevik legion, the Reich Commissioner published a decree to the effect that Dutchmen taking part in the fight against Russia shall not lose their Dutch citizenship.[8]

The provisions of the Polish Criminal Code whereby a judge is entitled to defer the execution of penalties involving loss of liberty or fines, or to exercise mercy in any other way, were declared invalid.[9]

Changes were also made in the family law of Luxemburg, especially as to illegitimate children.[10]

In the Netherlands, Articles 92–98 of the Netherlands Civil Code, requiring that a girl of Netherlands nationality who is under age should have the consent of her parents, grandparents, or local guardian to marry, were modified by the Reich Commissioner to the effect that if such person wishes to marry a German the consent of the Reich Commissioner shall be sufficient.[11] Substituting for the rights of the parents the rights of the Reich Commissioner is a flagrant disregard of family rights, which are under the protection of Article 46 of the Hague Regulations.

III. Departures from Law

The observance of the letter and spirit of the law is not mandatory according to German conceptions. The following institutions of German law furnish an illustration:

1. *The Principle of Analogy in Criminal Law.* On June 28, 1935, one of the most revolutionary innovations was introduced in the German Criminal

[8] *Verordnungsblatt*, 1941, No. 133.
[9] See order of February 19, 1940, on Polish jurisdiction in the Government General, below, p. 529.
[10] See order of March 22, 1941, below, p. 428.
[11] See order of February 28, 1941, below, p. 474.

Code. Until that time the principle *nulla poena sine lege* prevailed, namely, that no one could be punished for any act for which punishment was not prescribed by law. From then on a person could be punished if the act seemed merely analogous to any punishable act prohibited by law.[12] The judges could thus expand by analogy the field of criminal law. In order to determine what is an analogous case, the German judge had to guide himself by "sound popular feeling" and furthermore by Nazi literature, especially *Mein Kampf* and the Führer's speeches. This conception of the law represents an encroachment upon the rights of the individual,[13] because it subjects him to the arbitrary opinion of the judge as to what constitutes an offense. It destroys the feeling of legal security and creates an atmosphere of constant fear and terror.

A criminal law based upon the principle of analogy seemed to the Germans to provide an expedient instrumentality for the enforcement of the New Order in the occupied countries. German criminal law was therefore introduced in the incorporated areas,[14] and in the non-incorporated territories German criminal law is applied by German courts when they are trying inhabitants of the occupied countries.[15] This introduction of the German criminal law into the occupied countries is a violation of the Hague Regulations. If the occupant considered that the local law did not give sufficient protection to his military interests, he could lawfully introduce only the provisions of the German Criminal Code aiming at the protection of such

[12] The German law of June 28, 1935, provides: "Any person who commits an act which the law declares to be punishable or which is deserving of penalty according to the fundamental conceptions of a penal law and sound popular feeling, shall be punished. If there is no penal law directly covering an act it shall be punished under the law of which the fundamental conception applies most nearly to the said act." See Jerome Hall, "Nulla poena sine lege," in *Yale Law Journal*, Vol. 47 (1937), pp. 165–93.

[13] The German innovation provoked great criticism in legal circles outside Germany. The Second International Congress of Comparative Law, held at The Hague in 1937, formulated a resolution against analogy in criminal law. See particularly reports of Schaffstein and Dahm, representing the German view, and remarks representing the opposite view by Lord Justice du Parcq of the King's Bench Division, London; Abd-El-Fattah El-Sayed, member of the Supreme Court of Egypt; Ugo Aloisi, President of the Criminal Chamber of the Court of Cassation, Rome; Hanna, Justice of the High Court of the Irish Free State; and Hall (*Rapporteur*), Pella, Racine, Geesteranus, Glaser, Wolter, Hofmannstahl, Lemkin, Donnedieu de Vabres.

The following is the text of the resolution:

"Without expressing any preference upon the legal ideologies dominating in different countries which, especially in matters of criminal law, have their roots in the traditions, customs, moral values, and the political life of each nation,

"the Congress is in favour of the maintenance of the rule, 'nulla poena sine lege.'"— *Voeux et Résolutions du Deuxième Congrès International de Droit Comparé*, La Haye, 4–11 Août 1937, publié par les soins de M. Elemér Balogh, p. 69.

The IVe Congrès International de Droit Pénal, held in Paris in 1937, likewise discussed the problem of analogy in criminal law and adopted conclusions as to the inadmissibility of analogy. See *Revue internationale de droit pénal*, 1938, No. 1, p. 55.

[14] In the Polish territories, by decree of June 6, 1940, *Reichsgesetzblatt*, 1940, I, p. 844; in Eupen, Malmédy, and Moresnet, by decree of July 29, 1940, below, p. 315.

[15] In Belgium, by order of the Commander in Chief of the German Army of May 10, 1940, below, p. 319; in the Protectorate of Bohemia and Moravia, by order of April 14, 1939, below, p. 347; in the Netherlands, by order of July 17, 1940, below, p. 466; in Norway, by order of August 27, 1940, below, p. 501; in Yugoslavia, by order of the Commander in Chief of the Army promulgated at the front without date, below, p. 597.

interests. He certainly was not entitled to introduce the Criminal Code *in toto* relating to non-military matters such as family relations, morality, and property rights. On the other hand, if the occupant should decide to substitute some other law for the local law, he may do so only by substituting the one law for the other. However criminal codes of different countries may differ among themselves, it may safely be stated that they consist of strict rules of law and that they constitute essentially a strict delimitation on one side of the right of the state and, on the other side, of the right of the individual. But the German Criminal Code, because of the principle of analogy to which it adheres, cannot be treated as a rule of law. It does not furnish the elementary protection of law to which the inhabitants of the occupied territories are entitled by Article 43 of the Hague Regulations. That the German Criminal Code cannot be treated as a rule of law had been previously recognized. When provisions based on the Nazi-modified Criminal Code were introduced by decree in Danzig in 1935, a petition was presented by representatives of minority parties to the League of Nations High Commissioner protesting against the decrees as violating the Constitution of the Free City of Danzig. The petition was in turn presented to the Council of the League, which voted to submit the request to the Permanent Court of International Justice at The Hague. The Court delivered an advisory opinion on December 4, 1935,[16] which in effect held that the application of the German law of June 28, 1935 (introducing the principle of analogy) was in violation of the constitutional requirement that the government of the Free City be by rule of law.

2. *Other Departures from Law Ordered by the Occupant.* Because the principle of legality in determining offenses and criminal responsibility was destroyed, the occupant could introduce the principle of retroactivity and even punish on the presumption of future guilt, an innovation without parallel in modern law. In some instances the occupant has ordered that penalties shall be imposed for acts committed before the occupation.[17] In Belgium the order concerning factory trustees of April 29, 1941, was made effective retroactively as of February 1, 1941, violations of this order being punishable by fine or imprisonment.[18] In Luxemburg the decree of January 15, 1941, concerning insidious attacks on the Party and the Movement (German National Movement),[19] and providing the death penalty in serious cases, was made retroactive as of December 1, 1940.

Besides retroactivity, the presumption of future guilt mentioned above was introduced. According to the order of the Reich Commissioner for the Netherlands of July 4, 1940,[20] penalties of confiscation may be imposed in

[16] Series A/B No. 65; M. O. Hudson, *World Court Reports*, Vol. III (Washington: Carnegie Endowment for International Peace, 1938), pp. 516 ff.

[17] "The courts of the armed forces shall also have jurisdiction to try crimes committed before the occupation by the German forces." See undated order of the Commander in Chief of the Army in Yugoslavia, issued at the front, below, p. 597.

[18] See below, p. 325. [19] See below, p. 425. [20] See below, p. 478.

cases where "it must be assumed" that a person will in the future further activities hostile to the German Reich and to Germany.[21]

In some instances, the occupant has declared that the authorities shall not be bound by law at all or that some essentially legal matters shall be accomplished without judicial procedure. Thus the order of the Reich Commissioner for the Netherlands establishing administrative courts martial has created the institution of a special agent for the area in which the administrative court martial has been decreed. This special agent takes over the entire public administration and in the fulfilling of his duties he "shall not be bound by law."[22] Also, as mentioned in the preceding chapter, when the Governor General of Poland on January 24, 1940, introduced a decree on sequestration of private property, he exempted the police from observing the provisions of this decree in certain cases when they are ordering sequestrations.[23]

*

The divorce of administration from law in the occupied countries seems to be in line with the complete abolition of legality in German public life. On August 20, 1942, Hitler issued a decree granting special full powers to the Reich Minister of Justice, which reads: "A vigorous administration of justice is necessary for the fulfillment of the tasks of the Greater German Reich. I order and empower, therefore, the Reich Minister of Justice to organize a National Socialist administration of justice and to undertake all necessary measures, in accordance with my instructions and guidance, and in agreement with the Reich Minister and Chief of the Reich Chancellery, as well as the Chief of the Party Chancellery. The Reich Minister of Justice may hereunder deviate from existing law."[24]

The introduction of German law into the occupied countries cannot be justified by the occupant on the ground of military necessity. The purpose of the mass introduction of German law into the incorporated areas is dictated by the desire to assimilate these areas as soon as possible with the Greater German Reich. As incorporation is of itself a violation of international law, all actions tending to this end must also be considered as illegal. The introduction of German law and the changing of local law in the non-incorporated areas are dictated, as reflected in the character of the laws, by the occupant's plan to integrate these countries into the New European Order. Such introduction of German law cannot be justified by the occupant on the ground of military necessity (Article 43 of the Hague Regulations), because the integration of the occupied countries into the New Order is obviously a political objective and has no realistic relation to the needs of the army or the

[21] Basing penalties upon presumption of future guilt is an institution of mediaeval German law, especially as codified later in the *Constitutio Carolina criminalis*.

[22] See order of March 19, 1941, below, p. 475.

[23] See below, p. 534. As to deviations from law, especially by police, see above, chapter on "Police."

[24] *Reichsgesetzblatt*, 1942, No. 91.

successful conduct of the military operations. Hence it cannot be classified as a measure dictated by military necessity. It was not contemplated in the Hague Regulations that an occupant should undertake plans or actions which would enter into the post-war period.

Moreover, the ideological substance of German law should also be envisaged. One may state that German law is bereft of moral content and self-limitations, being predominantly utilitarian. Law to the Germans is that which is useful to them.[25]

German law is based upon the principle of discrimination and not of equality. It is subordinative to the state and not protective of the rights of the citizen. In this respect it denies the main principle and mission of law, because the individual, as the weaker party in his relations with the state, needs more protection by law than does the state. German law is not conceived as human justice. It invokes legal technique simply as a means of administrative coercion.[26]

German law is cruel in its content. It has not only revived the *jus talionis* —the principle of an eye for an eye and a tooth for a tooth—but has surpassed it by exacting penalties in the ratio of ten eyes for one, or punishments wholly without relation to guilt. It has divorced law from morality and mercy.[27]

Consequently, the introduction of German law in the occupied countries is not only in violation of the Regulations of the Hague Convention but also of the very principles of the law of nations and also of the laws of humanity.[28]

[25] At the session of the Academy of German Law in Berlin in November, 1939, Hans Frank, the President of this Academy and former Reich Minister of Justice, who was appointed as Governor General of Poland, declared: "We are proud that we have constructed our legal principles so that nothing is to be changed in war. Law is that which is useful and necessary for the German nation; that is unlawful which harms the interests of the German nation. These principles guide us in these times."—*Juristische Wochenschrift*, December, 1939.

[26] Address on "The Legal Framework of Totalitarian Control over Foreign Economies," by Raphaël Lemkin, before the Section of International and Comparative Law of the American Bar Association in Indianapolis, September 29–October 3, 1941.

[27] See decree of February 19, 1940, prohibiting Polish judges from exercising mercy and parole, below, p. 529; also the decree of December 22, 1941, providing the death penalty for sheltering Jews—a denial of the most humane of all human rights, that of giving help in distress, below, p. 601.

This ruthless character of German law and the implications therefrom for the legal life of the occupied countries gave rise to the adoption of a resolution of the American Bar Association at its Indianapolis session in October, 1941, as proposed by the late John T. Vance, Law Librarian of Congress, and Judge Keaton of Oklahoma:

"WHEREAS, Municipal law has been replaced in most of the continent of Europe by the *lex talionis;* and

"WHEREAS, The legal profession of those nations whose sovereignty has been ruthlessly despoiled by Axis powers, has been reduced to the status of servile dependence or completely abolished, and many of our colleagues have been executed, imprisoned, or forced to seek refuge in distant lands; now, therefore, be it

"*Resolved*, That the American Bar Association expresses to its European brethren in distress its profound sympathy and the hope that the day may soon come when their countries may be freed and they may be restored to their former place of trust and honor." —*American Bar Association Journal*, Vol. 27 (1941), p. 726.

[28] See the preamble to Hague Convention IV.

CHAPTER IV

COURTS

The occupant has introduced into the occupied countries important changes in the organization of the courts. A great part of the jurisdiction has been taken over by German courts, and their jurisdiction sometimes varies from country to country. Even within one country the vague delimitation of jurisdiction augments the feeling of legal insecurity.

I. German Courts

A common feature of German courts is that sufficient care is not taken in their procedure to safeguard the rights of the defendant. For example, no preliminary investigation is made in some cases, such as those tried before special courts or courts martial.[1] Furthermore, no appeal lies from the decisions of special courts, although in some countries, such as Poland, they are empowered to pronounce the death penalty. Notice is served on the defendant in so short a time as twenty-four hours before the trial, and he may have counsel appointed to defend him only if it seems "expedient."[2] Generally speaking, only German counsel may appear, although in exceptional cases, if the German authorities will admit them, members of the local bar in occupied countries may appear before German courts to defend their compatriots.

An especially severe régime as to legal recourse was established in the Ostland. According to the decree of the Reich Commissioner for the Ostland, Jews are allowed no legal recourse against the decision of a German court. Moreover, the Reich Commissioner for the Ostland may exclude at his discretion other entire groups of people from the right of legal recourse.[3]

The generally admitted principle that a judge of original jurisdiction cannot act as a judge in an appeal of the same case was violated by the order of July 17, 1940,[4] whereby the judge whose order has been attacked by a motion to set it aside is not disqualified from sitting with a full court of three in deciding on such a motion.

The insecurity of the defendant is further increased by the lack of finality of the decision. According to the above-mentioned order of the Reich Commissioner of the Netherlands, the Attorney General may, within one year after a judgment of a German court, file a petition to have such judgment declared void. If the Reich Commissioner sets aside the judgment, there is

[1] For Norway, see order of August 27, 1940, below, p. 501.

[2] For Poland, see decree of February 19, 1940, below, p. 525; for Norway, order of August 27, 1940, below, p. 501.

[3] *Verordnungsblatt*, 1941, p. 31.

[4] Order for the Netherlands territories, below, p. 466.

not only a trial *de novo*, but the court is "bound to follow" the Reich Commissioner's "mandate as to the applicable law contained in the reasons given for setting aside the original judgment."[5] Thus the Reich Commissioner not only supervises justice but also directs the decisions of the courts.

One of the striking features in the organization of these courts is the introduction of the principle of extraterritoriality for Germans in the occupied countries (see below), and also the fact that the courts are not the only institutions empowered to exercise judicial functions. The German military commanders of France, the district governors in Poland, and S.S. officers in Poland may inflict penalties upon the inhabitants. Because they are empowered to take such action without judicial procedure, the exercise of this power is referred to as "summary penal jurisdiction." An appeal lies within twenty-four hours to the superior of the officer who has passed the order of punishment.[6] In Yugoslavia military commanders, and in Poland S.S. officers, may order confiscations and sequestrations without judicial procedure, and without the right of review for the defendant.[7] In France the German commanders may inflict fines up to 30,000 Reichsmarks and, if the fine cannot be levied, imprisonment in lieu of the fine up to six weeks.[8]

The following types of tribunals prevail in the organization of courts in occupied Europe:

1. *Military Courts*, called also "courts of the armed forces" (*Wehrmachtsgerichte*). The military courts try cases involving military treason, offenses connected with army activities or directed against the German armed forces or their members, and even offenses committed in premises used by or for purposes of the German armed forces.

2. *Special Courts*. The jurisdiction of special courts varies from country to country. For the most part it is not defined beforehand but is provided for in every special decree issued by the German occupant for the protection of special interests, it being generally specified in these decrees that the offenses shall be tried by special courts. Thus special courts, in Poland for example, try cases involving violations of the law concerning use of the German salute,[9] of the law requiring the wearing of Jewish insignia,[10] of the law establishing a Bank of Issue in Poland,[11] of the various decrees concerning sequestration of property,[12] etc. In Norway, again, the special courts try cases involving violations of the law prohibiting political parties,[13] and also

[5] Order for the Netherlands territories, below, p. 470.

[6] See order for the district commanders in occupied France, of September 10, 1940, below, p. 394.

[7] See order of the Commander of the German Army in Serbia, of December 22, 1941, below, p. 598; and decree for the Government General of Poland of January 24, 1940, below, p. 534.

[8] See order by the Chief of Military Administration in France, of September 10, 1940, below, p. 394.

[9] *Verordnungsblatt*, 1939, p. 62.

[10] Order of November 23, 1939, *Verordnungsblatt*, 1939, No. 8, p. 61.

[11] Decree of December 15, 1939, below, p. 537.

[12] See decree of January 24, 1940, below, p. 531.

[13] See orders of September 25 and October 25, 1940, below, pp. 499, 503.

cases involving violation of the law concerning prohibition of activities on behalf of the Royal House of Norway;[14] while in Luxemburg the special court tries cases involving disturbances of public order or activities inimical to Germany or Germans, conversation with prisoners, ceasing work in disregard of German interests,[15] etc.

3. *Courts Martial.* These courts try cases involving attacks which are made against the German administration (and sometimes the German Army), as well as attacks made on individual Germans because of their nationality.[16] They are called "Administrative Courts Martial" in the Netherlands, and their jurisdiction there is very general, being defined as covering cases which involve intentional participation "in activities likely to disturb or to endanger public order and the safety of public life" or intentional violation of "special orders of the Reich Commissioner." Despite the general nature of this jurisdiction, however, the penalties to be imposed are quite definite, namely, death, and in less serious cases hard labor, either for life or for a period of not less than ten years.[17]

4. *German Courts of General Jurisdiction.* These courts are called German courts of original jurisdiction and German superior courts (acting mostly as appellate courts), and they have jurisdiction over both civil and criminal cases. Their criminal jurisdiction includes cases involving German nationals. Thus, if a German national commits a crime in any conspiracy with one or more inhabitants of the occupied country, the case must be tried by a German court.[18] German courts also try non-Germans in cases involving German interests. Such interests are defined as those involved in offenses committed against the Greater German Reich or the National Socialist Party, in acts against Germans or persons in the service of Germany, and in offenses committed during service for German authorities (or in premises used by German authorities), as well as in acts of pillage.[19] In the matter of civil jurisdiction, the principle adopted is that cases in which even one party is a German must be tried by German courts.

II. Local Courts of the Occupied Countries

The local courts of the occupied countries were either abolished completely or limited in their jurisdiction and organization. Thus the Supreme Courts

[14] See orders of October 7, and October 25, 1940, below, pp. 500, 503.

[15] See order of August 20, 1940, below, p. 421.

The special courts are German, except in Norway, where this type of tribunal is called "Norwegian Special Court" and where the Norwegian judges are appointed by the Commissioner of State for the Department of Justice or, more recently, by the Norwegian Minister of Justice. See order of October 25, 1940, below, p. 503.

[16] *Verordnungsblatt* for Poland, 1939, pp. 8, 10, 223.

[17] See order of March 19, 1941, below, p. 475.

[18] See decree of February 19, 1940, concerning German jurisdiction in the Government General, below, p. 525.

[19] As to Poland, see *ibid.;* as to the Netherlands, see order of the Reich Commissioner of July 17, 1940, below, p. 466.

of Poland, Austria, and Luxemburg were abolished. In incorporated western Poland, in Eupen, Malmédy and Moresnet, and in Austria, all local courts were abolished and German courts introduced in their stead; these pronounce sentences in the same way as do the courts in the Greater German Reich, namely, "in the name of the people" (*im Namen des Volkes*). In other occupied territories, the local courts were retained with a limited jurisdiction. These limitations derive from: (1) the granting of the privilege of extraterritoriality to German inhabitants, and (2) the stringent supervision of local courts by the German authorities.

The principle of *extraterritoriality* was introduced by the provision excluding German inhabitants of the occupied countries from the jurisdiction of the local courts.[20] If one party is a German, or if his nationality is not defined, then the case must be tried before a German court. A Polish court may not even hear a German witness.

As has been indicated, the supervision of the local courts by German authorities is very strict. In the order of the Reich Commissioner for the Netherlands of May 29, 1940,[21] it was declared that the judiciary is independent; but in the same decree it was stated that "the Reich Commissioner will determine which judgments are to be submitted for his confirmation before execution may be issued." In Poland the German authorities may withdraw any case from a Polish court and transfer it to a German court. Judgments of a Polish court may be disregarded by a German court and the case tried *de novo* by the German court.[22]

*

The organization of German courts and the changes in the organization of local courts have brought about a disintegration of the existing judicial organization. These changes brought about the abolition of legal security—a principle of judicial organization upon which the social structure of the nations in the areas now occupied has been based for centuries. In particular, the destruction of all safeguards for the defendant in criminal procedure must be considered as a retrogression to those times when life and liberty of a citizen were at the mercy of the arbitrary practice of issuing *lettres de cachet*. In this regard the present organization of the courts represents a violation of Article 43 of the Hague Regulations, of which the essential requirement is that the occupant respect the legal institutions of the occupied country—a requirement which also implies that he should respect the organization of the courts.

[20] As to the Protectorate of Bohemia and Moravia, see decree of April 14, 1939, below, p. 347.

[21] See below, p. 448.

[22] See decree of February 19, 1940, below, p. 529.

CHAPTER V

PROPERTY

I. New Methods in Treatment of Property by the Occupant

The occupant has introduced new methods in the treatment of property. They consist mainly of the unlimited expansion of the institution of sequestration and compulsory administration, and the handling of property not only as a means for enrichment of the occupant but also for political purposes in the enforcement of the New Order.

Sequestration by itself, according to the decree of the Commander in Chief of the German Army in Belgium, dated May 20, 1940, does not cancel ownership but restricts the right of the owner to dispose of his goods.[1] However, the principle of sequestration as applied by the German occupant is frequently a preliminary step to confiscation, although a sequestrated property may also in some cases be released. Transfer of the sequestrated property to other persons can be undertaken only by special permission of the authorities and on condition that such transfer is in the interest of the "general economic welfare." [2] Sequestrated property is as a rule put under the compulsory administration of special trustees (*Treuhänder*), who report to special trust agencies called *Treuhandstellen*. Sometimes, in exceptional cases, the owner is allowed to act as manager of his own sequestrated property.

That sequestration of property is considered by the occupant as a very important element of administration is obvious from the decree published in incorporated Poland on September 17, 1940.[3] According to this decree, severe penalties are imposed on persons withholding sequestrated items from German authorities. It is stated also in this decree that "if the culprit acts from opposition to the new political order, or if the case is particularly serious for some other reason, then the death penalty shall be imposed." [4] A decree for the Government General of Poland confers upon the Superior S.S. and Police Chief the right to order sequestrations, with the object "of increasing the striking power of the units of the uniformed police and armed S.S." [5]

To all practical purposes, sequestration for the duration amounts to confiscation because as a rule the owner is not allowed to participate either in the administration or in the profits of the property. Only in exceptional cases does he receive small amounts for subsistence, at the discretion of the administrator of the sequestrated property. As the owner may expect restitution only after the defeat of the occupant, the consequences of sequestra-

[1] See below, p. 321. [2] *Ibid.* [3] See below, p. 511.
[4] *Ibid.*, Section 20. [5] See decree of January 24, 1940, below, p. 534.

tion and of confiscation within the period of occupation are thus practically the same.

The new methods introduced by the occupant in this war consist in fact in creating a system of removing properties from whole groups of the population, and in vesting the titles either in the German State, in Germans, or in other persons collaborating with Germany. In this way properties of millions of Jews, Poles, Serbs, Frenchmen, Norwegians, Luxemburgers, Greeks, Czechs, and Belgians have been sequestrated and in great part confiscated.

1. *State Property.* The occupant has confiscated not only movable state property but also real property belonging to the state, which latter action is a violation of Article 53 of the Hague Regulations. Moreover, in confiscating state property the occupant has not limited himself to the use of the real property belonging to the state but has resorted to selling this property, which is also a violation of the above-mentioned Hague Regulations, Article 55, since an occupant has only the right under that article to act as administrator and usufructuary of realty belonging to the state; he cannot assume any title of ownership.

Notwithstanding this provision, however, the Reich Commissioner for the Netherlands issued a decree on October 4, 1940,[6] which provided for the selling of real property owned by the Dutch State. As under Dutch law [7] a secretary general of a ministry has no right to act as a seller of state property on his own authority, the Reich Commissioner has arbitrarily conferred such right upon the Secretary General of the Ministry of Finance and has thus changed the basic laws of the Netherlands in order to enable him to transact sales of Dutch state property under the direction of the German authority.[8] The above-mentioned change in the basic laws of the Netherlands is again a violation of Article 43 of the Hague Regulations, which states that the occupant shall respect the laws in force in the country "unless absolutely prevented." Obviously, no question of military necessity is involved when the occupant engages in illegal property transactions simply for political New-Order reasons. In this particular case, properties were being sold to Germans and to pro-Nazi Dutchmen as a partial reward for their pro-Nazi activities.

2. *Private Property.* As to private property, the methods adopted for the countries occupied in the west differ from those employed in the territories occupied in the east, especially Poland. In the former countries, private property is being sequestrated or confiscated mainly in order to force the population to collaborate with the New Order, whereas in Poland the aim of sequestration and confiscation is to deprive Poles of property and to give it to

[6] See below, p. 478.

[7] See act of August 29, 1848 (*Staatsblad*, No. 39), as revised by act of April 8, 1937 (*ibid.*, No. 403).

[8] Apparently the occupant was eager to have the Dutch headless government appear as a seller of the Dutch state property, in order to create more confidence with the buyer.

Germans. Thus, citizens of the Netherlands and of Luxemburg may be deprived of their property if they do not wish to promote Germanism, whereas the Poles are being deprived of their property for the mere reason that they are Poles and their property is needed for allocation to German settlers. The following decrees illustrate the above-mentioned methods:

In Luxemburg a decree was promulgated on March 1, 1941, by the *Gauleiter* and Chief of the Civil Administration, Section 1 of which reads:

> To enterprises of trade or industry whose management is unwilling to promote Germanism at all times and without any reservations, the Chief of the Civil Administration may issue orders which will ensure the establishment of conditions in harmony with the fact of a German administration in Luxembourg.
>
> The same shall apply if the management of an enterprise in trade or industry fails to fulfill its duties arising from the general principles of a National Socialist Works' Community or violates orders and instructions of the Chief of the Civil Administration or his designees.
>
> The Chief of the Civil Administration may by special order restrain managers of enterprises from exercising their authority, and by order define their legal position with regard to the enterprise, and may appoint in their stead commissioners who will exercise authority as required. These orders shall not be subject to review by courts of general jurisdiction. The cost arising from the activity of such commissioners shall be borne by the enterprise.[9]

In the Netherlands a decree was issued by the Reich Commissioner on July 4, 1940,[10] permitting confiscation of property not only for activities hostile to the German Reich or Germanism which are perpetrated or attempted but also in cases where "it must be assumed" that a person will in the future further activities hostile to the German Reich or Germany. Confiscation is thus based not on actual guilt only, but also upon the presumption of future guilt. This decree tends to create in the Dutch population a feeling of insecurity and fear, and a readiness to comply with every request of the occupant.

In the western part of Poland which was incorporated into the Reich, the lack of respect shown for private property is a mass phenomenon. The occupant is conferring on German nationals the ownership of Polish land, enterprises and even chattels, if the latter are sufficiently valuable. The decree of September 17, 1940,[11] permits mass sequestration and mass confiscation of property in Poland, under the assumption that the property is required for the "public welfare, particularly in the interests of Reich defense or the strengthening of Germanism." In taking over Polish properties, the Reich Commissioner for Strengthening Germanism has jurisdiction as regards agriculture, because the farms taken from the Poles are given to German settlers. That confiscation and sequestration tend to promote Germanism is obvious also from Section 13 of the above-mentioned decree of September 17, which states that sequestration must be suspended if the

[9] *Verordnungsblatt*, 1941, No. 17, p. 119.
[10] See below, p. 478. [11] See below, p. 511.

owner of the property asserts that he is a German national.[12] Upon comparison of the provision in Article 46 of the Hague Regulations—that private property must be respected and cannot be confiscated—with the texts of the above-mentioned German decrees on the treatment of property, the illegality of the confiscations and sequestrations becomes so obvious that further discussion is unnecessary.

3. *Control of Transactions in Property.* Because the occupant treats property as a means of political control, transactions in property, especially of the more important character, are licensed. Control introduced over such transactions embraces such items as food, raw materials, agricultural products, half-manufactured materials, and other supplies. The decree of the Commander in Chief of the German Army in the West of May 20, 1940, concerning sequestration, made transactions in these goods, with certain exceptions, subject to the consent of the Army Group in the territories of the Netherlands, Belgium, Luxemburg, and France.[13] In the territories occupied during the present Russo-German war, transactions in real estate as well as transactions involving acquisition of enterprises or shares therein are subject to license by German authorities.

4. *Buying Devices.* Because of the overvaluation of German currency in relation to local currencies, which were themselves inflated as a result of German economic pressure, the Germans acquired a predominant position in buying private enterprises. Thus, many enterprises belonging to inhabitants of the occupied countries were acquired by Germans either totally or to the extent of at least 51 per cent, in many instances by the use of duress. As freedom of contract, as well as the theory of just price (under the doctrine of *laesio enormis*), is an essential element of the laws in the various occupied countries, these buying devices are to be considered as a disregard of the rules relating to private property as defined in Article 46 of the Hague Regulations.

5. *The Occupant and the Communistic System of Property.* That private ownership is not an institution respected, as such, by National Socialism in general and by the German occupant in particular, is obvious from the treatment of private property in the Ostland. In the first proclamations issued by the German armies when they occupied Lithuania, Latvia, and Estonia (held at that time by Russia), the restoration of private property was promised to the local population as a "means of returning to the manner of life adapted to a civilized society." However, the occupant soon discovered that the collectivization of property which had in the meantime been introduced by Russia was useful to the Germans. The collective farms (*kolhozy*) or state farms (*sovhozy*) and the institutions of industrial concentration, such as the combines, cartels, and trusts, provided the German war economy with centralization of control. The occupant was therefore reluc-

[12] On the treatment of property, see also below, chapters on "The Legal Status of the Jews" and "Poland."

[13] See below, p. 321.

tant to accept the idea of restoration. In regulations issued under a decree of October 17, 1941,[14] the Commissioner General in Riga announced that in order to avoid excessive disturbances in the normal economic life by the measures taken for restoration of private property, the liquidation of the Bolshevik system should take place step by step only. Accordingly, an order of November 29, 1941, concerning economic reconstruction in the Ostland, declares it unlawful for economic enterprises, as well as for agricultural and forestry establishments, to separate themselves from their existing state economic organizations without permission. Nevertheless, a return to private property was later announced in the regulations issued by the Commissioner General in Riga, dated December 16 and December 23, 1941. The main purpose of these decrees and regulations is not, however, the establishment of the legal institution of private property but rather the creation of an incentive for the local population to serve German interests to a greater degree. Not every dispossessed owner may be reestablished in ownership; rather, he is to be so reestablished only if he proves to be a qualified manager of the enterprise who will be useful for the same enterprise in the German war economy. The candidate for admission to the right to hold private property must submit the necessary papers or otherwise prove that he has been active for at least five years in a given profession. In corroboration of professional suitability the candidate may be required to pass an examination.[14a]

*

As a result of the practices of the occupant, property in Europe has been deprived of legal foundations and has become an object of utilitarian administrative techniques. Therefore it may be stated that not only have the rules of the Hague Convention been violated, but also its main purpose, which consists in safeguarding the accepted principles of morality and social order, to which the people of most of the occupied countries adhered and of which respect for private property is an essential part. Social philosophers and statesmen must watch carefully the phenomenon of the destruction of the institution of private property in Europe in the present war, which may become even more extensive if the war is prolonged and may prove significant for future developments in the post-war period.

II. Plan for Restitution of Property after Liberation

Every military occupation has as a consequence changes in property relations, and after every war adjustments of titles have been necessary. The government of the occupied country, upon regaining control of its territory, enacts laws and regulations for the purposes of such adjustments. In the

[14] See below, p. 308.
[14a] See also "Return to Private Property" in chapter on the "Baltic States," below, pp. 120–23.

first World War, changes of title to ownership effected under political pressure or by reason of military contingencies in occupied France and in occupied Belgium were not recognized by French and Belgian authorities after the occupation, and special laws were passed invalidating contracts involving property entered into during the occupation period.[15] Illegal measures of dispossession, devices in buying up properties, as well as the use of duress in the reconveying of titles in territories under German occupation during the present war caused the United Nations to issue a declaration on January 5, 1943, in which they reserved their right "to declare invalid any transfers of, or dealings with, property, rights and interests" in territories under enemy occupation.[16] Even before that date several governments-in-exile had issued decrees to the effect that measures as to property adopted by the occupying power were to be considered null and void. Such decrees were issued by the Belgian Government on January 10, 1941, the Polish Government on November 30, 1939, and by the Yugoslav Government under date of May 28, 1942.[17]

The problem of the restitution of property[18] after the present war will be complicated because of the changes in title amounting to millions of cases and the great variety of the techniques and devices applied by the occupant. It is not too soon to prepare a detailed plan for the restitution of such property. The author sees the main features of such a plan as follows:

1. *Transactions with the Occupant and with Other Persons.* One should make an essential distinction between, on the one hand, transactions and transfers of property entered into by the inhabitants of an occupied country

[15] As to France, see "Loi relative aux saisies et ventes effectuées en pays ennemi, dans les territoires occupés par l'ennemi et en Alsace-Lorraine," November 8, 1917 (*Journal Officiel*, November 11, 1917), in *Législation de la Guerre de 1914* (Paris: L. Tenin, [1915–19]), Vol. 8, p. 123.

[16] Declaration regarding Forced Transfers of Property in Enemy-controlled Territory: "The Union of South Africa, the United States of America, Australia, Belgium, Canada, China, the Czechoslovak Republic, the United Kingdom of Great Britain and Northern Ireland, the Union of Soviet Socialist Republics, Greece, India, Luxembourg, the Netherlands, New Zealand, Norway, Poland, Yugoslavia and the French National Committee:

"Hereby issue a formal warning to all concerned, and in particular to persons in neutral countries, that they intend to do their utmost to defeat the methods of dispossession practiced by the governments with which they are at war against the countries and peoples who have been so wantonly assaulted and despoiled.

"Accordingly the governments making this declaration and the French National Committee reserve all their rights to declare invalid any transfers of, or dealings with, property, rights and interests of any description whatsoever which are, or have been, situated in the territories which have come under the occupation or control, direct or indirect, of the governments with which they are at war or which belong or have belonged, to persons, including juridical persons, resident in such territories. This warning applies whether such transfers or dealings have taken the form of open looting or plunder, or of transactions apparently legal in form, even when they purport to be voluntarily effected.

"The governments making this declaration and the French National Committee solemnly record their solidarity in this matter." Department of State, *Bulletin*, Vol. VIII, No. 185 (January 9, 1943), pp. 21–22.

[17] See, respectively, the *Moniteur Belge* (London), February 25, 1941; ***Dziennik Ustaw***, December 2, 1939, No. 102; and *Službene Novine*, June 18, 1942, No. 7.

[18] By property we mean also interests and rights.

with the occupant himself or persons vested by the occupant with special rights (as for example German citizens or *Volksdeutsche*) and, on the other hand, transactions and transfers entered into between inhabitants of the occupied countries among themselves.[19] In transactions of the first category the element of duress is usually to be presumed. In transactions of the second category more care must be taken in determining the real nature of the motives, because under occupation the inhabitants may carry on normal transactions in property as between themselves in accordance with pre-war standards. Therefore, transactions of the first kind should as a general rule be declared void *ex officio*, while transactions of the second kind may be declared void only on petition of the interested party and after special investigation.

Moreover, because of practical reasons, a distinction should likewise be made between properties carried into Germany and changes in properties within the limits of one occupied territory. This distinction is important because of its effect on the procedures to be adopted in the restitution.

2. *Restitution of Property Carried into Germany.* This property includes valuable chattels such as paintings and other objects of art, precious antiquities, libraries, scientific laboratories, valuable papers such as securities, and so on. Such objects should be taken away from the last possessor, whether that possessor is the German State or an individual. If the objects carried away cannot be traced to the actual possessor in Germany, the last-known German possessor should be given a fixed period of time within which to return the property or its equivalent in the form either of specie or a similar property which he should be compelled to provide. If there is evidence that the Germans took away from Poland, for example, art treasures from one of its galleries, they should be required to return them within a certain period of time, for example, three months. A German art gallery of similar value should in the meantime be seized as collateral. If within the given time these art treasures are not restored, then the collateral should be taken from Germany. Another example may illustrate such a plan. There is evidence, for instance, that a member of the Wehrmacht has taken valuable rugs from Greece. If this person can be traced, and the rugs are still in his possession, they should be taken from him. If the rugs cannot be traced, an attachment should be made on the property of the culprit in Germany until the rugs in question are restored or objects in kind of equivalent value are received. If the member of the German Wehrmacht does not own any property, attachment may be made at a given time on his earnings within the limitations of actual possibility. The reasons for advocating such a procedure are the following:

(*a*) German currency being based at present on political power, it will

[19] *Mutatis mutandis*, the same distinction should apply as to other occupants, as, for example, Hungarians, Italians, Rumanians, Bulgarians, and Albanians.

crumble on the day of Germany's defeat, and therefore reparations in money on the part of the state or of individuals would seem to be impractical.

(*b*) The looters should be subject to such a procedure for exemplary purposes. The removal of a valuable painting from the home of a looter may create in his family a lasting impression and feeling as to responsibility for loot and crime.

3. *Restitution of Property within the Limits of One Occupied Territory.* Although in the case of property carried away to Germany the nature of the title is irrelevant, and loot or duress in acquisition can be presumed as a rule, changes in title among inhabitants of the same occupied country must be considered from the point of view of whether political pressure or political considerations in general have prevailed in the transaction involved. One must distinguish between political pressure and political considerations as motives for given transactions. The following examples will serve to illustrate the need for this distinction: If a Quislingite has used his political connections in order to compel a fellow countryman to sell him his property, such an act was undertaken under political pressure and should be declared invalid. On the other hand, a situation may occur wherein a non-collaborationist, in anticipation of the probable confiscation of his property because of his political activities, has sold it in advance to a person not involved in political activities in any way whatsoever. In the latter instance, the original owner should be given the opportunity of rescinding the transaction by repaying the money, whereas in the case of the Quislingite it would be only just that the original owner repay the money, not to the Quislingite but to a special state fund to be established.

4. *Acquisition by Neutral Countries, Other Occupied Countries, or Axis Countries other than Germany.* During the present war, the German occupant or his agents have been engaged in selling properties and interests to neutral countries, to other occupied countries, or to other Axis countries. The rights of an occupant in occupied territory being governed by the Hague Regulations, to which most of the countries of the world have adhered, the validity of such transfers of property can be considered only within the framework of international law. The occupant, having violated the Hague Regulations, possesses an invalid title to those properties and rights which it thus illegally acquired and therefore cannot transfer any valid title to other persons. *Nemo plus juris transferre potest quam ipse habebat.* All countries which recognize international law, and especially the parties to the Hague Convention, cannot recognize any acts committed in violation of that Convention. Consequently, such properties ought to be restored to their owners.[20]

[20] See in this respect resolutions of the London International Law Conference, 1943, based, among others, upon a paper read by A. Raestad, "How far can belligerent occupation create a valid title of acquisition of rights transferable outside the occupied country and that of the occupant?" See W. R. Bisschop, "London International Law Conference 1943," *London Quarterly of World Affairs*, Vol. IX, No. 2 (October, 1943), pp. 73–77.

5. *The Problem of Good Faith in Acquisition and Repayment of the Price.* The question arises whether acquisition by the last possessor may involve the plea of good faith. In view of the fact that during the present war looting and other techniques of dispossession have become a mass practice and are of common knowledge, and that warnings on the part of the Allied Governments have also been issued,[21] the plea of good faith in the acquisition of such properties cannot be taken into consideration in the same way as would be the case under normal conditions.

It is advisable to amplify this summary statement of the reasons which militate against the admission of the plea of good faith in the situation created by the present war. Loot and other techniques of dispossession have become a mass phenomenon, as has been mentioned, and are of common knowledge not only to the inhabitants of one occupied country but also to the inhabitants of other occupied countries and of neutral countries, as well as of other Axis countries which are following the German pattern in the territories occupied by them. Such common knowledge is based upon concrete evidence and also upon laws promulgated by the occupant. In addition, one should take into consideration the fact that in every occupied country dealings in real estate and in securities labeled in foreign currency are prohibited except with permission of the occupant. Consequently, the person who offers to sell such property must be in possession of permission from the German authorities. Since such permission is given only to persons collaborating with the Germans or assisting them in their loot, the acquirer knows that the seller is an accomplice of the occupant. The number of other properties and chattels in which transactions are dependent on permission varies from country to country, but transactions in most valuable objects, such as paintings, jewelry, gold, silver, and platinum, are subject to such permission in all the occupied countries. If one combines the problem of common knowledge regarding loot and property devices with the regimentation of transactions in property, and if one takes into consideration also the warning issued by the United Nations as to the acquisition of such properties, one must come to the conclusion that the plea of good faith cannot be admitted. Only in exceptional cases could the last possessor invoke that plea on the ground of exclusion from common knowledge. For example, if a person had spent a long time in a hospital in a serious condition and had been offered such property for purchase the day he left the hospital, not knowing about the mass dispossession practices of the occupant, he might properly plead good faith in acquisition. The practical significance of such exception would obviously be nil.[22] In this

[21] See declaration on property, above, p. 41.
[22] That this seems to be the view of the London International Law Conference is indicated in its Resolution 7: "A person who acquires, even in good faith, any property, rights or interests which are or have been situated in occupied territory or are the property of nationals of that country will, if his acquisition of them is derived directly or indirectly from acts of

connection, the problem arises whether the last possessor is entitled to claim from the original owner reimbursement of the sum he has paid for the property involved. The Belgian law of May 31, 1917, concerning measures of dispossession effected by the enemy, provided that the owner could never be compelled to pay to the last possessor the price which that possessor had paid. The latter would have a claim only against the person who conveyed the title to him.[23] Such a provision would seem to provide an adequate solution also in the present situation.

6. *The Problem of the Colonists.* The problem of the colonists is specific because many thousands of them have been settled on properties of dispossessed persons.[24] The fact that many of them, especially those coming from the Baltic States, Transylvania, and Bukovina, were moved against their will, may exclude their penal responsibility in assisting the enemy in acts of dispossession but does not provide any valid title to the property on which they are settled. In cases where colonists have been settled on state property, the legal situation remains the same. The occupant has the right only to the usufruct of real property belonging to the state in the occupied country; he has no right to dispose of such property and convey title to it to other persons. Consequently, the property given by the occupant to the colonists should be returned to the original owners.

7. *The Responsibilities of the Administrators of Sequestrated Property.* The administrators (*Treuhänder*) of the property seized are predominantly of three groups: (1) Germans imported from Germany proper (*Reichsdeutsche*); (2) Germans who lived in the occupied country before the invasion (*Volksdeutsche*); and (3) local "Quislings." Because the first two types of persons were those in whom the occupant had particular confidence and because rewards had to be given to the traitors who constituted the third type, it was to these persons that the occupant entrusted the administration of the property of individuals who would not promote Germanism.[25] A voluntary element is unquestionably involved here, since there can be no doubt that most, if not all, such administrators have willingly accepted possession and control of the seized properties. This voluntary element in recruiting administrators must lead us to the conclusion that the administrators should not only be held responsible personally (for their participation in war crimes) but should also be held responsible in their property for damages to the se-

---

the occupant or his associates or agents, not acquire an internationally valid title thereto as against the true owner unless such title is valid by the law of the occupied country as applied by the reconstituted authorities after the liberation of the country." Bisschop, *op. cit.*, p. 74.

[23] See Article 3 of the decree-law of May 31, 1917, *Arrêté-loi relatif aux mésures de dépossession effectuées par l'ennemi*, in *Moniteur Belge*, May 27–June 2, 1917.

[24] During 1943 the number of colonists was increased by the fact of mass raids over Germany, which resulted in removing great numbers of German families from bomb-stricken areas, especially from Berlin to Poland. These newcomers were given properties which had been confiscated from Poles.

[25] See above, pp. 37–38.

questrated properties. It should be stated that in many instances, the administrators of sequestrated property are financially solvent men in their own right, and would therefore be in a position to make compensation for such damages. Attachments should be immediately entered on their real and personal property as soon as may be possible.

8. *Restitution Agencies and Tribunals.* As to the problem of the agencies which should be entrusted with the restitution of property and of the procedure to be adopted, the following factors should be taken into consideration:

The number of cases will be very high, surpassing all imaginable figures. Because of the magnitude of the problem, precedents based on the practice of the past will be of little avail in reaching a solution. It would be impossible to handle such a large task expeditiously through ordinary court action. Judicial procedure alone would be too slow; and in any event the courts and judges may well be insufficient in number and judicial systems badly disorganized.[26] In addition, the handling of property cases requires a great deal of preliminary investigation of a highly specialized nature, in the political, financial, and technical fields. On the whole, therefore, administrative procedure would be more appropriate for such investigations than judicial procedure.

Changes in property relations affect not only the inhabitants of one occupied country but also the inhabitants of other occupied, and even neutral, countries—and certainly the inhabitants of Germany itself. Therefore, it should not be overlooked that restitution of property is a problem of international dimensions.

9. *Property Restitution Agencies.* In consideration of these factors, the author proposes the creation of an international agency for handling the problems involving the restitution of property. Such an agency could be called "International Property Restitution Agency"[27] and should have national autonomous branch agencies in each country affected called "Property Restitution Agency of Country X." To the extent that the size of the country and the number of cases so required, the national agencies should have branch agencies in the cities and counties, which should apply the same rules of procedure as the national agencies.

A delimitation of the jurisdiction of the various national agencies, on the one hand, and of the international agency, on the other hand, should be

[26] It happens sometimes that as a result of military operations the judges are removed by the military power from a given territory. This happened, for example (although under different circumstances) during the occupation of Palestine by the British when the Turks removed all judges in order to hamper the administration of the country. See Norman Bentwich, "The Legal Administration of Palestine under the British Military Occupation," *British Yearbook of International Law, 1920–1921*, pp. 139–43.

[27] The author of this work has used the name International Trust Company in previous statements for the same institution. See *Proceedings of the Forty-Fourth Annual Session of the North Carolina Bar Association; held at The Carolina, Pinehurst, N. C., May 15, 16, 17, 1942*, p. 116.

carefully planned. The national agency should handle, as a rule, cases of restitution of property as between the inhabitants of its own country. The international agency should handle cases involving more than one country. It should certainly deal with all cases involving neutral countries and especially with those involving Germany, because Germany will be subject to claims from many countries. A special procedure should be elaborated for particularly close cooperation between the international agency and national agencies which are interested in a specific case of international importance involving the inhabitants of their respective countries. For example, property belonging to a Luxemburg citizen may have been transferred to France. The international agency should cooperate in this particular case with the Luxemburg national agency, and also with the French agency. If Belgian property has been transferred to Germany, the international agency should cooperate with the Belgian agency in handling this case. On the other hand, where an illegal transfer of property has taken place between the inhabitants of the Netherlands, for instance, only the Netherlands national agency should handle the case.

A specific problem arises as to the cooperation between the international agency and a neutral country. It would be desirable that the neutral countries should join an international plan for restitution of property. Indeed, collaboration of neutrals in the plan seems imperative because the German occupant has sold or otherwise transferred properties from occupied countries to neutral countries. Such a cooperation should be sanctioned by international agreement, which should provide also for the creation of property restitution agencies in neutral countries; or at least the neutral countries should allow the International Property Restitution Agency to establish its agents in their countries with special staffs to act as liaison officers between the agency and the authorities or inhabitants of the neutral countries.

The national and international property restitution agencies should employ administrative officials on their staffs and should apply administrative procedures. They should make investigations, through special investigators, into the background of the property transactions involved. In order to prevent changes in property before final decisions are made, the respective agency should be entitled to issue orders and regulations, especially concerning the freezing of property status for a given period. The agency should also be vested with the right to issue attachments on properties.

The procedure in the case of the national property restitution agencies, following the completion of the investigation, should be as follows: The investigator should submit the case to a special committee within the agency, which would then render a final decision on the restitution of title and rescission of the contract, as well as on other changes in the status of the property. Such a committee, which may be called "Property Restitution Committee," should be composed of three members, of which two should be members of the staff of the Property Restitution Agency and the third a judge who should be permanently connected with the committee and preside over it. However, provision should be made to the effect that, whereas the agency should not be limited in the scope of its investigations as to property relations, it should be limited as to the kind of cases in which it can render final decisions affecting the status of property. In the opinion of the author, it would be in accordance with the legal traditions of the respective countries if the Property Restitution Committee were empowered to render final decisions only in the smaller and simpler cases, whereas changes in title in the more complicated cases or in those representing larger amounts should be decided by the Restitution Tribunals described below. Moreover, in order to assure uniformity in judicial action and to stress judicial guaranties in the procedure of the property restitution committees, an arrangement should be made to the effect that the presiding judge of the Property Restitution Committee may always, at his discretion, refer the case before the committee to the respective Restitution Tribunal. Such a submission of the case could take place if the presiding judge does not agree with the opinion of the two lay members of the committee or if he thinks that the case is complicated for any reason, or if a matter of principle is involved.

The organization of, and procedure to be applied by, the International Property Restitution Agency should be similar to that of the national agency with one exception, that no Property Restitution Committee should be created in such agency because international cases by their nature are more complicated and they should always be determined by decision of the International Restitution Tribunal, described below, connected with the international agency.

10. *Property Restitution Tribunals.* As mentioned above, it seems to be appropriate that final decision as to all international cases, and the more involved national cases, should be rendered by tribunals composed of judges. These tribunals should be organized as autonomous benches within the international agency and the national property restitution agencies. The tribunal could have a small or large number of judges depending on the number of cases, but it should always render decisions in benches composed of three judges. As to the national agencies, the cases in which final decisions as to restitution should as a rule be rendered by such tribunals rather than by the committees, are, for example, in the view of the author, those involving the following: (*a*) real property; (*b*) corporations; (*c*) chattels of a high value (to be specifically defined); and (*d*) in addition, every other case that the presiding judge of the property restitution committee of the agency shall deem appropriate to transfer for final decision to the tribunal. As regards the International Agency, all property restitution decisions should be rendered by the International Tribunal. The International Tribunal should

be composed of experts in international law and persons who have had experience in international tribunals, international arbitration courts, etc.

To sum up: A National Property Restitution Agency would consist of three elements: (*a*) investigators; (*b*) Property Restitution Committee; (*c*) Property Restitution Tribunal. The International Property Restitution Agency would consist of two elements: (*a*) investigators; (*b*) the International Property Restitution Tribunal. The investigation as to property relations, as well as all attachments, would always be carried out by the national or international property restitution agency. In the case of a national agency, the final restitution decisions would be rendered in the less complicated cases by a property restitution committee of the agency, and in the more complicated cases, by a tribunal constituting an autonomous part of the agency. In cases before the International Property Restitution Agency, the tribunal of that agency would have exclusive jurisdiction in rendering final decisions in view of the more complicated nature of international cases. Moreover, if the international agency is cooperating with a national agency in cases involving that country and another country, the international tribunal, and not the national tribunal, should render the final decision.

Detailed procedural measures should be worked out in advance by an international commission. It is suggested that the following points of procedure should be borne in mind by such a commission:

(*a*) Time is of the essence in the post-war settlement of property cases, and, in order to heal as quickly as possible the wounds of war and not to disrupt the economic life by prolonged mass trials in civil cases, the decisions of property restitution committees and tribunals should be final.

(*b*) The records prepared by the investigators of the restitution agencies should be relied on as much as possible by the committees and tribunals, and the hearing of witnesses should be limited to the most essential questions.

CHAPTER VI

FINANCE

German Practices and the Plea of Military Necessity

Considered with reference to the well-established practices of civilized nations and the law as sanctioned by the letter and spirit of the Hague Regulations, the rôle of finance under German occupation has been completely reversed. An occupant is entitled, on the one hand, to undertake such measures in the financial field as will restore and ensure public order (which term also implies order in the financial relations of the population in question), and, on the other hand, to collect taxes, levies, and money contributions for the needs of the army or for the administration of the territory under occupation. The fact that such operations are sanctioned by law and custom presupposes that the financial resources of the occupied country—with the exception of "cash, funds, and realizable securities which are strictly the property of the State" (Article 53 of the Hague Regulations)—should be respected and serve the purposes of maintaining and ensuring order in the financial relations of its population. Accordingly, the financial resources of an occupied country as a whole should remain with the population of that country, and only a part of such resources may be appropriated by the occupant, subject to the above-mentioned limitations of the Hague Regulations. The German occupant, as stated above, has completely reversed this picture by taking over practically the whole of the financial resources of the occupied country and leaving to the population only a small part. In engaging in such practices the German occupant can hardly invoke the plea of military necessity because what he is undertaking is not merely a procedure of appropriation for the needs of the occupation forces but rather a mass exploitation and mass looting both for the needs of the German economy as a whole and for political purposes. That such is the case is seen from the application to the occupied countries of the German Four-Year Plan,[1] under which the administration of the economy of the occupied countries is mainly carried out. Formally speaking, the Four-Year Plan is a German institution developed in the pre-war period; it serves the economic needs of the German nation and not especially the needs of an occupying army in the sense of the Hague Convention.

In studying the actual financial setup under German occupation, it is not alone the measures relating to contributions, levies, and requisitions which

[1] See decree of the Führer and Chancellor of the Reich of October 12, 1939, for the Government General of Poland, below, p. 522.

are important; of even greater significance is the problem of the mechanism which has been created and developed in taking over the whole of the financial resources of the countries in question. The main elements of that mechanism are described in the paragraphs which follow.

I. Currency

1. *German Currency.* In the first period of occupation the German troops used special certificates as legal tender, called *Reichskreditkassenscheine,* in all the occupied countries.[1a] These certificates were used as legal tender in the occupied territories only, and there was a prohibition against importing them into Germany. They were issued by the Central Office of the Reich Credit Institutes (*Reichskreditkassen*), which is located in Berlin. This office is headed and managed by a directorial board consisting of at least two persons, and is supervised by a board of governors. The directorial board is appointed by the board of governors. Members of this board are: a deputy of the Minister of Finance, a deputy of the Minister of Economy, a deputy of the Supreme Commander of the Armed Forces (in order to keep in contact with the needs of the occupying armies), a representative of the commander in chief of each army of occupation, as well as members to be appointed by the President of the German Reichstag. The Reich Credit Institute in Berlin issues bills and coins. The bills and paper money are issued in denominations of fifty, twenty, five, and one Reichsmark, as well as fifty pfennigs. The coins are issued in amounts of ten and five pfennigs. An indication as to the amount issued may be found in the provision of the order of May 18, 1940, concerning Reich Credit Institutes,[2] to the effect that the Central Office may extend to the German Reich a loan not exceeding three billion Reichsmarks. Actually the Germans transgressed this limit as early as 1941, and in 1942 the amount of Reich Credit Institute notes issued was as high as five billion marks.[2a]

The local Reich Credit Institutes created in the occupied countries act as agencies of the Central Office in Berlin.[3] They are also authorized to regulate money and credit transactions in the occupied territories, and in particular to carry on the following business:

[1a] The German Reichsmark could not be used at all in Belgium. This shows a difference between the present occupation and that of 1914–18, when the Germans used also their own mark.

[2] Application of orders concerning the Reich Credit Institutes to the occupied territories of Belgium, Luxemburg, France, and the Netherlands. See below, p. 329.

[2a] See Bank for International Settlements, *Twelfth Annual Report, 1st April 1941–31st March 1942* (Basle, 1942), p. 129.

[3] The Reich Credit Institutes "which closely followed the German Army in the field, were manned by Reichsbank personnel (although the institutions were, of course, completely separate) and the management of the circulation of *Reichskreditkassenscheine* and their withdrawal were thus supervised by Reichsbank staff." Bank for International Settlements, *Eleventh Annual Report, 1st April 1940–31st March 1941* (Basle, 1941), p. 179.

a) Purchase and sell promissory notes and checks bearing the names of usually three, but not less than two, persons known to be solvent and assuming responsibility for these notes or checks. Notes shall mature not later than six months from the date of purchase.
b) Make loans for interest, usually for a period not exceeding six months, provided that due collateral is furnished.
c) Receive money without interest for purposes of transfer or deposit.
d) Transact any bank business, especially collection of promissory notes and other documents.
e) Accept for safe-deposit articles of value, especially securities.

The Reich Credit Institute currency was withdrawn at different periods in most of the occupied countries. The local central banking institutions were compelled by the occupant to exchange them into local currency. Thus, the local institutions of the occupied territories were forced to finance the invasion (see below).

2. *Local Currencies.* As to local currencies, a distinction was made between the incorporated areas and the non-incorporated areas. In the incorporated areas the local currencies were abolished and the Reichsmark was introduced as sole legal tender. The following exchange rates were set up in these areas for the exchange of the local currencies into German currency:

1 Reichsmark = 1.50 Austrian schillings
1 Reichsmark = 8.34 Czech crowns in the Sudeten
1 Reichsmark = 10.0 Czech crowns in the Protectorate of Bohemia and Moravia
1 Reichsmark = 2.0 Polish zlotys
1 Reichsmark = 1.43 Danzig gulden
1 Reichsmark = 2.50 Lithuanian lit[3a]
1 Reichsmark = 10.0 Luxemburg francs

In the non-incorporated countries the following rate was established:

1 Reichsmark = 2.0 Danish crowns
1 Reichsmark = 1.67 Norwegian crowns
1 Reichsmark = 0.75 Dutch gulden
1 Reichsmark = 12.50 Belgian francs
1 Reichsmark = 20.0 French francs
1 Reichsmark = 20.0 Yugoslav dinars
1 Reichsmark = 10.0 Slovakian crowns
1 Reichsmark = 20.0 Croatian kuna
1 Reichsmark = 10.0 Russian rubles
1 Reichsmark = 10.0 Ukrainian carbovanets

In comparison with pre-war exchange rates (before the invasion) the Reichsmark was generally overvalued in relation to the currencies of occupied countries.

[3a] As applied in Memel Territory.

This overvaluation creates for the occupant an additional purchasing power and allows him to obtain possession of the resources of the country at low prices. Moreover, the prices are also kept low through rigid price control. Thus the occupant, though he pays from time to time for goods and properties, enriches himself by the difference between the real prices and the artificial prices established through the above-mentioned devices. These devices amount, in consequence, to hidden contributions or requisitions, which are prohibited by Article 52 of the Hague Regulations.[4]

II. Central Banks and Currency Services

For the creation of legal tender in terms of local currency new banks of issue were instituted in the occupied countries as follows:

By the decree of December 15, 1939,[5] an issue bank was established in the Government General of Poland. The new bank is directed by a Polish president and deputies appointed by the Governor General, together with the German bank governor (*Bankdirigent*), who controls all the operations of the bank, especially with regard to the opening of credits and the fixing of interest rates. The bank issues its own notes, denominated in zlotys. The notes of the former Bank Polski and the notes issued by the Reich Credit Institutes have been gradually withdrawn. According to the decree concerning the Bank of Issue in Poland of December 15, 1939, coverage for the new notes was to include not only claims arising from discount and credit business, and German legal tender, as well as accounts maintained with the German Reichsbank or the German *Verrechnungskasse* (Clearing Office), but also a mortgage up to the amount of three billion zlotys on all real estate in the territory, with priority over all tax claims and other encumbrances.[6]

In Belgium a new bank of issue was constituted at Brussels on June 27, 1940, by a decree of the German military commander for Belgium and Northern France.[7] The bank, which is a joint stock company under Belgian law, has a capital of 150 million Belgian francs, subscribed by the Belgian commercial banks. It is noteworthy that the German currency, including notes of the Reich Credit Institutes, as well as credits with the German Reichsbank, are admitted as cover for the bank of issue in Brussels.

After the occupation of Yugoslavia and the division of the occupied territory into two states, Serbia (under German military administration) and Croatia (a puppet state previously under Italian protection and lately under German control), two new banks of issue were created in these terri-

[4] See the well-documented book of Ernst Feilchenfeld, *The International Economic Law of Belligerent Occupation* (Washington: Carnegie Endowment for International Peace, 1942), p. 82.

[5] See below, p. 537.

[6] *Ibid.*, p. 539.

[7] See below, p. 334.

tories to replace the former National Bank of Yugoslavia, which was forced into liquidation on May 29, 1941. On the same day a decree was issued establishing the Serbian National Bank, with headquarters in Belgrade. The new bank is under the direct control of the German Plenipotentiary for Economic Affairs, who appoints the Serbian governing directors; in addition, a German commissioner (*Bankdirigent*) acts in the Serbian National Bank, and without his approval no important transactions may be made. This bank proceeded to exchange all Yugoslav dinars and Reich Credit Institute notes for new Serbian dinars. The Serbian State handed over to the bank debt certificates to the amount of the notes exchanged. Thus the Serbian State, with the help of the Serbian National Bank, financed the first stages of German occupation, because the Reich Institute notes were exchanged, not into Reichsmarks but into new Serbian dinars.[8]

In the puppet state of Croatia, the Croatian State Bank was established by the decree of the Chief of the Croatian State under date of May 10, 1941.[9] The new bank issued a new currency (kuna). This bank also exchanged the old Yugoslav dinar notes and *Reichskreditkassenscheine* for the new kuna notes. Thus the Croatian State Bank was likewise compelled to finance the first stage of the German occupation.

In the Ostland the privilege of note issue remains with the Reich Credit Institutes. Thus the Reich Credit notes, as well as Russian rubles, are legal tender. All general business for the economic reconstruction of the Ostland is carried out by a specially created *Gemeinschaftsbank* with headquarters in Riga.

In the Reich Commissariat of the Ukraine a new Ukraine Central Bank was created on March 5, 1942, with headquarters at Rovno, in the Polish eastern province of Wolhynia. This bank issued a new currency, carbovanets (the old name of Ukrainian currency). The new notes are guaranteed, like the zlotys in the Polish Government General, by a general mortgage on land. In order to make the local population finance the military operations and the occupation, the new bank was compelled to exchange the Reich Credit Institute notes into the carbovanets.

For the purpose of absorbing the local currencies of the areas in the west incorporated into Germany, a *Landesbank und Girozentrale* was created by the amalgamation of five existing banks. Its head office is in Saarbrücken. The currency of this area consists, as mentioned above, of notes of the Reichsbank.[10]

The occupant has not only resorted to the creation of new central banks and sometimes also of auxiliary financial institutions but has also altered the statutes of the existing central banks, in order to make them more dependent on Germany. Thus, the law of 1937 governing the Nederlandsche

[8] See Bank for International Settlements, *Twelfth Annual Report*, p. 204.

[9] See below, p. 622.

[10] Bank for International Settlements, *Twelfth Annual Report*, p. 204.

Bank was altered in March, 1942. "As the bank's foreign bills and other foreign claims are almost exclusively in Reichsmarks this currency now ranks equally with gold as cover for the Dutch florin." [11]

*

The foregoing review of the central banks shows one common feature, namely, that they are not only called on to provide the population with legal tender but also mainly to finance the German war economy and the exports from the occupied countries to Germany. Evidence of this may be seen in the admission of the Reich Credit notes and clearing claims as cover for new issues. As to the item of clearing, it must be pointed out that because of the oppressive system of German trade in occupied Europe,[12] Germany owes huge amounts of money to the occupied countries.[13]

Furthermore, the central banks of the occupied countries, as mentioned above, were compelled to absorb the *Reichskreditkassenscheine*. This device amounts in fact to a contribution imposed upon the country, although it is not called by that name.

The specific organization of the central banks and their rôle in the administration of occupied Europe raises two essential problems, one in international law, the other in finance.

From the point of view of the Hague Regulations, the organization and functioning of the central banks represent a violation of international law. The occupant has the right and the duty to restore public order and safety in the occupied country. Obviously, public order also means order in economic and financial relations. It means the restoration of a currency system which functions in the orderly way necessary for the maintenance of a normal economic life in the occupied area. However, the occupant violates international law by creating a special currency system in order to enrich himself beyond the limits imposed by the Hague Regulations. He is entitled only to requisitions and contributions for the needs of the army, with due respect for the resources of the occupied country; he cannot legally strip the country of its financial and economic resources by a specially created financial mechanism.[14]

[11] See Bank for International Settlements, *Twelfth Annual Report*, p. 206.

[12] Lemkin, "The Legal Framework of Totalitarian Control over Foreign Economies," read before the Section of International and Comparative Law of the American Bar Association (1941). See also Lemkin, *Valutareglering och Clearing*, Stockholm University lectures (Stockholm: P. A. Norstedt & Söner, 1941); and below, section V of the present chapter.

[13] In the post-war picture, the interconnection of the cover of the banks of issue and the functioning of the clearing agreement concluded by Germany, as well as the clearing arrangements ordered by it, may be of importance. See below, section VIII of this chapter.

[14] The issues of local currency by specially created central banks in Belgium and Rumania during German occupation in the first World War gave rise to claims by the Belgian and Rumanian governments for indemnity because these governments, after the occupation, exchanged the new currencies for their own. These claims were settled as to Belgium and Germany by agreements between these two countries signed in Brussels on July 13, 1929, to the effect that Germany took over the obligation to pay Belgium 5,284,260,600 Belgian francs. As to Rumania, a convention was signed between Germany and Rumania on November 10, 1928, to the effect that both governments declared as settled the differences which

The fact that the gold foreign exchange reserves were removed from occupied Europe, in part by the governments-in-exile and in part through confiscation by Germany, as well as the fact that claims against Germany in the form of frozen clearing assets or *Reichskreditkassenscheine* were introduced as cover for the new issues of local currencies, makes it obvious that the new currencies have no financial foundations whatsoever. This dangerous situation is recognized not only by Germany's Axis partners [15] but also by Germany itself. Moreover, the Germans are trying to impress upon the occupied countries that this danger may be met only by a German victory in a war which Germany is fighting "in behalf of Europe." [16] Now this dependence of European currencies on German victory makes it obvious that after Germany is defeated the currencies of all the occupied countries and also of the dominated countries face a grave disaster.

III. Exchange Control

Exchange control was introduced in all the occupied countries.[17] An examination of the pattern of the German Exchange Control Law reveals two main aspects: (1) prohibition of the exportation of foreign currency, securities, and precious metals; and (2) surrender by the population of foreign exchange and gold to the state, which assumes a monopoly in dealing with foreign exchange.[18] Under these provisions the occupant introduced prohibition of free money circulation between Germany and the occupied countries, and ordered every inhabitant to turn in all foreign exchange, including gold as well as other precious metals. For such for-

arose from money issued by the Banca Generala under German occupation, and agreed that Germany should undertake to contribute to the stabilization of the Rumanian currency. The two above-mentioned treaties create a precedent for the legal obligation on behalf of the occupant to liquidate currencies issued by it during the occupation. See Boris Nolde, "La monnaie en droit international public," Académie de Droit International, *Recueil des Cours*, Vol. 27 (1929), pp. 306–12.

[15] As to Hungary, see *Südost Echo*, May 22, 1942: "The piling up of clearing balances has its limits in the danger for the currency which could arise from big advances given by central banks."

[16] "The European countries trading with Germany receive under the conditions of total European warfare somewhat fewer deliveries from Germany than they are exporting to Germany. Thus, a monetary indebtedness of Germany toward her neighbors is the result. Having a claim against a victorious Germany is no cause whatever for worry. In this way big amounts are frozen and will become liquid as soon as the war Germany is fighting for Europe has come to its victorious end. It is the same situation that exists with regard to our German non-saving accounts, which will be unblocked as soon as victory is achieved. Until then, however, the money is frozen and becomes as solid as iron." *Deutsche Allgemeine Zeitung*, May 14, 1942.

[17] Later on exchange control was abolished as between the incorporated areas and Germany as well as between the Netherlands and Germany.

[18] On different forms of exchange control, see Howard S. Ellis, *Exchange Control in Central Europe* (Cambridge: Harvard University Press, 1941); Lemkin, *La règlementation des paiements internationaux* (Paris: A. Pedone, 1939); also Lemkin, *Valutareglering och Clearing*, *op. cit.* As to the economic implications of exchange control on an international scale, see J. B. Condliffe, *The Reconstruction of World Trade* (New York: W. W. Norton & Co., 1940), containing also valuable materials on the twelfth session of the Bergen Conference of 1939, which was a most important conference on exchange control.

eign exchange and precious metals the occupant paid in inflated local money at official rates much below the actual equivalent of these valuables, and thus retained for himself the difference in value. All the inhabitants of the occupied countries were at the same time summoned to declare and to cede to the authorities the claims they had against foreigners or foreign states, even if non-belligerent. Thus the occupant became the owner of large amounts of foreign exchange and formally secured control of the financial claims of the inhabitants of the occupied countries against foreign countries.[19] The bank deposits were frozen and payments could be effected only by special permission. Such freezing served two purposes: (1) to check inflation by limiting spending; and (2) to use the unfreezing as a means of political pressure.

The status under international law of exchange control manipulations is the following: An occupant is entitled to prohibit the traffic of money between the occupied territory and countries abroad, because such traffic may be of assistance to the enemy, and because the flight of money abroad may result in a disruption of the monetary system and thus in a disruption of order and safety, which he is called upon to safeguard. An occupant may not, however, compel the inhabitants to cede to him privately owned valuables, because this amounts to a violation of the rules established for the protection of private property by the Hague Regulations.

IV. Confiscation of Gold Reserves and Foreign Exchange

The gold left in the vaults of the central banks of the occupied countries was immediately confiscated by the German occupant. Thus, the Germans have seized gold and foreign exchange reserves of the Bank of Austria in an amount equal to about 80 million dollars. The Germans also took possession of 25 million dollars in gold held in Czechoslovakia's account by the Bank of England in the Bank for International Settlements at Basle, Switzerland. This gold was released in 1939 on the promise of German authorities to transfer it to the Bank of the Protectorate of Bohemia and Moravia. However, Germany merely gave the bank of the Protectorate scrip in an equivalent amount in the form of gold deposit certificates, and never returned the gold itself. When a new bank of issue was created by the puppet state of Slovakia, that bank made a request for its share of Czechoslovakian gold but Germany did not accede to this request. Some gold was likewise seized in France, but accurate figures as to the amount seized in Paris are not available. The Germans also came into possession of some 228 million dollars in gold, which had been deposited in France by the National Bank of Belgium soon after the invasion of Belgium. When the fall of Paris was imminent, the Belgian Government

[19] Freezing legislation passed by the United Nations, and by the United States even before the creation of the United Nations, frustrated the German plans of obtaining control over many of the foreign assets belonging to the population of occupied territories.

ordered the French National Bank to send this gold to the United States, but, despite these orders, the gold was sent to Dakar. After the defeat of France, the German occupant demanded that this gold be brought back from Dakar and handed over to the Germans, which was actually done.[20] The assignees of the Bank of Belgium then obtained an attachment on French assets in the United States for the amount of this gold.[21] From the other countries occupied by Germany the gold was exported in due time to the United States and to Great Britain, so that the invader could not get hold of it. Freezing legislation concerning the assets of the occupied countries enacted by the United States and Great Britain prevented the German occupant from acquiring the gold and foreign exchange belonging to the occupied countries and deposited within the jurisdiction of the United States and of Great Britain.

The confiscation of gold and foreign exchange by the occupant raises the question of its validity under international law. According to the Hague Regulations, the occupant may only "take possession of cash, funds, and realizable securities which are strictly the property of the State" (Article 53). *A contrario*, the property of individuals (Article 46), as well as the property of municipalities (Article 56), cannot be confiscated. The problem of legality of the confiscations of gold from the central banks is connected with the legal question whether the central bank involved is a state bank or a privately owned corporation. As regards the four central banks from which the gold was seized by the Germans, that is, in Austria, Czechoslovakia, Belgium, and France, those of Austria, Belgium, and France are privately owned while of the bank of Czechoslovakia, two thirds are privately owned and one third is owned by the Czechoslovak Government. In the case of Austria, part of the shares belonged to municipalities, the rest to savings banks, commercial banks, and individuals. As the property of municipalities may not be confiscated, the seizure of the Austrian gold and foreign exchange was illegal. Similarly, the seizure of the Belgian, French, and Czechoslovak gold was in violation of international law.

V. Clearing as an Instrumentality of Exploitation of Foreign Trade and Labor

In organizing "foreign" trade in occupied Europe, Germany made use of clearing,—an instrumentality of payments in international trade,—which it had applied many years before the war, mainly in its economic penetra-

[20] See Ernest S. Hediger, "Nazi Exploitation of Occupied Europe," *Foreign Policy Reports*, June 1, 1942 (New York: Foreign Policy Association, Incorporated), Vol. XVIII, No. 6, pp. 70, 71.

[21] See Albany dispatch of March 5, 1942, to *New York Times*, stating that the Court of Appeals had ruled that the State Supreme Court has jurisdiction to hear and determine the action brought by the Bank of France against the assignees of the Bank of Belgium in the matter of some $228,000,000 in gold now in the possession of the Federal Reserve Bank. *New York Times*, March 6, 1942, p. 29, col. 6.

tion into southeastern Europe and Latin America. Clearing has had quite an evolution in German foreign trade practices, and one may distinguish three stages [22] thereof: (1) inducive stage; (2) oppressive stage; (3) spoliative stage. In the *inducive* stage of clearing Germany tried to penetrate into the markets of a foreign country by granting to that country especially favorable exchange rate conditions and also by establishing low prices for the articles exported. In the *oppressive* stage, Germany made a practice of freezing clearing assets and of unfreezing them later in consideration of further privileges in trade extorted thus from the country involved. In the last or *spoliative* stage, Germany uses clearing in order to import goods without paying at all. In this latter stage, which has now been reached, Germany has frozen the clearing assets of the occupied countries for the so-called "duration." In the present situation, German trade is backed in the occupied countries by political power, and therefore economic and financial considerations count only to the extent that they are useful to Germany.[23]

The occupant has integrated the occupied countries into the foreign trade which is conducted by Germany as the controlling power. Though clearings are mostly through Berlin, this trade is carried on in four directions: (1) between Germany and one occupied country; (2) between two different occupied countries; (3) between an occupied country and an Axis country other than Germany; and (4) between an occupied country and a neutral country, as, for example, between Norway or Belgium and Sweden. For all these transactions, the instrumentality of clearing has been adopted.

1. *Bilateral Clearing.* According to clearing procedure, no cash passes from one country to another for shipment of goods or for rendering services, but the payments for imports and exports in one country are set off against the payments for imports and exports in the other country participating in the trade transaction. The normal function of clearing presupposes the existence of four participants, two each in two trade transactions—viz., an importer and an exporter in each of the countries involved. To illustrate: A Dutchman exports butter to Germany. Another Dutchman imports coal from Germany. A German imports butter from the Netherlands and another German exports coal to the Netherlands. According to the normal procedure of clearing, the Dutch importer in effect pays the Dutch exporter through special accounts, and the German importer likewise pays the German exporter through special accounts. These trade accounts for such transactions are concentrated in special institutions called "clearing institutes" (the German Clearing Institute is called *Verrechnungskasse*), one in

[22] The evolution of clearing in German trade practices is described in Lemkin, "The Legal Framework of Totalitarian Control over Foreign Economies," *op. cit.*

[23] "National Socialist foreign trade could not go its own way, but had to get its direction from the political side. . . . It was the National Socialist foreign trade policy from the very beginning that the national economies of her neighbors should be coordinated with the needs of Greater Germany." *Der Deutsche Volkswirt,* June 12, 1942.

each country participating in the trade. Periodically, the balances of trade transactions between the two countries must be equalized, and only then can the clearing institutes of each country proceed to pay out to the parties the amounts due for their exports, which amounts are normally taken from the money which the importers pay into the clearing institute. Therefore, for the full normal functioning of clearings, the exports from one country as a whole must be equal in their value to the imports from the other country as a whole in given periods of time.

The above is an illustration of a normally functioning clearing. In the course of its occupation of various countries during this war, Germany has made clearings one of the most efficient institutions for financial and economic exploitation of the occupied countries. This was done by Germany's substitution of long-term and hopeless or so-called "frozen" credits for actual payments. Because Germany imports from the occupied countries more than it exports to them,—indeed, in great part it only imports, without exporting anything at all to such countries,—there is practically no possibility of balancing the payments within the clearing institutes. To illustrate by another example: A Dutchman exports butter to Germany, while a Dutch coal importer cannot get from Germany as much coal as he was promised, or he cannot get coal at all. In this situation, the German importer of butter pays to the German *Verrechnungskasse*, to the credit of the Dutch exporter of butter, the amount due; but since practically no coal is available for export to the Netherlands, the Dutch importer of coal for long periods has no occasion to pay for its import. Such being the case, the Dutch exporter of butter, who normally would have been paid by the Dutch clearing office out of the amount paid by the Dutch importer of coal, cannot be paid for his butter. But the German occupant is eager to have the exporting of Dutch butter to Germany continued; and since the continuation of the export is dependent upon the continuation of payments to the exporter, the German occupant compels the Dutch Clearing Institute to pay out the sum to the Dutch exporter anyway, and a credit therefor is entered in the German *Verrechnungskasse* in Berlin. Then, in order to meet such financial requirements, the Berlin Clearing Institute must get money from the National Bank of the Netherlands. As the National Bank of the Netherlands—like every bank in the world—has limited resources, new issues of Dutch currency must be undertaken in order to meet the German demands. Because of this procedure, which prevails in all the occupied countries to a greater or less degree, there is a vast scale of exploitation of the financial resources of the occupied countries by misuse of the institution of clearing. The function of the clearing institutes under these conditions amounts practically to the levying of large-scale contributions. Because the local clearing institutes must meet large currency requirements in order to finance exports to Germany, the bank of issue in each occupied country is called upon to expand the currency, which amounts to unchecked inflation.

This procedure creates for Germany advantages not only in the financial, but also in the political, field. In countries of forced collaboration, where the atmosphere of false peace is being fostered, the occupant is eager not to injure directly and openly the interests of the individual; what he does injure directly is the whole financial and economic structure of the country. For psychological reasons, the exporters in the occupied countries are less dissatisfied with such a procedure than they would be by a procedure denying them payments at all. The harm done to the economy of the occupied country must be determined by the exporter on the basis of a clear understanding of the financial implications of this procedure rather than by a feeling of immediate harm. He is paid for his exports by credits advanced by his national bank of issue, and when he receives the money from his own bank he does not realize how inflated it becomes because his own bank of issue has paid for his exports to Germany. Indeed, it is only when he understands the long-range effects of the transaction that he appreciates the true nature of the occupant's methods.

2. *Multilateral Clearing*. The trade of one occupied country with another occupied country, or even with a neutral or Axis country, is also being carried out through the instrumentality of clearing. In such cases, not one but three clearing institutes may be involved, namely, the clearing institute of the occupied country, the clearing institute of the neutral or Axis country, and the German institute in Berlin.[24] The German Clearing Institute by this means acquires control over all transactions in which the occupied countries are involved. Some authors call it *central clearing*. Germany's advantages from the central clearing are numerous. On the financial side, Germany controls the exchange rates throughout almost all of Europe. By controlling the clearing balances of the occupied countries, Germany is able to freeze credits entered in favor of one party to a transaction and to use such credits as a temporary compensation in its own transactions with occupied countries, which it exploits by overdrawing imports from them. For example, Germany has imported large quantities from Belgium without exporting to that country, with the result that the exporters from Belgium have not been paid by Germany. But Belgium has a clearing agreement with the Government General of Poland. When the Government General of Poland imports goods from Belgium in exchange for goods which the Government General sends to Belgium, the German Clearing

[24] In some cases, however, trade between an occupied country and a foreign country is functioning directly between these two countries. An example of such clearing is provided by Belgium and Russia (before the latter went to war with Germany). The clearing agreement between Belgium and the U.S.S.R., which was established by the decrees of the German commander in Belgium published in the *Verordnungsblatt*, 1941, No. 40, provides for direct clearing relations between the clearing office in Brussels and the State Bank of the Union of Soviet Socialist Republics in Moscow.

Institute transfers the credit of the Polish Clearing Institute into Germany's balance with Belgium. Thus a partial adjustment is made as to frozen Belgian clearing balances in Germany. But the burden of this adjustment is borne by the Government General of Poland.

It is obvious that the controlling power of the occupant is being exercised in such a way that the most important and essential products of the occupied countries are being excluded from trade and kept at the disposal of the occupant.

Consequently, on the commercial side clearing gives to Germany a dominant position, and Germany makes use of this advantage by offering products of the occupied countries to neutral countries and obtaining in such a way reciprocal economic and political advantages.

3. *Freezing of the Savings of Foreign Labor.* Clearing as established by Germany in occupied countries provided not only for the transfer of payments for goods, but also for the transfer of payments for services, such as savings of foreign laborers in Germany, transportation costs, patent rights, and so on. The foreign workers, after having spent a part of their wages for subsistence in their place of work, try to send home some savings in order to help their families or other relatives. However, the *Verrechnungskasse* treats these payments of foreign workers the same as it does the payments of German importers to exporters from occupied countries, that is to say, it freezes them. In some instances the German authorities order the clearing offices of the occupied countries to advance to the families of the workers sums corresponding to the savings, but even this is by no means the general practice. Thus the occupied countries not only finance the exports to Germany, but also pay their own people working in Germany.

4. *Clearing Legislation and International Law.* The occupant has adapted the existing legislation in the occupied country to the requirements of clearing as instituted by Germany. Some of these adaptations may be cited. Because clearing has been made the exclusive channel of "foreign" trade and foreign payments, an order was issued by the Dutch Secretary General of the Ministry of Finance on March 26, 1941, prohibiting any other way of payment than through the Netherlands Clearing Institute.[25] Furthermore, an earlier order of October 10, 1940, introduced the possibility of extending financial aid to enterprises "which find themselves financially embarrassed through their inability to enforce claims arising out of shipments abroad, as a result of the extraordinary circumstances prevailing or of orders freezing accounts abroad as a result of these conditions." [26] A similar decree as to the exclusion of other ways of payments abroad than through clearing was introduced in Denmark on June 25, 1940.[27]

The institution of clearing raises several questions under international law. Obviously, clearing has become a subtle device for extorting huge con-

[25] See below, p. 490. [26] See below, p. 489. [27] See below, p. 378.

tributions or forced loans in a disguised form from the populations of the occupied countries.[28] For the purposes of such exploitation, the occupant—as in the case of Denmark, for example—grants to the occupied country a certain kind of sovereignty in order to be able to present the clearing exploitation device before the population of that country in the form of an agreement. It is plain that agreements of this kind entered into under duress are invalid, because they do not represent the real will of the country. For purposes of clarification of the law in the future, the Hague Regulations should be amended to the effect that the occupant should not have the right to impose additional burdens upon the occupied country, even through arrangements having the form of international agreements entered into with the occupied country.

VI. Taxation

The occupant may collect taxes only for the purpose of covering the expenses of administration of the occupied territory. Article 48 of the Hague Regulations provides that the legal basis and assessment for taxation shall be, as far as is possible, the same as they were at the time when the national government ruled the country.

According to the underlying principle of taxation observed in the occupied countries before their occupation, every inhabitant had the right to equal treatment before the law, and the assessment of taxes could vary only according to the financial situation of the taxpayer. The occupant, however, has changed this principle, introducing the practice of political discrimination in taxation as in other fields. Particularly is this true in incorporated Poland, where taxation is an instrumentality of German colonization. On December 9, 1940, a decree concerning tax abatement for the benefit of the eastern incorporated areas was promulgated,[29] and the following measures were introduced decreasing taxes for German settlers in Poland: (1) Germans may deduct three thousand marks from income for tax purposes; (2) they are exempt from the war addition to the income tax; (3) they are exempt from the defense tax; (4) their exemption from the property tax may be tripled; (5) they are excused from a tax which may be levied on the acquisition of land; (6) they are exempt from the sales tax; (7) they are excused from the inheritance tax on property originating elsewhere in the Reich or abroad and transferred to the incorporated Polish areas for investment or settlement; (8) municipal taxes are reduced for Germans; and (9) German business establishments in the incorporated Polish areas are granted a number of other tax privileges.

[28] The sums extorted by the Germans in occupied Europe through the misuse of clearing in trade relations with occupied countries is estimated by the British Ministry of Economic Warfare at the amount of $5,200,000,000. *New York Times*, October 29, 1943, p. 3, col. 8.

[29] See below, p. 516.

It is true that the occupant may in exceptional cases change the rules of assessment, because Article 48 of the Hague Regulations, as mentioned above, uses the words "as far as is possible." However, such changes must be necessitated by the needs of the administration of the occupied country, and colonizing the occupied country by nationals of the occupant is not within the scope of such administration. Therefore the tax practices as to exemptions for Germans are illegal.

The rules of tax assessment were also changed in Belgium by the order concerning surrendering of non-ferrous metals, of October 20, 1941,[30] issued by the military commander. This order introduced tax credits for Belgians who surrender non-ferrous metals. The Belgian Treasury was compelled to collaborate in obtaining such metals for Germany and, as a result of the reduction in taxes incident to the surrender of scrap metals, it is actually the Belgian Treasury which pays for the scrap.

Moreover, the tax rates were substantially raised in many countries, especially in Poland.[31]

VII. Costs of Occupation

The occupant is levying contributions of considerable sums in the occupied countries in the form of so-called "costs of occupation." Not all the figures are available. According to the *World Economic Survey* of the League of Nations for 1939–41,[32] the figures available are the following:

	£ sterling (at pre-war rates)	*National currencies (000,000's omitted)*	*Reichsmark (at new rates)*
France	827	146,000	7,300
Belgium	75	2,062	825
Netherlands	54	475	630
Denmark	26	582	280
Norway	68	1,353	810
Total	1,050		9,845

Denmark, however, was not formally obliged to pay occupation costs, although it was in practice compelled to pay them, since the Danish National Bank had to make advances to the German authorities to cover all the expenditures of the latter in Denmark. As to the legality of the German occupation costs, it must be stated that, according to Article 49 of the Hague Regulations, contributions for occupation costs may be levied only "for the needs of the army or of the administration of the territory in question." Actually the Germans, especially in France, have been using the high contributions demanded for occupation costs not only for their strictly

[30] See below, p. 327. [31] See below, chapter on "Poland."

[32] (Geneva, 1941), p. 156. See also Ernest S. Hediger, "Nazi Exploitation of Occupied Europe," *op. cit.*, pp. 76, 77.

military expenditures but also for various other purposes, such as acquiring movable goods and capital assets, including real estate and shares in French enterprises." [33] Consequently, such a misuse of the institution of levying contributions for occupation costs is a violation of international law.

VIII. Liquidation Agency for Occupation Finance

The foregoing review of the financial mechanism created by the German occupant for the exploitation of Europe leads to one obvious conclusion. The financial institutions of the occupied countries and their whole financial system have been completely reversed and have not only been subjected to German control but have also been closely bound up with, and made dependent upon, German financial institutions. The currencies of the occupied countries have their cover mainly in German assets. Clearing claims against the *Verrechnungskasse* are a common plague of the financial structure of the occupied countries. Thus, a community of bitter experience in disaster and exploitation has created a similarity of interests in all the occupied countries. This interdependence and interconnection of the financial claims of all the occupied countries against the German occupant is stressed even more by the institution of multilateral or central clearing. The financial structure of occupied Europe has been forcibly "regionalized" by the occupant in relation to the rest of the world. Therefore, for practical reasons the liquidation of the financial side of the occupation must be carried out through an institution of a correspondingly regional character.

For a certain period after Germany's defeat, the financial situation of the countries under occupation should be treated as one whole for purposes of liquidation. The *Verrechnungskasse*, which is the greatest debtor of the occupied countries, may have claims against neutrals or even other Axis countries. The Reichsbank and the Reich Credit Institute, which have forced German currency upon the central banks as coverage, may have a certain amount of valuable assets. Such claims and assets as are available after German defeat should be placed at the disposal of the financial institutions of the occupied countries in order to cover German debts owed to these countries and their inhabitants. This summary and direct procedure is necessary in order to meet an emergency situation in the occupied countries, without awaiting the long-range plans for financial reconstruction to be undertaken on an international scale.

Certain examples may illustrate the emergency nature of the action pro-

[33] Concerning occupation costs, see also Thomas Reveille, *The Spoil of Europe* (New York: W. W. Norton & Co., 1941), pp. 103–9.

According to recent estimates by the British Ministry of Economic Warfare, the total amounts levied on the occupied countries of Europe by the German Government, whether for occupation costs or other charges, are estimated at £3,200,000,000. For the purposes of these calculations the mark is taken at 13⅓ to the pound sterling. London *Times*, October 27, 1943, p. 8, col. 2.

posed. As mentioned above, the Germans have blocked, in the form of frozen clearing assets, the savings of millions of imported foreign workers intended for their families left behind in misery and distress. In some instances the clearing institutes of the occupied countries were obliged to advance certain amounts to the families in inflated currency without sufficient purchasing power. In other instances even that was not done. In these situations it is only just that the assets of the *Verrechnungskasse*, for example, should be made immediately available to the families of the workers, which need the money for subsistence. If such action is delayed while the question of pooling assets for purposes of reparations is subjected to a highly political and controversial discussion, this will mean a retarding of a very useful and humane action.

Examples of this type may be multiplied. The author therefore proposes that a Liquidation Agency for Occupation Finance should be created. Such an agency, with branches in every occupied country, should in the main carry on the following activities:

1. Elaboration of a common plan for liquidation of financial measures of occupation.
2. Registration of all claims deriving from German measures of occupation.
3. Registration of German financial assets, especially of the clearing saldos (*Clearingspitzen*).
4. Liquidation of mutual trade claims between one occupied country and another as carried out through the *Verrechnungskasse.*
5. Distribution of German financial assets for the purpose of satisfying claims of the occupied countries against Germany as deriving from financial measures of occupation.
6. Collection and distribution of related information among the interested occupied countries.
7. Cooperation with property restitution agencies and other agencies to be established by the United Nations.

Because the activities of such an agency may encroach upon the province of general policies towards the defeated occupant, it should include representatives not only of the occupied countries but of certain other members of the United Nations as well. Finally, it should be emphasized that a Liquidation Agency for Occupation Finance would prove useful to every international institution which is planned for general reconstruction of international finance in that it would provide the first stepping-stone for such reconstruction.

CHAPTER VII

LABOR

Labor has been a subject of primary concern of the German occupant, and German labor policy in the occupied countries reveals several definite objectives. Thus, labor is mobilized in order to maintain and increase production in industry and agriculture to serve the German war effort. Deportation of labor to Germany also serves the purpose of replacing German workers to be released for the front.[1] By deporting millions of able-bodied men and women from the occupied countries, Germany moreover hopes to disrupt centers of political resistance to the occupant,[2] on the one hand; and on the other hand, by separating families and keeping the men far away from their homes, a policy of depopulation is being pursued.[3] In the introduction of a régime of forced labor for Jews under specially organized unhealthy conditions, the occupant endeavors thereby to liquidate physically a great part of the Jewish population. That the policy with respect to Jewish labor is not based primarily on economic considerations is admitted in the statement of the occupant that it serves educational purposes.[4] In order to carry out the above-mentioned policies, detailed legislation has been enacted by the German authorities and, under pressure of the occupant, also by puppet governments or headless governments.

CONTROL OF LABOR

Control of labor is in the hands of German authorities, who have special officials handling labor matters. Thus, in Poland, there is a special department for labor in the office of the Governor General, as well as special departments in the offices of the governors of districts, and labor offices in every city. In the Netherlands there is a special state labor office in the Ministry of Social Welfare. In Belgium control of labor for purposes of

[1] On November 6, 1941, before the Conference of the International Labor Organization, President Roosevelt said: "To replace Nazi workers shipped to the front and to meet the gigantic needs of her total war effort, Nazi Germany has imported about two million foreign civilian laborers."—*White House Press Release*, November 6, 1941.

[2] Considerations of military safety seemed to play an important rôle also in Germany's practice of deporting labor in the first World War from occupied Belgium. See statement by General Ludendorff: "The existence of a large mass of unemployed labour is a danger to public safety. With a view to averting that danger, men may be sent compulsorily to any place where they are needed; whether at home or abroad is immaterial."—*The General Staff and Its Problems*, by General Ludendorff, Vol. I, pp. 156, 157. Quoted from H. de Watteville, "The Military Administration of Occupied Territory in Time of War," *Transactions of the Grotius Society*, Vol. VII (London, 1922), pp. 146–47.

[3] See below, chapter on "Genocide."

[4] See order of December 12, 1939, below, p. 544; see also below, chapter on "The Legal Status of the Jews."

local industries is in the hands of labor offices. However, if labor is to be shipped to Germany, the control is exercised by the field commander having jurisdiction in the given district.[5]

Control over the indiviual laborer is effected by the use of a work book (*Arbeitsbuch*) or a work card (*Arbeitskarte*). The latter is a certificate on which the employment schedules of the bearer are listed and his employment status set forth. Work books or cards have been introduced in most of the occupied areas.[6]

Freedom to make and break labor contracts has been abolished throughout all occupied countries. Employment and separation in all enterprises must have the previous consent of the labor office. This provision applies in the Government General of Poland even with respect to the employment of relatives.[7] Wages were originally frozen at the level of the date preceding the invasion of the occupied country. Later the labor offices established wages at a certain level which could not be changed.

Dissolution of labor contracts and the changing of labor conditions, especially wages and hours, without permission of the labor office are subject to penalties. Especially severe is the punishment for lockouts and strikes. Employers conniving with employees to close down enterprises, as well as picketers, are liable to penalties of imprisonment or hard labor, and in serious cases even to the death penalty.[8]

PROCUREMENT OF LABOR

For the procurement of labor, different procedures are used. The most drastic, which is applied in Poland and in areas occupied during the present Russo-German war, consists of labor conscription. Polish inhabitants of the Government General between the ages of eighteen and sixty years are subject to compulsory public labor.[9] The district governor may at his discretion extend the compulsory labor requirements for the Polish inhabitants of the Government General to juveniles between fourteen and eighteen years of age.[10] In countries of "forced" collaboration such as the Netherlands, Norway, France, and Belgium, the puppet or headless governments

[5] See *Verordnungsblatt*, 1942, No. 87.

[6] In the Government General of Poland and Ostland work cards are mainly used for labor control purposes. The workers are required to give their cards into the keeping of their employers while employed and to report all changes of name or address for entry on their cards. Employers must retain the work cards of workers in their employ, permitting employees to inspect their cards once a month, and must enter on the cards the name, location, and type of enterprise in which they are engaged, the date of employment of each employee, changes in address or the type of work performed by him, and the date of separation. All entries on work cards must be reported to the labor office, and the cards must be relinquished to the labor office if the possessor is transferred, has died, or has reached eighty years of age. *Verkündungsblatt für das Ostland*, 1940, No. 15.

[7] See order of February 22, 1940, below, p. 547.

[8] Order of the Reich Commissioner for the Netherlands, May 19, 1941, below, p. 496. See also order of the military commander in France, of November 6, 1941, below, p. 392.

[9] See decree of October 26, 1939, below, p. 542.

[10] See decree of December 14, 1939, below, p. 545.

are compelled by the occupant to refuse unemployment relief to persons who are not willing to go to Germany to work. Also, the device of refusing ration cards for people who do not accept work in Germany is widely practised. However, later on, labor conscription was also gradually introduced in these countries. Thus, in the Netherlands, a decree was published stating that all the inhabitants of the occupied Netherlands might be required by the district labor offices to perform labor for a specified time.[11] The place of service was at first limited to the Netherlands, but this restriction was eliminated in March, 1942.[12] The implementation of this order specified that all Dutch youths of both sexes between the ages of eighteen and twenty-five years were to perform labor services for six months.[13] In October, 1942, labor conscription was introduced in Belgium for men between eighteen and fifty years of age and for women between twenty-one and thirty-five.[14] Labor conscription serves mainly the purpose of exporting labor to Germany.[15]

Another means of procurement of labor is through the so-called Reconstruction Services, which assign their members to service on public works. The Reconstruction Service is headed by a Labor Commandant and is supposed to be a service of honor on behalf of the nation. At the beginning it was presumed that members of the demobilized armed forces should be provided first of all with work through these services.[16]

WAGES

1. *Economic Background*. As stated above, wages were generally frozen on the level of the date preceding the invasion. Only slight increases were allowed in the different countries. In this connection, it is important to stress that the purchasing power of money has decreased because of inflationary processes, and prices in some countries have increased—especially in the "black market"—by very large percentages. A picture of wages is given, for example, in the wage scale order for the forest industry in the Government General of Poland, dated February 7, 1941.[17] According to this order the following wages per hour are paid:

[11] *Verordnungsblatt* for the Netherlands, 1941, p. 152.
[12] *Ibid.*, 1942, p. 155. [13] *Ibid.*, 1941, p. 370, and 1942, p. 178.
[14] See *Verordnungsblatt* for Belgium, 1942, No. 87.
[15] "They [the Nazis] have changed the occupied countries to great slave areas for the Nazi rulers. Berlin is the principal slave-market of the world."—President Roosevelt, *White House Press Release*, November 6, 1941.

According to figures given by Eugene M. Kulischer, *The Displacement of Population in Europe* (Montreal: International Labour Office, 1943), p. 160, the number of civilian workers from the occupied countries employed in Germany at various dates from the end of 1939 to the beginning of 1943 amounted to approximately 4,454,000. The figures given by country are as follows: Poland, 1,300,000; Denmark, 48,000; Netherlands, 300,000; Norway, 2,000; Belgium, 300,000; France, 400,000; Yugoslavia, 250,000; Greece, 34,000; U.S.S.R., 1,500,000; Protectorate of Bohemia and Moravia, 200,000; Slovakia, 120,000.
[16] See order concerning the Netherlands Reconstruction Service, July 30, 1940, below, p. 494. This service was dissolved fifteen months later (*Verordnungsblatt*, 1941, p. 376).
[17] See below, p. 550.

1. Male
   21 years or older .... 0.50 zloty
   17 years or older .... 0.40 zloty
   less than 17 years old .... 0.26 zloty
2. Female
   18 years or older .... 0.36 zloty
   16 years or older .... 0.26 zloty
   less than 16 years old .... 0.22 zloty

When one considers that the Polish zloty before the war was equal to 20 cents at the official rate and but 10 cents at an unofficial rate, it is seen that the workers in the highest-paid brackets receive in American money (computed at the unofficial rate) 5 cents per hour per man and 3.6 cents per hour per woman. In the lowest brackets a man receives 2.6 per hour and a woman 2.2. In Poland the prices of commodities are believed to have increased from 400 to 500 per cent and for some articles, such as butter and meat, approximately 1000 per cent. The cost-of-living index in Warsaw during the first ten months of occupation gives the following figures:[18]

	1939		*1940*		
Commodity Group	August	December	March	May	July
General	100	269	463	546	433
Foodstuffs	100	278	614	743	561

In 1942 the price for one kilogram or about two pounds of butter was around 35 zlotys and for one kilogram of pork, around 32 zlotys on the "black market." (The rations in these commodities are so low that they are practically non-existent for the local population.) According to this computation, a worker in the lower bracket would have to work eight and one-half days in order to buy one pound of butter, and to buy a pound of pork he would have to do six days' work. The foregoing details give a picture of starvation wages for Polish labor. The conditions in the countries occupied in western Europe are better but still under the normal level.

2. *Racial Differentiation.* In the countries occupied in the east, especially in Poland, there is a difference in the wages paid to local labor and to German labor, as evidenced in the decree of November 23, 1939,[19] concerning wage scales for craftsmen in public service in the Government General, and in the wage scale decree for German construction workers, of March 5, 1940.[20] According to the latter decree, such workers as come from Germany to work in the Government General are paid the same wages as they received in their places of employment at home.

In the Ostland the Jews are not allowed to receive wages, and employers of Jews must pay a special fee to the German authorities.[20a]

[18] *Concise Statistical Year-Book of Poland, September, 1939–June, 1941* (Glasgow: Polish Ministry of Information, 1941), p. 108.

[19] See below, p. 543. [20] *Verordnungsblatt*, 1940, II, p. 159. [20a] See below, p. 311.

Special regulations were issued on June 30, 1942,[21] for eastern workers imported to Germany, and on July 14, 1942,[22] for workers imported to Belgium, from the Reich Commissariat for the Ukraine, from the General Commissariat for White Russia, and from the territories to the east of the above-mentioned administrative units as well as to the east of the Baltic States. The above-mentioned decrees contain a special schedule for wages. According to the schedule, the eastern worker actually receives for himself only a small amount of what the employer pays out. A special sum from his wages is deducted to pay for his subsistence, and the employer pays the main equivalent of the work performed—and this is especially true with respect to the higher wage brackets—not to the worker himself but to the German State in the form of a special Eastern Worker's Tax (*Ostarbeiterabgabe*). Hence, under the wage scale schedule in question, which is attached to the above-mentioned decrees, the equivalent of the work is divided into three parts: (1) for subsistence; (2) allowance for the worker himself; and (3) the Eastern Worker's Tax for the state. To illustrate: Where a German worker receives wages ranging from 4.25 to 4.40 Reichsmarks a day, the eastern worker is paid 2.60 for work of a like nature (of which he actually receives 1.10 Reichmarks, since 1.50 are deducted for subsistence), and the approximate difference between the German's normal wage and the 2.60 wage of the eastern worker is paid to the German State by the employer (*Ostarbeiterabgabe*). This sum amounts, in effect, to a form of taxation for using foreign labor. The German State does not permit its citizen (the employer) to benefit from the low wages paid to imported cheap labor, but takes for itself such benefits. The amounts which the employer has to pay to the state increase in a special progression. Thus, while no such payments are required in connection with the six lowest wage brackets, they range upward in the higher brackets until they exceed the wages actually paid the eastern workers by 200 per cent and even more. Employers in agriculture, however, pay to the state only half of the normal Eastern Worker's Tax.

RESTRICTION ON SOCIAL LEGISLATION

The above-mentioned labor system introduced by the occupant superseded a considerable body of progressive labor legislation in many of the occupied countries. These institutions of progressive social legislation were abolished by the occupant. For example, by the orders of December 16, 1939, and March 7, 1940,[23] claims for payments under the Polish social security law were nullified. Instead of legally established claims, these two decrees introduced some unemployment benefits for which no legal claim can be made. Legal rights were replaced by the grace of the occupant, in order to enable him to use security benefits for political purposes.

[21] See below, p. 556. [22] *Verordnungsblatt* for Belgium, 1942, p. 966.
[23] See orders concerning social security in the Government General, below. pp. 546, 548.

Labor unions were abolished in Poland at the same time that all associations were suppressed. In the areas occupied in the west, labor unions were put under German control and were also Nazified from within.

THE LABOR RÉGIME UNDER INTERNATIONAL LAW

The labor legislation and labor practices introduced by the occupant are in violation of international law. According to Article 52 of the Hague Regulations, services may be demanded from the inhabitants under the following conditions:

(1) They must be for the needs of the army of occupation.

(2) They must be in proportion to the resources of the country.

(3) They must be of such a nature as not to involve the population in the obligation of taking part in the operations of the war against their own country.

The reservation that labor may be used only for the needs of the army of occupation makes it unlawful to use labor from the occupied country outside the area of occupation. Therefore the deportations of labor from occupied countries into Germany are unlawful.[24]

The occupant has no right to strip the country of all labor resources just as he has no right to strip the country of all economic resources. Millions of inhabitants of occupied countries, however, have been deported to Ger-

[24] In the first World War, Germans committed the same type of violations of international law by deporting Belgian laborers to Germany. The Belgian Government protested against these practices and the Government of the United States, at that time not a belligerent, also expressed its great concern over these practices of the German occupant. See the communication of Robert Lansing, Secretary of State, to Mr. Grew, Chargé d'Affaires in Berlin, of November 29, 1916, as printed in Department of State, *Diplomatic Correspondence with Belligerent Governments relating to Neutral Rights and Duties*, "European War, No. 4" (Washington, 1918), p. 358:

"The Government of the United States has learned with the greatest concern and regret of the policy of the German Government to deport from Belgium a portion of the civilian population for the purpose of forcing them to labor in Germany, and is constrained to protest in a friendly spirit but most solemnly against this action, which is in contravention of all precedent and of those humane principles of international practice which have long been accepted and followed by civilized nations in their treatment of noncombatants in conquered territory. Furthermore, the Government of the United States is convinced that the effect of this policy, if pursued, will in all probability be fatal to the Belgian relief work so humanely planned and so successfully carried out, a result which would be generally deplored and which, it is assumed, would seriously embarrass the German Government."

Writers also condemned these practices. See James W. Garner, *International Law and the World War* (New York: Longmans, Green and Co., 1920), Vol. II, p. 183:

"Whatever may be the technical merits of the German case, the enormous scale on which the policy of deportation was carried out and the harsh and indiscriminate, not to say cruel, way in which it was executed, makes it comparable to the slave raids on the Gold Coast of Africa in the seventeenth century. It appears to be without precedent in modern wars. In ancient times it was the practice of the Roman conquerors to carry back to Italy a portion of the inhabitants and hold them in captivity, and it is said to have been the practice of Attila to force the conquered tribes into his army, but not since the beginning of the modern age—not even during the Thirty Years' war—has any invader seized and virtually enslaved a large part of the civil population in order to carry on his own industries at home and to release his own able-bodied men for military service."

many without regard to the needs of labor for the economy of the occupied country. These practices, as has been indicated, are in violation of Article 52 of the Hague Regulations.

As stated above, the same Regulations stipulate that the occupant has no right to compel the inhabitants to render services involving the population in the obligation of taking part in the operations of the war against their country. Hyde observes that it is unlawful to requisition services "upon works directly promoting the ends of war, such as the construction of forts, fortifications and intrenchments." [25] In the present war, which is more a war of movement on the ground and in the air than a trench war, employment of inhabitants of occupied countries in plane factories or bomb factories must be considered as work directly promoting the ends of war. Moreover, labor from occupied countries is also extensively used by the Germans in building fortifications, especially on the Atlantic coast. Thus the kind of work performed by laborers from occupied countries is of a nature prohibited by the Hague Regulations.

Further disregard of the principles of international law with respect to the use of labor may be found in the conscription of children over fourteen, which amounts to a transgression of the laws of the occupied countries protecting child labor, and of the laws of humanity as well, especially if one takes into consideration the fact that these children have been undernourished and physically weakened through the ruthless food policy of the occupant.

The wage policy must also be considered as a violation of international law. The introduction of an especially low level of wages amounts to starvation practices—a violation of the laws of humanity, laws which are invoked in the preamble to Hague Convention IV. The occupant cannot present the argument that wages are kept on an especially low level in order to check inflation. If such were the case, there would be no differentiation of wages between Germans and non-Germans. The particularly low level of wages and this racial differentiation in wages create an undue enrichment for the occupant, particularly when the occupant is the employer. This enrichment amounts to the difference which is paid actually to the worker and what should be paid to him. The limits of this enrichment may be seen by comparison of the wages of German workers with the wages of the local population in the respective countries. Official evidence regarding exploitation of foreign labor with respect to wages is provided by the above-mentioned decrees and the attached schedules concerning eastern workers. As every worker is provided with a work card or work book in which his wages are enumerated, it is easy to establish, in the light of the above-mentioned decree, the exact amount which each foreign worker is underpaid

[25] Charles C. Hyde, *International Law* (Boston: Little, Brown, and Company, 1922), Vol. II, p. 384.

as compared with the amount paid a German worker engaged in the same kind of employment. The amount of this difference in the wages of imported workers represents the amount of future claims which may be made against the occupant. In other words, the amount of the differences between the daily wages paid to the German and the foreigner for performing identical work, multiplied by the number of days employed, represents the amount of each individual foreign worker's claim, and these individual claims, multiplied by the number of workers imported into Germany from a given country, represent the aggregate amount of a future claim which should be made by the home country of the workers against the occupant.

It should also be noted that the Germans have frozen the savings of the foreign laborers in Germany with the result that their families do not receive these savings at all or they receive them in the form of advances which the clearing institutes of the occupied countries are ordered by the Germans to pay out. In this case the occupied country is paying its own workers doing work in Germany.[26] Obviously such amounts are creating a justified claim against Germany.

The institution of the Eastern Worker's Tax shows that the occupant has introduced involuntary servitude, because the occupant not only uses foreign labor but trades in labor, collecting for the Reich specific amounts of money from employers using such labor. This involuntary servitude is also stressed by denial of wages to Jews and the paying of fees by their employers to the German authorities. Obviously, such regulations amount to a violation of the laws of humanity as invoked in the preamble to the Hague Convention.

[26] See above, section on Clearing, in chapter on "Finance."

CHAPTER VIII

THE LEGAL STATUS OF THE JEWS

A special status for the Jews was created by the occupant in every occupied country. The definition of a Jew was based mainly upon the Nuremberg Laws.[1] A Jew is any person who is, or has been, a member of the Jewish faith or who has more than two Jewish grandparents. Grandparents are to be considered as Jewish if they are, or have been, members of the Jewish faith.[2]

Regulations were issued pertaining to personal status, to freedom of movement, to property, labor, rationing, and the right to practice professions. From the beginning of the occupation, the conditions imposed on the Jews were not as severe in the countries occupied in the west as they were in the countries occupied in central and eastern Europe. But later on, when Jews from France, Norway, Belgium, and the Netherlands were removed from time to time *en masse* to Poland,[3] they were treated there in the same way as Polish Jews. Shortly after the occupation in the west, the German military commanders issued regulations forbidding Jews who had fled from the occupied territory to return to their homes.[4]

On November 23, 1939, a law was introduced in the Government General of Poland imposing upon all Jews and Jewesses over ten years of age an obligation to wear on the right arm an armband with the Star of David at least ten centimeters wide.[5] All Jewish enterprises and stores had to have special signs visible to the public.[6]

According to the decree of January 26, 1940, the Jews in the Government General of Poland were forbidden to use railways.[7] Later, in October, 1940, the Jews in Poland were compelled to live in ghettos, leaving the ghetto without permission being punishable by death. The administration of Jewish affairs in the ghettos was entrusted to Jewish councils, which are responsible to the German authorities for the carrying out of demands made by the latter upon the Jewish population.

All Jewish property in the Polish areas which were incorporated into the Greater Reich was ordered to be sequestrated by decree of September 17, 1940,[8] the same decree providing that sequestrated property could be con-

[1] See Section 5 of the law of November 14, 1935, *Reichsgesetzblatt*, I, p. 1333.
[2] See order concerning measures against the Jews, of September 27, 1940, promulgated by the Chief of the Military Administration in France, below, p. 399.
[3] In Denmark the Danish authorities successfully resisted German demands as to the introduction of anti-Jewish legislation. However, after the Germans took over complete control of Denmark in August, 1943, the German authorities rounded up the Jews and sent them to Poland. About a thousand Jews managed to escape to Sweden through the narrow water straits.
[4] As to France, see *ibid.*, Section 2. [5] *Verordnungsblatt*, 1939, No. 8, p. 61.
[6] *Ibid.* [7] *Ibid.*, 1940, p. 45. [8] See below, p. 511.

fiscated if the public welfare, particularly Reich defense or the strengthening of Germanism, so required. By an order of the Chief of Military Administration in France of October 18, 1940, Jewish property had to be declared and, if it was of some value, especially if it was real property, it could be put under the administration of trustees appointed by the occupant, which practically amounts to confiscation since the owner is not entitled to any allowances from property thus administered.[9]

In the Netherlands, the Reich Commissioner issued on August 9, 1941, a decree concerning the treatment of Jewish capital. According to this decree, Jews are prevented from disposing of their capital in the form of securities and bank accounts amounting to more than a thousand florins. Some exception was made in cases where capital did not exceed ten thousand florins and the yearly income did not exceed three thousand florins.[9a]

As to real property in the Netherlands, the Reich Commissioner issued a decree requiring the registration of all Jewish real property and authorizing the transfer of administration of such properties to managers appointed by the occupant.[10]

A special form of forced labor was introduced for Jews, with an essentially severe régime and under conditions deleterious to health. According to the decree on Jewish labor in the Government General of Poland, of December 12, 1939,[11] all Jewish inhabitants from fourteen to sixty years of age are subject to forced labor. The decree states that forced labor is normally for two years, but the German authorities may lengthen this period at their discretion in a given case by invoking the reason that the "educational purpose" of forced labor has not been attained in that particular case. The use of the word "educational" in the above-mentioned decree is evidence of the punitive character of the forced labor applied on a wholesale scale to large groups of the population in the occupied countries.[12]

In the areas occupied in the present Russo-German war (such as Ostland) the Jews are not allowed to receive wages. Employers of Jews must pay a special fee to the German authorities, and if Jews are employed in overtime work or on holidays or at night, the employer does not pay any extra fee to the German authorities.[12a] Jews do not receive unemployment relief.[13]

[9] Any enterprise is considered Jewish if the owners or lessees are: (*a*) Jewish; (*b*) a partnership with one Jewish partner; (*c*) a limited partnership in which more than one third of the partners are Jewish, or more than one third of the shares are owned by Jewish partners, or in which the manager is a Jew, or more than one third of the board of trustees are Jews; or (*d*) corporations in which the president of the board of directors or managing officer is a Jew, or in which more than one third of the board of directors are Jews. However, the authorities are free to declare an enterprise Jewish even if the above-mentioned factors do not occur. The authorities may declare as Jewish an enterprise which, according to their opinion, is predominantly under Jewish control. See order of October 18, 1940, promulgated by the Chief of the Military Administration in France, below, p. 400.

[9a] *Verordnungsblatt*, 1941, No. 148. [10] *Ibid*., No. 154. [11] See below, p. 544.

[12] A similar decree on forced labor was issued in Serbia for Jews and gypsies from fourteen to sixty years of age, for the purpose of repairing damages caused by the war. *Verordnungsblatt*, 1941, p. 85. [12a] See below, p. 311.

[13] See decree of December 16, 1939, for the Government General of Poland, below, p. 546.

The Jewish population in the occupied countries is undergoing a process of liquidation (1) by debilitation and starvation, because the Jewish food rations are kept at an especially low level; and (2) by massacres in the ghettos. In order to isolate the Jews from every source of help from the local population, severe penalties have been introduced for extending such help to them. In that part of Yugoslavia designated as Serbia, the military commander issued an order dated December 22, 1941, imposing the death penalty on any person who shelters or hides Jews or accepts any object of value from Jews for safekeeping.[14]

*

The treatment of the Jews in the occupied countries is one of the most flagrant violations of international law, not only of specific articles of the Hague Regulations, but also of the principles of the law of nations as they have emerged from established usage among civilized nations, from the laws of humanity, and from the dictates of the public conscience—principles which the occupant is equally bound to respect.[15]

The massacres of the Jews and wholesale confiscations are an obvious violation of Article 46 of the Regulations; and the institution of forced labor is a violation of Article 52, because the occupant, while he may demand the services of local labor for limited needs of the army of occupation, has no right to use them for so-called "educational purposes." Moreover the denial of wages to Jews amounts to involuntary servitude, which is a violation of the laws of humanity.

Family honor and rights of the Jewish population as protected by Article 46 were violated on a wholesale scale by separating families during deportations.

Starving the Jewish population by deliberately establishing low food rations, and exposing them to mass death by creating unhealthy conditions in the ghettos and the forced labor camps, amount to disregard of human life, which is prohibited by Article 46 of the above-cited Regulations.

Depriving the Jews of the right of free movement and the exercise of professions is a violation of Article 43 of the Hague Regulations. These rights were guaranteed by the constitutions of all occupied countries. The occupant is entitled only to make such changes in the laws of the occupied country as may be justified by military necessity. Obviously no military necessity is involved when the aim of the occupant is solely to deprive people of their elementary human rights. Moreover, the obligation of the occupant to restore public order embraces also the obligation to restore economic order, which means the right to work and to make a living.

The persecution of Jews in the occupied countries has given rise to many protests throughout the world by institutions, parliaments (House of Com-

[14] See below, p. 601.

[15] See preamble to Hague Convention IV respecting the Laws and Customs of War on Land.

mons, the Congress of the United States), and governments.[16] The Jews being one of the main objects of German genocide policy, their particular situation in occupied Europe has been additionally treated in the chapter on genocide.

[16] See chapter on "Genocide," below, p. 89, note 45.

CHAPTER IX

GENOCIDE

I. Genocide—A New Term and New Conception for Destruction of Nations

New conceptions require new terms. By "genocide" we mean the destruction of a nation or of an ethnic group. This new word, coined by the author to denote an old practice in its modern development, is made from the ancient Greek word *genos* (race, tribe) and the Latin *cide* (killing), thus corresponding in its formation to such words as tyrannicide, homocide, infanticide, etc.[1] Generally speaking, genocide does not necessarily mean the immediate destruction of a nation, except when accomplished by mass killings of all members of a nation. It is intended rather to signify a coordinated plan of different actions aiming at the destruction of essential foundations of the life of national groups, with the aim of annihilating the groups themselves. The objectives of such a plan would be disintegration of the political and social institutions, of culture, language, national feelings, religion, and the economic existence of national groups, and the destruction of the personal security, liberty, health, dignity, and even the lives of the individuals belonging to such groups. Genocide is directed against the national group as an entity, and the actions involved are directed against individuals, not in their individual capacity, but as members of the national group.

The following illustration will suffice. The confiscation of property of nationals of an occupied area on the ground that they have left the country may be considered simply as a deprivation of their individual property rights. However, if the confiscations are ordered against individuals solely because they are Poles, Jews, or Czechs, then the same confiscations tend in effect to weaken the national entities of which those persons are members.

Genocide has two phases: one, destruction of the national pattern of the oppressed group; the other, the imposition of the national pattern of the oppressor. This imposition, in turn, may be made upon the oppressed population which is allowed to remain, or upon the territory alone, after removal of the population and the colonization of the area by the oppressor's own nationals. Denationalization was the word used in the past to describe the destruction of a national pattern.[1a] The author believes, however, that this

[1] Another term could be used for the same idea, namely, *ethnocide*, consisting of the Greek word "ethnos"—nation—and the Latin word "cide."

[1a] See *Violation of the Laws and Customs of War: Reports of Majority and Dissenting Reports of American and Japanese Members of the Commission of Responsibilities, Conference of Paris, 1919*, Carnegie Endowment for International Peace, Division of International Law, Pamphlet No. 32 (Oxford: Clarendon Press, 1919), p. 39.

word is inadequate because: (1) it does not connote the destruction of the biological structure; (2) in connoting the destruction of one national pattern, it does not connote the imposition of the national pattern of the oppressor; and (3) denationalization is used by some authors to mean only deprivation of citizenship.[2]

Many authors, instead of using a generic term, use currently terms connoting only some functional aspect of the main generic notion of genocide. Thus, the terms "Germanization," "Magyarization," "Italianization," for example, are used to connote the imposition by one stronger nation (Germany, Hungary, Italy) of its national pattern upon a national group controlled by it. The author believes that these terms are also inadequate because they do not convey the common elements of one generic notion and they treat mainly the cultural, economic, and social aspects of genocide, leaving out the biological aspect, such as causing the physical decline and even destruction of the population involved. If one uses the term "Germanization" of the Poles, for example, in this connotation, it means that the Poles, as human beings, are preserved and that only the national pattern of the Germans is imposed upon them. Such a term is much too restricted to apply to a process in which the population is attacked, in a physical sense, and is removed and supplanted by populations of the oppressor nations.

Genocide is the antithesis of the Rousseau-Portalis Doctrine, which may be regarded as implicit in the Hague Regulations. This doctrine holds that war is directed against sovereigns and armies, not against subjects and civilians. In its modern application in civilized society, the doctrine means that war is conducted against states and armed forces and not against populations. It required a long period of evolution in civilized society to mark the way from wars of extermination,[3] which occurred in ancient times and in the Middle Ages, to the conception of wars as being essentially limited to activities against armies and states. In the present war, however, genocide is widely practiced by the German occupant. Germany could not accept the Rousseau-Portalis Doctrine: first, because Germany is waging a total war; and secondly, because, according to the doctrine of National Socialism, the nation, not the state, is the predominant factor.[4] In this German conception the nation provides the biological element for the state. Consequently, in enforcing the New Order, the Germans prepared, waged, and continued a war

[2] See Garner, *op. cit.*, Vol. I, p. 77.

[3] As classical examples of wars of extermination in which nations and groups of the population were completely or almost completely destroyed, the following may be cited: the destruction of Carthage in 146 B.C.; the destruction of Jerusalem by Titus in 72 A.D.; the religious wars of Islam and the Crusades; the massacres of the Albigenses and the Waldenses; and the siege of Magdeburg in the Thirty Years' War. Special wholesale massacres occurred in the wars waged by Genghis Khan and by Tamerlane.

[4] "Since the State in itself is for us only a form, while what is essential is its content, the nation, the people, it is clear that everything else must subordinate itself to its sovereign interests."—Adolf Hitler, *Mein Kampf* (New York: Reynal & Hitchcock, 1939), p. 842.

not merely against states and their armies [5] but against peoples. For the German occupying authorities war thus appears to offer the most appropriate occasion for carrying out their policy of genocide. Their reasoning seems to be the following:

The enemy nation within the control of Germany must be destroyed, disintegrated, or weakened in different degrees for decades to come. Thus the German people in the post-war period will be in a position to deal with other European peoples from the vantage point of biological superiority. Because the imposition of this policy of genocide is more destructive for a people than injuries suffered in actual fighting,[6] the German people will be stronger than the subjugated peoples after the war even if the German army is defeated. In this respect genocide is a new technique of occupation aimed at winning the peace even though the war itself is lost.

For this purpose the occupant has elaborated a system designed to destroy nations according to a previously prepared plan. Even before the war Hitler envisaged genocide as a means of changing the biological interrelations in Europe in favor of Germany.[7] Hitler's conception of genocide is based not upon cultural but upon biological patterns. He believes that "*Germanization* can only be carried out with the *soil* and never with *men*." [8]

When Germany occupied the various European countries, Hitler considered their administration so important that he ordered the Reich Commissioners and governors to be responsible directly to him.[9] The plan of genocide had to be adapted to political considerations in different countries. It could not be implemented in full force in all the conquered states, and hence the plan varies as to subject, modalities, and degree of intensity in each occupied country. Some groups—such as the Jews—are to be destroyed completely.[10] A distinction is made between peoples considered to

[5] See Alfred Rosenberg, *Der Mythus des 20. Jahrhunderts* (München: Hoheneichenverlag, 1935), pp. 1–2: "History and the mission of the future no longer mean the struggle of class against class, the struggle of Church dogma against dogma, but the clash between blood and blood, race and race, people and people."

[6] The German genocide philosophy was conceived and put into action before the Germans received even a foretaste of the considerable dimensions of Allied aerial bombings of German territory.

[7] See Hitler's statement to Rauschning, from *The Voice of Destruction*, by Hermann Rauschning (New York, 1940), p. 138, by courtesy of G. P. Putnam's Sons:

". . . The French complained after the war that there were twenty million Germans too many. We accept the criticism. We favor the planned control of population movements. But our friends will have to excuse us if we subtract the twenty millions elsewhere. After all these centuries of whining about the protection of the poor and lowly, it is about time we decided to protect the strong against the inferior. It will be one of the chief tasks of German statesmanship for all time to prevent, by every means in our power, the further increase of the Slav races. Natural instincts bid all living beings not merely conquer their enemies, but also destroy them. In former days, it was the victor's prerogative to destroy entire tribes, entire peoples. By doing this gradually and without bloodshed, we demonstrate our humanity. We should remember, too, that we are merely doing unto others as they would have done to us."

[8] *Mein Kampf*, p. 588.

[9] See "Administration," above, pp. 9–10.

[10] *Mein Kampf*, p. 931: ". . . the National Socialist movement has its mightiest tasks to fulfill: . . . it must condemn to general wrath the evil enemy of humanity [Jews] as the true creator of all suffering."

be related by blood to the German people (such as Dutchmen, Norwegians, Flemings, Luxemburgers), and peoples not thus related by blood (such as the Poles, Slovenes, Serbs). The populations of the first group are deemed worthy of being Germanized. With respect to the Poles particularly, Hitler expressed the view that it is their soil alone which *can and should be profitably Germanized.*[11]

II. Techniques of Genocide in Various Fields

The techniques of genocide, which the German occupant has developed in the various occupied countries, represent a concentrated and coordinated attack upon all elements of nationhood. Accordingly, genocide is being carried out in the following fields:

POLITICAL

In the incorporated areas, such as western Poland, Eupen, Malmédy and Moresnet, Luxemburg, and Alsace-Lorraine, local institutions of self-government were destroyed and a German pattern of administration imposed. Every reminder of former national character was obliterated. Even commercial signs and inscriptions on buildings, roads, and streets, as well as names of communities and of localities, were changed to a German form.[12] Nationals of Luxemburg having foreign or non-German first names are required to assume in lieu thereof the corresponding German first names; or, if that is impossible, they must select German first names. As to their family names, if they were of German origin and their names have been changed to a non-German form, they must be changed again to the original German. Persons who have not complied with these requirements within the prescribed period are liable to a penalty, and in addition German names may be imposed on them.[13] Analogous provisions as to changing of names were made for Lorraine.[14]

Special Commissioners for the Strengthening of Germanism are attached to the administration, and their task consists in coordinating all actions promoting Germanism in a given area. An especially active rôle in this respect is played by inhabitants of German origin who were living in the occupied

[11] *Ibid.*, p. 590, n. ". . . The Polish policy in the sense of a Germanization of the East, demanded by so many, rooted unfortunately almost always in the same wrong conclusion. Here too one believed that one could bring about a Germanization of the Polish element by a purely linguistic integration into the German nationality. Here too the result would have been an unfortunate one: people of an alien race, expressing its alien thoughts in the German language, compromising the height and the dignity of our own nationality by its own inferiority."

As to the depopulation policy in occupied Yugoslavia, see, in general, Louis Adamic, *My Native Land* (New York: Harper & Brothers, 1943).

[12] For Luxemburg, see order of August 6, 1940, below, p. 440.

[13] See order concerning the change of first and family names in Luxemburg, of January 31, 1941, below, p. 441.

[14] *Verordnungsblatt*, 1940, p. 60.

countries before the occupation. After having accomplished their task as members of the so-called fifth column, they formed the nucleus of Germanism. A register of Germans (*Volksliste*)[15] was established and special cards entitled them to special privileges and favors, particularly in the fields of rationing, employment, supervising enterprises of local inhabitants, and so on. In order to disrupt the national unity of the local population, it was declared that non-Germans, married to Germans, may upon their application be put on the *Volksliste.*

In order further to disrupt national unity, Nazi party organizations were established, such as the Nasjonal Samling Party in Norway and the Mussert Party in the Netherlands, and their members from the local population were given political privileges. Other political parties were dissolved.[16] These Nazi parties in occupied countries were also given special protection by courts.

In line with this policy of imposing the German national pattern, particularly in the incorporated territories, the occupant has organized a system of colonization of these areas. In western Poland, especially, this has been done on a large scale. The Polish population have been removed from their homes in order to make place for German settlers who were brought in from the Baltic States, the central and eastern districts of Poland, Bessarabia, and from the Reich itself. The properties and homes of the Poles are being allocated to German settlers; and to induce them to reside in these areas the settlers receive many privileges, especially in the way of tax exemptions.[17]

SOCIAL

The destruction of the national pattern in the social field has been accomplished in part by the abolition of local law and local courts and the imposition of German law and courts, and also by Germanization of the judicial language and of the bar.[18] The social structure of a nation being vital to its national development, the occupant also endeavors to bring about such changes as may weaken the national spiritual resources. The focal point of this attack has been the intelligentsia, because this group largely provides national leadership and organizes resistance against Nazification. This is especially true in Poland and Slovenia (Slovene part of Yugoslavia), where the intelligentsia and the clergy were in great part removed from the rest of the population and deported for forced labor in Germany. The tendency of the occupant is to retain in Poland only the laboring and peasant class, while in the western occupied countries the industrialist class is also allowed to remain, since it can aid in integrating the local industries with the German war economy.

[15] As to Poland, see order of October 29, 1941, below, p. 552.
[16] As to Norway, see order of September 25, 1940, below, p. 499.
[17] See above, chapter on "Finance."
[18] See above, chapters on "Law" and "Courts."

CULTURAL

In the incorporated areas the local population is forbidden to use its own language in schools and in printing. According to the decree of August 6, 1940,[19] the language of instruction in all Luxemburg schools was made exclusively German. The French language was not permitted to be taught in primary schools; only in secondary schools could courses in that language continue to be given. German teachers were introduced into the schools and they were compelled to teach according to the principles of National Socialism.[20]

In Lorraine general compulsory education to assure the upbringing of youth in the spirit of National Socialism begins at the age of six.[21] It continues for eight years, or to the completion of the grammar school (*Volksschule*), and then for three more years, or to the completion of a vocational school. Moreover, in the Polish areas Polish youths were excluded from the benefit of liberal arts studies and were channeled predominantly into the trade schools. The occupant apparently believes that the study of the liberal arts may develop independent national Polish thinking, and therefore he tends to prepare Polish youths for the rôle of skilled labor, to be employed in German industries.

In order to prevent the expression of the national spirit through artistic media, a rigid control of all cultural activities has been introduced. All persons engaged in painting, drawing, sculpture, music, literature, and the theater are required to obtain a license for the continuation of their activities. Control in these fields is exercised through German authorities. In Luxemburg this control is exercised through the Public Relations Section of the Reich Propaganda Office and embraces music, painting, theater, architecture, literature, press, radio, and cinema. Every one of these activities is controlled through a special chamber and all these chambers are controlled by one chamber, which is called the Reich Chamber of Culture (*Reichskulturkammer*).[22] The local chambers of culture are presided over by the propaganda chief of the National Socialist Party in the given area. Not only have national creative activities in the cultural and artistic field been rendered impossible by regimentation, but the population has also been deprived of inspiration from the existing cultural and artistic values. Thus, especially in Poland, were national monuments destroyed and libraries, archives, museums, and galleries of art carried away.[23] In 1939 the Germans burned

[19] See below, p. 440.

[20] "It is the task of the director to orient and conduct the school systematically according to National Socialist principles."—See announcement for execution of the order concerning the elementary school system, February 14, 1941, promulgated in Lorraine by the Chief of Civil Administration, below, p. 388.

[21] *Verordnungsblatt*, 1941, p. 100. See below, p. 386.

[22] As to organization of the Reich Chamber of Culture, see law of November 1, 1933, *Reichsgesetzblatt*, I, p. 979.

[23] See note of the Polish Minister of Foreign Affairs of the Polish Government-in-Exile to the Allied and neutral powers of May 3, 1941, in *Polish White Book:* Republic of Poland, Ministry of Foreign Affairs, *German Occupation of Poland—Extract of Note Addressed to the Allied and Neutral Powers* (New York: The Greystone Press [1942]), pp. 36–39.

the great library of the Jewish Theological Seminary at Lublin, Poland. This was reported by the Germans as follows:

For us it was a matter of special pride to destroy the Talmudic Academy which was known as the greatest in Poland. . . . We threw out of the building the great Talmudic library, and carted it to market. There we set fire to the books. The fire lasted for twenty hours. The Jews of Lublin were assembled around and cried bitterly. Their cries almost silenced us. Then we summoned the military band and the joyful shouts of the soldiers silenced the sound of the Jewish cries.[24]

ECONOMIC

The destruction of the foundations of the economic existence of a national group necessarily brings about a crippling of its development, even a retrogression. The lowering of the standard of living creates difficulties in fulfilling cultural-spiritual requirements. Furthermore, a daily fight literally for bread and for physical survival may handicap thinking in both general and national terms.

It was the purpose of the occupant to create such conditions as these among the peoples of the occupied countries, especially those peoples embraced in the first plans of genocide elaborated by him—the Poles, the Slovenes, and the Jews.

The Jews were immediately deprived of the elemental means of existence.[25] As to the Poles in incorporated Poland, the purpose of the occupant was to shift the economic resources from the Polish national group to the German national group. Thus the Polish national group had to be impoverished and the German enriched. This was achieved primarily by confiscation of Polish property under the authority of the Reich Commissioner for the Strengthening of Germanism. But the process was likewise furthered by the policy of regimenting trade and handicrafts, since licenses for such activities were issued to Germans, and only exceptionally to Poles. In this way, the Poles were expelled from trade, and the Germans entered that field.

As the occupant took over the banks a special policy for handling bank deposits was established in order to strengthen the German element. One of the most widely patronized Polish banks, called the Post Office Savings Bank (P.K.O.), possessed, on the day of the occupation, deposits of millions of Polish citizens. The deposits, however, were repaid by the occupant only to the German depositors upon production by them of a certificate of their German origin.[26] Thus the German element in Poland was immediately made financially stronger than the Polish. In Slovenia the Germans have liquidated the financial cooperatives and agricultural associations, which had for decades proved to be a most efficient instrumentality in raising the standard of living and in promoting national and social progress.

[24] *Frankfurter Zeitung*, Wochen-Ausgabe, March 28, 1941.
[25] See above, chapter on "Legal Status of the Jews."
[26] See ordinance promulgated by the German Trustee of the Polish Savings Bank published in *Thorner Freiheit* of December 11, 1940.

In other countries, especially in Alsace-Lorraine and Luxemburg, genocide in the economic field was carried out in a different manner. As the Luxemburgers are considered to be of related blood, opportunity is given them to recognize the Germanic elements in themselves, and to work for the strengthening of Germanism. If they do not take advantage of this "opportunity," their properties are taken from them and given to others who are eager to promote Germanism.[27]

Participation in economic life is thus made dependent upon one's being German or being devoted to the cause of Germanism. Consequently, promoting a national ideology other than German is made difficult and dangerous.

BIOLOGICAL

In the occupied countries of "people of non-related blood," a policy of depopulation is pursued. Foremost among the methods employed for this purpose is the adoption of measures calculated to decrease the birthrate of the national groups of non-related blood, while at the same time steps are taken to encourage the birthrate of the *Volksdeutsche* living in these countries. Thus in incorporated Poland marriages between Poles are forbidden without the special permission of the Governor (*Reichsstatthalter*) of the district; and the latter, as a matter of principle, does not permit marriages between Poles.[28]

The birthrate of the undesired group is being further decreased as a result of the separation of males from females [29] by deporting them for forced labor elsewhere. Moreover, the undernourishment of the parents, because of discrimination in rationing, brings about not only a lowering of the birthrate, but a lowering of the survival capacity of children born of underfed parents.

As mentioned above, the occupant is endeavoring to encourage the birthrate of the Germans. Different methods are adopted to that end. Special subsidies are provided in Poland for German families having at least three minor children.[30] Because the Dutch and Norwegians are considered of

[27] See "Property," above, p. 38.

[28] See Report of Primate of Poznań to Pius XII, *The Black Book of Poland* (New York: G. P. Putnam's Sons, 1942), p. 383.

[29] That the separation of males from females was preconceived by Hitler as an element of genocide is obvious from his statement:

"'*We are obliged to depopulate*,' he went on emphatically, 'as part of our mission of preserving the German population. We shall have to develop a technique of depopulation. If you ask me what I mean by depopulation, I mean the removal of entire racial units. And that is what I intend to carry out—that, roughly, is my task. Nature is cruel, therefore we, too, may be cruel. If I can send the flower of the German nation into the hell of war without the smallest pity for the spilling of precious German blood, then surely I have the right to remove millions of an inferior race that breeds like vermin! And by "remove" I don't necessarily mean destroy; I shall simply take systematic measures to dam their great natural fertility. For example, I shall keep their men and women separated for years. Do you remember the falling birthrate of the world war? Why should we not do quite consciously and through a number of years what was at that time merely the inevitable consequence of the long war? There are many ways, systematical and comparatively painless, or at any rate bloodless, of causing undesirable races to die out.'"—Rauschning, *op. cit.*, pp. 137–38, by courtesy of G. P. Putnam's Sons.

[30] See order concerning the granting of child subsidies to Germans in the Government General, of March 10, 1942, below, p. 553.

related blood, the bearing, by Dutch and Norwegian women, of illegitimate children begotten by German military men is encouraged by subsidy.[31]

Other measures adopted are along the same lines. Thus the Reich Commissioner has vested in himself the right to act as a guardian or parent to a minor Dutch girl if she intends to marry a German.[32] The special care for legitimation of children in Luxemburg, as revealed in the order concerning changes in family law of March 22, 1941,[33] is dictated by the desire to encourage extramarital procreation with Germans.

PHYSICAL

The physical debilitation and even annihilation of national groups in occupied countries is carried out mainly in the following ways:

1. *Racial Discrimination in Feeding.* Rationing of food is organized according to racial principles throughout the occupied countries. "The German people come before all other peoples for food," declared Reich Minister Göring on October 4, 1942.[34] In accordance with this program, the German population is getting 93 per cent of its pre-war diet, while those in the occupied territories receive much less: in Warsaw, for example, the Poles receive 66 per cent of the pre-war rations and the Jews only 20 per cent.[35] The following shows the difference in the percentage of meat rations received by the Germans and the population of the occupied countries: Germans, 100 per cent; Czechs, 86 per cent; Dutch, 71 per cent; Poles (Incorporated Poland), 71 per cent; Lithuanians, 57 per cent; French, 51 per cent; Belgians, 40 per cent; Serbs, 36 per cent; Poles (General Government), 36 per cent; Slovenes, 29 per cent; Jews, 0 per cent.[36]

The percentage of pre-war food received under present rations (in calories per consumer unit) is the following:[37] Germans, 93 per cent; Czechs, 83 per cent; Poles (Incorporated Poland), 78 per cent; Dutch, 70 per cent; Belgians, 66 per cent; Poles (General Government), 66 per cent; Norwegians, 54 per cent; Jews, 20 per cent.

As to the composition of food, the percentages of required basic nutrients received under present rations (per consumer unit) are as follows:[38]

[31] See order of July 28, 1942, concerning the subsidizing of children of members of the German armed forces in occupied territories, *Reichsgesetzblatt*, 1942, I, p. 488:

"To maintain and promote a racially valuable German heritage, children begotten by members of the German armed forces in the occupied Norwegian and Dutch territories and born of Norwegian or Dutch women will upon the application of the mother be granted a special subsidy and benefit through the offices of the Reich Commissioners for the occupied Norwegian and Dutch territories."

[32] See order of February 28, 1941, below, p. 474. [33] See below, p. 428.

[34] See *New York Times*, October 5, 1942, p. 4, col. 6.

[35] The figures quoted in this and the following two paragraphs have been taken, with the permission of the Institute of Jewish Affairs, from its publication entitled *Starvation over Europe (Made in Germany); A Documented Record, 1943* (New York, 1943), pp. 37, 47, 52.

[36] *Ibid.*, p. 37. [37] *Ibid.*, p. 47.

[38] *Ibid.*, p. 52. For further details, see League of Nations, *World Economic Survey* (Geneva, 1942), pp. 90–91.

Consumer Unit	*Carbohydrates* %	*Proteins* %	*Fats* %
Germans	100	97	77
Czechs	90	92	65
Dutch	84	95	65
Belgians	79	73	29
Poles (Incorporated Poland)	76	85	49
Poles (General Government)	77	62	18
Norwegians	69	65	32
French	58	71	40
Greeks	38	38	1.14
Jews	27	20	0.32

The result of racial feeding is a decline in health of the nations involved and an increase in the deathrate. In Warsaw, anemia rose 113 per cent among Poles and 435 among Jews.[39] The deathrate per thousand in 1941 amounted in the Netherlands to 10 per cent; in Belgium to 14.5 per cent; in Bohemia and Moravia to 13.4.[40] The Polish mortality in Warsaw in 1941 amounted in July to 1,316;[41] in August to 1,729;[42] and in September to 2,160.[43]

2. *Endangering of Health.* The undesired national groups, particularly in Poland, are deprived of elemental necessities for preserving health and life. This latter method consists, for example, of requisitioning warm clothing and blankets in the winter and withholding firewood and medicine. During the winter of 1940–41, only a single room in a house could be heated in the Warsaw ghetto, and children had to take turns in warming themselves there. No fuel at all has been received since then by the Jews in the ghetto.[44]

Moreover, the Jews in the ghetto are crowded together under conditions of housing inimical to health, and in being denied the use of public parks they are even deprived of the right to fresh air. Such measures, especially pernicious to the health of children, have caused the development of various diseases. The transfer, in unheated cattle trucks and freight cars, of hundreds of thousands of Poles from Incorporated Poland to the Government General, which took place in the midst of a severe winter, resulted in a decimation of the expelled Poles.

3. *Mass Killings.* The technique of mass killings is employed mainly against Poles, Russians, and Jews, as well as against leading personalities from among the non-collaborationist groups in all the occupied countries. In Poland, Bohemia-Moravia, and Slovenia, the intellectuals are being "liquidated" because they have always been considered as the main bearers of

[39] See *Hitler's Ten-Year War on the Jews* (Institute of Jewish Affairs of the American Jewish Congress, World Jewish Congress, New York, 1943), p. 144.
[40] League of Nations, *Monthly Bulletin of Statistics* (Geneva, 1942), Nos. 4, 5, 6.
[41] *Nowy Kurjer Warszawski* (Warsaw), August 29, 1941.
[42] *Die Nation* (Bern), August 13, 1942. [43] *Poland Fights* (New York), May 16, 1942.
[44] *Hitler's Ten-Year War on the Jews*, p. 144.

national ideals and at the time of occupation they were especially suspected of being the organizers of resistance. The Jews for the most part are liquidated within the ghettos,[45] or in special trains in which they are transported to a so-called "unknown" destination. The number of Jews who have been killed by organized murder in all the occupied countries, according to the Institute of Jewish Affairs of the American Jewish Congress in New York, amounts to 1,702,500.[46]

RELIGIOUS

In Luxemburg, where the population is predominantly Catholic and religion plays an important rôle in national life, especially in the field of education, the occupant has tried to disrupt these national and religious influences. Children over fourteen years of age were permitted by legislation to renounce their religious affiliations,[47] for the occupant was eager to enroll such children exclusively in pro-Nazi youth organizations. Moreover, in order to protect such children from public criticism, another law was issued at the same time imposing penalties ranging up to 15,000 Reichsmarks for any publication of names or any general announcement as to resignations from religious congregations.[48] Likewise in Poland, through the systematic pillage and destruction of church property and persecution of the clergy, the German occupying authorities have sought to destroy the religious leadership of the Polish nation.

MORAL

In order to weaken the spiritual resistance of the national group, the occupant attempts to create an atmosphere of moral debasement within this

[45] See the Joint Declaration by members of the United Nations, issued simultaneously in Washington and in London, on December 17, 1942:

"The attention of the Belgian, Czechoslovak, Greek, Jugoslav, Luxembourg, Netherlands, Norwegian, Polish, Soviet, United Kingdom and United States Governments and also of the French National Committee has been drawn to numerous reports from Europe that the German authorities, not content with denying to persons of Jewish race in all the territories over which their barbarous rule has been extended, the most elementary human rights, are now carrying into effect Hitler's oft-repeated intention to exterminate the Jewish people in Europe.

"From all the occupied countries Jews are being transported in conditions of appalling horror and brutality to Eastern Europe. In Poland, which has been made the principal Nazi slaughterhouse, the ghettos established by the German invader are being systematically emptied of all Jews except a few highly skilled workers required for war industries. None of those taken away are ever heard of again. The able-bodied are slowly worked to death in labor camps. The infirm are left to die of exposure and starvation or are deliberately massacred in mass executions. The number of victims of these bloody cruelties is reckoned in many hundreds of thousands of entirely innocent men, women and children.

"The above-mentioned governments and the French National Committee condemn in the strongest possible terms this bestial policy of cold-blooded extermination. They declare that such events can only strengthen the resolve of all freedom-loving peoples to overthrow the barbarous Hitlerite tyranny. They reaffirm their solemn resolution to insure that those responsible for these crimes shall not escape retribution, and to press on with the necessary practical measures to this end."—*The United Nations Review*, Vol. III (1943), No. 1, p. 1.

[46] *Hitler's Ten-Year War on the Jews*, p. 307.

[47] See order of December 9, 1940, below, p. 438.

[48] *Ibid.*

group. According to this plan, the mental energy of the group should be concentrated upon base instincts and should be diverted from moral and national thinking. It is important for the realization of such a plan that the desire for cheap individual pleasure be substituted for the desire for collective feelings and ideals based upon a higher morality. Therefore, the occupant made an effort in Poland to impose upon the Poles pornographic publications and movies. The consumption of alcohol was encouraged, for while food prices have soared, the Germans have kept down the price of alcohol, and the peasants are compelled by the authorities to take spirits in payment for agricultural produce. The curfew law, enforced very strictly against Poles, is relaxed if they can show the authorities a ticket to one of the gambling houses which the Germans have allowed to come into existence.[49]

III. Recommendations for the Future

PROHIBITION OF GENOCIDE IN WAR AND PEACE

The above-described techniques of genocide represent an elaborate, almost scientific, system developed to an extent never before achieved by any nation.[50] Hence the significance of genocide and the need to review international law in the light of the German practices of the present war. These practices have surpassed in their unscrupulous character any procedures or methods imagined a few decades ago by the framers of the Hague Regulations. Nobody at that time could conceive that an occupant would resort to the destruction of nations by barbarous practices reminiscent of the darkest pages of history. Hence, among other items covered by the Hague Regulations, there are only technical rules dealing with some (but by no means all) of the essential rights of individuals; and these rules do not take into consideration the interrelationship of such rights with the whole problem of nations subjected to virtual imprisonment. The Hague Regulations deal also with the sovereignty of a state, but they are silent regarding the preservation of the integrity of a people. However, the evolution of international law, particularly since the date of the Hague Regulations, has brought about a considerable interest in national groups as distinguished from states and individuals. National and religious groups were put under a special protection by the Treaty of Versailles and by specific minority treaties, when it became

[49] Under Polish law, 1919–39, gambling houses were prohibited; nor did they exist on Polish soil when it was under Russian, German, and Austrian rule before 1914. See *The Black Book of Poland*, pp. 513, 514.

[50] "No conqueror has ever chosen more diabolical methods for gaining the mastery of the soul and body of a people."—*Manchester Guardian*, February 28, 1941.

"We know that there is no war in all our history where such ruthless and deliberate steps have been taken for the disintegration of civilian life and the suffering and the death of civilian populations."—Hugh R. Jackson, Special Assistant to the Director of Foreign Relief and Rehabilitation Operations, U.S. Department of State, in an address before the National Conference of Social Work, New York, March 12, 1943; printed in Department of State, *Bulletin*, Vol. VIII, No. 194 (March 13, 1943), p. 219.

obvious that national minorities were compelled to live within the boundaries of states ruled by governments representing a majority of the population. The constitutions which were framed after 1918 also contain special provisions for the protection of the rights of national groups. Moreover, penal codes which were promulgated at that time provide for the protection of such groups, especially of their honor and reputation.

This trend is quite natural, when we conceive that nations are essential elements of the world community. The world represents only so much culture and intellectual vigor as are created by its component national groups.[51] Essentially the idea of a nation signifies constructive cooperation and original contributions, based upon genuine traditions, genuine culture, and a well-developed national psychology. The destruction of a nation, therefore, results in the loss of its future contributions to the world. Moreover, such destruction offends our feelings of morality and justice in much the same way as does the criminal killing of a human being: the crime in the one case as in the other is murder, though on a vastly greater scale. Among the basic features which have marked progress in civilization are the respect for and appreciation of the national characteristics and qualities contributed to world culture by the different nations—characteristics and qualities which, as illustrated in the contributions made by nations weak in defense and poor in economic resources, are not to be measured in terms of national power and wealth.

As far back as 1933, the author of the present work submitted to the Fifth International Conference for the Unification of Penal Law, held in Madrid in October of that year in cooperation with the Fifth Committee of the League of Nations, a report accompanied by draft articles to the effect that actions aiming at the destruction and oppression of populations (what would amount to the actual conception of genocide) should be penalized. The author formulated two new international law crimes to be introduced into the penal legislation of the thirty-seven participating countries, namely, the crime of *barbarity*, conceived as oppressive and destructive actions directed against individuals as members of a national, religious, or racial group, and the crime of *vandalism*, conceived as malicious destruction of works of art and culture because they represent the specific creations of the genius of such groups. Moreover, according to this draft these new crimes were to be internationalized to the extent that the offender should be punished when apprehended, either in his own country, if that was the situs of the crime, or in any other signatory country, if apprehended there.[52]

[51] The idea of a nation should not, however, be confused with the idea of nationalism. To do so would be to make the same mistake as confusing the idea of individual liberty with that of egoism.

[52] See Raphaël Lemkin, "Terrorisme," *Actes de la Ve Conférence Internationale pour l'Unification du Droit Pénal* (Paris, 1935), pp. 48–56; see also Lemkin, "Akte der Barbarei und des Vandalismus als *delicta iuris gentium*," *Internationales Anwaltsblatt* (Vienna, November, 1933).

This principle of universal repression for genocide practices advocated by the author at the above-mentioned conference, had it been accepted by the conference and embodied in the form of an international convention duly signed and ratified by the countries there represented in 1933, would have made it possible, as early as that date, to indict persons who had been found guilty of such criminal acts whenever they appeared on the territory of one of the signatory countries. Moreover, such a project, had it been adopted at that time by the participating countries, would prove useful now by providing an effective instrument for the punishment of war criminals of the present world conflict. It must be emphasized again that the proposals of the author at the Madrid Conference embraced criminal actions which, according to the view of the author, would cover in great part the fields in which crimes have been committed in this war by the members of the Axis Powers. Furthermore, the adoption of the principle of universal repression as adapted to genocide by countries which belong now to the group of nonbelligerents or neutrals, respectively, would likewise bind these latter countries to punish the war criminals engaged in genocide or to extradite them to the countries in which these crimes were committed. If the punishment of genocide practices had formed a part of international law in such countries since 1933, there would be no necessity now to issue admonitions to neutral countries not to give refuge to war criminals.[53]

It will be advisable in the light of these observations to consider the place of genocide in the present and future international law. Genocide is, as we have noted, a composite of different acts of persecution or destruction. Many of those acts, when they constitute an infringement upon honor and rights, when they are a transgression against life, private property and religion, or science and art, or even when they encroach unduly in the fields of taxation and personal services, are prohibited by Articles 46, 48, 52, and 56 of the Hague Regulations. Several of them, such as those which cause humiliations, debilitation by undernourishment, and danger to health, are in violation of the laws of humanity as specified in the preamble to the Hague Regulations. But other acts falling within the purview of genocide, such as, for example, subsidizing children begotten by members of the armed forces of the occupant and born of women nationals of the occupied area, as well as various ingenious measures for weakening or destroying political, social, and cultural elements in national groups, are not expressly prohibited by the Hague Regulations. The entire problem of genocide needs to be dealt with as a whole; it is too important to be left for piecemeal discussion and solution in the future. Many hope that there will be no more wars, but we dare not rely on mere hopes for protection against genocidal practices by ruthless conquerors. Therefore, without ceasing in our endeavors to make this the

[53] See statement of President Roosevelt, *White House Press Release*, July 30, 1943, Department of State, *Bulletin*, Vol. IX, No. 214 (July 31, 1943), p. 62.

last war, we must see to it that the Hague Regulations are so amended as expressly to prohibit genocide in any war which may occur in the future. *De lege ferenda*, the definition of genocide in the Hague Regulations thus amended should consist of two essential parts: in the first should be included every action infringing upon the life, liberty, health, corporal integrity, economic existence, and the honor of the inhabitants when committed because they belong to a national, religious, or racial group; and in the second, every policy aiming at the destruction or the aggrandizement of one of such groups to the prejudice or detriment of another.

Moreover, we should not overlook the fact that genocide is a problem not only of war but also of peace. It is an especially important problem for Europe, where differentiation in nationhood is so marked that despite the principle of political and territorial self-determination, certain national groups may be obliged to live as minorities within the boundaries of other states. If these groups should not be adequately protected, such lack of protection would result in international disturbances, especially in the form of disorganized emigration of the persecuted, who would look for refuge elsewhere.[54] That being the case, all countries must be concerned about such a problem, not only because of humanitarian, but also because of practical, reasons affecting the interest of every country. The system of legal protection of minorities adopted in the past, which was based mainly on international treaties and the constitutions of the respective countries, proved to be inadequate because not every European country had a sufficient judicial machinery for the enforcement of its constitution. It may be said, in fact, that the European countries had a more efficient machinery for enforcing civil and criminal law than for enforcing constitutional law. Genocide being of such great importance, its repression must be based not only on international and constitutional law but also on the criminal law of the various countries. The procedure to be adopted in the future with respect to this matter should be as follows:

An international multilateral treaty should provide for the introduction, not only in the constitution but also in the criminal code of each country, of provisions protecting minority groups from oppression because of their nationhood, religion, or race. Each criminal code should have provisions inflicting penalties for genocide practices. In order to prevent the invocation of the plea of superior orders, the liability of persons who *order* genocide practices, as well as of persons who *execute* such orders, should be provided expressly by the criminal codes of the respective countries. Because of the special implications of genocide in international relations, the principle of universal re-

[54] Adequate protection of minority groups does not of course mean that protective measures should be so stringent as to prevent those who so desire from leaving such groups in order to join majority groups. In other words, minority protection should not constitute a barrier to the gradual process of assimilation and integration which may result from such voluntary transfer of individuals.

pression should be adopted for the crime of genocide. According to this principle, the culprit should be liable to trial not only in the country in which he committed the crime, but also, in the event of his escape therefrom, in any other country in which he might have taken refuge.[55] In this respect, genocide offenders should be subject to the principle of universal repression in the same way as other offenders guilty of the so-called *delicta juris gentium* (such as, for example, white slavery and trade in children, piracy, trade in narcotics and in obscene publications, and counterfeiting of money).[56] Indeed, genocide should be added to the list of *delicta juris gentium*.[57]

INTERNATIONAL CONTROL OF OCCUPATION PRACTICES

Genocide as described above presents one of the most complete and glaring illustrations of the violation of international law and the laws of humanity. In its several manifestations genocide also represents a violation of specific regulations of the Hague Convention such as those regarding the protection of property, life, and honor. It is therefore essential that genocide procedures be not only prohibited by law but prevented in practice during military occupation.

In another important field, that of the treatment of prisoners of war, international controls have been established in order to ascertain whether prisoners are treated in accordance with the rules of international law (see Articles 86 to 88 of the Convention concerning the Treatment of Prisoners of War, of July 27, 1929).[58] But the fate of nations in prison, of helpless women and children, has apparently not seemed to be so important as to call for supervision of the occupational authorities. Whereas concerning prisoners of war the public is able to obtain exact information, the lack of direct-witness reports on the situation of groups of population under occupation gravely hampers measures for their assistance and rescue from what may be inhumane and intolerable conditions. Information and reports which slip out from behind the frontiers of occupied countries are very often labeled as untrustworthy atrocity stories because they are so gruesome that people simply refuse to believe them. Therefore, the Regulations of the Hague Convention should be modified to include an international controlling agency vested with specific powers, such as visiting the occupied countries and making inquiries as to the manner in which the occupant treats nations in prison. In the situation as it exists at present there is no means of providing for alleviation of the treatment of populations under occupation until

[55] Of course such an offender could never be tried twice for the same act.

[56] Research in International Law (Under the Auspices of the Faculty of Harvard Law School), "Part II. Jurisdiction with Respect to Crime," (Edwin D. Dickinson, Reporter), *American Journal of International Law, Supp.*, Vol. 29 (1935), pp. 573–85.

[57] Since not all countries agree to the principle of universal repression (as for example, the United States of America), the future treaty on genocide might well provide a facultative clause for the countries which do not adhere to this principle.

[58] League of Nations, *Treaty Series*, Vol. 118, p. 343.

the actual moment of liberation. It is then too late for remedies, for after liberation such populations can at best obtain only reparation of damages but never restoration of those values which have been destroyed and which cannot be restored, such as human life, treasures of art, and historical archives.

PART II

THE OCCUPIED COUNTRIES

CHAPTER X

ALBANIA[1]

When the Italian troops occupied Albania after a short but stubborn resistance during which King Zog I fled abroad, the occupant immediately started to organize a puppet régime to function under his own guidance. On April 12, 1939, a National Constituent Assembly was convoked which decided: (1) to proclaim the abrogation of the political régime theretofore in force as well as the abrogation of the constitution of December 1, 1928; (2) to create a government vested with full powers; (3) to express the desire for the creation of a union between Italy and Albania, and to offer the Crown of Albania to the King of Italy and to his successors in the form of a personal union.[1a]

On April 13, 1939, the Fascist Grand Council (*Gran Consiglio del Fascismo*) gave its approval to this union, and on April 16, 1939, a law was published in Italy authorizing and proclaiming the acceptance by the King of the Crown of Albania and the consequent creation of a union between the two states.[2]

On April 17, this acceptance was formally effected when a special Albanian mission, consisting of members of the Provisional Albanian Government, officially presented the Crown of Albania to the King of Italy.

By the royal decree of April 18, 1939,[3] there was established in the Italian Ministry of Foreign Affairs an Under Secretariat for Albanian Affairs.

In the further development of relations between Italy and Albania, a convention was signed in Tirana on April 20, 1939, to the effect that citizens of Albania in Italy and citizens of Italy in Albania shall enjoy all civil and political rights which they enjoy in their respective countries.[4]

On the same day there was signed in Rome a treaty on economic matters as well as matters pertaining to customs and exchange,[5] and on May 28, 1939, this treaty was completed by the addition of further details. By these two treaties a customs union was established between the two states, Italy being empowered to represent this union (see below).

[1] The present chapter was written and set up in print prior to the surrender of Italy, and much of the account of the Italian régime established in Albania was therefore cast in the present tense. Since it is the author's purpose to describe the Italian occupation and union with Albania rather than to discuss developments subsequent to the surrender, he has allowed the chapter to stand substantially as it was written.

[1a] See text of the decision of the Constituent Assembly of April 12, 1939, in the *Gazzetta ufficiale del Regno d'Albania*, April 12–July 15, 1939, numero straordinario, p. 10.

[2] See below, p. 267. [3] *Gazzetta ufficiale del Regno d'Italia*, April 29, 1939, No. 102.

[4] See *Gazzetta ufficiale del Regno d'Albania*, 1939, No. 27; and *Gazzetta ufficiale del Regno d'Italia*. 1939. No. 180.

[5] See *Gazzetta ufficiale del Regno d'Italia*, 1939, No. 178.

By a treaty signed in Rome on June 3, 1939, Italy assumed management of the foreign affairs of Albania and the representation of that country abroad.[6]

In addition, the union between the two states was carried out mainly through the creation of the office of a Vicegerent of Albania *Luogotenente Generale*, through the Albanian Fascist Party, and through the permanent Italian counselors with Albanian ministries. The Vicegerent was appointed by royal Italian decree of April 22, 1939. He represents in Albania the absent King and exercises in his name the rights of sovereignty.

A fusion of the Albanian and Italian armed forces was effected by Italian law No. 1115 of July 13, 1939,[7] and by the decree of the Vicegerent of Albania of December 11, 1939.

By the decree of the Vicegerent of June 2, 1939,[8] there were established permanent Italian counselors with the various Albanian ministries. Such permanent counselors were appointed not only in the ministries and in particular services but also in municipalities.[9]

BASIC STATUTE

On June 3, 1939, King Victor Emmanuel conferred a Basic Statute [10] upon the Albanian people, to replace the constitution of 1928 theretofore in force. Under this statute the Albanian State is ruled by a constitutional monarchic government. The throne is hereditary, according to the Salic law, in the dynasty of Victor Emmanuel III, King of Italy and of Albania, Emperor of Ethiopia. The executive power belongs to the King and is exercised by him through a Council of Ministers, who are appointed and dismissed by him. The King may appoint a Vicegerent, who exercises the royal powers, with the exception of those which the King expressly reserves to himself. The rôle of the former Parliament is assumed by the Fascist Upper Corporative Council, which is composed of the Central Council of the Albanian Fascist Party and of members of the Central Council of Corporative Economy. The Fascist Upper Corporative Council is convoked by the King, and the King, together with the Fascist Upper Corporative Council, exercises legislative power. When reasons of urgent and absolute necessity require it, the King may issue decrees having the force of laws. In this case, however, the royal decree must be presented to the Fascist Upper Corporative Council for conversion into law. Articles 45 to 52 deal with the

[6] *Gazzetta ufficiale del Regno d'Albania*, 1939, No. 38. In Italy this treaty was published by law of May 16, 1940, No. 636.

[7] See below, p. 272.

[8] *Gazzetta ufficiale del Regno d'Albania*, 1939, No. 39.

By the decree of the Vicegerent of September 18, 1939, No. 94, the functions of these counselors were defined. These functions are of a double character, to advise the ministry and to control its activities.

[9] Decree of Vicegerent of September 12, 1939, *Fletorja Zyrtare*, No. 86.

[10] See below, p. 267.

rights and duties of citizens. Formally, civil rights were granted the Albanians by this statute, but every article of the statute in this respect is qualified by such reservations as "except in cases otherwise provided for by law." These reservations make illusory the guaranties of individual rights mentioned in the Basic Statute.

ADMINISTRATION

1. *Italian Administration.* The supreme authority (under the King) is the Vicegerent, who represents the King in Albania. The Vicegerent promulgates decrees, called Vicegerent's decrees (*Decreti Luogotenenziali*).

Control over the Albanian Government is carried out by the exercise of the appointive power on the part of Italy, but the Albanian Government is also controlled from within by the permanent Italian counselors mentioned above, who are active in every ministry.[11]

A decree of September 18, 1939, defined the functions of these Italian counselors as follows: they advise the ministry on the one hand and control it on the other. Formally, the counselors are appointed by the Albanian Government, but the government must be authorized to do so by the Italian Vicegerent. The permanent counselors have a civil service rating in the Albanian administration and are paid from the Treasury of the Albanian State.

Beside this form of control of the Albanian administration through permanent Italian counselors, the Italian Government exercises an effective influence on Albanian administration by establishing directly Italian authorities in Albania. These authorities are controlled by the Under Secretary for Albanian Affairs in the Ministry of Foreign Affairs in Rome. In this way various Italian offices have been created in Albania, such as offices of civil engineering, offices for highway, tramway and automobile transportation, for railroads and for public works, as well as an office of Director of the Italian Day Dispensary of Tirana, and of an Expert for Albanian Youth and for After-Work Recreation Centers (*Dopolavoro*).[12] The salaries of such officials are paid by the Italian Treasury.

2. *Albanian Administration.* The Albanian Government is directed by a Council of Ministers, consisting of a president, the Minister Secretary of the National Fascist Party, Minister of Justice, Minister of the Interior, Minister of Public Works, Minister of Finance, Minister of Public Instruction, and Minister of National Economy. To these ministries a Ministry for Redeemed Territories was added when Albania annexed certain territories after the dismemberment of Yugoslavia by the Axis.[13] Every minister is

[11] See decree of the Vicegerent of June 2, 1939, *Gazzetta ufficiale del Regno d'Albania,* June 9, 1939, No. 39.

[12] See decree of January 29, 1940, below, p. 273.

[13] The organization in the annexed territories after Germany took over Albania is unknown to the author.

assisted by one or more under secretaries of state. The ministers and the under secretaries are nominated by the Vicegerent.

The provincial administration was not essentially changed. The country is divided into prefectures, and because of the war new authorities were created, such as, a Central Committee for Provisioning and Consumption (*Comitato Centrale Approvigiamenti e Consumi*), which takes care of the food situation in the country, and Provincial Economic Councils (*Consigli Provinciali dell'Economia*), which coordinate economic activities in the provinces with the respective ministries in the capital.

Among other new authorities the following are noteworthy: the authorities and committees for the confiscation of property and the committees for police internment (see below).

In the field of finance the same unit of currency, namely, the Albanian franc, remained in force. The Albanian franc, divided into 5 lek, is equivalent to 6.25 lire.

FASCIZATION

Fascization of Albania was carried out mainly through the Albanian Fascist Party, the Fascist Upper Corporative Council, and the Central Council of Corporative Economy.

Albanian Fascist Party. The Albanian Fascist Party, the only political party in Albania, was organized in the first month after the occupation of Albania by Italy. It was constituted in no sense as a separate organization but as a branch of the Italian Fascist Party. The unity of the two parties was indicated by the subordination of the Albanian branch to the Duce of Fascism.[14] The members of the Albanian Fascist Party took an oath to obey the orders of the Duce of Fascism.[15]

The organization of the Albanian Party provided that its secretary be appointed and dismissed by the Vicegerent on the recommendation of the President of the Council of Ministers, after consultation with the Secretary of the National Fascist Party in Rome. The Secretary of the Albanian Fascist Party was to have the title and function of Minister of State, and to receive orders of the Duce from the secretary of the party in Rome. The latter party was represented in the Albanian Fascist Party "by a National Fascist Party Inspector assisted by a Federal Secretary and by Federal inspectors of the National Fascist Party." In harmony with the Italian Fascist pattern, members of the party were called upon to fulfill administrative duties in the Albanian Government, as well as to participate in the corporative councils. Thus, the Secretary of the Albanian Fascist Party designated, with the approval of the Vicegerent, representatives of the

[14] Vicegerent's decree of June 2, 1939, Article I: "The Albanian Fascist Party is a voluntary civilian militia under the orders of Benito Mussolini, the Creator and Duce of Fascism." See below, p. 275.

[15] See text of the oath, *ibid*.

Albanian Fascist Party to serve in the Central Committee of Corporative Economy and in the councils, as well as in the central and local offices of each ministry.[16] The dependence of the Albanian branch on the Italian Party is to be seen in the provision of the statute that no modification may be made therein "without previous agreement with the National Fascist Party."[17]

Fascist Upper Corporative Council. In accordance with the provisions of the Basic Statute of the Kingdom, the Fascist Upper Corporative Council was established in place of the former Parliament, as indicated above. The main function of this council is collaboration with the government in the elaboration of laws. The ministers are *ex officio* a part of the council. Among other things, the council establishes the corporative order, the budget, and accounts. It discusses and votes on various subjects, including such important matters as international treaties involving changes in state territory and problems concerning the administration of justice. The Fascist Upper Corporative Council functions through a plenary assembly, a General Budget Committee, and legislative committees.[18]

Central Council of Corporative Economy. By the Vicegerent's decree of March 14, 1940, a Central Council of Corporative Economy in Albania was instituted. This council is called on to give its opinion on all matters relating to economics and labor. It is composed of a president, four vice-presidents, and twenty-four members of the Fascist Party. It includes four sections—agriculture, industry, commerce, and professions and arts.[19]

ITALIAN PROPAGANDA

In order to carry on Italian propaganda in the field of culture in Albania, a special institution called "Skanderbeg Foundation" was established with headquarters in Tirana. The Foundation is composed of two autonomous sections. The first section is called the Institute for Albanian Studies and has as its object the development of "philosophical, literary, artistic, and historic culture in Albania." The second section is called the Italo-Albanian Skanderbeg Club and has as its purpose the establishment, improvement, and furtherance of social relations between Albanians and Italians. The Foundation is based upon an endowment of eight million Italian lire granted by the Minister of Foreign Affairs of the Kingdom of Italy. The members of the Institute of Albanian Studies are appointed by the Vicegerent, on recommendation of the Minister for Public Instruction, from among Albanians, Italians, and even foreign scholars who have taken an interest in the

[16] See Article XXI of the statute of the Albanian Fascist Party, below, p. 276.
[17] Since the writing of the present chapter the Italian Fascist Party in Rome has been dissolved by the government of Badoglio. This event should bring about a dissolution also of the Albanian Fascist Party. At the close of this book, however, it is unknown to the author what repercussions the dissolution of the Fascist Party in Rome has had in Albania.
[18] See Vicegerent's decree No. 101, April 3, 1940, below, p. 277.
[19] See Vicegerent's decree No. 73, *ibid.*

cultural studies of Albania. Membership in the Skanderbeg Club is restricted to Italian and Albanian citizens.[20]

ECONOMIC CONTROL

Customs Union. By the treaty of April 20, 1939, as we have seen, a customs union between Italy and Albania was established. By the terms of this treaty the territory of both countries is considered, with respect to the application of tariffs and customs regulations, as one territory. All trade restrictions between the two countries, with the exception of those which may be dictated by sanitary considerations, are abolished. The Italian customs laws apply in both countries, and the customs administration is Italian. Treaties with third parties are concluded by Italy alone, though the effects of such treaties are also binding on Albania. However, Albanian representatives are to be admitted to treaty negotiations in order to take care of specific Albanian interests. According to the customs union treaty, Albania was to receive yearly fifteen million Albanian francs from Italy as compensation for the customs duties which Albania expected to lose because of the tariff union with Italy. A mixed Italo-Albanian committee was established in order to carry out this treaty.[21]

Although the term "tariff union" was used in the above-mentioned document, the conditions of the treaty justify rather the use of the term "absorption of Albanian tariff interests by Italy," because the Italian tariff system has superseded the Albanian system and because Italy is empowered to determine the tariff policy of both countries.

Italian Economic Penetration. Because of the control by the Vicegerent and the Italian counselors in the various ministries over the political and economic life of Albania, Italian capital is enabled to assume a dominant position in Albania. Such dominance has been conferred mainly by granting charters for monopolistic exploitation of natural resources, and for industrial and commercial businesses. In some instances mixed Italo-Albanian companies were created, for example, La Società Anonima Compagnia Commerciale Italo Albanese (S.A.C.I.A.); in other instances Italian companies took over directly economic interests in Albania. On March 14, 1940, the Albanian Government signed a mining covenant with the Italian Coal Company (A.Ca. I.) to the effect that this company shall receive for a period of ten years the exclusive right of search for and production of mineral combustibles in Albanian territory. The Italian company was given the right not only to extend its activities to areas free from mining concessions at the date of the signature of the agreement, but also to areas which subsequently might be freed, by relinquishment or by default on the part of

[20] See Statute of the Skanderbeg Foundation, Vicegerent's decree No. 114 of April 8, 1940, below, p. 278.

[21] *Rivista di diritto internazionale,* Vol. XIX (1940), pp. 271–83.

the present holders of permits or concessions.[22] The predominant position of the Italian Government in Albania gives to this company in fact very great opportunities for taking over the rights of actual concessionaires in the field of mining. Many other Italian or Italian-controlled mixed companies were given similar rights in exploiting other national resources of Albania.

CRIMINAL LAW

A considerable part of the Italian Criminal Code of 1930, namely, the chapter on *crimes against the personality of the state*, was introduced into Albania by a decree of the Vicegerent of January 6, 1940.[23] The Italian Criminal Code deals in a detailed manner with all forms of offenses against the state from the point of view of both internal and international relations. The Albanians were called upon to be faithful to both states, Albania and Italy, to the same extent as Italians were obliged to be faithful to Italy.[24] Treason in the sense of this decree is punished as a rule by the death penalty.[25]

Police Internment. Judicial guaranties as to *personal freedom* do not exist in the régime introduced by Italy. A person may be deprived of his freedom by way of police internment—equivalent to confinement in a certain type of concentration camp. Decisions in regard thereto are made by special committees for police internment. These include a central committee for police internment in Tirana and various provincial committees, of which representatives of the police and of the Fascist militia are members.[26]

In a country like Albania the safety of the roads and telecommunications services represents an important problem. It is along the roads that the Albanian patriots strike most frequently in their struggle against the Italian invader and the Albanians who are collaborating with Italians. Besides the provisions set forth in penal law, special additional administrative sanctions for such acts were introduced by the decree of November 13, 1942.[27] This order does not specify the offenses but speaks in general terms of acts which constitute "a menace to public safety on the roads and to telecommunications services." According to this decree, all inhabitants of villages included within a radius of five kilometers from the spot where any of the acts have been committed are collectively responsible for such acts. A collective fine of from 1,000 to 20,000 Albanian francs is to be imposed on such inhabitants, and heads of all families residing in the area are to be interned for one year. If the fine is not paid, the land produce, sheep, and other cattle of the inhabitants will be sold in order to cover the sum of the fine. The collective fine and the internment are decided upon by the committees for police internment mentioned above.

[22] See Vicegerent's decree, below, p. 280.
[23] See below, p. 281.
[24] It is unknown to the writer whether an amendment to the Italian Penal Code was enacted obligating Italians to be faithful to the Albanian State.
[25] Decree of January 6, 1940, below, p. 281.
[26] Decree of October 23, 1942, below, p. 282.
[27] See below, p. 282.

PROPERTY

Likewise there are no judicial guaranties as to protection of property. According to the decree of the Vicegerent of September 12, 1939, a special office (*Ufficio Beni Confiscati e Sequestrati*) was established for handling sequestrated and confiscated goods of persons who are suspected of activities "against the interests of the nation." This office is supervised by a Central Committee created within the Ministry of Finance. It consists of a counselor of the Ministry of Finance, of the permanent Italian counselors at the ministries of Justice, Finance, and National Economy, of the Commander of the Finance Guard, and of a representative of the Albanian Fascist Party. The Central Committee renders decisions regarding sequestration and confiscation, and the *Ufficio Beni Confiscati e Sequestrati* carries out the respective decisions. For confiscations throughout all the country provincial committees were created at every prefecture. These provincial committees make recommendations concerning confiscations to the Central Committee in Tirana.[28]

INTERNATIONAL STATUS OF ALBANIA

In official documents as well as by writers of Italian periodical literature the term "Union" is used to define the relationship between Italy and Albania. Whatever the modalities of a union may be, they essentially presuppose equality and coordination between the states, whereas in the relations between Italy and Albania there is rather inequality and subordination of Albania to Italy. This subordination is obvious from the fact that Italy assumed the representation of Albania in international relations; that the Albanian Government has been controlled from without and from within by the Italian Government; and that Albanian political life, even in the form of the Albanian Fascist Party, has been directed from Italy, that is, by the Secretary of the Italian Fascist Party, to which the Albanian Fascist Party was wholly subject.

Other Italian authors recognize this fact of complete subordination of Albania to Italy.[29] But still other writers advance the argument that no state of war existed between Italy and Albania and that Italy's occupation of Albania is in the nature of a pacific occupation.[30] The latter authors ignore not only the fact of the stubborn resistance of the outnumbered Albanian

[28] *Fletorja Zyrtare*, 1939, No. 99.

[29] See Giorgio Cansacchi, "L'Unione dell'Albania con Italia," *Rivista di diritto internazionale*, Vol. XIX (1940), pp. 113–32.

[30] Rizzo, "L'Unione dell'Albania con l'Italia e lo Statuto del Regno di Albania," *Rivista di diritto pubblico*, 1939, p. 18; Varanini, "L'Albania," *Gerarchia* (1939), pp. 299 ff.; Cataluccio, "L'Unione personale fra Italia e Albania," *Civiltà Fascista* (1939), pp. 285 ff.; Feroci, "L'Unione all'Italia del Regno d'Albania," *Il Tribunale*, November 30, 1939; La Torre, "L'Unione dell'Italia con l'Albania i suoi riflessi politici e giuridici," *Echi e Commenti* (1939), pp. 388 ff.; Marchitto, "L'Albania nell' aggregato imperiale Italiano," *Lo Stato* (1939), pp. 555 ff.

Army in April, 1939, but also the circumstance that Albanian patriots continued to fight a form of guerrilla warfare against the Italians. One must rather conclude that a protectorate was established over Albania by Italy in the course of a prolonged belligerent occupation, and that in fact the Italo-Albanian relationship cannot be properly described as either "pacific occupation" or "union."

In the war against Greece and Yugoslavia, Italy used Albania as an operational base against these two countries. For the services rendered by Quisling Albanians to the Axis Powers, Albania was allowed to annex parts of Yugoslavia and Greece.[31] The Allies have, however, recognized that Albania has been overrun by Italy by way of military action, and the continued resistance of the Albanian patriots has moved the Allies to issue statements on the restoration of Albania's independence after the defeat of the Axis.[32]

[31] See below, chapters on "Greece" and "Yugoslavia."

[32] See statement of Cordell Hull of December 10, 1942, Department of State, *Bulletin*, Vol. VII, No. 181 (December 12, 1942), p. 998; and statement by Winston Churchill of November 4, 1943, London *Times*, November 5, 1943, p. 8, col. 2.

CHAPTER XI

AUSTRIA

I. Pre-Invasion Period

One of the main points in Hitler's *Mein Kampf* concerned the absorption of Austria.[1] Before achieving that goal, however, many other important steps had to be taken, including the remilitarization of the Rhineland and the rebuilding of German economy in accordance with war plans (rearmament). In order to be able to carry out this program unhampered, it was necessary for Hitler to assure his neighbors of his peaceful intentions. A non-aggression treaty with Poland was signed in 1934; and in his speech of May 21, 1935, Hitler asserted: "Germany neither intends nor wishes to interfere in the internal affairs of Austria, to annex Austria or to conclude an Anschluss." At the time of the occupation of the Rhineland he announced that the German struggle for equality was concluded and that "we have no territorial demands to make in Europe."[2] On July 11, 1936, Germany signed a treaty with Austria, Articles 1 and 2 of which state that Germany "recognizes the full sovereignty of the Federal State of Austria"; and that both governments shall regard the internal political conditions existing in the country of the other signatory, including the problem of Austrian National Socialism, as an internal problem which concerns only the country involved and upon which the other signatory shall not take any direct or indirect action. According to Article 3 of the same agreement, the Federal Government of Austria declared itself to be ready to maintain its general policy, and especially its policy in relation to the German Reich, upon the basis of principles in harmony with the fact that Austria recognized herself to be a German state.[3]

In July, 1937, Hitler gave a specific pledge not to attack Austria, and on January 30, 1937, declared that "the period of so-called surprises is now over."[4] On February 8, 1938, Chancellor Schuschnigg was invited to an interview with Hitler at Berchtesgaden. The interview took place on February 12, 1938, at which time Hitler required from Schuschnigg a pledge that he would remove restrictions on the Nazi Party and admit Nazi sympathizers to ministerial posts. If that promise should not be complied with, Hitler threatened to invade Austria; if it should be complied with, he prom-

[1] "German-Austria must return to the great German motherland. . . . *Common blood belongs in a common Reich*." — *Mein Kampf*, p. 1.

[2] Edgar McInnis, *The Oxford Periodical History of the War* (Toronto: Oxford University Press, Canadian Branch, March 12, 1940), p. 20.

[3] *Völkerbund* (Geneva), VII, No. 11–12 (March, 1938), p. 150.

[4] Edgar McInnis, *op. cit.*, p. 20.

ised to reaffirm Austrian independence. In compliance with the request of Hitler, Schuschnigg formed a new cabinet, in which he gave the post of Minister of Interior and of Security to the Nazi leader Seyss-Inquart.[5] Another Nazi sympathizer, Dr. Skubl, was appointed Inspector General of all police and gendarmerie forces.[6] On February 20, Hitler made a pledge in the Reichstag, in which he declared himself protector of all Germans—without, however, mentioning Austria. Schuschnigg, who had evidence of a Nazi plot then in course of preparation, tried to extend the political basis of his cabinet by opening negotiations with the leaders of the working class; and he announced a referendum on the question of Austrian independence for March 13, 1938. Nazi demonstrations thereupon broke out in Austria and the German press started a campaign against "Austrian atrocities."[7] Hitler sent an ultimatum on March 11 demanding that the plebiscite be called off. The same day a second ultimatum demanded that Schuschnigg resign within three hours; if he should refuse, the country would be invaded. Schuschnigg resigned in order to avoid bloodshed. Then a Nazi member of the Schuschnigg cabinet formed a government and invited Hitler to send troops into Austria to preserve order.

II. The Anschluss

The invasion began on the morning of March 12, 1938; on March 13 President Miklas was forced out of office,[8] and by proclamation Hitler assumed office as Chief of State of Austria and took command of its armed forces.[9] A law of March 13, 1938 (published in the *Reichsgesetzblatt* the following day) provided for the annexation of Austria by Germany;[10] and from then on Austria became a province of the German Reich. (The name Ostmark was also temporarily used for the designation of Austria.) The same law likewise announced a plebiscite for April 10, 1938, "on the question of reunion with the German Reich." The act of annexation, however, had in effect converted the issue from a question to be decided by plebiscite into an affirmative fact.

[5] Seyss-Inquart now serves as Reich Commissioner of the Netherlands.

[6] *Bulletin of International News* (The Royal Institute of International Affairs), Vol. XV, No. 5 (March 5, 1938), p. 188.

[7] In order to create an atmosphere of appeasement in the United States, Walther Funk, the German Minister of Economics, on March 6 appealed to the United States for an improvement in American-German trade relations. He proposed an international plan as a basis of stabilizing currencies.

[8] See "The Occupation of Austria," in *The United States in World Affairs, an Account of American Foreign Relations, 1938*, by Whitney H. Shepardson in collaboration with William O. Scroggs, published by the Council on Foreign Relations (New York, 1939), especially p. 42.

[9] On the same date Göring warned Europe that the Reich extended protection to all Germans, whether or not they lived within German borders.

[10] See below, p. 283. This law embodied verbatim the Austrian Federal Constitutional Law of the same date concerning the reunion of Austria with Germany and providing for a plebiscite on April 10.

That the plebiscite, indeed, was conceived only as a formality to serve Hitler's purpose is clear from the fact that the incorporation occurred before the plebiscite and that no flexible or alternative clause was provided in the incorporating act in the event that the decision by plebiscite should be against the incorporation. On the same day, March 13, Hitler published a decree by which the Austrian Federal Army was incorporated into the German Wehrmacht and placed under Hitler's command.[11] All members of the former Austrian Federal Army were compelled without delay to take the oath of allegiance to him as their Commander in Chief. Thus, in anticipation of a "free" plebiscite, Austria was already absorbed and disarmed.

On March 15 a decree of the Führer was published by which the Austrian Federal Government was abolished and its name changed to Austrian Provincial Government. A governor was named for Austria to serve as head of the Provincial Government.[12]

On the same date Hitler issued a decree to the effect that all laws and decrees promulgated for the German Reich after March 13, 1938, should extend automatically to Austria, except in those cases in which an express reservation was made to the contrary.[13] Thus the sovereignty of German law was imposed upon Austria. Moreover, by the same decree a number of specific German laws were introduced, such as the Reich flag law of September 15, 1935; the law against the formation of new parties, which law provided that the only political party in Austria should be the National Socialist Party; the law for ensuring the unity of party and state; the *Reichsstatthalter* Act of January 30, 1935, which defines the duties and rights of the Reich governors; the order for implementation of the Four-Year Plan of October 18, 1936; and the law concerning compulsory registration of members of the German State abroad.

The Reich Minister of the Interior, on March 16, 1938, was entrusted by Hitler with the carrying out of "the reunion of Austria with the German Reich," and was authorized to delegate his authority to a special Reich Commissioner for Austria.[14]

By decree of March 17, 1938,[15] the Austrian National Bank was liquidated and its administration and assets transferred to the Reichsbank for the account of the Reich. Also on March 17, the Reichsmark was introduced as legal tender in addition to the Austrian schilling. The ratio of exchange between these two currencies was established as 1 Reichsmark to 1.5 schillings. The reserves of the Austrian National Bank, amounting to 422,000,000 schillings worth of gold and foreign exchange, were transferred to the Reichsbank.[16] On March 23, Hitler took command of the Austrian flotilla and ordered the building of a new war fleet on the Danube.[17]

[11] See below, p. 284. [12] See below, p. 285. [13] See below, p. 292.
[14] See below, p. 284. [15] See below, p. 287.
[16] Arnold J. Toynbee, *Survey of International Affairs, 1938* (London: Oxford University Press, 1941. Issued under the auspices of the Royal Institute of International Affairs), Vol. I, p. 77.
[17] *Current History*, May, 1938, p. 61.

A further evidence of the extension of German sovereignty before the plebiscite is the decree of March 22, 1938, providing that the Austrian courts should administer justice "in the name of the German people," [18] as well as the decree of March 15, in which it was stated that all civil servants in service at that time, or to be appointed in the future, had to take the following oath: "I swear that I shall be loyal and obedient to Adolf Hitler, the Führer of the German Reich and People, and that I shall observe the laws and conscientiously fulfill the duties of my office, so help me God." [19] Ten days before the plebiscite, namely, on March 31, 1938, a Reich Propaganda Office was created in Vienna.[20] Thus, having incorporated the Austrian Army on March 13, 1938, and having sworn in the entire civil administration, which was required to collaborate in the control of the plebiscite, Hitler could quietly await its results.

The plebiscite was carried out on April 10, 1938. Formally 99.08 per cent of the votes were given in favor of annexation. It is obvious that under these conditions the plebiscite was not carried out as an expression of the free will of the Austrian people.

III. Administration

In accordance with the law of April 14, 1939,[21] the territory of Austria was divided into districts (*Gaue*), in compliance with the German pattern of administration. Eight districts were created, namely, the District of Vienna, comprising the city of Vienna; the District of Carinthia, comprising the former Austrian province of Carinthia, with its seat in Klagenfurt; the District of the Lower Danube, comprising the former Austrian province of Lower Austria, with its seat in Krems-on-the-Danube; the District of the Upper Danube, comprising the former Austrian province of Upper Austria, with its seat in Linz; the District of Salzburg, comprising the former Austrian province of Salzburg, with its seat in Salzburg; the District of Styria, comprising the former Austrian province of Styria, with its seat in Graz; the District of Tyrol, comprising the former Austrian province of Tyrol, with its seat in Innsbruck. The former Austrian province of Vorarlberg was made a separate administrative district and autonomous corporation, to be supervised by the Reich Governor in Tyrol.

At the head of every district is a Reich governor (*Reichsstatthalter*). Within the area of the district the Reich governor conducts the administration under the supervision of the Reich Minister of the Interior and in accordance with directives of other Reich ministers in their respective spheres of jurisdiction. The authorities of the Reich special administrations within the area of the district, with the exception of the Reich justice, finance, railway, and postal administrations, are subordinated to the Reich governor.

[18] See below, p. 293. [19] See below, p. 286.
[20] See below, p. 287. [21] See below, p. 288.

The administration of the Reich District of Vienna is divided under a special provision into a state administration and a municipal administration. For administrative purposes the districts are in general divided into counties and municipalities. At the head of the county is the prefect (*Landrat*). At the head of the municipality is the burgomaster.

The Austrian administration of justice was merged with the German administration of justice. The Supreme Court of Austria in Vienna was abolished by decree of February 28, 1939,[22] and the jurisdiction of this court was transferred to the Reichsgericht in Leipzig. The duties of the Attorney General before the Supreme Court of Austria were transferred to the Attorney General at the Reichsgericht. The courts of lower jurisdiction received the same designations as in Germany. The provincial and circuit courts were designated *Landgerichte* and the precinct courts *Amtsgerichte*.[23]

A special state tribunal, the members of which were to be appointed by the Führer and Reich Chancellor, was created in Vienna by law of August 17, 1938,[24] in order to try members of the former Austrian Federal Government and their associates, as well as burgomasters of the city and their associates, for acts "inimical to the people." The indictment was to be filed "in the name of the German people" by the Reich Commissioner for the Reunion of Austria with the German Reich.[25] In addition to the penalties to be imposed by this tribunal, the Reich Minister of the Interior was authorized to act independently, that is, he was empowered to withdraw the civil rights of the persons found guilty, to deprive them of citizenship, and to confiscate their property.

In furtherance of the principle that vocational education should have preference over liberal arts education, an order was issued on May 31, 1940, elaborating Austria's system of vocational schools.[26] This emphasis upon vocational education may be explained by war conditions. However, in the particular case of Austria the preference given to vocational over general (liberal arts) education was designed to destroy humanistic thinking, which might give foundations for national thinking. Thus the new school system was only one of the instrumentalities intended for the intellectual and political absorption of Austria.

IV. International Status of Austria

The Anschluss of Austria involves several problems of international law:

1. Hitler displayed a disregard for the principle of non-intervention in the internal affairs of other countries by requesting that Nazi leaders should

[22] See below, p. 295. [23] See decree of August 2, 1938, below, p. 294.

[24] See below, p. 294.

[25] A temporary office, which lasted until the division of Austria into districts (*Gaue*). See above, pp. 110, 111.

[26] See below, p. 296. This decree relates also to the Sudetenland.

form a part of the Schuschnigg cabinet, by demanding that the Schuschnigg plebiscite should be prohibited, and by requesting the resignation of Schuschnigg himself.

2. Germany violated its treaty with Austria of July 11, 1936, by the terms of which it obligated itself to respect the sovereignty of Austria and to consider National Socialism as an internal problem of Austria. By this treaty the principle of non-intervention in the relations between the two countries was specifically strengthened, and therefore Germany's intervention in behalf of National Socialism in Austria became not only a violation of recognized principles of international law, but also a violation of a specific treaty.[27]

The third article of the above-mentioned treaty, stating that Austria's "general policy and its policy towards Germany in particular shall be constantly guided by the principle that Austria recognizes herself to be a German State," [28] requires some comment. It may be understood as a reference to the fact that the population of Austria is of German origin and speaks the German language. On the same basis, a German-speaking canton in Switzerland would be able to make a similar statement. By making such a statement, however, no implications would be created for that canton as to relationship or allegiance to other states of German culture. In somewhat the same sense any Latin American country would be able to declare itself a Latin American state, without infringing upon the idea of its sovereignty. The third article is thus irrelevant from the point of view of international law. It did not impose any particular obligations upon Austria. It has the character only of a generally conceived declaration without legal consequences. In the light of later developments, however, it would appear that Hitler, in concluding this agreement, made mental reservations in relation to Austria. From that point of view the article was a premeditated preparation on his part of pretexts for later declaring himself protector of "the whole German people, whose sons we all are, wherever we may have been born." [29]

3. The Anschluss of Austria was likewise a violation of Article 80 of the Treaty of Versailles,[30] as well as the Covenant of the League of Nations, which guaranteed the independence of all of its members, including Austria.[31] The fact that Germany had retired from the League of Nations be-

[27] See above, p. 108. [28] *Völkerbund* (Geneva), VII, No. 11–12 (March, 1938), p. 150.

[29] Hitler's speech in the Reichstag, February 20, 1938, *ibid.*, p. 151.

[30] "ARTICLE 80. Germany acknowledges and will respect strictly the independence of Austria, within the frontiers which may be fixed in a Treaty between that State and the Principal Allied and Associated Powers; she agrees that this independence shall be inalienable, except with the consent of the Council of the League of Nations."

[31] "ARTICLE 10. The Members of the League undertake to respect and preserve as against external aggression the territorial integrity and existing political independence of all Members of the League. In case of any such aggression or in case of any threat or danger of such aggression the Council shall advise upon the means by which this obligation shall be fulfilled."

fore the invasion of Austria did not change the obligation of other members of the League "to respect and preserve as against external aggression" Austrian territorial integrity and political independence.

4. Both plebiscites—that announced by Schuschnigg and that carried out by Hitler—are irrelevant from the point of view of international law. According to Article 88 of the Treaty of St. Germain,[32] the independence of Austria is inalienable and changes in its international status could be validly undertaken only with the consent of the Council of the League of Nations. Neither Austria itself nor another power could legally organize a plebiscite contrary to the Treaty of St. Germain, in order to decide as to Austria's sovereignty. Aside from the cited express provisions of international treaties, it is a clear violation of international law for one country to invade another country and to try to validate the incorporation of the invaded country into its own by a specially organized plebiscite under the protection of its invading armies.

5. Disregarding these legal considerations, it is obvious that under the conditions above set forth the plebiscite was not carried out as an expression of the free will of the Austrian people. If Hitler believed that a plebiscite was a solution of the problem involved, he should have awaited the results of the plebiscite announced by Schuschnigg for the 13th of March. Having two Nazi members in the Schuschnigg cabinet (Dr. Seyss-Inquart, now Reich Commissioner for the Netherlands, and Dr. Skubl), he would have been able to ascertain whether the plebiscite as ordered by Schuschnigg was conducted with fairness and accuracy. Moreover, as already noted, the law calling the plebiscite, by announcing the annexation of Austria, converted the issue in effect from a question to be decided by the free will of the people into an affirmative fact. And since the Anschluss law was promulgated before the plebiscite and did not contain a resilient clause to the effect that the incorporation would be invalid if the plebiscite were decided in favor of Austria's independence, one must consider that the plebiscite was conceived by Hitler as a mere formality, organized and prepared for the purpose of covering the real character of the invasion.

6. The recognition *de jure* of the Anschluss by some states was in violation of the Covenant of the League of Nations. In accordance with the provisions of Article 16, the members of the League of Nations were obliged to act against the aggressor and not help such aggressor by recognition. Setting aside the problem of whether and how far recognition of a state by other states is relevant as to the evaluation of its juridical existence or non-existence, the *de jure* recognition of the Anschluss was in violation of the Cove-

[32] "ARTICLE 88. The independence of Austria is inalienable otherwise than with the consent of the Council of the League of Nations. Consequently Austria undertakes in the absence of the consent of the said Council to abstain from any act which might directly or indirectly or by any means whatever compromise her independence, particularly, and until her admission to membership of the League of Nations, by participation in the affairs of another Power."

nant of the League of Nations. Guided by the principles of the non-recognition doctrine, the United States of America has not recognized the Anschluss *de jure*. The recognition was only *de facto*.[33] Other states have not only not recognized the Anschluss but have filed protests with the League of Nations against it.[34]

Thus, while the basic facts are that Austria was invaded and occupied by military action, it is submitted that the Anschluss was illegal from the point of view of international law; that the sovereignty of Austria has not been destroyed but only suspended;[35] and that as soon as the occupant is driven from the territory of Austria, that country's sovereignty will be automatically restored to it.[36]

[33] Garner, in an article on "Questions of State Succession Raised by the German Annexation of Austria," states that the United States could not recognize the incorporation of Austria because of the doctrine laid down in the convention on the rights and duties of states (Montevideo, 1933), the Anti-War Pact of Rio de Janeiro, also of 1933, and the convention on the fulfillment of existing treaties (Buenos Aires, 1936). *American Journal of International Law*, Vol. 32 (1938), p. 421. The author of the present work does not share this view. The Pan American treaties referred to are limited to territorial changes effected by force in the territories of the contracting states and do not apply to territorial changes which take place outside the territories of the contracting parties. See Articles 11, 2, and 1, respectively, of the above-mentioned treaties, *International Conferences of American States, First Supplement, 1933–1940* (Washington: Carnegie Endowment for International Peace, 1940), pp. 122, 497, and 193.

Austria, not being a party to the aforementioned treaties, was therefore not protected by them. Only the following European countries have deposited ratifications of adherence to the Anti-War Pact of 1933: Bulgaria, Czechoslovakia, Finland, Rumania, Spain, and Yugoslavia. See *Status of the Pan American Treaties and Conventions* (Revised to January 1, 1943, by the Juridical Division of the Pan American Union).

[34] See letter from the Mexican Delegation to the Secretary General of the League of Nations, Geneva, March 19, 1938:

"The Mexican Government, which has always upheld the principles of the Covenant and in accordance with its consistent international policy refuses to recognise any conquest made by force, enters the most emphatic protest against the external aggression of which the Austrian Republic has just been the victim. It informs the public opinion of the world that in its view the only means of securing peace, and preventing further international outrages such as those that have been committed against Ethiopia, Spain, China, and Austria, is for the nations to carry out the obligations laid upon them by the Covenant, the treaties they have concluded and the principles of international law. Otherwise it will not be long before the world is overwhelmed by a far worse conflagration than that which it is sought to avoid by attempted action outside the League system." — League of Nations, *Official Journal*, 19th Year, Nos. 3–4 (March-April, 1938), p. 239.

[35] See Hyde, *International Law*, Vol. I, p. 176: "Thus in practice, upon the withdrawal of a belligerent occupant, the normal government of the State resumes automatically the exercise of its rights as sovereign which are deemed to have been suspended rather than transferred during the period of occupation."

[36] After this chapter was completed the Conference of Foreign Secretaries of the United States of America, the United Kingdom, and the Soviet Union, which met at Moscow from the 19th to the 30th of October, 1943, issued a declaration concerning the restoration of an independent Austrian state. The text of this declaration, which was published November 1, 1943, follows:

"The Governments of the United Kingdom, the Soviet Union and the United States of America are agreed that Austria, the first free country to fall a victim to Hitlerite aggression, shall be liberated from German domination.

"They regard the annexation imposed upon Austria by Germany on March 15th, 1938, as null and void. They consider themselves as in no way bound by any changes effected in Austria since that date. They declare that they wish to see reestablished a free and independent Austria, and thereby to open the way for the Austrian people themselves, as well as those neighboring states which will be faced with similar problems, to find that political and economic security which is the only basis for lasting peace.

"Austria is reminded, however, that she has a responsibility which she cannot evade for participation in the war on the side of Hitlerite Germany, and that in the final settlement account will inevitably be taken of her own contribution to her liberation." Department of State, *Bulletin*, Vol. IX, No. 228 (November 6, 1943), p. 310.

The last paragraph of this text raises the question of Austrian responsibility for participation in the present war on the side of Germany. Here it may be observed that Austria, unlike Albania, Slovakia, or Croatia, was not organized by the Axis as a puppet state with a quasi-international personality, but was completely absorbed by Germany politically as well as administratively (see above). The Austrians who have been participating in this war on the side of Germany were mobilized under the German conscription laws. Thus it was by Germany, not by Austria, that these people were mobilized, and the question of the responsibility of Austria would not seem to arise. Those former Austrian citizens, however, who assisted Hitler in taking over the country, in Nazifying it, and in oppressing their fellow citizens, should be considered personally responsible for their acts.

CHAPTER XII

BALTIC STATES

(Lithuania, Latvia, Estonia)

The three Baltic States, Lithuania, Latvia, and Estonia, granted to Russia military bases on their own territories in November and December, 1939. In June, 1940, these states were occupied and incorporated into the Union of Soviet Socialist Republics as autonomous soviet republics of Lithuania, Latvia, and Estonia. A communist régime was gradually introduced into these countries up to the date of their occupation by Germany.

GERMAN ADMINISTRATION

After Germany occupied the Baltic States in June and July, 1941,[1] during the course of the war with Russia, each of these states was organized as a general commissariat, with headquarters in the capital of the respective state. Thus there were organized a General Commissariat for Lithuania,[1a] with headquarters in Kaunas, a General Commissariat for Latvia, with headquarters in Riga, and a General Commissariat for Estonia, with headquarters in Tallinn. These three general commissariats, together with a fourth called General Commissariat for White Russia,[2] composed one Reich Commissariat for the Ostland, with headquarters in Riga. The Reich Commissariat Ostland, as well as other territories occupied in Russia, was supervised by a specially created Ministry for the Territories Occupied in the East, with headquarters in Berlin. An intimate collaborator of Hitler, Alfred Rosenberg, author of the book *Der Mythus des 20. Jahrhunderts*, was named Reich Minister for the Territories Occupied in the East.

In the Baltic States the administration is in the hands of the Reich Commissioner for the Ostland. In each Baltic state there is also a Commissioner General who handles the administration in each individual state, chief commissioners who supervise administration of special regions or special branches, and district commissioners who are responsible for the administration in the smaller territorial units. However, the former administrative division was not continued but in its stead larger administrative districts or regions (*Gebiete*) were created with a chief commissioner at the head of each region.

[1] As to Lithuania, Germany had in March, 1939, occupied and incorporated Memel Territory, which had been theretofore under Lithuanian state sovereignty (see below, Chapter on "Memel Territory").

[1a] The territory of Lithuania was in the meantime increased, when, after the occupation of Poland by Germany and Russia in September, 1939, Russia turned over to Lithuania the Polish city of Wilno, together with the western part of the Wilno province.

[2] See below, chapters on "Poland" and "Union of Soviet Socialist Republics."

Thus in Lithuania the country's twenty-seven administrative districts were grouped in six larger *Gebiete*.[3]

ADMINISTRATION BY LOCAL POPULATION

To a certain extent the local population has been called upon to participate in the administration. Administration by the local population (*Landeseigene Verwaltung*) is headed in each of the states by a group of department chiefs, who have the title of general councillors in Lithuania, general directors in Latvia, and directors in Estonia. These departmental chiefs are appointed by the commissioners general in conjunction with the Reich Commissioner for the Ostland. The departmental chiefs receive directions from and are strictly supervised by the office of the Commissioner General in each state. The participation of the local population in the lower bracket, that is, in the districts, is effected by district elders (*einheimische Kreisälteste*). These district elders are appointed from the local population by the Commissioner General in each country, on the recommendation of the departmental chiefs. Just as the departmental chiefs receive directions from and are supervised by the German commissioners general, the district elders receive their instructions from and are supervised by the German district commissioners.

Administration in the urban and rural communities is carried out by special leaders, who are assisted in the towns by town councillors (*Stadträte*) and in the rural communities by parish councillors (*Gemeinderäte*). All these officials are appointed by the German administration, on recommendation of the district leaders, from the local administration.[4]

COURTS

A German Superior Court for all the Ostland was established at the headquarters of the Reich Commissioner, and at the headquarters of each Commissioner General a German court was established for his jurisdictional district. In addition a special court is associated with each German court. German courts have jurisdiction over all criminal cases except when these have been referred to another court for judgment; they have civil jurisdiction when a German citizen or a German by descent (*Volkszugehöriger*) is a party to the case. In addition the Reich Commissioner may in his discretion expressly define the jurisdiction of the German tribunals. From decisions of the lower German courts in the occupied areas an appeal lies to the German Superior Court. The special courts have such jurisdiction as is

[3] See mimeographed *Current News on the Lithuanian Situation.* Compiled by the Lithuanian Legation, Washington (June, 1943), Vol. II, 6 (30), p. 3.
[4] See *Latvia under German Occupation, 1941–1943.* With a Preface by Dr. Alfred Bīlmanis, Minister of Latvia to the United States (Washington: Press Bureau of the Latvian Legation, 1943), pp. 3–12.

expressly defined in the laws of the Reich or in the laws of the Ostland.[5] According to established principles, the jurisdiction of special courts is always defined by the decree, which fixes penalties. Thus, it is a jurisdiction *a casu ad casum*. There are also courts martial, with the normal jurisdiction of German courts martial.[6]

In the German court as described above only one judge is required for decisions; in the German Superior Court, three judges, except as otherwise prescribed; and in the special court, one presiding judge and two associates. The associates of the special court must, "as far as practicable have the qualifications for the office of judge." But the insertion of the phrase "as far as practicable" makes it obvious that the qualifications of a judge are not an absolute prerequisite. The associates are appointed by the Commissioner General for one year, from the ranks of German citizens or Germans by descent resident in the district of the special court. In some cases the presiding judge of the Superior Court may decide without oral process. Representation by counsel is not compulsory. Any Reich German or German by descent who "offers surety for an adequate defense" may be admitted as defense counsel. Thus it would appear that he need not be a practising lawyer.

The right of appeal is limited. In criminal cases it is allowed only when a more severe penalty than one month's imprisonment or five hundred marks' fine has been imposed; in civil cases, when the right of appeal "has been expressly granted by the judgment," the meaning of which is that a judge *a quo* decides whether his judgment may be reviewed by the Superior Court. Jews may not seek legal recourse against the decision of a German court.[7]

The local courts have been allowed to continue in so far as their activities are not in conflict with the organization of German justice. The verdicts of local courts are passed "in the name of the law"; and final decisions of such courts may be reexamined by the German Superior Court, on motion by the Commissioner General. The German Superior Court "may confirm the decision of the local courts, or itself decide the matter differently, or, after cancelling the decision, delegate the case" to a German court or to another local court.[8]

The German courts in the Baltic States apply German criminal law to the same extent as in other occupied countries. As the principle of analogy in criminal law was introduced in the German Criminal Code in 1935,[9] no legal guaranties have been given the local population as to previous knowledge of the criminal nature of an act. This provision regarding German criminal

[5] See order of October 6, 1941, below, p. 303. [6] See above, Part I, "Courts."

[7] See order of October 6, 1941, below, p. 304.

[8] Decree concerning the provisional administration of justice by the local judicial authorities in the General District of Latvia, issued March 13, 1942, quoted in *Latvia under German Occupation, op. cit.*, p. 16.

[9] See above, Part I, "Law."

law, in conjunction with the limitations regarding review and defense, creates in fact a state of lawlessness and places the population completely at the mercy of the German administration.

SEIZURE OF PROPERTY

The problem of property became complicated because of the special régime of property which was introduced in the Baltic States after their incorporation into the U.S.S.R. Since the bulk of the property under the communist régime belongs to the state or to collective economic associations, it was possible for the German occupant to seize immediately a large number of properties, organized in special forms of economic concentration (*sovhos*, *kolhos*, combine, trust).

By the order of August 18, 1941,[10] the Reich Commissioner for the Ostland declared that "the German Civil Administration takes over all of the real and personal property situated in the territories administered by the Reich Commissioner for the Ostland which belongs to the Union of Soviet Socialist Republics, its member states, public corporations, associations, and partnerships, including all claims, investments, rights, and interests of all kinds as of June 20, 1941." These properties were put under the administration of special trustees.[11] Because of the great number of such trustees an especially elaborate system of control became necessary. Special public records were established in which the names of the trustees are entered for the information of the public. For the duration of the sequestration of property no legal processes for the satisfaction of creditors of any given property are permitted. Severe penalties, including the death penalty, are to be imposed upon persons interfering with the administration of the sequestrated properties.

As to private property, which survived to a certain extent in the Baltic States, the occupant gave its first attention to Jewish owners. An order was issued on October 13, 1941,[12] to the effect that Jewish property would be subject to sequestration, trustee administration, and confiscation. Only the following were exempted from seizure: (*a*) that part of the household furniture which is used for essential personal needs; and (*b*) cash, bank, and savings credits up to a total of one hundred Reichsmarks.

RETURN TO PRIVATE PROPERTY

When the German Army moved into the then Russian-held territories in June, 1941, it found a communistic régime which had been entrenched more or less deeply according to the duration of the régime in a given area. The Baltic States of Lithuania, Latvia, and Estonia had been under a Russian

[10] See below, p. 301.
[11] Order concerning sequestration of the property of the U.S.S.R., August 19, 1941, below, p. 304.
[12] See below, p. 307.

régime for one year, from June, 1940, to June, 1941, while the eastern Polish territories had been under Russian administration since September, 1939; but the remainder of the territories had been under a communist régime since 1917 and 1918. It is thus obvious that this régime was more deeply entrenched in the latter territories and that private property was more communized in them than in the territories held by the U.S.S.R. for one or two years.

In his first proclamation to the population the Reich Commissioner for the Ostland denounced the communist system, stating in his proclamation of July 28, 1941,[13] that "Bolshevism was threatening all Europe. . . . If this world enemy had been rampant among you a few more years, nothing would have been left to you of your property and people." It was also stated in the proclamation that the Germans had made sacrifice of their blood in order to overthrow "the Bolshevik universal enemy" and that the German people have "therefore now assumed the duty and the right to make such arrangements that never again will a similar danger be able to threaten anew the traditions of the people of Europe, and indeed their whole existence." This proclamation therefore encouraged the hope on the part of the local population that their private properties would be restored to them. However, in the first executive regulation concerning the reorganization of handicrafts, issued on December 23, 1941, in connection with the decree of October 17, 1941,[14] concerning the reorganization of handicrafts, small industry and the retail trade, the Commissioner General in Riga announced that in order to avoid excessive disturbances in the normal economic life by the measures taken for restoration of private property, the abolition of the Bolshevik system should take place step by step only. The reason for the change in attitude of the occupant is the following: the communistic system seemed useful for the German war economy, since it provided for the German war effort a concentration of resources and wealth and a centralized form of control. The existing institutions of economic concentration, such as collective farms (*kolhozy*) and state farms (*sovhozy*) and industrial associations such as combines, cartels, and trusts, were considered by the occupant as appropriate instrumentalities for taking over immediately the whole economy of the area. Although in the Baltic States and eastern Poland communism had not, as already indicated, become deeply entrenched, because of the relatively short time in which those territories were held by Russia, and the inhabitants were keenly interested in regaining possession of their properties, the occupant nevertheless, for reasons of economic expediency, disregarded this socio-political element in dealing with property.

A return to private property was envisaged to a certain extent only in the Baltic States.[15] But even in the Baltic States a return of properties in the

[13] See below, p. 300. [14] See below, p. 308. [15] See above, Part I, "Property."

handicraft and other small industries and in the retail trade was made dependent upon two principles: (1) It must be in the "public interest" to return private property; and (2) the owner must be personally and professionally qualified to manage the property. Properties which would lose in efficiency and output in the hands of a private owner or by redistribution between or among the several owners were not to be handed over to those to whom they rightfully belonged.

The following procedure for the return to private property was provided for: A formal and detailed application is required, and in the event of a favorable decision the permit for restoration of the property specifies the date on which the property in question is to be separated from the collective or state institution (combine, trust, or public enterprise). Machinery and other equipment formerly belonging to the owners of small industrial establishments are to be returned to the owner free of charge. As to raw materials on hand in the plants and all products in process of manufacture, the following arrangement is made: Raw materials and products up to the value of one thousand Reichsmarks become the property of the owner to whom the plant is restored. Materials and products in excess of this amount may be acquired by the said owner upon payment therefor. He may also acquire finished products but he must pay for them at prices established by evaluation.

As to claims and obligations incurred during the combined or collective operation of the plant, no responsibility therefor is assumed by the owner to whom the plant is restored.

Regarding employment contracts, it is stated that they are unaffected by the change in ownership, and the new owner and the workers and employees must obtain permission from the district commissioner if they wish to terminate the contract. A special clause provides for the continuity of work by the stipulation that the termination of the employment contract cannot take effect before one month has elapsed from the time of the separation of the plant from the former combine or collective establishment.

That the occupant did not envisage primarily the principle of restoration of private property is obvious from regulations concerning reorganization of small industry issued in connection with the decree of October 17, 1941.[16] According to these regulations, an application for return of property to the previous owners shall not be approved when it involves the partition of a collective enterprise if there is reason to fear that the partition will result in the creation of small businesses unable to carry on. In those circumstances, however, a transformation is permitted of the communistically organized enterprise into a joint establishment based upon a partnership agree-

[16] For a general orientation as to the system of return to private property, see "Wie wird reprivatisiert?" in *Deutsche Zeitung im Osten*, February 17, 1942. See also *Latvia under German Occupation*, cited above.

ment. In such a case, the Director for Latvian Small Industry is authorized to issue provisional by-laws until the partnership agreement becomes final.

Special regulations were issued as to city buildings and dwelling houses by the decree of December 15, 1941,[17] of the Reich Commissioner for the Ostland, authorizing the district commissioner to deal with the rights of former owners of city buildings and houses. These regulations, however, did not proclaim the principle of reestablishment of former owners in their rights, but provided only that the district commissioners could grant to the former owners the right of management and use of their former properties consisting of city buildings, dwelling houses, and sites. If the former owner should not be present, such management and use could be ceded to a relative. District commissioners may not grant the use and administration of such property if they find that such an act would be contrary to the public interest, if there are no guaranties for an orderly administration and maintenance of the house, or if there are doubts as to the "integrity" of the interested person. This provision, granting wide discretionary power to district commissioners, makes it possible for them to use the rights of owners as an instrumentality of special policies within the limits, on the one hand, of economic expediency and, on the other hand, of political submission to the occupant. The right of the district commissioner to revoke the privilege of management and use once granted, increases not only the atmosphere of insecurity but also the absolute and constant dependence of the former owners on the German administration. Disadvantageous as this situation may be to the former owners, the occupant, in addition, has neglected no occasion to create fiscal advantages for himself through this institution of granted management and use. Although the owners are not restored in their ownership rights, they are obliged to pay public taxes devolving on such city buildings, houses, and sites.

LABOR

The exploitation of labor is one of the main objectives of the occupant. The local manpower is being exploited in a twofold way: first, by utilizing it in local industrial or farming establishments to supplement the German war economy; and second, by shipping millions of workers into Germany. In the Ostland all workmen, domestic workers, persons engaged in independent trades, and members of their families who are also in trade or in housework must possess work books.[18] Labor can be employed only with the permission of the German district commissioner.[19] Labor contracts may not be terminated by either party without authorization from the same source. It is prohibited to induce a worker to give up his job by offering higher

[17] See below, p. 310.

[18] First rules and regulations of January 31, 1942, under the order concerning the pooling of labor resources.

[19] Regulation of December 22, 1941, concerning engagement of and notice to workers as well as prevention of breach of contract and enticement.

wages or better working conditions elsewhere. As to farming, there is an obligation imposed on every farmer to utilize his own labor resources.[20] When Jews are employed, they do not receive any wages; but the employer of Jewish labor must pay a fee to the financial department of the district commissioner.[21]

ECONOMY

Because of the concentration and reorganization of economy by the Russian authorities during their stay of a year in the Baltic States, the German occupant was able to take hold immediately of all the economic resources of these countries. Having been taken over in a short time (by a real *Blitzkrieg*), no great disturbances occurred in the economy of these countries when the German occupant moved in. The occupant proceeded to make inventories of raw materials, agricultural products, and livestock. All transactions in these materials were prohibited. Agricultural products such as grain, sheep wool, and even poultry had to be delivered to the occupant according to especially elaborate orders and schedules.

[20] Regulation of February 10, 1942, concerning effective distribution of agricultural labor.

[21] Regulation of March 19, 1942, concerning remuneration to Jewish labor in the General District of Latvia. See below, p. 311.

CHAPTER XIII

BELGIUM

Belgium was invaded by Germany on May 10, 1940. When the King surrendered with his army, his legal status became, and has since remained, that of a prisoner of war. Thus the King does not participate in public affairs of the occupied country.

INCORPORATION OF EUPEN, MALMÉDY, AND MORESNET

Two provinces of Belgium which belonged to Germany before 1918, Eupen and Malmédy, as well as neutral Moresnet, were incorporated into Germany and assigned for purposes of administration to the District of Aachen by decree of May 18, 1940.[1] Since then the institutions of these three districts have undergone a régime of assimilation with German political and cultural institutions. Germans living in these districts are represented in the Reichstag.[2] Inhabitants of "related blood," i.e., those considered racially akin to Germans, were granted nationality of the inferior type (*Staatsangehörige*), and German inhabitants were granted nationality of the superior type (*Bürger*).[3] Gradually the whole body of German and Prussian law was introduced into these districts. The official language was made German and names were changed to a German form.

ADMINISTRATION

The remainder of Belgium was put under the administration of one military commander for the German armed forces in Belgium and Northern France, including Pas-de-Calais. Because of the strategic importance of the area,[4] the administration was entrusted to a military commander instead of to a civilian Reich Commissioner.

The general staff of the Military Commander is divided into two separate staffs: the military staff (*Militär-oder Kommandostab*) and the staff for military administration (*Militärverwaltungsstab*). The military staff, headed by the Chief of Staff, is in charge of purely military matters. The staff for military administration, headed by a Chief of Military Administration, handles economic and cultural matters of the occupied areas. This staff contains three divisions: Division of the Chief (*Präsidialabteilung*), Administrative Division (*Verwaltungsabteilung*), and Division for Economics (*Wirtschaftsabteilung*). The Division of the Chief handles general and political matters.

[1] See below, p. 313. [2] See Act of February 4, 1941, below, p. 315.

[3] See decree of May 23, 1940, below, p. 313.

[4] See Dr. Hailer, member of the staff of the Military Commander in Brussels, "Die Militärverwaltung in Belgien und Nordfrankfreich," *Deutsches Recht*, 1940, Vol. 45/46, p. 1916.

The Administrative Division is divided into sections for political administration, communal administration, social welfare, police, communications, press and radio, finance, justice, schools, culture, health, building of roads, and the administration of waterways. The Division for Economics deals with all matters pertaining to the economic life of the country.

In the cities of Brussels, Ghent, Liége, and Charleroi chief field commands (*Oberfeldkommandanturen*) were created for the administration of the respective cities and adjacent provinces. The chief field commanders act through subordinate field commands (*Feldkommandanturen*), usually three in number, and the latter in turn also have an average of three local commands (*Ortskommandanturen*) under them.

Special city commissioners were appointed for the administration of Brussels, Antwerp, Ghent, Ostend, and Liége.

Apart from the administrative agencies of the occupant, the Belgian administration is in the hands of the secretaries general of the former Belgian ministries.[5] The following secretaries general are functioning, namely, those of the Ministry of Justice, the Ministry of Finance, the Ministry of Labor and Social Welfare, the Ministry of Agriculture and Food, the Ministry of Communications, and the Ministry of Economic Affairs. The local authorities perform their functions mainly in accordance with the pre-war Belgian pattern. However, the elective element in government has been curtailed. A shakeup among officials was undertaken at the beginning by introducing an order that persons over sixty years of age could not hold office.[6] In this order the German military command referred especially to opening public offices to demobilized Belgian soldiers who wanted to "serve their country with energy and in full realization of their responsibility." In taking care of the demobilized soldiers of a defeated army, the occupant had two purposes in mind: first, the occupant wished to gain popularity; and secondly, by this policy an opportunity was afforded to the German authorities to scrutinize politically every candidate for a public office, even though the actual appointments were made through the channels of the secretaries general.

The local administration is supervised by representatives of the nearest German military command.

ECONOMY AND FINANCE

The occupant immediately organized a special system for taking over the economic resources of the country. Economic officers (*Wirtschaftsoffiziere*) followed the troops in order to take possession of the raw materials and factories. Sequestration was ordered of foodstuffs, raw materials, semi-fabricated products, as well as some finished products such as woolen clothing,

[5] The nature of this form of central government, which is called "headless" or "subcabinet" government, has been explained above, pp. 11–12.

[6] See order of March 7, 1941, below, p. 320.

jute bags, tires, industrial oils, and so on.[7] For purposes of industrial production commodity control agencies (*Warenstellen*) were organized, with wide powers to issue regulations concerning acquisition, distribution, storing, serving, and consumption, and to require the submission of reports. These commodity control agencies provided the factories with materials necessary for the manufacture of their products, if and when they were working for the German war economy. The factories also found themselves under the management of factory trustees appointed by the military commander.[8] It was the duty of the factory trustees to see to the maintenance of industrial production and to execute orders of the occupying authorities as well as to undertake all measures for the purpose of increasing output. Moreover, every enterprise in Belgium was made subject to audit by special orders of the Chief of Military Administration, in order to keep the production of the enterprises under constant control.

A special device was used in order to provide the occupant with non-ferrous metals. On October 20, 1941,[9] a decree was published to the effect that persons delivering non-ferrous metals are entitled to a certain tax exemption. Thus the Belgian Treasury was compelled to collaborate with the occupant in obtaining non-ferrous metals and it is in fact the Belgian Treasury which pays for the scrap.

A number of financial decrees gave to the occupant an especially privileged position in the field of finance. The proclamation of May 10, 1940,[10] established an especially favorable exchange rate—one belga to one-half Reichsmark. The mark was fixed at 10 francs at the time of the invasion, after which it was raised to 12½ francs. Occupation currency (*Reichskreditkassenscheine*) was put into circulation and later on the Belgian Bank of Issue was compelled to exchange this occupation currency into new Belgian francs. All Belgian banks were put under the control of a banking supervisory board.[11] This office controls the business of the banks, especially credit operations. In particular, the banking supervisory office sees to it that credit is given to enterprises working for Germany. A clearing office was established in Brussels in order to carry on trade with Germany and, through German intermediaries, with other countries. The clearing arrangements between Germany and Belgium on the one side and, on the other, between Belgium and other countries (which must be carried out through Berlin channels), are arranged by orders of the German military commander. Thus, German authorities decide which commodities Belgium shall export and import, what shall be the prices paid, and what exchange rate shall apply in every case. Clearings have been established between Belgium and the following countries: the Netherlands, Italy, the Protectorate of Bohemia and Moravia, Switzerland, Sweden, Yugoslavia, Bulgaria, Norway, Hun-

[7] See order of May 20, 1940, below, p. 321. See also, in general, Ardenne, *op. cit.*
[8] See order of April 29, 1941, below, p. 325. [9] See below, p. 327.
[10] See below, p. 317. [11] See order of June 14, 1940, below, p. 333.

gary, Denmark, the Government General of Poland, France, Rumania, Finland, and the Union of Soviet Socialist Republics[12] (the last was interrupted because of the Russo-German war).

For the regular functioning of clearing, it is necessary that exports shall be equal to imports on both sides, i.e., on the side of each party to the clearing agreement. But Germany imports from Belgium more than it exports there. Hence, in order to create a balance a credit item is entered in the central Clearing Institute (*Verrechnungskasse*) in Berlin in favor of the clearing office of Belgium. Germany thus becomes the clearing debtor of Belgium. The trade between Belgium and other countries is likewise carried out through the Clearing Institute in Berlin. However, this central clearing arrangement has not contributed to the unfreezing of Belgian credits by transferring to Belgium actual payments made to the Berlin Clearing Institute by the countries importing Belgian goods, because—as in the case of her trade with Belgium—Germany is importing from those countries also more goods than she is exporting to them.

The above-described economic and financial measures are facilitated by a complete control of all the economic life of Belgium, which was put into effect by the order concerning the organization of national economy, promulgated by the secretaries general on February 10, 1941.[13] This order created the framework for economic totalitarianism in Belgium and furnished a basis for integrating the Belgian economy into the Germany economy. It envisaged the creation of economic associations organized according to trades and regions. These associations are designated as sole official representatives of the trade or region concerned. For example, all mining enterprises in Belgium are organized into one central mining association, with headquarters in Brussels. Moreover, all enterprises engaged in any economic activity in a particular area—citing Charleroi for example—such as mining enterprises, retail trade and wholesale trade enterprises, handicraft associations, and banks, are organized in the Economic Chamber of Charleroi. Thus the economic life of Belgium is seized and controlled in a twofold manner: first, specific economic control of the "vertical" type, which directly affects the capital structure; and, secondly, general economic control organized horizontally on a geographic basis.

REPARATIONS

During the occupation of 1914–18, Germany tried to disintegrate Belgium by creating and exaggerating differences between the Belgians and the Flemings, and the latter collaborating with Germany were given special privileges. When the German occupant left Belgium, the Belgian Govern-

[12] See International Chamber of Commerce, *Clearing and Payments Agreements* (Looseleaf edition, Basel, Verlag für Recht und Gesellschaft AG.), *passim*.

[13] See below, p. 323.

ment passed legislation inflicting penalties upon persons who had collaborated with the Germans. During the present occupation, the German occupant has published two orders for the "restitution of the rights of persons persecuted in Belgium because of their collaboration with the German Army of Occupation during the war of 1914–18." [14] To understand this it is necessary to recall that according to Section 5 of the Belgian Penal Code,[15] a person sentenced to death or to forced labor is deprived forever of "honor rights," which means the right of employment in public office, right to be elected, right to decorations and title of nobility, right to be a member of a jury, a court witness, a member of family council, a guardian, a member of the judiciary council, and an administrator of estates, as well as the right to bear arms, to be a member of the civil guard, or to serve in the army. The above-mentioned orders provide that these rights shall be restored. Moreover, the interested persons may receive special damages for personal sufferings, for loss of freedom, for expropriations, and so on.

A special board, as an independent Belgian governmental institution, was created for allotting damages and reinstating such persons in their rights. The members of the board and their alternates are chosen with the consent of the German military commander. The costs of the reparations, as well as the expenses of the board, are to be borne by the Belgian State. The Belgian Secretary of the Treasury is obliged to hold the amounts currently required for these purposes at the disposal of the board. Thus the Belgian Treasury has been compelled to pay compensation for penalties inflicted upon those who had been traitors to the Belgian nation in 1914–18.

[14] See orders of September 6, 1940, below, pp. 338, 339.
[15] See Code Pénal in *Les XV Codes* (Brussels, 1928), p. 338.

CHAPTER XIV

CZECHOSLOVAKIA

In the course of 1938 and 1939 the territory of the Republic of Czechoslovakia was disposed of in the following way:

In accordance with the Munich Agreement, the Sudetenland was incorporated into Germany. Moreover, Germany also incorporated two areas in the neighborhood of Bratislava which dominated the strategic position of this city, namely, Devin and Petrzalka, inhabited by Slovaks.

The Protectorate of Bohemia and Moravia was created within the boundaries of the German Reich as an autonomous area comprising these two divisions.

Slovakia was made a separate state and a special treaty of protection between Germany and Slovakia put the latter under the protection of Germany. According to this treaty, the area delimited on its western side by the frontiers of the state of Slovakia and on its eastern side by a line formed by the eastern rims of the Lower Carpathians, the White Carpathians, and the Javornik Mountains, was put under the "military sovereignty" of the German armed forces.

By the Vienna arbitration award, Hungary incorporated the following Slovak[1] areas:[2] the entire districts of Stará Ďala, Feledince, Královský Chlumec, Komárno, Košice (city), Parkan, Dunajská Streda, Želiezovce; parts of the districts of Bratislava, Galanta, Modrý Kameň, Velké Kapušany, Košice, Krupina, Levice, Lučenec, Michalovce, Moldava nad Bodrou, Nitra, Revúca Rožňava, Rimavská Sobota, Šala, Šamorín, Tornaľa, Trebišov, Trstená, Vráble, Nové Zámky. In implementation of the Vienna award, the frontiers between Slovakia and Hungary were rectified, and it was announced by Order No. 102,473/1939 of the Hungarian Royal Ministry of the Interior of March 13, 1939, that the following communities "shall hereafter come under the authority of the Hungarian Holy Crown:[3] Vága (Váhovce), Alsójattó (Dolný Jatov), Nagycétény (Velký Cetín), Kalász (Kalaz), Nagyhind (Velké Hyndice), Bori (Bory), Hévmágyarád, Felsözellö (Hornie Saliby), Alsopokorágy (Nižna Pokoradz), Pádár (Padarovce), Felsöfalu (Chvalová), Rekenyevitálu (Rekeňa), Andrási (Andra-

[1] One should bear in mind that after Munich the Republic of Czechoslovakia continued as a federative state, consisting of three autonomous divisions, Bohemia and Moravia, Slovakia, and Subcarpathia. This arrangement was helpful for the Germans during the final dismemberment of Czechoslovakia.

[2] *Seznam obci a okresů Republiky Československé* (Stav ke dni 28. listopadu, 1938). Praha, 1938, pp. 17 ff.

[3] The names of the additionally incorporated communities are given herein in the Hungarian version according to the Hungarian decree. The Czech version is given in parenthesis following the Hungarian names. The author is indebted to Dr. V. Palic, First Secretary of the Czechoslovak Embassy in Washington, for assistance in identifying the Czech names of these localities.

šovce), Aifalucska, Jászo (Jasov), Jászomindszent (Poproč), Rudnok (Rudnik), Aranyida—Reka (Zlatá Idka), Mészpest, Bajánháza (Bajany).

Moreover, the Vienna arbitration allotted to Hungary the following entire districts or parts of districts belonging to Carpathian Ruthenia, or Subcarpathia: the entire district of Berehovo; the city districts of Mukačevo and Užhorod; parts of the districts of Iršava, Mukačevo, Sevluš, and Užhorod.

The rest of Subcarpathia was also occupied and incorporated by Hungary in March, 1939.

Parts of the following districts were ceded to Poland on October 2, 1938: from Moravia—Fryštát, Frýdek, Český Těšín;[4] from Slovakia—Čadca, Kežmarok (Javorina), Stará Ľubovna, and Spišska Stárá Ves.

After the occupation of Poland by Germany, the first group of these areas was incorporated into Germany, namely, into the district of Silesia; the second group was allegedly turned back to Slovakia.

Sudetenland

THE MUNICH AGREEMENT

The Sudeten were incorporated into the Greater German Reich following the Munich Agreement of September 29, 1938, which was signed by Germany, Italy, Great Britain, and France under threat of a German invasion of the Sudeten. Under the terms of this agreement, the Sudeten were incorporated into Germany and the new boundaries of the Czechoslovak State were to have been guaranteed by the four signatory powers.[5] This guaranty, however, was given neither by Italy nor by Germany. During the war of nerves which preceded the Munich Agreement Hitler declared that the Sudeten represented the last territorial demand that he had to make in Europe.

The Munich Agreement was never recognized by the United States and Russia,[6] and it was subsequently denounced by Great Britain[7] and the

[4] See below, chapter on "Poland."

[5] See Agreement and Annex, Great Britain, Foreign Office, Misc. No. 8 (1938), Cmd. 5848.

[6] Russia, however, recognized Slovakia and denied diplomatic status to the Czechoslovak Legation in Moscow during the winter 1939–40 and until after the German attack upon Russia, when the relations between the two countries were resumed. Hubert Ripka, *The Repudiation of Munich* (London: Czechoslovak Ministry of Foreign Affairs Information Service, 1943), p. 17.

[7] See letter of Anthony Eden to M. Masaryk, "Exchange of Notes between His Majesty's Government in the United Kingdom and the Government of the Czechoslovak Republic concerning the Policy of His Majesty's Government in the United Kingdom in regard to Czechoslovakia," Great Britain, *Treaty Series*, No. 3 (1942), p. 2:

"Foreign Office, London, *August 5, 1942*.

"Your Excellency,

"In the light of recent exchanges of view between our Governments, I think it may be useful for me to make the following statement about the attitude of His Majesty's Government in the United Kingdom as regards Czechoslovakia.

French National Committee.[8] It has been stated on other occasions that the Munich Agreement is invalid for the following reasons:

1. The guaranty of the new Czechoslovakian boundaries, which was an essential element of the agreement, was not given by Germany and Italy, as mentioned above.

2. This agreement was violated by the German invasion of Czechoslovakia.[9]

3. No consent of the Czechoslovak Parliament was obtained for the cession of the territories, as is required by Article 64 of the Czechoslovak Constitution of February 29, 1920.

ADMINISTRATION

In matters of administration, the Sudeten were disposed of in the following manner: From the main part was created a special district (*Reichsgau Sudetenland*); the parts in the neighborhood of the districts of the Upper Danube (*Oberdonau*) and Lower Danube (*Niederdonau*)—formerly part of Austria—were incorporated into these districts; and other parts were incorporated into Prussia and Bavaria, respectively.[10]

The district of Sudetenland is headed by a Reich Governor (*Reichsstatthalter*), having his official residence in Reichenberg. The Reich Governor is under the supervision of the Reich Minister of the Interior. He is also subject to the instructions of the several Reich ministers for the respective branches of administration. All agencies of the special administrative serv-

---

"In my letter of the 18th July, 1941, I informed your Excellency that The King had decided to accredit an Envoy Extraordinary and Minister Plenipotentiary to Dr. Benes as President of the Czechoslovak Republic. I explained that this decision implied that His Majesty's Government in the United Kingdom regarded the juridical position of the President and Government of the Czechoslovak Republic as identical with that of the other Allied heads of States and Governments established in this country. The status of His Majesty's representative has recently been raised to that of an Ambassador.

"The Prime Minister had already stated in a message broadcast to the Czechoslovak people on the 30th September, 1940, the attitude of His Majesty's Government in regard to the arrangements reached at Munich in 1938. Mr. Churchill then said that the Munich Agreement had been destroyed by the Germans. This statement was formally communicated to Dr. Benes on the 11th November, 1940.

"The foregoing statement and formal act of recognition have guided the policy of His Majesty's Government in regard to Czechoslovakia, but in order to avoid any possible misunderstanding, I desire to declare on behalf of His Majesty's Government in the United Kingdom that as Germany has deliberately destroyed the arrangements concerning Czechoslovakia reached in 1938, in which His Majesty's Government in the United Kingdom participated, His Majesty's Government regard themselves as free from any engagements in this respect. At the final settlement of the Czechoslovak frontiers to be reached at the end of the war they will not be influenced by any changes effected in and since 1938.

"I have, &c.

ANTHONY EDEN."

[8] Ripka, *op. cit.*, pp. 13–14.

[9] See Edvard Táborský, "'Munich,' the Vienna Arbitration and International Law," *Czechoslovak Yearbook of International Law* (London, 1942), pp. 21–38; Quincy Wright, "The Munich Settlement and International Law," *American Journal of International Law*, Vol. 33 (1939), pp. 12–32.

[10] See Harry v. Rozycki, "Ueber den Geltungsbereich des Reichsrechts im Grossdeutschen Reich," in *Deutsche Verwaltung*, 1941, p. 55.

ices of the Reich within the Reich District Sudetenland are under the Reich Governor, with the exception of justice, railways, and postal services. The Reich Governor is empowered to promulgate law with the consent of the Reich ministers involved. The Reich Governor has two deputies, namely, for general administration a so-called Government President, and for autonomous administration of the district a District Chief (*Gauhauptmann*).[11]

REPARATIONS TO GERMANS

After the incorporation of the Sudeten, the Germans in the Sudeten who were active under their leader Henlein, and who had brought about the Munich crisis, were rewarded in the form of reparations. A law signed by the Führer, of October 20, 1939,[12] provided such reparations for Germans who incurred physical or property damages because they belonged to the Sudeten German party or because of their National Socialist convictions, or if the damages occurred in connection with the fight for the incorporation of the Sudetenland into the Reich. Such damages must have been caused through action of members of the armed forces or officials of the Czechoslovak State or of political adversaries before January 1, 1939.

Protectorate of Bohemia and Moravia

ESTABLISHMENT OF THE PROTECTORATE

On March 14, 1939, Hitler requested Prime Minister Hácha of the Czechoslovak Government to come to see him. During that visit Hitler placed before Hácha a memorandum which contained a renunciation of independence by Czechoslovakia and placed the country under the protectorate of Germany. These proposals were accompanied by threats of invasion and reprisals. Hácha signed this agreement,[13] but, as facts have since shown,

[11] Act of April 14, 1939, below, p. 341. [12] *Reichsgesetzblatt*, 1939, I, p. 2119.

[13] The conditions under which Hácha and his Foreign Minister Chvalkovsky signed the agreement surrendering the sovereignty of their country are described in a report of M. Coulondre, French Ambassador in Berlin, to M. Georges Bonnet, French Minister of Foreign Affairs, on March 17, 1939, as follows:

"Upon their arrival in Berlin, M. Hácha and his Minister were received with military honors and immediately taken to the Chancellery, where Herr Hitler, Field Marshal Göring, von Ribbentrop, and Keppler awaited them. On the table lay the document to be signed in its final form and a memorandum concerning the proposed statute for Bohemia and Moravia. Hitler stated briefly that the Czech Ministers were invited, not for negotiations but in order to be informed of Germany's decisions, which were irrevocable; that Prague would be occupied on the following day at nine o'clock, Bohemia and Moravia would be incorporated within the Reich as a Protectorate, and whoever attempted to resist would be 'trodden under foot' (*zertreten*). Then the Führer signed his name to the document and left the room. It was then about 12:30 a.m.

"A tragic scene followed between the Czech Ministers and the three Germans. For many hours Dr. Hácha and M. Chvalkovsky protested against the outrage and refused to sign the document, stating that should they do so they would be eternally cursed by the Czech people. Dr. Hácha opposed the statute with all his energy, remarking that such a condition of servitude had never before been imposed upon a white nation.

"The German Ministers were merciless in their insistence. They literally followed Dr. Hácha and M. Chvalkovsky around the table where the documents lay, thrusting them

even during his conversation with Hitler German troops were already on the march into Czechoslovakia and had completed the occupation of the country.[14]

On March 16, 1939,[15] a decree of the Führer and Reich Chancellor was published concerning the Protectorate of Bohemia and Moravia, the preamble to which states that "the Bohemian-Moravian countries belonged for a millennium to the living space (*Lebensraum*) of the German people," and that there was danger that out of this area "would arise a new, stupendous menace to European peace." Moreover, the Czechoslovak State was declared to have "demonstrated its inherent inability to exist and therefore now has fallen into actual dissolution." Since "the German Reich cannot tolerate everlasting disturbances in these areas," it was held to be "only an act of compliance with the law of self-preservation if the German Reich is resolved to take decisive action for the reestablishment of the foundations of a Central European Order." Moreover, "the millennial historic past of the German Reich has proven that it alone is chosen by virtue of its greatness and the qualities of the German people to solve this problem." By Article 3 of the decree the Protectorate of Bohemia and Moravia was declared to be autonomous, and it was described as possessing certain "sovereign rights." These sovereign rights, however, must be exercised "in conformity with the political, military, and economic interests of the Reich."

The decree contains provisions to the effect that the Protectorate shall act through its own government and that it shall even have the right to accredit a minister to the Government of the Reich. But it is also provided that the German Government shall appoint as guardian of its interests an official with residence in Prague, whose title is "Reich Protector of Bohemia and Moravia." Thus the autonomous status in fact proves to be a mere illusion, since the Reich Protector has almost supreme power in the Protectorate.

The Reich maintains police and military forces in the "autonomous" Protectorate and supervises directly such essential agencies as traffic, posts,

---

before their eyes and placing pens in their hands, at the same time repeating that if the Czech Ministers refused to sign the documents, half of Prague would be laid waste by airplanes within two hours. The German Ministers declared that hundreds of bombers were awaiting the command to take off, and unless the signatures were forthcoming by six o'clock in the morning, the order would be given.

"President Hácha was in such an exhausted condition that he frequently needed medical attention from physicians who had been in attendance since the beginning of the conference. On the statement of the Czech Ministers that such a decision could not be made without the consent of their government, they were informed that there already existed a direct telephone line to the Cabinet of Ministers then meeting in Prague and that the Cabinet could therefore be reached immediately. Such a line, it seems, had been laid in Czech territory by members of the German minority, unknown to Czech authorities.

"At 4:30 in the morning, Dr. Hácha, who was in a state of total collapse and was kept on his feet only by means of medical stimulants, resigned himself to the inevitable and signed the document. M. Chvalkovsky declared on leaving the Chancellery: 'Our people will curse us, and yet we have saved their existence and have preserved them from a horrible massacre.'" *Documents Diplomatiques*, 1938–1939, No. 77.

[14] *Völkerbund*, March 23, 1939, No. 12, p. 151. [15] See below, p. 342.

and telegraph. The members of the Czech autonomous government are subject to confirmation by the Reich Protector.

It is stated in the decree of March 16, 1939, that the Reich may undertake any changes it deems necessary in the so-called autonomous Czech administration. In implementation of this provision the decree of the Führer concerning administration in the Protectorate of Bohemia and Moravia of May 7, 1942,[16] delegated to the Reich Protector powers which enable him to make further limitations on the rights of the autonomous Czech administration. It is broadly stated in this decree that the Reich Protector is empowered "to undertake measures"—within the limits of the decree of March 16, 1939—"in order to make possible the adaptation of the administration of Bohemia and Moravia to any situation which may arise." Thus practically the Reich Protector may limit the meager autonomy of the Protectorate as much as he deems it necessary to do so.

ADMINISTRATION

In execution of the decree of March 16, 1939, two central authorities were established in Prague—the office of the Reich Protector (German) and the government of the Protectorate (Czech).

The German Protector acts through nineteen German district prefects for the twelve districts in Bohemia and the seven districts in Moravia. These German prefects, each of whom has authority over one district, control German administrative agencies and handle matters relating to general administration and citizenship, as well as other matters concerning Germans living in their districts. The Czech autonomous administration carries out its functions through local Czech authorities. As a result of the parallelism thus created throughout the Protectorate, there are two types of authorities, viz., German and Czech, but on every level of administration the German authorities control the Czech authorities. The office of the Reich Protector, for example, controls the government of the Czech "autonomous" Protectorate, the German district governors control the Czech district administrative authorities, and the same situation exists in the cities and smaller communities.

CITIZENSHIP

Citizens of German origin were granted citizenship of the German Reich, whereas the Czechs became citizens of the Protectorate.[17] In order to create for Germans an influential position in Czech political institutions as well, Germans were granted in addition all the rights deriving from Czech citizenship in the Protectorate, without any requirement that they should assume obligations pertaining to such citizenship. Moreover, Czech pa-

[16] See below, p. 347.

[17] See order concerning the acquisition of German citizenship by former Czechoslovak citizens of German origin, of April 20, 1939, below, p. 346; also decree of March 16, 1939, below, p. 343.

triots who were abroad were deprived of the citizenship of the Protectorate. The decree of the Reich Protector of October 3, 1939, stated that citizens of the Protectorate who were abroad and who had committed acts detrimental to the interests or reputation of the Reich or who did not comply with an order to return to the Protectorate would lose citizenship of the Protectorate and their property would be confiscated for the benefit of the Reich.[18]

COURTS

The judicial system is based upon the principle of extraterritoriality for Germans. As a rule Germans may not be tried by Czech courts. Czechs, however, are subject not only to the criminal law of the Protectorate but also to the Criminal Code of the Reich in cases in which the political interests of Germany are involved, as, for example, cases involving treason, attacks against the Führer, disrespect for German national emblems, and libel of the National Socialist Party or similar National Socialist organizations.[19]

CONTROL OF INDUSTRIES

The areas included in the Protectorate being highly industrialized, the Reich Protector was eager to take over the control of all industries. On June 23, 1939, a decree was published creating a framework for the totalitarian reorganization of the economy of the Protectorate.[20] An order implementing this decree dated August 29, 1939, provided for the organization of the industries.[21] And finally an announcement by the Minister for Industry, of November 4, 1939, provided for the creation of twenty-three groups, which included all persons engaged in specific industries. The acquisition of raw materials by these groups, as well as the production and sale of their products, is controlled. The above-mentioned decree created the following industrial groups: (1) mining, (2) production of sugar, (3) production of alcohol, (4) production of beer, (5) malt industry, (6) flour mills, (7) food industry, (8) meat and poultry industry, (9) metal industry, (10) electrical works, (11) lumber mills, (12) lumber manufacturing, (13) paper and graphic industry, (14) chemical industry, (15) ceramics, (16) construction industry, (17) glass industry, (18) textile industry, (19) clothing industry, (20) leather industry, (21) film industry, (22) gas and water works, (23) manufacture of precious metals and precious stones.

CONTROL OF TRADES AND OCCUPATIONS

The most efficient instrumentality for subduing the Czechs to the will of the German ruler was provided by a decree which the government of the

[18] *Verordnungsblatt des Reichsprotektors in Böhmen und Mähren*, No. 36, 1939.
[19] See order of April 14, 1939, below, p. 347.
[20] Decree of January 23, 1939, concerning basic organization of economy. *Sammlung der Gesetze und Verordnungen des Protektorats Böhmen und Mähren*, No. 61, 1939.
[21] *Ibid.*, No. 78, 1939.

Protectorate (Hácha) was forced by the Reich Protector to promulgate. It was dated November 4, 1939, and entitled, "Government decree concerning temporary restrictions on trade and other gainful occupations."[22] It is specifically stated in this decree that the authorities may deny permission to exercise a trade or occupation, even if all necessary requirements are met with. The right to grant or to deny permission is based upon vague and indefinite premises. It is stated that such permission will be granted by the authorities only when it appears that no objections arise against it, either from the point of view of the "extraordinary economic conditions or in general because of reasons of public interest." Practically, no Czech can make a living without being compelled to comply with the "new order" imposed upon his country by the occupant.

PROPERTY

A great part of Czech property, as well as almost all Jewish property, was taken over by the Germans. The main instrumentalities for taking over such properties are the following: A decree of October 4, 1939, gave the Reich Protector the right to confiscate property of persons and associations which had promoted "tendencies inimical to law" (*Rechtsfeindliche Bestrebungen*). As political pressure on and persecutions of the Czechs and Jews increased, many of them endeavored to obtain permission to leave the country. Such permission was granted only when the applicant agreed to pay a high tax, amounting to a substantial part of his property, for the benefit of the Reich.[23] Such a tax is called "emigration tax," amounting in practice to a profit taken by Germans on persecutions they organized against the inhabitants of the invaded country. Moreover, many of the Czechs, especially those possessing larger industrial undertakings, were compelled to sell their property to persons indicated by the Reich Protector.

THE PRIVILEGED SITUATION OF THE GERMANS

Czechoslovak citizens of German origin (*Volksdeutsche*) who before the invasion played the rôle of fifth columnists became the privileged element in the Protectorate. They were entitled not only to dual citizenship and to the right of extraterritoriality in courts (see above), but to a great many other privileges as well. First of all, they were granted rewards for their preinvasion activities in behalf of Germany, in the form of reparations for damages incurred by them when they were fighting the Government of the Czechoslovak Republic. In order to increase the number of Germans in the Protectorate, the German laws on subsidies for marriages and children

[22] *Sammlung der Gesetze und Verordnungen des Protektorats Böhmen und Mähren*, No. 94, 1939.

[23] See decree of November 23, 1939, concerning emigration tax. *Sammlung der Gesetze und Verordnungen des Protektorats Böhmen und Mähren*, No. 103, 1939.

were extended to German officials, members of the Gestapo and of the S.S., and to members of the *Reichsarbeitsdienst*.[24]

The German language was introduced as a compulsory subject to be taught in the grammar schools.[25]

A great part of the food supplies from the Protectorate is shipped to Germany. Moreover, the Protectorate has become a vacation ground for Germans and men on leave from military service. All of them have looked to the Protectorate for better food and better beer. Therefore the Minister of Agriculture of the Protectorate issued a decree on January 15, 1941, to the effect that ration cards of Germans on leave or on vacations should be valid in the Protectorate.[26]

JEWS

The status of the Jews in the Protectorate was established both by legislation of the Reich Protector and by the puppet Czech government. On June 21, 1939, Jewish property was ordered registered. Jewish employees were eliminated from enterprises by decrees of October 23, 1939, and September 14, 1940. On January 26, 1940, the Reich Protector issued a decree concerning the elimination of Jews from the economy of the Protectorate. Two orders, of January 26, 1940,[27] and February 7, 1940, implemented this elimination decree. Jews were, in fact, excluded from economic enterprises of every kind. Even peddling was prohibited. A period of grace up to April 30, 1940, was given to those engaged in the manufacture of textiles and shoes. Jews were forced to declare all of their gold, platinum, silver, and pearls. They were initially allowed to sell these valuables to a German company in Prague (Hadega—Handelsgesellschaft in Prague). On February 16, 1942, a decree was published concerning measures for the allocation of Jews in closed settlements. In implementation of this decree, thousands of Jews were concentrated in the prison fortress of Terezín.

GENOCIDE AND RESISTANCE

Throughout all the Protectorate Czech nationhood is under persecution. Czech teachers may not refer to Czech national heroes, and may not give an interpretation along national lines. Revision of Czech textbooks has been required. Books by authors representing the national spirit, such as Masaryk, Beneš, and Karel Čapek, as well as others, were prohibited. Books which emphasized national elements were initially burned. Later on the Germans changed this practice and made them into pulp to provide

[24] See decree of October 25, 1939, *Verordnungsblatt des Reichsprotektors*, No. 36, 1939.

[25] See decree of October 5, 1939, *Sammlung der Gesetze und Verordnungen des Protektorats Böhmen und Mähren*, No. 93, 1939.

[26] See *Sammlung der Gesetze und Verordnungen des Protektorats Böhmen und Mähren*, No. 8, 1941.

[27] *Verordnungsblatt des Reichsprotektors*, No. 7, 1940.

material for papermaking. Also plays and operas were censored. Dvořák's opera *Jakobín*, which was composed over fifty years ago was prohibited on the ground that it contains a tune starting with the words "Adolf, you are mad!"[28] The intellectuals, who are considered by the Germans as standard bearers of the Czech national spirit and consequently as dangerous elements to Germanism, are persecuted and kept in prisons and in labor battalions. Because of the patriotic feelings and activities of the students of Czech universities, all of those institutions were closed. The leaders of the students have been "liquidated" and thousands of others were sent into labor camps. The persecutions, however, seem only to stiffen the national resistance of the Czechs. Sabotage in the factories and in communications, the slaying of Gestapo members, and of Deputy Reich Protector Heydrich, are evidence of such increasing resistance. Even such wholesale retaliation as the complete destruction of a Czech town (Lidice) does not seem to stop the liberty-loving Czechs.

Slovakia

ESTABLISHMENT OF THE STATE

As in Yugoslavia, the Germans took advantage of some difficult population problems within the Czechoslovak Republic in order to foster the dismemberment and division of that country. For this purpose they directed their attention particularly to Slovakia, a nation of about two and a half million people. The Slovaks and Czechs are of the same ethnic group, but political differences arose between them during the period of the Czechoslovak Republic, the Slovaks claiming that they were not duly represented in the public affairs of the republic. At the time of the Munich crisis Hitler, through his agents, played upon these political differences. The majority of the Slovaks, however, and also such prominent statesmen as Monsignor Hlinka, seemed to prefer to remain within the framework of the Czechoslovak Republic. Thus the Germans found followers only among the extremists of the Slovak population. Meanwhile an autonomous status, with a special Slovak Diet, was granted to Slovakia by the government in Prague on November 19, 1938.[29] The Slovak Diet opened at Bratislava on January 20, 1939, and Monsignor Tiso was appointed Premier by the President of the Republic.[30]

The Germans who swarmed over Slovakia worked against the consolidation of the good relations between the two federated countries. Especially active in this field was the German leader Karmasin. On March 10, 1939, the Prague government, being aware of the separatist activities in

[28] See Eugene V. Erdely, *Germany's First European Protectorate* (London: Robert Hale, Limited, 1942), p. 210.
[29] *Bulletin of International News*, Vol. XV, No. 24 (December 3, 1938), p. 1139.
[30] *Ibid.*, Vol. XVI, No. 2 (January 28, 1939), p. 68.

Slovakia, dismissed the Slovak Premier, Monsignor Tiso, and the next day appointed Sidor as the new Premier.[31] On March 13, Monsignor Tiso was summoned to Berlin by Hitler and was accompanied on his visit by Karmasin. On his arrival in Berlin the former was given the honors due a prime minister. At the same time a Vienna broadcasting station was used by members of the Slovak faction advocating the separation of Slovakia from Czechoslovakia.[32] On March 14 the Slovak Diet, which had functioned as the federal Diet of the Slovak part of the Czechoslovak Republic, after hearing Monsignor Tiso's account of his visit to Hitler, voted for the creation of an independent State of Slovakia.[33] By the same vote the Slovak Diet was transformed into the legislative Diet of the State of Slovakia. The presiding committee of this Diet having been authorized to appoint a government, this was done on March 15, 1939, when a decree was issued establishing the following offices: President of the Government, Ministry of Foreign Affairs, Ministry of the Interior, Ministry of Finance, Ministry of Schools and Public Education, Ministry of Justice, Ministry of Economy, Ministry of Transportation and Public Works, Ministry of National Defense.[34]

After the occupation of Bohemia and Moravia and the proclamation regarding a protectorate for those territories, the German Army occupied the western part of Slovakia, "the Valley of Váh, with its arms and munitions factories—Dubnica, Považská Bystrica, Nové Mesto nad Vahom—hydro-electric plants at Púchov and Ladce, and the most important railroads, linking the capital, Bratislava, with the rest of the country, and with Bohemia-Moravia."[35] Thus Germany controlled the railway communications between Bratislava and the eastern part of Slovakia, as well as the communications with Poland, Rumania, and Hungary. Afterward it sought to legalize this unlawful occupation by a treaty between it and Slovakia.

On March 24, 1939,[36] a declaration was issued by the Reich Minister of Foreign Affairs, announcing that the German and Slovak governments had signed a treaty extending protection by the German Reich to the State of Slovakia. This treaty states that the Slovak State "has placed itself under the protection of the German Reich." The German Reich undertook the protection of the political independence of the State of Slovakia and of the integrity of its territory. For the purpose of making effective the protection thus undertaken, Germany was given an area "delimited on its western side by the frontiers of the State of Slovakia, and on its eastern side by a line formed by the eastern rims of the Lower Carpathians, the White Carpathians and the Javornik Mountains." In this area which had been, *nota bene*,

[31] *Bulletin of International News*, Vol. XV, No. 6 (March 25, 1939), pp. 255–56.
[32] *Ibid.*, pp. 235–36, 256, 257, 258. [33] *Ibid.*, p. 258. [34] See below, p. 353.
[35] Eugene V. Erdely, *Germany's First European Protectorate* (London: Robert Hale, Limited, 1942), p. 53.
[36] See below, p. 353.

previously occupied by Germany according to a preconceived plan, the German Reich was to have the right to construct military installations and to keep them garrisoned by German troops in the strength which Germany deemed necessary. The Government of Slovakia obligated itself to provide the land for such military installations. Moreover, the Slovak Government agreed to grant exemptions from customs duties on imports from the Reich for the maintenance of the German troops and the supply of all military installations. Article 4 of the same treaty states that "the Government of Slovakia will at all times conduct its foreign affairs in close agreement with the German Government." The treaty was signed for a period of twenty-five years, and a final clause contains a provision for its extension "in due time."

CONSTITUTION AND ADMINISTRATION

On July 21, 1939, the Slovak Diet voted a constitution.[37] This constitution is preceded by a preamble based upon the principle of the solidarity of social classes. It states in particular that the Slovak State endeavors to coordinate all moral and economic forces of the nation in one Christian national community and to avoid all conflicts between social classes.

The Slovak State is a republic headed by an elected president. The legislative power in the republic is exercised by the Diet, consisting of eighty members directly elected for a term of five years through universal elections in which equal suffrage and the secret ballot are prescribed. Every citizen twenty years of age has a right to vote, and every citizen thirty years of age has a right to be a candidate for election. Among the exclusive rights of the parliament are the election of the president, the drafting and enacting of the laws pertaining to the constitution and the establishing of the budget, the receiving of accounts of government expenditures, the establishment of courts, and the conclusion of treaties. The president is elected for seven years. He is the supreme representative of the state and supreme commander of the army. He appoints the members of the cabinet and higher officials and orders the promulgation of laws. The president is not responsible for the way in which he carries out his office. He may be indicted by the Council of State, but only for treason. The Council of State is composed as follows: The president of the republic appoints six members; the Slovak Hlinka (Popular) Party delegates ten members; every national group within Slovakia delegates one member; and each professional class within Slovakia also delegates one member. The president of the government and the president of the Diet are members *ex officio* of the Council. The Council of State has the following jurisdiction: it determines whether the president of the republic is permanently unable to fulfill his presidential

[37] *Slovenský Zákonník*, 1939, No. 41, p. 375. For a German text of this constitution, see the *Zeitschrift für Ausländisches Öffentliches Recht*, Vol. IX, No. 3, 1939, p. 759.

functions; it has the right to indict the president of the republic, as well as members of the government; it recommends candidates for election to the Diet; it introduces bills in the Diet and advises the president of the republic on political, cultural, and economic matters. The period of functioning by the Council of State is three years.

In accordance with the Fascist pattern a corporate professional organization was introduced. Every citizen must belong to and may practice a profession only if he is a member of one of the following organized groups: (*a*) agriculture, (*b*) industry, (*c*) trade and manufacture, (*d*) banking and insurance business, (*e*) free professions, (*f*) public servants, and (*g*) national educators.

As to the rights of citizens, they are only formally patterned according to democratic principles, for almost every civil right formulated in the constitution is qualified by reservations. Thus, while Article 81 states that the inhabitants shall enjoy the protection of their lives, liberties, and property, without regard to their racial origin, religion, or profession, the same paragraph adds that limitations of these rights may be enacted by law. Therefore it was possible to promulgate the anti-Jewish Code, despite Article 81 of the constitution.[38]

As to property, it must, according to the constitution, fulfill a social function, and hence the owner is obliged to administer his property in the interest of the common weal.

Slovak political life is organized along monoparty lines. The Hlinka (Popular) Party is the only one permitted to represent the Slovaks themselves in political life. But other national groups, such as Hungarians and Germans, are entitled to their own political parties and to participation in the political life of the country. Thus, parties are established according to ethnographic, but not political, principles.

Because of the presence in Slovakia of German and Hungarian minorities, the constitution provides for organization of racial minority groups. These groups have their own national registers and have the right to exercise their own cultural and political activities. They may also communicate with the states in which the main bulk of their national group is living. This provision as to the maintenance of contacts outside the boundaries of Slovakia should be considered as a concession, imposed by Germany and Hungary.

LAW AND COURTS

The new Slovak State has inherited from the Czechoslovak Republic a great body of basic laws pertaining to civil and criminal law and procedure, as well as administrative law. The new constitution and the totalitarian

[38] It may be noted also that in the elections to the Diet held as early as December 18, 1938, neither Czechs nor Jews were permitted to nominate their candidates, and the Jews were required to place their ballot papers in a separate urn. *Bulletin of International News*, Vol. XV, No. 26 (December 31, 1938), p. 1243.

trends in the new state required an adaptation of the law to the totalitarian pattern, especially to the Nazi pattern. Thus a law on concentration camps was promulgated as early as March 24, 1939. The reasons for confinement in a concentration camp are defined in a very broad way, and thus a great discretionary power is given to the administrative authorities in fighting political adversaries. It is stated that "the Minister of the Interior shall be authorized to order protective custody for persons who by their activities up to the present time have warranted and still warrant reasonable fear that they will be an obstacle to the upbuilding of the State of Slovakia."[39]

The organization of the courts remained much the same as in the time of the Czechoslovak Republic, except for the introduction of special courts to punish political crimes. The creation of the state necessitated also the establishment of a Supreme Court in Bratislava,[40] and of a Supreme Administrative Court. This latter court decides "all cases in which a party alleges that its right has been violated by an illegal decision or order issued by an administrative authority."[41]

GENOCIDE LEGISLATION

As has been indicated, in accordance with the German pattern anti-Jewish legislation was introduced, involving deprivation of citizenship, confiscation of property, prohibition of the exercise of professions, forced labor, and deportations. From Slovakia, 130,000 Czechs were removed to Bohemia and Moravia; 60,000 Jews to Eastern Galicia in the Government General of Poland; and 10,000 Jews to Hungary.[42] The new state considered its anti-Jewish policy to be of such importance that all anti-Jewish measures were codified in one Jewish Code consisting of as many as 270 articles.

FINANCE

On April 4, 1939,[43] a decree was published establishing a Slovak National Bank. This bank was authorized to issue bank notes for the State of Slovakia. The new currency unit was established as a Slovak crown, divided into 100 haliers. For purposes of exchange the Slovak crown was made equal to the Czech crown. A special provision required that the total amount of small coins issued must not be higher than 200 crowns per capita of population.[44]

CONTROL OF PROPERTY

As in other parts of occupied or Axis-dominated Europe property plays a dual rôle: first, that of affording economic resources to the state; and second, that of serving as an instrumentality of political pressure. A decree was introduced on March 30, 1939,[45] to the effect that "the County Court

[39] See below, p. 355. [40] See decree of April 4, 1939, below, p. 356.
[41] See law of May 7, 1940, below, p. 356. [42] Kulischer, *op. cit.*, p. 114.
[43] See below, p. 357. [44] See decree of April 4, 1939, below, p. 358. [45] See below, p. 359.

shall establish a temporary control of those estates over thirty hectares in extent where farming is for any reason jeopardized." The mayor and the secretary of each community are directed "to watch the farming in their districts" and report the state of farming to the county administration. If the farming situation is unsatisfactory, the court "shall, on motion of the county administration or the Minister of Economy, place the estate in the hands of a trustee," who shall take over the farming. This decree gives *prima facie* the impression of a tendency on the part of the government to intensify agricultural production; but on the other hand it confers on the administration the right to take over properties of people who are not in sympathy with the new political régime.

Of a definitely political nature is the decree of April 24, 1939.[46] This decree states that the property of persons "which was obtained through their own political activities, through political influence, or through the political activities or influence of other persons or political parties during the period from October 30, 1918, to October 6, 1938, shall be forfeited to the independent State of Slovakia regardless of whether the property is situated in this country or abroad." This decree is evidence of the intent of the present government to seize the property of the Slovak statesmen who collaborated with the Prague government during the period in which the Slovaks considered that they had suffered from the political predominance of the Czechs.

THE HIGHLAND TERRITORIES AND SUBCARPATHIA

(Incorporated into Hungary)

Hungary has occupied and incorporated, from among territories which it had lost to Czechoslovakia by virtue of the Trianon Treaty of 1921, two provinces, one with a Hungarian majority of population, the so-called Highland Territories; and the other, with a Ruthenian majority of population, Subcarpathia. Because of the fact that these territories represent a different historic and ethnographic picture and also because they were occupied and incorporated at different times, they are treated separately below. The claim to these territories by Hungary being based on a specific Hungarian institution called the "doctrine of the Holy Crown," the author has deemed it necessary to devote a section to this problem.

The Doctrine of the Holy Crown

The doctrine of the Holy Crown is a very essential element of Hungarian history vitally affecting the political life of Hungary. Even before the present war, this doctrine had been especially expressed in the agitation for

[46] See below, p. 360.

the acquisition of formerly owned territories and their incorporation into the Hungarian Holy Crown.

The doctrine may be said to date from the coronation of St. Stephen as King of Hungary on Christmas day in the year 1000,[47] by Pope Sylvester II, who previously, in a letter of March 27, had announced that he took the people of Hungary under the protection of the Church.[48]

In the succeeding centuries the Crown, consecrated by the Church, has symbolized kingship and royal prerogatives. But at an early date it also assumed further attributes, with the result that throughout the long period of Hungarian history reference is made to the Holy Crown as a legal entity, possessing dignity, glory, property, and benefits, but also subject to injuries and grievances. It acquired a transcendental character because of its religious origin and because of the fact that it had been "worn by the saintly king who founded the Hungarian State."[49]

Later on, the "Holy Crown" became the first sign of the evolution of a state personality independent of the king's person. For example, the small towns of Dalmatia appealed for protection, not to the king but to the Crown of Hungary, and in the period of the fifteenth century when Hungary was without a king, the Hungarian magnates declared that the Holy Crown alone could exercise the powers of the state. After the Estates were developed, the election of the king and his coronation ceased to be a Church function and became a prerogative of the Estates, the person of the king fading more and more into the background and the Holy Crown becoming the symbol of the whole territory of the Hungarian Kingdom, while the subjects of the kingdom were called subjects of the Crown. As stated by the great Hungarian historian Verbőczi, every noble was a member of the "Holy Crown." "The criterion of citizenship was also whether the person in question belonged to the Holy Crown."[50]

As the Holy Crown came to be considered the legal owner of the territory, it was therefore regarded as entitled to claim territories lost by it to other countries. When such lands were lost, it was the "Holy Crown," not Hungary, which figured in speeches of members of Parliament regarding the lost territory. After the creation of the dual monarchy of Austria-Hungary, "the defective character of the country's sovereignty was felt,"[51] and the doctrine of the Holy Crown was used as an argument against encroachments by the monarchy upon the rights of the Hungarian Parliament.

[47] See Dominic G. Kosáry, *A History of Hungary* (Cleveland and New York: The Benjamin Franklin Bibliophile Society, 1941), p. 21.

[48] See William E. Lingelbach, *Austria Hungary*, in the series "The History of Nations," Henry Cabot Lodge, Editor-in-Chief (New York: P. F. Collier & Son Company [1928]), Vol. XVII, p. 47.

[49] Gyula Szekfü, "The Doctrine of the Holy Crown," *Danubian Review* (Budapest and London), Vol. IX, No. 2 (July, 1941), p. 3.

[50] *Ibid.*, pp. 3–6.

[51] *Ibid.*, p. 6.

Following the Treaty of Trianon, the doctrine of the Holy Crown was again invoked in treaty revision activities which were subsequently carried on. The Hungarians claimed, in the name of the Holy Crown, the restoration of all territories which had belonged to the Crown in the past. In particular they claimed territories lost to Czechoslovakia under the Treaty of Trianon, namely, Subcarpathia and the so-called Highland Territories, situated in the highlands along the northern borders of Hungary, which are the southern borders of Czechoslovakia. They claimed also territories lost to Yugoslavia and to Rumania (Transylvania). Because of the persistence of the doctrine of the Holy Crown in Hungarian history, the laws on reincorporation of these territories, as cited below, refer always to the return of these territories to the "Hungarian Holy Crown." [52]

The Highland Territories

INCORPORATION (VIENNA AWARD)

During the Munich crisis Hungary renewed its claims to the territories situated in Czechoslovakia to the north of the mountainous Hungaro-Czechoslovak frontiers. As Germany and Italy took over at that time the factual control of Central Europe, they decided to settle by arbitration this claim of Hungary against Czechoslovakia, and accordingly the Foreign Ministers of Germany and Italy met in Vienna and issued the so-called Vienna Award of November 2, 1938,[53] under which a number of districts were allotted to Hungary (see above).

These regions, referred to as the "Highland Territories," [54] were incorporated into Hungary by the law of November 12, 1938, enacted by the Hungarian Royal Parliament. In this law the doctrine of the Holy Crown found its full expression in the solemn words: "The Hungarian Parliament devoutly expresses its gratitude to Divine Providence that after twenty years' separation, trial, and heroic resistance against foreign rule, one part of the torn-away Highland Territories returns to the realm of the Hungarian Holy Crown. The Hungarian fatherland greets with the deepest joy, and clasps to its heart with the affection of a loving mother, these returning children who have suffered so much." [55] By the incorporation of the Highland Territories Hungary acquired a territory of 11,927 square kilometres (4,605 square miles) and a population of 1,044,438. Of these inhabitants,

[52] See, as to the Highland Territories: Law XXXIV of November 12, 1938; decree of December 18, 1938, No. 9330/1938; and Law V of June 22, 1939, below, pp. 361, 366, 370. As to Subcarpathia, see Law VI of June 22, 1939, below, p. 363.

[53] See *Documents on International Affairs, 1938*, Monica Curtis, ed. (London, etc.: Oxford University Press), Vol. II (1943), p. 351.

[54] The Hungarians used to refer to all of Slovakia and Carpathian Ruthenia as *Felvidék* (Highland Territories). After November, 1938, this designation applied in Hungary to that part of Slovakia annexed to Hungary by the Vienna arbitration.

[55] See Law XXXIV of 1938, below, p. 361.

the main groups consisted of the following: 587,692 Hungarians, 51,578 Jews, 288,803 Slovaks, and 35,261 Subcarpathian Ruthenians (figures of the 1930 census).

REPRESENTATION IN PARLIAMENT

The Parliament of Hungary consists of two houses, the Upper House and the Lower House. Under the provisions of Law XXII promulgated November 15, 1926,[56] membership in the Upper House is based on (1) dignity of office, (2) election, and (3) nomination, and consists of the following groups: high dignitaries, such as judges and high state officials; clerical dignitaries of the various confessions; elected representatives of former hereditary members of the House of Magnates; members elected by the county and municipal authorities; members elected by organizations and representative bodies of agriculture, industry, commerce, science, arts and other professions; male members of the former reigning dynasty who have completed their twenty-fourth year and are residing permanently in the country; and members appointed by the head of the state. The Lower House consists mainly of representatives of rural constituencies elected by ballot.

After the incorporation of the Highlands, the Hungarian Government was eager to introduce into the Parliament representatives of the incorporated territories as a means of signalizing the return of these territories to Hungary. There was a prevailing tendency however to have only persons acceptable to the Budapest Government join the Parliament. Therefore Law XXXIV of 1938[57] provided that the Hungarian Parliament, on the motion of the Prime Minister, and with both houses consenting, should nominate those who, "from among those persons elected by the population of the Highland Territories as senators and national or provincial representatives," were to become members of the Hungarian Parliament. Law V of 1939[58] contained a similar provision, to be in effect "until such time as it may be possible to hold parliamentary elections" in the reincorporated territories. It further stipulated that elections should take place before June 30, 1940. Another law was enacted in 1942 (Law XXI),[59] which listed the number of members eligible to the Upper House from all the counties of Hungary.

The denial to the reincorporated territories of the right of free elections after reincorporation is evidence of the fact that the Hungarian Government was not sure of the attitude and feelings of the population, although the incorporation law referred to this population as faithful returning sons.

ADMINISTRATION

A special ministry without portfolio was instituted in Budapest for the administration and supervision of the Highland Territories. Since the Hun-

[56] *British and Foreign State Papers*, Vol. 123, p. 903. [57] See below, p. 361.
[58] See below, p. 366. [59] See below, p. 367.

garians regarded the incorporated areas as returning to them, and since the loss of these territories had been considered by the Hungarians as a national disaster, they were anxious to introduce as soon as possible in the reacquired territories the type of administration which existed in them before the Trianon Treaty. Not only was the Hungarian type of administrative agency introduced but also the Hungarian geographical divisions of the counties. The boundary lines of the old counties before their acquisition by Czechoslovakia were thus restored.

The county or comitatus is an essential element of Hungarian administration in the middle bracket, based upon a long historical evolution. All the country is divided into counties and, for the larger cities, town-counties. The administration of the counties is carried on by a County Chief (*Főispan*), appointed by the government. The County Chief is assisted by a representative body, half of which consists of elected members and half of citizens who pay the highest taxes. By the decree of the Hungarian Royal Prime Minister of December 18, 1938,[60] the organization of the Hungarian comitatus was reintroduced into the Highland Territories with certain essential changes limiting the elective form of government. This decree stated that the County Chief should appoint members of the representative assemblies of the comitatus from among the members of the representative assemblies of the former Czechoslovak counties. Special provisions were made for members of representative bodies in the town-counties. Thus, the members of the assembly of the autonomous city of Kassa (Košice) were to be appointed in the number of fifty-six by the Minister of the Interior, in agreement with the Minister without portfolio for Highland Affairs. In the cities of Ungvár and Munkács (which are a part of Subcarpathia), the members of the representative assemblies were to be appointed by the mayors. In the surrounding communities the members of the assemblies were to be appointed by the judges.

As no elections to Parliament were to take place for the time being, the representative assemblies of the counties could not function as electors of members of Parliament. The above-mentioned law expressly suspended this function of the county assemblies.

The officials necessary for the functioning of the representative assemblies, the decree states, were to be appointed by the Minister of the Interior, in agreement with the Minister without portfolio for Highland Affairs, and possibly other ministers interested. In certain counties (Esztergom, Nógrád, Abauj-Torna and Zemplén) special advisers to the county chiefs were to be appointed by the Minister of the Interior, in agreement with the Minister without portfolio for Highland Affairs. These advisers were to assist the county chief in supplying information relative to the affairs of the Highland Territories, and in reaching decisions upon all matters relating to these territories.

[60] See below, p. 370.

Czech officials were dismissed and replaced by Hungarian officials. Since there were not sufficient numbers of Hungarian candidates for these posts, the civil service requirements for appointive officials in the incorporated Highland Territories were lowered by decree No. 9330/1938 of December 18, 1938. Such lowering of the civil service requirements imposes a hardship on the population, particularly in times of political change and tension, when the culture and skill of government officials are of great importance.

It is true that the Minister of the Interior instructed the Hungarian authorities, in a decree of March 13, 1939 (which established definitively the Hungarian-Czechoslovakian frontier in the area between the Danube and the Ung), to refrain from any measures in connection with "acts caused by the present political tension until the day of the actual return of the territories." [61] Discrimination in the treatment of the population was, however, introduced by order of the Minister of the Interior of January 24, 1939, to the effect that only persons who prove their Hungarian citizenship may engage in certain trades and occupations.[62] The local Czech and Jewish population were principally affected by this order. Moreover, the legal status of the Jews in the incorporated Highland Territories was adjusted to the anti-Jewish laws which had been in force in all Hungary.[63]

ANNULMENT OF AGRARIAN REFORMS

Before the present war the Hungarians claimed in many instances that the Czechoslovak agrarian reforms were directed mainly toward the liquidation of land ownership by Hungarians, the Hungarian landowners representing the focus of political influence in the given area. Consequently, under the reincorporation a decree was promulgated [64] by the Hungarian Royal Cabinet to the effect that all transfers of real property which took place in the Highland Territories under Czechoslovak regulations dealing with agrarian reform should be investigated and might be declared null and void. Exceptions were to be made only in the case of acquisitions by municipalities, the Church, or former seigniorial landowners, or by associations and institutions of agricultural training. The ownership of the landed estates the acquisition

[61] Below, p. 363. [62] *Belügyi Közlöny*, February 5, 1939, Order No. 45700.

[63] The main laws of this type are the following: the law of May, 1938, which provided for a gradual reduction over a course of five years of the percentage of Jews in commerce and industry; the complicated law of May 4, 1939, which concerned converts and exemptions of certain categories of Jews from anti-Jewish laws and established deadlines for the elimination of Jewish employees; a decree of the Minister of Education of January, 1940, dismissing all Jewish teachers; a decree of the Minister of Commerce of November 16, 1940, to the effect that only those Jewish tavern- and inn-keepers who employed Gentile help would be permitted to keep their licenses until the final date provided by law; law of October, 1940, which deprived Jews from Transylvania of representation in the Upper House of the Parliament; decree of May 15, 1941, which provided that if a Jewish employee was called into military service his civilian position was to be filled by a Gentile; decree of August, 1941, prohibiting marriages between Gentiles and Jews under penalty of five years' imprisonment for both parties. For details, see *Hitler's Ten-Year War on the Jews*, pp. 68–77.

[64] See decree of March 12, 1939, below, p. 372.

of which has been voided is, from the time of such voiding, vested in the Hungarian State free of every incumbrance and with the land servitudes intact. As to the voided transactions, the former owner has a right to reimbursement for the amounts which he or his legal predecessor paid to the Czechoslovak Ministry of Agriculture or to the previous owner. Compensation is paid for improvements in landed estates only in exceptional cases. The execution of this decree was entrusted to a special commissioner appointed by the Ministry. The decisions of this commissioner as to voiding and compensation are to be final. The commissioner functions under the supervision of the Minister of Agriculture, with headquarters in Budapest. In this connection it should be stated that, aside from racial considerations (Czechs *versus* Hungarians, and *vice versa*), the Czechoslovak reform was a work of democratization of landed property. The annulment of this reform and the cancellation of the measures taken thereunder signify a return to a socially more backward system of land ownership in the incorporated territories.

CURRENCY

By a decree of the Council of Ministers, Hungarian currency became legal tender in the Highland Territories as of November 19, 1938. Currency in denominations of 20, 50 and 100 Czechoslovak crowns was exchanged at the rate of 100 pengő to 700 Czechoslovak crowns, and 100 crowns to 14.28 pengő. Claims owned by the Czechoslovak National Bank were taken over by the Hungarian National Bank under the decree of the Council of Ministers of November 27, 1938.[65]

Subcarpathia

INCORPORATION

Subcarpathia, a country inhabited in large majority by Ruthenians and only in the minority by Hungarians, was also claimed by Hungary on the ground that it had once belonged to the Hungarian Holy Crown. At the time of the occupation of the remaining parts of Czechoslovakia, Subcarpathia or Carpatho-Ukraine, as it was also called, which was then a federative unit within Czechoslovakia, decided through its National Council that this province should declare its independence. The following resolution was passed by the Council: "We stand for an ethnographic settlement of the frontiers between Hungary and Ruthenia. We decisively reject any form of plebiscite, as the political allegiance of Ruthenia has already been definitely settled. We are in favour of the federal form of the State of the Czechs, Slovaks, and Ukrainians (Ruthenians)." [66] A new cabinet was formed with

[65] Order No. 7,210/1938, *Belügyi Közlöny*, November 27, 1938, pp. 1152–53.
[66] Resolution of the Ukrainian National Council, quoted by Monsignor Vološín, Minister for the Administration of Ruthenia, October 26, 1938. See *Documents on International Affairs, 1938, sup. cit.*, Vol. II, p. 349.

Father Vološín as Prime Minister, but in the meantime, on March 14, 1939, Hungarian troops had crossed the border and had begun the occupation of Subcarpathia.[67] Vološín telegraphed to Berlin for assistance, and when his appeal failed he and his ministers fled to Rumania.[68]

On the same day that Hungarian troops were marching into the territory, the Hungarian Government sent an ultimatum to Prague demanding the withdrawal of all Czech troops within twelve hours. The Czech Government complied partially with this ultimatum, and later on Hungary occupied all Subcarpathia.

Subcarpathia was incorporated into Hungary by Law VI of 1939 enacted by the Hungarian Parliament on June 22 of that year, in which law the doctrine of the Holy Crown again found expression. In this law of incorporation Parliament welcomes the returned territory and its inhabitants in the following words:

> The Hungarian Parliament devoutly expresses its gratitude to Divine Providence that, after the return in the last quarter of the year 1938 of a part of the torn-away Highland Territories, Carpathia also returned to the realm of the Hungarian Holy Crown in the month of March of the year 1939. The Hungarian fatherland greets with the deepest joy, and with the affection of a loving mother clasps to its heart, its faithful sons who have suffered so much and who have returned together with the territory of the northeastern Carpathians, delimited by their 1,000-year-old boundaries.[69]

By the incorporation of Subcarpathia Hungary acquired a territory of 12,146 square kilometres (4,690 square miles) and a population of 671,962 persons. From Subcarpathia, 20,000 to 30,000 Czechs and Slovaks were moved to Bohemia and Moravia and Slovakia.[70]

REPRESENTATION IN PARLIAMENT

Law VI of 1939 provided that elections should take place before June 30, 1940. In the meantime, in accordance with the provisions of this law, the Prime Minister was to propose as members of Parliament not more than ten persons "from among those elected by the population of the Carpathian territories as senators and national or provincial representatives, or candidates listed on the register of the Hungarian parties as elected substitute representatives, or members of the national council elected by the original population of Subcarpathia." These names were to be subject to the approval of both houses of Parliament. Subsequently, Law XXI of 1942 indicated the number of representatives eligible to the Parliament from Sub-

[67] *Bulletin of International News*, Vol. XVI, No. 6 (March 25, 1939), p. 259.

[68] Some authors do not treat seriously the endeavors toward independence of Subcarpathia. Michael Winch describes with distrust these endeavors of "half a million backward mountain shepherds and lumbermen who cared only about the price of timber and the possibility of earning a few shillings." See *Republic for a Day: An Eye-Witness Account of the Carpatho-Ukraine Incident* (London: Robt. Hale & Co., Ltd., 1939).

[69] See Law VI of 1939, below, p. 363.

[70] Kulischer, *op. cit.*, p. 114.

carpathia, and, in addition, Section 8 of the same law provided that three members of the Upper House should be appointed from Subcarpathia, beginning January 1, 1943.[71]

ADMINISTRATION

Law VI of 1939 authorized the Prime Minister to introduce in the Parliament a bill providing for the autonomy of Carpathia. However, the same law provided in Section 7, that the Cabinet "is authorized . . . to issue such orders in regard to the Carpathian Territories as may be necessary in order to adjust the administration, legislation, economy and generally the whole legal system, to the legal structure of the country or to harmonize the two." The Cabinet was authorized to issue these orders even though they dealt with matters falling normally within the jurisdiction of the Parliament. They were required subsequently to be confirmed by Parliament. Thus, the idea of autonomy, although proclaimed, was from the beginning very greatly restricted by the provisions concerning assimilation of administration and law with the governmental régime of Hungary. The administration of Subcarpathia was originally in the hands of the Hungarian military authorities but this system was soon changed to administration by civil authorities. The Hungarian Government appointed a commissioner for Subcarpathia, with the title "Commissioner of the Regent," who is assisted by an adviser.

The promised autonomy is limited to local administrative matters, while in the political and cultural fields the government endeavors to impose the Hungarian pattern upon the population. Education, especially in secondary schools, follows the Hungarian system. The land which had been distributed among the peasants by the Czechoslovak law on agrarian reform has been reallocated to Hungarian landowners from whom it was taken. Moreover, landed properties have been taken from Jews and distributed among Hungarians repatriated from Rumania. The Ruthenian youth is pressed into the "Levente" organization (a kind of Hungarian fascist youth organization). A pro-Hungarian local politician by the name of Kurtyak[72] is collaborating with the Hungarian authorities, while other Ruthenian leaders have left the country or are hiding to escape persecution.

The Hungarians instituted a severe church policy, usually directed against the union of free churches, which had a considerable number of adherents and which were regarded as centers of Anglophile influence. The union was dissolved and church property confiscated.[73]

[71] The Subcarpathian deputies to the Parliament, in the number of seven, have formed a special group in the Parliament called the "Group of Subcarpathian Deputies."

[72] *Czechoslovakia Fights Back. A Document of the Czechoslovak Ministry of Foreign Affairs*. Introduction by Jan Masaryk (Washington: American Council on Public Affairs, 1943), p. 171.

[73] George Hronek, "Subcarpathian Russia—a Forgotten Country," *Central European Observer*, Vol. XVIII, No. 19 (September 19, 1941), p. 263.

CITIZENSHIP

Hungarian citizenship was granted *ipso jure* [74] to inhabitants of the Subcarpathian territory who had lived continuously for ten years (from March 15, 1929, to March 15, 1939) in this territory, and who were Hungarian citizens on July 26, 1921 (day of the exchange of ratifications of the Trianon Treaty). Hungarian citizenship granted under these rules was extended to wives and to children under twenty-four years of age. A child born out of wedlock, if not over twenty-four, follows the citizenship of its mother. A full orphan or a fatherless orphan born after July 26, 1921, as a Czechoslovak citizen acquired Hungarian citizenship if the father was a Hungarian citizen on that date, or the grandfather, if the father was born later. The essential condition is, however, that the orphan himself shall have lived for ten years continuously from March 15, 1929—or since his birth (if born later)—in the territory of Subcarpathia.

The law provided further that any person whose ancestor acquired Czechoslovak citizenship by option on the basis of Article 64 of the Treaty of Trianon should not be entitled to Hungarian citizenship.

CURRENCY

By decree No. 3,670/1939 of April 23, 1939,[75] Hungarian currency was made legal tender in Subcarpathia. The exchange rate was established as follows: 100 pengő equals 700 Czech crowns; 100 crowns equals 14.28 pengő.

[74] Law VI of June 22, 1939, below, p. 364.
[75] *Belügyi Közlöny*, April 23, 1939, No. 18, p. 476.

CHAPTER XV

DANZIG

BACKGROUND

The port of Danzig, founded by the Poles, was for centuries a goal in the German *Drang nach Osten*. In 1308 it was conquered from Poland by the Teutonic Knights, who carried out a mass slaughter of the Polish population.[1] When Pope Clement V, in his Bull dated at Avignon June 19, 1310, denounced the massacre of more than 10,000 people in the city of Gdańsk (Polish name for Danzig), the procurators of the Teutonic order alleged that "the mentioned citizens destroyed the houses of the town of their own free will and went to live in other parts." [2]

About the middle of the fifteenth century, a Prussian League, formed at that time, which included Danzig, appealed to the ancient Polish sovereign against the Teutonic Order of Knights. After a twelve-year war Danzig was restored to the Polish Crown. The city received from the Polish king full self-government and entered on a period of great economic prosperity because it served as the only port for all the exports from Poland. The subsequent partitions of Poland have destroyed Polish sovereignty over Danzig. After the Peace Conference of 1919 the economic interdependence of Poland and Danzig was recognized.[3]

The Conference initially intended to incorporate Danzig into Poland, but finally decision was reached to create from Danzig (with an area of nearly eight hundred square miles and a population of 400,000) a Free City under the protection of the League of Nations and with special rights for Poland. The provisions for the establishment of the Free City are contained in Articles 100 to 108 of the Treaty of Versailles, and these provisions were further

[1] "No person of Polish nationality was spared, whatever his condition, sex or age might be, but they put to death without mercy individuals of age and under age, including children and infants at the breast, so that the news of this cruelty should spread and break the nerve of others who would fear to offer resistance in other towns and fortified places, and thereby render secure their occupation of the said land. Seldom was the spilling of Polish blood attending the conquest of any place more profuse, seldom the slaughter more inhuman." *Dlugosii Joannis canonici Cracoviensis Historiae Polonicae*, libri XII, Cracoviae, 1876, III, p. 44 s.

[2] *Lites ac res gestae inter Polonos Ordinemque Cruciferorum I*, Posnaniae, 1890, pp. 423, 428.

[3] The importance of Danzig for Poland was recognized in past centuries by German leaders as well. Frederick the Great once said: "Whosoever possesses the mouth of the Vistula and the city of Danzig will be more master of Poland than the King who reigns there." Quoted from Casimir Smogorzewski, *Poland's Access to the Sea* (London: Allen & Unwin, Limited, 1934), p. 229.

When Bismarck was out of the government, he headed in Germany an anti-Polish movement. In 1893 he declared to a delegation of followers: "For a Polish State with Warsaw, Danzig is a greater necessity than Poznań." *Bismarck: Die gesammelten Werke*, Vol. XIII, ed. by W. Schüssler (Berlin, 1930), p. 544.

See also *Poland and Danzig*, edited by the Polish Research Centre (London: The Cornwall Press, Ltd., 1941).

implemented by two conventions between Poland and the Free City of Danzig which were signed, one in Paris on November 9, 1920, the other in Warsaw on October 24, 1921.[4] The mutual rights of Danzig and Poland as formulated in the above-mentioned documents were in the main as follows: The Free City of Danzig was included within the Polish customs frontiers and a free area was established in the port. Poland received the free use and service of the whole railway system, the waterways, docks, basins, wharves, and other works within the territory of the Free City necessary for Polish imports and exports. The railways and docks of the port were to be administered by a commission of Poles and Danzigers, with a neutral chairman. Poland received also the control and administration of postal, telegraphic, and telephonic communication between Poland and the port of Danzig. The Polish Government was granted the right to conduct the foreign affairs of the Free City of Danzig and was entrusted with the diplomatic protection of the citizens of that city when abroad. No discrimination could be undertaken within the Free City of Danzig to the detriment of Polish citizens.

A constitution was drawn up for the Free City of Danzig, providing for a popular Assembly (Volkstag) as a parliament, and for an executive body called the Senate, which was elected for a period of four years by the Volkstag. Danzig had its own currency (gulden), and its own courts. The official language was German.

The League of Nations was represented in Danzig by a High Commissioner, whose main task was to coordinate and maintain good relations between the Free City and Poland. For the safeguarding of Polish interests, the office of a Polish Commissioner was established in Danzig.

INCORPORATION

On April 28, 1939, Hitler declared in a speech before the Reichstag that Danzig must return to German sovereignty. After four months of great political tension, Germany launched an attack on Poland on September 1, 1939, and occupied Danzig.

On the same day, the *Gauleiter* of the Nazi Party in Danzig, Förster, signed a statute abolishing the Constitution of the Free City of Danzig and declaring the city, with its territory and its citizens, incorporated into the German Reich. All legislative and executive power was vested exclusively in the Head of the City. On the same day an act was passed by the Reichstag embodying the Danzig statute and making it an "Act of the Reich." Under this statute of the Reichstag, citizens of the Free City of Danzig were to become "German citizens in accordance with provisions to be issued," and provision was made for "the entire body of Reich law and Prussian law" to "take effect as of January 1, 1940." The Reich Minister of the Interior

[4] Ian F. D. Morrow, "The International Status of the Free City of Danzig," *British Year Book of International Law*, Vol. XVIII (1937), pp. 114, 118, 120.

was entrusted with all matters connected with the incorporation of Danzig into the German Reich.[5]

Later, on October 8, 1939, Danzig was incorporated into the District (*Gau*) of Western Prussia and served as headquarters for the Reich Governor. Poles living in Danzig, even if they were formerly citizens of the Free City, were treated just as were the Poles in the incorporated parts of western Poland. They were excluded from German citizenship and their property was sequestrated in Danzig in the same way as in the Polish Incorporated Territories.[6]

The German Reichsmark was made exclusive legal tender and the local Danzig gulden were exchanged into Reichsmarks at the rate of 1 Reichsmark to 1.43 Danzig gulden.

[5] See below, p. 375.
[6] See decree of September 17, 1940, below, p. 511.

CHAPTER XVI

DENMARK

I. Invasion

Without warning and in violation of the non-aggression pact between Germany and Denmark signed less than a year before,[1] and on which the Government of Denmark strongly relied,[2] German troops marched into Denmark and took possession of the country in the early morning hours of April 9, 1940.[3] At the same time German cruisers entered the harbor of Middelfart on the west coast of Fyn. Other ships landed troops on the east coast of Fyn and at the Korsor.[4]

At the very moment when the German Army began its invasion of the country, the German Minister to Denmark informed the government that German troops had occupied Denmark's most important military objectives. He then handed over a memorandum which stated that the territory of Denmark had been occupied in order to forestall violations of Denmark's neutrality by the Allies. In this memorandum the Danish Government was requested to cooperate with the German troops and a solemn promise was given by the German Government that neither the territorial integrity nor the political independence of Denmark would be challenged.[5]

After receiving notice of these events, as well as the memorandum, King Christian met with the government to consider the situation. The conclusion was reached that since a large part of the military objectives were already occupied, resistance would result only in bloodshed and destruction.

[1] The Danish-German Non-Aggression Pact was signed on May 31, 1939. Article 1 of this treaty reads as follows:

"The Kingdom of Denmark and the German Reich will in no case resort to war or any other use of force against each other.

"In case any third power should take action of the nature described in the first paragraph against either contracting party, the other contracting party will not in any way render support to such action." *Nordisk Tidsskrift for International Ret* (Copenhagen, etc.), Vol. 10 (1939), Fasc. 1 "Scandinavian Documents," p. 66.

[2] In introducing the Danish-German Non-Aggression Pact to the Rigsdag on June 1, 1939, the Danish Foreign Minister, Dr. Munch, stated:

"This agreement, therefore, is in close conformity with the policy pursued by Denmark for a long time. The Government are convinced that in the troubled conditions prevailing in the world it will be of considerable value. . . ." *Ibid.*, p. 68.

As to the interpretation of the Danish-German Non-Aggression Pact, see Erik Brüel, "Den Dansk-Tyske Ikke-Angrebspagt," *ibid.*, Vol. 10, Fasc. 1, p. 50. English text, *ibid.*, Fasc. 4, p. 157.

[3] The first German units crossed the frontier at Aabenraa at 4:30 a.m.

[4] "The Nazi Invasion of Denmark," *Notes on Denmark: Before and After the German Invasion* (American Friends of Danish Freedom and Democracy, New York, 1941), p. 56.

[5] A memorandum containing the same text, *mutatis mutandis*, was presented on April 9, 1940, to the Norwegian Government. (See "Norway," below.) See *Nordisk Tidsskrift for International Ret*, Vol. 11 (1940), Fasc. 3-4, D-45-48. English text, *ibid.*, "Scandinavian Documents," p. 143.

A protest was presented to the German authorities against the invasion. Then the King gave orders to Danish troops everywhere to cease resistance; but before orders were received fighting had taken place along the border.

On the same day a proclamation was issued to the people of Denmark signed by the King and Prime Minister, which reads as follows:

To the Danish People! German troops last night crossed the Danish frontier and have landed in various places. The Danish Government have decided under protest to arrange the affairs of the country with a view to the occupation which has taken place, in pursuance whereof the following announcement is made:

The German troops which are now present in the country enter into contact with the Danish defence force, and it is the duty of the population to refrain from any resistance to these troops. The Danish Government will endeavour to safeguard the Danish people and our country against the disasters resulting from war conditions and therefore urge the population to adopt a calm and restrained attitude to the conditions which have now arisen. Quiet and order must prevail in the country and a loyal attitude must be displayed to all who have authority to exercise.[6]

The King added the following personal warning:

Under the present conditions which are so momentous for our fatherland, I beg you all in town and country to maintain a perfectly correct and dignified behaviour, remembering that any ill-considered deed or word may entail the gravest consequences. God keep you all! God keep Denmark![7]

On the same day both houses of the Rigsdag met in joint session; the Prime Minister made a full report on the situation; and the Rigsdag approved the government's action.

II. Occupation

ADMINISTRATION

On April 9, 1940, the commander of the German troops (Kaupisch) issued a proclamation to the Danish Army and the Danish nation stating that England and France had declared war on Germany without reason and in opposition to the sincere wishes of the German Government and people. He accused England of violating Danish as well as Norwegian neutrality and of preparing for a battle off the Danish and Norwegian coasts. In order to "forestall" the English attack, the German armed forces assumed "the protection of the neutrality of the Kingdoms of Denmark and Norway." The proclamation also referred to the agreements in course of negotiation with the Danish Government, the purpose of which was "to make sure that the Danish Kingdom shall continue to exist, that the fleet shall be maintained, that the liberty of the Danish people shall be respected, and that the future independence of that country shall be secured."[8] The Danish

[6] *Ibid.*, p. 146. See also *Notes on Denmark*, pp. 57–58.
[7] *Notes on Denmark*, p. 58.
[8] See proclamation, below, p. 377.

military and civil authorities were asked to enter into contact with the German commanders and the people were requested to continue to work and to preserve order.

In the first stage of occupation, as it developed from April 9, 1940, until August 29, 1943, the structure of the occupation was as follows: Danish governmental institutions remained essentially unchanged. The King carried out his royal functions. Even elections to Parliament took place on March 3, 1943.[9] The administration of the country and legislation were in the hands of the Danish Government. Requests of the German Government or of the occupation authorities were presented to the Danish Government by the German Minister or by the commander of the German forces in Denmark. The Danish Government tried, through negotiations, through meeting some requests of the occupation authorities and rejecting others, to make the occupation as little of a burden as possible to the population. In their negotiations the German representatives used mainly the threat that if their requests should not be complied with, they would not be bound by the promise of April 9, 1940, as to safeguarding the Danish Government and institutions; and also, as Denmark was dependent on German coal and fuel, they threatened to cut off the importation of these essential commodities.

Although the administration was left to the Danish Government, the Germans displayed a particular interest in the police. They required that the Danish police force be increased and trained according to German methods. In the autumn of 1941 the *Polizeiverwaltung Dänemark* was established. The army of occupation also succeeded in having appointed a police minister acceptable to it. The Gestapo assumed control of news and information channels. Censorship was established, but handled by Danish authorities under German guidance. Movement into and out of the country was also controlled. In the summer of 1940 the Germans suggested a customs and currency union and a kind of common citizenship. The Danish Government rejected this proposal.[10]

At the end of 1940 the Germans asked the Danish Cabinet for the retirement of Premier Stauning and five other members of the cabinet. This request was also rejected.

When the German Minister made a demand for ten of the modern torpedo boats which formed the larger part of the Danish fleet, the demand was refused and attention called to the German promise of April 9, 1940, that the Danish Navy was to be maintained. The answer of the German Minister was that Germany wished to hire the boats for use in training crews for patrol in the Baltic, to which the Danes replied that their Navy was not for hire. Then the German Minister declared that if the demand was not complied with, the boats would be expropriated and delivery of German

[9] *Bulletin of International News*, Vol. XX, No. 7 (April 3, 1943), p. 309.

[10] Gunnar Leistikow, "Denmark under the Nazi Heel," *Foreign Affairs* (Council on Foreign Relations, Inc., New York), Vol. 21 (1943), pp. 346, 347.

coal would cease. Under these circumstances the boats were delivered after being disarmed and partly dismantled by the Danes.[11]

ACCESSION TO THE ANTI-COMINTERN PACT AND ANTICOMMUNISTIC LEGISLATION

Since the beginning of the occupation German authorities have exercised strong pressure upon the Danish Government to introduce, first, anti-Jewish legislation and regulations for deporting the 5,000 Danish Jews from Denmark; and, second, anticommunist legislation after Denmark's accession to the Anti-Comintern Pact. The Danish Government, especially King Christian, categorically opposed the first request, so that no anti-Jewish legislation was enacted.[12]

The pressure regarding anticommunistic legislation was continuous. Hitler succeeded in getting accessions to the Anti-Comintern Pact by his Axis partners Italy and Japan, and also by Hungary, Spain, Finland, Bulgaria, Croatia, Rumania, Slovakia, Manchukuo, and puppet China. This pact, signed initially November 25, 1936, provided that common action should be taken by the signatory parties against communism, and that they should furnish one another with information as to the activities of the Communist International. Under the terms of the Anti-Comintern Pact, a permanent Executive Committee for its implementation was provided, with headquarters in Berlin. After Germany marched into Russia the pressure on Denmark was increased and it finally acceded to the pact on November 25, 1941.[13] As a result of this signature a law was issued prohibiting communistic associations and activities in Denmark.[14] All such associations were dissolved and conduct or propaganda in favor of communism was prohibited. Communist activities were made punishable by fines, detention, or imprisonment up to one year. Of particular interest is Section 2 of this law, which provides for taking persons into custody who give reason for the presumption that "they intend to take part in communistic activities or propaganda." Those who are charged with such acts or intentions may be interned by decision of the Minister of Justice when it is deemed necessary "for the sake of the security of the state or of its relations with foreign states." However, every person taken into custody under the above-mentioned conditions must be brought within twenty-four hours before the City Court of Copenhagen, which decides whether custody shall be continued. Internment shall last as long as is deemed "necessary for the

[11] Gunnar Leistikow, "Denmark under the Nazi Heel," *Foreign Affairs* (Council on Foreign Relations, Inc., New York), Vol. 21 (1943), p. 348; *Bulletin of International News*, Vol. XVIII, No. 4 (February 22, 1941), p. 229.

[12] After the Germans requested the adoption of anti-Jewish laws, the King attended services in a synagogue in Copenhagen. He is reported to have explained to the German officials that there was no Jewish question in Denmark because Danes "never had had any minority feelings toward the Jews." Leistikow, *op. cit.*, p. 352.

[13] For accession of Denmark to the Anti-Comintern Pact, see *Lovtidenden-C*, No. 2, July 2, 1942.

[14] Law No. 349, August 22, 1941, below, p. 381.

security of the state or of its relations with foreign states." The Minister of Justice is required to report every third month to a special committee created within the Rigsdag concerning the persons interned and the reasons for such action.

LABOR

There is no law on compulsory labor or conscription, but Danish workers are being compelled to accept work in Germany because of the occupant's pressure upon the Danish Government, exerted chiefly through the requirement that the government withhold unemployment relief from those Danes who do not accept offers of work in Germany.[15] The government has also been compelled to permit several exemptions or privileges for Danish workers leaving for Germany.

SELLING POLICY

From the beginning the occupation of Denmark resulted in the draining of the natural resources and stocks of commodities from the country by the occupant.[16]

Because of the behavior of the German armed forces, the Danish Government felt compelled to enact a law regulating the sale of merchandise to them.[17] By this means the Danes, who were not strong enough to prevent completely German purchases, endeavored to organize them through intergovernmental channels, wherein they could maintain a certain control over such transactions. This law stated that the German armed forces in Denmark "as a rule receive all supplies of food, forage, and all other commodities from Germany." That this statement, however, was in the main illusory is evident from the further content of the same law, which provided among other things for the sale of butter, meat, lard, milk, eggs, and cheese without restriction except that such sales must be made through Danish export agencies controlled by the Danish Government. Other goods could be sold by the Danes to the German armed forces only by special permission issued by the Ministry of Foreign Affairs, although such permission was not required when the price of the commodities did not exceed 200 kroner in each individual case.[18] Under the pressure of the occupant, the Danish Government was forced to agree that in sales to the German armed forces or to in-

[15] According to various sources, about 50,000 Danes have had to leave Denmark and work for Germany, either inside Germany or in other occupied countries. See Leistikow, *op. cit.*, pp. 350, 351.

[16] The army was "on the hunt," so to speak, for food. "In the first days of the occupation you could see big, serious-looking fellows in uniform standing outside dairy-shops and licking up half a pound of butter, without bread, like ice-cream. . . ." Joachim Joesten, "Denmark Under the Jackboot," *The Fortnightly* (London), Vol. 148, New Series (1940), pp. 567–68.

[17] Law No. 639 of December 11, 1940, below, p. 380.

[18] Since 200 kroner is equivalent to about $40, the aggregate value of these exempted transactions may well have been large.

dividual units thereof "the Danish seller is entitled only to receive payment in the form of checks." In sales involving less than 200 kroner, however, payments may be made in cash. This specific regulation as to payment by checks in larger transactions was a special form of forced long-term borrowing from the Danes.

As the war continued, the curtailing of German buying became one of the main concerns of the Danish Government, because the Germans wished to purchase everything they could lay their hands on. They tried to buy or lease Danish merchantmen and smaller transport ships from Danish shipping firms, and the Danish Government was therefore compelled to issue several laws making such sales or leases dependent on the permission of the government.[19] After the occupation of the Ukraine, which was stripped by the retreating Russian armies of all agricultural implements,[20] the occupant sought to buy agricultural implements from Denmark. The Danish Government then promulgated a law [21] to the effect that sale to foreign countries of agricultural machinery or implements without permission of the Danish Directorate for Supply of Commodities is prohibited.

In order to further reduce German purchases, a law was enacted prohibiting the Danes, without the permission of the Danish National Bank, from receiving payments in any form from persons who are not residents of Denmark.[22] Because, in particular, of the German endeavors to penetrate into Danish companies, the transfer of Danish securities to foreigners was forbidden.[23]

CLEARING ARRANGEMENTS

The main exploitation of Denmark is carried out through the institution of clearing.[24] Under a clearing arrangement with the Danish National Bank, all trade settlements between Germany and Denmark are made through the *Verrechnungskasse* in Berlin and the Clearing Institute in Copenhagen. Under the mechanism of clearing,[25] the balances of imports and exports must be equal; but Germany is constantly overimporting from Denmark without counterexporting the equivalents. In 1942 Germany owed to Denmark on account of the clearing trade "two and one-half billion kroner, equivalent to nearly one-fourth of the national wealth."[26]

In order to continue the exports from Denmark, the occupant is forcing the Danish National Bank to advance sums to the Danish exporters. To

[19] See Law No. 482, September 14, 1940, *Lovtidenden-A*, No. 99, September 17, 1940; Law No. 148, March 31, 1941 (*ibid.*, No. 20, March 31, 1941); Law No. 205, April 25, 1941 (*ibid.*, No. 29, April 30, 1941).

[20] See below, chapter on "Union of Soviet Socialist Republics."

[21] Law No. 61, February 26, 1943, *Lovtidenden-A*, No. 14.

[22] Law No. 415, October 2, 1941, below, p. 379.

[23] *Ibid.*

[24] See Section 17 of Law No. 337 of June 25, 1940, below, p. 378.

[25] See above, chapter on "Finance."

[26] Leistikow, *op. cit.*, p. 350. It is obvious that at the time this book is written the amount of the debt has considerably increased—according to some information, to about four billion kroner.

meet the increasing currency requirements, the volume of Danish currency is being expanded, and this in turn is causing inflation.[27]

ADMINISTRATION OF JUSTICE

The problem of administration of justice in Denmark is of particular importance and has been one of the main topics of negotiations and the cause of strained relations between the Danish Government and the army of occupation. The question arose as to which courts, German or Danish, should try Danish citizens libeled or accused of sabotage and attacks upon the German Army. One of the German commanders agreed that a group of Danish citizens should not be tried by German justice, provided alterations were made in the Danish Penal Code. With some exceptions these cases were tried by Danish courts under a law of January 18, 1941, until a new military commander was appointed.

PRESSURE ON LEGISLATION

As the occupation authorities did not legislate at all in Denmark, pressure was brought on the Danish Government as above stated to introduce legislation which would meet the requirements of the occupying power. Accordingly, the following Danish enactments were published: a law requiring deposit of certain naval and radio apparatus;[28] a law prohibiting the photographing of German military establishments;[29] a law to control the private possession of firearms;[30] a law on importation of or trade in firearms and munitions;[31] a law concerning movement in military zones;[32] a law prohibiting photographing of bombed areas and damaged ships.[33] The Penal Code was supplemented by provisions establishing penalties for giving information on military establishments and military forces and for aiding opponents of the military forces occupying Denmark,[34] and by several laws concerning navigation,[35] etc.

Another addition to the Danish Penal Code provided that Danish courts may impose sentence of imprisonment of from one year to life for sabotage, espionage, and other acts which may prejudice the relations between Denmark and the occupying power "under agreement." Under a proclamation dated June 9, 1941, any acts or demonstrations which may disrupt relations with the occupying troops are punishable by imprisonment up to two years, if more severe penalties are not already provided by law. In May, 1942, the maximum penalty for the dissemination of rumors was in-

[27] Leistikow, *op. cit.*, p. 350.
[28] Law No. 190, April 16, 1940, *Lovtidenden-A*, No. 41, April 17, 1940.
[29] Law No. 220, May 1, 1940, *ibid.*, No. 47, May 1, 1940.
[30] Law No. 246, May 10, 1940, *ibid.*, No. 53, May 11, 1940.
[31] Law No. 266, May 23, 1940, *ibid.*, No. 59, May 24, 1940.
[32] Law No. 562, October 31, 1940, *ibid.*, No. 110, November 5, 1940.
[33] Law No. 633, December 4, 1940, *ibid.*, No. 118, December 9, 1940.
[34] Law No. 14, January 18, 1941, *ibid.*, No. 3, January 20, 1941.
[35] Law No. 346, August 16, 1941, *ibid.*, No. 53, August 20, 1941; Law No. 359, August 22, 1941, *ibid.*, No. 55, August 29, 1941.

creased to three years' imprisonment. Where military information is involved, life sentence may be imposed.

As regards prosecutions under these provisions, a law of May, 1941, provides that documents may be withheld, choice of counsel may be denied, lay assessors may be excluded from the lower court, and appeal may be made directly to the Supreme Court, thus avoiding trial by jury in the upper court. The German occupant insists on these cases being tried secretly, in order not to stir up public opinion.

III. The Revolt of August, 1943

As acts of sabotage increased during the summer of 1943, the German Minister to Denmark, Werner Best, made an official request, in the form of an ultimatum, that saboteurs should be tried by German military courts. The Danish Government did not accept this ultimatum and resigned. In the meantime the population, backing the government, showed signs of unrest; acts of sabotage occurred, and in the first days of September open clashes occurred between the German armed forces and Danish patriots. The German commander thereupon declared martial law, and interned the government and the King. The German Army took over control of various localities in Denmark. At the same time the German military commander assumed control of the administration of the country and made an appeal to the different agencies of government to continue work, under threat of penalties for strikes. When the occupying power endeavored to take over the Danish Navy, part of it was scuttled by Danish patriots and part of it escaped to Sweden.[36]

IV. Effect of German Occupation of Denmark on Iceland and Greenland

1.—*Iceland*

In accordance with the Danish Act of Union of November 30, 1918, Iceland and Denmark have been since 1918 two fully sovereign states united by a common King. In this document Denmark expressly admits that the status of Iceland is that of a free and sovereign state on a footing of complete equality with Denmark.[37]

[36] At the time of writing the above, the actual situation in Denmark is in a state of instability, fluctuating from day to day, under the influence of the strengthened Danish resistance and German measures of oppression.

[37] See the following provisions of the Act of Union:

"Part 1.—Sec. 1. Denmark and Iceland shall be free and sovereign States united under a common King, and by the agreement contained in this Law of Union; the names of both States shall be included in the King's title.

. . .

"Part 7.—19. Denmark shall give notice to foreign Powers that, in agreement with the contents of this Law of Union, Iceland has been recognized as a sovereign State, and shall also give notice that Iceland declares herself permanently neutral and has no naval flag." *British and Foreign State Papers*, 1917–1918, Vol. 111, pp. 703, 706.

When Denmark was occupied by German forces, the Iceland Parliament (Althing), on April 10, 1940, conferred upon the Icelandic Government the powers of the King with respect to Iceland, in the following resolutions:

> Having regard to the fact that the situation created makes it impossible for the King of Iceland to execute the royal power given to him under the Constitutional Act, the Althing declares that the Government of Iceland is for the time being entrusted with this power.
>
> Having regard to the situation now created, Denmark is not in a position to execute the authority to take charge of the foreign affairs of Iceland, nor can it carry out the fishery inspection within Icelandic territorial waters. Therefore the Althing declares that Iceland will for the time being take the entire charge of these affairs.[38]

This was done in conformity with Article 4 of the Constitution of Iceland of May 18, 1920, in which it is provided that should the King be unable to discharge his constitutional functions, "the rules in force in Denmark on the 1st December, 1918" shall apply likewise to Iceland.[39] In the Danish Act of February 11, 1871,[40] it is provided that in case the King is ill or absent or unable to make decisions as to succession, the cabinet shall immediately convoke the Rigsdag, which shall decide who shall carry on the government. Consequently the Althing felt authorized to take over governmental functions and to provide for carrying on the government while the King of Denmark was unable to do so.

The Act of Union of 1918 gives each country, among other things, the right to demand the commencement of negotiations for revision of the agreements therein contained on the expiration of the year 1940, and in the event that agreement is not reached within three years from the date of the petition, the law may be annulled by action of the Danish Rigsdag and the Icelandic Althing, respectively.[41] The relationship between Iceland and Denmark is characterized by some authors as being of a contractual character, in which case, according to the principle *clausula rebus sic stantibus*, either partner has the right to rescind the contract on the ground of changed conditions.[42]

On May 17, 1941, the Althing took further steps toward gaining independence by the passage of the following resolution:

> The Althing considers that Iceland has acquired the right to sever entirely the Act of Union with Denmark, as Iceland has had to take into its own hands the conduct of all its affairs, Denmark not being in a position to conduct such affairs as it undertook to deal with on Iceland's behalf under the Danish-Icelandic Act of Union of 1918.

[38] *Bulletin of International News*, Vol. XIX, No. 17 (August 22, 1942), p. 744. See also Sveinbjorn Johnson in "Iceland and the Americas," *American Bar Association Journal*, Vol. 26 (1940), p. 508.

[39] *British and Foreign State Papers*, Vol. 125, p. 851.

[40] Holger Federspiel, *Kongeriget Danmarks Love* (Copenhagen, 1910), p. 725.

[41] See Part 6 of Act of Union, *British and Foreign State Papers*, Vol. 111, p. 706.

[42] Some authors believe that the Act of Union was neither a statute nor a treaty but a *tertium quid*. See Philip E. Mosely, "Iceland and Greenland: An American Problem," *Foreign Affairs*, Vol. 18 (1940), p. 742.

On the part of Iceland there shall be no question of renewing the Act of Union with Denmark, although it is not thought expedient in present circumstances to accomplish the formal severance of the Union and settle the Constitution of the State in its final form; this, however, is to be postponed no longer than until the end of the war.

A Regent shall be elected for one year at a time, such power being vested in him as was vested in the Government of Iceland by a Resolution of the Althing of April 10, 1940, concerning the supreme power in the affairs of the State.

A Republic shall be established in Iceland as soon as the Union with Denmark has been formally dissolved.[43]

On June 17, 1941, the Althing elected the Regent of Iceland in the person of Mr. Sveinn Björnsson. He was reelected for another year on April 21, 1943.[44]

In the meantime, while these constitutional changes were taking place in Iceland, the Allies were taking military steps in order to forestall an extension of the German occupation to Iceland. On May 10, 1940, British forces occupied the island.[45] Later, on July 1, 1941, an exchange of messages took place between the Prime Minister of Iceland and the President of the United States. It was stated by the Prime Minister that it would be in the interest of Iceland if the United States would undertake the protection of that country during the war by sending troops to Iceland to supplement and eventually replace the British forces, which were required elsewhere. Iceland was ready to entrust such protection to the United States subject to the conditions, among others, that the United States would promise to withdraw these forces on conclusion of the present war, and would promise to recognize the absolute independence and sovereignty of Iceland and to exercise its best efforts at the time of negotiation of a peace treaty to the end that such treaty should likewise recognize the absolute independence and sovereignty of Iceland; a further condition was that the United States would not interfere with the Government of Iceland, either while the armed forces remained in the country or afterward. In his reply the President of the United States accepted all the conditions set forth in the Prime Minister's message.[46] In accordance with the understanding so reached, forces of the United States Navy arrived in Iceland on July 7.[47] On July 11, 1941, the Althing, by 39 votes to 3, approved the landing of the United States forces and sanctioned the agreement made with the President.[48]

[43] *Bulletin of International News*, Vol. XIX, No. 17 (August 22, 1942), p. 745.

[44] *Ibid.*, Vol. XX, No. 9 (May 1, 1943), p. 408.

[45] The Faroe Islands were also occupied by the British.

[46] H. R. Doc. 307, 77th Cong., 1st Sess., pp. 1–5; Department of State, *Bulletin*, Vol. V, No. 106 (July 5, 1941), pp. 15–17; *Bulletin of International News*, Vol. XVIII, No. 15 (July 26, 1941), p. 948.

[47] See message of the President to Congress, dated July 7, 1941, Department of State, *Bulletin*, Vol. V, No. 106 (July 5, 1941), p. 15.

[48] Prime Minister Churchill explained that Great Britain adhered to such an agreement, that under it both governments recognized the independence of Iceland and that her status was improved "by the change from occupation by a belligerent to defense, at her own invitation, by a non-belligerent." *Bulletin of International News*, Vol. XVIII, No. 15 (July 26, 1941), p. 987.

2.—*Greenland*

Greenland, the largest island of the world, with a native population of approximately 17,000 people (including 400 Danes), was cut off from the Danish metropolis through the German occupation of Denmark in 1940.

A year later, on April 9, 1941, an executive agreement was signed by the Secretary of State of the United States of America, Cordell Hull, and Henrik de Kauffmann in his capacity as Envoy Extraordinary and Minister Plenipotentiary of H.M. the King of Denmark at Washington, to the effect that the government of the United States was entitled to establish military bases in Greenland. On this occasion the United States Government reiterated its recognition of and respect for the sovereignty of the Kingdom of Denmark over Greenland. The reasons for this agreement are given in its preamble as follows:

ONE. After the invasion and occupation of Denmark on April 9, 1940 by foreign military forces, the United Greenland Councils at their meeting at Godhavn on May 3, 1940 adopted in the name of the people of Greenland a resolution reiterating their oath of allegiance to King Christian X of Denmark and expressing the hope that, for as long as Greenland remains cut off from the mother country, the Government of the United States of America will continue to hold in mind the exposed position of the Danish flag in Greenland, of the native Greenland and Danish population, and of established public order; and

TWO. The Governments of all of the American Republics have agreed that the status of regions in the Western Hemisphere belonging to European powers is a subject of deep concern to the American Nations, and that the course of military events in Europe and the changes resulting from them may create the grave danger that European territorial possessions in America may be converted into strategic centers of aggression against nations of the American Continent; and

THREE. Defense of Greenland against attack by a non-American power is essential to the preservation of the peace and security of the American Continent and is a subject of vital concern to the United States of America and also to the Kingdom of Denmark; and

FOUR. Although the sovereignty of Denmark over Greenland is fully recognized, the present circumstances for the time being prevent the Government in Denmark from exercising its powers in respect of Greenland.[49]

After the signature of the agreement Minister de Kauffmann was informed by the Danish Government in Copenhagen that it did not approve the agreement which he had made with the United States and that he was recalled as Danish Minister to Washington. This act of the Danish Government under occupation was considered both by Minister de Kauffmann and the United States Government as performed under duress. The Minister of Denmark was informed by the State Department that it continued to

[49] Agreement between the United States of America and Denmark, signed April 9, 1941. Executive Agreement Series 204, *Defense of Greenland* (Department of State Publication 1602, 1941), pp. 1–2.

recognize him as the duly authorized Minister of Denmark in Washington.[50]

In the course of the execution of this agreement, an American-Danish Greenland Commission was created in New York in order to carry on economic relations between Greenland and the United States.

[50] Department of State, *Bulletin*, Vol. IV, No. 95 (April 19, 1941), p. 471.

The validity of the Greenland agreement has been questioned by some authors on the ground that neither de Kauffmann nor the Greenland Councils had capacity to make international agreements. See editorial comment of Herbert W. Briggs, *American Journal of International Law*, Vol. 35 (1941), p. 512.

As the purpose of this volume is to deal with Axis rule in Europe, however, the author does not consider it as within his province to discuss here the validity of the Greenland agreement.

CHAPTER XVII

ENGLISH CHANNEL ISLANDS

The Channel Islands, which are situated off the northwest coast of France, are the only portions of the Dukedom of Normandy now belonging to the English Crown, to which they have been attached since the Norman Conquest. There are four principal islands: Jersey (area, 45 square miles; population, 49,701); Guernsey (area, 24.5 square miles; population, 38,283); Alderney (area, 3.06 square miles; population, 1,598); and Sark (area, 2 square miles; population, 614).

After the fall of France and the British military reverses, the British Government removed all troops from the Channel Islands and declared them to be demilitarized. A considerable number of inhabitants—about 40,000—left for England on ships which were sent over from England for their embarkation.[1] The Germans, however, ignored the proclamation of demilitarization and bombed the harbors of St. Helier and St. Peter Port, and the next day invaded the islands by air.[2] Guernsey was occupied by German military forces on June 30, 1940, and Jersey on July 1, 1940.

Administration. The Channel Islands are administered by a German local military commander, who is under orders of the military commander in France. On August 23, 1940, an order was published by the Chief of the Military Administration in France to the effect that "the general orders issued or to be issued by the Supreme Commander of the Army for the area of the Chief Command of the Military Administration in France are applicable, by way of analogy, to the occupied English Channel Islands."[3] Thus the Channel Islands, though still belligerent territory, and the occupation régime which was established in French territory affected by the Armistice Agreement of June 22, 1940, are under the same German military commander.

French having been the official language of the islands before the occupation (although English is the main language of business and religion and is familiar to all), it is possible for the population to become acquainted with the orders of the military commander in France, which are published in both German and French.

Finance. The branches of the English banks were evacuated. The Germans have recreated a local currency and put into circulation notes of 3d., 6d. and 2/6d., and have issued an order to open the local banking institutions. Advances equivalent to several million pounds sterling have been made by them to the local states.[4]

[1] Sixty Channel Island societies have been formed in England in different parts of the country to help refugees from the islands. London *Times*, June 30, 1943, p. 3.
[2] *Ibid.* [3] See below, p. 384. [4] London *Times*, June 30, 1943, p. 3.

Deportations to Germany. In the autumn of 1942, a great number of the islanders, men and women of ages up to 70 years, were deported to camps in France and Germany. As the inhabitants, because of their insular life, dwelt in closer association than is usual among peoples of the mainland—almost like one big family—these deportations were a great shock to the population. Farewell services were held in the churches and the deportees were presented with clothing and food by those remaining behind.[5] Among the deportees was the Seigneur of the Island of Sark, American-born R. W. Hathaway, who became a British citizen, and acquired the title of "Seigneur" through his marriage to Dame Sibyl Mary Beaumont, ruler of Sark under charter of Queen Elizabeth.[6]

[5] London *Times*, June 30, 1943, p. 3.
[6] See *New York Times*, April 30, 1943, p. 6, col. 1. On the relationship of the Channel Islands to the British Empire and their historic connection with the Duchy of Normandy, see "The Channel Islands," by Dr. R. R. Marett, in *The British Isles*, "The Oxford Survey of the British Empire" (Oxford: Clarendon Press, 1914), pp. 481 ff.

CHAPTER XVIII

FRANCE

The Territorial Administrative Division

After the armistice agreements which France signed with Germany and Italy,[1] the following administrative setup was created: Northern France and Pas-de-Calais were placed under the administration of the same German military commander as Belgium. Both for Alsace and Lorraine special civil administrations (*Zivilverwaltungen*) were established within the framework of the neighboring German Reich districts (*Reichsgaue*) into which they were incorporated. Thus, Lorraine was incorporated into Westmark [2] and Alsace into Moselland. The district of Mentone was occupied by Italian forces. In November, 1942, Italian occupation was extended to the Alpes-Maritimes, Haute-Savoie, and the Rhône valley.[3] The areas, apart from Alsace-Lorraine, which were included under the armistice agreement in the territory known as Occupied France were administered by a German military commander in Paris. The rest of France (known as unoccupied France) was administered from Vichy. When the German troops occupied all France in November, 1942, the Vichy régime was not displaced, the German authorities exercising only supervision and Gestapo activities.

On the grounds of military security, a special régime was established along the coastline to which outsiders are not permitted access (prohibited zone), as well as in the cities of Marseilles and Toulon.

I. Alsace-Lorraine

The régime in Alsace-Lorraine [4] is directed toward the complete assimilation of the political, cultural, and social institutions, as well as the economy of the two provinces, with those of the Greater German Reich. These tasks are in the hands of specially appointed Chiefs of Civil Administration, one for Lorraine and another for Alsace. These Chiefs of Civil Administration have the title of *Gauleiter*. Thus Alsace and Lorraine represent for the time being special administrative units, but they are incorporated into the normal German administrative districts (*Gaue*). Alsace, as has been stated, is thus incorporated into the District of Moselland, and Lorraine into the Dis-

[1] Armistice between France and Germany, June 22, 1940; Armistice between France and Italy, June 24, 1940. *American Journal of International Law, Supp.*, Vol. 34 (1940), pp. 173, 178.

[2] *Bulletin of International News*, Vol. XVII, No. 26 (December 31, 1940), p. 1679.

[3] After the collapse of Italy in the summer of 1943, the Italian troops evacuated French territory, and were replaced by German troops.

[4] The legislation promulgated in Alsace is similar to that promulgated in Lorraine, and hence it seems sufficient here to refer only to the decrees relating to Lorraine.

trict of Westmark. Alsace and Lorraine have been barred from communication with the rest of France by a customs frontier. Communications between Alsatians and Lorrainers on one side and Frenchmen on the other side of the customs frontier are allowed only within the limits of the so-called small frontier traffic, involving persons living in the immediate neighborhood of the frontier.[5] The policies of the Chief of the Civil Administration are designed, as indicated above, to promote the complete assimilation of Alsace and Lorraine with the other parts of the German districts, so that in the future a special administration for Alsace and Lorraine will not be necessary. At the time of the completion of this volume no express provision of law as to the annexation of Alsace-Lorraine by Germany is known to the author. Apparently the occupant has refrained from any such express provision because of collaboration with Vichy. However, the treatment of these territories may justify a statement that they have been *de facto* annexed to Germany. This seems to be the opinion of Frenchmen. One of the French leaders, General Giraud, stated in his address of March 14, 1943: "Alsace and Lorraine have been *de facto* incorporated into Germany. No voice of protest has been heard in France. Here, we protest. All the world must know that France does not accept this annexation. Alsace and Lorraine will again become French in a completely liberated France."[6]

In carrying out the policies of assimilation above mentioned, the occupant introduced into Lorraine, as of January 1, 1941, the German Municipal Code of January 30, 1935.[7] French citizens of German origin were granted German citizenship. The official language in administration, as well as in courts and business, was declared to be German. A decree was issued requiring that the names of persons be written with the German spelling. German equivalents must be used for French given names, and where no such equivalent exists a German given name is to be adopted.[8] Towns were also given equivalent German names.[9] With the exception of business firms, associations and organizations of all kinds have been dissolved, in order that reorganization on National Socialist principles may take place.[10] The education of the youth was put under Nazi control. In the order of December 6, 1940,[11] the Chief of the Civil Administration in Lorraine stated: "In order to assure the uniform institution of National Socialist schooling for youth, as well as adaptation to the school system of the Reich, . . . all private schools and school camps shall be closed." Grammar schools were made public and German; and only persons of German or re-

[5] Decree of March 26, 1941, *Verordnungsblatt*, 1941, p. 224.

[6] "L'Alsace et la Lorraine, de fait, viennent d'être incorporées à l'Allemagne. Aucune voix en France ne s'est élevée pour protester. Ici, nous protestons. Le monde entier doit savoir que la France n'accepte pas cette annexion. L'Alsace et la Lorraine redeviendront françaises dans une France complètement liberée." *Pour la Victoire* (New York), March 20, 1943, p. 2, col. 4.

[7] *Verordnungsblatt*, 1940, p. 445.

[8] Decree of September 28, 1940, *ibid.*, p. 60.

[9] Decree of January 25, 1941, *ibid.*, 1941, p. 139.

[10] Decree of October 16, 1940, *ibid.*, 1940, p. 160.

[11] See below, p. 385.

lated blood may be teachers in public elementary schools. The school must be actuated by the spirit of National Socialism in all its work. Permission must be obtained to give religious instruction, and such permission is to be withheld if the instructor-clergyman or his wife is not of German or related blood.[12] The Reformed and Lutheran churches were combined with the *Pfaelzische Landeskirche* (United Protestant-Evangelical Christian Church of Pfalz), so that the powers of the Reformed Synod in Alsace-Lorraine and of the Directorium of the Church of the Augsburg Confession in Alsace-Lorraine passed to the Protestant Provincial Church Council of Pfalz.[13] The courts were Germanized, and the requirement laid down that sentences be pronounced "in the name of the German people." German criminal law has been introduced,[14] and published materials relating to judicial matters appear only in the Official Gazette of the Chief of Civil Administration.[15] In order that Germans alone may acquire real property, a decree was passed on October 10, 1940, to the effect that permission is necessary for acquiring farm, forest, or business properties, and for buying, renting, starting, building, or enlarging enterprises. Moreover, the same decree authorized German authorities to close enterprises without allowing claims for indemnity.[16]

The economy of Alsace and Lorraine was organized according to the totalitarian pattern. Essential goods, foods, and products were requisitioned by decree of June 23, 1940, and are administered under German control.[17] Control of prices and of wages was introduced by the decree of August 9, 1940.[18]

According to the German genocide philosophy, the imposition of the German cultural and political pattern upon Frenchmen was not sufficient. The Frenchmen themselves must be removed and replaced by Germans in order to make Alsace-Lorraine German "forever." The occupant then resorted to mass transfers of the French population. According to an elaborate plan of replacing French population by a German imported population, about 270,000 persons (including 22,000 Jews) were removed from Alsace-Lorraine to unoccupied France, and 200,000 to the Reich.[18a]

II. The Occupied Zone

ADMINISTRATION

The Armistice Agreement of June 22, 1940, established the limits of the so-called Occupied Zone as distinguished from the non-occupied zone administered by Vichy. A demarcation line was introduced between the two zones and a decree of April 28, 1941,[19] provided penalties of imprisonment or fine

[12] See order of February 14, 1941, concerning the elementary school system, below, p. 387; and the announcement for the execution of that order, below, p. 388.
[13] See decree of September 28, 1940, below, p. 385.
[14] *Verordnungsblatt*, 1940, p. 5.
[15] See decree of September 10, 1940, *ibid.*, p. 52.
[16] *Ibid.*, p. 71.
[17] *Ibid.*, p. 5.
[18] *Ibid.*, p. 22.
[18a] See Kulischer, *op. cit.*, p. 115.
[19] See below, p. 391.

for persons who without permission crossed the demarcation line between the Occupied Zone and unoccupied France, or carried goods from one zone to another. On the occupation of all France by Germany on November 11, 1942,[20] the demarcation line was retained, but more facilities for traffic between the two zones were introduced. The Vichy zone remained thereafter under the administration of Vichy, the Germans taking over the administration of strategic points and acting in other places mainly through the Gestapo.

According to Article III of the Armistice Agreement, Germany acquired in the Occupied Zone the right of an occupying power. This zone has two types of administration. The German administration is in the hands of a German military commander. For purposes of military administration, the Occupied Zone is divided into five chief military field commands (*Oberfeldkommandanturen*). Each of these chief military field commands is divided into field commands (*Feldkommandanturen*) and every field command is divided into local commands (*Ortskommandanturen*). Officers of civil sections of the military commands supervise the French authorities. For a certain time the German Ambassador to Paris, whose office has been continued, coordinated the activities of the central German authorities with those of the local German authorities, as well as with those of the central French authorities. The main body of French authorities has been retained. These authorities are not only supervised by the German military authorities, but they also receive instructions from beyond the demarcation line. Moreover, the legislative power of the Vichy government extends over the Occupied Zone.

PUNITIVE FUNCTIONS OF MILITARY COMMANDERS

Because the German military commanders play such an important rôle in controlling the country, they have been vested with extensive powers, among them judicial powers which in some respects supplement the functions of the courts.[21] Not only the commanders of the chief field commands but also the heads of the ordinary field commands may issue orders regarding summary punishment against persons not subject to the Military Penal Code, and they may impose penalties up to 30,000 Reichsmarks or, in lieu thereof, imprisonment for a term not exceeding six weeks. Moreover, the same offense, if it seems to be sufficiently serious, may be tried later by a court. This provision is a violation of the principle *ne bis in idem*, even though in such cases it is required that the court take account of the punishment already imposed and mitigate its sentence accordingly. However that may be, it is clear that the primary purpose of the order is to give increased authority to the military commanders so as to enable them to act as the first and main protectors of the established German order.

[20] See the *New York Times*, November 12, 1942, p. 1, col. 8.
[21] See order of September 10, 1940, below, p. 394.

SERVICES AND LABOR

Among the other powers vested in military commanders is that of requiring members of the local population to serve as military guards,[22] failure to fulfill such duties being punishable by death. This is a violation of Article 52 of the Hague Regulations, which prohibits the requisitioning of services of inhabitants of an occupied country in activities involving military operations.

The personal responsibility of the inhabitants to the occupant was still further extended by the decree of January 31, 1942, under which the failure to perform personal services or comply with requisitions in kind which were ordered by the authorities for the German Army was made punishable by fine, imprisonment, hard labor, or, "in grave cases," even by the death penalty.[23] Because all economic and industrial enterprises were put into the service of the German war economy, any interference with employment in such enterprises was also made punishable. Thus, for interruption of work or any aggressive actions by workers against employers, penalties of imprisonment, fine, hard labor, or even death may be imposed.[24] Even before labor conscription was introduced, the occupant tried to induce the French workers to accept work in Germany, and a decree of June 22, 1942, introduced special privileges for persons accepting work there. The courts are required to adjourn cases of such persons if the military commander so requests. Moreover, no execution of contracts of rent and no notice thereof may be effectuated during the absence of workers in Germany.[25] Later on a labor conscription law was published by Vichy in order to provide Germany with labor.[26]

ECONOMY AND FINANCE

As mentioned above, the whole economic life is being controlled and channelled into the German war economy. If an enterprise is not important enough for the German war economy, it may be closed by the military commander, the reason given for such closing being the requirements of "economic conditions" and "particularly the supply of raw materials and equipment."[27]

That the local economic life is subordinated to the interests of the occupant is to be seen from the decree of May 22, 1942,[28] according to which all construction projects exceeding 100,000 francs in cost require the permission of the German military commander. Applications for such permission are to be filed with the French authorities, who in turn submit them to the German commander.

[22] See order of October 10, 1940, below, p. 395.
[23] See below, p. 398.
[24] See decree of November 6, 1941, below, p. 392.
[25] *Verordnungsblatt*, 1942, pp. 395–96.
[26] See below, section IV of this chapter; see also *New York Times*, September 14, 1942, p. 1, col. 6; p. 4, cols. 5–6, 6–8 (text of law).
[27] See decree of February 25, 1942, below, p. 398.
[28] *Verordnungsblatt*, 1942, pp. 380–81.

In the field of finance, the same instrumentalities were applied as in Belgium, namely, Reich Credit Institute notes were issued and clearing agreements with Germany and other countries were arranged through the German clearing office in Berlin. Exchange control was introduced prohibiting the transfer of currency out of the Occupied Zone in any dealings in exchange, forbidding transactions of an international character, and requiring the surrender of foreign exchange and gold.[29] The exchange control was carried out by a special institute called *Devisenschutzkommando Frankreich* (Commando France for the Protection of Holdings of Foreign Exchange).

A special Banking Supervisory Board controls French banks, especially the Banque de France.[30] This bank is compelled to expand its issues in order to meet the requirements of the occupant.

BOOKS AND ART

Not only is the press regimented and subjected to preventive censorship but also text books of history published before the war are suppressed if they contain "unjustifiable attacks on the German people and its armed forces."[31]

Works of art, which represent in France a considerable part of the national wealth, immediately attracted the attention of the occupant. On July 15, 1940, an order was issued by the Supreme Commander of the Army freezing such works of art.[32] Thus, movable works of art may not be removed from their present location or changed in any manner without the written authorization of the military commander. Legal transactions involving the transfer or sale of movable works of art are invalid without the consent of the military commander. Owners or possessors of such objects of art that are worth more than 100,000 francs are required to register them with the field commander's office. The purpose of these provisions is apparent: because the distressed owners could not receive the permission of the military commander to sell works of art to private persons at their real value, they were compelled to sell them at much lower prices to Germans, who could obtain the required permission.

The above-mentioned decree on works of art is in violation of Article 46 of the Hague Regulations, which requires that private property be respected. Respect for private property implies not only freedom from confiscation but also non-interference with the enjoyment of the full rights of property, including the right to dispose of it.

RESISTANCE

The occupant apparently does not enjoy a feeling of security in the occupied area despite the policy of "forced collaboration" imposed upon the

[29] See above, chapter on "Finance."
[30] Order of July 22, 1940, *Verordnungsblatt*, July 26, 1940. See also Paul Jacob, *Les lois de l'occupation en France* (New York, 1942), p. 14.
[31] See order of August 10, 1940, below, p. 391.
[32] See order of July 15, 1940, below, p. 390.

French population. Evidence thereof is to be found, among other things, not only in the large extent of sabotage and the taking of hostages, but also in such a decree as that of February 5, 1942, forbidding medical personnel, such as doctors, dentists, and nurses who are not serving in the German Army, to treat members of the German armed forces or civilians of German nationality in the service of such forces. French medical personnel is allowed to take care of Germans only in emergency cases.[33]

Recently, the security of the occupant has been gravely challenged not only by a well-organized French underground but also by a special type of guerrilla fight which is going on in the southeastern part of France, especially in Haute-Savoie. Young Frenchmen who escaped deportation to labor camps in Germany have been crossing the demarcation line between the occupied and unoccupied zone and fleeing into the mountains. The German troops who try to capture these young Frenchmen often meet with strong resistance. The French population has organized a service of clandestine help for these people, whose hiding places are called *maquis*.

III. Italian Zone

Following its Armistice Agreement with France of June 24, 1940, Italy assumed the rights of an occupying power over several localities on the French side of the frontier.[33a] In these localities Italian civil commissioners were established for purposes of administration. However, the main institutions of French administration remained. This is also true as to the local courts, except that trials for serious offenses committed by the inhabitants of the occupied territories may be referred to the Court of Assizes in Turin, under the law of December 5, 1940.[34] The same law provides that appeals from civil or criminal sentences pronounced by French courts shall be referred to the Court of Appeals of Turin or to the Supreme Court of the Kingdom. The Italian rules for judicial proceedings are to be observed in regard to the form of processes before the courts of the Italian Kingdom. The reasons for this provision are to be found in the comparatively insignificant number of localities occupied by Italy, and the absence of higher judicial French authorities in the occupied area.

The law of December 5, 1940, also empowered the military occupation authorities to extend Italian regulations concerning customs to the occupied territory in order to make them applicable to the traffic in goods across the new border line.

In the occupied zone the Italian lira was made legal tender in addition to the French franc by proclamation of June 21, 1941,[35] the rate of exchange being set at 100 francs to 38 lire.

[33] See decree of February 5, 1942, below, p. 393.
[33a] As to other areas subsequently occupied by Italy and Germany, see above, section on The Territorial Administrative Division, p. 171.
[34] See below, p. 402.
[35] See below, p. 404.

Because the areas occupied by Italy were cut off from more important French administrative centers, difficulties arose in dealing with certain activities normally administered under the direction of higher French authorities whose offices are outside the zone of occupation. Such a difficulty occurred, for example, with regard to the issuing of diplomas for graduates of schools in the occupied territory. Therefore, on May 22, 1941,[36] a proclamation was issued to the effect that such diplomas might be issued by the competent civil commissioner.

IV. Vichy France

"NATIONAL REVOLUTION"

After the collapse of France, the political leaders who gathered around Marshal Pétain believed that they could restore the self-confidence of the French people by proclaiming a "national revolution" in political, social, economic, and even private life. The program of this "revolution" consisted mainly of such slogans as the strengthening of the executive power, the increase of production through proclaimed solidarity of the classes, a return to the land,—which amounts to stressing the social importance of agriculture,—the strengthening of the family unit, education of the youth in the national spirit, and racialism, which resulted in the promulgation of anti-Jewish laws. Only the future historian will be able to determine to what extent these slogans are a product of the minds of the Vichy leaders and to what extent they have infiltrated French life through the channels of collaboration with Germany.[36a]

DELEGATION OF POWERS TO PÉTAIN

On July 10, 1940, Albert Lebrun, President of the French Republic, promulgated a constitutional law adopted by the National Assembly, to the effect that the National Assembly had vested in Marshal Pétain all powers in the Government of the Republic and empowered him, as President of the Council of Ministers, to promulgate a new constitution. It was stressed that this future constitution should guarantee the rights of labor, of the family, and of the fatherland.[37] It was further stressed that the new constitution must be ratified by the nation and applied by "assemblies which it shall create," i.e., by a new parliament.

CONSTITUTIONAL ACTS

The Constitutional Law of July 10, 1940, provided for the creation of a new constitution by "one or several acts." Pétain has chosen the second

[36] See below, p. 403.
[36a] The collaboration between Vichy France and Germany is a well-known fact and therefore will not be discussed here.
[37] See below, p. 405.

method. He has promulgated several constitutional acts, directed mainly to the strengthening of the authority of the Chief of State and to the abolition of the representative element in government.

By Constitutional Act No. 1,[38] Pétain declared that he assumed "the functions of Chief of the French State." In the same act he abrogated Article 2 of the Constitutional Law of February 25, 1875, which provided that the President of the Republic should be chosen by a National Assembly composed of the Senate and Chamber of Deputies.

By Constitutional Act No. 2 of July 11, 1940,[39] Pétain assumed sweeping powers, not only in the executive branch of the government, but also in the legislative branch. The provisions of the French law of 1875 that "ministers shall be collectively responsible to the chambers for the general policy of the government, and individually for their personal acts" were made void by the provision that ministers and state secretaries shall be responsible only to the Chief of the French State. Moreover, by the above-mentioned law, the Chief of State assumed legislative power, which he exercises in cooperation with the Council of Ministers only; he also promulgates the laws, and may negotiate and ratify treaties. He may not, however, declare war without the previous consent of the legislative assemblies.

FÜHRER PRINCIPLE

To a certain extent, an imitation of the *Führer* principle was introduced by Constitutional Act No. 7.[40] Pétain has introduced the element of personal leadership, not only in relation to the state but also in relation to officials, especially those of higher rank. Under the above-mentioned act, these officials must swear allegiance to the person of the Chief of State, and they are made *personally* responsible to him. This responsibility—a responsibility which, in the language of the act, "shall apply to their person and their property"—is implemented by the Chief of State himself, who may institute inquiries concerning any breach of faith on the part of such officials "by means of a procedure upon which he shall decide." He may require them to make reparations and may also impose such penalties as "loss of political rights; surveillance of residence in France or in the Colonies; administrative internment; detention in a fortress."

The elements of personal leadership and authoritarian doctrine are in a sense emphasized by the fact that the provision as to the imposition of penalties by the Chief of State for breach of faith in personal allegiance to him is superimposed upon the normal machinery of prosecution and punishment; for the same act provides that persons upon whom such penalties have been imposed may also be punished "under normal judicial procedure" for crimes or offenses which may have been committed by them.

[38] See below, p. 405. [39] See below, p. 406.
[40] Act of January 27, 1941, below, p. 406.

PARLIAMENTARY ISSUES

As mentioned above, the Constitutional Law of July 10, 1940, mentions the Assemblies which the proposed new constitutional document was to create, and Constitutional Act No. 3 of July 11, 1940,[41] states that the present Senate and Chamber of Deputies "shall continue to exist until the Assemblies anticipated by the Constitutional Law of July 10, 1940, have been formed."

On January 22, 1941, Pétain promulgated a law creating a National Council.[42] Under this law the Council was to be composed of members appointed by the Chief of State from among representatives of the different legislative assemblies of the departments, municipalities, and professions, and from among "other competent persons or persons who have rendered special services to the state." The sessions are non-public. They are called only for the purpose of expressing opinions on matters submitted to the Council by the Chief of State. Obviously the National Council, as conceived by the law of January 22, 1941, cannot be considered as a parliamentary institution representing the French nation.

On August 25, 1942,[43] Pétain promulgated another law, by which the bureaus of the Chamber of Deputies and of the Senate were abolished as of August 31, 1942. Thus, the Parliament of France, an institution in which throughout French history the people had taken great pride, has been formally eliminated from the public life of France.

TRIAL OF POLITICAL OPPONENTS

From the beginning the new régime fixed its attention on the problem of dealing with political opponents. Since the persons who left France without permission after the collapse were treated as adversaries of Pétain, a decree was signed on July 23, 1940, to the effect that property of Frenchmen who, without authority, had fled the country between May 10 and June 30, 1940, might be confiscated and their citizenship withdrawn.[44] In addition, Pétain has instituted criminal proceedings against members of former governments, the purpose of this procedure being, on the one hand, to destroy political opponents, and, on the other hand, to create the feeling in the future that the disaster which befell France was due only to the machinations and mistakes of its political leaders. Germany, too, was interested in the removal of French statesmen who were opposed to Hitler.

To this end a special Supreme Court of Justice—to be seated in Riom from August 8, 1940—was established by act of August 1, 1940.[45] The act especially states that the court shall try persons who have committed offenses or have violated their duties "by acts which contributed to passing from a state of peace to a state of war before September 4, 1939, and also those

[41] *Journal officiel*, 1940, No. 168. [42] *Ibid.*, 1941, No. 24.
[43] *Journal officiel de l'Etat français*, 1942, No. 204.
[44] *Bulletin of International News*, Vol. XVII, No. 16 (August 10, 1940), p. 1030.
[45] *Journal officiel*, 1940, No. 189.

persons who later on have aggravated the consequences of the situation thus created."

Such a formulation of criminal responsibility represents *ex-post-facto* legislation and is a violation of well-recognized principles of criminal law.

CORPORATIVE SYSTEM AND LABOR

The principles of the corporative system were laid down in a report by Admiral Darlan, Vice President of the Council of Ministers,[46] which served as a preamble to the law of October 4, 1941, concerning the social organization of occupations. In this report it was stated that solidarity between workers and industrialists should supplant the old system of struggle of classes. In order to further the national interests, the report continued, members of occupational groups should collaborate closely among themselves and with other professional groups.

The law of October 4, 1941,[47] created several new institutions for the enforcement of these principles. The most important among them are: industrial or commercial "families," occupational unions, social committees for enterprises and for occupational families, and labor tribunals.

Occupational families are composed of members of various industries and trades. Practically speaking, all French economic activities are to be divided into large "occupational families," every occupational family representing a separate branch of economic activity. A separate organization is to be established for each of these occupational families and also, if necessary, for every industry and occupation within the framework of the occupational family. In accordance with the provisions of the above law, various occupational families have already been established, such, for example, as an occupational family for the chemical industry,[48] for buildings and public works,[49] for insurance,[50] for banking, finance and exchange,[51] and so on.[52]

The occupational family comprises, then, every person engaged in a given economic occupation, irrespective of his particular rôle and position, each occupational family comprising both employers and employees. Thus the element of economic solidarity in production is stressed. According to the above-mentioned law of October 4, 1941, the occupational families have as their purpose "joint administration of the occupational interests of their

[46] *Journal officiel*, 1941, No. 293.
[47] See below, p. 407. See also "The French Labour Charter," *International Labour Review* (Montreal: International Labour Office), Vol. XLV, No. 3 (March, 1942), pp. 269 ff.
[48] *Journal officiel*, March 1, 1942.
[49] *Ibid.* [50] *Ibid.*, June 4, 1942. [51] *Ibid.*
[52] The following will give an idea as to the framework of an occupational family: "The occupational family for the manufacture of textiles and similar industries comprises the spinning, weaving or manufacture, finishing and dyeing of yarn, cloth, textiles, knitwear and similar products, the production of artificial fibres, and the trades supplying the industries."—"Establishment of Occupational 'Families' under the Labour Charter," *International Labour Review*, Vol. XLVI, No. 3 (September, 1942), p. 329.

members of every category and . . . contribution to the support of the national economy in accordance with directions given by the public authorities."

Occupational unions (*syndicats professionnels*) are reminiscent to a certain extent of the former class organization in economic life because they are organized according to different categories of members: (1) employers, (2) workers, (3) clerical staff, (4) foremen, (5) engineers and administrative and commercial personnel. A single occupational union is to be formed in each area for each occupation, industry, or occupational family and for each category of members. Since the occupational union bears traces of class distinction, its rôle has been made less important and is mainly reduced to technical matters, such as enlistment and representation of its members, execution of corporative decisions, study of occupational questions, and the solving of problems affecting the members of its territorial unit. Any activity of a political or religious nature is expressly excluded. The local occupational unions are to be represented in regional occupational unions and the regional occupational unions in a national federation of occupational unions.

Social committees for enterprises are provided by Article 23 of the law, which requires that in every enterprise with a staff of not less than one hundred workers or employees, a Works Social Committee is to be created in order to ensure collaboration between employers and employees. Such a committee is to be composed of the head of the enterprise and representatives of every category of personnel. The works social committee has no authority to interfere with the management and operation of the undertaking. Subject to this reservation, however, it has wide functions as regards advising the management concerning all questions affecting the life and the work of the staff, providing information on the social life of the staff and their families, and organizing mutual aid institutions.

Social committees for occupational families or occupations are also provided by the same law. These social committees are local, regional, and national in character. Each local social committee consists of from twelve to twenty-four members, chosen from among the officers of the occupational union and divided into three equal groups: (1) employers, (2) workers and salaried employees, and (3) other categories. The regional and national social committees, like the local committees, are tripartite in character. The officers, however, are appointed. Through these appointments on a regional and national scale, the government keeps control of and has an opportunity to shape the policy of the social committees. The functions of social committees are twofold, occupational and social. Political and religious questions are excluded. In the occupational field, they deal with wages, collective agreements, vocational training, trade practices, and so on; in the social field, with social security and employment, mutual aid, improvement of living conditions, sport, recreation, and so on. The local social committees control the works social committees of the enterprises.

Labor disputes are to be settled, first of all, by the occupational bodies of the respective groups. If it is found impossible to avoid such disputes or to settle them by this means, then the differences should be submitted to conciliation boards, or, if they do not exist, to justices of the peace, "if individual differences are involved"; but if the differences are of a collective character, then labor tribunals shall decide the case. These labor tribunals are of two kinds, regional and national. Regional tribunals are composed of two judges—of whom one shall exercise the functions of the president—and of three members of the regional social committee. Appeals from decisions of regional labor tribunals shall be submitted to a national labor tribunal, which shall render final decisions.

OTHER LABOR ISSUES

Labor has become one of the main concerns of the Vichy régime for two reasons: It was believed, first, that an increased production, especially in agriculture, might help to solve the economic crisis; and secondly, the Germans have made constant demands on French labor, to be engaged for work in Germany.

In this atmosphere, labor efficiency became of paramount importance. In order to foster this efficiency, a National Order of Labor was created, conferring distinction upon persons who display "unusual technical ability in the exercise of their occupation, a high sense of responsibility to the community, or a particular and sustained devotion to the occupation and the nation." [53]

On September 4, 1942,[54] a government decree was promulgated relative to the utilization and organization of labor. Labor compulsion was introduced for males between 18 and 50 years of age and for unmarried persons of the female sex between the ages of 21 and 35. Any dismissal of labor or any cancellation of a labor contract, without previous authorization of labor inspection services, was forbidden in all industrial and commercial enterprises. Every Frenchman between 18 and 50 years of age "whose physical qualification has been medically recognized" must be able to prove that he is engaged in work useful to the country. Any person from the above category who cannot furnish such proof may be subject to employment on any work designated by the Secretary of State for Labor. By this law an obligation was imposed upon employers to provide technical and professional educational facilities in order to create a skilled manpower for those professions which lack labor. Severe penalties were introduced for violating the law,

[53] See Law No. 439 of April 1, 1942, below, p. 411.
[54] *Journal officiel*, 1942, p. 3122. See also *New York Times*, September 14, 1942, p. 1, col. 6; p. 4, cols. 5–6, 6–8 (text of law).

namely, imprisonment up to five years and fines up to 30,000 francs. These punishments may be doubled in case of repetition of such violations.

The law of October 4, 1941, concerning the social organization of occupations envisages an organization in which all persons engaged in economic activities are to form a pyramid of different groups, controlled and checked one by another (in particular, the employees are checked and controlled by the employers), and then controlled at the pinnacle by the state. Labor in this pyramid has a clearly subordinate rôle. The decrees on mobilization of labor stress even more this subordinate rôle, which makes it impossible for the workers to defend themselves against the well-established Vichy policy of trading in French labor with Germany.

CHAPTER XIX

GREECE

On October 28, 1940, at 3:00 a.m., an ultimatum was handed by the Italian Minister to the Prime Minister of Greece in which demand was made by Italy of the right to occupy certain strategic points of Greek territory. The time for the expiration of the ultimatum was set for six o'clock the same morning. Early in the same morning the Italians started the attack against the Greeks.[1]

The campaign against Greece was not successful in 1940, but was successful in 1941, when Germany joined in the attack. During the Italo-German operations Bulgaria joined the Axis, and as a result of this common action Greece was occupied by Italy, Albania, Bulgaria, and Germany, and was divided into four zones of occupation. The Bulgarians were given Western Thrace (Aegean region), Eastern Macedonia up to the Struma River, and the islands of Thasos and Samothrace. The Germans occupied Central Macedonia, including Salonika, parts of the Aegean region, and the islands of Lemnos, Mytilene, and Chios. In addition the Germans supervised and gave instructions to the Greek Governor of the province of Evros, near the frontier of European Turkey. The Italians occupied the remainder of the country and most of the islands, including a small part of Crete, which, however, was in greater part occupied by Germany. The Albanians were allowed to occupy the provinces of Yanina, Thesprotia, and Prenza, an area of 7,821 square kilometers, with a population of 300,573.

Whereas the Bulgarian zone of occupation was relatively more stabilized, there were frequent changes in the zones occupied by Germany and Italy. Thus, when it seemed that the military situation in Greece was well in hand and German troops were required for the Russian front, the Italian zone of occupation was extended. During this extension the German zone was limited principally to strategic points such as ports, communication lines, and airdromes.[2] But when the military situation in this section deteriorated because of guerrilla warfare and the menace of an Allied invasion, the Germans took under their control more and more territories. Finally, after the collapse of Italy in the summer of 1943, Germany took over control of the areas previously occupied by Italy. The Bulgarian occupation area was also extended.

I. Italian Occupation

ADMINISTRATION

On Italy's occupation of Greece, a special Office of Civil Affairs was established on the staff of the High Commander of the Troops in Albania.

[1] *Italy's Aggression against Greece* (Royal Ministry for Foreign Affairs, Athens, 1940), pp. 133–37.

[2] *Bulletin of International News*, Vol. XVIII, No. 15 (July 26, 1941), p. 986.

The first orders on military occupation were issued by the commanding general of the troops in Albania. The proclamation of October 28, 1940,[4] states that the Office for Civil Affairs is to coordinate civilian services and exercise the necessary control over them. The Royal Carabinieri were called on to play an essential rôle in the administration of the territories in the initial stages of the occupation. They took over the enforcement of the orders and the supervision of the local police. The occupied territory was completely shut off from Albanian territory and only with the permission of the Royal Carabinieri could persons enter the occupied zone.

In 1941, when all Greek territory had been occupied by the Axis, the office of High Commissioner was established for the civil administration of the territory of the Greek peninsula occupied by units attached to the High Command of the Troops in Albania. The functions of the High Commissioner are fixed by the proclamation of the Duce of July 2, 1941.[5] According to this proclamation, the High Commissioner is the highest civil authority of that part of the Greek peninsula occupied by Italian forces. He is appointed and recalled by order of the Supreme Military Command, and is responsible to that command, although a provision is also included according to which the Supreme Command may specify that the High Commissioner, in the exercise of particular powers or of all his powers, shall be responsible to the High Command of the Armed Forces in Albania. The order also conferred upon the High Commissioner the right to replace local officials and to make new appointments. The area under Italian occupation is divided into civil commissariats with Italian civil commissioners at the head.

ECONOMY

In economic matters not only the Royal Carabinieri but also the Royal Finance Guards had jurisdiction. It was required under the proclamation of the commanding general of October 30, 1940,[6] that persons among the local population in the occupied territory owning flour, macaroni products, vegetables, barley, wheat and fodder, beef, poultry, goats, and pigs must make and submit an inventory thereof to the Royal Carabinieri or the Royal Finance Guards. The proclamation stated that failure to make such a report or the making of an incorrect report would be punished by arrest and a sentence of from six months to two years, and that the unreported produce would be sequestrated. The same proclamation introduced penalties of imprisonment up to fifteen years for the destruction, damaging, or spoiling of food products, fodder, building or fire wood, coal or peat, gasoline, and other articles of prime necessity to the civilian population or useful to the occupying army. The occupant took over the Greek monopoly services for salt, tobacco, matches, cigarette boxes, automatic lighters and flints.[7]

[4] See Proclamation No. 10, below, p. 412. [5] See below, p. 415.
[6] See below, p. 413. [7] See proclamation of May 4, 1941, below, p. 414.

CURRENCY

In the Italian-held areas the Italian lira and Albanian franc were introduced as an additional currency by the proclamation of the Duce of June 21, 1941. According to this order 100 drachmae are to be equivalent to 12.50 lire and to 2 Albanian francs.[8] Later on the Italians issued the liretta in the Ionian Islands and the Mediterranean drachmae on the mainland of Greece.[9]

MISCELLANEA

As horses, mules, and donkeys are considered a necessary means of transportation in the mountainous regions, especially severe penalties (imprisonment of from one to five years) were fixed for killing such animals or so harming them as to render them unfit for further use. The damaging and destroying of vehicles of any kind, including wagons or carts, was made punishable by imprisonment of from six months to three years.[10]

On October 29, 1940,[11] the commanding general issued an order which was directed mainly against landing planes. According to this order any person with knowledge of the landing of enemy planes in occupied territory was required to give immediate notice thereof to the Royal Carabinieri or to other authorities. The same applied to crashing planes.

The fortunes of all Greek army officers who have left the country have been confiscated and their families exiled to remote parts of Greece.[12]

II. Bulgarian Occupation

Bulgaria has annexed Eastern Macedonia, Thrace (Aegean region), and Samothrace, this territory comprising 16,682 square kilometers and including the provinces of Serrai, Drama, Cavalla, and Rhodope. Thus Bulgaria augmented its population by about 590,000 as a result of the annexation of Greek territory.[13] The Bulgarians claim that the Aegean is necessary for their living space; the seacoast especially is supposed to be necessary for their overseas trade.

ADMINISTRATION

The Greek administrative agencies were abolished and Bulgarian institutions introduced instead. The provincial administration of the occupied areas is headed by Bulgarian governors.

For purposes of colonization special additional agencies were created: (1)

[8] See below, p. 415.
[9] At the time of completing this book the author does not possess any official text introducing this new type of currency.
[10] See Proclamation No. 7 of October 30, 1940, below, p. 414.
[11] See Proclamation No. 6, below, p. 413.
[12] *Bulletin of International News*, Vol. XIX, No. 11 (May 30, 1942), p. 498.
[13] Stephen G. Xydis, *The Economy and Finances of Greece under Axis Occupation* (Pittsburgh, Pa., 1943), p. 10.

a regional director for colonization in every region; (2) a central committee for land grants (the activities of this committee are described below).

The personnel of the administration was Bulgarized completely, a procedure which follows the well-established Balkan pattern of changing all officials upon taking over new territories. This seems to be justified because of national antagonisms, which have always been rife in the Balkans. During the present war former Greek officials have been replaced by Bulgarian officials to a larger extent than in any other occupied country in Europe, these replacements involving all grades, from the higher officials down to janitors. By thus replacing officials the Bulgarian occupant intended to achieve an additional goal, namely, to increase the numbers of the Bulgarian population in the occupied areas. The Bulgarian officials were summoned to come to Thrace with their families. If they brought their families along, they were entitled to receive land grants and dwelling-houses. The Council of Ministers, on October 9, 1942,[14] issued a decision establishing the conditions for granting lands and dwelling-houses to Bulgarian officials moving in from Bulgaria, such as mayors of villages, agents of the police, guards of the fields, janitors, and supervisors of breeding stations. According to this decision lands are not granted to unmarried officials or public servants who do not have families at the place of their employment nor are they granted to married functionaries whose families do not live at the place of their employment. In order to induce public servants to live permanently in the Aegean region with their families, land and dwelling-houses are granted at the start only on a temporary basis. The temporary grant lasts up to the completion of three years' uninterrupted service in the Aegean region. After the servant has completed three years' service, the grant becomes permanent.

TRANSFER OF POPULATION

The policy pursued by the Bulgarian occupant in Eastern Macedonia was entirely different from the one adopted in the Aegean region. Whereas in Macedonia a policy of rehabilitation was followed, the Macedonians being considered by the occupant as of Bulgarian origin, "freed from the Greeks," a real genocide policy was applied to the Greeks in the Aegean region. Greek churches and schools were closed and the Bulgarian language was made the official language. These measures aimed at changes in the composition of the population in accordance with the German pattern. First of all, the Greeks who had come as immigrants from Anatolia and settled in Greece after the exchange of populations in 1922–23 were expelled from Thrace into that part of the Greek territory which was left under a Greek puppet government.[15]

[14] See below, p. 416.
[15] *Bulletin of International News*, Vol. XVIII, No. 18 (September 6, 1941), p. 1175. From Western Thrace, 80,000 Greeks were removed to the remaining territory of Greece, and 25,000 to Old Bulgaria. Kulischer, *op. cit.*, p. 115.

Various other devices were also used in order to compel the Greeks to leave. Thus, a general licensing system for trades and professions was introduced.[16] No one could engage in trades who had not received a special license from the Bulgarian Chamber of Commerce and Trade. The refusal of such a license was equivalent to condemning the applicant to starvation. Again, the property of the wealthier classes was confiscated.[17] Furthermore, pre-invasion bank deposits were not returned to Greeks (see below). Consequently, many of the Greeks preferred to leave the territory rather than to starve. More than 100,000 Bulgarians have been brought from Bulgaria proper to Thrace for purposes of colonization, mainly in the areas between the Struma and Mesta rivers.

In the autumn of 1942, a decree was issued whereby "all private estates indispensable for the building of residences for immigrants in the Aegean province are to be expropriated."[18] The immigrant colonists in this region received credits, land, and dwelling-houses. The colonization and the granting of land and houses was handled by regional directors in the respective regions and by a central committee for land grants. A deficiency budget of 12,000,000 leva was appropriated by the Sobranje (Parliament) for the construction and repair of dwelling-houses for colonists in the Aegean region.[19]

FINANCE

In accordance with the decision of the Council of Ministers of May 26, 1941,[20] all private persons and firms with domicile and residence in territories occupied by the Bulgarian authorities heretofore belonging to Greece, namely, Western Thrace and Eastern Macedonia, were ordered to declare from June 6 to 19, 1941, in agencies of the Bulgarian National Bank or in branches of the Bulgarian Agricultural and Cooperative Bank all drachmae in their possession in bank notes of 100 drachmae and higher denominations. Declaration of bank notes of less than 100 drachmae denomination was not required. The drachma was declared invalid after June 19, 1941, and the deposits were to be changed into leva. Moreover, the Bulgarian National Bank was entrusted with the collection in leva or drachmae of the claims of the Greek Bank and the Greek National Bank against private persons and firms in Western Thrace and Eastern Macedonia.

As to bank deposits dating from the pre-invasion period, the Bulgarian authorities in occupied Greece proceeded in the same way as in that part of Yugoslavia occupied by Bulgaria. The same decision of the Council of Ministers[21] settled the problem of bank deposits in both the Yugoslav and

[16] Xydis, *op. cit.*, p. 19.
[17] *Bulletin of International News*, Vol. XIX, No. 11 (May 30, 1942), p. 498.
[18] *Ibid.*, Vol. XX, No. 7 (April 3, 1943), p. 319.
[19] 36th Decision of the Council of Ministers, October 14, 1942, below, p. 417.
[20] Decision No. 2012, below, "Yugoslavia," p. 633.
[21] No. 3121, August 1, 1941, Protocol No. 130. See below, "Yugoslavia," p. 635.

Greek areas under Bulgarian occupation. According to this decision, all accounts existing and all amounts to be collected by the National Bank of Greece, the Bank of Greece, and the Agricultural Bank of Greece were to be centralized in the central account of the Ministry of Finance with the Sofia branch of the Bulgarian National Bank. Payments to depositors of the above-mentioned institutions could be made only to persons of *Bulgarian origin* who had not emigrated from these regions during the year 1941. Most of these payments, however, could take place only in instalments. Thus, for amounts up to 2,000 leva payment is permitted in full, but for amounts above 2,000 leva, the payments must be at the rate of only 2,000 monthly. By this procedure the Greek population was deprived of all its bank deposits.

III. German Occupation

As mentioned above, the area of the German occupation has varied according to the military situation. Since the beginning of the invasion Germany has held under administration Central Macedonia, with the town of Salonika and the islands of Lemnos, Mytilene, and Chios. The Commander in Chief of the German Army in Greece has a special staff for civil administration. This staff acts through local military commands throughout all the occupied military area. The existing Greek authorities are supervised by German officers.

Immediately after the occupation the Germans started to requisition all food and fruits.[22] A special arrangement was made for German soldiers to send air-mail packages of food to their homes. Food production since the beginning of the occupation has been directed toward the needs of the German war economy. For example, in May, 1942, all the milk production in this area was requisitioned in order to be transformed into cheese and butter to be sent to Germany. Fresh fruit was also requisitioned sometime later.[23]

One of the main problems of German administration consists in recruiting labor and preventing sabotage. All males between sixteen and fifty years of age are liable for labor conscription for work in Greece or for work in Germany.[24] Strikes and lockouts were outlawed and severe penalties threatened for resort thereto. Persons who organize and direct a strike are liable to the death penalty. Strikers, as well as saboteurs, are tried by military courts. For the prevention of sabotage the German occupant has resorted very widely to the practice of taking hostages. Following the sabotaging of

[22] *Bulletin of International News*, Vol. XIX, No. 3 (February 7, 1942), p. 118.

[23] Xydis, *op. cit.*, p. 10.

It was reported that German and Italian food controllers requisitioned foodstuffs in quantities far exceeding the needs of the army and sold the surplus at enormous prices. *Bulletin of International News*, Vol. XVIII, No. 15 (July 26, 1941), pp. 986–87.

[24] Xydis, *op. cit.*, p. 20.

the postal, telegraph, and telephone services, the Germans introduced the death penalty for retarding work.[25]

IV. The Area of the Greek Puppet Government

The Greek mainland, Thessaly and the Peloponnesos, representing a total of 60,263 square kilometers, with a population of 3,546,185 people, is administered by a Greek puppet government, which was established by the Axis in Athens and was controlled by them.

Administration. Ostensibly the former ministries are functioning. A special German plenipotentiary and also an Italian plenipotentiary maintain their offices in Athens, however, where they act as representatives of the Reich and of Italy to the Greek puppet government. A considerable authority is concentrated in the person of the Minister of Finance, who is a kind of economic dictator, having control over the ministries of Agriculture, Food, and Labor. The Minister of Finance has the right to supervise these ministries, to determine their jurisdiction and control their services, to create or abolish positions, and to supervise trade, supplies, prices, and rationing. Even the so-called "soup kitchens" are within his jurisdiction.

Finance. More than any other country Greece has been stricken by inflation. The volume of currency has risen from 6,721 million drachmae on January 1, 1938, to 110,000 million drachmae on August 15, 1942.[26] The reason is the unchecked printing of currency by the Greek National Bank, which was put under the dual control of two commissioners; one being Herr Hahn, sent to Athens by the Reichsbank; the other Signor Forte, from the Banca d'Italia.[1] Under the pressure of these two commissioners the volume of the currency was further expanded in order to meet currency requirements of the German and Italian armies.

Barter. Although price regulations have been enacted, they cannot in practice fulfill their purpose because of the complete disintegration of the currency and the pressure of the black market. Therefore in some instances currency has practically ceased to fulfill its mission of being a measure of value. Goods are exchanged against goods and even government officials are paid sometimes in goods, especially in food provided them by the soup kitchens. Some taxes are paid by farmers in agricultural products.

When requisitions fail, the Axis authorities exchange manufactured objects for agricultural products of the farmers.[28]

Feeding the Population. In view of the particularly bad food situation in Greece, the United Nations agreed to make an exception with respect to the blockade and to send food to Greece, with the cooperation of the Swedish Government.

[25] *Bulletin of International News*, Vol. XIX, No. 10 (May 16, 1942), p. 455.
[26] Xydis, *op. cit.*, p. 9.
[27] *Free Europe*, Vol. 4, No. 53 (November 14, 1941), p. 274. [28] Xydis, *op. cit.*, p. 15.

A considerable rôle in feeding the population is played by the soup kitchens, which hand out food to the population on the streets. As mentioned above, the soup kitchens are under the Ministry of Finance and they are handled by a Central Soup Kitchen Committee.[29] Soup kitchens are dispersed throughout all the country. Various professions or groups, such as government employees, bank employees, and students, have their own soup kitchens.

[29] Xydis, *op. cit.*, p. 13.

CHAPTER XX

LUXEMBURG

ADMINISTRATION

On May 10, 1940, the Germans crossed the frontiers of the Grand Duchy of Luxemburg.[1] When the government was forced to leave the country, an Administrative Commission was set up by a number of government officials for the purpose of establishing order and for carrying on current administrative affairs. After a short time, however, this Administrative Commission was abolished by the German occupant.

Immediately after the occupation, a German *Feldkommandantur*, and shortly afterward an *Oberfeldkommandantur*, took over the administration of Luxemburg. Early in August, 1940, the office of a *Stadtkommandantur* was established. On August 7, 1940, a German Civil Administration was set up in the Grand Duchy and the District Leader (*Gauleiter*) of Koblenz-Trier (Gustav Simon) was appointed its chief.[2] On August 30, 1942, it was announced by the *Gauleiter* that Luxemburg had been incorporated into the German District of Moselland.

Since the beginning of the occupation local institutions of administration and communal life have been gradually abolished and replaced by German institutions. The Chamber of Deputies and the Council of State established under the Constitution of Luxemburg of October 17, 1868, were dissolved.[3] The German Municipal Code of January 30, 1935, was introduced.[4] As that Code is based upon the principle of leadership (*Führerprinzip*), the Luxemburg form of elective government was abolished, and municipalities are now headed by mayors and aldermen, who are not elected by the population but appointed by the German authorities. The Mayor constitutes the local police authority. Communities are divided into (1) municipal districts, headed by mayors, and (2) county districts, headed by county chiefs. The mayors and county chiefs are supervised by the Chief of the German Civil Administration.

NAZI PARTIES

An order was published on January 15, 1941,[5] placing the National Socialist Party under special protection. By this order persons who voice utterances against the German Reich and the National Socialist Party and

[1] *Bulletin of International News*, Vol. XVII, No. 10 (May 18, 1940), p. 622.

[2] *The Luxembourg Grey Book — Luxembourg and the German Invasion Before and After.* Based upon Official Documents, with a Preface by M. Joseph Bech, Foreign Minister of the Grand-Duchy of Luxembourg (London: Hutchinson & Co., Ltd. [1942]), p. 54.

[3] *Ibid.*, pp. 18, 54.

[4] Order of November 14, 1940, below, p. 420.

[5] See below, p. 425.

its leading personalities—even though not made in public—also are punishable. Not only deliberately malicious but also careless statements of this character render the speaker liable to penalties; it is sufficient that the judge shall find that the person involved has been guilty of negligence. Legal insecurity is augmented by the provision that prosecution under this law shall be subject to the consent of the Chief of the Civil Administration.

The main instrumentality of Germanism, aside from the Civil Administration, is the National German Party (*Volks-Deutsche Bewegung*).[6] Only persons who have joined this party are considered as being willing to promote Germanism and as such they are privileged.

LAW AND COURTS

The Supreme Court of Luxemburg has been abolished and its functions assigned to chambers of the Provincial Court of Appeals.[7] The courts have been Germanized, and a German Special Court (Criminal Court) has been established in Luxemburg with very broad jurisdiction over matters supposedly opposed to German interests, ranging from gatherings in the streets to ceasing work in factories. Moreover, the German prosecuting attorney may always send any case to the Special Court by removing it from the jurisdiction of the local courts. This court has created an atmosphere of legal insecurity in the country, because the jurisdiction is vague and the penalties not adjusted to specific offenses. These penalties are severe, ranging from fine and imprisonment to hard labor and even death.

THE BAR

Not only the judicial system, but also the bar, was Germanized. In order to make Luxemburg barristers comply with the New Order, a Special Honor Court (*Ehrengericht*) for practising attorneys was established.[8] The jurisdiction of this court is practically unlimited and is formulated in the following manner: "The Special Honor Court shall have jurisdiction to try acts which constitute a violation of the duties arising from the organization of a German administration in Luxemburg." The agent initiating proceedings before the Special Honor Court is the Chief of the Civil Administration himself. The jurisdiction being vague and undefined, as in the case of the Special Court, the Chief of the Civil Administration has thus practically unlimited authority over the bar in Luxemburg. He alone may determine what constitutes a "violation of the duties arising from the organization of a German administration in Luxemburg." The aim of the above-mentioned order is to break the resistance of the Luxemburg Bar, to make its mem-

[6] "The Luxembourg Professor Kratzenberg—himself of German origin—was made leader of the *Volks-Deutsche Bewegung*." — *Luxembourg Grey Book*, p. 55.

[7] Order of November 9, 1940, below, p. 423.

[8] Order of February 12, 1941, below, p. 427.

On the continent of Europe "honor courts" for attorneys usually deal with matters involving professional activities of the bar.

bers subservient to the German administration, and to deprive the persecuted Luxemburg population of its natural legal protectors[9] and intellectual leaders.

ECONOMY

The economy of Luxemburg was organized according to the principle of economic totalitarianism, e.g., the grouping of all persons and enterprises involved in economic activities into professional and regional organizations controlled by the central authority of the Chief of the Civil Administration.[10] Participation in economic life and the right to work and to own property are made dependent upon the willingness of the person concerned to promote Germanism in Luxemburg. According to the decree of February 21, 1941,[11] the Chief of the Civil Administration may restrain managers of enterprises from their activities if they are not willing to "promote Germanism at all times without any reservations," or if they violate duties "arising from the general principles of a National Socialist Labor Community (*Arbeitsgemeinschaft*)." All measures undertaken by the occupant in Luxemburg show but one aim, namely, the destruction of the Luxemburg nationhood and the promotion of Germanism.

CURRENCY

When the German Army occupied Luxemburg, it was provided with Reich Credit Institute notes (*Reichskreditkassenscheine*), which the population were compelled to accept in payment for goods purchased by members of the army. By order of August 26, 1940,[12] the Reichsmark was introduced as additional legal tender in Luxemburg. However, on January 29, 1941,[13] the Reichsmark was made exclusive legal tender. Luxemburg francs, as well as Belgian francs[14] and Reich Credit Institute notes, were withdrawn and exchanged for Reichsmarks. This exchange procedure was closed on March 1, 1941, the rate of exchange being established as follows: 1 Belgian franc equals 0.08 Reichsmark; 1 Luxemburg franc equals 0.10 Reichsmark. After the above date Luxemburg and Belgian francs were considered as foreign exchange. Claims for Belgian and Luxemburg francs by residents of Luxemburg, Alsace-Lorraine, the Protectorate of Bohemia and Moravia, and the Greater German Reich on other residents had to be changed into claims for Reichsmarks. Thus Luxemburg was completely incorporated into the Reichsmark area.

[9] The Luxemburg Bar displays an especially stubborn attitude toward the German Administration. According to the *Luxembourg Grey Book* (pp. 63–64): "All the members of the Luxembourg Bar who had, up till May 23rd, 1941, refused to associate themselves with the activities carried out by the Germans against the independence and the Constitution of the Grand-Duchy were condemned to forced labour."

[10] See order of November 12, 1940, below, p. 431.

[11] See below, p. 433. [12] See below, p. 434. [13] See below, p. 435.

[14] Belgian francs, as well as Luxemburg francs, were legal tender in the Grand Duchy. — *Annuaire Officiel* (Luxemburg, 1940), p. 206, par. c.

By the proclamation of September 13, 1940,[15] all residents of Luxemburg were required to sell their United States of America dollar notes, Swiss francs, Swedish crown notes, French franc notes, gold coins, and gold, pure and unalloyed, to the German authorities acting through specified banks. In addition, claims in foreign and home currency against non-residents were subject to registration.

LABOR

The manpower of Luxemburg was mobilized for German purposes through workbooks issued by the Labor Office in Luxemburg.[16] By order of February 12, 1941,[17] youths and girls were compelled to enter the Reich Labor Service. Originally they were required to work within the District of Moselland, of which Luxemburg is a part, but later on they were sent to work in Germany.

GENOCIDE

The Grand Duchy of Luxemburg has been for centuries bilingual (French and German). Nevertheless, the Chief of the German Civil Administration on August 6, 1940,[18] issued an order in which he stated that "the language of Luxemburg and of its inhabitants is, and always has been, German. . . .[19] The German language shall be the exclusive official language," as well as the language in commercial life. All names of streets and localities were made German.[20] Luxemburgers having non-German first names were required to assume in lieu thereof the corresponding German first name, or, if that were impossible, to select a German first name. Nationals of Luxemburg having a family name of German origin which later had been given a foreign or non-German form were required to resume the original German form. If the person involved did not apply for a change of name before February 15, 1941, the occupant himself conferred a German name upon him.[21]

An order was issued in Luxemburg concerning legitimation of illegitimate children, in which it was declared that an illegitimate child shall, in relation to its mother or her relatives, have the legal status of a legitimate child.[22]

[15] See below, p. 434. [16] See order of September 30, 1940, below, p. 436.
[17] See below, p. 437. [18] See below, p. 440.
[19] Since the earliest days of Luxemburg's national existence both languages have been spoken. Charters written in Latin after the thirteenth century were later generally worded in French. Only seventy charters were written in German, while more than 280 were drawn up in French. Because of affinity with French culture, the French language was the official language of the country. The population also speaks "Letzeburgesch," a homely dialect based on Teutonic origins, with extensive borrowings from Celtic, Roman, and French. Neither Germans nor Frenchmen understand the Luxemburg dialect. Therefore, the statement of the Chief of the Civil Administration of Luxemburg to the effect that German has always been the language of Luxemburg is untrue. French had always remained the official legislative, administrative, and judicial language. — *Luxembourg Grey Book*, p. 24.
[20] See above, chapter on "Genocide." [21] Order of January 31, 1941, below, p. 441.
[22] See order of March 22, 1941, below, p. 428.

Although this provision does not expressly mention German fathers, one may infer by comparison with other genocide laws issued by the occupant [23] that the order had as a goal the procreation of children by German fathers.[24]

RESISTANCE

Despite oppression, however, the Luxemburg people remain faithful to their country and nationhood. During the census of population on October 10, 1941, ordered by the occupant, forms to be filled in and signed contained the usual entries—surnames, Christian names, age, nationality, language. A special order was issued to the effect that where German nationhood did not apply, foreign nationhood, such as Italian or French, could be indicated, but in no case could Luxemburg nationhood be admitted. The Luxemburg language was excluded under the pretext that the Luxemburg dialect was only a branch of the German language. In spite of these orders, however, 96 per cent of the population in towns and 99 per cent in the country stated their nationality to be that of Luxemburg and their native language to be Luxemburgisch.[25]

[23] See above, chapter on "Genocide."

[24] See the speech of Adolf A. Berle, Jr., at the reception held at the Luxemburg Legation in August, 1941, as quoted in the *Luxembourg Grey Book*, p. 50: "A conqueror, claiming to establish a 'new order,' has put its young men at forced labour; and has taken its girls from their homes, has forced them into German industry, and proposes to make them, if possible, mothers of alien children."

[25] *Luxembourg Grey Book*, p. 57.

CHAPTER XXI

MEMEL TERRITORY

BACKGROUND

Under Article 99 of the Treaty of Versailles, Germany renounced in favor of the Principal Allied and Associated Powers the port of Memel, with a small territory surrounding it.

Upon the ratification of the treaty, the Allies occupied and administered this territory for three years. Meanwhile, the suggestion had been made that Memel might be given a status in regard to Lithuania similar to that which had been accorded Danzig in relation to Poland. The administration of Memel was in the hands of a French High Commissioner, with the old German Direktorium retained as the executive organ,[1] which, according to Lithuanian claims, pursued a policy hostile to the Lithuanians. On January 9, 1923, the Lithuanians seized Memel by a surprise attack.[2] After negotiations between the Lithuanian Government and the Conference of Ambassadors, and action taken by the League of Nations, a convention was signed in Paris on May 8, 1924, between Great Britain, France, Italy, and Japan, on the one side, and Lithuania on the other, by the terms of which Memel Territory was placed under the sovereignty of Lithuania. An annex was attached to the convention constituting the statute for Memel Territory, which provided that Memel was to enjoy "legislative, judicial, administrative and financial autonomy" within the limits prescribed in the statute, with a governor appointed by the President of the Lithuanian Republic. In a second annex to the convention the port of Memel was described "as a port of international concern," to which recommendations adopted by the Barcelona Conference of 1921 should apply, and it was placed under a Harbor Board, which was to include among its members a technical expert of neutral nationality appointed by the League of Nations.[3]

INCORPORATION

In the atmosphere of international terror created after the sudden occupation and dismemberment of Czechoslovakia by Germany, Hitler made a request to the Lithuanian Government that it cede Memel to Germany.

[1] *The Question of Memel. Diplomatic and Other Documents* . . . (1919–1923), (London: Lithuanian Information Bureau, 1924), pp. 7–8, 43.

[2] *Ibid.*, p. 8.

[3] *Convention and Transitory Provision concerning Memel, signed at Paris, May 8th, 1924.* Extract No. 28 from the League of Nations *Official Journal* (Geneva, 1924), pp. 2, 5, 10, 11. See also Jacob Robinson, *Kommentar der Konvention über das Memelgebiet vom 8. Mai, 1924* (Kaunas, 1934), 2 vols.; League of Nations, *Treaty Series*, Vol. 29, p. 85.

Lithuania complied with this request, and on March 22, 1939, a treaty was signed with Germany regarding the cession of this territory.[4]

On March 23, Hitler arrived in Memel on board the battleship *Deutschland*, and the whole of the German Baltic fleet entered the harbor. In a speech in the city Hitler thanked the Memellanders for their loyalty during the separation from Germany, and among other remarks spoke as follows: "We know what we have to expect from another part of the world. We have no intention of imposing suffering on that other world, but merely of making good the suffering which it has imposed on us, and I believe that to a great extent we have come to the end of this unique reparation."[5]

Aboard the *Deutschland*, Hitler signed the "law concerning the reunion of Memelland with the German Reich."[6] Under the terms of this law, Memel Territory was incorporated into the German Reich and included within the province of East Prussia, namely, in the district of Gumbinnen. Inhabitants of Memelland were declared German citizens if they were German citizens on July 30, 1924, and if on March 22, 1939, they had their domicile in the territory of Memel or in the German Reich. According to this law, the whole body of German law, and also Prussian law, was to be enforced in Memel Territory as from May 1, 1939, with such exceptions as the proper German ministers might decide. The Reich Minister of the Interior was authorized to carry out the incorporation.

On March 23, 1939, a decree was published by which the Reichsmark was made legal tender and Lithuanian currency was replaced by the Reichsmark at the rate of 1 Lithuanian lit to 40 Reichspfennigs.[7]

[4] *Reichsgesetzblatt*, 1939, II, p. 608.
[5] *Bulletin of International News*, Vol. XVI, No. 7 (April 6, 1939), p. 348.
[6] See below, p. 444. [7] See below, p. 445.

CHAPTER XXII

THE NETHERLANDS

GERMAN ADMINISTRATION

On the occupation of the Netherlands after a short but stubborn fight, Germany took over the administration of the country. Hitler appointed a Reich Commissioner in the person of Seyss-Inquart, the same individual who, as a member of the last "Austrian Government," had invited Hitler to "protect" Austria against internal disorders.[1] The Reich Commissioner was made responsible directly to Hitler.

In his first proclamation to the Netherlands population, the Reich Commissioner stated that as a result of "the magnanimity of the Führer and the power of the German armed forces," an order of public life had been restored within a few days "after the catastrophe brought about by the former leadership of the Netherlands." Because the German people "are fighting a decisive battle for their survival or destruction, a struggle which the hatred and envy of their enemies have forced upon them," the exigencies of that struggle compelled the German nation "to exert all its strength" and gave it "the right to avail itself of all means within its reach."[2] A reference to the blood kinship of Dutchmen and Germans suggested that Dutchmen were to be treated in a favorable way by the occupant.

It was stated in the Reich Commissioner's order of May 29, 1940,[3] that "to the extent required for the fulfillment of his duties, the Reich Commissioner for the occupied Netherlands territories assumes all powers, privileges, and rights heretofore vested in the King and the government in accordance with the Constitution and the laws of the Netherlands." Under the decree of June 3, 1940,[4] the Reich Commissioner acts through a staff consisting of general and special commissioners. The general commissioners head the following sections: (*a*) General Administration and Judiciary; (*b*) Public Safety (Superior S.S. and Police Chief); (*c*) Finance and Commerce (Economics); (*d*) Special Matters. The section on General Administration and Judiciary embraces matters relating to: (1) general orders and legislation, constitutional law, and the Official Gazette;[5] (2) planning; (3) civil administration, especially the supervision of municipalities, with the exception of municipal police forces; (4) administration of justice, with the exception of the Reich police forces;[6] (5) culture, and matters relating to schools

[1] See above, chapter on "Austria."

[2] See proclamation of May 25, 1940, below, p. 447.

[3] See below, p. 448.

[4] See below, p. 450.

[5] *Verordnungsblatt für die besetzten niederländischen Gebiete.*

[6] The exception of the Reich police forces is explained by the fact that the police also participate in the administration of justice. See above, chapter on "Courts."

and churches; (6) public health and "cultural and social welfare of juveniles." [7]

The Commissioner for Public Safety, who is at the same time Superior S.S. and Police Chief, commands the units of the military S.S. and German police forces stationed in the Netherlands; he supervises also the Netherlands central and municipal police. The General Commissioner of Finance and Commerce supervises all matters relating to: (1) the Ministry of Finance; (2) the Ministry of Economics (Commerce); (3) the Ministry of Waterways; (4) the Postal Administration; and (5) the Ministry of Public Welfare (with the exception of public health and "cultural and social welfare of juveniles").

The General Commissioner for Special Matters is entrusted with the political aspects of administration. His duties are, among other things, "the molding of public opinion" and the controlling of non-profit associations.

Besides the general commissioners there are also special commissioners, who are appointed by the Reich Commissioner, either for the several provinces and cities or for specific purposes as need arises.

DUTCH ADMINISTRATION

For purposes of local administration, a subcabinet or headless government was organized consisting of the secretaries general of the existing Dutch ministries.[8] Secretaries general are functioning in the following ministries: Ministry of Trade, Industry, and Shipping; Ministry of Agriculture and Fisheries, Ministry of Waterstaat,[9] Ministry of the Interior, Ministry of Finance, Ministry of Social Welfare (labor matters belong also to this ministry), Ministry of Justice, and Ministry of General Affairs.

To the Ministry of Trade, Industry, and Shipping is attached the office of a Price Commissioner, appointed by the Secretary General of that ministry.[10] His authority extends especially to prices for "all articles of every-day need, to rentals for chattels and real property, and to tariffs for transportation, gas, and electricity, and to interest rates." The Price Commissioner is assisted by a board consisting of members representing: (1) the Ministry of Trade, Industry, and Shipping; (2) the Ministry of Agriculture and Fisheries; (3) the Ministry of Waterstaat; (4) the Ministry of the Interior; (5) the Ministry of Finance; (6) the Ministry of Justice; and (7) the Ministry of Social Welfare.

Powers and duties relating to food problems are vested in the Director General for the Food Supply, who is assisted by a Commission for Securing

[7] "Culture and social welfare of juveniles" refers, apparently, to Nazi indoctrination of youth.

[8] See order of June 21, 1940, below, p. 453.

[9] The Ministry of Waterstaat supervises the waterways and waterworks, the ports, and generally all communications. There has never been a special ministry for communications in the Netherlands.

[10] See order of November 11, 1940, below, p. 485.

the Food Supply. The members of this commission are appointed by the Secretary General in the Ministry of Agriculture and Fisheries.[11]

For the regulation of transportation and traffic, the office of the Inspector General of Traffic was established under the supervision of the Ministry of Waterstaat. The Inspector General of Traffic is appointed by the Secretary General of the Ministry of Waterstaat to control all matters pertaining to transportation. As transportation of goods for personal requirements, even on public highways, is prohibited without permits, one of the functions of the Inspector General is to receive and act on applications for such permits. Furthermore, the unauthorized use of motorcycles or any motor vehicles (with the exception of motor busses) having been prohibited in order to save gasoline, it falls within the jurisdiction of the Inspector General to decide on the granting of permits for the use of such vehicles.[12]

A Netherlands Reconstruction Service was established by the order of July 30, 1940,[13] with the objective of affording employment to members of the former Netherlands armed forces. This service is headed by a Labor Commandant and by an Administrative Director. Both are under the orders of the Secretary General in the Ministry of Social Welfare.

To deal with labor problems in general, as well as with public occupational guidance and the apprenticeship placement service, a State Labor Office was created within the Ministry of Social Welfare.[14] The State Labor Office is headed by a General Director. Labor procurement having been monopolized for the needs of the German war economy, the continuation of licenses issued to private employment agencies for trade and industry is made dependent on the decision of the Ministry of Social Welfare. Favorable decisions are made with respect to agencies collaborating with the German authorities in procurement of labor for Germany.

All the above-mentioned Dutch agencies are under the control of German authorities, especially of the four general commissioners who are members of the staff of the Reich Commissioner. Their powers are divided in such a way that each general commissioner controls a different ministry and agency, according to the jurisdictional division set forth in the decree of June 3, 1940.[15]

In his order of August 20, 1940,[16] the Reich Commissioner stated that he would appoint certain categories of Dutch officials (these categories, the most important ones, being named), leaving to the secretaries general the right to appoint all others. But by the same order this right of appointment of the secondary officials by the secretaries general was made illusory by the further provision that the Reich Commissioner likewise reserved to himself

[11] See order of September 10, 1940, below, p. 484.

[12] See four orders of June 17 and 18, 1940, concerning transportation of persons and goods, below, pp. 480–82.

[13] See below, p. 494.

[14] Order of September 24, 1940, below, p. 495.

[15] See below, p. 450.

[16] See below, p. 455.

the right to exercise, if he saw fit, the power of appointment granted to the secretaries general in the immediately preceding section of the order.

The following basic institutions of Dutch self-government were suspended by the orders of June 21, 1940, and August 11, 1941,[17] implementing the order of May 18, 1940:[18] (1) the two chambers of the States-General (*Generalstaaten*) comprising the parliament of the Netherlands, which is divided into upper and lower chambers as in some other countries; (2) the State Council;[19] (3) the Provincial States (*Provinzialstaaten*), which are representative bodies for the provinces; (4) the municipal councils in the cities.

The local administration was reconstructed. Members of the merely advisory councils which have been created are not elected by the population as in the case of the previous local bodies, but are appointed by the mayors, who are strictly supervised and act according to the instructions of the supervising administrative authority.[20]

By the decree of July 4, 1941,[21] political parties were dissolved. Later on the Nazi Mussert Party was created for the purpose of promoting collaboration.

CITIZENSHIP

Disrespect for the exclusiveness of Netherlands nationality was displayed by the order of the Reich Commissioner which provided that a Dutchman acquiring German nationality shall not be deemed to have lost Netherlands nationality unless he renounces it within one year after acquisition of German nationality.[22]

Dual nationality was unknown in the Netherlands, but the occupant was eager to create a privileged class of fifth columnists who would be protected by German nationality and at the same time enjoy the rights of Dutch nationals and thus be able to perform political tasks for the benefit of the occupant within the Dutch national community.

The law on citizenship was changed further by the occupant for recruiting reasons. According to Dutch law, a Dutchman serving in a foreign army loses his citizenship. When the creation of the Anti-Bolshevik Legion was proclaimed by the occupant, the law on citizenship was changed in such a way that service against Russia does not deprive one of Dutch citizenship.[23]

DAMAGES AND CIVIL CLAIMS

Especial significance is to be attached to the decree of February 7, 1941,[24] to the effect that German nationals are to be indemnified for damages to

[17] See below, pp. 453, 461. [18] See below, p. 446.

[19] The State Council is an advisory body to the Crown, composed of members appointed by the Queen. The State Council also handles conflicts of jurisdiction between administrative authorities.

[20] See order of August 11, 1941, below, p. 461. [21] See below, p. 459.

[22] See order of August 8, 1941, below, p. 460.

[23] Decree of July 25, 1941, *Verordnungsblatt*, No. 133, July 28, 1941. [24] See below, p. 473.

property which they have suffered or may suffer in the occupied Netherlands territories as a result of the war. A special fund, called "Reconstruction Fund," was created for this purpose under the administration of the Secretary General of the Ministry of Finance. The income and expenditure of this fund are "established by an annual budget" and are financed by funds supplied by the Dutch Government. Thus the Dutch Treasury is paying for war damages caused by the German Army to German residents in the Netherlands. If Dutch Government funds are insufficient, the order provides that the Treasury may incur short- or long-term loans.[25]

Significance is also to be attached to the order concerning certain measures relating to civil claims. This order deals with the problem of civil claims which may arise from orders of the Reich Commissioner.[26] For example, an order from the Reich Commissioner may undertake the reallocation of property. The party aggrieved by such an order, or his successor, is excluded from relief in the courts. Such person may apply only to the Reich Commissioner himself. Thus the same authority which has issued an order aggrieving a party decides upon the right of appeal from such order. Moreover, the same decree states that suit on civil claims shall not be brought against Germans or corporations having their domicile in the Greater Reich if the cause of action shall have arisen directly or indirectly as a result of the events of war. Thus, Dutchmen are precluded from suing for war damages, yet they must provide money to pay Germans for such damages caused by Germans.

FINANCE

With regard to finance, the same technique was adopted in the Netherlands as in other western countries which had been occupied. *Reichskreditkassenscheine* were issued and later on the Bank of the Netherlands had to exchange them for gulden. The exchange rate between the Reichsmark and the gulden was established as follows: 1 gulden equals 133 Reichspfennigs.[27]

A clearing arrangement was established between the Netherlands and Germany, as well as between the Netherlands and other countries, through the German *Verrechnungskasse* (Clearing Institute).

As the occupant was unwilling to maintain a balance of trade between the Netherlands and Germany, Dutch exporting firms had difficulties when their claims were frozen in Germany. Disruption of Dutch economic life was the result. The Secretaries General in the Ministry of Trade, Industry, and Shipping, and in the Ministry of Finance, were then compelled by the occupant to issue an order authorizing Dutch banks to extend loans to the exporting firms "which find themselves financially embarrassed

[25] See order of June 21, 1940, below, p. 487.
[26] See order of December 19, 1940, below, p. 471.
[27] See order of July 16, 1940, below, p. 488.

through their inability to enforce claims arising out of shipments abroad."[28] An instrumentality was thus created whereby the Dutch banks financed further exports to Germany, with consequent inflationary effect upon the Dutch currency.

A peculiar evolution occurred in the field of exchange control. At the beginning of the occupation the Netherlands was divided from Germany by a customs frontier and by exchange control restrictions. Later on, because of the relatively strong and well organized Dutch economy, the occupant saw the advantage of incorporating the Netherlands totally into the economy of the Greater German Reich. A logical consequence of such incorporation was the abolition of customs frontier and exchange control restrictions between these two countries, especially as to the transfer of money from one country to another. Germany, however, had owed large sums of money to individuals in the Netherlands for many years before the war. These sums had been since 1931 under the protection of the German Exchange Control Law, so that all the demands of Dutch creditors were met with the answer that the German debtor was not allowed to pay his money because of exchange control restrictions. However, the exchange control restrictions had to be abrogated and this took place on March 31, 1941.[29] Theoretically, money could then be transferred from Germany to the Netherlands. But on the same day a decree was published to the effect that every Dutchman withdrawing money from the Greater Reich to the Netherlands should pay a tax for the benefit of the Dutch Treasury, this tax amounting to 72 per cent of the sum withdrawn.[30] Both of the decrees—on the removal of the exchange control frontier, as well as the taxation of blocked Dutch funds—went into effect on the same day, April 1, 1941. Although the taxes were to be paid to the Dutch Treasury, the interested persons were not eager to pay such a high percentage and thus the taxation decree made illusory the relief granted by the removal of the exchange control frontier.[31]

AMERICAN PROPERTY

On September 11, 1941, the Reich Commissioner issued an order concerning the declaration of United States assets in the Netherlands. According to this decree, real and personal property situated in the occupied Netherlands had to be declared, if owned or even controlled by the Government of the United States, by citizens of the United States, by corporations, private associations, foundations, endowments, trusts, or other forms of organizations which have their seat or principal place of business in the

[28] See order of October 10, 1940, below, p. 489.
[29] *Verordnungsblatt*, No. 65, April 1, 1941. Such a move may be explained by a desire to manifest a community of the economies of the two countries.
[30] See decree of the Reich Commissioner of March 31, 1941, *ibid.*, No. 66, April 1, 1941.
[31] Later, as of September 1, 1941 (*ibid.*, No. 169, August 30, 1941), this decree on taxing money transfers was abolished as a too obvious device to nullify the effect of the other decree.

United States or which have been incorporated under the laws of the United States. Moreover, the order embraces also other persons (beside those mentioned above) if beside the real and personal property situated in the occupied Netherlands, such persons have business branches in the United States.[32]

RESISTANCE

The resistance of the Dutch population to the occupant is strong, despite the fact that some Dutchmen are forced into collaboration, especially as regards the German war economy. The activities of Dutch patriots gave rise to the creation by the occupant of a system of severe punishments for any inimical act. On October 16, 1941, an order was issued concerning defense against acts of sabotage, in which the Reich Commissioner declared that "Germany is engaged in a fight against the enemy powers," "on behalf of Europe's future."[33] Although for every act of sabotage the death penalty was prescribed, the Reich Commissioner did not give an exact definition of sabotage. According to his order, any person will be punishable by death as a saboteur who wilfully perpetrates "an act punishable under existing statutes and intended or liable to endanger public order or security of public life." If one considers that any violation of administrative regulations pertaining to public order may be interpreted as endangering that order, the possibility is presented of practically unlimited application of the death penalty, even for offenses which are essentially of a purely administrative character. Moreover, attempt is punished in the same way as perpetration. No judicial guaranties are given as to trial of such offenses. For example, the date of trial shall be fixed "without the usual restriction as to the time within which such date may be set." The indictment "may be preferred orally." In such cases a German Superior Court, acting as a special court, has exclusive jurisdiction.[34]

Not only are the lives and personal liberties of Dutchmen held in pawn, so to speak, against non-compliance with the New Order, but also their property. By the order of July 4, 1940,[35] the property of persons and associations which have furthered "activities hostile to the German Reich or Germanism, or of whom it must be assumed that they will further such activities in the future" may be confiscated. The same applies to property and rights which have been used for the furtherance of activities hostile to the German Reich or Germanism, "or which are capable of being thus used." The effect of this order is therefore to create, and it was doubtless so intended, an attitude not only of complete compliance with the orders of the occupant but also of complete dependence and even subservience. As mentioned above,[36] such a provision is without parallel in law, for, according to

[32] As to details, see decree below, p. 492. [33] See below, p. 477.
[34] See above, p. 33. [35] See below, p. 478. [36] See above, chapter on "Law."

well-established principles of criminal law, a person may be punished only for acts which have been committed or attempted, not for acts which may be committed in the future.[37]

[37] As to other institutions of German occupation in the Netherlands, see references to these in the several chapters in Part I of the present work.

CHAPTER XXIII

NORWAY

THE INVASION

In connection with the invasion and occupation of Norway certain governmental acts of the occupying power and of the King and Government of Norway must be considered, since they influenced to some extent the institutions of military occupation.

It was apparently Germany's intention to occupy Norway rather by using threats than by actual fighting. In order to create a menacing atmosphere, the German Minister to Norway, Dr. Bräuer,[1] on April 5, 1940, invited a group of distinguished guests, including members of the Norwegian Government, to the legation to see a German film. The guests were horrified at the film, which showed the German conquest of Poland, with gruesome pictures of the bombing of Warsaw, accompanied by the caption: "For this they could thank their English and French friends."[1a]

The invasion began on the night of April 8. Several hours later the German Minister in Oslo presented to the Minister of Foreign Affairs an ultimatum stating that Great Britain and France were violating Norway's neutrality and intended to occupy that country; that the German Government had therefore begun "certain military operations which will result in the occupation of strategically important points in Norwegian territory"; and that the "German Government therewith takes over the protection of the Kingdom of Norway during this war."[2] The German Minister expressed the hope that Norway would not resist, using the words of the film showing the bombing of Warsaw: "For such horrors you would have to thank your English and French friends."[3] The document ended with certain demands. Thus the Germans insisted that all places (in particular, all the coastal forts or military establishments) which the German troops wanted to take should be surrendered to them without any resistance. The Norwegian troops were requested to cooperate and were told that if they behaved well, they

[1] Dr. Bräuer appeared to be the main agent for the invasion inside Norway, and he acted through German agents and Norwegian fifth columnists headed by Quisling. It is believed that the Germans did not expect any serious opposition. Dr. Bräuer was seen at three o'clock in the night of the invasion on the docks of the harbor apparently waiting for the German fleet. On the same night the transatlantic telephonic communication was also in the hands of German fifth columnists. When the American Minister to Norway, Mrs. Harriman, attempted to place a call to Washington, a voice with a German accent informed her that it would perhaps not get through. The fifth columnists were even more active in disrupting other means of communication. See F. J. Harriman, *Mission to the North* (Philadelphia: J. B. Lippincott Company, 1941), p. 252.

[1a] See Halvdan Koht, former Foreign Minister of Norway, *Norway—Neutral and Invaded* (New York: The Macmillan Company, 1941), pp. 57–58.

In connection with this film performance, Koht remarks: "Undoubtedly it was intended to show the Norwegians what would be the result of resisting Germany." — *Ibid.*

[2] *Ibid.*, p. 66.

[3] *Ibid.*, p. 69.

might be permitted to keep their arms. Under the conditions laid down in this ultimatum the Germans would have at their disposal, in addition to military points, the railways and steamers, the pilots and the lighthouses, the mail, telegraph, and telephone services, the wireless, the radio, and the press; [4] the whole country was to be blacked out and the publication of weather reports was to cease. In addition, it was demanded that all communications between Norway and the countries to the west, including America as well as Europe, be severed.

The reply of the Norwegian Government was in the negative. In the midst of the severe bombing of Oslo, the government and the King, as well as the Storting, left the capital. At the last moment the gold assets of the Bank of Norway were saved.

On April 9 the Storting held meetings at Hamar, at which all but five of the 150 members were present. The Nygaardsvold government [5] informed the King that they placed their resignations at his disposal in order to permit a new government to be formed representing all the political parties. The Storting summoned the Nygaardsvold government to remain in power and, on the motion of Mr. Hambro, president of the Storting, unanimously adopted the proposal to grant to the government complete authority to safeguard the interests of the Kingdom, such authority to continue in effect until the government and the Presidential Board of the Storting should agree to call the Storting into session again. President Hambro also stated that if the then existing government should be compelled to establish itself in a foreign country, that government alone would remain "the legal Government of Norway, and the international symbol of the independence of the kingdom." [6]

In the meantime, Major Vidkun Quisling, the head of the pro-Nazi fifth columnists in Norway, formed a cabinet in Oslo.

On April 10 the German Minister asked for an appointment with the King, and, on being received by the King and the Minister of Foreign Affairs, proposed that the fighting cease and that the King appoint Quisling as his Prime Minister. After consulting the government and members of the Storting, the King refused.[7]

On April 11 an emissary from Quisling, a Captain Irgens, appeared at Nybergsund (where the King took refuge after the bombing of Hamar) and invited the King to come to Oslo. No one, however, wished to receive the emissary. On the same day a message was received from Dr. Bräuer that he would like to see the King again; but the King decided that if any new German proposals were to be made, they should be conveyed to the Minister of Foreign Affairs, Mr. Koht, and word to that effect was sent to Dr. Bräuer. No reply was received from the German authorities, but

[4] Koht, pp. 69, 218–20.
[5] Nygaardsvold was Prime Minister of Norway at that time.
[6] Koht, pp. 75–77.
[7] *Ibid.*, pp. 79–84.

instead Nybergsund, a small village without military significance where the King and government had taken refuge, was bombed by air.[8] During the bombing the King and the population fled to the neighboring forest, where the King spent several hours in the snow in conversation with the citizens and giving comfort to them.

When all Norway was occupied, the King and the government went to England, wherefrom they are continuing the war against Germany.

ADMINISTRATION

When the fifth-column activities of Quisling were displayed in the form of open treachery, public opinion in Norway was so strongly opposed to him that the Germans felt it necessary to dismiss the puppet government formed by Quisling and to look for other forms of collaboration with Norwegians.

In the latter part of April, 1940, an Administrative Council was established with the collaboration of the Supreme Court of Norway,[9] and I. E. Christensen was chosen as its president. The duty of this Council was to carry on the current administrative functions of government in the occupied areas, while the northern part of Norway was still defending itself under the leadership of King Haakon. In a letter approved by the Cabinet Council on April 19, 1940, King Haakon made it clear, however, that although the Administrative Council was necessary under the circumstances, it could not represent the King or his government, because the Council was controlled by the occupying power.[10]

On April 24, 1940,[11] the Führer promulgated a decree in which he appointed a Reich Commissioner to administer the occupied Norwegian territories. By this decree the Reich Commissioner was made "guardian of the interests of the German Reich and, within the domain of civil administration," was "vested with supreme governmental authority"; he was also authorized to call on the Norwegian Administrative Council and the Norwegian civil authorities for collaboration in the administration of the country. The law and statutes theretofore in force were declared to continue in effect "in so far as is compatible with the fact of occupation."

The Reich Commissioner has offices in Trondheim, Bergen, Harstad, Hammerfest, and Kirkenes. He is assisted by his staff, the Reich Commissariat, which is divided into three main sections: Administration, Economy, and Propaganda. In addition, a ranking S.S. police officer supervises the police forces within Norway. The German police are active in all the communities.

Although the central Norwegian administration has passed through various stages (having been directed, first, by the Quisling Government; second,

[8] Koht, pp. 85–86. [9] *Ibid.*, pp. 132, 134.

[10] Monica Curtis, ed., *Norway and the War, September 1939–December 1940*, "Documents on International Affairs" (London, etc.: Oxford University Press, 1941. Issued under the auspices of the Royal Institute of International Affairs), p. 76; Koht, *op. cit.*, p. 134.

[11] See below, p. 498.

by the Administrative Council; third, by the State Council; and fourth, again by a government with Quisling as Minister-President),[12] the Norwegian administration has remained essentially the same; however, control by the Nasjonal Samling has been gradually tightened. The country is divided into twenty districts known as *Fylke*, of which Oslo and Bergen are city Fylke (*Stadt-Fylke*). Every Fylke is headed by higher administrative officials called *Fylkesmenn*. Under these Fylkesmenn are subordinate *lensmenn*. There is a Norwegian police force under the direction of the Norwegian Minister of Police. Directly responsible to him are fifty-five Chiefs of Police (*Politimester*), and the lowest police authority is represented by the lensmenn.[13]

The higher administrative officers are predominantly members of the Nasjonal Samling Party.

Beside the Reich Commissioner, who was vested with supreme civil authority, the Commander of the German Forces in Norway was vested "with supreme military authority." The jurisdiction was divided between the Reich Commissioner and the military commander. If it should be necessary for the military commander to issue orders relating to the civil domain, these orders were to be enforced exclusively by the Reich Commissioner. Both the Reich Commissioner and the military commander in Norway were to be supervised by, and receive orders from, their respective authorities, i.e., the Reich Commissioner, by the Reich Minister and Chief of the Reich Chancellery; the military commander in Norway, by the Chief of the Supreme Command of the Wehrmacht. The Reich Commissioner was declared to be directly responsible to the Führer, and as the military authorities are also responsible to the latter, any conflict of jurisdiction between the Reich Commissioner and the military commander has to be decided by the Führer.[14]

Attempts to Dethrone the King. The fact that the King enjoyed great popularity with the people and was continuing resistance from London was a disturbing element in the administration of the country. The Reich Commissioner therefore endeavored to bring about the dethroning of the King by the Storting. Under pressure from the Reich Commissioner, the Presidential Board of the Storting (a kind of Speaker's Committee, which has no constitutional functions) notified the King of its request that he abdicate; but the King, in a letter dated July 3, 1940, declined to resign his royal duties for the reason that the request emanated from a body which was subject to the control of the occupying authorities and was not the free expression of the will of the Norwegian people.[15]

[12] As to the evolution of the central government under occupation, see below.

[13] See Great Britain, Foreign Office, *Secret German Documents Seized during the Raid on the Lofoten Islands on the 4th March, 1941*, Norway No. 1 (1941), pp. 4–5.

[14] See decree of April 24, 1940, below, p. 498.

[15] For correspondence between the Presidential Board and the King of Norway, see Annex 1 to the present chapter.

Later on the members of the Storting were summoned to meet in September (those who had left the country being expressly excluded), for the purpose of dethroning the King, which action by statute required a majority of two thirds. Two texts of resolutions were proposed, one in Norwegian, the other in German. During the voting procedure it was discovered that the two texts differed substantially.[16] The Board of the Storting advised the members that an agreement had been reached with the German authorities to the effect that in consideration of their dethroning the King, a Norwegian National or State Council (*Riksraad*) would be formed to carry on independently the administration of internal affairs without interference by German authorities. In the trial vote, the highest total reached for suspension—not dethroning—was 92 votes for and 52 against.[17] Under these conditions, the efforts of the German authorities to bring about the dethronement of the King failed.

However, the Reich Commissioner announced on September 25 that the Royal House of Norway had been repudiated by a two-thirds majority of the Storting; that the King had no further importance and would not return to Norway. The Supreme Court of Norway had declared the dethroning of the King unlawful; and the action of the occupant aroused great sympathy for the King, with the result that his popularity rose even higher. The Reich Commissioner therefore felt compelled to issue an order on October 7, 1940, concerning the prohibition of activities on behalf of the Royal House of Norway. Violations of this order were to be punished by forced labor for a period up to three years, or by imprisonment, as well as by fine.[18]

From the point of view of the Hague Regulations, this attempt by the occupant to dethrone the King was a violation of international law. The occupant has the right and the duty to restore order and safety in an occupied territory but this right does not include measures for dethroning the local sovereign such as were attempted in Norway.

Implementation of the New Order. Following these measures designed to divest the King of his office and authority, the Reich Commissioner terminated the activities of the Administrative Council and appointed a State Council (*Riksraad*) in its place. The latter consisted of thirteen members, six of whom had been members of Quisling's original cabinet, Quisling himself not being included. An order was issued to the effect that all political parties and any other political organizations, with the exception of the Nasjonal Samling (the Quisling Party), were dissolved.[19] Under this order the Reich Commissioner was to appoint trustees for the liquidation of the affairs of the organizations so dissolved. As the order did not apply, however, to the Nasjonal Samling, a monoparty system was thus created in

[16] See Koht, *op. cit.*, pp. 157–58.
[17] *Bulletin of International News*, Vol. XVIII, No. 2 (January 25, 1941), p. 62.
[18] See below, p. 500.
[19] See order of September 25, 1940, below, p. 499.

Norway in harmony with the Nazi pattern. At the same time political persecutions were begun against members of the preexisting political parties who were opposed to the New Order.

A special rôle under the New Order was given to the party guards of the Nasjonal Samling. These party guards, who considered it their duty to punish members of the opposition by measures outside the law, were called *Hird*,[20] and were protected by the police authorities.

In the further evolution of events, Quisling was made Minister-President of the Norwegian puppet government, and ostensibly proceeded to the integration of Norway into the New Order. He organized a Norwegian Legion and a Regiment Nordland, consisting of Norwegian volunteers serving in cooperation with the German Army. In order to induce Norwegians to join these militaristic organizations, various privileges were granted to them. Particular reference may be made to a decree published by Quisling on February 26, 1942, postponing foreclosure sales of the property of such volunteers.[21]

GENOCIDE LEGISLATION

The Norwegians, as representatives of the Nordic race, were declared to be of related German blood, and therefore Norwegian blood was declared to be a "racially valuable" contribution to German blood; hence the interest of the occupant in promoting procreation by Germans in Norway. A decree was published by the Führer on July 28, 1942, to the effect that children begotten by members of the German armed forces in Norway and born of Norwegian women should be granted special subsidies through the office of the Reich Commissioner for the occupied Norwegian territories, these benefits including costs of delivery of such children, payment to the mothers of maintenance benefits for the time before and after delivery, payment of maintenance benefits for the children, the sheltering of mothers in clinics or homes, and similar care. As an additional means of encouraging such unions it was declared that the mother of a child begotten by a member of the German armed forces should be given suitable employment.[22]

Undesirable books were banned from libraries. Among others, were included as a rule all books by Jewish and Polish authors and all books on psychoanalysis.

[20] Koht, *op. cit.*, p. 177.

[21] See below, p. 503.

[22] See below, p. 504.

As the Dutch were also declared to be of related German blood, the decree above cited was likewise made applicable to the Netherlands.

The Norwegian population resists the endeavors on the part of the occupant to promote "friendly relations" between Norwegian women and German soldiers, as is seen from an order of the German Chief Police Inspector in Solvaer which is among the documents seized in the British-Norwegian raid on the Lofoten Islands on March 4, 1941. In this order the Police Inspector instructs his subordinates how to act when a Norwegian girl of friendly disposition toward Germans has her hair cut short by her indignant compatriots. This Norwegian practice of cutting the hair of such girls was announced several times in the press. *Secret German Documents, op. cit.*, p. 13.

COURTS

The New Order was especially protected by two courts, a Norwegian Special Court and a German Court. The Norwegian Special Court was established to try cases concerning the prohibition of political parties in Norway and activities in behalf of the Royal House of Norway.[23] This court is composed of a presiding judge and two associate judges, appointed by a commissioner of state for the Department of Justice. No appeal lies from the decision of the Special Court. The German Criminal Court has an almost unlimited jurisdiction, since the president and its members are directly under the supervision of the Reich Commissioner. No preliminary investigation by the court is required, and it may issue notice and summons within so short a time as twenty-four hours before the trial. There is no appeal from the decision of the German Court.[24]

The Attitude of the Norwegian Supreme Court. The Supreme Court of Norway, which played an important rôle in the creation of the Administrative Council, hoped to insure a regular administration under military occupation. When it became clear, however, that administration by Germany was being carried out in violation of international law, the Supreme Court blamed these practices on the members of the Administrative Council (called "state councillors"), as well as on the Reich Commissioner himself.

The Supreme Court declared that the dethroning of the King was unlawful.[25] The open conflict between the court and the occupying authorities started, however, with the issue of a decree by the Department of Justice to the effect that the State Councillor should have authority to appoint and dismiss members of Conciliation Commissions, to remove from the panels jurors, expert witnesses, and assessors, and to appoint others in civil as well as criminal proceedings. The Supreme Court saw in this decree an attempt to interfere in the composition of the courts, and especially a violation of the principle of the independence of courts, which is guaranteed by the Constitution of Norway and which was also proclaimed in the first decree of the Reich Commissioner. In a letter sent out by the Norwegian Supreme Court to the Department of Justice dated November 19, 1940,[26] the Supreme Court gave expression to its concern regarding this violation of international law, pointing out also that the independence of courts is prescribed by the Constitution and that the Führer's decree of April 24, 1940, declared that the Norwegian law would continue in force so long as this was consistent with the occupation.[27] Consequently the Supreme Court requested that the order of the Department of Justice should not be carried into effect. The Reich Commissioner replied that neither the Supreme Court nor other Norwegian courts were justified in raising the question of the validity of decrees issued

[23] See order of October 25, 1940, below, p. 503.
[24] Order of August 27, 1940, below, p. 501.
[25] Koht, *op. cit.*, p. 142.
[26] See Annex 2 to the present chapter.
[27] See below, p. 498.

by him or his councillors,[28] whereupon the Supreme Court again stated that it could not adopt this point of view, reiterating its former statement that under the Norwegian Constitution the courts have the duty of testing the validity of laws and administrative orders, and adding that in its opinion the courts may, during a military occupation, test the validity under international law of decrees which are issued by the organs of the occupying power.[29] Such being the considered opinion of the Court, it further stated that its members felt themselves unable, in the light of the views expressed by the Reich Commissioner, to remain in office, and they accordingly resigned on December 23, 1940.[30]

ANNEX 1[31]

CORRESPONDENCE BETWEEN THE PRESIDENTIAL BOARD OF THE STORTING AND THE NORWEGIAN GOVERNMENT[32]

(a) *Letter from the Presidential Board of the Storting to H. M. the King of Norway, June 27, 1940*

After Oslo and the surrounding districts had been occupied by German troops on April 9, and the following days, and Hr. Vidkun Quisling, in the absence of the Government, had considered himself entitled to form a Government, the necessity of having an order established which secured the population against unnecessary sufferings occurred to Norwegians of all occupations and classes of society in the occupied territory. For this reason the Administrative Council was appointed, with the approval of the German occupation authorities, on April 15 to conduct the civil administration in the occupied territories. An attempt was made beforehand to get into communication with Your Majesty to have this order approved. When this did not succeed, the Supreme Court considered that it ought to undertake the nomination of the Council. This step helped in creating orderly conditions and has given the population such security as has been possible under the existing circumstances.

After the whole country was occupied by German troops and the King and Government had left the country the question arose of changing this arrangement. The members of the Presidential Board of the Storting who have been able to meet, were therefore assembled in Oslo on June 14 together with representatives of the four great political parties and the workers' trade union organization, and held discussions, in some of which the Administrative Council took part. On the basis of these discussions between the above representatives the following arrangement was concluded with the German authorities:

"Since the King and his Government are outside Norway and are therefore prevented from carrying out the functions imposed upon them by the Constitution,

[28] Koht, *op. cit.*, p. 179.
[29] Letter of December 12, 1940, in Annex 2 to the present chapter.
[30] *Ibid.* See also Curtis, *op. cit.*, p. 14.
[31] The texts of the documents printed in annexes 1 and 2 to this chapter are reproduced from translations printed in Curtis, *Norway and the War—September 1939–December 1940*, *op. cit.*, pp. 129–34, 144–45. The author is indebted to the Royal Institute of International Affairs and to the Oxford University Press for permission to include these translations in the present volume.
[32] Texts from *Ny Norsk Kvitbok*.

the Presidential Board of the Storting regards it as its duty to the country and people to nominate a National Council (*Riksraad*).

"The Storting is therefore being summoned to give its consent to this step and to reach further agreement about the authority of the National Council as regards the administration of the country. The Presidential Board of the Storting is laying before the Government proposals to include the following resolutions:

"I. The authority which was given to the Nygaardsvold Government at the meeting of April 9 is no longer valid.

"II. The Nygaardsvold Government can no longer be recognized as a Government.

"III. Since the King is outside the frontiers of the country he is not in a position to exercise his constitutional functions.

"Note: on this point the Presidential Board reports that in consideration of the situation it has asked the King to resign his constitutional functions for himself and his House.

"IV. The National Council takes over until further notice the business of the Government and the King's constitutional functions. A new Parliamentary election is postponed till after the conclusion of peace, while it is an instruction to the National Council to arrange a new election as soon as conditions permit, but at latest three months after the conclusion of peace.

"V. The members of the Storting who at present are abroad shall not be summoned during the rest of the period of the Storting's functions and shall be given no opportunity to take part in its meetings.

"VI. Until a new election the National Council has authority, in conformity with Point IV, to take all decisions which are required for the good of the country.

"VII. Norway's constitutional form of government as a monarchy shall still continue in the future."

As will be understood, it is a condition of this arrangement that the King resigns for himself and his House his constitutional functions. And out of consideration for the prosperity of the people and the future of the country we address, painful as it may be felt by Norwegian minds, an urgent prayer to Your Majesty to accede to our request on this point.

Trusting that Your Majesty will understand our action, we ask to have a report of Your Majesty's decision by July 12 at latest.

With deep respect,

MAGNUS NILSSEN, GABRIEL MOSEID, P. THORVIK, NERI VALEN, IVAR LYKKE (added to the Presidential Board by the Conservative Group).

(*b*) *Reply from H. M. the King of Norway to the Presidential Board of the Storting, London, July 3, 1940* [33]

I have received a communication of June 27, 1940, from the Storting's Presidential Board, and have with the full realization of my personal responsibility and of the seriousness of the situation conscientiously considered the resolution so fateful for our country which is dealt with in the letter of the Presidential Board.

I came to Norway in 1905 on an invitation from the Norwegian people, and I have in the years that have passed sought to the best of my ability to fulfil the duties which were thus imposed upon me.

My new Fatherland became infinitely precious to me, and I became bound to the Norwegian people by intimate ties. My motto, "All for Norway", has always been

[33] *Ny Norsk Kvitbok.*

and still is the guide of my actions, and if I could be persuaded at this time that I should best serve my people by resigning my royal task, or if I could be sure that behind the Storting's Presidential Board in this matter there was a majority of the Norwegian people, I would—however deeply it would pain me to be separated from Norway—comply with the request that the Presidential Board has addressed to me. I see from the letter of the Presidential Board that the proposal which the Presidential Board has thought of laying before the Storting has been arrived at through an agreement with the German occupation authorities in Norway. It is thus not an expression of a free Norwegian decision, but the result of a compulsion exercised by foreign military occupation.

It appears further from the letter that those members of the Storting who have evaded this compulsion by taking up their abode outside the frontiers of Norway are not to have an opportunity to take part in the meetings which are to come to a decision on the proposal in question.

The Storting in 1814 maintained an entirely opposite principle, since it refused to recognize the mandate of those members of the Storting who came from districts occupied by foreign military power. It founded itself on the logical consideration that such an occupation must fetter the freedom of decision of the members: *now* the representatives—including even the President of the Storting—who still retain their freedom of decision are to be excluded from the Storting, while those who are living under the pressure of foreign power are alone to decide the fate of the country.

I should be failing in my constitutional duties by accepting a decision made by a Storting summoned under such conditions.

In Point III of the Presidential Board's proposal it is said, "Since the King is outside the frontiers of the country he is not in a position to exercise his constitutional functions." Section 11 of the Norwegian Constitution provides expressly that the King can be as much as six months outside the country without the consent of the Storting, and *with* such consent still longer. If the King is abroad on *active service* the provision in Section 41 of the Constitution suggests that special consent is on the whole not required.

At the meeting of the Storting at Elverum on April 9, 1940, the President, with the unanimous approval of the Storting, said that the King and the Government, if it should be necessary out of consideration for a free and independent Government, should be able to take up their abode outside the country, without any limit of time being suggested in this connexion. There is thus no constitutional foundation for the assertion that I cannot carry out the task which the Constitution lays upon me.

The present Norwegian Government under the leadership of Prime Minister Nygaardsvold was nominated on March 19, 1935; the composition of this Government has later undergone a number of changes, the latest being the appointment of Ministers belonging to other political parties than that which the Government originally came from. Thus a National Government has been created, which has had the unanimous confidence of the Storting, expressly recognized by its vote in its meeting of April 9 of this year.

In accordance with Norwegian constitutional practice, the Storting is fully entitled to revoke a vote of confidence which has been given; but in such case this must be done by a Storting which acts with full constitutional freedom, and has not been arbitrarily deprived of a number of its members. Neither of these conditions is fulfilled by the assembly which the Presidential Board is now to summon.

In the agreement between the Presidential Board and the German occupation authorities it is said that neither can the Norwegian Government carry out its constitutional functions, since it is outside Norway. I and the Government have no higher wish than to be able to exercise our functions within the country; it is merely foreign power which has forced the Government, together with myself, to leave the country. We have done this in conformity with the resolution of the Storting, in order so far as possible to preserve a free and independent control of the Norwegian kingdom.

If such conditions could be created in Norway that I and the Government could return to the country to continue our activities in full liberty, it would be done immediately. The obvious condition for this must be that all foreign military forces should leave the country. The arrangement, however, with the German authorities on which the Presidential Board has come to an agreement assumes the continued maintenance of the German occupation, and in these circumstances I see no possibility for the existence of a free Government of Norway within the frontiers of Norway.

When in the proposal of the Presidential Board it is remarked that fresh elections to the Storting can first be held "after the conclusion of peace", it is thereby assumed that Norway will not come to enjoy peace before the war between the Great Powers is carried to a conclusion. The Presidential Board is doubtless right in this, but that being so it is also clear that the proposed arrangement does not help the Norwegian people to the peace for which it so deeply longs.

Nor does the agreement with the German occupation authorities serve to promote several of the economic interests which are so important to the welfare of our people. I recall that the German demands to the Norwegian Government, at the time of the attack on the country on the night of April 9, involved *inter alia* a complete economic blockade of Norway in relation to all Western countries in and outside Europe. And important economic interests would, under a new Government such as is proposed by the appointment of a new "National Council", come to suffer even greater damage than at present, since it could not take charge of the vitally important interests abroad which are now looked after by the present Government.

I will further indicate an aspect of the question at issue which is not touched on in the letter of the Presidential Board, but which throws a vivid light on the arrangement now in question. I refer to the scope of the authority which the proposed National Council is to have. I will say no more of the fact, manifest to every one, that the National Council in practice will have to follow German directions as long as the German occupation of Norway lasts; but I will emphasize what follows from the resolution published at this time by the German Government in Berlin, that no foreign States are to have diplomatic representation in Oslo, and that the foreign policy of Norway will be conducted by the Department of Foreign Affairs in Berlin.

This clearly means that the new National Council in Oslo does not represent an independent kingdom, but merely a German dependency. An abdication on my part would therefore not even formally be to the advantage of an independent Government in Norway; the National Council would not acquire all the constitutional functions appertaining to the King. I cannot see that the Presidential Board of the Storting has any constitutional basis whatsoever for modifying the lawful decisions of the Storting which have hitherto been taken. It is on the contrary quite evident that the whole of the proposed arrangement conflicts with the Constitution.

I cannot see that I should be acting in the interests of the country by submitting to the demand addressed to me by the Presidential Board, whereby I should approve an arrangement which conflicts with the Constitution of Norway, and which it is sought to impose by force upon the Norwegian people. By doing so I should abandon the principle which has guided my actions throughout all my reign, viz.: to keep myself strictly within the framework of the Constitution.

The liberty and independence of the Norwegian people are to me the first commandment of the Constitution, and I consider I am obeying this commandment and watching over the interests of the Norwegian people best by adhering to the position and the task which a free people gave me in 1905.

ANNEX 2[34]

CORRESPONDENCE BETWEEN THE NORWEGIAN SUPREME COURT AND THE DEPARTMENT OF JUSTICE

(*a*) *Letter from the Norwegian Supreme Court to the Department of Justice, November 19, 1940*[35]

The Department of Justice has, on November 14, 1940, prepared an Ordinance giving the Constituted State Councillor[36] authority, *inter alia*, to appoint and dismiss members of Conciliation Commissions, and to remove from the panels jurors, expert witnesses and assessors, and to appoint others. This Ordinance applies equally to civil and criminal proceedings. It gives the Constituted State Councillor the opportunity of interfering in the composition of the Courts of Justice in a way which is in manifest conflict with the principles on which the constitution of our courts is founded. The Ordinance exceeds the limits of the authority enjoyed by the Constituted State Councillor as representative of the power in occupation, according to the Hague Convention of 1907, with the regulations which it contains for the conduct of war on land, especially Article 43, according to which the authority in occupation is to "respect the laws applying in the country unless absolute impediments exist". The Ordinance also exceeds the authority given to the Constituted State Councillors by paragraph 3 of the Reich Commissioner's Ordinance of September 28, together with paragraph 3 of the *Führer's* Ordinance of April 24,[37] which lays down that laws heretofore valid remain in force, so long as this is consistent with the occupation. The independence of the Courts is prescribed in the Constitution, and is expressly recognized in accordance with international law, in the Reich Commissioner's ordinance of September 28, paragraph 5. If the Ordinance should be carried into effect it would have fateful effects on the administration of justice. To maintain this independence is of fundamental importance to the security of justice. As the highest representative of the judicial power, the Supreme Court must request that the Department's Ordinance shall not be carried into effect.

(*b*) *Letter from the Norwegian Supreme Court to the Department of Justice, December 12, 1940*[38]

The Reich Commissioner on December 3 sent the Chief Justice of the Supreme Court a letter, copy of which is attached.[39] The letter was received on December 7. After the Supreme Court had sent the Department of Justice its letter of December 9 regarding the Ordinance concerning the age limit, the members of the Court considered the Reich Commissioner's letter. Judges Broch and Stang were not able to be present. As will be seen, the Reich Commissioner has stated that neither the Supreme Court nor other Norwegian Courts can adopt an attitude towards the question of the validity of directions issued by the Reich Commissioner, or by the Constituted State Councillors by virtue of his Ordinance of September 28, since it is exclusively the province of the Reich Commissioner to settle what regulations can serve to promote public order and the interests of public life in Norway. We wish to maintain that the Courts according to Norwegian constitutional law have the duty to test the validity of laws and administrative Ordinances. During a military occupation the Courts in our opinion may in the same way take up an attitude as to the validity in international law of Ordinances

[34] Texts from Curtis, *op. cit.*, pp. 144–45. [35] *Norsk Tidend*, December 27, 1940.
[36] I.e., the Head of the Department appointed by Herr Terboven.—Translator's note.
[37] See below, p. 498.—Ed. [38] *Norsk Tidend*, December 27, 1940.
[39] Not available.

which are issued by the organs of the occupying power, in settling questions of law which come before them in a case, to such an extent as international law allows. We cannot follow the view of the authority of the Courts which the Reich Commissioner's letter expresses, without acting in conflict with our duties as judges of the Norwegian Supreme Court. We therefore find that we are unable to continue in our office. We anticipate a further conference with the Department of Justice on the subject of the date for our resignation.

CHAPTER XXIV

POLAND

Poland was dismembered by the occupant in the following way:

Western and northern Poland, as well as the Białystok area in the east, were incorporated into Germany.

The Government General was established from territories of central and southern Poland.

Other eastern territories were made part of the General Commissariat of White Russia, and the southeastern province of Wolhynia and parts of the province Polesie were incorporated into the Reich Commissariat of the Ukraine.

I. Polish Incorporated Territories [1]

ADMINISTRATION

By an order of October 8, 1939,[2] the western parts of Poland were incorporated into Germany. The following administrative units were created:

1. The Reich district Danzig-West Prussia, embracing the Free City of Danzig and the Polish districts of Pomerania, Lipno, and Ripin, as well as the German district of Marienwerder (formerly a part of the province of East Prussia) and some counties belonging formerly to the province of West Prussia.

2. The Reich district Wartheland, embracing the Polish province of Poznań (Posen), and the Polish city of Łódź (called now Litzmannstadt) with surrounding areas.

3. The northern Polish district of Ciechanów was incorporated into the province of East Prussia. The eastern Polish district of Suwalki was also incorporated into East Prussia as part of the county of Gumbinen. The Polish industrial city of Białystok, with large surrounding areas, as well as most of the Polish district Grodno, was attached to East Prussia as a separate administrative unit (*Regierungsbezirk*).

4. The industrial city of Katowice with a large surrounding area and also the Cieszyń district were incorporated into the district of Silesia.

Every Reich district (*Gau*) is administered by a Reich governor (*Reichsstatthalter*) and is divided into government districts, which in turn are divided into counties and municipalities. The governor is at the same time head of the Nazi Party in each district (*Gauleiter*).[3]

[1] Referred to in German legislation as incorporated Eastern Territories (*Eingegliederte Ostgebiete*) because of their geographical position in regard to Germany.

[2] See below, p. 506.

[3] See above, chapter on "Administration."

The office of the Reich governor is divided into the following sections: General Financial and Organizational Matters; Public Health and Hygiene; Education, Instruction, Furtherance of Cultural and Communal Life; Agriculture, Settlement, Reallocation of Realty and Waterways; Economics and Labor; Forestry and Hunting; Private and Public Construction.[4]

To the office of the Reich governor is attached the ranking S.S. and Police Chief, who is at the same time the agent of the Reich Commissioner for the Strengthening of Germanism. This officer is mainly responsible for the destruction of Polish nationhood and its supplanting by German elements.

The Reich Minister of the Interior is designated as the responsible agency for the reorganization of the incorporated territories.[5]

The incorporated areas are subject to an especially severe régime, involving genocide for the Polish population. On short notice Poles were removed from their homes [6] and replaced by German settlers. Institutions of Polish administration were abolished and replaced by German institutions. Polish cultural institutions were closed, and the German language was made the language of education in the schools.

THE LEGISLATIVE SETUP

The Reich Minister of the Interior was designated to introduce German law in the incorporated territories. He in turn has delegated some of his powers to the governors and even to the police.

The Reich Minister of the Interior has gradually introduced a great body of German statutes in these territories, starting with the Conscription Law for military service, the Nuremberg Laws, and the Four-Year Plan. A great many German decrees were declared applicable in the territory.[7]

The replacement of civil law was difficult because in these incorporated areas there is the following variety of civil codes: In the districts which

[4] Second order of November 2, 1939, below, p. 507.

[5] See decree of October 8, 1939, below, p. 507.

[6] See above, chapter on "Genocide."

[7] Already in 1940 the following decrees had been introduced: administration of economy (*Reichsgesetzblatt*, June 8, 1940, No. 120); regulations regarding the common weal in housing (*ibid.*, June 28, 1940, No. 126); introduction of family alimony statutes (*ibid.*, July 4, 1940, No. 119); regulations concerning production of energy (power) (*ibid.*, July 6, 1940, No. 121); administration of contributions to the Cattlemen's Association (*ibid.*, July 9, 1940, No. 129); introduction of air-raid prevention measures (*ibid.*, July 18, 1940, No. 125); introduction of real estate taxes (*ibid.*, July 18, 1940, No. 132); carrier doves (*ibid.*, July 13, 1940, No. 128); emergency service (labor service) (*ibid.*, July 14, 1940, No. 132); determination of damages (*ibid.*, July 25, 1940, No. 134); combatting contagious diseases (*ibid.*, July 28, 1940, No. 135); vinegar brandy and vinegar production (*ibid.*, July 29, 1940, No. 147); introduction of the police regulations of the Reich Minister (*ibid.*, July 31, 1940, No. 137); public seed management (*ibid.*, July 31, 1940, No. 139); introduction of the German medicine book (*ibid.*, June 8, 1940, No. 141); training for the professional forestry service (*ibid.*, August 7, 1940, No. 140); introduction of mining law (*ibid.*, August 10, 1940, No. 143); transportation of police officers (*ibid.*, August 13, 1940, No. 143); regulations concerning chimney sweepers (*ibid.*, August 13, 1940, No. 149); manpower (*Arbeitseinsatz*) (*ibid.*, August 13, 1940, No. 150); promotion of tourism (*ibid.*, August 19, 1940, No. 149); protection of trade (*ibid.*, August 20, 1940, No. 149); diseases of animals and protection of animals (*ibid.*, August 29, 1940, No. 157); meetings and meeting localities (*ibid.*, August 31, 1940, No. 161); protection of labor (*ibid.*, August 5, 1940, No. 164).

belonged to Germany before 1918, there is still in force a great part of the German Civil Code (*Bürgerliches Gesetzbuch*). In other parts which did not belong to Germany before 1918 but which formed the so-called "Congress Poland," the Code Napoléon was and is still in force. In the districts of Suwalki and Białystok, the Russian Civil Code of 1864 is still in effect.

THE JUDICIARY

The decree of June 13, 1940,[8] has introduced in the incorporated eastern areas the German basic law on organization of courts (*Gerichtsverfassungsgesetz*), as well as subsidiary laws concerning the judiciary such as: the law on the jurisdiction of courts, with respect to changes in the division of courts, of December 6, 1933;[9] the decree concerning a uniform organization of courts of March 20, 1935;[10] the law concerning the distribution of functions in the courts of November 24, 1937;[11] the decree concerning qualifications for the office of judge, prosecuting attorney, notary, and attorney, of January 4, 1939;[12] decree concerning preparation for the office of judge and of prosecuting attorney of May 16, 1939;[13] decree concerning certain measures in the organization of courts and the administration of justice, of September 1, 1939;[14] and the implementing orders issued on September 8 and October 4, 1939;[15] decree concerning simplification of the legal examinations of September 2, 1939.[16] Polish courts have ceased to exist. German judges have been appointed; and Polish judges are used only as clerks in the transitional period for translating Polish records in cases still pending in the courts. By the introduction of the decree concerning qualifications for attorneys of January 4, 1939, Polish barristers were practically barred from the courts.

CURRENCY AND FOREIGN EXCHANGE

By decree of November 22, 1939,[17] the Reichsmark was declared the sole legal tender. By the same decree the German Treasury and Reichsbank offices which had been established in these territories, and other delegated agencies, were directed to exchange the notes of the Bank Polski and the Polish Government coins for all residents at a rate of exchange of two zlotys for one Reichsmark.

SEQUESTRATION AND CONFISCATION

According to the decree of September 17, 1940,[18] the property of Polish citizens was subject to sequestration, trustee administration, and confiscation. This does not apply to the property of persons who have acquired German nationality. Sequestration *must* be ordered in regard to the property of Jews and those persons who have fled or are not merely temporarily

[8] See below, p. 510. [9] *Reichsgesetzblatt*, I, p. 1037. [10] *Blatt*, p. 403.
[11] *Ibid.*, p. 1286. [12] *Ibid.*, p. 5. [13] *Ibid.*, p. 917. [14] *Ibid.*, p. 1658.
[15] *Ibid.*, pp. 1703, 1994. [16] *Ibid.*, p. 1606. [17] See below, p. 521. [18] See below, p. 511.

absent. Sequestration may be ordered if the property is required "for the public welfare," particularly in the interests of Reich defense or the strengthening of Germanism, or if the owners had immigrated, after October 1, 1918, into the territory which had belonged to the Reich until the end of the war of 1914–18. Excluded from such sequestration are movable objects for personal use, and cash, bank or savings bank balances, or securities of less than one thousand Reichsmarks. Trustee administration may be ordered in regard to all property that is subject to sequestration, "if orderly administration requires it." The legal transactions of such administrators are limited by Section 7 of the above-mentioned decree.[19] Sequestrated property may be confiscated for the benefit of the Reich, if the public welfare, particularly Reich defense or the strengthening of Germanism, so requires. If a person maintains that he is a German citizen and therefore his property is not subject to sequestration or management by a trustee, the procedure must be suspended immediately, pending a decision by the competent German authorities.

All measures concerning sequestration, administration, and confiscation coming under this decree are carried out through a special trustee agency (*Haupttreuhandstelle Ost*), under the authority of the Commissioner for the Four-Year Plan; and, as regards agriculture, through the Reich Commissioner for Strengthening Germanism. The trustee agency appoints administrators or trustees for the administration—and subsequently the liquidation—of the properties seized from Poles and Jews. The procedure of expropriating the property of Poles and Jews is considered as a primary matter of policy. Severe penalties are imposed for interfering with such procedure. "If the culprit acts from opposition to the new political order, or if the case is particularly serious for some other reason, then the death penalty shall be imposed."[20]

ECONOMY AND TAXATION

The Four-Year Plan has been introduced in the incorporated territories by orders of October 30, 1939, and July 9, 1940.[21] These territories have thus been integrated into the economy of the Greater German Reich. Poles have been in great part expelled from economic life, such as trade, handicrafts, banking, and especially from agriculture. Special divisions in the office of the respective Reich governors in the Polish incorporated territories, such as the Division of Agriculture, Settlement, Reallocation of Realty and Waterways, and the Division of Economics and Labor, are responsible for uprooting Poles from economic life and putting Germans in their place. The colonization policy is being carried out chiefly by the first of the two divisions above mentioned in connection with its functions relating to settle-

[19] See below, p. 512. [20] See Section 20 of the decree, below, p. 516.
[21] See below, pp. 521, 522.

ment and reallocation of realty, as well as by the Special Agent of the Reich Commissioner for the Strengthening of Germanism.

To induce Germans to settle in the Polish territories, numerous tax privileges were granted to them.[22] An order concerning tax abatement was issued on December 9, 1940, introducing a great number of essential tax exemptions for German nationals and persons of German origin in the incorporated Eastern Territories. This order begins with a blunt statement of its purpose: "In the effort to establish and promote Germanism (*Deutschtum*) in the incorporated Eastern Territories through taxation measures, as well as by other means, we order. . . ."[23] Thus, Germans with an income of 25,000 Reichsmarks or less may deduct 3,000 Reichsmarks from their income when calculating and paying income taxes. The exemption of 3,000 Reichsmarks is increased by 300 Reichsmarks for each minor child belonging to the household. The regular tax exemptions provided for in the German property tax law are tripled for Germans. Germans are released from real estate acquisition tax, while a person selling property to a German is released from the sales tax. There are also provisions for release from inheritance and gift taxes if the acquisitor is a German. During the calendar years 1940–50, German retailers and partnerships may claim exemption from income tax on as much as 50 per cent of the net profit or 20 per cent of the gross profit of the enterprises. The corporation tax is lowered for Germans to 20 per cent of incomes not exceeding 300,000 Reichsmarks, and 30 per cent of incomes above that amount. Property of Germans which belongs to a farm and lumber business or to an industrial enterprise or plant is to be taken into account in the assessment of property tax only in so far as its value exceeds 250,000 Reichsmarks. By these tax exemptions and many others, the German settlers were immediately placed in a stronger and more advantageous position than the Poles, who were destined, in accordance with the occupant's plans, to suffer a general liquidation.

II. The Government General

ADMINISTRATION

The Government General of Poland was established by the decree of the Führer of October 12, 1939.[24] The Governor General has the title of Reich Minister and is responsible directly to the Führer. The headquarters of the government are in Cracow. The office is divided into six sections (chancellery, legislation, territorial organization, personnel, organizational matters, business) and fifteen divisions (finance, economy, interior, labor, agriculture and food, justice, enlightenment and propaganda, foreign exchange, educa-

[22] As to transfer of Polish population and German colonization, see above, chapter on "Genocide."

[23] See order of December 9, 1940, below, p. 516.

[24] See below, p. 522.

tion, health service, building, forestry, post, railroads, and trustee administration).[25] In addition there is a liaison office for relations with the army and with the administration of the Four-Year Plan. The Chief of Police coordinates his activities with those of the office of the Governor General.

The Government General is divided into the following districts: Cracow, Warsaw, Radom, and Lublin; and after the occupation of Lwów in 1941 (up to which time it had been held by the Russians), an additional district was formed consisting of Lwów and Eastern Galicia. Each district is under a governor. The title of "Governor" is, however, complimentary, so that a district under a governor is not called "government." The districts in turn are divided into counties and municipalities. The municipal administration is in the hands of mayors, the Governor General appointing those officials in communities of over 20,000 inhabitants, while in smaller communities they are appointed by the governor of the district. In communities of less than 10,000 inhabitants, the mayor selects five advisers, and in communities of over 10,000 inhabitants he selects ten advisers to assist him in the administration of the municipalities. The district governor may in his discretion appoint a special commissioner to act with the mayor. This commissioner supervises the community, being empowered to suspend, change, or invalidate any order of the mayor and to issue orders of his own. The community may not contract debts without the previous consent of the Governor General.

COURTS

There are two main types of courts, German courts and Polish courts. Germans may be tried only by German courts, but Poles are regularly tried by Polish courts, unless a case against the interests of the German Reich or of a German is involved.

1. *German Courts.* German courts of general jurisdiction function as follows:

(*a*) German courts of original jurisdiction try criminal cases, if one of the parties is a German, or if the offense involves "the security and authority of the German Reich and people," or if the offense was committed on the premises of a German authority or in connection with activities of German authorities. The German courts have jurisdiction in civil cases if a German is involved or if the case pertains to matters concerning German commercial records.

(*b*) German Superior Courts try, mainly, appeals from the court of original jurisdiction. They function in Cracow, Rzeszów, Lublin, and Lwów.[26]

(*c*) German Special Courts. Every district has one special court, whose jurisdiction is defined in every case by orders and decrees promulgated by

[25] See Adami, "Die Gesetzgebungsarbeit im Generalgouvernement," in *Deutsches Recht*, Vol. 16 (1940), p. 605.

[26] See decree of February 19, 1940, below, p. 526.

the Governor General. For example, they try cases involving offenses against banking, against the order of confiscation of private property, against the order requiring Jews to wear special signs, etc.

2. *Polish Courts.* The jurisdiction of Polish courts is permitted with respect to those cases which do not come within the jurisdiction of a German court.[27] These courts apply Polish law. The types of Polish courts which are allowed to deal with judicial business are municipal courts, district courts, and appellate courts. The Supreme Court of Poland is not functioning.

SEQUESTRATION OF PRIVATE PROPERTY

A comparison of the decree on sequestration of private property issued in the Government General [28] with the analogous decree issued in the incorporated territories [29] is worth while. In the decree on sequestration in the incorporated areas, one of the chief reasons given for confiscations and sequestrations is the "strengthening of Germanism." The decree in the Government General states that sequestration may be ordered in connection with the performance of tasks "serving the public interest." In particular, in the Government General property may be liquidated because it is "financially unremunerative" or "anti-social." Since the occupant has the right to define these terms, he has likewise the opportunity to use this decree for purposes of loot and political pressure. Under both decrees, sequestrated property may be given to trustees for administration. As sequestration is a mass phenomenon in the Government General, a special Trustee Administration (*Treuhandstelle*) has been organized. The decree for the Government General provides that when the trustees take over property, the rights of third parties in the sequestrated property are suspended. However, the trustee may claim debts owed to the property by third parties. By this decree, also, abandoned property may be seized, in which case the rights of third parties abate, although it should be noted that the director of the Trustee Administration has the right to grant exemptions from such abatement. This power is given to the German authorities as a weapon for political purposes. The same tendency is displayed by the provision that compensation may be granted for losses arising from the implementing of the decree, although legal processes are precluded. These provisions mean in effect that the interested person may always hope to get some compensation in consideration for services to the occupant.

TAXATION AND ECONOMY

Another source of loot is taxation. Despite the economic distress of the inhabitants, taxes were raised. Thus the Polish property tax for the fiscal

[27] See decree of February 19, 1940, below, p. 529.
[28] Decree of January 24, 1940, below, p. 531.
[29] Decree of September 17, 1940, below, p. 511.

year 1940 was increased by 50 per cent,[30] and registration fees were raised to 200 per cent,[31] in comparison with the pre-invasion rates. A new tax was introduced, namely, a head tax, which communities are required to collect from their inhabitants.[32]

The occupant is also drawing heavily in other ways on the meager finances of the population. The budget for Poland, a country of 35,000,000 inhabitants, amounted in normal times to around 2,500,000,000 zlotys. An order concerning the budget of the Government General for the fiscal year 1940 [33] shows that the Government General alone had a budget of 1,004,004,440 zlotys for a population which then numbered hardly a third [34] of the former population of Poland and which was deprived of normal conditions of life and income.

The Four-Year Plan was introduced into the Government General by the decree of October 12, 1939.[35] The Commissioner for the Four-Year Plan, together with other German authorities, is especially called upon to "make the arrangements required for the planning of German life and the German economic sphere."[36] Within the framework of the Four-Year Plan, offices for the control of commodities were created and practically all raw materials and agricultural products were seized and administered by German authorities. Among the offices thus established were raw material control boards such as (1) an office for iron and steel, to control the production, utilization, and trade in these products; (2) an office for coal, to control the production, distribution, storing, and consumption of coal; (3) an office for metals, to control the production, distribution, storing, and consumption of metals; (4) an office for leather and furs, to control the trade in hides and furs.[37] The most important Polish industries were taken over by a specially created corporation presided over by Göring and called "Göring A.G. Werke."

The anti-German attitude of the Polish population led the occupant to use special devices to get agricultural products from the Polish farmers. The Germans began first of all to destroy private trade, with Polish currency as their first target. A decree was published inviting every Pole to deposit for six months with certain banks under German control all Polish currency with the exception of two hundred zlotys. After the six months had elapsed, the money was to be stamped and returned to the depositors. There was also a provision that the money which was not deposited should lose its value. The Germans knew that the Poles mistrusted them and would not deposit their money. There were, indeed, very few deposits, and after six

[30] Decree of March 16, 1940, below, p. 540.
[31] Decree of February 14, 1940, below, p. 540.
[32] Decree of June 27, 1940, below, p. 540. [33] Order of March 3, 1941, below, p. 541.
[34] This was prior to the enlargement of the Government General through the inclusion of Eastern Galicia. In 1941 and 1942 the budget was more than doubled.
[35] See the decree, below, p. 522.
[36] As to labor, Jews, and other topics, see respective chapters in Part I, above.
[37] Adami, *op. cit.*, p. 613.

months the greater part of the Polish currency in circulation was destroyed. With the destruction of currency no trade could be carried on. Then the Germans proceeded toward their immediate goal. There were in Poland special cooperative agricultural societies for trade with the peasants. The Germans took these societies under their control, and provided them with manufactured goods for the needs of the peasants. Any peasant could buy all he wanted upon presentation of a certificate from one of the cooperative associations testifying that he had sold a part of his agricultural products to that association. Through the destruction of Polish currency and through the lack of manufactured goods in the towns, private trade was destroyed, the peasants being compelled to trade with the German-controlled agricultural associations. Thus the Germans came into control of the agricultural products of the country.[38]

EDUCATION AND CULTURAL MATTERS

Education has been completely reorganized. It is controlled by a special section under the Governor General in Cracow. Corresponding sections for education have been created under every district governor.

The immediate administration of schools is directed by an educational council in the several cities and counties. The officials of the school administration must, however, be Germans, although the city and county educational councils may appoint Poles and Ukrainians as school supervisors for a period of two years.

German and Polish children are being educated in different schools. German children may attend only German schools and be taught only by German teachers, whereas Polish children may attend only Polish schools. In places where there are at least ten German school children a German school must be opened.[39] Polish grammar and professional schools have been to a certain extent reestablished. Private Polish schools, however, require a license from the district governor before they may be reopened.

The budget as announced by the Government General provides a comparatively large amount for educational purposes. This does not mean, however, that the occupant is doing much for Polish liberal education but rather that trade schools are being favored in order to prepare Polish youth for physical work and to develop in them technical skills. Such an educational policy is in compliance with the general plan to use the Polish population mainly as a source of manpower.[39a]

The universities and liberal art schools were closed. Libraries, labora-

[38] *German Organization of Distribution in Poland,* "Documents relating to the Administration of Occupied Countries in Eastern Europe," No. 3, published by Polish Information Center (New York), pp. 6 ff.; Lemkin, "The Legal Framework of Totalitarian Control over Foreign Economies," cited above.

[39] "Ein Jahr Generalgouvernement," *Deutsches Recht* (1940), p. 1797.

[39a] See above, chapter on "Labor."

tories, and art galleries, as well as paintings belonging to individuals, were carried into Germany.

In the year 1940, on the birthday of the Führer, the Governor General opened, at the premises of the Polish University of Cracow, an Institute for German Eastern Work (*Institut für Deutsche Ostarbeit*). According to the by-laws of this institute, its main task is to continue and increase the hitherto completed German research work in the East, to do research in actual problems of the Government General and to publicize the results of the research. The Governor General stated in his opening speech that "the establishment of the Institute means the resumption of the historical mission that Germanism is to fulfill in this place" and the "restitution of all that which the Poles took away from the German spirit and German influences in this place." [40]

RESISTANCE

From the first days of the occupation the Polish population has displayed an attitude of stubborn and uncompromising resistance to the occupant. The Germans not only failed to organize a puppet or sub cabinet government in Poland as they partially succeeded in doing in Western Europe, but they feared this resistance so much as not to allow Polish agencies in the middle brackets of administration. The services of Poles are used only in the lowest branches of administrative agencies in the cities and communes. Occupied Poland is covered by a network of Gestapo and S.S. units whose business it is to trace Polish patriotic activities, particularly the strong underground movement. This movement is headed by a Directorate of Civilian Resistance which directs the underground press and propaganda as well as organized acts of sabotage and even open hostilities carried on by the units of a secretly organized National Army. The Directorate of Civilian Resistance has organized special Polish tribunals which are trying Germans and occasional Polish traitors. The sentences are issued in the name of the Polish Republic and they are normally communicated to the culprit before the penalty is executed, even if he is tried *in absentia*.[40a]

[40] It is important to state that German cultural influences were never significant in the Polish University City of Cracow. The University of Cracow, one of the oldest in Europe, was founded in 1364, and was a spiritual center for central and southern Europe at that time. German students used to come to this university to study because education in Germany at that time was on a low level. The following is a statement from an American author about the University: "In 1364 the University of Krakow was founded, its formulation being strengthened by a large gift from Queen Jadwiga just at the end of the century. It quickly rose to such importance as a centre of learning and culture that in 1416 it had sufficient standing to justify it in 'forwarding an expression of its views in connection with the deliberations of the Council of Constance.' By the end of the 15th Century it 'was in high repute as a school of both astronomical and humanistic studies,' in these capacities helping form the mind of the great Polish astronomer Copernicus, who entered the university in 1491."—Paul Super, *The Polish Tradition* (London: George Allen & Unwin, Ltd., 1939), p. 94.

[40a] The following is a sample of such a verdict: "In the name of the Polish Republic! On February 12, 1943, the Special Tribunal in Warsaw, after having considered the case of Her-

The distrust and the fear of patriotic conspiracy go so far that no opportunity for Poles to assemble, even for social events, is allowed. On April 9, 1941,[41] an order was published introducing a general prohibition of dancing in the Government General. The prohibition is absolute and no exceptions are made in the form of special permissions. It applies likewise to private parties. Only dance performances in public may be licensed.

III. The Eastern Polish Territories [42]

The eastern territories of Poland were disposed of and are administered in the following way: The city of Wilno, together with the western part of the province of Wilno, is administered as part of the General Commissariat of Lithuania.[43] Other territories between the pre-war Polish-Russian frontier and the area of Białystok (which was incorporated as a separate unit into East Prussia) are administered as part of the General Commissariat of White Russia. The southeastern Polish province of Wolhynia and the Southern part of the province of Polesie [44] are administered as part of the Commissariat for the Ukraine.[45]

---

man Gleist, chief of the Arbeitsamt (Labor Office) in Warsaw, born on July 2, 1901, in Berlin, and accused in 1942 in Warsaw (*a*) of being, as chief of the Arbeitsamt, the main organizer of the street raids and one of the promoters of the action to deport the Polish population to Germany, and of showing cruelty in the performance of his duties in relation to the Poles; (*b*) of taking advantage of his position and obtaining personal profit by threatening the persons involved with deportation to forced labor in Germany — has passed the following verdict: Herman Gleist, born on July 2, 1901, chief of the Arbeitsamt, is deemed guilty of the crimes of which he is accused and is condemned to the penalty of death."—*Tygodnik Polski*, 1943, Nr. 42, 43, 44.

[41] See decree of April 9, 1941, below, p. 555.

[42] The eastern Polish territories are to be distinguished from the incorporated Eastern Territories referred to in the German legislation.

[43] The Wilno area was occupied in September, 1939, and handed over to Lithuania by Russia in October, 1939. In June, 1941, the same area was occupied by Germany.

[44] For further details on the administration of these territories, see, in part, chapter on the Union of Soviet Socialist Republics, below, p. 232.

[45] The industrial city of Białystok with its surrounding area, as well as the province of Wolhynia, was occupied by Russia in September, 1939, and later on in June–July, 1941, was occupied by Germany in the course of the Russo-German war.

CHAPTER XXV

UNION OF SOVIET SOCIALIST REPUBLICS[1]

(Partially under German and Rumanian Occupation)

The Reich Ministry for the Territories Occupied in the East, which was created in Berlin shortly after the war with Russia started in June, 1941, extends its control not only to eastern Poland and the Baltic States, occupied in the course of the Russo-German war, but also to the territories of the U.S.S.R. to the east of the eastern borders of the Baltic States, Poland, and Rumania as they existed at the outbreak of the war in 1939. The part of Russia between the rivers Dniester and Lower Bug is under Rumanian occupation (see below).

ADMINISTRATION

The territories occupied in Russia are included partly in the General Commissariat for White Russia, headquarters of which are in Minsk, and partly in the Reich Commissariat for the Ukraine. Both commissariats include also Polish territories to the west of the Polish-Russian border as it existed at the outbreak of the war in 1939. The eastern parts of the Polish provinces (*województwa*) Nowogródek, Wilno, and Polesie were included in the General Commissariat for White Russia, and the main part of the Polish province of Łuck, as well as the southern part of the Polish province of Polesie, was included in the Reich Commissariat for the Ukraine.

The General Commissariat for White Russia forms part of the Reich Commissariat for the Ostland, which has its headquarters in Riga, and is supervised by the Ministry for the Territories Occupied in the East, with headquarters in Berlin. It consists of ten regional districts (*Landgebiete*), namely, Minsk-Land, Wilejka, Głębokie, Borisow, Słuck, Lida, Słonim, Baranowicze, Nowogródek, and Hancewicze. The first five districts are grouped in the general region Minsk (*Hauptgebiet Minsk*). The other five districts are grouped in the general region Baranowicze (*Hauptgebiet Baranowicze*).

The Reich Commissariat for the Ukraine, with headquarters in Równe, is divided into six general commissariats: Zitomir, Kiev, Nikolajev, Tshernigov, Dniepropetrovsk, and Crimea.[1a] It also is supervised by the Ministry for Occupied Territories in Berlin.

[1] See also chapter on the Baltic States, above, p. 117.
[1a] At the time this chapter is written the Russo-German front line is being moved westward, obviously necessitating changes in the administrative divisions.

The areas under administration by the General Commissariat for White Russia and the Reich Commissariat for the Ukraine are in the hands of German non-military administrators, while those areas to the east of these commissariats, approaching the zone of military operations, are in the hands of military commanders.

PROPERTY

In the territories occupied in Russia which were part of the U.S.S.R. in accordance with the frontier of 1939, the problem of private property presents various aspects. In the first stage of the occupation the occupant maintained completely the communistic status of ownership. The collective farms were continued. But since the leaders of these farms had fled with the Russian Army, the occupant was faced with serious problems because of lack of leadership in farming.[2] On the other hand, the farms were disorganized because of the scarcity of implements and sometimes even of manpower. The task of reorganizing and supervising agriculture in those areas was entrusted to German agricultural leaders (*Landwirtschaftsführer*) specially trained in Germany. In order to increase their authority, they were vested with some administrative powers, and with the right to punish farmers for not carrying out the agricultural program.

The occupant was reluctant to return to the system of private property in those areas for the following reasons: such a redistribution of property—especially of land property—would require capital, implements, and a great many technical and legal formalities (such as measurements and recording by courts), and difficulties would arise in tracing titles of former owners, particularly as to city property. The problem of finding criteria for establishing new property titles had also to be solved. In order to instil fear the German occupant relied largely on the principle of collective responsibility in Russian cities and farms, a principle which found its natural basis in the institution of collective ownership and work among the Russian people. If a collective farm, for example, failed to deliver its products, the occupant could punish collectively all the members of the farm.

However, apparently for propaganda purposes, a change in the forms of ownership was envisaged by the decree of Reich Minister Rosenberg issued on February 28, 1942,[3] which was designed to "guide the agricultural population back to individual farming." The decree states that collective farms (*kolhozy*) will be transformed into joint-farming establishments (*Gemeinwirtschaften*). The latter are considered, according to the decree, to

[2] It should be stated that in a collective farm (*kolhoz*) the leader plays an important rôle because of his special qualifications of professional skill and training in methods of organization.

[3] See "Occupied U.S.S.R.," *Free Europe*, Vol. 5, No. 63 (April 10, 1942), p. 124; see also Lazar Volin, "The 'New Agrarian Order' in Nazi-Invaded Russia," *Foreign Agriculture* (Washington: Department of Agriculture), April, 1943, p. 79.

be of a merely transitional nature. From these an individual farming system, combining, as the decree puts it, the principle of cooperative farming with that of individual farming, is to be developed.[4]

Thus far, the following three forms of agricultural organizations have been created by the occupant in the territories occupied in Russia proper:

(*a*) *The Joint-Farming Establishment* (Gemeinwirtschaft). The members of a joint-farming establishment are peasant farmers employed in the labor of plowing, sowing, and harvesting, and they receive wages. Full property rights in the small plots surrounding their houses are granted them, and individual cattle breeding is permitted. The difference between a joint-farming establishment and a collective farm is not of an essential nature, but several minor differences may be noted. The income in kind and in cash is distributed on a collective farm to the farmers on the basis of so-called "labor days," which are not actually working days but abstract accounting units used to calculate the amount of work performed by individual workers. In a joint-farming establishment the farmers receive wages. A further difference between these establishments and collective farms lies in the above-mentioned individual right to breed cattle granted now to managers of joint-farming establishments. As to property rights in the small plots surrounding the houses of the farmers, the innovation consists in the granting of full property rights in these plots, whereas in the *kolhoz* system the farmers had individual use of the plots only as long as they were members of the collective farm.

(*b*) *The Farming Association* (Landbau-Genossenschaft). This is an association of individual farmers who receive merely the usufruct of the land. They are engaged in collective labor for only part of the year: for example, for plowing, sowing, and harvesting, and presumably because machinery for large-scale operations cannot be assigned for individual use in most areas. Members do not receive wages. The crops they harvest are divided among them, after deduction of compulsory deliveries in kind to the German administration. Here, as well as in the joint-farming establishment, the prospect is held out to the members that the land may in the future be conveyed to them in full ownership.

(*c*) *Individual farms* (Einzelwirtschaft). Individual farming is permitted only in exceptional cases by German authorities. Individual farms are granted as a reward for cooperation with the Germans against Soviet guerrillas as well as for demonstrated efficiency in farming.

As to other farming institutions, it is worthy of note that state farms (*sovhozy*) have been maintained and taken over by the occupant. The rôle played by the machine-tractor stations in the Soviet communistic system has also been important to the occupant in connection with this institution.

[4] At the time when the present book was completed further material on this problem was not available to the author.

The machine-tractor stations are the central point in the organization of Soviet agriculture, because they hold the monopoly of mechanized implements and lease these implements to collective farms. The services of machine-tractor stations are paid for in kind in grain, sunflower seed, etc., at rates fixed by the government for different types of operations. By monopolizing the mechanized implements in the machine-tractor stations, the Soviet Government was enabled to control and impose its will upon the collective farms. The occupant took over this institution completely because it served only too well his own purposes—the promotion of the German war economy, as well as of political control.[5]

On the whole it may be stated that the new or modified institutions of agricultural life have not abolished the communist system, despite the slight changes mentioned above.

In the same manner as in territories occupied in the Baltic States and in eastern Poland "return to private property in the territories occupied in the U.S.S.R." proper was used only as a propaganda slogan or as a reward for treachery on the part of Russians toward their own country. Under such a system the counterpart for reward is punishment, which is being applied extensively to Russian and Ukrainian peasants who are reluctant to cooperate with the occupant or are not efficient enough in their work.

LABOR

Russian workers are used to a great extent by the occupant in the occupied territories and are also shipped abroad. An especially severe régime has been established for such workers in the occupied Russian area. Reluctance to work or inefficiency in work is being punished, such punishment ranging from flogging to the death penalty.[6]

Special provisions regarding wages were made for workers imported into Germany from the Reich Commissariat for the Ukraine, from the General Commissariat for White Russia, and from the territories to the east of the above-mentioned administrative units as well as to the east of the Baltic States. Thus, according to the decree of June 30, 1942,[7] issued by Göring, President of the Council of Ministers for the Defense of the Reich, the workers imported from these eastern territories (called *Ostarbeiter*) were given a special employment status (*Beschäftigungsverhältnis eigener Art*). The eastern workers receive wages under these provisions only for work actually performed. In case of sickness they receive only free shelter and subsistence. No leave is granted.

[5] Lazar Volin, *op. cit.*, pp. 77–81.

[6] See "Note of The People's Commissar of Foreign Affairs of the USSR, V. M. Molotov, to the ambassadors and envoys of all countries with which the USSR has diplomatic relations," April 27, 1942, *Information Bulletin*, Embassy of the Union of Soviet Socialist Republics (Washington, 1942), p. 14.

See also E. Jaroslavskij, *Vielikaja otjetshestviennaja vojna sovjetskavo naroda protiv hitlerovskoj Germanii* (Moskwa, 1942), p. 155.

[7] See below, p. 556.

However, the most important feature of their legal status is shown by a comparison of wages paid German workers with the wages allowed eastern workers for similar work in accordance with the official wage scale schedule. As this schedule shows, the eastern worker actually receives for himself only a small amount of what the employer pays out in employing him. A special sum is deducted to pay for his subsistence, and the main part (especially in the higher brackets of wages) is paid by the employer to the state in the form of a special tax (*Ostarbeiterabgabe*).

As the Belgian industries were working for the German war economy they were allowed to import workers from the Ukraine. However, they could not profit without reservations from this cheap labor as they were also obliged to pay this special tax for using Russian labor.[8]

In addition to what is said above in the chapter on "Labor" regarding violations of international law, it should be stated that the occupant, by publishing the above labor decree and the attached schedules, has provided official evidence regarding Germany's illegal exploitation of foreign labor as to wages.

JUSTICE

The problem of organizing justice in the Ukraine created many difficulties. The local courts (so-called "People's Courts"), based upon the principles of communistic justice, could not be used for political reasons. On the other hand, because of the fact that the communist régime has been retained in its essential features, the need for courts to deal with civil matters was not so urgent as it would be in an area with a prevailing private-ownership régime. The occupant has resolved the problem of civil justice in the following way: An institution of local arbitrators (*einheimische Schlichter*) has been established to take care of civil disputes arising between members of the local population. These arbitrators are appointed by the Reich Commissioner for the Ukraine, upon the recommendation of the respective district commissioners. The decisions of the arbitrators must be enforced.[9] For criminal cases there exist German courts patterned along the same lines as those in other occupied countries.

GENOCIDE AND RESISTANCE

The treatment of the Russian population during occupation reminds one of a punitive expedition in continuous operation. The Russian population has been engaged since the beginning of the occupation in constant guerrilla fighting with the occupant. Widespread collective penalties have been inflicted by the occupant in the form of mass executions and mass destruction

[8] See decree of July 14, 1942, issued by the German military commander in Belgium, *Verordnungsblatt*, 1942, p. 966.

[9] At the time when the present book was completed, further material on this problem was not available to the author.

of property. Especially has the scorched-earth policy carried out by the retiring German armies enlarged the extent of the destruction. In implementing the decisions of the Moscow Conference to the effect that war criminals should be tried by local courts of the countries where the crimes have been perpetrated, the Government of the U.S.S.R. ordered the first trials of German war criminals in December, 1943. These trials have revealed a gruesome picture of war atrocities.

Bessarabia, Bukovina, and Transnistria
(Occupied and Incorporated by Rumania)

BACKGROUND

1. *Political and Territorial Changes.* Rumania joined Germany in its attack on Russia in June, 1941, as a result of an internal transformation of the state under German influence and also as a result of specific relations with Russia as they had developed since 1940, when Rumania was compelled to cede North Bukovina and Bessarabia to Russia.

For several years Hitler had endeavored to penetrate Rumanian political and economic life, because Rumania occupied a strategic position, and also because it is a country rich in raw materials. Through his agents he fostered the Rumanian Fascist Iron Guard and organized it as his fifth column against King Carol. Carol resisted these disintegrating influences at first, by the execution in 1938 of the Chief of the Iron Guard (Codreanu), as well as his assistants, while they were "attempting to escape" from Bucharest one morning at dawn. The King was, however, undermined by Hitler, who forced him to give up a part of Transylvania to Hungary under the Vienna "arbitration" award rendered by Germany and Italy on August 30, 1940.[10] The popularity of King Carol was also weakened by two other losses of territory. In June, 1940, as stated above, he had ceded North Bukovina and Bessarabia to Russia, when the latter, having mobilized, made a request for these territories. Bessarabia had constituted part of Russia until the end of the first World War, when it became incorporated into Rumania. Under the treaty of September 7, 1940, Rumania had also ceded Southern Dobruja to Bulgaria.[11] In the same month, King Carol was forced to abdicate by the new leader of the Iron Guard, General Antonescu, who declared himself Leader of the Rumanian State (*Conducătorul Statului Român*), the state being organized on Fascist lines. Antonescu placed King Carol's son Michael on the Rumanian throne and forced Carol to leave the country and to go into exile.

2. "*Rumanianization.*" This term refers mostly to Rumanianization of economic life, and it means that property and the most important branches of

[10] For text, see *Affaires danubiennes*, 1940, No. 8, pp. 81–82. [11] *Ibid.*, pp. 84 ff.

economic life, such as business, professions, and other occupations, may be exercised only by persons of Rumanian ethnic origin. Two trends paved the way for this process: the anti-Jewish trend, which became accentuated in Rumania several years before the war; and the territorial changes, which brought into Rumania masses of Rumanian refugees from Transylvania, Dobruja, Bessarabia, and Northern Bukovina. In this situation, the Rumanian Government introduced Rumanianization laws providing for the taking over of properties and businesses from Jews and distributing them among Rumanians. The first important laws of this nature were promulgated on October 4, 1940, and November 12, 1940. The law of October 4 introduced the institution of Rumanianization commissioners in Jewish enterprises, and the November law ordered the ouster of Jewish employees from private concerns. On May 2, 1941, two further decrees were published which established a new organizational framework for Rumanianization, under one of which [12] an Undersecretariat for Rumanianization, Colonization, and Inventorization (*Subsecretariatul de Stat al Românizării, Colonizării şi Inventarului*) was created and established in connection with the presidency of the Council of Ministers. It is a central body which lays down policies concerning colonization of Rumanian refugees and the reallocation of property in Rumania. By the second law of this date a National Center for Rumanianization was established. This center is attached to the undersecretariat and is supervised by the latter. The center is an operational agency, which deals with and takes over principally Jewish properties and actually distributes them among persons of Rumanian origin.[13]

North Bukovina and Bessarabia

Bessarabia and Bukovina were occupied by Rumania and Germany in the first weeks of the war. After a short period of military administration the Leader of State, Antonescu, introduced civil administration in the form of two governorships,[14] one for each province. To the governorships were attached directorates of various administrative services, which services were to be coordinated in each case by a special coordinating committee of the directorates concerned. Specific importance is attached to the directorate for Rumanianization, Colonization, and Inventorization, which has been given the right to have a special budget.[15] The governorship was divided into districts, with heads of administration called prefects.

Rumanian administration was faced with many difficulties growing out of the sudden territorial changes. Here again the main attention of the government was directed toward Rumanianization. The proclamation of July 25, 1941,[16] by the Presidency of the Council of Ministers, provided for a re-

[12] *Monitorul oficial*, No. 102. [13] See below, p. 563.
[14] Law No. 790, *Monitorul oficial*, 1941.
[15] See decree-law of October 15, 1942, *ibid.*, No. 241, p. 8974. [16] See below, p. 565.

turn of refugees to Bessarabia and Bukovina. However, only Rumanians and Germans by origin could obtain permission to return to these provinces. In order to strengthen the Rumanian element, Rumanian agriculturalists received 80 per cent tax exemptions and Rumanian business men and industrialists were completely freed from taxation until March 31, 1943.[17] Jews were expressly excluded from the benefits of this law.

A decree-law of May 26, 1942,[18] restored Rumanian citizenship in principle to the inhabitants of Bessarabia and Northern Bukovina, if they were Rumanian citizens under the provisions of the revised law on Rumanian citizenship of June 28, 1940. Such citizenship was denied to three categories of persons: (*a*) persons who requested permission to return from Rumania to Bessarabia when it was occupied by Russia, with the exception of demobilized soldiers who were returning home; (*b*) persons who after June 28, 1940, acquired another citizenship than that of one of the republics of the Soviet Union; and (*c*) persons who left the territory occupied by Russia before it was reoccupied by Rumania. However, Rumanians by origin were not denied citizenship even if they came within this latter category.

Because of the war, the records concerning real property were either lost or destroyed. The local courts were given great discretionary power in reproducing such records, which amounted to the formulation of new titles of ownership. Since under the Fascist form of government prevailing in Rumania the courts are subordinated to the executive power, large opportunities were thus created for a reallocation of real property for political reasons. Obviously, persons of Rumanian origin were the beneficiaries of such a law.

Transnistria

Transnistria[19] is the name of the Russian territory between the pre-June 1940 Russo-Rumanian border and the Lower Bug, delimited on the west side by the Dniester River, on the east side by the Lower Bug, on the north side by a line running approximately from Zhmerinka to Mogilev Podolsk, and on the south by the Black Sea. This territory was handed over by the Germans to Rumania for administration. A Rumanian governor was appointed by Marshal Antonescu, with his headquarters in Odessa. German advisers were delegated to his staff by German authorities. The territory was divided into territorial districts and sixty-four counties (*rayons*), corresponding approximately to Soviet administrative divisions. Rumanian prefects were put in charge of the districts. At the head of the counties were two higher officials, one Rumanian and one from the local population.

In this territory, which had been under a communist property system since the Russian Revolution, the property relations under Rumanian admin-

[17] See law of April 1, 1942, *Monitorul oficial*, No. 78. [18] *Ibid.*, No. 119.
[19] The author uses the spelling "Transnistria" as given in the *Monitorul oficial*.

istration were not changed to any great extent. Land ownership was granted for the most part as a reward for pro-Rumanian activities and zealous work.

After the introduction of Rumanian currency (lei), the following exchange rate was established: 60 lei = Reichskreditkassenschein = 10 rubles.

This territory became a large center to which Rumanian Jews were deported, in the same way that Poland was made a center for west European Jews. The deported Jews were forced to work under inhumane conditions in labor camps. Several hundred thousand Rumanian Jews of both sexes above fifteen years of age were deported to Transnistria from Bessarabia and North Bukovina.[20]

Special decrees were promulgated concerning these deportees. Conditions in Transnistria being very difficult for them, they escaped in some cases to Rumania. A special law published by Antonescu, Marshal of Rumania, Leader of State, fixed the death penalty for Jewish deportees who returned illegally to Rumania, and persons who helped them to escape were to be punished by imprisonment up to twenty-five years.[21]

Another decree-law [22] instituted severe penalties for using secret mails and packages in communications with Transnistria, because the deportees, under Rumanian regulations, were to be completely isolated from their homes and friends in Rumania.

Moral debasement in administration of justice is displayed by the decree-law of July 9, 1941,[23] by which the death penalty was provided even for such offenses as non-declaration of property left by the retreating enemy. Trial and execution had to take place within twenty-four hours. Unparalleled in legislation is the following paragraph of the above-mentioned law: "In case of *flagrante delicto*, the culprit shall be executed on the spot."

[20] See Kulischer, *op. cit.*, p. 115, and *Krakauer Zeitung* of August 13, 1942.
[21] Law No. 698, September 19, 1942, below, p. 567.
[22] See decree-law No. 252, March 28, 1942, below, p. 566. [23] See below, p. 566

CHAPTER XXVI
YUGOSLAVIA

BACKGROUND

Of all the countries occupied in this war Yugoslavia has been the most dismembered and has been divided into the greatest number of administrative units. Its territory has been occupied by Germany, Italy, Bulgaria, Hungary, and Albania. Parts of its territories were formed into the new puppet state of Croatia.[1] Even the idea of the pre-Versailles state of Montenegro was revived, although the state itself was not set up in a definite form.

This dismemberment of Yugoslavia serves not only the immediate political purposes of the occupant but also the purpose of disintegrating and dividing the political forces in the occupied areas so far as to make difficult in the future the unification of all the political elements within the framework of one state.

In the process of dismemberment, the German and Italian occupants have taken advantage of the fact that the country had difficult population problems. The population consisted of three main national groups (Slovenes living in the northwest, Croats in the central northern part, and Serbs living in the east and south); also of smaller groups such as Moslems (in Bosnia-Herzegovina), Macedonians (in the part of Macedonia which was taken in previous wars from Bulgaria and incorporated into the Kingdom of the Serbs, Croats, and Slovenes by the Treaty of Neuilly), Germans living in the so-called Banat and scattered in other parts of Slovenia, Italians scattered over Dalmatia and near Fiume, Jews, Albanians, and a number of gypsies.

Among these groups there were many differences and conflicts, the relations between the Serbs and Croats being especially hostile. The Croatian grievances consist mainly of the following: that the Treaty of Versailles had created a Kingdom of Serbs, Croats, and Slovenes, implying in this name the idea of a three-nation state, whereas, according to the Croats, the Serbs have unilaterally endeavored to create an integrated Yugoslav state under Serbian leadership, without granting the Croats equal representation in the government. The Croats refer particularly to the Geneva agreement of 1918 between them and the Serbs to the effect that the Croats should have equal representation in the government with the Serbs; and they maintain that

[1] When the Yugoslav Government protested, on May 12 and 24, against the dismemberment of Yugoslavia and the creation of the State of Croatia, Under Secretary of State Sumner Welles declared that he wished "to reiterate the indignation of this Government and the American people at the invasion and mutilation of Yugoslavia by various member states of the Tripartite Pact."—The Under Secretary of State to the Minister of Yugoslavia, May 28, 1941, Department of State, *Bulletin*, Vol. IV, No. 102, June 7, 1941, p. 683.

the terms of this agreement were not observed by the Serbs.[2] In addition, the Croats assert that the constitution which was adopted in 1921 was not patterned along federative lines, and that the Croatian population was not duly represented in the making of this constitution. Furthermore, the fact that the constitution was changed by King Alexander in 1929 by means of a *coup d'état* augmented the Croatian grievances. And when the King changed the name of the Kingdom of Serbs, Croats, and Slovenes to "Yugoslavia," the Croats saw in this change of name a new pattern for political homogeneity and a danger to their own national aspirations.

The Croatian political parties at the time differed in their policies. The Peasant Party under Radić, and later under Maček, opposed the centralizing tendencies of the Belgrade government, and Radić visited the capitals of the Allies in order to try to win them over to the Croatian cause. When a pro-Serbian radical party, created in Zagreb in 1929, approved the changes in the constitution, the Croats claimed that this party represented only a slight minority of the Croatian population, 95 per cent being organized in the opposition or Peasant Party. Upon Radić's return to Zagreb after his unsuccessful political mission abroad, he and other members of the Peasant Party made an arrangement with the Serbs for participation in the Parliament. However, in 1928 Radić was shot during one of the sessions of the Parliament by an extremist Serb nationalist deputy.

About the same time another Croatian party called the "Ustaše" or Croatian Liberation Movement, was developing its activities along more radical and more revolutionary lines. Whereas Radić had endeavored to win the Allies of 1914–18 for the Croatian cause, the leaders of the Ustaše movement—Pavelić and Kvaternik—collaborated with the countries dissatisfied with the Versailles and Trianon treaties, namely, Germany, Hungary, the Macedonian Irredenta, and especially Italy, which had made claims to the Adriatic coast and was pursuing expansionist policies in the Balkans. These countries gave their support to the separatist program of Ustaše. In Italy, Pavelić and Kvaternik were given every support in training Ustaše men for future military and terroristic action.

In 1934, King Alexander of Yugoslavia was assassinated in Marseilles by members of the Ustaše. The assassins took refuge in Italy and no extradition was granted.[3]

In 1938, the Croats participated in elections to the Belgrade Skupština but subsequently the Croatians who were elected refused to enter the Parliament, the elections having been used only for the purpose of displaying the political strength of the Croatian Nationalist Party.

The Ustaše leaders, who were collaborating with the Axis Powers, took

[2] Dr. August Kossutitch, "The Croatian Problem," *International Affairs*, Vol. XII, No. 1 (January–February, 1933), p. 79.

[3] In the second trial by the Court of Justice in Aix-en-Provence (France) of the murderers of Alexander, they were sentenced on February 11, 1936, *in absentia* to death.

over the organization of a puppet state of Croatia when the Axis invaded Yugoslavia. On April 8, 1941, in the course of the invasion, Ante Pavelić broadcast from abroad an appeal to the Croats to secede from the Serbs and to support Germany and Italy.[4]

The manner in which the Axis proceeded to divide Yugoslavia is shown in the following sections.

NEW TERRITORIAL DIVISIONS

I. THE DIVISION OF SLOVENIA

Slovenia, with a population of about 2,000,000 Slovenes, has been divided between Germany and Italy in accordance with an agreement signed in Berlin on July 8, 1941, by Dino Alfieri, Italian Ambassador, and von Weiszäcker, German State Secretary for Foreign Affairs.[5] Hungary was also given a few small towns and villages with less than 100,000 inhabitants. Under the agreement between Germany and Italy, Germany annexed approximately three fourths of Slovenia, with a population of about 900,000 inhabitants, these parts being incorporated into Germany as a special district called Südsteiermark and including Lower Styria, parts of Carinthia, and Upper Carniola. Italy annexed the province of Ljubljana, with about 350,000 inhabitants.[6] The Slovenes, being the immediate neighbors of Greater Germany and of Italy (the Slovenes dwell also in the neighborhood of Trieste and Fiume), have been considered by both countries as creating a natural barrier to their expansion in the Balkans. The division of this highly cultured Slavic nation has, especially with respect to German policy, a definite genocide purpose.

A. Lower Styria, Carinthia, and Carniola
(German Occupation)

Immediately after the occupation the occupant proceeded with the destruction of the national Slovene pattern in the occupied area.

The German language was proclaimed as the only official language.[7] All Slovene signs on offices and principal buildings were removed and replaced with German signs. The names and surnames of the population were permitted to be used only in the German form, both in speech and in writing. A great number of Slovenes were removed to Croatia and other parts of

[4] *Bulletin of International News*, Vol. XVIII, No. 6 (April 19, 1941), p. 518.

[5] See *New York Times*, July 10, 1941, p. 1, col. 4; *Bulletin of International News*, Vol. XVIII, No. 15 (July 26, 1941), pp. 979, 999.

[6] Boris Furlan, *Fighting Jugoslavia* (New York: Yugoslav Information Center, [1943]), p. 4.

[7] Furlan, *op. cit.*, p. 7.

Yugoslavia, in order to make room for German colonists. The latter are recruited from the Reich and from Germans who were removed to Germany from Rumania (Bessarabia and Dobruja), from Italy (Southern Tyrol) and from Italian-occupied Slovenia. The process of colonization is called by the Germans *Heimholung* (bringing into the homeland), the Germans claiming that these territories belong to the German living space. A special bureau (*Gaugrenzlandamt*) sees to it that the vacated farms, after removal of the Slovenes, are colonized by German peasant families that are politically reliable.[8]

German teachers, together with other administrative personnel, were put in charge of Slovene schools and introduced teaching methods in harmony with the principles of National Socialism. In his endeavors to destroy all traces of Slovene culture, the occupant has demanded the surrender of Slovene books, including even prayer-books.[9]

The highly cultured Slovene population had developed an efficient system of financial cooperatives which were carrying on useful activities in agriculture and trade among the Slovenes. The cooperatives improved the standard of living of the Slovenes and provided means for the creation of useful national cultural institutions. Hence the Slovenes cherished them as an instrumentality of social and national progress. Realizing the importance of these cooperatives in strengthening the Slovene national spirit, the German occupant, as one of the first steps after the occupation, proceeded to liquidate them. As early as May 19, 1941, a decree was issued in Lower Styria closing all cooperatives, savings banks, and agricultural associations.[10] German banking institutions alone were allowed to function. In fact, only the Creditanstalt-Bankverein A. G. and the Länderbank in Vienna were permitted to open branches, in Marburg and Celje, although, in addition, a number of German savings banks were established. As the savings banks also had a political mission (i.e., the exercise of political discrimination in granting credits and withholding the repayment of deposits), special political commissioners were entrusted with the business of those institutions.[11]

It is stated in the last-mentioned decree that the repayment of deposits made prior to occupation shall be dependent upon the orders of the Chief of Civil Administration. When one realizes how the German occupant has handled bank deposits in other countries, especially Poland, one may see in this order an obvious instrumentality of racial discrimination and political oppression, the employment of which means that the Germans are privileged and the Slovenes underprivileged in receiving their deposits.

Not only the banking system but also the monetary system was Germanized. German currency was introduced by the decree of May 28, 1941, effective as of June 1, 1941, in Lower Styria. As to Carinthia and Carniola,

[8] Furlan, *op. cit.*, p. 19. [9] *Ibid.*, pp. 20–21. [10] See below, p. 582.
[11] See decree of June 5, 1941, below, p. 583.

German currency was introduced as legal tender by the decree of May 23, 1941, to become effective on June 1, 1941.[12] The rate of the dinar was established as follows: 1 dinar equals 0.05 Reichsmark.

Thus it is plain that the Germans are pursuing a genocide policy in Slovenia. This policy is evident not only from the measures taken but also from public statements. The *Stajerski Gospodar*, a German newspaper which is appearing in the Slovene language in order to promote the policies of Germanism, stated on April 11, 1942: "The most important task has been to prove that the inhabitants of Lower Styria are not Slovenes but Styrian patriots and thus [are] qualified to be an integral part of the great German national community and able to graduate as perfect Germans. When in the near future Lower Styrians are serving in the German army, they will be yet one step nearer the supreme ideal of becoming totally German."[13]

B. Ljubljana
(Italian Occupation)

Of the remaining Slovene areas, the major part was organized as the province of Ljubljana, while some of the smaller areas in the neighborhood of the province of Fiume were incorporated directly into that province.

The province of Ljubljana was annexed to Italy by royal decree-law of May 3, 1941.[14] The decree in question envisaged autonomy for this province which should take "into consideration the racial characteristics of the population, the geographical position of the territory, and its special local needs." The powers of the Italian government were exercised by a High Commissioner appointed by royal decree on the motion of the Duce of Fascism, Mussolini, and it was further provided that the High Commissioner should be assisted by a council consisting of fourteen representatives chosen from among the "productive" classes of the Slovene population. As the decree states that the annexed territory has a "uniformly Slovene population," the Slovene language was made "obligatory" in the elementary schools, while in secondary and higher education, instruction in the Italian language was made optional. All official documents must be printed in both languages. Although a slight freedom was permitted in the cultural field (such as schools and language), in the economic field a system of exploitation was embarked upon. An illustration of this tendency may be seen in the decree-law of May 19, 1941, establishing Italian monopoly services in this province.[15]

As regards the legal system, the courts of original jurisdiction remain essentially unchanged, but appeals from these courts, in so far as they were

[12] See below, p. 583.
[13] See quotation from *Stajerski Gospodar*, in Joseph Kalmer, "Slovenes and Slovenia," *Free Europe*, Vol. 5, No. 68 (June 19, 1942), p. 202.
[14] See below, p. 584.
[15] See below, p. 585.

directed previously to the Court of Appeals of Zagreb (now the capital of Croatia) have been transferred to the Court of Appeals in Fiume (on Italian territory). Because cases arising in the Slovene territory require a particular knowledge of local law, a special branch for the appeal of cases from the province of Ljubljana has been created within the Court of Appeals in Fiume.[16]

II. Dalmatia

(Italian Occupation)

The territories along the Adriatic known as Dalmatia, as well as most of the Adriatic islands, with the exception of Pag, Brač, and Hvar, were annexed by Italy.[17] Dalmatia was organized as a province with the capital in Zadar (Zara). By the proclamation of Mussolini of July 11, 1941,[18] a governorship for Dalmatia was created and Giuseppe Bastianini, Italian Under Secretary of Foreign Affairs, was appointed first governor and made directly responsible to the Duce. Italian currency [19] and various Italian economic laws were introduced gradually into Dalmatia.

On the annexation of Dalmatia, the former Croat administrative authorities were replaced by Italians. All municipal councils were dismissed and Italian commissioners appointed instead. Croat schools were gradually changed into Italian and Italian teachers were imported from Italy. In the political, social, and economic field Fascist institutions were introduced.[20] The Italian policy in Dalmatia was based upon the idea of keeping both shores of the Adriatic under control by elements upon which Italy could rely.

By the proclamation of the Duce of April 29, 1941,[21] tariffs and customs laws in force at the time of occupation remained unchanged, but this provision refers only to trade other than that between the occupied territories and the Italo-Albanian Customs Union. No customs duties are to be paid on goods originating in and shipped from the area of the Italo-Albanian Union into the occupied territories, or on goods shipped from those territories into the area of the Italo-Albanian Union or into the free zones of Carnaro and Zara.

The manner in which the local population was treated by the Italians is shown in a letter of protest sent to the Vatican by the Catholic Bishop Josip Srebrenic in Dalmatia. The Bishop charges the Italian authorities with mis-

[16] See proclamation of June 2, 1941, below, p. 586.
[17] See decree of May 18, 1941, below, p. 587; *Free Europe*, Vol. 4, No. 53 (November 14, 1941), p. 274.
[18] *Gazzetta ufficiale*, 1941, No. 197.
[19] See proclamation of April 16, 1941, below, p. 577.
[20] Marko Pavičić, "Italian Barbarities in Dalmatia and Croatia," *The Central European Observer*, September 4, 1942, p. 283.
[21] See below, p. 573.

treating the Croatian population, shooting people without trial after having drawn them by lot from a crowd, and burning houses of innocent inhabitants.[21a]

III. Montenegro

(Italian Occupation)

Montenegro, or Crna Gora, which existed as a separate state before and during the first World War, was absorbed by Yugoslavia (then the Kingdom of the Serbs, Croats, and Slovenes) after 1918. When the Italian forces occupied Montenegro, it was planned that this area should receive special treatment, involving not only military aspects but diplomatic aspects as well, as became obvious when Mussolini, in issuing a proclamation appointing a High Commissioner for the Montenegrin territory, ordered such commissioner, in his exercise of civilian authority, to communicate directly with the Italian Minister of Foreign Affairs. Two underlying factors no doubt had a bearing on these arrangements: on the one hand, there had existed traditionally well-established relations between the last King of Montenegro, Nicholas, and the Royal House of Savoy because Victor Emmanuel married the daughter of Nicholas; and, on the other hand, the fact that Montenegro was abolished as a state and absorbed into the Kingdom of Yugoslavia was sufficient to cause the Italian occupant to treat it in a more favorable way.

For these reasons, therefore, a certain hesitancy was manifested in the policy of the occupant as to the status of Montenegro. At the beginning the tendency was marked not to apply to Montenegro the basic Italian decree on military occupation of May 17, 1941. In particular, the decree of July 26, 1941,[22] provided that the Supreme Command could, for the territory of Montenegro, refrain from establishing a civil commissioner, as provided for in other territories. However, in a later decree of October 3, 1941,[23] creating a governorship for Montenegro, the Governor was empowered to establish a civil commissariat headed by a civil commissioner. Thus the organization of Montenegro in the terms of the latter decree is as follows: It is headed by a Governor, who reports on political, civil, and administrative matters to the Minister of Foreign Affairs (which shows that Montenegro represents special political aspects). The handling of these matters is entrusted to the civil commissioner, who reports to the Governor in Cetinje. As to military matters, the Governor communicates with the Supreme Command.

[21a] This letter stresses the following point: "Yes, it is true that the German Nazis too commit such acts, but they profess pagan and materialistic ideas whereas both the Italian army and the Italian people are faithful Catholics."—Letter of Josip Srebrenic, Catholic Bishop of the Island of Krk, Italian occupied Dalmatia, sent on June 14, 1942, to Luigi Maglione, Secretary of State of the Holy See. *Inter-Allied Review*, Vol. II, No. 12 (December 15, 1942), pp. 331–32.

[22] *Gazzetta ufficiale*, 1941, No. 185, p. 3143. [23] See below, p. 590.

By the proclamation of October 6, 1941, Italian legal tender was introduced and dinars were exchanged by a special committee at the rate of 38 lire for 100 dinars.[24]

IV. Serbia

(German Occupation)

In the process of disintegration Serbia was left with 4,500,000 inhabitants —28 per cent of the population of the original Kingdom of Yugoslavia—and was subjected to German military occupation. In this German-controlled territory, a Serbian puppet government was established under General Nedić, who acts through his ministers and local Serbian authorities. The ministers are called commissarial directors of the ministries.

ADMINISTRATION

The German administration is in the hands of a German military commander and local military commanders. The German military commander supervises the Serbian Government and local authorities. However, the German occupation authorities are themselves legislating extensively, their legislation aiming at the complete political, economic, and social subordination of Serbia to the occupant. The Serbian puppet government is also issuing orders and decrees.

LAW

As the territory has not yet been completely subdued, the Partisans and the army of General Mikhailović continuing to fight, the German occupant has met this resistance by the creation of a semilegal system of terror. German military courts with vast powers have been introduced. In one of the first decrees promulgated by the German Commander in Chief of the Army in the *Verordnungsblatt* for the occupied Yugoslav territories, it was stated: "Any person who commits an act punishable according to German law and is brought to trial before courts of the armed forces, shall be subject to German criminal law." [25] Thus a foreign legal code of the greatest complexity was introduced in the first days of occupation, and it took effect immediately without giving the population an opportunity to become acquainted with it. In this connection one must distinguish between the promulgation of a particular order issued in the language of the local population and a reference made in a specific order to the legal code of the home country of the occupant which is unknown to the population of the occupied country. Whereas in the first case it is possible for the population to become

[24] *Gazzetta ufficiale*, 1941, No. 241, p. 4035.

[25] See order concerning the application of German criminal law and criminal statutes in the occupied Yugoslav territories, below, p. 597.

acquainted with the law and act accordingly, in the second case the population has no opportunity to obtain exact knowledge of what is right and what is wrong under the code. Moreover, the above-mentioned order also gave the German courts jurisdiction to impose punishment for acts committed before the German occupation, prosecution of such offenses to be "at the discretion of the prosecuting authorities." Thus the occupant has created a state of legal uncertainty and constant fear among the local inhabitants, who have been made completely dependent on the occupant for a determination of the consequences of their acts. The Hague Regulations endeavored to create a rule of law to be applied in occupied territories, but the German occupant has established instead a state of facts and force, using legal channels only as an instrumentality of administrative coercion. Therefore, one must consider the above-mentioned order a most flagrant violation of both the letter and spirit of the Hague Regulations.

PROPERTY

In the same spirit was conceived an order concerning the confiscation of property for activities hostile to the state, dated December 22, 1941, which gives to the chief of the administrative staff of the German military commander in Serbia the right to "decide by order, without formal judicial procedure: (*a*) on the penalty of confiscation, (*b*) on the use to be made of the property thus confiscated." Not only is the property of the defendant liable to confiscation but also the property of the members of his family—a procedure which creates possibility of punishing persons without establishing their individual guilt.[26]

ANTI-GUERRILLA LEGISLATION

Anti-guerrilla legislation was introduced to cope with the Partisans and with the Chetniks of General Mikhailović. As the guerrilla fighters used cornfields extensively for hiding places, the German military commander issued an order on October 9, 1941, providing for an early harvesting of the corn and the cutting of the cornstalks. Not only the persons in possession of the cornfields and their owners but also the mayors having jurisdiction in the respective localities were made responsible for the early harvesting of the crops. Non-compliance with this order was punishable by death or, under extenuating circumstances, by hard labor.[27]

GENOCIDE LEGISLATION

To the same extent as in other occupied countries legislation regarding racial discrimination was introduced. The fate of the Jews was shared in Yugoslavia by the gypsies, both being excluded from practising professions. The liquidation of the Jews—an essential element of German policy—was of

[26] See below, p. 598. [27] See below, p. 602.

primary importance in Serbia. Accordingly, the Serbs were forbidden to help Jews by the order of December 22, 1941, which provided the death penalty for sheltering or hiding Jews or for accepting from them objects of value of any description, such as furniture and money, or even for buying such objects from them.[28] Jewish accounts in the banks were blocked (see below).

FINANCE

By the decree of May 29, 1941,[29] the military commander in Serbia ordered the liquidation of the National Bank of the Kingdom of Yugoslavia, and the German Plenipotentiary for Economic Affairs in Serbia was entrusted with the execution of this liquidation decree. Two days later a decree was published establishing a new Serbian National Bank as the bank of issue, with an initial capital of 100 million Serbian dinars, divided into 10,000 shares of 10,000 Serbian dinars each. It was stated in this decree that the shares should be paid up at least 50 per cent at the time of subscription. As in other banks of issue created under German occupation, it was provided in this decree that the clearing debts in favor of Serbia should serve also as one of the cover items for the new issue.[30] The creation of huge clearing debts through overimportation from occupied countries is one of the exploitation devices of the German occupant. Thus one exploitation device is being used by the occupant for double exploitation purposes. The German Plenipotentiary for Economic Affairs has been given a decisive rôle in the organization of the new bank. He appoints the governor of the bank and his deputies, as well as a governing board consisting of ten persons. The German commissioner appointed by the economic plenipotentiary is attached to the administration of the bank in order to report on its activities to the economic plenipotentiary.

The new currency, called the Serbian dinar, was divided into 100 para. In addition the bank was permitted to issue a subsidiary currency in the form of coins not exceeding twenty Serbian dinars. It was stated that the total amount of the subsidiary currency may not exceed 250 dinars per head of the population.

The opening business of the new Serbian issue bank was the exchange of all Yugoslav dinar notes and Reich Credit Institute notes for new Serbian dinars, the state handing over to the bank all debt certificates to the amount of the notes exchanged. The fact that the new bank was compelled to call in and to exchange the Reich Credit notes issued by the German occupation troops has imposed a new and heavy burden upon Serbia.[31]

On May 29, 1941, a decree was published freezing all balances in the banks and allowing payments only according to special schedule.[32] Where the balance of the account was not more than 2,000 dinars, the whole

[28] See below, p. 601. [29] See below, p. 600. [30] See above, chapter on "Finance."
[31] Bank for International Settlements, *Twelfth Annual Report* (1942), p. 204.
[32] *Verordnungsblatt des Militärbefehlshabers in Serbien*, May 31, 1941.

amount could be repaid. For other amounts monthly payments were provided for according to the following schedule:

For a balance of from 2,000 to 25,000 dinars, a monthly repayment of 3,000 dinars;
From 25,000 to 50,000, a monthly repayment of 4,000 dinars;
From 50,000 to 100,000, a monthly repayment of 5,000 dinars;
From 100,000 to 250,000, a monthly repayment of 6,000 dinars;
And for amounts of more than 250,000, a monthly repayment of 7,000 dinars.

Balances belonging to Jews were blocked completely.

V. The Banat

(German Occupation)

A part of the Danube Province with a considerable German population,[33] descendants of those who had come as immigrants from the Rhine provinces, from Bavaria, and from Alsace under Maria Theresa, was organized by the German occupant as a separate administrative unit called the Banat. Because the Banat forms only a part of the territory of the Danube Province, it is headed by a Vice Governor, with the title of Vize-Banus ("Banus" is the title of the Governor). The office of the Vice Governor is formally subordinated to the Ministry of the Interior within the puppet government in Belgrade. The Banat is divided into the following administrative districts: Pančevo, Vršac, Bela Crkva, Kovin, Jaša Tomić, Veliki Bečkerek, Velika Kikinda, Novi Becej, Nova Kanjiža, Kovačica, and Alibunar, as well as the city of Pančevo. The higher officials in the Banat are appointed by the puppet government in Belgrade, on recommendation of the Vice Governor.

The administration of the Banat is mainly in the hands of local Germans, from the Vice Governor down to the lower officials. The requirements of the existing Civil Service Code have been lowered in order to enable great numbers of local Germans to procure civil service appointments. Judges and notaries public are Germans.

The administration of posts, railways, and finance, and of the other branches is also in the hands of local Germans. Taxes and revenues in the territory of the Banat go to the central Treasury in Serbia, but the revenues from provincial taxes and duties are used for the needs of the provincial administration.

As the major part of the population of the Banat is Serbian, both German and Serbian are the official languages.[34]

The civil administration of the Banat being in the hands of local Germans, there are also in this territory German military forces under a German military commander.

[33] Numbering about one third.
[34] See ordinance concerning the internal administration of the Banat, below, p. 602.

Apparently the Germans do not consider the situation in the Banat as definitely settled.[35]

VI. The State of Croatia

When German troops entered Zagreb three days after the broadcast by Ante Pavelić on April 8, 1941, referred to above, Kvaternik proclaimed Croatia a free and independent state. This state was to have a population of around six million and a half, including about two million Serbs.

ESTABLISHMENT OF THE STATE

On April 11, 1941, Kvaternik, as Deputy Chief of State, ordered that until the establishment of the government of the State of Croatia its administrative affairs should be "discharged by the divisional offices of the Provincial Government of Croatia."[36] In the meantime Pavelić had arrived in Zagreb, and, after issuing a proclamation as Chief of the new state (*Poglavnik*), established the first Croatian government by decree of April 16, 1941.[37] This government consisted of Pavelić as presiding minister and at the same time Minister of Foreign Affairs, of a Vice President, and of a Commander of the Armed Forces and Minister of Defense (Kvaternik, who was also appointed Deputy of the Chief of State). By the same decree there were created the offices of Minister of Justice, of the Interior, of Public Health, of National Economy, of Religion and Education (one ministry), of Forestry and Mines (one ministry), and of Corporations; in addition, the decree established a Legislative Committee with a president appointed by Pavelić.

INTERNATIONAL RELATIONS

On April 15 Germany and Italy granted recognition to Croatia. The Croatian State was subsequently recognized by Hungary and Slovakia (April 16), Bulgaria (April 22), Rumania (May 7), and Japan (June 7).[38]

On May 18, 1941, three agreements were signed in Rome by Italy and Croatia: a treaty fixing the frontiers between Croatia and Italy, a military agreement, and a treaty of guaranty and collaboration which was to last twenty-five years.[39] By the terms of the latter treaty Italy guaranteed the political independence and territorial integrity of Croatia, while in order to

[35] It is reported that Hitler intends to create a Donaustaat in which he would settle German minorities living in Hungary, Rumania, and Croatia. In that case, the whole of the Banat, including the Rumanian part, would become a kind of Balkan East Prussia. *Free Europe*, November 14, 1941.

[36] See below, p. 606. [37] See below, p. 606.

[38] *New York Times*, April 17, 1941, p. 8; May 8, p. 13; June 8, p. 16.

[39] *New York Times*, May 19, 1941, p. 1, col. 6; *Bulletin of International News*, Vol. XVIII, No. 26 (December 27, 1941), pp. 2009–10. A German-Croatian Treaty had been signed on May 13 fixing the boundaries between Germany and Croatia. See *ibid.*, p. 2009.

safeguard the "protective" rights of Italy Croatia obligated itself not to contract any obligations incompatible with such guaranties. The treaty also stressed the aim of both parties to enter into fuller and closer relationship in customs and currency affairs, and provided for future agreements on other matters of mutual interest. It would seem, however, that the military clauses, taken in conjunction with the military agreement of the same date, were actually the provisions of a determining character in the treaty; in fact the intent of those provisions was to put the "independent" Croatian State in a position of complete military dependence on Italy. In Article 3 of the treaty, the Croatian Government declared that it would use Italians in the organization and instruction of its armed forces as well as in the establishment of the military defenses of the country. The military agreement provided that the Dalmatian shore and islands of the Croatian State were not to be fortified (Article 1), which means that in military matters Italy was to have a free hand in relation to Croatia. This presumption is strengthened by the provisions of the agreement that Croatia was not to have a navy—except for specialized units necessary for police and customs services (Article 2)—and that Italy should have the right of military transit across Croatian territory.[40] Following the signing of the treaties on May 18, King Victor Emmanuel, on the request of Pavelić, designated his nephew, Aimone Savoy-Aosta, Duke of Spoleto, to be King of Croatia, and in Rome the latter was proclaimed King in the presence of Pavelić and one hundred Croat delegates. However, he never assumed his functions.[41]

COUNCIL OF STATE

The Council of State was created as a substitute for parliament. The decree on its establishment, dated January 24, 1942,[42] is based upon two premises: (1) that although the Croatian State was dissolved centuries ago, the national traditions lasted throughout the centuries and there is a historical constitutional law which affords a basis for the present constitution of the Independent State of Croatia; (2) that not only the Ustaše movement but also other political groups and persons who were active in the cause of Croatian independence are responsible for the activities of the Council of State. Apparently the rulers of Croatia wished to be able to present evidence in the future that the creators of independent Croatia were acting not on a narrow but on a broader national basis, particularly in the formation of

[40] Angelo Piero Sereni, "The Status of Croatia under International Law," *American Political Science Review*, Vol. XXXV (1941), p. 1147.

[41] *New York Times*, May 19, 1941, p. 1, col. 6; *Bulletin of International News*, Vol. XVIII, No. 26 (December 27, 1941), p. 2010.

On orders from King Victor Emmanuel, the Duke of Aosta (formerly Duke of Spoleto) resigned the throne of Croatia on July 31, 1943. He is "reliably reported not to have wanted the Croatian throne, and he never visited the state from the time of its founding. . . ."—*New York Times*, August 1, 1943, p. 3.

[42] See below, p. 608.

the first Council of State.[43] In this broader basis of the Croatian Council of State it was deemed necessary to include surviving representatives—Croats—of the last Croatian Diet of 1918, surviving representatives—Croats—of the Skupština (parliament in Belgrade) elected in 1938, the founders and life members of the Central Committee of the former Croatian Agrarian Party, and members of the council of the former Party for the Acquisition of Rights for the Croats, elected in 1919. Because of Axis affiliations, representatives of the German national minority were accorded the right to send their representatives to the first Council of State. According to Section 5 of the decree members of the Council of State enjoy rights of immunity. The president of the Supreme Court is charged with the execution of the decree (Section 7). By including a provision on rights of immunity, an endeavor was made to create the impression that the Council of State is a parliament in the strict sense of the word.

MONOPARTY SYSTEM

The main political feature of the new state is the monoparty system and the exclusion of other parties. The only party entitled to represent the political idea of Croatia is the Ustaše Party. This party, as mentioned above, proclaimed the independence of Croatia by revolutionary means. It is a radical, nationalistic movement with socialistic inclinations. Labor is proclaimed as a basis for any reward. The party consists of adult members and special youth groups. However, two additional elements are involved, the union of professional organizations and special party guard Ustaše troops, which represent the executive element of the party.[44]

CHURCH

The religion of the predominant part of the Croat population is Roman Catholic, while the Serbs included within the boundaries of the new state belong to the Serb Orthodox Church. Before the dismemberment of Yugoslavia all Serbs belonging to the Orthodox faith were united in the Eastern Orthodox Church with headquarters in Belgrade. After the creation of the new state, the Croatian authorities looked unwillingly at the fact that their own citizens might seek religious leadership in a foreign country and hence they were eager to sever relations between their new citizens and the Eastern Orthodox Church in Belgrade. Therefore a Croatian Orthodox Church was established in the territory of Croatia by the law of April 3, 1942.[45] A little later a special statute was enacted for the new Croatian Orthodox Church.[46] It is declared in this statute that the Croatian Orthodox

[43] However, it should not be overlooked that the régime in Croatia is based upon a single party, representing the Ustaše liberation movement, and that the admission of other persons to the Council of State can be treated only as an exception serving a specific purpose.
[44] See regulations of August 11, 1942, below, p. 611.
[45] See below, p. 617. [46] June 5, 1942, *ibid.*

Church is indivisible in its unity, that it is autocephalous, and that it shall be guided dogmatically and canonically by the principles of the Holy Eastern Orthodox Church. The new church was given the status of a patriarchy, with its seat at Zagreb.

The language of the Eastern Orthodox Church of Yugoslavia since 1918, and in former times back to the earliest days, had been Serbian. The lettering in its literature and other written materials had also been Serbian (Cyrillic alphabet). Despite this, the above-mentioned statute declared that the official language as well as the official lettering of the Croatian Orthodox Church should be Croatian, which, in the existing circumstances, must be felt by the Serbs to be an infringement upon their religion.

In order to connect the new church officially and visually with the new state, it was provided that the flag of the church should have the colors of the Croatian state (red, white, and blue).

As already noted, it was officially declared in the statute that the new church is autocephalous, but this autonomy is illusory when one considers the complete subordination of the clergy to the state in matters of appointments as well as of financial support. Thus, as regards the procedure for appointments, a Council of Electors is established, consisting of all bishops of the new church, of a government official (the Chief of the Eastern Orthodox Division in the Ministry of Justice and Cults), of the Dean of the Orthodox Faculty of the University of Zagreb, and of five members of the Eastern Orthodox Church appointed for each election by the chief of the state, upon the recommendation of the Ministry of Justice and Cults. The bishops themselves are to be appointed by the chief of the state, upon the recommendation of the Minister of Justice and Cults, from among three candidates presented by the Synod of Bishops. In order to elect the Patriarch of the church, the Council of Electors must nominate from among the bishops three candidates, whose names must be presented to the chief of the state through the Minister of Justice and Cults. Thus it is the chief of the state who has the final decision in the matter of appointments of the bishops and of the Patriarch. According to Section 116 the chief of the state shall himself directly appoint the first Patriarch and the first bishops.

As to the financial status of the church, it should be stated that the religious officers of the church are paid by the state in the same manner as government officials and that their civil service ratings are determined in accordance with the general principles of the Croatian Civil Service. The money for the expenses of the church is collected by local tax authorities from parishes of the Croatian Orthodox Church. Later the Treasury passes on the payments to the church authorities. Thus the new church is made dependent financially as well as otherwise on the Croatian State.

LABOR

The labor legislation of Croatia stresses the importance of labor in society. The law regulating labor relations [47] proclaimed that "it is the right and duty of every citizen to work, and work alone should be the basis of his existence and the measure of his usefulness." The state has the right to supervise not only the nature of work but also wages. Moreover, penalties are imposed for workers' failures in accomplishment and for actions making work impossible or difficult. Both employers and employees are called upon to conduct their mutual relations primarily "upon the principle of the welfare of the nation and the state as a whole," and only secondarily "with regard to individual profit." However, collective bargaining is permitted.

The Croatian Union of Workers was established as a professional organization of workers covering all fields of labor in Croatia. According to the statute of the Croatian Union of Workers,[48] this union is a part of the Ustaše liberation movement. It embraces all workers and their societies and all trade unions, the highest office of the union being that of the leader, who is appointed by the government. Thus the workers are controlled politically by the Ustaše Party and in an administrative way by their leader, a government appointee. As not only labor but also all trades and economic activities are controlled by the government, it is thus possible for the government to exercise a decisive control over both employers and employees and to decide their disputes by fiat.

CONTROL OF TRADES

On April 18, 1942,[49] a Fascist corporate system was introduced. The purpose of this decree was to seize and develop the national resources, to organize and protect trades, and to eliminate competition in economic activities. The underlying aim is to strengthen the nation and the state. The decree provides for the establishing of chambers of handicrafts, industry, commerce, and banking and insurance throughout all the country. All the chambers are to be supervised by the Minister of Handicrafts, Industry, and Commerce. No person can engage in economic activities without having a trade license or membership in a particular chamber. Even governmental enterprises and establishments and enterprises belonging to the local government must also be members of the respective chambers. The chambers are required to organize a regular association under the name, "Representatives of Croatian Trade Chambers," to serve as a consultative body to the government.

Besides the trade chambers, professional associations are also to be established under this law.

[47] See law of April 30, 1942, below, p. 624.
[48] Dated January 23, 1942. See below, p. 623. [49] See decree of that date, below, p. 609.

The Minister of Handicrafts, Industry, and Commerce and the Minister of Finance are charged with the execution of the law, and the former is authorized "to amend, change, correct, abolish, and interpret" all rules and regulations issued thereunder, and to issue new ones.

COURTS

When the territory of Croatia was a part of the Yugoslav Kingdom, the Supreme Court of Yugoslavia was the highest court of the whole kingdom. After the creation of the Independent State of Croatia, a Supreme Court for the entire Croatian territory was established in Bania Luca.[50] At the same time the office of a national Attorney General was established in Bania Luca, as well as offices of state attorneys in Zagreb and Sarajevo. The Supreme Court in Bania Luca has final jurisdiction in civil and criminal cases as well as in non-trial cases. This court has one president, one vice president, and an appropriate number of judges. The president—or in his absence the vice president—is vested with power to suspend any decision of individual benches in civil cases, "if such decision is in contradiction to previous important or basic decisions of the Supreme Court" or "in obvious contradiction to the contents of the record in the case, or if it is in obvious violation of the law." The same decree states that "whenever the president exercises this right, the case must be brought before the plenary session of the Supreme Court." However, there is no statement to the effect that the plenary session may overrule the president.

PENAL LAW

On July 20, 1942,[51] a law was published concerning the suppression "of violent crimes against the state, individuals, and property." This law provides for special treatment of political and certain common criminals. It does not, however, define in a detailed manner the offenses for which especially harsh treatment is established, but speaks generally of persons "who violate public order and safety or threaten the peace and quiet of the Croatian people, or who undertake some violent crime against the state, individuals, or property." For such crimes two types of treatment were introduced: (1) confinement in concentration camps for a period of not less than three months nor more than three years; and (2) confiscation of property. Although the law provides for deprivation of liberty and property, it is not carried out by way of judicial procedure but merely by a division of the Ministry of the Interior designated as "Administration of Public Order and Safety." A peculiar provision states that if the culprits have fled, the members of their families may be confined in concentration camps and their property confiscated. This provision is in contradiction to the principle of individual responsibility under modern criminal law. However, the most

[50] See law of January 7, 1942, below, p. 614.

[51] See below, p. 615

drastic penal law was published on April 17, 1941.[52] This law imposes the death penalty for the most serious political crimes. The acts for which that penalty may be imposed, however, are defined quite vaguely, namely, as harm done "to the honor and vital interests of the Croatian nation" or as acts endangering the "existence of the Independent State of Croatia or its government authorities." These cases are tried by extraordinary People's Courts, consisting of three judges, applying a summary procedure.

PROPERTY

An especially severe régime for property was established in Croatia. Transactions of transfer and mortgaging of real property may take place only with the permission of the Minister of Justice.[53]

According to the law of August 2, 1941, practically every productive establishment may be expropriated "whenever necessary for the needs of the state and nation."[54] Of especial political importance is the law concerning investigation of the origin of property and the forfeiture of property illegally acquired.[55] This law is directed mainly against statesmen (ministers, representatives, or senators) who have collaborated with the Yugoslav Government, and its aim is to deprive such persons of their property. A National Committee for Investigation of the Origin of Property was created, and ministers, representatives, or senators who occupied their respective offices during the period from December 1, 1918, to April 10, 1941, must, in accordance with Section 1 of this law, submit to such committee "a declaration concerning the status and origin of their property and of that of their wives and children." This committee has also the right to ask any Croatian national or citizen to submit within one month of the effective date of the law a statement regarding the status and origin of his property and of that of his wife and children. According to Section 6, paragraph 2, it is assumed that property was acquired illegally "if it is in obvious and considerable disproportion to the plausible income of the suspected person, his wife and children, and to their expenses; or if he acquired the property through the use of political or family influence, by intermediation with the national or local authorities."

This decree operates on the presumption that the property was acquired illegally; and the person called upon has the burden of proof to the contrary. If the proof fails, the property in question is condemned by the committee to be transferred to the Treasury or to persons or institutions which were injured "by such illegal acquisition."

FINANCE

By the decree of May 10, 1941, a Croatian State Bank was established in Zagreb as the bank of issue. A new monetary unit was introduced for Croa-

[52] See below, p. 613.
[53] See decree-law of April 18, 1941, below, p. 620.
[54] See below, p. 620.
[55] See law of August 30, 1941, below, p. 621.

tia, namely, the kuna. The kuna contains 100 banica. It was stated that the value of the kuna should be 17,921 milligrams of fine gold. The Croatian State Bank was authorized to exchange at par dinar notes of 1,000, 500, 100, and 50 denomination of the former National Bank of the Kingdom of Yugoslavia for new bank notes issued by the bank of the Independent State of Croatia.[56]

The Croatian State Bank has a share capital of 300 million kuna divided into 60,000 shares, to be registered in the names of the holders and to be held only by Croat nationals. The notes of the bank are to be covered by gold, foreign exchange, bills, checks, securities, and debt certificates representing the liabilities taken over from the Yugoslav National Bank. The authorities of the bank consist of a president, a vice president, and three directors appointed for three years by the chief of the state. Two more directors and a board of governors, consisting of five persons, are elected by the shareholders.[57]

GENOCIDE

Genocide policy is directed predominantly against Jews and Serbs.

a) Jews. Even in the first stage of the formation of the state a differentiation in treatment of the population was introduced in accordance with the racial principles laid down in the German Nuremberg legislation. According to the German pattern heretofore described, nationality was divided into two classifications. The higher type created a full right of relationship between individual and state and was granted only to persons of Aryan origin.[58] The inferior type of nationality does not confer rights to participate in political life but does give a certain protection to the person involved, such as the right to be granted a passport and the right to participate in economic activities within certain limitations. This latter type of nationality is granted to Jews and even to non-Jews who are not considered as completely reliable politically.

In Croatia Jewish property was seized. By a decree-law of April 14, 1941, all transactions between Jews and between Jews and third parties entered into within two months before the independence of the State of Croatia was proclaimed, were to be declared null and void if the value thereof exceeded 100,000 dinars.[59] This law was later made applicable to legal transactions entered into after independence was proclaimed.

Several other limitations relating to the exercise of professions and economic activities have reduced the Jewish population in Croatia to a state of degradation.

b) Serbs. The Serbian population living in Croatia is affected mainly in its political and cultural aspects. Its national pattern is being destroyed by

[56] See below, p. 622; see also decree-law of July 7, 1941, *ibid.*
[57] Bank for International Settlements, *Press Reviews*, May 17, 1943, Issue 95, p. 1.
[58] See law of April 30, 1941, below, p. 626. [59] See below, p. 625.

genocide legislation. Since the main difference between the Serbian and Croatian languages consists in the use by the Croats of the Roman lettering and by the Serbs of the Cyrillic lettering, the use of the latter has been prohibited. By this prohibition the Serbs are practically obliged to use the Croatian language in writing.[60] If one considers that the Cyrillic lettering is an essential part of the ritual of the Eastern Orthodox Church, one must conclude that the compulsion as to the use of the Roman lettering amounts to interference with religion.

It is reported that the Serbian population in Croatia is being subjected to massacres and tortures. Allegedly several hundred thousand Serbs have been killed by the Ustaše.[60a]

VII. Kossovo, Dibrano, and Struga (Albanian Occupation)

On June 9, 1940,[61] King Victor Emmanuel promulgated a royal decree to the effect that the Kingdom of Albania considered itself at war with those states with which the Kingdom of Italy was at war. By the same decree the Albanian Fascist Militia and Forestry Militia and the Armed Police Force and all other Albanian armed units were put under the orders of the Supreme Commander of the Italian Armed Forces. Thus Albania was automatically involved in the war with Yugoslavia when Italy started military action. It received for itself a part of the spoils of Yugoslavia.

By the proclamation of Mussolini of June 29, 1941,[62] it was declared that in the territories of Kossovo, Dibrano, and Struga occupied by Italian forces in Yugoslavia, the rights of the military occupant are "transferred to the Albanian Government." These territories were later annexed by the Albanian Government by the law of September 12, 1942,[63] and Albanian administration was introduced into them.

A special Ministry for Redeemed Territories was created in Tirana, the capital of Albania, but was later abolished.

On July 22, 1942, the Vicegerent published a decree establishing offices for public works in the redeemed territories at Prishtina, Peja, Dibrano, and Tetova.[64]

In these territories a genocide policy in relation to Serbs is being carried out. Yugoslav schools have been closed, with the exception of some schools belonging to Serbian religious bodies. In their stead Albanian schools have been opened. Those pupils of Albanian nationality who had previously attended the discontinued Yugoslav schools were given every fa-

[60] See decree of April 25, 1941, below, p. 626.
[60a] *Martyrdom of the Serbs*. Prepared and issued by the Serbian Eastern Orthodox Diocese for the United States and Canada (1943), *passim*.
[61] See below, p. 272.
[62] See below, p. 627.
[63] See below, p. 629.
[64] See below, p. 629.

cility to continue their studies in the new Albanian schools. The Minister of Education was empowered to take possession of the buildings and equipment, archives, and all scientific endowments of the former Yugoslav schools.[65] By so doing, the occupant has violated Articles 46 and 56 of the Hague Regulations, which prohibit the seizure of property of institutions dedicated to education and science. The discontinuance of the Yugoslav schools is also an encroachment upon the right to education, which is protected by customs of international law and by the principles of humanity which form part of the Hague Regulations.

The Albanian franc was made legal tender, and Yugoslav dinars were exchanged at the rate of 6.08 Albanian francs for 100 dinars. For transactions in connection with conversion of currency, a special committee of three persons was created, of which the president is designated by the civil commissioner (Italian), one member is appointed by the National Bank of Albania, and the third is elected from among the population.

As the Serbian population in the annexed territories displayed a hostile attitude toward the Albanian occupant, drastic measures were applied. There existed in Albania a law of 1930 providing for severe collective penalties for members of families of offenders in hiding. These penalties included the internment of families, sequestration of property, and setting fire to the houses of culprits. This law has a special practical importance in these areas, where hiding in the mountains is prevalent. The penalties imposed upon the innocent members of families are intended to cause the culprits to leave their hiding places and appear before tribunals of justice. The Albanian occupant proceeded to promulgate this law on collective penalties in the occupied areas.[66] The introduction of such a provision in occupied territory is a violation of Article 50 of the Hague Regulations, which prohibits the inflicting of collective penalties upon the population because of the acts of individuals, for which acts the population cannot be regarded as jointly and severally responsible.

VIII. Baranja, Bačka, Prekomurje, and Medžumurje (Southern Territories)

(Hungarian Occupation)

BACKGROUND

After the Treaty of Trianon, Hungary claimed a revision of the frontiers with Yugoslavia, not only with a view to restoring Hungarian ethnographic regions but also regions which had belonged to Hungary in the past, such as Croatia. Here again, the doctrine of the Holy Crown[67] was invoked.

[65] See Vicegerent's decree of November 12, 1941, below, p. 627.
[66] See Vicegerent's decree of October 2, 1942, extending law of August 29, 1930, to redeemed territories, below, p. 630.
[67] See above, chapter on Czechoslovakia, section on the doctrine of the Holy Crown, p. 144.

Therefore, during the intervening years the relations between the two countries were greatly strained and Hungary was often accused by Yugoslavia of fostering separatist movements in Yugoslavia. In particular, charges were brought that the Hungarians were training Croatian terrorists in Hungary. A change in the relations of the two countries occurred on December 12, 1940, when their respective foreign ministers met in Belgrade and signed a treaty of perpetual amity. Article I of this treaty expressly provided: "Permanent peace will reign and eternal friendship will exist between the Kingdom of Yugoslavia and the Kingdom of Hungary." And Article II stated: "The Signatory parties agree to consult on all problems which, in their opinion, affect their mutual relations."[68]

Four months later, during the German invasion of Yugoslavia in April, 1941, Hungarian troops marched into Yugoslavia and occupied the regions of Medžumurje, Prekomurje, Baranja, and Bačka. This occupation coincided with the proclamation of Croatia as an "independent" state.[69]

INCORPORATION

On December 27, 1941, the territories so occupied, referred to as "Southern Territories," were by law formally incorporated into Hungary.[70] As was the case with the Highland Territories and Subcarpathia, the law referred to the Hungarian Holy Crown as the legal entity into which the Southern Territories were incorporated, and thus in an official document gave expression anew to the doctrine of the Holy Crown.

REPRESENTATION IN PARLIAMENT

Law XX of 1941 provided for representation in Parliament of the incorporated Southern Territories. However, during the period when the citizens' electors could not choose representatives "by normal procedure," the members of the Upper House were to be nominated, on motion of the Prime Minister, by the Parliament, both houses concurring. Law XXI of 1942[71] provided further that the county assemblies should elect representatives to the Upper House, the number of such members for every county and autonomous city in the Southern Territories being fixed in advance.[72]

ADMINISTRATION

In the beginning these territories were administered by Hungarian military commanders of the occupying forces. Later on Hungarian civil administration was extended to them. The Hungarian authorities have introduced a

[68] Hungaro-Yugoslav Treaty of Amity, December 12, 1940, printed in London *Times*, December 13, 1940, p. 3, col. 2.

[69] See above, section on Croatia, p. 252. [70] See Law XX, 1941, below, p. 631.

[71] See above, chapter on Czechoslovakia, p. 147.

[72] The above law provides material for comparison of the number of representatives fixed for the Southern Territories with the number of other counties in Hungary proper, as well as in the incorporated Highland Territories and Subcarpathia.

genocide policy by endeavoring to impose a Hungarian pattern upon these territories. As Prekomurje and Medžumurje are inhabited also by Slovenes and Croats, the genocide policy affects those races; in Bačka and Baranja it affects the Serbs and Jews.

On May 6, 1942, the Yugoslav Government in London delivered to the Allied Governments a memorandum concerning mass destruction of the Serbian population in the occupied territories. In addition to the details concerning the many atrocities that had taken place under Hungarian occupation, the memorandum stated that concentration camps had been established in every town, the largest being in Subotica, Novi Sad, Pechuj, and Baja. That of Novi Sad contained about 13,000 men, women and children, Serbs and Jews. The memorandum further charged that churches had been looted and destroyed and that the celebration of all Orthodox holy days was prohibited by the Hungarian authorities.[73]

CITIZENSHIP

According to Law XX, 1941, the inhabitants of the incorporated Southern Territories were given the right to reacquire Hungarian citizenship as from April 11, 1941, if they were beyond question Hungarian citizens on July 26, 1921, under Hungarian law and became citizens of the Kingdom of the Serbs, Croats, and Slovenes by virtue of the Treaty of Trianon. Such persons must have lived continuously, however, in the incorporated Southern Territories for ten years, that is, from June 1, 1931, to June 1, 1941. Persons who had exercised the right of option and obtained foreign citizenship are excluded from the benefits of this law. That the Hungarian Government apparently does not feel sure of the loyalty of the population in the Southern Territories is to be seen from the provision instituting a procedure for voiding citizenship granted under the above-mentioned law. This law states (Section 4) that citizenship "reacquired or acquired" may be recalled by the Minister of the Interior within five years from the effective date of the law, if the new citizen has during the period of separation from Hungary "seriously injured the interests of the Hungarian nation by a hostile attitude."

CURRENCY

Serbian dinar notes and coins ceased to be legal tender on July 12, 1941, by which date all dinars had to be exchanged for pengo. The exchange rate was established of 1 pengő to 10 dinars. According to the twelfth Annual Report of the Bank of International Settlements, Hungary used about 191 million pengő to replace the Yugoslav currency.[74]

[73] See text of the memorandum in *New York Times*, May 19, 1942, p. 4, col. 1. See also *Martyrdom of the Serbs*. Prepared and Issued by the Serbian Eastern Orthodox Diocese for the United States of America and Canada (Chicago, [1943]), pp. 265–68; *Inter-Allied Review*, Vol. II, No. 5 (May 15, 1942), p. 102.

[74] See Bank for International Settlements, *Twelfth Annual Report* (1942), p. 209.

IX. Macedonia, Morava, Skoplje, and Bitolia Regions (Bulgarian Occupation)

A considerable part of Yugoslavia was occupied also by Bulgaria. The occupied areas include the long-disputed territory of western Macedonia and the regions of Skoplje, Bitolia, and parts of the Morava regions. Different policies were adopted by the occupant in the respective regions. Macedonia, which had been claimed by Bulgaria for many years, was considered after its occupation as Bulgarian territory returning to the homeland. Therefore a policy of rehabilitation and reconstruction was adopted there in relation to the Macedonians, who are considered by the Bulgarians as of Bulgarian origin. As to the other groups of the population, especially Serbs, a policy of national oppression (genocide) was adopted. From Macedonia 120,000 Serbs were removed to Old Serbia.[75] In order to carry out the rehabilitation policy, a special budget was voted by the Sobranje in Sofia.

Yugoslav administration was abolished and Bulgarian administration introduced in its stead. Because of an old feud between the Serbs and the Bulgarians in this region, most of the officials were superseded by Bulgarians.

Yugoslav currency, the dinar, was replaced by the Bulgarian lev.[76] By Decision No. 2012 of the Council of Ministers,[77] all private persons and firms with domicile and residence in Macedonia, Morava, and the western regions were ordered to deposit, within fourteen days as from June 6, 1941, in the respective agencies of the Bulgarian National Bank, notes of one hundred dinars and higher denominations. It was declared that after the expiration of the period prescribed for deposits dinars would cease to be legal tender.

Decision No. 3121 of the Council of Ministers has temporarily frozen all bank accounts. Bank accounts were transferred from dinars into leva but payments were to be made only to persons of Bulgarian origin who had not emigrated from these regions during the year 1941.[78] In order to limit spending of money and to check inflation, special arrangements were made as to repayment of deposits of Bulgarians. If the deposit amounted to less than 2,000 leva, it was repaid immediately, but deposits above 2,000 leva were repaid in monthly instalments of 2,000 leva.

All agricultural enterprises were ordered to declare the quantities of products which they had harvested within the last year.[79]

[75] Kulischer, *op. cit.*, p. 115. [76] The exchange rate adopted is unknown to the author.
[77] See below, p. 633. [78] See below, p. 635. [79] *Durjaven Vestnik*, No. 185, p. 3.

PART III

LAWS OF OCCUPATION

Statutes, Decrees, and Other Documents

ALBANIA

1. UNION ACTS AND BASIC STATUTE

Law No. 580 regarding Acceptance of the Crown of Albania by the King of Italy, Emperor of Ethiopia, April 16, 1939 [1]

Victor Emmanuel III, by the grace of God and by the will of the People King of Italy, Emperor of Ethiopia.

The Fascist Grand Council having expressed its opinion;

The Senate and the Chamber of Fasces and Corporations having approved;

We have authorized and we promulgate as follows:

ARTICLE 1. The King of Italy, having accepted the Crown of Albania, assumes for himself and his heirs the title of King of Italy and of Albania, Emperor of Ethiopia.

ARTICLE 2. The King of Italy and of Albania, Emperor of Ethiopia, shall be represented in Albania by a Vicegerent, who shall reside in Tirana.

We order that the present law, with the seal of the state affixed thereto, be inserted in the official collection of the laws and decrees of the Kingdom of Italy, and we direct whomsoever it may concern to obey it and cause it to be obeyed as a law of the state.

Given in Rome this day, April 16, 1939–XVII.

VICTOR EMMANUEL

MUSSOLINI

Seen: The Keeper of the Seal, SOLMI.

Decree concerning the Basic Statute of the Kingdom of Albania, June 3, 1939 [2]

Victor Emmanuel III, by the grace of God and by the will of the People King of Italy and of Albania, Emperor of Ethiopia.

In accepting the Crown of Albania, tendered by the Constitutional Assembly which met in Tirana on April 12, 1939–XVII, we have assumed the high duties of providing for the care of our Albanian sons and also of leading this noble People, renewed under the symbol of the Lictors, toward its highest destiny.

[1] *Leggi e decreti*, 1939, No. 580; published in the *Gazetta ufficiale del Regno d'Italia*, April 19, 1939, No. 94.

[2] *Fletorja Zyrtare*, 1939, No. 40, p. 1.

Considering that to achieve these ends it is indispensable to determine the structure of the state in conformity with supreme national interests, we have decided to grant to our beloved Albanian People a basic statute, a token also of our affection and of our paternal solicitude.

Inspired by these sentiments we have decreed and we decree:

BASIC STATUTE OF THE KINGDOM OF ALBANIA

I. General Provisions

ARTICLE 1. The Albanian State shall be ruled by a constitutional monarchic government.

The throne shall be hereditary, according to the Salic law, in the dynasty of His Majesty Victor Emmanuel III, King of Italy and of Albania, Emperor of Ethiopia.

ARTICLE 2. The Albanian flag shall be red, bearing in the center the black double-headed eagle with the emblem of the Lictors' Fasces (*Fascio Littorio*).

ARTICLE 3. The official language of the state is Albanian.

ARTICLE 4. All religions shall be respected. The free exercise of worship and of the outward practices thereof are guaranteed, in conformity with the laws.

ARTICLE 5. The legislative power shall be exercised by the King with the collaboration of the Fascist Upper Corporative Council.

ARTICLE 6. The executive power shall belong to the King.

ARTICLE 7. Justice shall emanate from the King and shall be administered in his name by the judges whom he shall appoint.

ARTICLE 8. The implementation of the laws, with the object of imposing obligation on all, shall lie exclusively with the legislative power.

ARTICLE 9. The organization of communal and provincial institutions shall be established by law.

II. The King

ARTICLE 10. The person of the King shall be sacred and inviolable.

ARTICLE 11. The King shall attain majority on completion of eighteen years of age.

During the minority of the King, or in the event that the King, being of age, is incapable of reigning because of physical incapacity, the powers of the King shall be exercised by a regent. The regency will fall to the Regent of the Kingdom of Italy.

ARTICLE 12. The King may appoint a Vicegerent (*Luogotenente Generale*).

The Vicegerent shall exercise all the powers of the King, with the exception of those which the King shall expressly reserve to himself.

ARTICLE 13. The King is the supreme head of the state; he commands the armed forces, declares war, concludes peace, and makes international treaties, giving notice thereof to the Fascist Upper Corporative Council, in so far as the interest and the security of the state permit.

ARTICLE 14. The King shall make appointments to all the positions of the state.

ARTICLE 15. The King shall promulgate the decrees and the regulations necessary to execute the laws, and to discipline the organization and functioning of the authorities of the state.

When reasons of urgent and absolute necessity require it, the King may issue rules having the force of laws. In this case, the royal decree must be presented to the Fascist Upper Corporative Council for conversion into law.

ARTICLE 16. The function of proposing laws shall belong to the King and to the Fascist Upper Corporative Council. But the proposing of laws which are of a constitutional nature or which involve increases in expense shall rest with the King alone.

ARTICLE 17. The King shall sanction laws and promulgate them.

ARTICLE 18. The King may grant clemency and commute sentences.

The Vicegerent shall exercise all the powers of the King, with the exception of those which the King shall expressly reserve to himself.

ARTICLE 19. The King may create orders of knighthood and prescribe the statutes thereof.

ARTICLE 20. The King may confer titles of nobility.

ARTICLE 21. No one may receive decorations, titles, or pensions from a foreign power without the authorization of the King.

III. The King's Government

ARTICLE 22. The King shall appoint and dismiss his ministers of state. They shall be responsible for all the actions and measures taken by their ministries.

ARTICLE 23. The King, should he consider it necessary, may convoke and preside over the Council of Ministers.

ARTICLE 24. The ministers of state shall always have access to the Fascist Upper Corporative Council and must be heard on request.

ARTICLE 25. The laws and acts of the government shall not be effective unless they bear the signature of a minister.

IV. The Fascist Upper Corporative Council

ARTICLE 26. The Fascist Upper Corporative Council shall be composed of members of the Central Council of the Albanian Fascist Party and of the active members of the Central Council of Corporative Economy.

The composition of the Central Council of the Albanian Fascist Party and of the Central Council of Corporative Economy cannot be modified except by law.

ARTICLE 27. It is requisite that councillors [i.e., members of the Fascist Upper Corporative Council] shall:

a) Have reached the age of 25 years.
b) Enjoy civil and political rights.
c) Comply with other requirements.

ARTICLE 28. A committee composed of the president and the vice presidents of the Fascist Upper Corporative Council shall decide whether these requisites for the office of councillor have been fulfilled.

ARTICLE 29. Before being admitted to the exercise of their official functions the councillors shall take oath to be loyal to the King, to observe faithfully the Statute and laws of the state, and to exercise their official functions with the sole purpose of serving the welfare of the King and that of the country, which are inseparable.

ARTICLE 30. Councillors shall receive an annual compensation to be determined by law.

ARTICLE 31. Councillors shall be relieved of their office on the cessation of the duties exercised by them in the councils which cooperate in the formation of the Fascist Upper Corporative Council.

ARTICLE 32. The Fascist Upper Corporative Council shall be convoked by the King. The King shall also call sessions and postpone them.

ARTICLE 33. The presidents and vice presidents of the Fascist Upper Corporative Council shall be appointed by the King.

The president of the Fascist Upper Corporative Council shall make the necessary appointments to other positions established in the regulations of the Upper Council.

ARTICLE 34. No subject may be placed on the agenda of the Fascist Upper Corporative Council without the authorization of the King.

ARTICLE 35. The sessions of the Fascist Upper Corporative Council shall be public. But when the ministers so request, they may be held in secret.

ARTICLE 36. Voting shall always occur openly.

ARTICLE 37. Bills approved by the Fascist Upper Corporative Council shall be presented for the sanction of the King.

The King may refuse his sanction. He can also ask for a second discussion of bills.

ARTICLE 38. The Fascist Upper Corporative Council shall determine by its own internal regulation the manner in which it is to exercise its functions.

ARTICLE 39. The Fascist Upper Corporative Council shall have the right to bring accusations against the King's ministers for offenses committed in the exercise of their duties and to call them before the High Court of Justice.

V. Judicial Order

Article 40. The organization and the responsibilities of tribunals shall be established by law.

Article 41. Judges, in the exercise of their judicial functions, shall be independent. They shall be irremovable, in accordance with the law on judicial organization.

Article 42. No one may be deprived of the natural right of trial. No extraordinary tribunals may therefore be created, except in cases specified by law.

Article 43. A High Court of Justice shall be instituted for the trial of ministers accused by the Fascist Upper Corporative Council.

It shall be composed of nine members appointed by the King. The rules on organization of the High Court of Justice and the exercise of its functions shall be established by law.

Article 44. The hearings of the tribunals in civil matters and arguments in penal matters shall be public, in accordance with the law.

VI. The Rights and Duties of Citizens

Article 45. All citizens shall be equal before the law: they shall enjoy civil and political rights and shall be admissible to civil and military positions, with such exceptions as are provided by law.

Article 46. They shall contribute without distinction, in proportion to their means, to the burdens of the state.

Article 47. No tax may be imposed if it has not been established by law.

Article 48. Military service shall be compulsory for all, in accordance with the laws on military conscription.

Article 49. Personal liberty is guaranteed. No one may be arrested or brought before courts of justice except in cases provided for by law and in the form prescribed thereby.

Article 50. The home shall be inviolable. No search of houses can take place except by virtue of the law and in the form prescribed thereby.

Article 51. The press shall be free, but the abuse of such freedom shall be curbed by law.

Article 52. All property, without any exception, shall be inviolable. Nevertheless, when it shall be legally ascertained that the public interest so demands, a person may be required to surrender his property in whole or in part, with just indemnification therefor, in accordance with the laws.

VII. FINAL PROVISIONS

ARTICLE 53. All laws contrary to the present statute are abrogated.

ARTICLE 54. The present Statute shall come into effect on June 4, 1939–XVII.

Given in Rome, June 3, 1939–XVII.

VICTOR EMMANUEL

SH. VERLACI, *President of the Council and Minister of Public Works ad interim;* T. MBORJA, *Minister Secretary of the National Fascist Party;* XHAFER YPI, *Minister of Justice;* MALIG BUSHATI, *Minister of the Interior;* FEJZI ALIZOTTI, *Minister of Finance;* ERNEST KOLIQI, *Minister of Public Instruction;* ANTON BEÇA, *Minister of National Economy.*

Law No. 1115 regarding the Fusion of the Albanian Armed Forces with the Corresponding Italian Armed Forces, July 13, 1939 [3]

[EXCERPTS]

Victor Emmanuel III, by the grace of God and by the will of the People King of Italy and of Albania, Emperor of Ethiopia.

The Senate and the Chamber of Fasces and Corporations, through their legislative committees, having approved;

We have authorized and We promulgate as follows:

ARTICLE 1. In view of the union of the destinies of the Italian People and the Albanian People, the Albanian armed forces shall be fused with the corresponding Italian armed forces.

ARTICLE 2. The government of the King shall be authorized to issue the necessary regulations for the implementation of the present law.

. . . . . .

Given at San Rossore this day, July 13, 1939–XVII.

VICTOR EMMANUEL

MUSSOLINI—CIANO—DI REVEL

Seen: The Keeper of the Seal, GRANDI.

Royal Decree No. 194 concerning Discipline of War, June 9, 1940 [4]

[EXCERPTS]

ARTICLE 1. The Kingdom of Albania shall consider itself at war with those states with which the Kingdom of Italy may be at war.

[3] *Leggi e decreti*, 1939, No. 1115; published in the *Gazzetta ufficiale*, August 11, 1939, No. 187.
[4] *Fletorja Zyrtare*, 1940, No. 93.

ARTICLE 2. The Supreme Commander of the Italian Armed Forces shall exercise his authority over all the armed forces which may operate in the territories, waters, and skies of Albania.

The Albanian Fascist Militia, the Albanian Forestry Militia, the Armed Police Force, and any other armed force which may be formed in Albania, shall, in the event of war, be subject to the orders of the aforementioned Supreme Commander.

. . . . .

Rome, June 9, 1940–XVII.

VICTOR EMMANUEL III

SH. VERLACI

2. ADMINISTRATION

Vicegerent's Decree No. 43 concerning the Order for the Promotion and Appointment of New State Employees, January 25, 1940 [5]

[EXCERPTS]

ARTICLE 1. Promotions shall normally take place from the lower grade to that immediately above, in accordance with the decisions, expressed by votes, of a committee composed of the minister in charge (who shall preside), the permanent counselor, the secretary general, and department heads of each ministry.

. . . . .

Tirana, January 25, 1940–XVIII.

FRANCESCO JACOMINI

SH. VERLACI—I. MBORJA—XHAFER YPI
M. BUSHATI—E. KOLIQI

Royal Decree concerning Personnel on Mission in Albania January 29, 1940 [6]

[EXCERPTS]

We have decreed and We decree:

To each of the following personnel not belonging to the administration, on mission in Albania to discharge special technical duties entrusted to them by the Ministry of Foreign Affairs, there is granted for the duration of the mission the annual salary indicated beside each name:

[5] *Fletorja Zyrtare*, 1940, No. 22, p. 6.

[6] *Gazzetta ufficiale*, 1940, No. 68.

Surname and Name	*Position*	*Amount of Annual Salary*
Califano, Dott. Simmaco	Director of the Italian Day Dispensary of Tirana	56.000
Bellavitis, Ing. Guisto	Organization of Public Works in Albania	56.000
Cannobio, Ing. Antonio	Do.	56.000
Bertè, Ing. Giulio	Do.	56.000
Gonfalonieri, Ing. Corrado	Do.	56.000
Giro, Comm. Giovanni	Expert in After-Work Recreation Centers for Albanian Youth	56.000

Given in Rome, this day, January 29, 1940–XVIII.

VICTOR EMMANUEL

MUSSOLINI—CIANO—DI REVEL

Seen: The Keeper of the Seal, GRANDI.

Vicegerent's Decree No. 163 concerning Employment of Counselors, July 16, 1942 [7]

[EXCERPTS]

ARTICLE 1. The Minister of Finance is hereby authorized to employ as many as four persons from the register of the Italian administration as counselors for his department.

Such persons shall be allowed salaries in accordance with their grades, together with the Albanian allowance and travel and per diem expenses.

. . . . .

Tirana, July 16, 1942–XX.

FRANCESCO JACOMINI

SHUK GURAKUQI

Vicegerent's Decree No. 176 concerning Regulations with respect to the Appointment and Jurisdiction of Under Secretaries of State, November 4, 1942 [8]

[EXCERPTS]

ARTICLE 1. At every ministry there may be nominated one or more under secretaries of state.

The under secretaries of state shall be nominated by decree of the Vicegerent on the suggestion of the President of Ministers.

[7] *Gazzetta ufficiale del Regno d'Albania*, 1942, No. 93.

[8] *Ibid.*, 1942, No. 130, pp. 7–8.

ARTICLE 2. The secretaries of state, aside from exercising the functions delegated to them by the minister, shall preside over administrative councils; shall supervise the application of the laws and regulations and the prompt execution of the orders of the minister; shall control the outlying offices under their jurisdiction; shall, if delegated, represent the minister before the legislative committees of the Fascist Upper Corporative Council; shall attend the meetings of the Council of Ministers when summoned by its president.

. . .

Tirana, November 4, 1942–XXI.

FRANCESCO JACOMINI

M. KRUJA—SHUK GURAKUQI

3. FASCIZATION

Vicegerent's Decree Creating the Albanian Fascist Party, June 2, 1939 [9]

[EXCERPTS]

THE STATUTE OF THE ALBANIAN FASCIST PARTY

I. The Albanian Fascist Party is a voluntary civilian militia under the orders of Benito Mussolini, the Creator and Duce of Fascism.

II. The Fascist Party shall be the only party in Albania.

III. The Albanian Fascist Party aims at the political education of the Albanians for the achievement of an ever higher degree of social justice, according to the principles of the Fascist Revolution.

. . .

IX. The Fascist, when admitted to the party, shall take the oath and sign his name to the text thereof.

The text of the oath is as follows: "I swear to carry out the orders of the Duce, Founder of the Empire and Creator of the New Albania, and to serve with all my strength, and if necessary with my blood, the cause of the Fascist Revolution."

. . .

XIV. The organizations of the Albanian Fascist Party shall be the following:

The Fascist University Groups.
The Littorio Youth (Group).
The Feminine Fascists.
The After-Hour Recreational Centers (*Dopolavoro*).
The Fascist Relief Organization.

Labor organizations shall be directly dependent on the Albanian Fascist Party.

. . . .

[9] *Fletorja Zyrtare*, 1939, No. 39.

XVII. The hierarchy of the Albanian Fascist Party shall be the following:

1. The Secretary of the Albanian Fascist Party.
2. The Members of the Central Directorate.
3. The Federal Secretaries.
4. The Members of the Federal Directorate.
5. The Political Secretary of the Fasces.
6. Members of the Fascio Directorate.
7. The Trustee of the regional Fascist Group.
8. The members of the regional Fascist Council Group.
9. The Sector Head.
10. The Nucleus Head.

XVIII. The collegiate organs of the Albanian Fascist Party shall be:

1. The Central Directorate.
2. The Central Council.
3. The Directorate of the Federation of Fascist Groups.
4. The Directorate of the Fascio.
5. The Council of the regional Fascist Group.

XIX. The Secretary of the Albanian Fascist Party shall be appointed and dismissed by the Vicegerent of His Majesty the King Emperor on the proposal of the President of the Council of Ministers, after consultation with the Secretary of the National Fascist Party.

To the Secretary of the Albanian Fascist Party shall pertain the title and functions of Minister of State.

. . . . .

XX. The Secretary of the Albanian Fascist Party shall receive the directives and orders of the Duce from the Secretary of the National Fascist Party, who shall be represented in the Albanian Fascist Party by a National Fascist Party Inspector, assisted by a Federal Secretary and by Federal inspectors of the National Fascist Party.

XXI. The Secretary of the Albanian Fascist Party shall propose to the Vicegerent of His Majesty the King Emperor the appointment and dismissal of members of the Central Directorate of the Albanian Fascist Party, among whom he shall designate two vice secretaries and the administrative secretary; he shall designate, subject to the approval of His Majesty the King Emperor, the representatives of the Albanian Fascist Party in the Central Committee of Corporative Economy and in the councils, as well as in the central and local offices of each ministry;

. . . . .

XLVII. No modification may be made in the present statute without previous agreement with the National Fascist Party.

JACOMINI, *Vicegerent*
VERLACI, *President of the Council of Ministers of Albania*

STARACE, *Secretary of the Party*

Vicegerent's Decree No. 73 concerning the Institution of the Central Council of Corporative Economy, March 14, 1940[10]

[EXCERPTS]

ARTICLE 1. The Central Council of Corporative Economy is hereby instituted. It shall be called upon to give its opinion on all matters relating to economics and labor on which the government may be questioned.

ARTICLE 2. The Central Council of Corporative Economy shall be composed of a president, four vice presidents, and twenty-four active members, and shall include four sections: *a*) agriculture; *b*) industry; *c*) commerce; *d*) professions and arts.

ARTICLE 3. It is required that the members of the Central Council of Corporative Economy shall:

a) Have reached the age of twenty-five years.
b) Enjoy civil and political rights.
c) Be members of the Fascist Party.

. . . . .

Tirana, March 14, 1940–XVIII.

FRANCESCO JACOMINI

SH. VERLACI—T. MBORJA—FEJZI ALIZOTTI

Vicegerent's Decree No. 101 concerning Attributions and Functioning of the Fascist Upper Corporative Council, April 3, 1940[11]

[EXCERPTS]

ARTICLE 1. Pursuant to item IV of the Basic Statute of the Kingdom, a Fascist Upper Corporative Council shall be established in place of the Parliament, which has been abolished.

ARTICLE 2. The Fascist Upper Corporative Council shall collaborate with the government in the formulation of laws.

ARTICLE 3. The ministers of state shall be members *ex officio* of the Central Council of Corporative Economy and hence of the Fascist Upper Corporative Council.

. . . . .

ARTICLE 5. Members of the Fascist Upper Corporative Council, before being admitted to the exercise of their legislative functions, shall take the oath in plenary assembly in accordance with the formula indicated in Article 29 of the Statute of the Kingdom.

. . . . .

ARTICLE 8. The Fascist Upper Corporative Council shall exercise its functions through its plenary assembly, the General Budget Committee, and the legislative committees.

For specific matters special committees may be appointed.

. . . . .

[10] *Fletorja Zyrtare*, 1940, No. 40, p. 8.

[11] *Ibid.*, 1940, No. 52, p. 6.

ARTICLE 11. The following bills shall be discussed and voted on by the Fascist Upper Corporative Council in plenary assembly, on the report of the respective committees in charge: those concerning the composition and functioning of the Fascist Upper Corporative Council; the right of the executive power to issue judicial rules; the corporative order; international treaties involving changes in the boundaries of state territories; the budget and expenses relating thereto; rules concerning judicial orders and the duties of judges; orders of the Council of State and of the Court of Accounts; questions of guaranties for magistrates and for other irremovable officials; legislative appointments of a general character; the general accounts rendered by the state as to state institutions and administrative bodies of any nature whatsoever, if directly or indirectly subsidized by the state budget.

. . . . .

Tirana, April 3, 1940–XVIII.

FRANCESCO JACOMINI

SH. VERLACI

4. ITALIAN PROPAGANDA

Vicegerent's Decree No. 114 concerning the Statute of the "Skanderbeg Foundation," National Body for Cultural Growth in Albania, April 8, 1940[12]

[EXCERPTS]

ARTICLE 1. The institution of a national body for cultural growth in Albania, with headquarters in Tirana, under the name "Skanderbeg Foundation," is approved.

ARTICLE 2. The Skanderbeg Foundation shall be composed of two autonomous sections having distinct aims:

1. The first section shall consist of the "Institute for Albanian Studies," the purpose of which shall be to encourage and continue the development of philosophical, literary, artistic, and historic culture in Albania;

2. The second section shall consist of the "Italo-Albanian Skanderbeg Club," whose objective shall be the improvement of social relations between Albanians and Italians.

Each of these two sections shall be subject to its own statutes, approved by decree of the Vicegerent.

. . . . .

ARTICLE 4. The endowment of the "Skanderbeg Foundation" shall consist of the following:

[12] *Fletorja Zyrtare*, 1940, No. 58, p. 6.

1. The capital granted by the founder, who is the Minister of Foreign Affairs of the Kingdom of Italy, amounting to eight million Italian lire, of which six million are invested in the building located in Tirana, and two million lire in corresponding money of the country.
2. Bequests, gifts, and other contributions which may come to the Foundation without other specific purpose.
3. Credit balances, of which annual provisions as to investment shall be made.

. . . . .

ARTICLE 6. The Institute of Albanian Studies shall be composed of active Albanian and Italian members, corresponding Albanian and Italian members, and foreign corresponding members in unlimited number, chosen from among scholars who have most distinguished themselves or who have taken an interest in the cultural studies of Albania.

ARTICLE 7. All members of the Institute of Albanian Studies shall be appointed by decree of the Vicegerent on the proposal of the Minister for Public Instruction.

. . . . .

ARTICLE 10. The general rules of administration of the Foundation and special rules concerning the individual sections shall be established by another decree.

. . . . .

Tirana, April 8, 1940–XVIII.

FRANCESCO JACOMINI

E. KOLIQI—M. BUSHATI

5. ITALIAN ECONOMIC CONTROL

Vicegerent's Decree No. 53 concerning Authorization of Operation for the S.A.C.I.A., February 14, 1940 [13]

[EXCERPTS]

We, Vicegerent of His Majesty Victor Emmanuel III, by the grace of God and by the will of the People King of Italy and of Albania, Emperor of Ethiopia.

By virtue of the authority vested in us;

Pursuant to the deliberations of the Tirana Tribunal under date of December 30, 1939–XVIII, on the matter of the act of establishment and of the Statute of the Italo-Albanian Commercial Company Limited (Società Anonima Compagnia Commerciale Italo-Albanese [S.A.C.I.A.]) in accordance with existing provisions of the law;

[13] *Fletorja Zyrtare*, 1940, No. 27, p. 9.

On the proposal of the Ministry for National Economy;

We have decreed and we decree:

The Italo-Albanian Commercial Company, Ltd. (S.A.C.I.A.) is authorized to carry on its activities in the territory of the Kingdom, with due respect to the laws in effect therein.

. . .

Tirana, February 14, 1940–XVIII.

FRANCESCO JACOMINI

A. BEÇA

Vicegerent's Decree No. 83 concerning the Covenant with the Italian Coal Co. (Azienda Carboni Italiani [A.Ca. I.]), March 14, 1940 [14]

[EXCERPTS]

We have decreed and we decree:

ARTICLE 1. The order on execution of the Covenant stipulated between the Albanian Government and the Italian Coal Co. (A.Ca.I.) is attached to the present decree.

. . . . .

Tirana, March 14, 1940–XVIII.

FRANCESCO JACOMINI

SH. VERLACI—F. ALIZOTTI A. BEÇA

MINING COVENANT

BETWEEN THE ROYAL ALBANIAN GOVERNMENT, REPRESENTED BY HIS EXCELLENCY A. BEÇA, MINISTER OF NATIONAL ECONOMY, AND THE "ITALIAN COAL CO." (A.CA.I.), REPRESENTED BY NATIONAL COUNSELOR INGENIERE UMBERTO CATTANIA (AS PER THE ATTACHED DOCUMENT)

. . .

ARTICLE 1. The Royal Albanian Government grants to the Azienda Carboni Italiani for the period of ten (10) years, the exclusive right of search for and production of all mineral combustibles for all areas of the Albanian territory which are free from permits of search or mining concessions as of the date of the present Covenant.

ARTICLE 2. The Azienda Carboni Italiani shall have the right to extend its activity to the areas held under permits or concessions up to the date mentioned, but which subsequently may be freed by relinquishment or by the default of the present holders of permits or concessions.

. . . .

Tirana, March 1, 1940–XVIII.

A. BEÇA, *Minister of National Economy*

ING. UMBERTO CATTANIA, *Delegated Administrator of the A.Ca.I.*

[14] *Fletorja Zyrtare*, 1940, No. 43, p. 1.

6. LAW

Vicegerent's Decree No. 228 concerning Crimes against the Personality of the State, January 6, 1940[15]

[EXCERPTS]

ARTICLE 1. *Acts against the Integrity, Independence and Unity of the State.* Whoever commits an act with the aim of subjecting the Albanian State, or the Italian State, or a part of either, to the sovereignty of a foreign state, or jeopardizing the independence of the two states, shall be punishable with death.

Whoever commits an act with the aim of dissolving the unity of the Albanian State or of the Italian State, or of detaching, even temporarily, from the sovereignty of the mother country a colony or some other subject territory, shall be liable to the same penalty.

ARTICLE 2. *Citizen Bearing Arms against the Albanian or the Italian State.* A citizen who bears arms against the Albanian State or against the Italian State, or gives aid to the armed forces of a state at war with the Albanian State or the Italian State, shall be punishable by imprisonment. If he is charged with a high command or a directive function, he shall be punishable by death.

Any such citizen who, finding himself during hostilities within the territory of the enemy state, has committed the act under compulsion imposed upon him by the laws of that state itself shall not be punishable.

A person who for any reason has lost Albanian citizenship shall also be considered liable to the effects of the provisions of this decree.

. . . . .

ARTICLE 25. *Political Defeatism.* Whoever in time of war spreads or communicates rumors or false, exaggerated, or colored reports which arouse public alarm or lower public morale or otherwise jeopardize the resistance of the Albanian Nation or of the Italian Nation concerning the enemy, or carries on anywhere activity that might bring damage to the interests of the two nations, shall be punishable with imprisonment for not less than five years.

The sentence shall be for a period of not less than fifteen years:

1. If the act was committed by propaganda or direct communications to soldiers.
2. If the culprit has acted following an understanding with foreigners.

The sentence shall be for life imprisonment if the culprit has acted following an understanding with the enemy.

. . . . .

Tirana, December 31, 1939–XVIII.

FRANCESCO JACOMINI

XHAFER YPI

[15] *Fletorja Zyrtare*, 1940, No. 14, p. 13.

Vicegerent's Decree No. 266 concerning New Members of the Provincial Committee for Police Internment, October 23, 1942[16]

[EXCERPTS]

ARTICLE 1. The Commander of the Albanian Cohort of Fascist Militia shall attend meetings of the Provincial Committee for Police Internment in accordance with Article 142 of the Police Code, and the Commander of the Albanian Legion of Fascist Militia shall also attend as a member of the Central Committee, in accordance with Article 143 of the same code.

. . . . .

Tirana, October 23, 1942–XX.

FRANCESCO JACOMINI

M. KRUJA—SHUK GURAKUQI

Vicegerent's Decree No. 287 concerning Rules with respect to Persons Who Commit Acts Constituting a Menace to Public Safety on the Roads and to Telecommunications Service, November 13, 1942[17]

[EXCERPTS]

ARTICLE 1. For any act which constitutes a menace to public safety on the roads and to telecommunications services, the administrative sanctions which are set forth in these articles shall be enforced irrespective of the existing penal laws which may be applicable to individual acts.

ARTICLE 2. A collective fine of from 1,000 to 20,000 Albanian francs shall be imposed by final decision of the committee referred to in Article 142 of the Police Code in effect, against the inhabitants of villages included within a radius of five kilometers from the spot where any of the acts described in Article 1 have been committed.

Also, the heads of all families residing in the area mentioned in the foregoing paragraph shall be interned by the aforementioned Committee for the period of a year.

. . . . .

ARTICLE 5. The interned heads of families mentioned in the second paragraph of Article 2 shall be set free, even before the completion of their term, when the authors of the offense have been captured through the efforts of the inhabitants of the area mentioned in the first paragraph of Article 2.

. . .

Tirana, November 13, 1942–XXI.

FRANCESCO JACOMINI

M. KRUJA—SHUK GURAKUQI

[16] *Gazzetta ufficiale del Regno d'Albania*, November 12, 1942, No. 128, p. 12.
[17] *Ibid.*, November 21, 1942, No. 136, p. 15.

AUSTRIA

1. ANSCHLUSS ACTS

Law concerning the Reunion of Austria with the German Reich, March 13, 1938[1]

The Reich Government has ordained the following law, which is hereby proclaimed:

ARTICLE I. The Federal Constitutional Law of March 13, 1938, ordained by the Austrian Federal Government, concerning the reunion of Austria with the German Reich, hereby becomes a law of the German Reich. It has the following text:

By virtue of Article 3, Section 2, of the Federal Constitutional Law concerning extraordinary measures in the constitutional field (*B.G.Blatt*, I, No. 255, 1934), the Federal Government has ordained:

ARTICLE 1. Austria is a province of the German Reich.

ARTICLE 2. On Sunday, April 10, 1938, a free and secret plebiscite shall be held for German men and women of Austria over twenty years of age on the question of reunion with the German Reich.

ARTICLE 3. In the plebiscite the majority of the votes cast shall decide the issue.

ARTICLE 4. The necessary regulations for the implementation and supplementing of this Federal Constitutional Law shall be provided by decree.

ARTICLE 5. This Federal Constitutional Law shall enter into force on the day of its proclamation.

The Federal Government is entrusted with the execution of this Federal Constitutional Law.

Vienna, March 13, 1938.

ARTICLE II. The laws at present in force in Austria shall remain in force until further notice. The introduction of Reich law into Austria will be effected by the Führer and Reich Chancellor or by the Reich Minister to whom he may delegate this power.

ARTICLE III. The Reich Minister of the Interior, in consultation with the other Reich Ministers concerned, is empowered to issue the legal and administrative regulations necessary for the implementation and supplementing of this law.

ARTICLE IV. This law shall enter into force on the day of its proclamation.

Linz, March 13, 1938.

ADOLF HITLER, *Führer and Reich Chancellor;* GÖRING, *General Field Marshal, Reich Minister of Aviation;* FRICK, *Reich Minister of the Interior;* VON RIBBENTROP, *Reich Minister of Foreign Affairs;* R. HESS, *Deputy Führer.*

[1] *Reichsgesetzblatt*, 1938, I, No. 21, p. 237.

Instruction of the Führer and Reich Chancellor concerning the Austrian Federal Army, March 13, 1938 [2]

1. The Austrian Federal Government has just resolved by law upon the reunion of Austria with the German Reich. The Government of the German Reich has by a law of this date recognized this resolution.

2. By virtue thereof I give this instruction: The Austrian Federal Army, as a component part of the German armed forces, shall be placed under my command as of this date.

3. I commission Infantry General von Bock, Commander in Chief of the Eighth Army, to assume command of what are now the German armed forces within the borders of the Austrian province.

4. All members of the former Austrian Federal Army shall without delay take an oath of allegiance to me as their supreme commander. Infantry General von Bock shall immediately issue the necessary orders.

ADOLF HITLER.

Order pursuant to the Law concerning the Reunion of Austria with the German Reich, March 16, 1938 [3]

By virtue of the law of March 13, 1938, concerning the reunion of Austria with the German Reich (*RGBl.* I, p. 237), I order:

SECTION 1. (1) The Reich Minister of the Interior shall be the central authority for carrying out the reunion of Austria with the German Reich.

(2) He may delegate his authority to a commissioner, who shall have his headquarters in Vienna and whose office shall be designated as that of the "Reich Commissioner for Austria."

SECTION 2. The Commissioner for the Four-Year Plan may delegate authority to the Reich Commissioner for Austria.

SECTION 3. The Reich Commissioner for Austria shall therefore be appointed by the Reich Minister of the Interior together with the Commissioner for the Four-Year Plan.

Munich, March 16, 1938.

ADOLF HITLER, *Führer and Reich Chancellor*
FRICK, *Reich Minister of the Interior*
GÖRING, *General Field Marshal, Commissioner for the Four-Year Plan*

[2] *Dokumente der deutschen Politik*, VI, 1, p. 150.
[3] *Reichsgesetzblatt*, 1938, I, No. 25, p. 249.

Decree of the Führer and Reich Chancellor concerning the Appointment of the Reich Commissioner for the Reunion of Austria with the German Reich, April 23, 1938 [4]

ARTICLE I. As Reich Commissioner for the Reunion of Austria with the German Reich, I appoint Gauleiter Buerckel-Saarpfalz.

ARTICLE II. The Reich Commissioner shall undertake measures for political reconstruction and for accomplishing the political, economic, and cultural reincorporation of Austria into the German Reich.

ARTICLE III. The Reich Commissioner shall have his headquarters in Vienna. He shall be directly responsible to me, and shall have until May 1, 1939, to fulfill his commission in accordance with my instructions. On that date his commission shall terminate.

ARTICLE IV. The Reich Commissioner is authorized to issue instructions to Reich offices in the province of Austria, to offices of the province of Austria and of the former Austrian federal provinces, as well as to offices of the National Socialist German Workers' Party, its branches and affiliated associations in the province of Austria. He may exercise supervision over public agencies and institutions in the province of Austria.

ARTICLE V. (1) The Reich Minister of the Interior, as the central authority for implementation of the reunion of Austria with the German Reich, shall consult with the Reich Commissioner concerning the measures to be taken, especially in questions of legal interpretation.

(2) The office of the Reich Commissioner for Austria (Section 1, subsection 2, of the order of March 16, 1938, pursuant to the law concerning the reunion of Austria with the German Reich, *RGBl.* I, p. 249) shall be combined with that of the Reich Commissioner for the Reunion of Austria with the German Reich.

Berlin, April 23, 1938.

ADOLF HITLER, *Führer and Reich Chancellor*
FRICK, *Reich Minister of the Interior*
DR. LAMMERS, *Reich Minister and Chief of the Reich Chancellery.*

2. ADMINISTRATION

Decree of the Führer and Reich Chancellor concerning the Austrian Provincial Government, March 15, 1938 [5]

By virtue of Article II of the law of March 13, 1938, concerning the reunion of Austria with the German Reich (*RGBl.* I, p. 237), and of Section 2, para-

[4] *Reichsgesetzblatt*, 1938, I, No. 61, p. 407. [5] *Ibid.*, No. 25, p. 249.

graph 4, of the first decree of March 15, 1938, concerning the introduction of Reich laws into Austria (*RGBl.* I, p. 247), I order:

SECTION 1. (1) The Austrian Federal Government shall be designated as the "Austrian Provincial Government."

(2) I commission the Reich Governor in Austria to assume direction of the Austrian Provincial Government. He shall have his headquarters in Vienna.

SECTION 2. The Reich Governor is empowered to arrange, with the approval of the Reich Minister of the Interior, the administrative organization of the Provincial Government.

SECTION 3. This decree shall enter into force on the day of its proclamation.

Vienna, March 15, 1938.

ADOLF HITLER, *Führer and Reich Chancellor*
FRICK, *Reich Minister of the Interior*

Decree of the Führer and Reich Chancellor concerning the Administration of Oath to the Officials of the Province of Austria, March 15, 1938 [6]

By virtue of Article II of the law of March 13, 1938, concerning the reunion of Austria with the German Reich (*RGBl.* I, p. 237), I issue the following order:

SECTION 1. Public officials of the province of Austria shall take an oath of office upon entrance into service.

SECTION 2. The oath of office of public officials reads: "I swear that I shall be loyal and obedient to Adolf Hitler, the Führer of the German Reich and People, and that I shall observe the laws and conscientiously fulfill the duties of my office, so help me God."

SECTION 3. The officials at present in office shall be sworn in forthwith in accordance with Section 2.

Jewish officials shall not be sworn in.

SECTION 4. A person is Jewish if he is descended from at least three racially full-blooded Jewish grandparents. A grandparent is automatically considered a full-blooded Jew if he belonged to the Jewish congregation.

A Jewish half-breed descended from two full-blooded Jewish grandparents is considered a Jew:

a) If he belonged to the Jewish congregation on September 16, 1935, or became a member of it thereafter.

b) If he was married to a Jew on September 16, 1935, or entered into marriage with one thereafter.

[6] *Reichsgesetzblatt*, 1938, I, No. 24, p. 245.

SECTION 5. Anyone who refuses to take this oath shall be removed from office.

SECTION 6. The legal and administrative regulations necessary to the implementation of this law shall be issued by the Reich Governor (Austrian Provincial Government).

SECTION 7. This decree shall enter into force on the day of its proclamation.

Vienna, March 15, 1938.

ADOLF HITLER, *Führer and Reich Chancellor.*

Order for the Transfer of the Austrian National Bank to the Reichsbank, March 17, 1938 [7]

By virtue of Article II of the law of March 13, 1938, concerning the reunion of Austria with the German Reich (*RGBl.* I, p. 237), I order:

SECTION 1. The administration of the Austrian National Bank shall be transferred to the Reichsbank.

SECTION 2. The Austrian National Bank shall be liquidated, and its assets placed by the Reichsbank to the account of the Reich.

SECTION 3. In taking over operations, the Reichsbank shall transfer to its staff the entire personnel of the Austrian National Bank, with due regard for legal and contractual rights.

SECTION 4. This order shall enter into force upon its proclamation.

Berlin, March 17, 1938.

ADOLF HITLER, *Führer and Reich Chancellor*
FRICK, *Reich Minister of the Interior*
Count SCHWERIN VON KROSIGK, *Reich Minister of Finance*
DR. HJALMAR SCHACHT, *Reich Minister and President of the Reichsbank*

Order concerning the Establishment of a Reich Propaganda Office in Vienna, March 31, 1938 [8]

By virtue of Article III of the law of March 13, 1938, concerning the reunion of Austria with the German Reich (*RGBl.* I, p. 237), it is ordered as follows:

[7] *Reichsgesetzblatt*, 1938, I, No. 27, p. 254. [8] *Ibid.*, No. 46, p. 350.

For the territory of the province of Austria a Reich Propaganda Office shall be established with its seat in Vienna.

Berlin, March 31, 1938.

Reich Minister for Public Enlightenment and Propaganda
DR. GOEBBELS
Reich Minister of the Interior
By deputy: PFUNDTNER
Reich Minister of Finance
By deputy: REINHARDT

Law concerning the Reorganization of the Administration in the Ostmark, April 14, 1939 [9]

The Reich Government has ordained the following law, which is hereby proclaimed:

ARTICLE I.—*The Reich Districts*

SECTION 1. (1) In the territory of the province of Austria the following Reich districts (*Reichsgaue*) shall be constituted:

the Reich District of Vienna, comprising the city of Vienna;

the Reich District of Carinthia, comprising the former Austrian province of Carinthia; the administration of the district shall have its seat in Klagenfurt;

the Reich District of the Lower Danube, comprising the former Austrian province of Lower Austria; the administration of the district shall have its seat in Krems-on-the-Danube;

the Reich District of the Upper Danube, comprising the former Austrian province of Upper Austria; the administration of the district shall have its seat in Linz;

the Reich District of Salzburg, comprising the former Austrian province of Salzburg; the administration of the district shall have its seat in Salzburg;

the Reich District of Styria, comprising the former Austrian province of Styria; the administration of the district shall have its seat in Graz;

the Reich District of Tyrol, comprising the former Austrian province of Tyrol; the administration of the district shall have its seat in Innsbruck.

(2) The former Austrian province of Vorarlberg shall constitute until further notice a separate administrative district and an autonomous corporation which shall be supervised by the Reich governor in Tyrol.

[9] *Reichsgesetzblatt*, 1939, I, No. 74, p. 777.

SECTION 2. The Reich districts shall be state administrative districts and autonomous corporations.

SECTION 3. (1) The Reich governor (*Reichsstatthalter*) shall be at the head of the Reich district.

(2) The Reich governor is authorized to obtain information from the authorities of the special Reich administrations, from the divisions of the organization of industrial economy and of the transportation industry, from the offices of the Reich Food Authority and of the Reich Culture Chamber, and from the offices of other corporations within the Reich district, and to bring to their attention the authoritative point of view and the necessary measures in accordance with it. In the sphere of law and of the directives of the superior Reich authorities he may impart to them instructions for the domain of his Reich district; the proper superior Reich authorities may suspend directives of the Reich governor.

(3) The powers indicated in subsection 2 may not be delegated by the Reich governor to the officials associated with him.

SECTION 4. (1) Within the area of the Reich district, the Reich governor shall conduct the state administration as a Reich administration under the official supervision of the Reich Minister of the Interior and in accordance with the departmental directives of the Reich ministers in their spheres of jurisdiction.

(2) The authorities of the Reich special administrations within the area of the Reich district, with the exception of the Reich justice, finance, railway, and postal administrations, shall be subordinated to the Reich governor. The Reich governor shall be at the head of these administrations and shall be represented in them by their directors.

(3) If the intermediate domain of Reich special administrations subordinated to the Reich governor by subsection 2 should include several Reich districts, the Führer and Reich Chancellor shall determine to which Reich governor these special authorities shall be subordinate.

(4) Subsections 2 and 3 shall likewise be applicable to the Provincial Farmers' Association and to the Provincial Security Institute, with the provision that the Reich governor shall be represented by the provincial farmers' leader in the direction of the Provincial Farmers' Association and by the district chief in the direction of the Provincial Security Institute.

(5) The duties and powers of the superior agencies of the former Austrian provinces shall be transferred to the Reich governor, except in so far as the Reich Minister of the Interior, in consultation with the superior Reich authorities concerned, may delegate powers to the latter.

SECTION 5. (1) The Reich governor, with the approval of the Reich minister concerned and of the Reich Minister of the Interior, may establish laws by executive order, so far as they are compatible with the sovereign law of the Reich.

(2) The powers of the Reich governor under the Reich law of January 30, 1935 (*RGBl.* I, p. 65) concerning the powers of such governors shall remain otherwise unaffected.

SECTION 6. (1) The Reich governor shall direct the autonomous administration of the Reich district under the supervision of the Reich Minister of the Interior.

(2) As an autonomous corporation, the Reich district will have public duties to fulfill on its own responsibility.

(3) The Reich district may regulate its own affairs by statute.

(4) The Reich governor shall be assisted by counsellors of the district as advisers in the sphere of its autonomy.

SECTION 7. The Reich governor shall be represented in the state administration by a general deputy whose office shall be designated as that of president of the government and who shall be a Reich official in his own right, and in the autonomous administration by a general deputy whose office shall be designated as that of district chief and who shall be an official of the Reich district as an autonomous corporation.

SECTION 8. (1) The administration of the Reich District of Vienna shall be divided into the state administration and the municipal adminstration.

(2) The Reich District of Vienna, as an autonomous corporation, shall be a municipal unit and at the same time shall have the duties of municipality associations of a higher order.

(3) The Reich governor shall be represented in the state administration by a general deputy whose office shall be designated as that of president of the government, and in the municipal administration by the first assistant of the city of Vienna, whose office shall be designated as that of burgomaster.

(4) The Reich governor shall be assisted by counsellors as advisers in the municipal administration.

(5) In other respects, for the municipal administration of the city of Vienna, the German Municipality Code (DGO) of January 30, 1935 (*RGBl.* I, p. 49) shall be valid.

ARTICLE II.—*Administration of Counties and Municipalities*

SECTION 9. (1) The Reich district shall be divided into counties and municipalities.

(2) The counties shall be state administrative units and autonomous corporations; the municipalities shall be autonomous corporations.

(3) The prefect (*Landrat*) shall be at the head of the county; the burgomaster, with the title of chief burgomaster, at the head of the municipality.

SECTION 10. (1) The county prefect shall conduct the entire state administration within the area of the county in the limits of the former regular jurisdiction.

(2) The Reich Minister of the Interior, in consultation with the superior Reich authorities concerned, shall delegate duties and powers of the former special administrations to the county prefect.

SECTION 11. Governmental administration in the municipalities shall be under the direction of the chief burgomaster, except in so far as other arrangements shall have been made or may be made for police matters. Section 10, subsection 2, shall also be considered applicable to such administration.

SECTION 12. (1) The county prefect shall direct the autonomous administration of the county, and in this administration he shall be assisted by county counsellors as advisers.

(2) As an autonomous corporation, the county will have public duties to fulfill on its own responsibility.

(3) The county may regulate its affairs by statute.

(4) Direct supervision over the county as an autonomous corporation shall be maintained by the Reich governor, with ultimate supervision by the Reich Minister of the Interior.

ARTICLE III.—*Final Provisions*

SECTION 13. (1) The authorities and institutions of the Reich district—except in so far as they are authorities and institutions of the Reich district as an autonomous corporation, of municipalities or associations of municipalities, or of corporations, institutes, and foundations of public law—shall be Reich authorities and Reich institutions.

(2) The officials and instructors serving with these authorities and institutions shall themselves be Reich officials.

SECTION 14. (1) The Reich districts shall be established by September 30, 1939.

(2) The Reich districts shall be the legal successors of the former Austrian provinces as indicated in Section 1.

SECTION 15. The regulation of property rights made necessary by the execution of this law shall be effected upon the basis of information supplied by the Reich governors concerned, by the Reich Minister of the Interior and the Reich Minister of Finance, or by the authorities designated by them.

SECTION 16. The Reich Minister of the Interior, in consultation with the superior Reich authorities concerned, shall transfer to the Reich governors the duties and powers [formerly exercised by] the Reich governor in Austria (Austrian Provincial Government) and by the superior Austrian provincial authorities in so far as they shall not have been transferred to the superior Reich authorities.

SECTION 17. (1) Until the appointment of the Reich governors, the former provincial chiefs shall conduct the administration of the Reich districts according to Sections 4 and 6 and shall exercise the right to issue executive orders as defined in Section 2 of the order concerning the right of legislation in the province of Austria of April 30, 1938 (*RGBl.* I, p. 455). The same powers shall be exercised for the city of Vienna by the Reich Commissioner for the Reunion of Austria with the German Reich; he shall be represented by the burgomaster of the city of Vienna.

(2) From May 1, 1939, until the transfer of the duties and powers of the Reich governor in Austria (Austrian Provincial Government) as provided in Section 16, the Reich Commissioner for the Reunion of Austria with the German Reich shall exercise the powers of the Reich governor in Austria (Austrian Provincial Government).

(3) The privilege of passing provincial legislation in accordance with Section 1 of the order concerning the right of legislation in the province of Austria of April 30, 1938 (*RGBl.* I, p. 455), shall expire for those branches of law in respect to which the transfer of powers indicated in Section 16 has been effected; in so far as such transfer shall have been made to the former provincial chiefs, Section 5, subsection 1, shall be applicable.

(4) The effective duration of the decree of the Führer and Reich Chancellor concerning the appointment of the Reich Commissioner for the Reunion of Austria with the German Reich of April 23, 1938 (*RGBl.* I, p. 407), shall be extended to September 30, 1939.

SECTION 18. The Reich Minister of the Interior shall issue the legal and administrative regulations necessary for the implementation and supplementing of this law.

SECTION 19. This law shall enter into force on May 1, 1939.

Berchtesgaden, April 14, 1939.

ADOLF HITLER, *Führer and Reich Chancellor;* FRICK, *Reich Minister of the Interior;* R. HESS, *Deputy of the Führer;* GÖRING, *General Field Marshal, Premier of Prussia, Commissioner for the Four-Year Plan;* Count SCHWERIN VON KROSIGK, *Reich Minister of Finance;* Dr. LAMMERS, *Reich Minister and Chief of the Reich Chancellery.*

3. LAW AND COURTS

First Decree of the Führer and Reich Chancellor concerning the Introduction of German Reich Law in Austria, March 15, 1938 [10]

By virtue of Article II of the law of March 13, 1938, concerning the reunion of Austria with the German Reich (*RGBl.* I, p. 237), I order:

SECTION 1. (1) The sphere of validity of the official gazettes of the Reich shall be extended to the province of Austria.

[10] *Reichsgesetzblatt*, 1938, I, No. 25, p. 247.

(2) Reich laws which are proclaimed after the effective date of the law of March 13, 1938, concerning the reunion of Austria with the German Reich (*RGBl.* I, p. 237), shall be valid for the province of Austria unless their application to the province of Austria is expressly held in abeyance.

SECTION 2. From the effective date of this decree, the following shall be applied in substance in the province of Austria:

1. The Reich flag law of September 15, 1935 (*RGBl.* I, p. 1145), with the provision that Jews shall be forbidden to raise the Reich and National Flag and to display the Reich colors;

2. The law against formation of new parties of July 14, 1933 (*RGBl.* I, p. 479);

3. The law for the preservation of unity of party and state of December 1, 1933 (*RGBl.* I, p. 1016), as amended by the law of July 3, 1934 (*RGBl.* I, p. 529);

4. The law concerning Reich governors of January 30, 1935 (*RGBl.* I, p. 65), with the provision that instructions of Reich ministers to the Reich Governor in Austria shall require, until further notice, the approval of the Reich Minister of the Interior;

5. The order for implementation of the Four-Year Plan of October 18, 1936 (*RGBl.* I, p. 887);

6. The Reich law concerning the compulsory registration of members of the German State abroad of February 3, 1938 (*RGBl.* I, p. 113).

SECTION 3. (1) Regulations for effecting the transition shall be issued by the Reich Minister of the Interior or by the Reich Governor in Austria with the approval of the Reich Minister of the Interior.

(2) By this means regulations of the Reich and regulations of the province of Austria can be assimilated to one another.

(3) Incompatible regulations of the province of Austria shall be invalidated.

SECTION 4. This decree shall enter into force on the day of its proclamation.

Vienna, March 15, 1938.

ADOLF HITLER, *Führer and Reich Chancellor*
FRICK, *Reich Minister of the Interior*

Order concerning the Administration of Justice in Austria, March 22, 1938 [11]

By virtue of Article III of the law of March 13, 1938, concerning the reunion of Austria with the German Reich (*RGBl.* I, p. 237), together with the order of March 16, 1938 (*RGBl.* I, p. 249), we order:

[11] *Reichsgesetzblatt*, 1938, I, No. 36, p. 301.

SECTION 1. The courts in the province of Austria shall administer justice in the name of the German people.

SECTION 2. (1) The judges, state attorneys, and other officials of the judicial administration in the province of Austria entitled to wear robes of office shall display the emblems of the state on the right breast of their robes of office.

(2) Provisions for the implementation of the present order shall be issued by the Reich Minister of Justice.

Berlin, March 22, 1938.

DR. GUERTNER, *Reich Minister of Justice*
FRICK, *Reich Minister of the Interior*

Order concerning a Change in the Designation of Courts in the Province of Austria, August 2, 1938 [12]

By virtue of the law of March 13, 1938, concerning the reunion of Austria with the German Reich (*RGBl.* I, p. 237), it is ordered that:

In the province of Austria the provincial and circuit courts shall be designated as "Provincial Courts" (*Landgerichte*), and the precinct courts as "District Courts" (*Amtsgerichte*).

Berlin, August 2, 1938.

The Reich Minister of Justice
By deputy: DR. SCHLEGELBERGER
The Reich Minister of the Interior
By deputy: PFUNDTNER

Law concerning the Accountability of Members of the Former Austrian Federal and Provincial Governments and Their Associates, August 17, 1938[13]

The Reich Government has ordained the following law, which is hereby proclaimed:

SECTION 1. (1) Members of the former Austrian Federal Government who during their activity in public life have been guilty of a violation of the law or of an act inimical to the people may with their associates be brought to trial before a State Tribunal in Vienna.

(2) This provision shall be valid also for the members of the former local governments (burgomasters of the city of Vienna) and their associates.

[12] *Reichsgesetzblatt*, 1938, I, No. 126, p. 998. [13] *Ibid.*, 1938, I, No. 131, p. 1045.

(3) The State Tribunal in Vienna shall determine whether the law has been violated or an act inimical to the people has been committed.

SECTION 2. The indictment shall be filed in the name of the German people by the Reich Commissioner for the Reunion of Austria with the German Reich.

SECTION 3. The Reich Minister of the Interior may withdraw their provisional civil rights from persons who are guilty according to the decision of the State Tribunal; he may also deprive them of citizenship in the German Reich. He may in addition confiscate their property on behalf of the German Reich for the purpose of indemnification.

SECTION 4. Trials before other courts and before administrative authorities on the same charges shall be adjourned pending the decision of the State Tribunal. The findings of fact by the State Tribunal shall be binding upon the courts and upon the administrative authorities.

SECTION 5. The members of the State Tribunal shall be appointed by the Führer and Reich Chancellor upon the nomination of the Reich Minister of the Interior.

SECTION 6. The detailed arrangements for the establishment of the State Tribunal, its procedure, and other measures for the implementation of this law shall be issued by the Reich Minister of the Interior.

Berlin, August 17, 1938.

ADOLF HITLER, *Führer and Reich Chancellor*
FRICK, *Reich Minister of the Interior*
DR. GUERTNER, *Reich Minister of Justice*
DR. LAMMERS, *Reich Minister and Chief of the Reich Chancellery*

Order for the Further Adaptation of the Administration of Justice in the Province of Austria and in the Sudeten German Territories, February 28, 1939 [14]

[EXCERPTS]

By virtue of Article III of the law of March 13, 1938, concerning the reunion of Austria with the German Reich (*RGBl.* I, p. 237), of Section 9 of the decree of the Führer and Reich Chancellor concerning the administration of the Sudeten German territories of October 1, 1938 (*RGBl.* I, p. 1331), and of Section 10 of the third law for the transfer of the administration of justice to the Reich of January 24, 1935 (*RGBl.* I, p. 68), it is ordered as follows:

. . . . .

SECTION 1. *Abolition of the Authorities.* The Supreme Court and the office of the attorney general in Vienna are abolished.

[14] *Reichsgesetzblatt,* 1939, I, No. 37, p. 358.

SECTION 2. *Transfer of Jurisdiction to the Reich Court.* Except as otherwise prescribed in this law, the former jurisdiction of the Supreme Court shall be transferred to the Reichsgericht, and the duties of the attorney general to the Attorney General at the Reichsgericht.

. . .

Berlin, February 28, 1939.

The Reich Minister of Justice
By deputy: Dr. SCHLEGELBERGER
The Reich Minister of the Interior
By deputy: Dr. STUCKART

4. EDUCATION

Order concerning Preliminary Regulation of the Vocational School System in the Reich District of Sudetenland and in the Reich Districts of the Ostmark, May 31, 1940 [15]

By virtue of Section 7 of the decree of the Führer and Reich Chancellor concerning the administration of the Sudeten German territories of October 1, 1938 (*RGBl.* I, p. 1331), and by virtue of Article II of the law concerning the reunion of Austria with the German Reich of March 13, 1938 (*RGBl.* I, p. 237), it is ordered:

ARTICLE I.—*Introduction of Compulsory Schooling into the Reich District of Sudetenland*

SECTION 1. The provisions concerning compulsory vocational schooling of the law concerning compulsory schooling in the German Reich (Reich Compulsory Schooling Law) of July 6, 1938 (*RGBl.* I, p. 799), shall be valid in the Reich District of Sudetenland.

ARTICLE II.—*Legal Status of Vocational School Teachers*

SECTION 2. The principal instructors of public vocational schools shall be Reich officials.

ARTICLE III.—*Regulation of the Support of Schools*

SECTION 3. (1) The agencies responsible for schools (*Schulträger*) shall be charged with the establishment and maintenance of public vocational schools.

(2) Such responsibility for schools shall lie with the city and rural county.

(3) In exceptional cases the school supervisory board may also admit others who will share in the responsibility for the schools.

[15] *Reichsgesetzblatt*, 1940, I, No. 97, p. 832.

(4) The school supervisory board shall comprise the superior administration authorities.

SECTION 4. Municipalities and associations of municipalities may group themselves, or may be grouped, into local administrative unions for the maintenance of one or more municipal vocational schools, according to the provisions of the law regarding the formation of local administrative unions of June 7, 1939 (*RGBl.* I, p. 979).

SECTION 5. (1) The establishment of a vocational school must have the approval of the school supervisory board.

(2) Before the establishment of a vocational school, representatives of those engaged in the vocations shall be consulted.

SECTION 6. (1) If an agency responsible for schools does not meet its obligation as defined in Section 3, subsection 1, the school supervisory board, in consultation with the municipal supervisory authorities, shall determine the extent of the obligation, taking into consideration the needs of the school and the financial ability of the agency in question.

(2) Against this decision an appeal may be made within two weeks to the Reich Minister for Science and Education. He shall make the final decision in consultation with the Reich Ministers of the Interior and of Finance.

(3) If the agency responsible for schools fails to comply with this decision (subsection 1), then application shall be made of the procedure set forth in Sections 110 *et sqq.* of the German Municipality Code of January 30, 1935 (*RGBl.* I, p. 49).

SECTION 7. (1) The personnel costs for the teaching staff of public vocational schools shall be borne by the Reich.

(2) Personnel costs in the sense of this provision include items of salary and maintenance, expense for substitutes, emergency assistance, grants, transfer expenses, travelling expenses, and contributions to the social security funds.

(3) The Reich shall also bear the expense of instruction by the subordinate, non-official personnel.

SECTION 8. (1) The agency responsible for schools shall bear the material expenses, as well as the personnel expenses of the officials, employees, and workers other than teachers engaged by them.

(2) It shall refund to the Reich a part of the expenses enumerated in Section 7, the amount of which is determined by the Reich Minister for Science and Education in consultation with the Reich ministers of the Interior and of Finance.

(3) The number of compulsory pupils shall be the basis for the amount of refund.

SECTION 9. The agency responsible for schools shall refund to the Reich in full those personnel expenses for teachers which it considers necessary in excess of the provisions for the staff contained in the Reich budget (i.e., additional staff).

SECTION 10. (1) The Reich shall furnish additional allowances (supplementary grants) to school agencies of limited resources in order to lighten the burden of the personnel and the essential expenses of vocational schools.

(2) Supplementary grants shall be fixed annually by the Reich budget; they shall amount to at least 5 per cent of the personnel expenses as defined in Section 7, subsections 2 and 3.

SECTION 11. The services of the local treasuries may be utilized without charge in dealing with payments.

ARTICLE IV.—*School Counsellors*

SECTION 12. The Reich Minister for Science and Education, in consultation with the Reich ministers concerned, shall issue statements concerning the summoning of counsellors for vocational schools.

ARTICLE V.—*Transition Measures for the Reich Districts of the Ostmark*

SECTION 13. (1) In the Reich districts of the Ostmark, with the exception of the Reich District of Vienna and the administrative district of Vorarlberg, the agency responsible for schools shall be the vocational or technical School Fund Administration up to a date to be determined by the Reich Minister for Science and Education in agreement with the Reich Minister of the Interior, in accordance with the vocational or technical school laws of the former Austrian provinces. In the administrative district of Vorarlberg the agency responsible for the schools shall be the vocational or technical school organization. The scope of activities of the vocational or technical school fund administrations shall be extended to cover the Reich districts within their present boundaries.

(2) The vocational and technical school councils shall be dissolved. The administration of the vocational and technical school funds and the duties of the vocational and technical school councils shall be transferred to the Reich Governor (State Administration).

SECTION 14. (1) The Vienna vocational and technical School Fund Administration shall be dissolved. Its property shall be transferred with all rights and obligations to the Reich District of Vienna (Municipal Administration) in its capacity as agency responsible for the schools.

(2) The property transferred, as well as all legal acts involved therein, shall be free from public fees and taxes.

SECTION 15. Those responsible for the vocational school system in the Reich districts of the Ostmark may levy vocational school assessments in the form of percentages, which are calculated on the basis of the assessment for the license tax on income and capital.

ARTICLE VI.—*Final Provisions*

SECTION 16. This order shall not apply to agricultural vocational schools.

SECTION 17. The stipulations necessary for the implementation and supplementing of this order shall be issued by the Reich Minister for Science and Education in consultation with the Reich ministers concerned.

SECTION 18. (1) This order shall be effective as of April 1, 1940.

(2) The provisions concerning the levy of vocational school assessments (Section 15) shall be effective as of April 1, 1939.

Berlin, May 31, 1940.

The Reich Minister for Science and Education
RUST
The Reich Minister of Finance
Count SCHWERIN VON KROSIGK
The Reich Minister of the Interior
By deputy: PFUNDTNER

BALTIC STATES

LITHUANIA, LATVIA, ESTONIA

1. ADMINISTRATION

Proclamation of July 28, 1941 [1]

By decree of July 17, 1941, the Führer of the Greater German Reich, Adolf Hitler, has appointed me Reich Commissioner for the Ostland. In this area the former free state of Lithuania is also included.

By a decree of the same date the Führer has likewise appointed Herr Dr. Adrian von Rentelen as Commissioner General for the former free state of Lithuania. Commissioner General Dr. von Rentelen shall be responsible to me, as the representative of the Reich Government for the Reich Commissariat of the Ostland, for the execution in Lithuania of all decrees and orders issued by the Reich Government or by myself. His own decrees and orders shall likewise be obeyed in every instance within this territory.

I first address to the inhabitants of the territories south of the Dwina and as far as the boundaries of the former free state of Lithuania, inclusive, the appeal to cooperate uniformly and with all their energy in carrying out the task assigned to me, namely, to restore order and work in these territories.

Bolshevism was threatening all Europe. It was on the march to attack Germany, and it has also inflicted most terrible wounds upon you. If this world enemy had been rampant among you a few more years, nothing would have been left to you of your property and people. The Bolshevik leaders would have carried you off to Siberia, robbed, and murdered you.

At the cost of their blood the armed forces of the German people have overthrown the Bolshevik universal enemy; and so everyone will understand that this German people has therefore now assumed the duty and the right to make such arrangements that never again will a similar danger be able to threaten anew the traditions of the people of Europe, and indeed their whole existence.

Those who in the past twenty years promised you so much freedom believed themselves under the necessity of following a policy based upon playing off the Soviet Union against the German Reich. But the moment the German Reich, in view of an English attack, renounced certain territories in the east as its sphere of interest, this attitude, so fraught with consequences for you all, was revealed in its true form. The Soviet Union was able to fall upon you without opposition.

[1] *Verkündungsblatt für das Ostland*, 1941, No. 1, p. 1.

In spite of everything which has been done to injure Germans and the attacks which have been made upon the National Socialist German Reich, the Reich Government will take pains, in the interest of your welfare, to assure you work, bread, and continued development. However, the German administration must demand that its orders be unconditionally obeyed, for they serve only this single purpose: the safety of the country and security of your lives. The German administration will call upon your representatives in the communities and in the cities for collaboration. It will in case of necessity appoint deputies from your people through whom your wishes may be transmitted to the Reich Commissioner, the Commissioner General, and the district commissioners, and it will permit you to form police organizations for the security of your work and your lives.

I expect the entire population to obey my directions, in order to heal the grave wounds which the universal Bolshevik enemy has inflicted upon you also. Only then will culture and wellbeing again be established in the future; only then will you all be able to live in peace. The German Reich offers you the opportunity. It is now for you to make use of this opportunity.

Kaunas, July 28, 1941.

LOHSE
Reich Commissioner for the Ostland

Order pursuant to the Assumption of the Administration by the Reich Commissioner for the Ostland, August 18, 1941 [2]

SECTION 1. With the assumption of the administration, the executive power is transferred to the Reich Commissioner for the Ostland.

The exercise of superior military power and authority has been transferred by the Führer to the Commander of the Armed Forces in the Ostland; and his authority is not affected by this order.

SECTION 2. Regulations for the civil population in the territories administered by the Reich Commissioner for the Ostland will be issued by the offices of the German Civil Administration.

The authority of the offices of the Commander of the Armed Forces in the Ostland to requisition contributions for the tasks of the Reich defense is not affected by the present provisions.

SECTION 3. Officers of the German Civil Administration are: the Reich Commissioner for the Ostland; the Commissioner General; the Chief Commissioner; and the District Commissioners.

SECTION 4. The German Civil Administration takes over all of the real

[2] *Verkündungsblatt*, 1941, No. 1, p. 3.

and personal property situated in the territories administered by the Reich Commissioner for the Ostland which belongs to the Union of Soviet Socialist Republics, its member states, public corporations, associations, and partnerships, including all claims, investments, rights, and interests of all kinds as of June 20, 1941, in a manner to be determined in detail by further regulations.

Dispositions, alterations, and registrations of title made after July 20, 1941, shall be unlawful if they have not been made through German agencies. Measures already taken by German officers shall remain irrevocably in force.

Arrangements concerning the status of property and possessions shall remain subject to change.

The German armed forces shall have the power of disposal over the property of the Soviet Russian armed forces.

SECTION 5. The official language in the Reich Commissariat of Ostland shall be German. In each general district the language of the province shall be permitted.

SECTION 6. This regulation shall be effective on the day of its publication.

Kaunas, August 18, 1941.

LOHSE
Reich Commissioner for the Ostland

2. COURTS

Order concerning the Establishment and Organization of the German Judiciary System in the Ostland, October 6, 1941 [3]

Since the German armed forces have freed the Ostland from the Bolshevik terror, it is now the first task of the civil administration to begin the reconstruction of the judiciary system in the Ostland which was destroyed by the Bolsheviks. I therefore direct:

SECTION 1. (1) There shall be established in the Ostland: at the seat of the Reich Commissioner a "German Superior Court" for his jurisdictional district; at the seat of each Commissioner General a "German Court" for his jurisdictional district.

(2) With each German Court shall be associated a Special Court.

(3) The office of prosecutor to be established in each German Court and in the German Superior Court shall be charged with the prosecution of offenses.

[3] *Verkündungsblatt*, 1941, No. 7, p. 31.

(4) The Reich Commissioner may establish branch offices of the courts and of the prosecutors and arrange that court sessions be held away from the seat of the court.

SECTION 2. (1) The German Courts shall have jurisdiction over all criminal cases, except when these have been referred to another court for judgment; over civil law proceedings when a Reich German or German by descent (*Volkszugehöriger*) is a party to the case; over all other legal processes when their jurisdiction is expressly so defined by directive of the Reich Commissioner.

(2) The German Superior Court shall have jurisdiction to decide upon appeals and complaints against decisions of the German Courts in criminal and civil proceedings.

(3) The Special Courts shall have such jurisdiction as is expressly defined in the orders of the German administration, and such jurisdiction shall include also cases in which the office of the prosecutor brings indictments before the Special Court. They shall give judgment also in proceedings for the rehearing of a criminal case which has been decided by them.

(4) The jurisdiction of the court martial remains unaffected.

SECTION 3. (1) Cases shall be decided: in the German Court, with one judge sitting; in the German Superior Court, with three judges sitting, except as otherwise prescribed; in the Special Court, with one judge presiding and two associates.

(2) The associates of the Special Court shall as far as practicable have the qualifications for the office of judge. They shall be appointed for one year by the Commissioner General from the ranks of the Reich Germans or Germans by descent resident in the district of the Special Court, and shall be summoned by the presiding judge to the sessions in an order to be determined in advance.

(3) In criminal cases decisions in other than primary proceedings shall be handed down by the presiding judge of the Superior Court and of the Special Court alone. In other cases decisions which are reached without oral process may be handed down by the presiding judge of the Superior Court alone.

SECTION 4. (1) The prosecutor may also be represented in the primary proceedings by a district attorney or by a higher official of the government service.

(2) Representation by counsel shall not be compulsory. As defense counsel any Reich German or German by descent shall be deemed to be qualified who offers surety for an "adequate" defense.

(3) German Courts may commission responsible Reich Germans or Germans by descent to settle cases involving collections of all kinds (namely, of foreclosures and forced executorships). These should be, as far as possible, in government service.

SECTION 5. (1) Appeal against judgments of the German Courts shall be permissible only:

a) In criminal cases, when a more severe penalty than one month's imprisonment or 500 marks' fine has been imposed.
b) In civil cases, when the right of appeal has been expressly granted by the judgment.

No legal recourse shall be available against decisions of the German Courts which confirm a summary penalty imposed by the District Commissioner and decisions of the German Superior Courts.

(2) Jews may not seek legal recourse against the decision of a German Court; they may enter no petition for the reconsideration of a process nor refuse trial before a German judge on the grounds of prejudice.

(3) The Reich Commissioner may stipulate by directive that other groups of people be excluded from the use of legal recourse except in those individual cases in which the Commissioner General, upon the initiative of the prosecutor, grants authorization for the use of legal recourse.

SECTION 6. (1) If there are important legal or factual considerations against the correctness of a legally valid decision by a German Court or by a Special Court, and the Reich Commissioner for the Ostland, on account of the particular significance of the decision, considers a new process and decision imperative, he may within a year after the effective date of the decision propose the reconsideration of the process in civil cases, or bring petition for nullification in criminal cases.

(2) The proposal for reconsideration and the petition for nullification shall be decided by the German Superior Court. If it grants the reconsideration proposal or the nullification petition, it shall hand down a new judgment in the case. This decision shall be final.

SECTION 7. This regulation shall be effective on the day of its publication.

Riga, October 6, 1941.

LOHSE
Reich Commissioner for the Ostland

3. PROPERTY

Order concerning the Sequestration of the Property of the Union of Soviet Socialist Republics in the Territory of the Reich Commissioner for the Ostland, August 19, 1941[4]

It is intended to restore private property completely. In order to be able to carry out this measure and restore an orderly system of legal rights,

[4] *Verkündungsblatt*, 1941, No. 2, p. 5.

seizure of the property of the Union of Soviet Socialist Republics becomes of immediate necessity. The following regulations shall apply with respect to this seizure:

SECTION 1. (1) All real and personal property situated in the territories administered by the Reich Commissioner for the Ostland belonging to the Union of Soviet Socialist Republics, its member states, public corporations, associations, and partnerships, including all claims, investments, rights, and interests of all kind, shall be sequestrated as of June 20, 1941.

(2) This property shall be seized for the purpose of sequestration. With this sequestration the former holders of title shall lose the power of disposal over this property, except as otherwise prescribed in Section 3.

SECTION 2. All persons, natural or legal, who as deputies, lessors, usufructuaries, or by virtue of another legal or factual circumstance, have mediately or immediately in possession or administer sequestrated property shall report this property to the District Commissioner, unless it has already been seized and registered by the local authorities. A special summons for the submission of these reports will be issued by the district commissioners. The report shall contain:

a) A precise statement of where the property is situated.
b) A brief description of the property, its value or its amount.
c) A statement of the legal or factual circumstances by virtue of which the person reporting considers himself obliged to report.

SECTION 3. (1) Anyone who holds sequestrated property in his possession or in trust shall administer it until further notice. Alterations or disposals of the property or its proceeds shall be permissible only within the limits of regular business.

(2) All further measures, especially for disposal of real estate, shall require the consent of the Reich Commissioner for the Ostland or of the authorities commissioned by him. Particularly shall consent be required for the leasing of industrial, business, and agricultural enterprises and real estate.

SECTION 4. Persons obliged to report by virtue of Section 2 shall, upon the demand of the Reich Commissioner for the Ostland or of authorities commissioned by him, yield sequestrated property to the German Civil Administration. This obligation shall include also the submission of any records available—and especially of books and documents—on administration or claims to property rights.

SECTION 5. Under conditions to be determined by the Reich Commissioner for the Ostland, the officers of the German Civil Administration may delegate to other officers or to special trustees the administration and employment, within the limits of regular business, of sequestrated property.

SECTION 6. The sequestration, and the appointment and withdrawal of trustees, as well as their names, shall be entered in a public record or register at the request of the Reich Commissioner for the Ostland or of the officers commissioned by him.

SECTION 7. (1) For the duration of the sequestration, no legal process for the satisfaction of creditors (forced executorship, forced auction, forced administration, bankruptcy, or arbitration process) will be held.

(2) Legal actions for payment and settlement which are based upon claims on sequestrated property shall not be permissible. The examination and satisfaction of these claims will be effected by the Reich Commissioner for the Ostland or by the officers commissioned by him.

SECTION 8. The Reich Commissioner for the Ostland and the officers commissioned by him, in the execution of the duties specified in this order, may require any person to give information.

SECTION 9. (1) Imprisonment and fine, or either of these penalties, shall be imposed upon any person:

1. Who attempts to deprive the German Civil Administration, or the officers or trustees commissioned by it, of any portion of sequestrated property, or who in any other manner attempts to frustrate, evade, or influence the operation of the sequestration.
2. Who with intent or by negligence fails to fulfill or fulfills incorrectly or incompletely the obligation to register property or to give information imposed upon him by this order.

(2) In grave cases the imprisonment shall be at hard labor (*Zuchthaus*): and if an especially grave case of disobedience is presented, the death penalty shall be pronounced.

SECTION 10. The Reich Commissioner for the Ostland will issue the regulations necessary for the execution of this measure.

SECTION 11. Special regulations will be issued concerning the registration of property situated in the territory of the Reich Commissioner for the Ostland and seized under Section 1, when it:

a) Was being used, or was destined for use, by the Soviet Russian armed forces, or
b) Has been taken over by the German armed forces for Reich defense purposes.

SECTION 12. This regulation shall be effective on the day of its publication.

Riga, August 19, 1941.

LOHSE
Reich Commissioner for the Ostland

Order concerning the Treatment of Jewish Property in the Reich Commissariat Ostland, October 13, 1941 [5]

SECTION 1. All real and personal property of the Jewish inhabitants in the territories administered by the Reich Commissioner for the Ostland shall be subject to sequestration, trustee administration, and confiscation according to the terms of the following regulations.

SECTION 2. Property is defined as real and personal goods together with all appurtenances, claims, shares, rights, and interests of all kinds.

SECTION 3. (1) Sequestration shall be effected by the Reich Commissioner for the Ostland or by the officers commissioned by him. It may be effected by writ upon individual persons or by general proclamation, and may be limited to particular possessions.

(2) The following shall be exempted from sequestration:

a) That part of the household furniture which is used for essential personal needs.

b) Cash, bank, and savings credits, as well as notes, to a total value of one hundred Reichsmarks.

SECTION 4. (1) Upon sequestration, the former holders of title shall lose the right of disposal over the sequestrated property.

(2) Anyone who holds sequestrated property in his possession or in trust shall administer it until further notice. Alterations or disposal of the property or its proceeds shall be permissible only within the limits of regular business. All further measures shall require the consent of the Reich Commissioner for the Ostland or of the officers commissioned by him.

SECTION 5. (1) Trustee administration may be ordered for property subject to sequestration, when necessary for regular business operations.

(2) The order for trustee administration shall be considered as equivalent to sequestration.

(3) The Reich Commissioner for the Ostland will issue regulations concerning the establishment and execution of trustee administration.

SECTION 6. (1) Sequestrated property may be confiscated by the Reich Commissioner for the Ostland or by the officers commissioned by him.

(2) The right of disposal over confiscated property shall lie with the officers authorized to confiscate it.

(3) These officers shall make final decisions concerning the settlement of mortgages upon confiscated property. The liability shall be limited to the total market value of the confiscated property.

SECTION 7. Registration of property subject to sequestration may be required by public proclamation.

SECTION 8. The competent authorities, in the execution of their duties, may require any person to give information.

[5] *Verkündungsblatt*, 1941, p. 27.

SECTION 9. (1) Imprisonment and fine, or either of these penalties, shall be imposed upon any person:

a) Who attempts to deprive the officers of the German Civil Administration or the authorities appointed by them of any portion of property sequestrated, or in any other manner to frustrate, evade, or influence the operation of the sequestration.

b) Who with intent or by negligence fails to fulfill or to fulfill promptly or completely the obligation to register property or to give information imposed upon him by this order, or by an implementation measure or other regulation issued for its execution.

(2) In grave cases the imprisonment shall be at hard labor (*Zuchthaus*). If the perpetrator has acted out of insubordination or if the case is otherwise particularly grave, the death penalty shall be pronounced.

SECTION 10. The Reich Commissioner for the Ostland will issue the necessary regulations for the implementation of this order.

SECTION 11. This order shall be effective on the day of its publication.

Riga, October 13, 1941.

LOHSE
Reich Commissioner for the Ostland

Decree on the Reorganization of Handicrafts, Small Industry, and the Retail Trade, October 17, 1941[6]

In the belief that only the free development of initiative and responsibility of action can safeguard a sound and workable economy, handicrafts, small industry, and the retail trade shall be liberated from the fetters of the Bolshevik system and reorganized on the solid basis of private initiative.

PROVISIONS CONCERNING HANDICRAFTS

SECTION 1. Only suitable persons possessing the necessary qualifications and provided with a handicraft card may engage in handicrafts.

SECTION 2. If no public need exists for the continuation of a handicraft establishment, it may be closed down.

SECTION 3. The handicraft establishments which had been incorporated into combines and trusts shall be converted into independent establishments and transferred to private ownership. Collective enterprises shall be separated into single establishments as they existed previously. The creation of inefficient small establishments shall be prevented. If contrary to the public interest, conversion to independent ownership, as well as partition into single establishments, shall not be considered.

[6] *Verkündungsblatt*, 1941, No. 41, p. 29. See also *Latvia under German Occupation, op. cit.*, pp. 44–46.

SECTION 4. All artels, cartels, or associations of collectively responsible craftsmen, the further existence of which is economically unjustified, shall be broken up and liquidated. The separated members shall, in accordance with the provisions of Sections 1 and 2, be permitted to open their own establishments. The remaining cartels shall be converted into cooperative societies.

SECTION 5. Machinery, tools, and other equipment which have been brought into the cartels shall, on the conversion of these cartels, revert to the previous owners in so far as the latter become independent craftsmen. Artisans who do not become independent shall be paid for such equipment in money.

SECTION 6. Artisans who, in addition to manufacturing goods independently, also sell other goods, must obtain permission in accordance with the regulations concerning retail trade, if their retail trade is of considerable extent.

PROVISIONS CONCERNING SMALL INDUSTRIAL ESTABLISHMENTS

SECTION 7. Small industrial establishments, i.e., establishments employing an average of no more than twenty workmen, shall be subject to license.

SECTION 8. A small industrial establishment shall be permitted only if justified by public need and if the owner or manager is qualified and personally suitable.

SECTION 9. The small industrial establishments incorporated in combines and trusts shall be converted into independent establishments reverting to private hands. Collective enterprises shall be partitioned into single establishments as they existed previously. The creation of inefficient small establishments shall be prevented. (Section 3 to be applied.)

This regulation shall not apply to existing establishments for the amelioration of the food economy, nor to enterprises dealing in lumber.

PROVISIONS CONCERNING RETAIL TRADE

SECTION 10. Retail trade establishments shall be subject to license. Public houses, as well as places serving meals, shall be regarded as retail trade establishments.

SECTION 11. Such an establishment shall be permitted only (*a*) if there is public need for it, and (*b*) if the owner or responsible manager is qualified and personally suitable.

SECTION 12. Nationalized retail trade establishments shall, in principle, revert to private ownership, provided this is not contrary to the public interest.

SECTION 13. If such an establishment reverts to private ownership, the available stock shall be sold at present market value to the person taking it over.

SECTION 14. Retail traders who, in connection with their establishment, also have a handicraft establishment, must obtain a license in accordance with existing regulations, provided the business of the handicraft establishment is of considerable extent.

JOINT REGULATIONS

SECTION 15. In the process of return to the system of private property, establishments shall, as far as possible, be handed back to their private owners.

SECTION 16. Machinery, tools, and other implements, as well as equipment, shall be transferred to the previous owners free of charge, or upon payment of the value thereof, to persons taking over the establishment. The provisions of Section 5 shall not be affected hereby.

SECTION 17. The premises and plots of land necessary for the above-mentioned establishments shall be made available on hire and lease.

SECTION 18. The funds required for the execution of this regulation shall be granted by way of credits.

SECTION 19. All arbitrary measures aiming at the restoration of private property which have been taken since June 20, 1941, shall be null and void.

SECTION 20. The Reich Commissioner may, by way of exception, order deviations from this regulation.

SECTION 21. Further regulations in implementation of this order will be issued.

SECTION 22. This regulation shall become effective for the time being in the former free states of Latvia and Lithuania upon the day of its publication.

Riga, October 17, 1941. LOHSE

Reich Commissioner for the Ostland

Regulations concerning the Administration of City Buildings and Houses, December 15, 1941 [7]

SECTION 1. (1) The District Commissioners shall be authorized, in accordance with further regulations concerning the ownership of property, to grant to former owners the right of administration and use of the city dwelling houses, and sites appurtenant thereto, which were removed from their administration as the result of mass nationalization under the Bolshevik rule.

(2) Should the address of the former owner be unknown or should he have died after the nationalization of the property, this right of administration and use may be ceded to a relative (the nearest of kin). As such relatives shall be considered only the husband or wife, direct descendants, and parents.

[7] *Verkündungsblatt*, December 20, 1941.

(3) If the previous conduct of the interested person does not presuppose an orderly administration and maintenance of a house or site, he shall not be entrusted with such administration and use. Likewise, no assignment shall take place if the integrity of the applicant is in doubt or if such an assignment is contrary to public interest.

SECTION 2. The use and management of such houses and sites shall be granted by a written order of installation.

SECTION 3. (1) The person to whom the administration and use of the property is granted shall be responsible for the orderly administration and maintenance of the building or site assigned to him.

(2) The right of administration and use of property, once granted, may be revoked at any time.

It may also be revoked if the person involved fails to carry out the duties incumbent on him according to subparagraph 1.

SECTION 4. (1) The person who is given the right of administration and use of property shall have the usufruct of premises and sites.

(2) If the administration and use is assigned to a relative of the person previously holding rights therein, according to subparagraph 2 of Section 1, the former is liable before the latter or the latter's heir as an agent.

SECTION 5. The person installed shall be obliged to bear the public taxes devolving on the property.

SECTION 6. The Reich Commissioner for the Ostland shall issue the legal and administrative regulations necessary to execute and implement the present order.

SECTION 7. This order shall become effective upon the day of publication. It shall not apply to the General District of White Russia.

Riga, December 15, 1941. LOHSE

Reich Commissioner for the Ostland

4. LABOR

[EXCERPTS]

Regulation concerning Remuneration to Jewish Labor in the General District of Latvia, March 19, 1942 [8]

The question of remuneration to Jewish labor in the General District of Latvia shall be regulated as follows:

SECTION 1. The Jews themselves shall not receive any wages.

SECTION 2. (1) Employers of Jewish labor shall pay a fee to the Financial Department of the competent District Commissioner, which shall be in ac-

[8] *Deutsche Zeitung im Osten*, March 31, 1942.

cordance with the wage rates established in the General Decree of the Reich Commissioner for the Ostland of November 21, 1941, concerning Local Workmen in Public Services and in Trade (*Verkündungsblatt des Reichskommissars für das Ostland*, 1942, p. 45). The District Commissioners will issue special provisions concerning these payments.

(2) For overtime work, or for work on Sundays, holidays and at night, which may be required only with the consent of the District Commissioner (through the Labor Office), no extra fee shall be paid.

SECTION 3. Violation of this regulation shall be punishable by imprisonment or fine, or by both.

. . . . .

Riga, March 19, 1942.

Commissioner General in Riga
Acting Deputy: DORR

BELGIUM

I. TERRITORIES INCORPORATED INTO GERMANY

Decree of the Führer and Reich Chancellor concerning the Reunion of the Districts of Eupen, Malmédy, and Moresnet with the German Reich, May 18, 1940 [1]

The districts separated from the German Reich by the Versailles dictate and incorporated into Belgium are again in German possession. At heart they have always remained united with Germany. They are therefore not even temporarily to be regarded and treated as occupied enemy territory. I therefore order immediately:

ARTICLE I. The districts of Eupen, Malmédy and Moresnet, separated from the German Reich by the Versailles dictate, are again a component part of the German Reich.

ARTICLE II. The above-mentioned districts are assigned to the Reich Province (Government District of Aachen).

ARTICLE III. I reserve to myself measures concerning the implementation of this order.

ADOLF HITLER
Führer and Reich Chancellor

Decree of the Führer and Reich Chancellor for the Implementation of the Reunion of the Districts of Eupen, Malmédy, and Moresnet with the German Reich, May 23, 1940 [2]

To implement my decree of May 18, 1940, concerning the reunion of the districts of Eupen, Malmédy, and Moresnet with the German Reich (*RGBl.* I, p. 777), I order as follows:

SECTION 1. To the districts named in Article I of the decree belong the former Prussian provincial districts of Eupen and Malmédy, including neutral Moresnet, and in addition the adjacent portions which fell to Belgium in consequence of the boundary settlements of the Versailles dictate. In other respects the Reich Minister of the Interior shall determine in detail the course of the Reich boundaries.

SECTION 2. The inhabitants of German or related blood in the districts named in Section 1 shall become German nationals (*Staatsangehörige*) as

[1] *Reichsgesetzblatt*, 1940, I, p. 777. [2] *Ibid.*, p. 803.

shall be provided in detail by further measures. Germans by descent (*Volksdeutsche*) shall become Reich citizens (*Bürger*) as provided by the Reich Citizenship Code.

SECTION 3. I. In the districts named in Section 1 the whole body of Reich law and Prussian provincial law shall become valid on September 1, 1940.

II. The competent Reich or provincial minister, in consultation with the Reich Minister of the Interior, may stipulate that Reich law or Prussian provincial law shall not become valid or shall become valid at a later date, or with special restrictions. Such a stipulation as regards Reich law shall require publication in the *Reichgesetzblatt*, and as regards Prussian provincial law, in the Prussian *Gesetzsammlung*.

III. Until August 31, 1940, the Reich Minister of the Interior, in consultation with the competent Reich or provincial ministers, may introduce Reich law or Prussian provincial law by order.

IV. Until the introduction of Reich law or Prussian provincial law, the law previously valid shall remain in force, in so far as consistent with incorporation into the German Reich.

SECTION 4. I. The necessary arrangements in regard to property rights occasioned by the execution of this decree shall be made by the Reich Minister of the Interior and the Prussian Minister of Finance.

II. Issues in the field of financial settlement which may be raised by this decree shall be arranged by the Prussian Minister of Finance in consultation with the Reich Minister of the Interior.

III. The Reich Minister of Finance shall act in the place of the Prussian Minister of Finance when arrangements made under subsections I and II affect the Reich.

SECTION 5. I. The central authority for the reunion of the districts named in Section 1 with the German Reich shall be the Reich Minister of the Interior.

II. The Reich Minister of the Interior shall issue the legal and administrative regulations necessary for implementing and supplementing this decree. In particular, he shall regulate the regional organization within the general provincial administration as made necessary by the reunion and shall determine the administrative headquarters.

ADOLF HITLER
Führer and Reich Chancellor

Order concerning the Provisional Administration of Justice in the Districts of Eupen, Malmédy, and Moresnet, July 29, 1940[3]

[EXCERPTS]

By virtue of the decree of the Führer and Reich Chancellor of May 23, 1940, for the implementation of the decree concerning the reunion of the districts of Eupen, Malmédy, and Moresnet with the German Reich (*RGBl.* I, p. 803), it is ordered:

. . . . .

SECTION 3. Sections 1 to 7 and 17 of the order concerning the introduction of German criminal law in the incorporated Eastern Territories of June 6, 1940 (*RGBl.* I, p. 844), shall be applied *mutatis mutandis*. In Section 7, subsection 2, the date September 1, 1939, shall be replaced by May 21, 1940.

. . . . .

SECTION 8. The process of transition with respect to cases pending at the time of the reunion shall be regulated in an administrative way by the Reich Minister of Justice.

SECTION 9. Decisions and other regulations of the judicial authorities which are made in the course of the administration of justice for the districts of Eupen, Malmédy, and Moresnet before the effective date of this order shall not be invalid or contestable in themselves if in deviating from the law previously in force they conform at least to the spirit of this order.

The Reich Minister of Justice
By proxy: DR. SCHLEGELBERGER
The Reich Minister of the Interior
By proxy: PFUNDTNER

Act concerning the Representation of the German Nationals Resident in the Territories of Eupen, Malmédy, and Moresnet in the Greater German Reichstag, February 4, 1941[4]

In order to give a visible expression to the reunion of the Territories of Eupen, Malmédy, and Moresnet with the Greater German Reich and in order to afford the German nationals resident there a representation in the Greater German Reichstag, the Reich Government has passed the following act which is hereby published.

SECTION 1. The Reichstag of Greater Germany, elected on April 10 and December 4, 1938, and enlarged by the acts of April 13, 1939, and January 29, 1940, shall be increased by as many members as the number 60,000 is contained in the total number of German nationals resident in the territories of Eupen, Malmédy, and Moresnet who are over twenty years of age.

[3] *Reichsgesetzblatt*, 1940, I, p. 1059. [4] *Ibid.*, 1941, I, p. 73.

SECTION 2. The members entering the Greater German Reichstag in accordance with Section 1 shall be selected by the Führer and Reich Chancellor from among the German nationals residing in these territories who are over twenty-five years of age.

Berlin, February 4, 1941.

ADOLF HITLER, *Führer and Reich Chancellor*
GÖRING, *Reich Marshal, President of the Council of Ministers for the Defense of the Reich*
FRICK, *Reich Minister of the Interior*
DR. LAMMERS, *Reich Minister and Chief of the Reich Chancellery*

Decree concerning the Nationality of the Inhabitants of Eupen, Malmédy, and Moresnet, September 23, 1941[5]

[EXCERPT]

By virtue of Section 2 of the decree of the Führer and Reich Chancellor of May 23, 1940, for the implementation of the reunion of the territories of Eupen, Malmédy, and Moresnet with the German Reich (*RGBl.* I, p. 803), it is ordered as follows:

SECTION 1. (1) Effective May 18, 1940, German nationality shall be acquired as a legal right by:

a) Persons who acquired Belgian citizenship through Article 36 of the Versailles Treaty.
b) Persons who as residents of neutral Moresnet acquired Belgian citizenship on January 10, 1920.
c) Legitimate offspring of the persons enumerated under letters *a* and *b* and the illegitimate offspring of females falling under *a* or *b* who according to Belgian law share the citizenship of the mother.
d) The wives of the persons enumerated under letters *a* through *c*, even if the status of marriage no longer existed on May 18, 1940.

(2) German nationality shall not be acquired, however, by:

a) Persons who after the acquisition of Belgian citizenship became citizens of a state other than Belgium or who became stateless persons.
b) Women who, after the effective date of the Versailles Treaty, married Belgians who had not acquired Belgian citizenship under Article 36 of the Versailles Treaty or under the Belgian law of September 15, 1919.
c) Children who were born out of wedlock, after the effective date of the Versailles Treaty, of a Belgian father who had not acquired Belgian citizenship under Article 36 of the Versailles Treaty or

[5] *Reichsgesetzblatt*, 1941, I, p. 584.

under the Belgian law of September 15, 1919, and who (1) were legitimated during their minority or before their declaration of majority by a subsequent marriage, or (2) before or together with the acknowledgment by their mother were acknowledged voluntarily or through court action by the father.

d) Jews (Section 5 of the first order in pursuance to the Reich citizenship law of November 14, 1935—*RGBl.* I, p. 1333) or gypsies.

(3) Decisions through which persons of German or related blood who satisfy the conditions of subsection 1 were deprived of their citizenship by virtue of the Belgian law of July 30, 1934, shall be considered as not having been issued. From such decisions for nullification of citizenship no legal consequences may be drawn under subsection 2*a*.

SECTION 2. (1) Effective May 10, 1940, probational German nationality shall be acquired by:

a) Belgian citizens of German descent who had their residence in the territories of Eupen, Malmédy, and Moresnet on May 18, 1940, and are not already qualified for German nationality under Section 1 of this order.

b) Stateless persons of German descent who had their residence in the territories of Eupen, Malmédy, and Moresnet on May 18, 1940.

(2) The probational acquisition of German nationality may be revoked only within a period of ten years.

. . . . .

Berlin, September 23, 1941.

The Reich Minister of the Interior
By deputy: Dr. STUCKART

II. NON-INCORPORATED TERRITORIES

1. ADMINISTRATION

Proclamation to the Occupied Territory, May 10, 1940 [6]

By virtue of the authority vested in me by the Supreme Commander of the Army, I hereby proclaim:

I. The German armed forces guarantee the inhabitants full safety of person and property. Whoever behaves quietly and peacefully has nothing to fear.

II. Acts of violence and sabotage are punishable by the most severe penalties. The following, among others, will be considered as acts of sabotage:

[6] *Heeresgruppen-Verordnungsblatt für die besetzten Gebiete*, Issue No. 1, May 10, 1940, p. 4.

injury to, or withholding of, crops, supplies, and installations of every description essential to the conduct of the war, and the tearing down and damaging of official posters. The following are placed under the special protection of the German armed forces: gas, water and electric works, railways, sluices, and art treasures.

III. The surrender of weapons and other implements of war has been ordered by special proclamation. Weapons constituting souvenirs or antiques and no longer usable need not be surrendered. Hunting guns are to be surrendered to the mayor, who shall be held responsible for their custody; name, profession, and residence of the owner shall be indicated.

IV. Acts punishable according to military law are:

1. Aiding non-German soldiers in the occupied territories.
2. Aiding civilians to escape into the unoccupied territory.
3. Transmitting news to persons or authorities outside the occupied territory if such transmittal is prejudicial to the interests of the German armed forces and the Reich.
4. Communicating with prisoners of war.
5. Insulting the German Army and its Commanders.
6. Street meetings, distribution of leaflets, arrangement of public assemblies and parades without previous approval by the German Commander, as well as any other manifestation of hostility towards Germany.
7. Inducing work stoppages, malicious stoppage of work, strikes, and lock-outs.

V. The state and municipal agencies, police forces, and schools are required to continue operations. They serve thereby their own population. The heads of the several agencies and institutions shall be held responsible for loyal conduct toward the occupying power. Persons employed in public service shall receive the same remuneration as before.

VI. All shops, plants, stores, banks, etc., shall remain open in the interests of the population. Any closing without sufficient reason shall be punishable.

VII. In the interests of orderly and equitable distribution of supplies among the population, any hoarding of goods of everyday need (any undue accumulation of supplies) is forbidden. Hoarding shall be considered sabotage. Traffic necessary for supplying daily needs of the civilian population (including the market traffic) shall not be suspended unless for military reasons. Producers and sellers of goods for daily needs shall continue their business and furnish goods to consumers.

VIII. Any increases in prices, remunerations of any kind, and salaries above the level of the day of occupation are prohibited, unless exceptions have been expressly permitted.

IX. The rate of exchange is: for the Netherlands, 1 gulden equals 1.50 Reichsmarks; for Belgium, 1 belga equals 0.50 Reichsmark. The use of any other rate of exchange is punishable. Every person shall be required to accept German currency as well as that of his own country.

X. The Army and its members shall pay cash for purchases, services, etc. Only when the amount involved exceeds five hundred Reichsmarks shall certificates for goods received or services be given in lieu of cash, and these certificates shall be paid by the German military administration.

THE COMMANDER IN CHIEF OF THE ARMY GROUP (*Heeresgruppe*)

Order concerning the Application of German Penal Law and Statutes in the Territories of the Netherlands and Belgium Occupied by the German Armies, May 10, 1940 [7]

By virtue of the authority vested in me by the Supreme Commander of the Army, I hereby order as follows:

SECTION 1. German criminal law shall be applicable whenever a person committing an act punishable according to German law is tried by the courts of the German armed forces or by special courts.

THE COMMANDER IN CHIEF OF THE ARMY GROUP (*Heeresgruppe*)

Ordinance concerning the Selling and Lending of Books and Pamphlets Hostile to Germany in Belgium, August 13, 1940 [8]

On the basis of the power conferred on me by the Supreme Commander of the Army, I order the following for the occupied Belgian territory:

ARTICLE 1. Any sale of books and pamphlets hostile to Germany is forbidden. Booksellers and librarians must select and lock away all publications hostile to Germany no later than September 1, 1940.

ARTICLE 2. All publications are considered hostile to Germany that hold up to derision the German people, the German Reich, or the National Socialist Movement; publications written by such people as emigrated from Germany are considered hostile to Germany in any case.

In cases of doubt, the booksellers and librarians must for the time being decide on their own responsibility whether or not publications are hostile to Germany.

ARTICLE 3. The prohibition concerning lending applies to all private and public libraries. In the case of special libraries of scientific books, the directors, as an exception, may permit the use of individual publications falling under the prohibition within the precincts of the library, if the user

[7] *Heeresgruppen-Verordnungsblatt für die besetzten Gebiete*, Issue No. 1, May 10, 1940, p. 7.

[8] *Verordnungsblatt des Militärbefehlshabers in Belgien und Nordfrankreich für die besetzten Gebiete Belgiens und Nordfrankreichs*, No. 10, August 13, 1940.

gives in advance a written declaration that he is using the publication exclusively for his own scientific work.

THE MILITARY COMMANDER IN BELGIUM AND NORTHERN FRANCE

An Order Directed Against the Holding of Office by Over-Aged Persons in the Public Administration of Belgium, March 7, 1941 [9]

In the present condition of Belgium the administration of the country is facing extraordinary tasks. New ways must be found for their accomplishment. Able persons of youthful age are ready to assume office. Among the great number of discharged Belgian soldiers especially are many who wish to serve their country with energy and in full realization of their responsibility. To these men access to public office shall be made possible.

In pursuance of the authority vested in me by the Supreme Commander of the Army, it is therefore ordered as follows:

SECTION 1. Persons holding public office in Belgium as defined in Section 3 of this order shall be retired from such office at the end of the month in which they complete their sixtieth year of life. Persons who have completed their sixtieth year of life at the effective date of this order shall thus be retired at the end of March, 1941.

SECTION 2. Whenever, in individual instances, it is in the public interest to retain the official in office beyond the age limit, the head of the ministry concerned shall be authorized, with the consent of the Military Governor, to exempt such official from retirement. The order of exemption may be revoked at any time.

The authority to issue such an order or to give such consent in accordance with the preceding paragraph may be delegated to officials of inferior rank.

SECTION 3. Holders of public office in accordance with this order shall be deemed to be:

a) The heads of the ministries and all other high government officials (first category).
b) The prosecuting attorneys and the members of the Court of Audit.
c) The provincial governors, district commissioners, members of the permanent committees, and the provincial "greffiers."
d) The mayors, lay judges, municipal secretaries, and police commissioners.

Special arrangements will be made for the judiciary.

SECTION 4. This order shall take effect upon publication.

THE MILITARY COMMANDER IN BELGIUM AND NORTHERN FRANCE

[9] *Verordnungsblatt des Militärbefehlshabers in Belgien und Nordfrankreich*, etc., Issue No. 34, March 8, 1941, p. 529.

2. PROPERTY

Order concerning Sequestration in the Occupied Territories of the Netherlands, Belgium, Luxemburg, and France (Sequestration Order), May 20, 1940[10]

Foods, raw materials, and half-manufactured materials are of vital importance for the economic life of the occupied territories. From a long range view, a sufficient supply of these will be endangered by the enemy blockade. It is therefore necessary to economize present supplies. Economical use and just distribution will assure stable operation of the factories. In the interests of the occupied territory, all scarce agricultural products, foods, raw materials, half-manufactured materials, and other supplies shall be seized and officially administered.

Sequestration does not cancel ownership, but restricts the right of using and disposing of the goods. Transfer of property to other persons or firms shall be ordered only if such transfer is in the interest of the general economic welfare.

By reason of the authority vested in me by the Führer and Supreme Commander of the Armed Forces, I order as follows:

SECTION 1. (1) Goods designated in the appendix[11] shall be considered seized as of the effective date of this order.

(2) Normal supplies in private houses shall be exempt from seizure.

SECTION 2. Sequestration has the effect of making all legal transactions involving the goods seized and any work performed upon them, with the general exceptions enumerated in Section 3, subject to the consent of the Army Group (*Heeresgruppe*) or its designees. The same applies to all legal process by way of execution of judgments or attachments.

SECTION 3. (1) No consent in accordance with Section 2 shall, until further notice, be required for the following transactions:

a) Goods (especially raw materials, foods, feed, and half-manufactured goods) may be processed in the same amount as in the corresponding month of the preceding year.

b) Goods may be supplied to a factory which has insufficient supplies on hand for processing according to subsection 1*a*.

c) Factories producing and/or processing agricultural products, foods and animal feed, and hotels and restaurants, shall be allowed to buy or sell agricultural products in quantities necessary for the ordinary needs of their customers.

d) All shopkeepers and artisans shall be required to continue delivery to consumers to meet their ordinary needs.

e) Logs and by-products of forestry may be prepared for shipment or cut as lumber or sold to the lumber industry.

[10] *Verordnungsblatt des Militärbefehlshabers in Belgien und Nordfrankreich*, etc., Issue No. 2, June 17, 1940, p. 23.

[11] The Appendix is not reproduced.—ED.

(2) The Army Groups or their designees may determine the amount of goods that may be processed according to subsection 1*b*.

SECTION 4. (1) A person having sequestrated goods in his custody shall be required to inventory them according to kind, quantity, and place where they are kept, on the first day of every month, the first such inventory to be made immediately after this order takes effect. In this inventory the goods shall be listed according to kind and described by their usual trade designation.

(2) Agricultural and food processing plants and factories, and shops dealing with foods and agricultural products, shall deliver such lists to points designated by the Army Groups or those authorized by them. They shall also determine the time at which the inventories shall be submitted.

(3) Farms and other agricultural producers and retail shops shall not be subject, until further notice, to the duties specified in subsections 1 and 2.

SECTION 5. (1) The Army Groups and their designees may demand information from any person concerning economic data, supplies, consumption, storage, purchase, and sale of goods, products, and wares of every kind. They may demand that books, papers, receipts, and samples be shown and that anyone required to furnish information appear in person.

(2) Information may be requested by an oral or written special order or by public proclamation.

(3) Information shall be given free of charge.

(4) The authorities named in subsection 1 may, at any time, inspect factories, plants, and rooms where goods are, or are presumed to be, stored, manufactured, or offered for sale.

SECTION 6. Any person having wares in his possession, must handle them with the utmost care and must to the best of his ability prevent their destruction.

SECTION 7. (1) A person who intentionally or negligently violates this order, or implementing rules or regulations issued hereunder, shall be liable to imprisonment or fine or both.

(2) The goods involved in the violation may be confiscated in favor of a person or agency designated in the sentence. If punishment of the person or persons guilty is not possible, confiscation alone may be ordered.

SECTION 8. (1) There shall be no reparation for damages arising from the execution of this order.

(2) The Army Groups may issue rules and regulations for the enforcement and implementation of this order.

(3) The order shall take effect as of the date of its publication.

Headquarters, May 20, 1940.

THE COMMANDER IN CHIEF OF THE ARMY

Order concerning the Confiscation of Property by Way of Summary Order of Punishment, April 24, 1941[12]

By virtue of the authority delegated by the Supreme Commander of the Army, and with reference to the order of the Supreme Commander of the Army of May 18, 1940 (*Verordnungsblatt des Militärbefehlshabers*, 2d edition, No. 3), concerning the authority of the local commanders to impose summary penalties in Belgium and Northern France, it is hereby ordered as follows:

(1) By summary order of punishment, the commanders may further order the confiscation of articles of personal property in all cases where such confiscation is lawful.

(2) Whenever punishment of an individual is not possible confiscation may be ordered by special order.

On behalf of the Military Commander in Belgium and Northern France:

THE CHIEF OF THE MILITARY ADMINISTRATION

3. ECONOMY

Order concerning the Organization of the National Economy, February 10, 1941[13]

[EXCERPTS]

The Secretary General of the Ministry of Justice,
The Secretary General of the Ministry of Finance,
The Secretary General of the Ministry of Labor and Social Welfare,
The Secretary General of the Ministry of Agriculture and Food,
The Secretary General of the Ministry of Communications,
The Secretary General of the Ministry of Economic Affairs.

Whereas an orderly administration of the country makes it absolutcly necessary that, in view of the present circumstances, the national economy be organized in such a manner as to assure a just distribution of raw materials and an efficient coordination of the means of production; whereas it is further necessary to assure unity in the representation of the interests of the various trades, occupations, professions, etc., and to impose the same discipline on all interests within the framework of their occupational or professional organizations; by virtue of the law of May 10, 1940, concerning the delegation of powers, and in view of the emergency and the impossibility of action by the higher authority, the above-mentioned hereby order as follows:

[12] *Verordnungsblatt des Militärbefehlshabers in Belgien und Nordfrankreich*, etc., Issue No. 40, April 26, 1941, p. 580.
[13] *Moniteur Belge*, February 13, 1941.

SECTION 1. In order to promote the national economy and assure its organization the head of the Ministry of Economic Affairs shall be authorized to make any and all orders for the regulation of economic matters and to take all steps necessary to enforce such orders, especially:

1. To create economic associations, organized according to trades, etc., or regions, and to designate them as sole official representatives within their sphere of economic activity. These economic associations shall be agencies of public law.
2. To reorganize into agencies of public law existing trade or occupational associations or to unite several into one such organization, to establish by-laws for it, and, if necessary, to make rules for the management and transfer of its assets.
3. To subject to the orders of these economic organizations all industrial, commercial, or trade enterprises. This shall apply to Belgian enterprises, and to foreign and colonial enterprises having a branch establishment in Belgium, and to any enterprise under public administration.
4. To establish the objectives, the powers, rights, privileges, and obligations of the said economic organizations and of their members.
5. To appoint and dismiss directors and members of the governing boards of these economic organizations.

SECTION 2. If rules and regulations are required for the enforcement of the provisions of Section 1, the Head of the Ministry of Economic Affairs may request existing organizations, individual persons, or special committees appointed by him for such purpose to prepare drafts of such rules and regulations.

SECTION 3. If the promotion of public welfare so requires, the Head of the Ministry of Economic Affairs may order a group or an organization representing trade or similar interests, to discontinue any activity for the furtherance of such interests.

If such an order has been issued, the assets of the group or the organization shall be disposed of as provided for in by-laws or by agreement. In the absence of such a provision, the liquidator or liquidators shall transfer the assets to a similar organization of the kind provided for in Section 1 of this order.

SECTION 4. (1) For rights affected by the application of this order or by measures taken for the purpose of its execution, no indemnity shall be granted.

(2) Notwithstanding the provision of subsection 1, the Head of the Ministry of Economic Affairs may grant an indemnity wherever he deems it equitable.

. . . . .

SECTION 5. The directors of the organizations contemplated in Section 1 may impose on persons negligently violating orders issued for the enforcement of this order, administrative fines not exceeding 10,000 francs.

Appeal from such an order imposing a fine may be made to the Head of the Ministry of Economic Affairs. The appeal shall be made, by registered letter, within five days of the service of the order imposing the fine.

. . . . . .

SECTION 7. Wilful violations of orders issued for the enforcement of this order shall be punished by imprisonment of not less than eight days but not exceeding two years, or a fine of not less than 200 francs but not exceeding 700,000 francs, or both.

All provisions of Book 1 of the Penal Code, with the exception of Section 85, are applicable to violations described in paragraph 1.

The penalties herein provided shall be imposed after complaint by the Head of the Ministry of Economic Affairs. Any case founded on such a complaint may be discontinued at any stage of the proceedings.

SECTION 8. This order shall not apply to enterprises engaged in agriculture, horticulture, or forestry, and to their trade associations. The authority of the Head of the Ministry of Agriculture and of Food, with regard to measures to be taken for the regulation of production, marketing, and consumption, in accordance with Article 2 of the order of August 12, 1940, shall not be limited in any manner by this order.

. . . . . .

SECTION 9. This order shall take effect within three days after publication in the *Moniteur Belge*.

Order concerning Factory Trustees, April 29, 1941 [14]

By virtue of the authority vested in me by the Supreme Commander of the Army, I hereby order as follows for Belgium and Northern France:

SECTION 1. (1) For the purpose of maintaining industrial production the Military Commander or his designee shall be authorized to appoint factory trustees in industrial plants. The factory trustees shall be individual persons. They are appointed subject to dismissal without notice.

(2) The appointing authority shall issue to the factory trustee a certificate of appointment and guiding instructions concerning the scope of his duties. He shall be obligated to fulfill conscientiously his duties and to treat all information obtained as confidential.

SECTION 2. (1) The factory trustee shall be responsible for the resumption or continuance of operations of the plant to which he has been appointed, for the orderly execution of orders and, in general, for all measures to be taken for the purpose of increasing the output.

[14] *Verordnungsblatt des Militärbefehlshabers in Belgien und Nordfrankreich*, etc., Issue No. 42, May 7, 1941, p. 599.

(2) The trustee shall also decide whether to pass on applications for admission of visitors to the plant.

SECTION 3. (1) The activities of the factory trustee shall not be deemed to affect the responsibility of the management and its authority to act on behalf of the enterprise. The management, however, shall be required to grant to the trustee access to all business transactions, documents, and plant operations, to give him all information required and to comply with his orders issued within the scope of his official duties. The trustee shall be authorized to participate in meetings of the management devoted to matters concerning business or plant operation.

(2) The factory trustee shall not be authorized to act on behalf of the enterprise.

SECTION 4. The enterprise shall be required to bear the costs arising through the appointment and activity of a factory trustee unless the appointing authority shall otherwise provide. The appointing authority shall also establish the compensation to be paid to the trustee.

SECTION 5. Violations of this order shall be punishable by fine or imprisonment or both unless by virtue of other provisions more severe penalties shall be incurred.

SECTION 6. This order shall take effect as of February 1, 1941.

THE MILITARY COMMANDER IN BELGIUM AND NORTHERN FRANCE

Order concerning an Audit of Enterprises, May 8, 1941 [15]

By virtue of the authority vested in me by the Supreme Commander of the Army, I hereby order as follows for Belgium:

SECTION 1. Enterprises of every description shall be subject to audit by order of the Chief of the Military Administration. The audit shall be made by experts competent to fulfill the duties incumbent upon them. The order to make such an audit shall be in writing.

SECTION 2. The auditors shall be required to treat as confidential with regard to third parties all facts learned in the course of their audit. They shall not be called as witnesses or experts concerning such facts unless consent of the Chief of the Military Administration to such call shall have been obtained.

SECTION 3. All persons who direct or manage the enterprise or act on its behalf or have previously so acted, shall be required to furnish the auditors all information which the latter may deem necessary for the making of the

[15] *Verordnungsblatt des Militärbefehlshabers in Belgien und Nordfrankreich*, etc., Issue No. 43, May 19, 1941, p. 605.

audit. On request books of account and correspondence of the enterprise shall be made accessible for inspection by the auditors.

SECTION 4. The cost of the audit shall be borne by the enterprise audited.

SECTION 5. Violations of this order shall be punishable by fine or imprisonment or both.

SECTION 6. This order shall take effect as of January 1, 1941.

On behalf of the Military Commander in Belgium and Northern France:

THE CHIEF OF THE MILITARY ADMINISTRATION

Order concerning the Surrender of Non-Ferrous Metals, October 20, 1941 [16]

Pursuant to the authority vested in me by the Supreme Commander, I hereby order as follows for Belgium:

SECTION 1. (1) All persons, excepting corporations which are subject to tax in accordance with their tax reports for the years 1939 or 1940, shall be required to surrender a quantity of non-ferrous metals as determined in subsection 2 of Section 4.

(2) All persons, including corporations engaged in industry or manufacture, shall surrender (on behalf of their shop or factory) a quantity of non-ferrous metals as determined in subsection 3 of Section 4, notwithstanding the duty to surrender non-ferrous metals as determined in subsection 1. In the case of corporations, the persons acting on their behalf or their agents shall be held responsible for full compliance with this duty.

(3) Non-ferrous metals shall be surrendered not later than November 30, 1941, at the public collection centers. The place and time of surrender for each person subject to such duty shall be determined by local proclamation.

SECTION 2. (1) Non-ferrous metals shall be deemed to include, for the purposes of this order, the following: copper, tin, nickel, lead, and their alloys, such as brass, bronze, tombac (pinchbeck), antimonial lead, german silver, alpaca, argenton, etc.

(2) Precious metals, zinc, aluminum, and their alloys shall not be deemed to be non-ferrous metals for the purposes of this order.

SECTION 3. (1) The persons subject to the duty of surrender may determine which non-ferrous metals and which objects made therefrom shall not be included in the quantity of non-ferrous metals surrendered if such metals consist of:

[16] *Verordnungsblatt des Militärbefehlshabers in Belgien und Nordfrankreich*, etc., Issue No. 59, October 27, 1941, p. 743.

1. Stocks of non-ferrous metals held in industrial plants or shops for purposes of resale, processing or metal production; or
2. Non-ferrous metals subject to Belgian provisions concerning the keeping of stock books and public registration duty (ore, raw material, semi-manufactured goods, and scrap).

(2) In complying with the duty of surrender the following objects need not be included:

1. Objects having a special historical, scientific, artistic, or folklore value;
2. Objects indispensable for daily use or for the continued operation of the factory or shop, or those for which other materials cannot be substituted.

SECTION 4. (1) The quantities of metals to be surrendered shall be determined according to the following key:

1 kg red copper or bronze	100 points
1 kg brass or yellow copper	50 points
1 kg tin	200 points
1 kg nickel	200 points
1 kg lead	50 points
1 kg of different alloys of copper, tin or lead	50 points

(2) Persons subject to the duty of surrender in accordance with subsection 1 of Section 1 shall be required to surrender the quantities determined according to the appendix[17] attached, which is graded in accordance with income.

(3) Persons subject to the duty of surrender in accordance with subsection 2 of Section 1 shall surrender an amount of metal equivalent to 100 points for each worker or employee employed on May 1, 1940.

SECTION 5. (1) Any person thus surrendering a quantity of metals shall receive a certificate of tax credit made out in his name which he may use as a credit toward his taxes due in 1942.

(2) The amount of credit shall be arrived at by crediting 3 Belgian francs for any 100 points as expressed in metals thus surrendered; for objects of pure copper, 6 Belgian francs, and for objects of pure tin or pure nickel, 12.50 Belgian francs, shall be credited for any 100 points as expressed in metals surrendered.

SECTION 6. Persons who fail to surrender in whole or in part the quantity of metals as determined by Section 4, shall make a substitute payment, the amount of which shall be determined in accordance with Appendix 2.

SECTION 7. (1) The penalties of imprisonment or fine or both shall be applied to a person:

[17] The appendices to this order are not reproduced.—ED.

1. Who fails to surrender metal as provided in Section 4, or does not surrender it at the time appointed though he possesses metals or objects made of such metals which should have been surrendered.
2. Who violates in any other way this order or the rules or regulations published for its enforcement, or intentionally endangers or hinders the activities directed toward the collection of these metals.
3. Who hides non-ferrous metals or objects made therefrom with the intention of withholding them from surrender; or
4. Who unlawfully appropriates non-ferrous metals or objects made therefrom which have been surrendered.

(2) In addition to the sentence, all objects found in the possession of the defendant and made in whole or part of non-ferrous metals may be confiscated by administrative order.

SECTION 8. The central authorities of Belgium concerned shall issue all rules and regulations required for the enforcement of this order.

THE CHIEF OF MILITARY ADMINISTRATION IN BELGIUM AND NORTHERN FRANCE

4. FINANCE

Order concerning Reich Credit Institutes, May 18, 1940[18]

By virtue of the authority vested in me by the Führer and Supreme Commander of the Armed Forces, I order as follows:

CHAPTER I

In the territories of Belgium, France, Luxemburg, and the Netherlands, occupied by the German army, the order concerning Reich Credit Institutes of May 3, 1940, as published by the Secretary of the Treasury of the Reich on May 15, 1940, and the order concerning the establishment and the scope of business of Reich Credit Institutes in the occupied territory, as published on May 15, 1940, shall be applicable.

The texts of these orders are as follows:

AN ORDER CONCERNING REICH CREDIT INSTITUTES, OF MAY 3, 1940

SECTION 1. (1) Bills and coins of the Reich Credit Institutes shall be issued for the purpose of purchasing supplies for the German Army and administrative agencies in Denmark, Norway, Belgium, France, Luxemburg, and the Netherlands, and for the purpose of maintaining the circulation of money and economic life in these countries.

[18] *Verordnungsblatt des Militärbefehlshabers in Belgien und Nordfrankreich*, etc., Issue No. 3, June 27, 1940, p. 58.

(2) Issue shall be made through the Central Office of the Reich Credit Institutes. This office shall be located in Berlin.

(3) A Board of Governors shall be formed, with its seat in Berlin. This board shall be composed of the following members: a deputy of the Minister of Finance, a deputy of the Minister of Economy, a deputy of the Supreme Commander of the Armed Forces and one of the Commander in Chief of the Army, as well as members to be appointed by the President of the German Reichsbank, one of whom shall be chairman.

SECTION 2. The Central Office of the Reich Credit Institutes shall be headed by a Directorial Board consisting of at least two persons. This board shall be appointed by the Board of Governors.

Written declarations of the Central Office shall be binding if signed by two members of the Directorial Board. They may be signed by deputies appointed by the Board of Governors.

SECTION 3. The Board of Governors shall at all times be kept informed of the measures taken by the Central Office. The Central Office of the Reich Credit Institutes shall, at the end of every calendar month, submit to the Board of Governors a report concerning the paper and coin money issued by the Reich Credit Institute and the cover on hand for the currency thus issued.

SECTION 4. The Central Office of the Reich Credit Institutes shall extend to the German Reich a loan not exceeding three billion Reichsmarks, for the purpose mentioned in Section 1.

SECTION 5. The bills (paper money) of the Reich Credit Institutes shall be issued in denominations of 50, 20, 5, 2, and 1 Reichsmark as well as 50 pfennigs. The coins of the Reich Credit Institutes shall be issued in amounts of 10 and 5 pfennigs. Before this money is issued, an exact description of it shall be furnished to the public through the Central Office of the Reich Credit Institutes.

SECTION 6. The Central Office shall replace bills worn, soiled or torn in circulation, by new bills.

The Central Office shall give full value for torn bills, provided that the owner produces a part of the bill larger than half the bill, or produces evidence that the remainder of the bill of which he produces half or less, has been destroyed. The Central Office shall decide whether or not the evidence is sufficient. This decision shall not be subject to judicial review.

The calling in and withdrawal of paper money shall take place through the Central Office, which shall make and publish further rules and regulations for this purpose. Bills which are called in shall be invalid after the lapse of a period determined by the Central Office.

The Central Office shall not be obligated to pay the value of bills which are lost or destroyed, or which have become invalid.

SECTION 7. Whoever forges or falsifies bills of the Reich Credit Institutes, with the purpose of using them as genuine bills, shall be sentenced to forced labor or, if there are extenuating circumstances, to imprisonment.

The same penalties shall apply to persons putting into circulation, or aiding in the distribution of, forged or falsified bills. If the accused has accepted the bill without knowing that it was forged or falsified, but has passed it on after he had gained knowledge of this fact, he shall be liable to punishment by imprisonment of not exceeding two years, or by a fine. The attempt to circulate such bills shall likewise be punishable.

In addition to punishment, the forged or falsified bills may be confiscated. If it is impossible to prosecute or sentence the guilty individual, the bill shall be confiscated.

The provisions governing the forging and falsification of paper money shall also apply to the forging and falsifying of coined money.

SECTION 8. The Central Office of the Reich Credit Institutes shall be exempt from taxes and fees of every kind.

SECTION 9. The accounts of the Central Office of the Reich Credit Institutes shall be audited according to rules and regulations to be issued by the Board of Governors.

SECTION 10. The surplus of the Central Office shall, after deduction of the cost of administration, be used for covering losses.

SECTION 11. The Ministers of Finance and of Economics, in agreement with the High Command of the Army, shall make the rules and regulations necessary for implementing and enforcing this order. In so doing they may deviate from the provisions contained in this order.

SECTION 12. This order shall take effect as of the date of publication.

AN ORDER CONCERNING THE ESTABLISHMENT AND SCOPE OF BUSINESS OF THE REICH CREDIT INSTITUTES IN THE OCCUPIED TERRITORY, MAY 15, 1940

(*RGBl.*, 1940, I, p. 743)

By virtue of Section 11 of the Order concerning Reich Credit Institutes of May 3, 1940, the following is ordered in agreement with the High Command of the Armed Forces.

SECTION 1. Reich Credit Institutes may be established in the territories enumerated in Section 1 of the order of May 3, 1940, as published by the Reich Minister of Finance on May 15, 1940 (*RGBl.* I, p. 743).

The Central Office of the Reich Credit Institutes shall appoint the directors and the necessary deputies of the Reich Credit Institutes. It shall determine the location and establishment of the Reich Credit Institutes and shall regulate their business procedure.

SECTION 2. (1) The Reich Credit Institutes shall be represented in court and elsewhere by their directors. Declarations of a directorial board of a Reich Credit Institute shall be binding if made by at least two members of the directorial board or their deputies within the usual scope of business of that Institute.

(2) The names and signatures of the authorized representatives shall be posted in the offices of the Institute.

(3) Notice to be given to the Reich Credit Institutes may be given to any one of the representatives of the Institute.

SECTION 3. (1) The Reich Credit Institutes shall be authorized to regulate money and credit transactions in the territories enumerated in Section 1 [of the Order of May 3, 1940].

(2) They shall be authorized to carry on the following business in accordance with regulations to be issued by the Central Office:

a) Purchase and sell promissory notes and checks bearing the names of usually three, but of not less than two, persons known to be solvent and assuming responsibility for these notes or checks. Notes shall mature not later than six months from the date of purchase.

b) Make loans for interest, usually for a period not exceeding six months, provided that due collateral is furnished.

c) Receive money without interest for purposes of transfer or deposit.

d) Transact any bank business, especially collection of promissory notes and other documents.

e) Accept for safe-deposit articles of value, especially securities.

(3) Business other than the above-mentioned shall only be transacted with the express consent of the Central Office. Acceptance of drafts shall not be permitted.

SECTION 4. (1) The following may be accepted as collateral:

a) A pledge of promissory notes satisfying the requirements of Section 3.
b) A pledge of securities from among those listed by the Central Office of the Reich Credit Institutes.
c) A pledge of goods of every description, not subject to deterioration, if possession of them can be obtained.
d) A pledge of bonds or other instruments of indebtedness, or of property of agencies of public law for loans to be made to such agencies.

(2) The Reich Credit Institutes may demand or admit, in addition to the above, other forms of security, especially guaranty or suretyships.

(3) If goods are pledged to a Reich Credit Institute, actual transfer of goods may be replaced by specially marking them, as, e.g., by posting of signs.

(4) If the pledgor states in writing that the goods pledged are his exclusive property, or that he, as merchant, is authorized by the owner to dispose of them without restriction, the rights of third persons existing in the pledged goods shall be recognized by the Reich Credit Institute only if the said Institute shall have received notice thereof.

SECTION 5. (1) The pledge shall secure capital, interest, and cost. Cost and interest may be deducted from the loan before it is paid out.

(2) If the loan secured by the pledge is not repaid when due, the Reich Credit Institute shall have the right to sell the pledge at a public auction or in the open market or to appropriate it without further notice, warning, or authorization by courts, at the usual exchange or market price or for a price deemed appropriate. The Reich Credit Institute shall have this right also with regard to other creditors or toward the debtor in case of bankruptcy.

The Reich Credit Institute may demand repayment of the loan without pursuing its rights arising from the pledge.

SECTION 6. The Central Office of the Reich Credit Institutes shall fix the rates of interest for the transactions of the Reich Credit Institute.

SECTION 7. The Reich Credit Institute bills in circulation shall be covered:

a) By bills and checks in accordance with Section 3, held by the Reich Credit Institute.
b) By claims from loans made in accordance with Section 3.
c) By German and foreign currency in accordance with regulations of the Board of Governors; by credits in the German Reichsbank and by credit balances in clearing transactions and treasury bonds of the Reich.
d) By the claim from the loan made to the German Reich in accordance with Section 4 of the order concerning Reich Credit Institutes of May 3, 1940, as published by the Reich Minister of Finance, May 15, 1940 (*RGBl.*, I, p. 774).

SECTION 8. This order shall take effect as of May 8, 1940.

Berlin, May 15, 1940.

Count SCHWERIN VON KROSIGK, *Reich Minister of Finance*
WALTHER FUNK, *Reich Minister of Economics*

CHAPTER 2

SECTION 1. Reich Credit Institute bills and coins issued by virtue of the order concerning Reich Credit Institutes as published by the Reich Minister of Finance, of May 15, 1940, are legal tender in the territories mentioned in Chapter 1 of this order.

SECTION 2. Bills of the Reichsbank and of the Rentenbank are not legal in the territories mentioned in Chapter 1 of this order.

CHAPTER 3

This order shall take effect as of the day of occupation.

Headquarters, May 18, 1940.

THE COMMANDER IN CHIEF OF THE ARMY

Order Establishing a Supervisory Board for Banking in Belgium, June 14, 1940 [19]

[EXCERPTS]

By virtue of the authority vested in me by the Führer and Supreme Commander of the Armed Forces, I hereby order as follows:

SECTION 1. For the purpose of supervising banking in Belgium a Supervisory Board with its official seat in Brussels shall be established.

SECTION 2. (1) All enterprises and their branch offices conducting banking or deposit business (accepting and paying of money, purchase and sale or safekeeping and administration of securities on behalf of others) shall be required to register their business through the local commander with the Supervisory Board.

. . . . .

SECTION 3. Banking businesses extending credit as described in Section 2 shall be subject to supervision by the Supervisory Board. They shall be required to comply with orders issued by the board.

SECTION 4. The board shall have especially the right:

a) To inspect the books and papers of the banking businesses subject to its supervision; to examine the assets on hand in the form of cash, securities, bills of exchange, etc., to require information on all business matters, and to make important business transactions subject to the approval of the board.

b) To inspect or require the production of balance sheets and underlying data.

c) To forbid all or some business transactions, especially the transfer of assets, payments of obligations, and the sending out of business letters or circulars.

d) To order the deposit or transfer of assets of the banking business under supervision.

e) To revoke the powers of legal representatives of the banking business under supervision and to transfer such powers to others.

SECTION 5. Legal transactions which have been declared subject to the approval of the Supervisory Board in accordance with Section 4*a* shall be void unless such approval has first been obtained.

[19] *Verordnungsblatt des Militärbefehlshabers in Belgien und Nordfrankreich*, etc., Issue No. 2, June 17, 1940, p. 47.

SECTION 6. The costs of the Supervisory Board shall be borne by the banking businesses supervised.

SECTION 7. Rules and regulations necessary for the enforcement and implementation of this order shall be issued by the Military Governor for Belgium.

. . . . .

SECTION 9. This order shall take effect as of the date of publication.

Headquarters, June 14, 1940.

VON BRAUCHITSCH
Supreme Commander of the Army

Order Establishing a Bank of Issue in Brussels, June 27, 1940 [20]

[EXCERPTS]

By virtue of the authority vested in me by the Supreme Commander of the Army, I order the following:

I. ORGANIZATION

SECTION 1. In order to maintain financial and credit business, the Bank of Issue in Brussels shall be established.

The bank shall be a corporation established under Belgian law and shall have its seat in Brussels.

The capital shall consist of 150 million Belgian francs, divided into fifteen thousand shares of ten thousand francs each.

Twenty per cent of the face amount of these shares shall be paid in cash.

The bank shall be authorized to establish branch offices.

The by-laws of the bank are subject to the approval of the Commissioner of the National Bank of Belgium.

SECTION 2. The bank shall be directed and managed by a president and two deputies. These shall be elected by a general meeting of the shareholders.

If required, additional deputies may be appointed for office in the same manner. The election, the contracts of service, and the salaries shall be subject to the approval of the Military Commander in Belgium and Northern France. If the Military Commander twice refuses to approve persons thus elected, he may appoint such persons as he deems fit. The approval may be revoked at any time.

A person who has been appointed may be discharged at any time.

SECTION 3. The Commissioner of the National Bank of Belgium shall at all times be kept informed on all measures taken by the Bank of Issue. He may require information on all transactions of the bank.

[20] *Verordnungsblatt des Militärbefehlshabers in Belgien und Nordfrankreich*, etc., 1940, p. 89.

At the end of each calendar month a statement on the bank notes issued, and the available cover, shall be submitted to the Commissioner.

All important measures, especially the extension of credits and the fixing of the rate of interest for bank transactions, shall be subject to the approval of the Commissioner. The Commissioner may issue any rules concerning the conduct of business by the bank. Neither the bank nor its officers shall be subject to Royal Order No. 185, of July 9, 1935, concerning the Supervision of Banks.

SECTION 4. The administrative board shall consist of the president, his deputy, and twenty members elected at a general meeting of the shareholders. The Military Commander of Belgium and of Northern France must approve the election, the contracts of employment, and the salaries of these members. If the Military Commander twice refuses to approve the persons elected, he may appoint such persons as he may deem fit. The confirmation may be revoked at any time. An officer who has been elected may be discharged at any time.

At the end of each financial year the president shall submit an annual report to the administrative board, and this board shall confirm the report.

SECTION 5. The branches of the bank shall be managed by a director and the necessary number of deputies in accordance with regulations issued by the president. The directors and the deputies shall be chosen by the president with the consent of the Commissioner of the National Bank of Belgium.

. . . . .

II. OPERATIONS OF THE BANK

SECTION 8. The bank shall be authorized to engage in the following operations:

Purchase and sell securities issued by the treasury of the state, and by provinces, communities, and monopolies of the state, provided that the securities fall due within a year of the date of purchase.

Discount bills and checks, provided they are signed or endorsed as a rule by three, but by at least two guarantors known to be solvent, and provided the bills shall mature within six months from the date of discount; and grant credits at interest against suitable securities, usually for not longer than six months.

Accept non-interest-bearing deposits and carry current accounts; from employees of the bank interest-bearing deposits may also be accepted.

Transact all kinds of banking operations, and, particularly, collect notes and other documents.

Accept articles of value for safekeeping and administration, particularly securities.

Enter into transactions involving foreign exchange, and issue and honor letters of credit.

SECTION 9. Transactions other than those named above may only be entered into with the express consent of the Commissioner. Acceptance of drafts is not permitted.

III. Issue of Notes and Cover

Section 10. The bank shall be authorized to issue notes in Belgian currency. The notes of the bank shall constitute the sole and unrestricted legal tender in the occupied Belgian territory.

Section 11. The following shall be permitted as cover for the notes issued by the bank and for the balances kept by it:

1. Claims arising from discount and credit business in accordance with Section 8, paragraphs 1–3.
2. Claims on the National Bank of Belgium as well as coins in circulation for the account of the treasury of the Belgian State.
3. Foreign exchange, especially German currency, including notes of credit of the Reich Credit Institute as well as credits with the German Reichsbank, German Clearing Institute, and German Credit Institutes.

Brussels, June 27, 1940.

The Military Commander for Belgium and Northern France

Order concerning the Calling in and Retirement of Coins Issued by the Reich Credit Institutes, April 28, 1941[21]

By virtue of special authority vested in me by the Supreme Commander of the Army, I hereby order as follows for Belgium and Northern France:

Section 1. Coins of ten and five Reichspfennigs issued by the Reich Credit Institutes shall cease to be legal tender after April 30, 1941.

Section 2. The Central Office shall be authorized to issue rules and regulations concerning the calling in and withdrawal of the coins issued by the Reich Credit Institutes.

Section 3. (1) The coins of the Reich Credit Institutes called for retirement shall be invalid after the time fixed by the Central Office of the Reich Credit Institutes for their retirement.

(2) The Central Office shall not be required to make compensation for coins of the Reich Credit Institutes thus invalidated.

The Military Commander in Belgium and Northern France

[21] *Verordnungsblatt des Militärbefehlshabers in Belgien und Nordfrankreich*, etc., Issue No 41, April 29, 1941, p. 583.

Proclamation concerning the Establishment of a Clearing System for Payments to be made by Residents of Belgium and Denmark, January 21, 1942 [22]

I. The monetary exchange between Belgium and Denmark shall be resumed, to a limited extent, by the establishment of a clearing system. This clearing system shall operate through the German Clearing Institute in Berlin. Its agents shall be, in Belgium, the Bank of Issue in Brussels, and in Denmark, the National Bank in Copenhagen.

II. The following payments due from Danish debtors to Belgian creditors and from Belgian debtors to Danish creditors shall be subject to clearing regardless of the time when such claims arose:

First, payments arising from the importation of goods from Denmark into Belgium and from Belgium into Denmark.

Second, payments for all incidental costs of Belgian-Danish imports and exports.

Third, payments for patent fees, licenses, and similar fees for the grant of incorporeal rights.

Fourth, in special cases of hardship, payments for support, pensions, legacies, etc.

Fifth, payments in all other instances, in addition to those enumerated in numbers 1–4, provided that the Clearing Office in Brussels so agrees.

III. Belgian debtors who, in accordance with the provisions of this clearing arrangement, are required to make payments to residents of Denmark shall pay, through the offices of the Bank of Issue in Brussels, the amounts due into "Special Account I" of the Denmark National Bank with the German Clearing Institute in Berlin. The German Clearing Institute shall transmit to the Denmark National Bank the amounts credited in accordance with the German-Belgian clearing arrangement. The Denmark National Bank shall then make payment to the Danish creditors.

IV. Danish debtors who, in accordance with the provisions of this clearing arrangement, are required to make payments to residents of Belgium shall pay, through the offices of the Denmark National Bank, the amounts due into the "Reichsmark Account" of the Bank of Issue in Brussels with the German Clearing Institute in Berlin. The German Clearing Institute shall transmit to the Bank of Issue in Brussels the amounts credited in accordance with the German-Danish clearing arrangement. The Bank of Issue in Brussels shall then make payment to the Belgian creditors.

V. The calculation of the exchange of Danish crowns, belga, and other currencies into Reichsmarks shall take place at the official Berlin average rate of exchange of the day preceding the day of payment. The Bank of Issue in Brussels shall be authorized to establish special rates of exchange for the exchange calculation of claims arising before December 21, 1940.

[22] *Verordnungsblatt des Militärbefehlshabers in Belgien und Nordfrankreich*, etc., Issue No. 31, January 29, 1941.

VI. Payments made in pursuance of this arrangement shall not be subject to foreign exchange licenses. However, payments or the acceptance of such payments arising out of the imports and exports of goods and made through the Bank of Issue in Brussels shall not be lawful unless a copy of the invoice bearing a license of the Clearing Office at Brussels, 11 rue du Gentilhomme, shall first have been submitted. For payments and acceptances of payment not connected with imports or exports of goods, a license of the Clearing Office shall be required whenever the amount shall exceed the sum of one thousand Belgian francs.

On behalf of the Military Governor in Belgium and Northern France:

THE CHIEF OF THE MILITARY ADMINISTRATION

5. REPARATIONS

Order concerning the Restitution of the Rights of Persons Persecuted in Belgium because of their Collaboration with the German Army of Occupation during the War 1914–1918, September 6, 1940 [23]

Wrong demands restitution. In the war of 1914–1918, inhabitants of this country tried to adopt a loyal attitude toward the German Army of Occupation and to obey its rules. For this they were persecuted by the state and certain sections of the population. They suffered penalties of death, hard labor, and imprisonment. They were deprived of public rights, suffered from robbery, arson, expropriation, withdrawal of sustenance, and bodily as well as mental torment. This took place despite the fact that the regulations of the German Army of Occupation complied with the valid international law of that time, and were therefore lawful. At that time, as today, these regulations had to be enforced just as did the Belgian laws. And so the persecuted people were acting in a way that was by no means unlawful.

The honor of Germany demands reparation for the violated regulations.

By virtue of the authority vested in me by the Supreme Commander of the Army, I issue the following orders for Belgium:

ARTICLE I. Any damage or injury to honor, liberty, person, life, goods, money, or other property of those who have been unlawfully persecuted shall be made good.

ARTICLE II. A board under the presidency of Dr. A. Borms, as an independent governmental institution, shall carry out these reparations. The members of this board shall serve without pay.

[23] *Verordnungsblatt des Militärbefehlshabers in Belgien und Nordfrankreich*, etc., 1940, Issue No. 14, p. 203.

ARTICLE III. Rules and regulations for the enforcement of this ordinance will be made by a special order.

THE MILITARY COMMANDER IN BELGIUM AND NORTHERN FRANCE

Order concerning the Enforcement of the Reparations Order, September 6, 1940 [24]

For the purpose of enforcing the Reparations Order of September 6, 1940 (*Verordnungsblatt des Militärbefehlshabers*, 14th Issue, No. 1), I hereby order as follows:

SECTION 1.—*Scope of Reparations*

(1) Measures for the restoration of all honor rights shall be taken in accordance with the gravity of the individual case. Especially, any persecuted person who has lost his position may regain the right of using his previous title or the designation of his former rank or honorary title.

No person has the right to demand reinstatement in his former position. But every persecuted person may be recommended for a similar position, according to his qualifications.

(2) Whoever suffered innocently the loss of freedom, or physical or other torment, may receive special indemnity in addition to other indemnities. The amount need not be measured by the amount necessary for sustenance or economic readjustment.

(3) Economic and financial damages shall be compensated as equity demands, with due regard to the present economic situation of the persecuted person.

Included in the list of compensable damages are: damages caused by robbery, arson, and open or veiled expropriation as well as sequestration of goods of political exiles or fugitives.

(4) Fines, cost of proceedings, seized goods, and like payments rendered by the persecuted person to the state, to the community, or to officials elsewhere, may be restored.

(5) The testate or intestate heirs may obtain the rights of the deceased.

(6) Claims and damages established in accordance with this ordinance can not be assigned, nor are they subject to execution by creditors.

SECTION 2.—*Procedure*

(7) The board designated in Article 2 of the Reparations Order shall consist of a president and one member chosen by the president and one member

[24] *Verordnungsblatt des Militärbefehlshabers in Belgien und Nordfrankreich*, etc., September 10, 1940, No. 14.

as a representative of the Belgian State. The members of the board and their alternates shall be chosen with the consent of the military commander.

The military commander may delegate a representative to the sessions of the board.

The board shall determine its procedure and its personnel as well as the positions of this personnel; its members shall receive compensation for expenditures in accordance with the rules applicable to officials.

The board may hear witnesses and experts and take other evidence in accordance with the rules of criminal procedure. The officials of the state, the communities and public corporations shall assist upon request. In case of delay the board itself shall make the necessary investigations at the expense of the official whose help was requested, reserving the right to hold liable the person responsible for the delay.

(8) The Secretary of Justice shall deliver a list of the persons concerned, and the files of the cases, to the board. Those persecuted may themselves report to the board up to December 31, 1941. The board shall proceed on the basis of the list of the claims or on its own knowledge.

The board shall decide according to law and equity in regard to the situation of the persons involved. It shall transmit its decisions to the officials concerned either for immediate execution, or as a suggestion if the case arises under subsection 2 of Section 1. The decisions shall be final and shall not be subject to judicial review.

(9) The cost of the reparations as well as the expenses of the board shall be borne by the Belgian State. The Belgian Secretary of the Treasury shall hold the amounts currently required at the disposal of the board.

(10) The work of the board shall begin on September 15, 1940.

THE MILITARY COMMANDER IN BELGIUM AND NORTHERN FRANCE

CZECHOSLOVAKIA

I. SUDETENLAND

An Act concerning the Administration of the Reich District Sudetenland, April 14, 1939 [1]

[EXCERPTS]

The Reich Government has passed the following act, which is hereby published.

SECTION 1. The Reich District (*Reichsgau*) Sudetenland shall constitute a unit of the Reich administration and an autonomous public corporation.

SECTION 2. (1) The Reich District shall be headed by the Reich Governor (*Reichsstatthalter*); his official residence shall be in Reichenberg.

(2) [The Reich Governor may request information from all public agencies within the district and issue instructions in accordance with law and orders of the supreme authorities of the Reich. Such instructions may be cancelled by the supreme authorities of the Reich.] [2]

(3) The authority conferred on the Reich Governor may not be delegated by him to other officials.

SECTION 3. (1) The Reich Governor shall be the head of the administration for the Reich District and as such shall be subject to the supervision of the Reich Minister of the Interior. He shall be subject to the instructions of the several Reich ministers for the respective branches of the administration.

(2) The agencies of the special administrative services of the Reich within the Reich District, with the exception of the agencies for the administration of justice, the railways, and the postal services which have their official residence in the Reich District, shall form part of the office of the Reich Governor. The Reich Governor shall head these administrative agencies and shall be represented in them by the chiefs of the several bureaus.

. . . . .

SECTION 4. (1) The Reich Governor may promulgate law by means of orders with the consent of the Reich ministers concerned and the Reich Minister of the Interior, provided that such orders do not violate the basic law of the land.

(2) Otherwise, the authority of the Reich Governor as established in the Act concerning the Reich Governors (*Reichsstatthaltergesetz*) of January 30, 1935 (*RGBl.* I, p. 65), shall remain in full force and effect.

SECTION 5. (1) The Reich Governor shall direct the autonomous administration of the Reich District under the supervision of the Reich Minister of the Interior.

[1] *Reichsgesetzblatt*, 1939, I, p. 780. [2] Summary by the translator.

(2) As an autonomous public corporation the Reich District will have administrative duties to fulfill under its own responsibility.

(3) The Reich District may regulate its own affairs by special statutes.

(4) For the purposes of autonomous administration, a district counsellor shall assist the Reich Governor in an advisory capacity.

SECTION 6. The Reich Governor shall be represented in the sphere of the Reich administration by a general deputy with the official designation of Government President (*Regierungspräsident*), who shall be a Reich official; and in the sphere of autonomous administration of the Reich District, by a general deputy with the official designation of Chief of the District (*Gauhauptmann*), who shall be an official of the district as an autonomous public corporation.

SECTION 7. The governmental presidents (*Regierungspräsidenten*) in Aussig, Eger, and Troppau shall be subject to the orders of the Reich Governor.

. . . . .

SECTION 14. The Reich Minister of the Interior shall promulgate rules and regulations necessary for the enforcement and implementation of this act.

SECTION 15. This act shall take effect as of May 1, 1939.

Berchtesgaden, April 14, 1939.

ADOLF HITLER, *Führer and Reich Chancellor;* FRICK, *Reich Minister of the Interior;* R. HESS, *Representative of the Führer;* GÖRING, *General Field Marshal, Premier of Prussia, Commissioner for the Four-Year Plan;* Count SCHWERIN VON KROSIGK, *Reich Minister of Finance;* LAMMERS, *Reich Minister and Chief of the Reich Chancellery.*

II. PROTECTORATE OF BOHEMIA AND MORAVIA

1. ADMINISTRATION

Decree of the Führer and Reich Chancellor concerning the Protectorate of Bohemia and Moravia, March 16, 1939 [3]

The Bohemian-Moravian countries belonged for a millennium to the living space of the German people. Violence and want of judgment have torn them arbitrarily from their old, historic environment and finally created, through their inclusion in the artificial structure of Czechoslovakia, a center of continuous unrest. Year after year the danger increased that out of this area—as once before in the past—would arise a new, stupendous menace to European peace. For the Czechoslovak State and its rulers had not succeeded in organizing in a reasonable manner the coexistence of the national

[3] *Reichsgesetzblatt*, 1939, I, No. 47, p. 485.

groups arbitrarily comprised within it, and thus they failed to awaken and to preserve the interest of all concerned in the maintenance of the state common to them. Thereby this state has demonstrated its inherent inability to exist and therefore now has fallen into actual dissolution.

The German Reich cannot tolerate everlasting disturbances in these areas, areas so decisively essential not only to its own peace and security but also to the general welfare and the general peace. Sooner or later the German Reich would have had to suffer the most serious consequences because it is the power which is most vitally interested and concerned by history as well as by geographical position. It is therefore only an act of compliance with the law of self-preservation if the German Reich is resolved to take decisive action for the reestablishment of the foundations of a Central European Order based on reason and to resort to measures impelled by this aim. For the millennial historic past of the German Reich has proven that it alone is chosen by virtue of its greatness and the qualities of the German people to solve this problem.

Imbued with the earnest desire to serve the true interests of the nations settled in this living space, to safeguard the national life of the German and Czech nations, to promote peace and the social welfare of all, I therefore order, in the name of the German Reich, the following as foundations on which the inhabitants of these areas can live side by side in the future:

ARTICLE 1. (1) The territories of the erstwhile Czechoslovak Republic, occupied by the German Armies in March, 1939, are hereby incorporated into the territory of the Greater German Reich and are placed under its protection as the "Protectorate of Bohemia and Moravia."

(2) In so far as the defense of the Reich requires it, the Führer and Reich Chancellor may issue, for specified areas of these territories, orders at variance with these articles.

ARTICLE 2. (1) The residents of the Protectorate of German origin are hereby declared to be German nationals and German citizens, in accordance with the provisions of the Reich Nationality Code (*Reichsbürgergesetz*) of September 15, 1935 (*RGBl.*, I, p. 1146). Therefore, the provisions for the protection of German blood and German honor shall apply to them. They shall be subject to the jurisdiction of German courts.

(2) The other residents of Bohemia and Moravia are hereby declared to be citizens of the Protectorate of Bohemia and Moravia.

ARTICLE 3. (1) The Protectorate of Bohemia and Moravia is declared to be autonomous and shall govern itself.

(2) It shall exercise the sovereign rights to which it is entitled within the framework of the Protectorate in conformity with the political, military, and economic interests of the Reich.

(3) The Protectorate shall exercise these sovereign rights through its own political agencies, authorities, and officials.

ARTICLE 4. The head of the autonomous administration of the Protectorate of Bohemia and Moravia shall be entitled to the protection and the full honors of the head of a sovereign government. The head of the Protectorate must enjoy, in the exercise of his high office, the confidence of the Führer and Reich Chancellor.

ARTICLE 5. (1) The Führer and Reich Chancellor will appoint as a guardian of the interests of the Reich a "Reich Protector of Bohemia and Moravia." His official residence shall be in Prague.

(2) It shall be the duty of the Reich Protector, as representative of the Führer and Reich Chancellor and as the agent of the Government of the Reich, to assure compliance with the political instructions issued by the Führer and Reich Chancellor.

(3) The members of the government of the Protectorate shall hold office subject to confirmation by the Reich Protector. A confirmation made may be later revoked.

(4) The Reich Protector may demand information concerning all acts of the government of the Protectorate and may offer his counsel to the government. He may protest against measures which may be harmful to the Reich, and, in cases of emergency, may take all steps necessary to the common welfare.

(5) The publication of statutes, orders, and other general rules and regulations, and the enforcement of administrative measures and execution of judicial decisions which have become final, shall be suspended upon notice of protest given by the Reich Protector.

ARTICLE 6. (1) The foreign affairs of the Protectorate, especially the protection of its citizens abroad, shall be entrusted to the Reich. The Reich shall take charge of the foreign affairs in such manner as shall conform with the common interest of both countries.

(2) The Protectorate shall have a representative with the Government of the Reich officially designated as Minister.

ARTICLE 7. (1) The Reich shall extend military protection to the Protectorate.

(2) For the purpose of extending such protection the Reich shall maintain garrisons and military establishments in the Protectorate.

(3) The Protectorate may establish its own units for the maintenance of home security and protection. The Government of the Reich shall determine the form of organization, the number of the forces, and the armament to be employed.

ARTICLE 8. The Reich shall directly supervise all traffic, posts, and telegraphs.

ARTICLE 9. The Protectorate shall form part of the German customs area and shall be subject to its customs authority.

ARTICLE 10. (1) In addition to the Reichsmark the Krone shall constitute legal tender until further notice.

(2) The rate of exchange for the two currencies shall be determined by the Government of the Reich.

ARTICLE 11. (1) The Reich may issue orders having the force of statutes for the Protectorate, in so far as required by the common welfare of both of them.

(2) In so far as there is a common need, the Reich may take over branches of the administrative services and may establish the necessary Reich agencies in their stead.

(3) The Government of the Reich may take all measures necessary for the maintenance of security and order.

ARTICLE 12. The laws and statutes presently in effect in Bohemia and Moravia shall remain in effect unless incompatible with the purposes of protection by the German Reich.

ARTICLE 13. The Reich Minister of the Interior shall, in agreement with the Reich ministers concerned, issue all rules and regulations, general and administrative, required for the enforcement and implementation of this decree.

Prague, March 16, 1939.

ADOLF HITLER, *Führer and Reich Chancellor*
FRICK, *Reich Minister of the Interior*
VON RIBBENTROP, *Reich Minister of Foreign Affairs*
DR. LAMMERS, *Reich Minister and Chief of the Reich Chancellery*

Order concerning the Rate of Exchange in the Protectorate of Bohemia and Moravia, March 21, 1939 [4]

By virtue of subsection 2 of Article 10 of the decree of the Führer and Reich Chancellor for the Protectorate of Bohemia and Moravia of March 16, 1939 (*RGBl.* I, p. 485), it is hereby decreed:

SECTION 1. The rate of exchange of the Reichsmark and Krone is hereby established as follows: 1 Krone equals 10 Reichspfennigs.

SECTION 2. The Reich Minister of Economic Affairs and the Reich Minister of Finance shall, in mutual agreement, issue rules and regulations for the implementation and enforcement of this order.

SECTION 3. This order shall take effect as of March 22, 1939.

Berlin, March 21, 1939.

GÖRING, *Commissioner of the Four-Year Plan*
WALTHER FUNK, *Reich Minister for Economic Affairs*
FRICK, *Reich Minister of the Interior*
Count SCHWERIN VON KROSIGK, *Reich Minister of Finance*

[4] *Reichsgesetzblatt*, 1939, I, No. 53, p. 555.

An Act concerning the Representation in the Reichstag of Greater Germany of German Nationals Resident in the Protectorate of Bohemia and Moravia, April 13, 1939 [5]

In order to afford to the German nationals resident in the Protectorate of Bohemia and Moravia a representation in the German Reichstag the Government of the Reich has passed the following act which is hereby published:

SECTION 1. The Reichstag of Greater Germany, elected on April 10 and December 4, 1938, is hereby increased by as many members as the number 60,000 is contained in the total number of German nationals resident on March 16, 1939, in the Protectorate of Bohemia and Moravia who are over twenty years of age.

SECTION 2. The members joining the Reichstag of Greater Germany in conformity with Section 1 shall be designated by the Führer and Reich Chancellor from among the German nationals resident in these territories who are over twenty-five years of age.

Berchtesgaden, April 13, 1939.

ADOLF HITLER, *Führer and Reich Chancellor*
FRICK, *Reich Minister of the Interior*

Order concerning the Acquisition of German Citizenship by Former Czechoslovak Citizens of German Origin, April 20, 1939 [6]

[EXCERPTS]

By virtue of the decree of the Führer and Reich Chancellor concerning the Protectorate of Bohemia and Moravia of March 16, 1939 (*RGBl.* I, p. 485), and of the act concerning the reunion of the Sudeten German territories with the Reich of November 21, 1938 (*RGBl.* I, p. 1641), the following is hereby ordered:

SECTION 1. The former Czechoslovak citizens of German origin who were entered in the birth records of a community within the former Czechoslovak countries of Bohemia and Moravia-Silesia on October 10, 1938, shall acquire, as of March 16, 1939, German citizenship unless they have acquired it previously as of October 10, 1938, by virtue of Section 1 of the German-Czechoslovak Nationality and Option Agreement of November 20, 1938 (*RGBl.* II, p. 895).

SECTION 2. German nationals who have their residence in the Protectorate of Bohemia and Moravia, shall also enjoy the rights of nationals of the Protectorate of Bohemia and Moravia.

. . . . .

Berlin, April 20, 1939.

FRICK
Reich Minister of the Interior

[5] *Reichsgesetzblatt*, 1939, I, No. 72, p. 762.

[6] *Ibid.*, No. 77, p. 815.

Decree of the Führer concerning the Administration in the Protectorate of Bohemia and Moravia, May 7, 1942 [7]

The coordination of all forces because of the war has made it necessary to introduce further simplifications in the administration of Bohemia and Moravia. In implementation of my order concerning the Protectorate of Bohemia and Moravia of March 16, 1939 (*RGBl.* I, p. 485), I have empowered the Reich Protector, in consultation with the Reich Minister of the Interior, to undertake measures within the limits of the above-mentioned decree, in order to make possible the adaptation of the administration of Bohemia and Moravia to any situation which may arise, and in order to issue the regulations necessary for this purpose.

Headquarters of the Führer, May 7, 1942.

THE FÜHRER

Dr. LAMMERS, *Reich Minister and Chief of the Reich Chancellery*

2. LAW AND COURTS

Order concerning the Exercise of Criminal Jurisdiction in the Protectorate of Bohemia and Moravia, April 14, 1939 [8]

[EXCERPTS]

By virtue of the decree of the Führer and Reich Chancellor concerning the Protectorate of Bohemia and Moravia, of March 16, 1939 (*RGBl.* I, p. 485), the following is hereby ordered:

SECTION 1. (1) German nationals in the Protectorate of Bohemia and Moravia shall be subject to:

1. The Criminal Code of the German Reich.
2. [Enumeration of statutes supplementing that code.]

SECTION 2. German authorities entrusted with the administration of justice in the Protectorate shall be subject to:

1. The Code of Criminal Procedure of the German Reich.
2. [Enumeration of statutes supplementing that code.]

. . . . .

SECTION 4. Fines collected through sentences passed by the German Courts in the Protectorate shall be paid into the German Treasury. . . .

. . . . .

SECTION 14. (1) Crimes committed by persons other than German nationals shall be tried by the courts of the Protectorate in conformity with the criminal law of the Protectorate. The procedure applicable in

[7] *Reichsgesetzblatt*, 1942, I, No. 54, p. 329.

[8] *Ibid.*, 1939, I, No. 71, p. 754.

these cases shall also be in conformity with that law, subject to such modifications as are contained in Sections 15 to 18 inclusive.

(2) In criminal proceedings before the courts of the Protectorate the provisions of the Code of Criminal Procedure of May 23, 1873 (*Oesterreichisches Reichsgesetzblatt*, No. 119), concerning the right of the person injured to join the proceedings as party plaintiff and to file a public complaint and proceed to trial in lieu of the public prosecutor shall not be applicable where the person injured is a German national.

SECTION 15. (1) Persons other than German nationals shall be subject to the following German criminal statutes:

a) Criminal Code for the German Reich:
Sections 80 to 93 *a* (Treason).
Section 94 (Attacks against the Führer and Reich Chancellor).
Sections 102 to 104 (Hostile acts against friendly nations).
Section 110 (Incitement to disobedience of laws).
Section 112 (Incitement of soldiers to insubordination).
Sections 134 *a*, 135 *b* (Libel of the Reich and the Party).
Section 135 (Disrespect for National Emblems).
Section 141 (Inducement to desertion).
Section 141 *a* (Recruiting for service with foreign armies).
Section 143 *a* (Damage to weapons).
Section 239 *a* (Kidnaping).
Sections 353 *b* and 353 *c* (betrayal of secrets) in so far as important public interests of the Reich have been jeopardized.

b) . . . .

c) Sections 49 *a* and 139 of the Reich Criminal Code (preparation of a crime, failure to report a planned crime) with regard to the crimes enumerated above.

(2) German criminal law shall also apply if the crime is directed against the German armed forces, or against a person holding a German office or an office of the N.S.D.A.P. (National Socialist Party of Germany), a member of the armed forces or their auxiliaries, or members of the S.A., the S.S., the N.S.K.K. (National Socialist Driver Corps), the N.S.F.K. (National Socialist Women Corps), who are present in the Protectorate on official business or by order of the Reich, provided that the crime was committed for political motives or because of official activities of the person or persons attacked.

(3) In so far as, according to the preceding subsections, German criminal law applies, the general principles of German criminal law shall likewise apply.

. . . .

SECTION 19. (1) If a German Court finds that a court of the Protectorate has jurisdiction, it shall declare itself to be without jurisdiction; or if a court of the Protectorate finds that a German Court has jurisdiction, it shall make a like declaration. There can be no appeal from such decisions.

(2) On demand of the German prosecuting attorney, the offices of the prosecuting attorneys and the courts of the Protectorate shall be required to transfer proceedings pending before them if, according to the opinion of the German prosecuting attorney, the German Court has jurisdiction. If the court or agency concerned in the Protectorate is of the opinion that the German Courts have no jurisdiction, it may request a decision by the prosecuting attorney attached to the German Circuit Court of Appeals (*Oberlandesgericht*).

SECTION 20. If the Reich Protector files protest against a final judgment of a court of the Protectorate (in accordance with subsection 5 of Article 5 of the decree of the Führer and Reich Chancellor concerning the Protectorate of Bohemia and Moravia of March 16, 1939, *RGBl.* I, p. 485), the German prosecuting attorney may file an indictment before a German Court. If the German Court passes a judgment and such judgment becomes final, the decision of the court of the Protectorate shall be voided. The Reich Protector shall determine further details.

. . . . . .

Berlin, April 14, 1939.

DR. GÜRTNER, *Reich Minister of Justice*
PFUNDTNER, *Acting Reich Minister of the Interior*

Order concerning the Exercise of Jurisdiction in Civil Proceedings in the Protectorate of Bohemia and Moravia, April 14, 1939 [9]

[EXCERPTS]

By virtue of the decree of the Führer and Reich Chancellor concerning the Protectorate of Bohemia and Moravia, of March 16, 1939 (*RGBl.* I, p. 485), it is hereby decreed:

SECTION 1. The jurisdiction of German Courts in civil matters in the Protectorate of Bohemia and Moravia shall extend:

1. To civil cases and controversies, exclusive of the execution of judgments, if one of the parties to the proceedings is a German national; to proceedings involving the status of the parties also, if none of the parties is a citizen of the Protectorate.
2. To proceedings for the enforcement of judgments, bankruptcy, and composition proceedings if the judgment debtor, or the debtor in bankruptcy, or the debtor applying for a composition, is a German national; if the proceedings against several debtors are inseparable, then the German Courts shall have jurisdiction where one of the judgment debtors or other debtors is a German national.

[9] *Reichsgesetzblatt*, 1939, I, No. 71, p. 759.

3. To court proceedings of non-litigious character provided that according to German law the citizenship of the person involved determines the law applicable and that this person is not a citizen of the Protectorate.

. . . . .

SECTION 4. The jurisdiction of, and the proceedings before, the German Courts in the Protectorate of Bohemia and Moravia in civil matters shall be determined, in so far as it is not provided otherwise and until further notice, by the law heretofore in force in the Protectorate; the provisions of the order concerning the further transfer of judicial administration in Austria and the Sudeten German Territories of February 28, 1939 (*RGBl.* I, p. 358), in so far as they apply to the procedure in civil matters originating in Austria, shall be applicable in the Protectorate of Bohemia and Moravia by way of analogy; instead of the reference to the Circuit Court of Appeals in Vienna the provisions shall be read to refer to the Circuit Court of Appeals in Prague.

SECTION 5. For the procedure to be observed by German notaries and prothonotaries in the Protectorate of Bohemia and Moravia in their official acts, the statutes and general instructions heretofore in force in the Protectorate of Bohemia and Moravia shall continue in effect unless otherwise provided.

. . . . .

Berlin, April 14, 1939.

DR. GÜRTNER, *Reich Minister of Justice*
PFUNDTNER, *Acting Reich Minister of the Interior*

Order concerning the Exercise of Military Jurisdiction in the Protectorate of Bohemia and Moravia, May 8, 1939[10]

[EXCERPTS]

By virtue of the decree of the Führer and Reich Chancellor concerning the Protectorate of Bohemia and Moravia, of March 16, 1939 (*RGBl.* I, p. 485) the following is decreed until further notice:

SECTION 1. (1) Crimes of persons who are not German nationals shall be tried by courts of the German armed forces if they constitute:

1. Military treason, that is,
   a) crimes in violation of Sections 88 to 90 *e* of the German Criminal Code in so far as these sections refer to state secrets of a military character.
   b) crimes in violation of Sections 91 *a*, 91 *b*, 92 *a* to 92 *c*, 92 *e*, and 92 *f* of the German Criminal Code.

[10] *Reichsgesetzblatt*, 1939, I, No. 89, p. 903.

c) crimes in violation of Section 92 of the German Criminal Code, in so far as the crime referred to in the conspiracy, incitement, or offer, would be, according to subsection 1 (a) or (b), under the jurisdiction of the courts of the German armed forces.
2. Incitement of soldiers to insubordination (Section 112 of the German Criminal Code).
3. Inducement to desertion (Section 141 of the German Criminal Code).
4. Recruiting for military service in a foreign country (Section 141 *a* of the German Criminal Code).
5. Damage to property of the Army which is used for combat (Section 143 *a* of the German Criminal Code).
6. Crimes which are
   a) directed against the German armed forces, their members or auxiliary forces, or
   b) committed in a building, a room or installation which is used by or for purposes of the German armed forces.
7. Incitement or offer (Section 49 *a* of the German Criminal Code) to commit a crime or the failure to report (Section 139 of the German Criminal Code) crimes which would be under the military jurisdiction according to Nos. 1, 5, and 6.

. . . . .

SECTION 4. If a court of the German armed forces sentences a defendant, who is not a German national, in accordance with Section 1, to a prison term or imposes upon him a punitive measure combined with deprivation of liberty for purposes of correction or segregation, the execution of the sentence is to be assigned to the German prosecuting attorney.

. . . . .

KEITEL, *Chief of the Supreme Command of the Armed Forces*
Dr. GÜRTNER, *Reich Minister of Justice*
Dr. STUCKART, *Acting Reich Minister of the Interior*

Order concerning the Authority to Promulgate Laws in the Protectorate of Bohemia and Moravia, June 7, 1939 [11]

[EXCERPTS]

By virtue of Article 13 of the decree of the Führer and Reich Chancellor concerning the Protectorate of Bohemia and Moravia, of March 16, 1939 (*RGBl.* I, p. 485), for the implementation and enforcement of subsection 4, Article 5, subsection 1, Article 11, and Article 12 of that decree, the following is hereby ordered:

SECTION 1. (1) The Reich Protector may by order change the local law in so far as required by the common interest of the Reich and the Protectorate.

[11] *Reichsgesetzblatt,* 1939, I, No. 110.

(2) In an emergency the Reich Protector may issue general orders of every kind having the force of laws.

. . .

SECTION 3. The Reich Protector shall decide which law [according to Article 12 of the decree of the Führer and Reich Chancellor concerning the Protectorate of Bohemia and Moravia] is incompatible with the purposes of protection by the German Reich.

. . . . .

Berlin, June 7, 1939.

ADOLF HITLER, *Führer and Reich Chancellor*
FRICK, *Reich Minister of the Interior*
Dr. LAMMERS, *Reich Minister and Chief of the Reich Chancellery*

III. SLOVAKIA

1. ESTABLISHMENT OF THE STATE

Law concerning the Sovereign State of Slovakia, March 14, 1939 [12]

The Slovak Diet has adopted the following law:

SECTION 1. The Slovak country votes for a sovereign and independent State of Slovakia. The Slovak Diet is transformed into the legislative Diet of the State of Slovakia.

SECTION 2. Until the issue of the Constitution of the State of Slovakia the entire governmental and executive power shall be in the hands of the government which shall be appointed by the presiding body of the Diet.

SECTION 3. All laws, decrees, and regulations hitherto in force shall remain in effect, with modifications which follow from the spirit of sovereignty of the State of Slovakia.

SECTION 4. The government shall be authorized to take, through legislative action, all necessary steps for maintenance of order and protection of the interests of the State of Slovakia.

SECTION 5. This law shall take effect today and the government shall execute it.

Dr. SOKOL — SIVÁK
Dr. TISO — Dr. PRUŽINSKÝ
Dr. TUKA — Dr. FRITZ
Dr. DURČANSKÝ — MEDRICKÝ
SIDOR — ČATLOŠ

[12] *Slovenský Zákonník* (Slovak Law Collection), No. 1, March 1, 1939, Text 1.

Decree of the Government concerning the Establishment and Competence of the Individual Ministries of the State of Slovakia, March 15, 1939 [13]

The Government of the State of Slovakia, on the basis of Section 4 of the law of March 14, 1939, concerning the independent State of Slovakia (*Slovenský Zákonník*, No. 1), ordains as follows:

SECTION 1. The following central offices shall be established for the discharge of the state administration:

1. Office of the President of the Government.
2. Ministry of Foreign Affairs.
3. Ministry of the Interior.
4. Ministry of Finance.
5. Ministry of Schools and Public Education.
6. Ministry of Justice.
7. Ministry of Economy.
8. Ministry of Transportation and Public Works.
9. Ministry of National Defense.

SECTION 2. The jurisdiction of these offices shall extend to all affairs pertaining to the life of the state.

SECTION 3. This decree shall take effect on the day of promulgation. It shall be executed by all members of the government.

DR. TISO	SIVÁK
DR. TUKA	DR. FRITZ
DR. DURČANSKÝ	MEDRICKÝ
SIDOR	STANO
DR. PRUŽINSKÝ	ČATLOŠ

Declaration concerning the German-Slovak Treaty of Protection concluded between the German Reich and the State of Slovakia, March 24, 1939 [14]

Between the German Government and the Slovak Government, a treaty was signed extending protection by the German Reich to the State of Slovakia.

The treaty became effective on March 23, 1939; its text is published hereinafter.

Berlin, March 24, 1939.

VON RIBBENTROP
Reich Minister of Foreign Affairs

[13] *Slovenský Zákonník*, No. 2, March 16, 1939, Text 4.
[14] *Reichsgesetzblatt*, 1939, II, No. 4, p. 606.

Treaty of Protection to be extended by the German Reich to the State of Slovakia

The German Government and the Slovak Government have agreed, after the Slovak State has placed itself under the protection of the German Reich, to regulate by treaty the consequences resulting from this fact. For this purpose the undersigned representatives of the two governments have agreed on the following provisions.

ARTICLE 1. The German Reich undertakes to protect the political independence of the State of Slovakia and the integrity of its territory.

ARTICLE 2. For the purpose of making effective the protection undertaken by the German Reich, the German armed forces shall have the right, at all times, to construct military installations and to keep them garrisoned in the strength they deem necessary, in an area delimited on its western side by the frontiers of the State of Slovakia, and on its eastern side by a line formed by the eastern rims of the Lower Carpathians, the White Carpathians and the Javornik Mountains.

The Government of Slovakia will take the necessary steps to assure that the land required for these installations shall be conveyed to the German armed forces. Furthermore the Government of Slovakia will agree to grant exemption from custom duties for imports from the Reich for the maintenance of the German troops and the supply of military installations.

Military sovereignty will be assumed by the German armed forces in the zone described in the preceding paragraph.

German citizens who, on the basis of private employment contracts, are engaged in the construction of military installations in the designated zone shall be subject to German jurisdiction.

ARTICLE 3. The Government of Slovakia will organize its military forces in close agreement with the German armed forces.

ARTICLE 4. In accordance with the relationship of protection agreed upon, the Government of Slovakia will at all times conduct its foreign affairs in close agreement with the German Government.

ARTICLE 5. This treaty shall become effective as of the date of its signature and shall be valid for a period of twenty-five years. The two governments will reach an understanding on the extension of this treaty in due time before the expiration of that period.

In witness whereof the representatives of the two parties have signed the above treaty in duplicate.

Vienna, March 18, 1939. Berlin, March 23, 1939.

For the German Government:
VON RIBBENTROP

For the Slovak Government:
DR. JOZEF TISO
DR. VOJTECH TUKA
DR. F. DURČANSKÝ

2. POLITICAL PARTIES

Law concerning Political Parties of Racial Groups, May 15, 1940 [16]

[EXCERPTS]

The Diet of the Slovak Republic has passed the following law:

PART I.—*General Provisions*

SECTION 1. The political parties (called in the following text "parties"), by means of which racial groups shall under Section 59 of the Constitution take part in the government, shall be registered by the Ministry of the Interior upon a decision to that effect by the government.

SECTION 2. Only the citizens of the Slovak Republic belonging to a given racial group may be members of a party.

PART II.—*Foundation of Parties and Their Registration*

SECTION 3. Persons who wish to found a party must present their project to the Ministry of the Interior before they begin organization activities and must submit the statute of the party within two months. . . .

SECTIONS 4 and following. [Registration means granting of monopoly for representatives of a given racial group. The party's activity may be limited or discontinued by the government.] [17]

. . . .

SECTION 29. This law shall take effect on the day of its promulgation. It shall be executed by the government.

DR. TISO	SIVÁK
DR. SOKOL	DR. FRITZ
DR. TUKA	MEDRICKÝ
DR. DURČANSKÝ	STANO
DR. PRUŽINSKÝ	ČATLOŠ

3. LAW AND COURTS

Decree of the Government concerning Protective Custody for the Enemies of the State of Slovakia, March 24, 1939 [18]

SECTION 1. The Minister of the Interior shall be authorized to order protective custody for persons who by their activities up to the present time have warranted and still warrant reasonable fear that they will be an obstacle to the upbuilding of the State of Slovakia.

[16] *Slovenský Zákonník*, No. 25, May 29, 1940, Text 121.
[17] Summary by the translator.
[18] *Slovenský Zákonník*, No. 7, March 25, 1939, Text 32.

SECTION 2. For this purpose the Minister of the Interior shall organize a protective camp in which the prisoners must perform commonly useful work.

SECTION 3. This decree shall take effect on the day of promulgation.

DR. TISO	DR. FRITZ
DR. TUKA	MEDRICKÝ
DR. DURČANSKÝ	STANO
PRUŽINSKÝ	ČATLOŠ
SIVÁK	

Decree of the Government concerning the Establishment of a Slovakian Supreme Court, April 4, 1939 [19]

[EXCERPTS]

SECTION 1. A Slovak Supreme Court (*Slovenský Najvyšší Súd*), with its seat in Bratislava, shall be established for the entire territory of the State of Slovakia. . . . .

The present decree shall take effect on the day of promulgation. It shall be executed by the Minister of Finance.

DR. TISO	DR. FRITZ
DR. DURČANSKÝ	MEDRICKÝ
DR. PRUŽINSKÝ	STANO
SIVÁK	ČATLOŠ

Constitutional Law concerning the Supreme Administrative Court, May 7, 1940 [20]

[EXCERPTS]

The Diet of the Slovak Republic has adopted the following law:

PART I

SECTION 1. *Organization of the Supreme Administrative Court and its Seat.* For the territory of the Slovak Republic a Supreme Administrative Court shall be established in Bratislava.

SECTION 2. *Jurisdiction.* (1) The Supreme Administrative Court shall decide all cases in which a party alleges that its right has been violated by an illegal decision or order issued by an administrative authority.

[19] *Slovenský Zákonník*, No. 11, April 6, 1939, Text 49.
[20] *Ibid.*, No. 25, May 29, 1940, Text 120.

(2) The administrative authorities whose decisions or orders may be attacked by an appeal to the Supreme Administrative Court are the agencies of the national, provincial, and communal governments.

(3) The Supreme Administrative Court shall decide claims against the state, provinces, and communities if all the competent administrative authorities have already passed on such claims in consecutive hierarchical order.

. . . . .

SECTION 53. This law shall take effect on the day of promulgation. The government shall execute it.

Dr. TISO	SIVÁK
Dr. SOKOL	Dr. FRITZ
Dr. TUKA	MEDRICKÝ
Dr. DURČANSKÝ	STANO
Dr. PRUŽINSKÝ	ČATLOŠ

4. FINANCE

Decree of the Government concerning the Slovak National Bank, April 4, 1939[21]

[EXCERPTS]

The Government of the State of Slovakia, on the basis of Section 4 of the law of March 14, 1939 (*Slovenský Zákonník*, No. 1), enacts the following:

SECTION 1. (1) In accordance with the present decree, the Slovak National Bank (*Slovenská Národnā Banka*) shall exercise the prerogatives of the state in the matter of issuance of bank notes.

(2) It shall be the duty of the bank to insure the stability of currency, to regulate all payments, and to extend credits as required by the national economy.

SECTION 2. (1) The Slovak National Bank is granted the exclusive right to issue bank notes in the State of Slovakia. The state renounces the right to issue government notes or to authorize anyone to issue money of any kind. Government coins shall be issued under an agreement with the bank.

(2) Bank notes shall be issued in Slovak crowns (Ks) and shall be, with the exception of the government's gold coins, the only unlimited legal tender.

(3) Foreign currency cannot be used for payments in the State of Slovakia.

(4) The Slovak National Bank may be authorized by a special law to supervise all banks, savings banks, and other banking establishments.

[21] *Slovenský Zákonník*, No. 11, April 6, 1939, Text 44.

SECTION 3. (1) The value of the Slovak crown shall be equivalent to 31.21 milligrams of pure gold.

(2) The Slovak National Bank shall buy and sell gold for this price. It may add as commission no more than ½ per cent.

. . .

SECTION 36. The present decree shall take effect on the day of promulgation except for the provisions of Section 24,[22] which shall be put into effect by the Minister of Finance.

This decree shall be executed by the Minister of Finance.

Dr. TISO — Dr. FRITZ
Dr. TUKA — MEDRICKÝ
Dr. DURČANSKÝ — STANO
Dr. PRUŽINSKÝ — ČATLOŠ
SIVÁK

Decree of the Government concerning Slovakian Currency, April 4, 1939 [23]

[EXCERPTS]

SECTION 1. (1) The Slovak crown shall be the unit of currency of the State of Slovakia and the basis on which coins shall be issued. It shall be divided into 100 haliers.

(2) The Minister of Finance shall, in agreement with the Slovak National Bank, issue coins as business needs may require.

. . . . .

SECTION 4. The total amount of small coins issued must not be higher than 200 crowns per capita of population.

. . . . .

SECTION 8. The Czechoslovakian currency (metal and bank notes) now in circulation in the territory of the State of Slovakia shall remain in circulation until it is withdrawn from circulation by a special order. One Czechoslovakian crown (Kč) shall be equivalent to one Slovak crown (Ks).

SECTION 9. The present decree shall take effect on the day of promulgation. It shall be executed by the Minister of Finance.

Dr. TISO — Dr. FRITZ
Dr. TUKA — MEDRICKÝ
Dr. DURČANSKÝ — STANO
Dr. PRUŽINSKÝ — ČATLOŠ
SIVÁK

[22] This section provides for periodical publication of the accounts of the bank.
[23] *Slovenský Zákonník*, No. 11, April 6, 1939, Text 45.

5. CONTROL OF PROPERTY

Decree of the Government concerning the Establishment of Provisional Supervision and Trusteeship of Large Estates, March 30, 1939 [24]

[EXCERPTS]

On the basis of Section 4 of the Constitutional Law of March 14, 1939 (*Slovenský Zákonník*, Text 1), the government ordains as follows:

SECTION 1. (1) The County Court shall establish a temporary control of those estates over thirty hectares in extent where farming is for any reason jeopardized.

(2) It shall be the duty of the mayor of the community and the community secretary to watch the farming in their districts, and if conditions such as those mentioned in the preceding paragraph exist the said officers shall report them without delay to the county administration, stating the reasons for such report.

SECTION 2. If such action fails to improve the situation, the County Court shall, on motion of the county administration or the Minister of Economy, place the estate in the hands of a trustee.

SECTION 3. The Ministry of Economy must be advised of the establishment of the temporary control or of the appointment of a trustee.

SECTION 4. . . . (3) The trustee shall manage the estate in accordance with the rules of the Code of Enforcement Procedure and regulations issued by the Minister of Economy.

SECTION 5. Temporary control shall last three months and trusteeship one fiscal year, and such control may be prolonged if necessity arises therefor.

SECTION 6. [The owner, tenant, subtenant, or usufructor of the estate shall give to the temporary supervisor all required information and place at the disposal of the trustee all implements and other equipment necessary for proper farming; otherwise the court will order this by injunction.] [25]

. . . . .

SECTION 8. [On motion of the Minister of Economy, the court may on its own initiative discontinue control or trusteeship before expiration of the term stated in Section 5.]

. . . . .

SECTION 10. This decree shall take effect on the day of promulgation and shall cease to be effective on September 30, 1941. It shall be executed by the Minister of Agriculture, in agreement with the Ministers of the Interior and Justice.

Dr. TISO
Dr. TUKA
Dr. DURČANSKÝ
Dr. PRUŽINSKÝ
SIVÁK
Dr. FRITZ
MEDRICKÝ
STANO
ČATLOŠ

[24] *Slovenský Zákonník*, No. 9, March 31, 1939, Text 39.
[25] Summary by the translator.

Decree of the Government concerning Those Gaining Wealth through Politics, April 24, 1939 [26]

[EXCERPTS]

On the basis of Section 4 of the law of March 14, 1939 (*Slovenský Zákonník*, No. 1), the Government of the State of Slovakia enacted as follows:

SECTION 1. (1) The property of persons, as defined in accordance with Section 4 hereof, which was obtained through their own political activities, through political influence, or through the political activities or influence of other persons or political parties during the period from October 30, 1918, to October 6, 1938, shall be forfeited to the independent State of Slovakia regardless of whether the property is situated in this country or abroad.

(2) The same regulation shall be applied to individuals who acquire property from persons mentioned in the preceding paragraph by inheritance, donation, or a transaction which conceals a donation.

SECTION 2. (1) Property received as payment for employment, as wages and additional allowances for performance of duties, and similar lump-sum compensation received from the treasury, do not fall within the provisions of this decree.

(2) Likewise this decree does not apply to property or a part thereof mentioned in Sections 1 and 2 which was obviously spent for public, charitable, or commonly useful purposes before this decree came into effect.

. . . . .

SECTION 4. The government shall determine those persons whose property shall be forfeited to the state under Section 1.

. . . . .

SECTION 7*a*. (1) The value of the property mentioned in Section 1 shall be determined in accordance with the procedure established for the assessment of direct taxes.

. . . . .

SECTION 10. (1) This decree shall take effect on the day of promulgation and shall be executed by all members of the government.

(2) Proceedings under this law may be instituted only before December 31, 1941.

DR. TISO	DR. FRITZ
DR. DURČANSKÝ	MEDRICKÝ
DR. PRUŽINSKÝ	STANO
SIVÁK	ČATLOŠ

[26] *Slovenský Zákonník*, No. 17, April 26, 1939, Text 73.

IV. THE HIGHLAND TERRITORIES AND SUBCARPATHIA

1. REINCORPORATION LAWS

Law XXXIV of 1938 concerning the Reincorporation into the Country of the Highland Territories Returned to the Hungarian Holy Crown, November 12, 1938[27]

I hereby announce to all whom it may concern that the Lower and Upper Houses of the Parliament of Hungary have by mutual consent enacted the following law:

The Hungarian Parliament devoutly expresses its gratitude to Divine Providence that after twenty years' separation, trial, and heroic resistance against foreign rule, one part of the torn-away Highland Territories (*Felvidék*) returns to the Hungarian Holy Crown. The Hungarian fatherland greets with the deepest joy, and clasps to its heart with the affection of a loving mother, these returning children who have suffered so much.

SECTION 1. The Hungarian Parliament takes note of the fact that the Hungarian Royal Government requested the Government of the German Reich and the Italian Royal Government to arbitrate the fate of the regions to be separated from the territory of the Czechoslovak Republic and reincorporated into Hungary, and, remembering with gratitude the painstaking activities of the governments of these friendly nations, accepts the award of the two governments delivered on November 2, 1938, concerning the territories to be reincorporated, and reincorporates the Highland Territories adjudicated to Hungary into the territory of the Hungarian State, in conformity with the terms of the arbitration award.

SECTION 2. The Parliament, on the motion of the Prime Minister, and with both houses concurring, shall decide who, from among those persons elected by the population of the Highland Territories as senators and national or provincial representatives, shall by virtue of the present law become members of the House of Representatives of the Hungarian Parliament convoked for the 27th day of the month of April, 1935.[28]

SECTION 3. The number of the members of the Upper House whose appointment for life is based upon the 23d Section of Law XXII of 1926 (1926: XXII, Section 23) shall be raised to forty-four.

SECTION 4. The Hungarian Royal Cabinet shall be authorized to issue, until further parliamentary measures are taken, such orders in respect to the reincorporated Highland Territories as may be necessary for the adjustment of the administration, legislation, economy, and, in general, the whole legal system of the reincorporated Highland Territories, to the existing legal system of the country.

[27] *Évi Országos Törvénytár*, 1938, p. 617.

[28] The Parliament's session began on that date.

The Hungarian Royal Cabinet shall be free to promulgate regulations, even when such regulations otherwise fall within the jurisdiction of the Parliament.

The Hungarian Royal Cabinet shall be authorized to cover the expenses relating to the reincorporation and administration of the Highland Territories, so far as may be necessary, even by means of extraordinary credit transactions; and the expenses, as well as the income resulting from the reincorporation of the Highland Territories, must be indicated in the final balance report.

Regulations promulgated under the authorization of the present section, which otherwise belong to the jurisdiction of the Parliament, shall be presented to Parliament for confirmation within six months of the date of promulgation.

Until the time that Parliament, or by the present authorization the Hungarian Royal Cabinet, shall otherwise decree, the laws existing in the reincorporated territories on November 2, 1938, shall remain in force, except in cases where application thereof is impossible because of the change of sovereignty.

SECTION 5. Of the silver coins to be minted in accordance with the existing law, two million pieces of two-pengő coins commemorating the reincorporation of the Highland Territories shall be minted.

SECTION 6. Regulations of the Hungarian Royal Cabinet and of individual ministers that were issued in regard to the reincorporation of the Highland Territories prior to the promulgation of the present law are hereby confirmed.

SECTION 7. The present law shall become valid on the day of its promulgation. The Hungarian Royal Cabinet shall be charged with its execution.

I hereby order the promulgation of this law. I shall obey it as the will of the nation and shall enforce its observance by others.

Given in Budapest, on November 12, 1938.

NICHOLAS HORTHY, *Regent of Hungary*
Vitéz BÉLA IMRÉDY, *Hungarian Royal Prime Minister*

Order No. 102,473/1939 B.M. of the Hungarian Royal Ministry of the Interior concerning the Territories to be Reincorporated as a Consequence of the Delimitation of the Hungarian-Czechoslovak Frontier and the Extension of the Czechoslovak-Hungarian Amnesty Agreement. March 13, 1939[29]

In execution of the Vienna arbitration, the frontiers between Hungary and Czechoslovakia, between the Danube and the Ung, have been finally

[29] *Belügyi Közlöny*, March 19, 1939, No. 12, p. 341.

agreed upon. In consequence the following localities hereafter shall come under the authority of the Hungarian Royal Crown: Vága, Alsójattó, Nagycétény, Kalász, Nagyhind, Bori, Hévmágyarád, Felsözellö, Alsopokorágy, Pádár, Felsöfalu, Rekenyevitálu, Andrási, Aifalucska, Jászo, Jászomindszent, Rudnok, Aranyida (Reka), Mészpest, Bajánháza.

The transfer of the territories shall take place before March 14, 1939.

Both governments have agreed that stipulations of the agreement of December 23, 1938, shall be applied to the population of the territories reciprocally taken over.

In accordance with Order No. 296,000,1938 B.M. [Ministry of Interior] of December 30, 1938, I call on the County Deputy Chief to instruct the chiefs of the superior police authorities in the respective communities that no administrative or police measures may be taken against acts caused by the present political tension until the day of the actual return of the territories.

I have taken the necessary steps toward the administration of the territories returned. In consideration, however, of the particular psychological atmosphere existing among the inhabitants of the territories reciprocally taken over, I particularly enjoin the County Deputy Chief to do everything in his power, and also enjoin the minor authorities to protect the population so annexed from every harm and to show toward them in every instance the greatest courtesy and friendliness.

This order shall take effect on March 14, 1939.

Dated in Budapest, March 13, 1939.

Vitéz Ferenc Keresztes-Fisher
Hungarian Royal Minister of Interior

Law VI of 1939 concerning the Union with the Country of the Carpathian Territories Reincorporated into the Hungarian Holy Crown, June 22, 1939 [30]

I hereby give notice to all whom it may concern that the Lower and Upper Houses of the Parliament of Hungary have in agreement enacted the following law:

The Hungarian Parliament devoutly expresses its gratitude to Divine Providence that, after the return in the last quarter of the year 1938 of a part of the torn-away Highland Territories, Carpathia also returned to the realm of the Hungarian Holy Crown in the month of March of the year 1939. The Hungarian fatherland greets with the deepest joy, and with the affection of a loving mother clasps to its heart, its faithful sons who have suffered so

[30] *Évi Országos Törvénytár*, 1939, p. 105.

much and who have returned together with the territory of the northeastern Carpathians delimited by their 1,000-year-old boundaries.

SECTION 1. The Hungarian Parliament takes cognizance of those laws by which the Hungarian Royal Government took possession of Carpathia in March, 1939, and expresses its gratitude to the Hungarian Royal Army (*Honvéd*) for its self-sacrificing and enthusiastic fulfillment of its duties.

Parliament reincorporates the territories into the territory of the Hungarian State.

SECTION 2. Until the time when the holding of parliamentary elections becomes possible in Carpathia, those persons from among those who were elected by the population of the Carpathian territories as senators and national or provincial representatives, or candidates listed on the register of the Hungarian parties as elected substitute representatives, or members of the national council elected by the original population of Subcarpathia, and who, on the motion of the Prime Minister, are nominated by the Parliament as parliamentary representatives, both houses concurring, shall, by virtue of this law, become members of the Parliament convoked for the 10th day of the month of June, 1939. The number of those so nominated shall not be more than ten.

SECTION 3. The number of lifetime members of the Upper House to be appointed in accordance with the 23d Section of Law XXII of 1926 (1926: XXII, Section 23) shall be raised to forty-six.

SECTION 4. The Cabinet is ordered to see that the parliamentary elections in the Carpathian territories shall be held not later than June 30, 1940.

SECTION 5. Inhabitants of the Carpathian territories who on July 26, 1921, were beyond question Hungarian citizens under the provisions of the then valid Hungarian laws, and who by the Treaty of Trianon, included in Law XXXIII of 1921, became Czechoslovak citizens, shall, beginning on March 15, 1939, regain their Hungarian citizenship without any administrative measures if, since March 15, 1929, they have lived continuously in the Carpathian Territories or in the Highland Territories reincorporated into the Hungarian Holy Crown by Law XXXIV of 1938.

The Hungarian citizenship regained under the preceding paragraph shall extend to the wife of the person who so regains his Hungarian citizenship and to their children who are not yet twenty-four years of age. A child born out of wedlock, if not over twenty-four, shall follow the citizenship of its mother.

A full orphan or a fatherless orphan born after July 26, 1921, as a Czechoslovak citizen shall acquire Hungarian citizenship effective March 15, 1939, if the father was a Hungarian citizen on July 26, 1921 (or the grandfather, if the father was born later) and the orphan himself has lived continuously since March 15, 1929—or since his birth, if born later—in the territory of Carpathia or in the Highland Territories reincorporated into Hungary by

Law XXXIV of 1938. A child born outside of wedlock shall follow the citizenship of the mother, or that of the grandfather.

The Hungarian citizenship acquired in accordance with the preceding paragraph shall extend to the wife and child of the man who became a Hungarian citizen, as well as to the child born out of wedlock to a woman who became a Hungarian citizen.

The regulations contained in the preceding paragraphs shall not extend to any person whose ancestor acquired Czechoslovak citizenship by option on the basis of Article 64 of the Treaty of Trianon as enacted in Law XXXIII of 1921.

SECTION 6. The Prime Minister shall introduce in Parliament a separate bill dealing with the regulation of the autonomy of Carpathia.

SECTION 7. The Cabinet shall be authorized, until further instructions from the Parliament, to issue such orders in regard to the Carpathian Territories as may be necessary in order to adjust the administration, legislation, economy, and in general the whole legal system, to the legal structure of the country or to harmonize the two.

The Cabinet may issue these orders even if they otherwise belong to the jurisdiction of the Parliament.

The Cabinet shall be authorized to cover expenses connected with the reincorporation and administration of the Carpathian Territories, if necessary, even through extraordinary credits.

Those regulations promulgated under the authorization of the present section, which otherwise belong to the jurisdiction of the Parliament, must be presented to the Parliament within six months from the date of publication.

SECTION 8. Regulations of the Hungarian Royal Cabinet and of the individual ministers that were issued in regard to the reincorporation of the Carpathian Territories previous to the promulgation of the present law are confirmed.

The present law shall become valid on the day of its promulgation. Its execution shall be the duty of the Hungarian Royal Cabinet.

I hereby order the promulgation of this law. I shall obey it as the will of the nation and shall enforce its observance by others.

Dated at Kenderes, June 22, 1939.

NICHOLAS HORTHY, *Regent of Hungary*
Count PAUL TELEKI, *Hungarian Royal Prime Minister*

2. REPRESENTATION IN PARLIAMENT

Law V of 1939 concerning Nomination of the Representatives of the Highland Territories Reincorporated into the Hungarian Holy Crown, to the House of Representatives of the Parliament Convoked for the 10th Day of the Month of June, 1939, June 22, 1939 [31]

I hereby give notice to all whom it may concern that the Lower and Upper Houses of the Parliament of Hungary have by mutual consent enacted the following law:

SECTION 1. Until such time as it may be possible to hold parliamentary elections in the territories reincorporated into the Hungarian Holy Crown by Law XXXIV of 1938, the House of Representatives of the Parliament convoked for the 10th day of the month of June, 1939, will seat as its members, by virtue of the present law, from among the persons who were elected by the population of the reincorporated Highland Territories as senators and national or provincial parliamentary representatives or substitute representatives listed on the register of the Hungarian political parties, those who, on motion of the Prime Minister, are nominated by the Parliament, both houses concurring, to membership in the House of Representatives of the Parliament. The number of those nominated may not be more than twenty-six.

SECTION 2. The Cabinet is ordered to see that the parliamentary elections in the Highland Territories reincorporated into the Hungarian Holy Crown shall take place not later than the 30th day of the month of June of the year 1940.

SECTION 3. The present law shall become valid on the day of its promulgation. Its execution is the duty of the Prime Minister but more particularly of the Cabinet.

I hereby order the promulgation of this law. I shall obey it as the will of the nation and shall enforce its observance by others.

Dated at Kenderes, June 22, 1939.

NICHOLAS HORTHY, *Regent of Hungary*
Count PAUL TELEKI, *Hungarian Royal Prime Minister*

[31] *Évi Országos Törvénytár*, 1939, p. 103.

Law XXI, 1942, concerning the Modification and Completion of Law XXII, 1926, relating to the Upper House of Parliament, as well as concerning the Necessary Transitory Modifications in the Organization of the Upper House resulting from the Reincorporation of Territories, November 25, 1942 [32]

[EXCERPTS]

I hereby give notice to whomsoever it may concern that the Upper and Lower Houses of the Parliament of Hungary by mutual agreement have enacted the following law:

CHAPTER I

SECTION 1. The first paragraph of Section 9 of law No. XXII, 1926, shall be modified to the effect that the elective group specified in paragraph (1) of Section 6, Law XXII, 1926, as well as other groups specified in other laws, shall at each election elect a number of additional members equal to the number of representatives to which the group, authority, or association is entitled in the Upper House.

. . . .

SECTION 3. (1) The first paragraph of Section 13 of Law XXII, 1926, shall be modified to the effect that the elective group designated in paragraph 1 of Section 6 of Law XXII, 1926, shall have the right to elect forty-four members of the Upper House, without regard to the number of members the counties and town-counties are permitted to elect.

(2) The second paragraph of Section 13, Law XXII, 1926, shall be completed by the following: When deciding upon taxes, consideration shall be given to those land estates situated in the territories, separated or reincorporated, which the owner had lost under a decision of a foreign authority or by administrative action.

If the person who lost his property under such circumstances has died in the meantime, his land estate shall go to his legal descendants; in case there are several descendants, it shall go to each in proportion to his legal right of succession, within ten years of the date the present law shall go into effect.

SECTION 4. The Regent of Hungary, on the basis of Section 23, Law XXII, 1926, of Section 3, Law XXXIV, 1938, of Section 3, Law VI, 1939, of Section 2, Law XXVI, 1940, and of Section 2, Law XX, 1941, which provide for nomination of members of the Upper House, may, upon the proposal of the Ministry, designate twenty-five additional members of the Upper House.

CHAPTER II

SECTION 5. (1) In the territories reincorporated into the Hungarian Holy Crown, newly created representative assemblies, as well as like repre-

[32] *Évi Országos Törvénytár*, 1942, p. 149.

sentative bodies of counties whose territories have been changed owing to such reincorporation, shall elect the number of members of the Upper House designated in subsection 2 as long as the number of members of the Upper House elected by the county assemblies has not yet been fixed, Section 18 of Law XXII, 1926, not yet having been adapted to the new conditions.

(2) The number of eligible Upper House members under subsection 1, shall be as follows:

Abauj-Torna (county)	2
Bács-Bodrog (county)	5
Baranya (county)	3
Bars and Hont (administratively united counties)	2
Bereg (county)	2
Beszterce-Naszód (county)	2
Bihar (county)	3
Csík (county)	2
Csongrád (county)	1
Esztergom (county)	1
Gömör and Kishont (county)	1
Háromszék (county)	2
Kolozs (county)	2
Komárom (county)	2
Máramaros (county)	2
Maros-Torda (county)	2
Nógrád (county)	2
Nyitra and Pozsony (administratively united counties)	2
Szatmár (county)	3
Szilágy (county)	2
Szolnok-Doboka (county)	2
Udvarhely (county)	2
Ugocsa (county)	1
Ung (county)	1
Vas (county)	3
Zala (county)	4
Zemplén (county)	2
Kassa (autonomous city)	1
Kolozsvár (autonomous city)	1
Komárom (autonomous city)	1
Marosvásárhely (autonomous city)	1
Nagyvárad (autonomous city)	1
Szabadka (autonomous city)	1
Szatmárnémeti (autonomous city)	1
Újvidék (autonomous city)	1
Ungvár (autonomous city)	1
Zombor (autonomous city)	1

SECTION 6. (1) The term of the elected Upper House members from Komárom and Esztergom, Nógrád and Hont, Borsod, Gömör and Kishont, Ugocsa and Bereg, counties administratively united (Law XXXV, 1923),

shall expire on December 31, 1942, without regard to the normal duration of their terms under Section 41, Law XXII, 1926.

(2) The Upper House members elected by the county assemblies of Szabolcs and Ung (administratively united) shall be considered as having been designated by the county of Szabolcs.

(3) The present law shall not affect the Upper House members of the following counties, elected in accordance with Section 7, Law XXII, 1926: Abauj-Torna, Bács-Bodrog, Baranya, Bihar, Csongrád, Vas, Zala and Zemplén.

. . . . .

SECTION 8. (1) From the incorporated Carpathian territory three Upper House members shall be nominated by the Parliament, both houses concurring, from the ranks of the population of that territory, beginning January 1, 1943.

(2) At the time the Upper House members are nominated, substitutes shall also be nominated. The order regarding substitutions shall be provided by act of Parliament.

(3) The nominating proposal shall be made in the Upper House of Parliament by the Prime Minister.

(4) The term of such members and substitutes shall end five years from the day fixed in subsection 1.

(5) The members designated in this section shall be subject in other respects to the provisions of Law XXII, 1926, concerning members of the Upper House.

CHAPTER III

SECTION 9. (1) In accordance with the provisions of the second paragraph of Section 3, Law XXII, 1926, and of the second paragraph of Section 13, the right to be elected as members of the Upper and Lower Houses from among the inhabitants of Transylvania, as well as of the reincorporated Southern Territories, shall be granted only to persons who meet the requirements of the regulations concerning voting and eligibility to membership in Parliament under Law XIX, 1938.

(2) Pursuant to subsection 1, the provision of Law XIX, 1938, requiring that the voters must have been Hungarian citizens for at least ten years before they acquire the right to vote, shall not be applied to those who prove that they have met the necessary legal requirements, namely, that they became Hungarian citizens in consequence of the change of sovereignty without special action of the authorities.

SECTION 10. Contrary to Section 8 of Law XXII, 1926, immediately after this law goes into effect the duration of the period prior to which elections shall be held may be fixed by the Minister of the Interior; but a period of at least twenty days must elapse before the elections.

SECTION 11. Paragraph 1 of Section 3 of Law XXVII, 1937, is abolished.

SECTION 12. This law shall go into effect on the day of publication.

I order the publication of this law. I will observe it as the will of the people and shall cause its observance by others.

Given in Budapest, November 25, 1942.

NICHOLAS HORTHY, *Regent of Hungary*
NICHOLAS KÁLLAY, *Hungarian Royal Prime Minister*

3. ADMINISTRATION

Decree No. 9330/1938 M.E. of the Hungarian Royal Cabinet concerning Administration of the Highland Territories Reincorporated into the Hungarian Holy Crown, December 18, 1938 [33]

[EXCERPTS]

I. [List of Cities]

II. ORGANIZATION OF THE AUTONOMOUS ADMINISTRATIVE BODIES

The following regulations shall be applicable as to representative bodies and autonomous administrative organizations of the cities and communities in the counties of the reincorporated Highland Territories, provided their reorganization is possible under the respective rulings.

1. *The Representative Body of the County*

SECTION 4. (1) In the administratively united counties of Komárom and Esztergom, Nógrád and Hont, Borsod, Gömör and Kishont, Szatmár, Ugocsa and Bereg, the members of the Representative Body or assembly elected from among individuals paying the highest taxes, and furthermore the members who represent religious communities and special interests, shall be apportioned, owing to the change of territories, in accordance with Section 2, subsections 2, 3, 4, 5, and 6.

. . . . . .

SECTION 5. (1) After the reapportionment of members under the preceding section, in the counties of Komárom, Esztergom, Nógrád, Gömör and Kishont, the representative assembly shall be completed by the representation of the other inhabitants of the remaining counties of the reincorporated Highland Territories. Thus shall the representative assembly of the counties of Abaúj-Torna and Zemplén be completed.

(2) For the representation of the population of the reincorporated Highland Territories, in accordance with the preceding paragraph, members of

[33] *Belügyi Közlöny* December 25, 1938, No. 56, p. 1200.

the representative assembly shall be designated from among the elected members of the Czechoslovak county representations who have their domicile in the territory of the respective counties.

(3) The persons mentioned in subsection 2 will be appointed to the representative assembly by the County Chief, who will announce the appointments to the assembly.

SECTION 6. In the counties of Nyitra and Pozsony, Bars and Hont, and Ung, members of the representative assembly will be appointed from among the elected members of the Czechoslovak county representations of such counties who have their domicile in the territory of the respective counties.

2. *Municipal Representative Bodies (Town-Counties)*

SECTION 7. The representative assembly of the autonomous city of Kassa (Košice) shall be created by the nomination of fifty-six members. The members of this assembly shall be appointed by the Minister of the Interior in accordance with the recommendation of the Minister without portfolio for Highland Affairs.

. . . .

6. *Representative Bodies of Counties, Towns, and Communities*

SECTION 12. (1) The representative assemblies of Ungvár and Munkács (capitals of counties), as well as of the communities of the Highland Territories, shall be composed of those persons who had theretofore been elected members of such municipal or communal assemblies.

(2) In accordance with the preceding paragraph, such persons will be appointed by the mayor in each city and by the communal judge in each community.

(3) In those communities where the representative assembly had been dissolved by the action of the Czechoslovak Government, the representative assembly shall be created by the nomination of members to conform numerically to those of the last elected assembly. The members of the assembly shall be appointed by the communal judge and shall be appointed, first, from among the duly elected members of the dissolved body; but, if it is deemed necessary, a certain number of members may be appointed also from among those individuals who have not been members previously.

. . . . . .

III. ORGANIZATION AND APPOINTMENT OF OFFICIALS

SECTION 15. (1) For such period as the respective representative assemblies are not created in accordance with previously existing regulations, the organization and appointment of officials for the functioning of the assemblies, referred to in Sections 5, 6 and 7, as well as of the cities and communities of the reannexed Highland Territories (also the autonomous city of Komárom) will be decided, in accordance with the respective laws, by the

Minister of the Interior, in cooperation with the Minister of Finance, the Minister without portfolio for Highland Affairs and, possibly, with other ministers interested.

. . . . .

SECTION 17. (1) For such period as the representative assembly is not formed under previously existing regulations, the County Chiefs of Esztergom, Nógrád, Abauj-Torna, and Zemplén are required to have advisers appointed to assist them in supplying information relative to the affairs of the reincorporated Highland Territories.

(2) The adviser to the County Chief shall be appointed by the Minister of the Interior, in cooperation with the Minister without portfolio for Highland Affairs, and may be recalled at any time.

(3) The County Chief shall decide as to matters pertaining to the Highland Territories in agreement with his appointed adviser.

. . . . .

V. GENERAL RULINGS

SECTION 30. For the time being, the laws concerning election of members to the Lower or Upper Houses shall not apply in the reincorporated Highland Territories.

. . . . .

Budapest, December 18, 1938.

Vitéz BÉLA IMRÉDY
Hungarian Royal Prime Minister

4. AGRARIAN REFORM

Order No. 2550/1939 of the Royal Hungarian Ministry, concerning the Transfer of Landed Estates in the Territories Reincorporated into the Hungarian Holy Crown, March 12, 1939 [34]

[EXCERPTS]

Pursuant to the authority granted under Section 4 of Law XXXIV of 1939, the Hungarian Royal Cabinet orders as follows:

SECTION 1. Transfer of real property which took place under decrees of the authorities concerning real property acquired in accordance with the Czechoslovak regulations on agrarian reform (law of April 16, 1919, No. 215) or by a transaction under private law in consequence of a decree of such authority, shall be investigated and may be declared null and void, so that the injustice done to the autochthonous inhabitants under regulations

[34] *Belügyi Közlöny*, March 12, 1939, No. 11, p. 296.

regarding agrarian reform may be corrected. So far as possible, there may be no voiding of acquisition of landed estates in the following cases:

1. If the acquirer was a municipality, the Church, a social community, or a former seigniorial property.
2. If the property was acquired by societies whose members had permanent domicile in the reincorporated territories and which have cultivated the land themselves.
3. If it was acquired by institutions of agricultural training, the upkeep of which is necessary in accordance with the decision of the Ministry of Agriculture.

In furtherance of the provisions specified in Section 1, control may be exercised over memberships in agricultural associations, distilleries, or other agricultural enterprises which were acquired under Czechoslovak agricultural decrees, and such memberships, as well as the rights exercised thereunder, shall be voided as necessity may arise.

SECTION 2. The ownership of landed estates of which the acquisition has been voided under the provisions of Section 1 shall be vested in the state.

Such landed estates shall be vested in the state free of every incumbrance and with the land servitudes intact. The previous lease agreements may be cancelled at the end of the agricultural year. As concerns creditors and other persons interested therein (in so far as Section 3 hereof provides reimbursement therefor or return thereof in favor of the owner), Law XXVII, paragraphs 31–36, shall be applicable, except that the usufruct beneficiary shall not receive compensation for the cancellation of the contract of usufruct.

SECTION 3. In so far as the acquisition of landed estate membership is voided under Section 1, the former owner shall have a right to reimbursement for the amounts which he or his legal predecessor paid to the Czechoslovak Ministry of Agriculture, or to the previous owner, either directly or through the intermediaries of the financial authority in question. Amounts paid for interest and expenses will not be reimbursed.

No compensation will be paid for improvements in real estate; in exceptional cases, however, especially if it seems to be appropriate for the satisfaction of creditors or for the satisfaction of family requirements of the persons whose property has been expropriated, compensation of amounts paid for necessary and useful improvements may be provided for.

SECTION 4. As to the acquisition of landed estates, as well as the voiding of rights under Section 1 and the compensation permitted under Section 3, the verdict of the commissioner appointed by the Ministry shall be decisive.

The estates which become state property shall be recorded by a notary in accordance with the decision of the commissioner.

SECTION 5. The estates which have become state property under Section 2 shall be utilized for agricultural-political purposes, and the voidings in accordance with Section 1 shall be decided by a judge with the consent of the Minister without portfolio for Highland Affairs.

As to the necessary personal requirements for participation in the landed estates the provisions of Law XXVII of 1936 shall be applicable.

. . . . .

SECTION 8. As to landed estates situated in the reincorporated Highland Territories, which had been taken over by the Czechoslovak Government, the compensation due to the former owner of such estates utilized for agricultural-political purposes, or utilized in accordance with the decision of the commissioner and the measure of service rendered in general, shall be decided according to Czechoslovak law. In other cases such estates shall be treated according to Hungarian law.

SECTION 9. The commissioner shall function under the supervision of the Minister of Agriculture, with headquarters in Budapest. For the execution of the duties of his office the necessary clerical assistance (such as investigators, secretaries, accountants) shall be paid from credits obtained in accordance with the order of the Minister of Finance and of the Minister without portfolio for Highland Affairs. The directives for the work of the commissioner shall be issued by the Prime Minister, in cooperation with the Minister of Agriculture and the Minister without portfolio for Highland Affairs.

SECTION 10. Orders for the implementation of the present law shall be issued by the interested ministers in accordance with the request of the Minister without portfolio for Highland Affairs.

Budapest, March 12, 1939.

Count PAUL TELEKI,
Royal Hungarian Prime Minister

DANZIG

An Act concerning the Reunion of the Free City of Danzig with the German Reich, September 1, 1939 [1]

The Reichstag has unanimously passed the following Act which is hereby published:

SECTION 1. The statute issued by the head of the Free City of Danzig concerning the reunion of Danzig with the German Reich is hereby made an Act of the Reich. Its text is as follows:

ARTICLE I. The Constitution of the Free City of Danzig is hereby abolished.

ARTICLE II. All legislative and executive power is vested exclusively in the Head of the City.

ARTICLE III. The Free City of Danzig, with its territory and its citizens, is hereby incorporated into the German Reich.

ARTICLE IV. Until the introduction of German Reich law is finally decreed by the Führer, all laws and statutes in force at the time the present Statute is issued shall remain in force with the exception of the Constitution.

Danzig, September 1, 1939.

ALBERT FÖRSTER

SECTION 2. The citizens of the former Free City of Danzig shall become German citizens in accordance with provisions to be issued.

SECTION 3. In the territory of the former Free City of Danzig the law heretofore in force, with the excepton of the Constitution of the Free City of Danzig, shall remain in effect until further notice.

SECTION 4. (1) In the former Free City of Danzig, the entire body of Reich law and Prussian law shall take effect as of January 1, 1940.

(2) The Reich Minister concerned may, in agreement with the Reich Minister of the Interior, determine that certain Reich laws or Prussian laws shall not take effect or shall take effect at a later date or subject to certain modifications. Any such decree shall be published in the *Reichsgesetzblatt*.

(3) The Reich Minister of the Interior, in agreement with the Reich ministers concerned, may, by means of orders, introduce Reich law and Prussian law before January 1, 1940.

SECTION 5. (1) The Reich Minister of the Interior is the officer chiefly responsible for matters connected with the reunion of Danzig with the German Reich.

(2) The Reich Minister of the Interior is hereby authorized to promulgate general rules and regulations necessary for the enforcement and implementation of this Act.

[1] *Reichsgesetzblatt*, 1939, I, p. 1547.

SECTION 6. This Statute shall take effect as of September 1, 1939.

Berlin, September 1, 1939.

ADOLF HITLER, *Führer and Reich Chancellor;* FRICK, *Reich Minister of the Interior;* R. HESS, *Representative of the Führer;* GÖRING, *General Field Marshal, Minister President of Prussia, Commissioner for the Four-Year Plan;* VON RIBBENTROP, *Reich Minister of Foreign Affairs;* DR. LAMMERS, *Reich Minister and Chief of the Reich Chancellery.*

DENMARK

Proclamation of the German Commander in Copenhagen to the Danish Army and the Danish People, April 9, 1940 [1]

Without reason and in opposition to the sincere wishes of the German Government and the German people to live in peace and friendship with the English and French peoples, the rulers of England and France declared war on Germany in September of last year. Their aim was and is to make decisions in theaters of war which lie far away and are therefore less dangerous for France and England; they hope thereby that it will be impossible for Germany to oppose them with sufficient forces. For this reason England has always, among other things, violated Danish and Norwegian neutrality and their territorial waters. They have always tried to make Scandinavia a theater of war. As further opportunities seemed not to be available after the Russo-Finnish peace, they have now officially declared and threatened that they will no longer tolerate the operation of the German commercial fleet in Danish territorial waters, in the North Sea, and in Norwegian waters. They have announced that they will take over the policing there themselves. All preparations have been made, in order to seize by surprise all strategic points on the coast of Norway, by the greatest warmonger of this century, Churchill, who in the first World War said openly, to the disaster of all humanity, that he would not be restrained by "legal decisions or neutral rights, which are written on scraps of paper." He has prepared for battle off the Danish and the Norwegian coasts. Some days ago he was appointed responsible chief for the whole British conduct of the war.

The German Government has up to now merely observed this man's preparations, but can no longer tolerate the creation of a new war theater to meet the wishes of the English-French warmongers. The Danish and Norwegian governments have for months known about these attempts. Their attitude also is no secret to the German Government. They are neither willing nor capable of making effective resistance against the English invasion. Therefore Germany has decided to forestall the English attack and with its own forces assume the protection of the neutrality of the Kingdoms of Denmark and Norway. It is not the intention of the German Government to obtain strategic points for the battle against England; its exclusive aim is to prevent Scandinavia from becoming a battlefield for the extension of the British war. For this reason strong German military forces have this morning taken possession of the most important military objectives in Denmark and Norway. Beside these measures, agreements are at the present

[1] *Nordisk Tidsskrift for International Ret* (Copenhagen, etc.), Vol. 11 (1940), Fasc. 3–4, D—48–50.

time being negotiated between the Government of the Reich and the Royal Danish Government. The purpose of these agreements is to make sure that the Danish Kingdom shall continue to exist, that the fleet shall be maintained, that the liberty of the Danish people shall be respected, and that the future independence of that country shall be secured. Until these negotiations have been concluded, it is expected that the Army and Navy will understand this; also that the people and all municipalities will evidence their good will by avoiding either passive or active resistance. Such resistance will be useless and will be broken by all means in our power. All military and civil authorities are therefore asked to enter into contact with the German commanders. The people are requested to continue their daily work and to see to it that tranquillity and order are maintained. From now on the German Army and Navy safeguard the security of the country against British violations.

KAUPISCH, *German Commander*

Decree No. 337 concerning Importation and Exportation of Money and Securities, *et cetera,* June 25, 1940 [2]

[EXCERPTS]

Pursuant to the regulations in Law No. 342 of December 22, 1937, concerning redemption of currency of the National Bank of Denmark and concerning measures to safeguard the Danish currency (see Law No. 459 of December 22, 1939, and Law No. 314 of June 14, 1940), it is hereby ordered:

SECTION 1. Importation of Danish or foreign securities, including coupons, from abroad may take place only through the banks and members of the Stock Exchange in Copenhagen who have obtained permission from the National Bank of Denmark to trade in foreign exchange, and only when permission has been obtained from the National Bank for each such importation.

On the entry of the money, the permission of the National Bank shall be presented to the custom authorities to be stamped.

. . . .

SECTION 17. If an agreement has been concluded between Denmark and a foreign country to the effect that payments between the two countries shall be effected by clearing or by other arrangements for payment, the National Bank of Denmark shall be authorized to conclude more detailed agreements with the foreign agency concerned regarding the execution of the agreement and, from the Danish side, to undertake the necessary control of the execution of such agreement; also care shall be taken that no other payments are

[2] *Lovtidenden-A*, No. 72, June 28, 1940.
See also proclamation concerning clearing, above, p. 337.

settled than those defined or stipulated by the agreement with the foreign country concerned.

In order to maintain Danish exports to countries with which no clearing agreement has been concluded, private clearings or special payment arrangements may be entered into with the approval of the Danish National Bank and of the Central Exchange Control Authority.

• • •

SECTION 20. This law shall take effect immediately.

At the same time, Law No. 143 of April 2, 1940, concerning importation and exportation of money and securities, *et cetera*, is repealed.

The present law is hereby publicly proclaimed.

Ministry of Commerce, Industry, and Shipping, June 25, 1940.

JOHS. KJAERBØL

Law No. 415 amending Law No. 337 of June 25, 1940, concerning Importation and Exportation of Money and Securities, *et cetera*, October 2, 1941 [3]

Pursuant to Section 7 of Law No. 406 of August 3, 1940, concerning economic measures, supply of commodities, *et cetera* (see Law No. 133 of March 29, 1941), it is hereby ordered:

SECTION 1. To Section 14 of Law No. 337 of June 25, 1940, concerning importation and exportation of money and securities, *et cetera*, are added as new paragraphs numbered 2 and 3:

Persons, firms, or juridical persons who are resident here or carry on a profession in this country may not, without the permission of the National Bank of Denmark, receive capital (in cash, in merchandise, or otherwise) or a guarantee from persons, firms, or juridical persons who are not residents.

Persons, firms, or juridical persons who are residents in this country may not, without the approval of the National Bank of Denmark, transmit or pledge Danish securities to persons, firms, or juridical persons who are not resident in this country. Transactions which are undertaken in violation hereof shall be invalid.

SECTION 2. This law shall take effect immediately.

It is hereby publicly proclaimed.

The Ministry of Commerce, Industry, and Shipping, October 2, 1941.

H. HENDRIKSEN

[3] *Lovtidenden-A*, No. 63, October 9, 1941.

Law No. 639 concerning the Sale of Merchandise to the Armed Forces and to Individual Members Thereof, December 11, 1940 [4]

Pursuant to Law No. 406 of August 3, 1940, concerning economic measures, supply of merchandise, etc., after negotiation with the Ministry of Foreign Affairs and the Ministry of Agriculture and in accordance with the agreements made with the German armed forces in Denmark, it is ordered as follows:

SECTION 1. As the German armed forces in this country as a rule receive all supplies of food, forage, and all other commodities from Germany, the sale of merchandise to the German armed forces or individual units thereof—directly or through intermediaries—shall take place in accordance with the following rules:

SECTION 2. 1. Sale of goods for use by the German armed forces or individual units thereof may take place in the following cases:

a) Butter, meat, lard, milk, eggs, and cheese may be sold without special permission, when the sale is made through the respective Danish export agency in accordance with the regulations concerning such transactions laid down by the Ministry of Agriculture.

b) Merchandise containing iron, steel, other metals, or rubber may be sold in accordance with the rules of Law No. 578 of November 4, 1940.

c) Other goods may be sold, if written permission in each instance has been given by the Ministry of Foreign Affairs. Such permission, however, is not required for every single sale in individual cases, where the price does not exceed 200 kroner.

2. In the cases mentioned in paragraph 1, where sale to the German armed forces or to individual units thereof is permissible, the Danish seller is entitled only to receive payment in the form of checks. For minor amounts, which do not exceed 200 kroner, payment in Danish coins or notes may be received.

SECTION 3. Sale of commodities to individual members of the German armed forces (commissioned officers, non-commissioned officers, officials, privates, and civilians, who are connected with the armed forces) may take place in the following cases:

a) Rationed goods may be sold only on delivery of ration coupons, in accordance with the established regulations concerning the rationing of individual goods.

b) Other commodities may be sold—directly or through intermediaries—only when the purchase does not exceed reasonable limits according to fair judgment.

SECTION 4. 1. Persons who knowingly sell or deliver goods in violation of the regulations set forth in this law or against the conditions set forth in

[4] *Lovtidenden-A*, No. 120, December 16, 1940.

the licenses, or who may be presumed to know that their transactions are in violation thereof, shall be punished, in accordance with Law No. 406 of August 3, 1940, concerning economic measures, supply of merchandise, *et cetera*, by fine, detention, or imprisonment for a period up to two years.

2. The proceeds derived from actions which are liable to the penalties provided in paragraph 1, or an amount which may be considered as the equivalent thereof, and objects with which the offense was committed or attempted, or, if these objects no longer exist, their value or price, may be confiscated by court sentence in favor of the Treasury. The person who is found guilty under paragraph 1 may by court sentence be deprived of his right to practice a profession for a definite period or permanently.

SECTION 5. This law shall take effect immediately.

It is hereby publicly proclaimed.

Ministry of Commerce, Industry, and Shipping, December 11, 1940.

H. HENDRIKSEN

Law No. 254 concerning the Prohibition of Certain Demonstrations, June 9, 1941[5]

Pursuant to Section 2 of temporary Law No. 219 of May 1, 1940, relating to increasing penalties for certain violations of the penal code, and concerning amendments to the police regulations, it is hereby ordered:

Demonstrations, by word or act, which are apt to injure relations with foreign military forces, which according to agreement with the Danish Government are in this country, are punishable by fine, detention, or imprisonment up to two years, if they are not subject to more severe punishment by other legislation.

This law shall take effect immediately.

It is hereby publicly proclaimed.

Ministry of Justice, June 9, 1941.

HARALD PETERSEN

Law No. 349 concerning the Prohibition of Communistic Associations and Communistic Activities, August 22, 1941[6]

[EXCERPTS]

We, Christian the Tenth, by the grace of God King of Denmark and Iceland, of the Vandals and Goths, Duke of Slesvig, Holstein, Stormann,

[5] *Lovtidenden-A*, No. 36, June 9, 1941. [6] *Ibid.*, No. 54, August 23, 1941.

Dytmarshen, Lauenborg, and Oldenborg, promulgate . . .; the Rigsdag has passed and We with Our consent have confirmed the following law:

SECTION 1. All communist organizations and associations are prohibited, and existing communistic organizations and associations shall immediately be dissolved.

Communistic activities or propaganda of any kind are prohibited. This applies regardless of whether there is any affiliation with another organization.

Violation of the present regulation shall be punished by fine, detention, or imprisonment up to eight years.

SECTION 2. Persons whose conduct has given special reason for the presumption that they intend to take part in communistic activities or propaganda may, in accordance with the decision of the Minister of Justice or with his approval, be taken into custody when it is deemed necessary for the sake of the security of the state or of its relations with foreign states.

Whoever is taken into custody pursuant to paragraph 1 shall within twenty-four hours be brought before the City Court of Copenhagen, which shall decide whether the accused person shall continue to be held in custody. The request concerning the continuance of custody must be acted upon when the decision or approval of the Minister of Justice is obtained, unless it can be presumed that an obvious mistake has been made regarding the identity or previous participation in communistic activity or propaganda of the person in question.

If within twenty-four hours it proves impossible to bring before the City Court of Copenhagen the person who has been taken into custody, he should within the same period be brought before a judge of a lower court, which shall receive his explanations. Decision concerning custody shall also be rendered in such cases as soon as possible by the City Court of Copenhagen.

After the decision of the City Court the person who has been taken into custody, as well as the public authorities, may appeal to the Supreme Court. Appeal by the public authorities shall stay the proceedings.

Custody shall cease as soon as it is no longer deemed necessary for the security of the state or of its relations with foreign states. Decision in regard thereto shall be made by the Minister of Justice.

The Minister of Justice shall report every third month to a committee created by one of the two chambers of the Rigsdag concerning those persons who have been taken into custody in the preceding period, in accordance with the above decisions, indicating the reason for which they have been taken into custody.

SECTION 3. Property which may belong to communistic organizations and associations, as well as archives, protocols, and similar material belonging to them shall be taken over by the public authorities.

SECTION 4. This law, which does not apply to the Faroes,[7] shall take effect immediately.

All concerned shall observe this law. Given at Amalienborg, August 22, 1941.

Under Our Royal Hand and Seal

CHRISTIAN R.

E. THUNE JACOBSEN

[7] Occupied by the British.—ED.

ENGLISH CHANNEL ISLANDS

Order concerning the Laws Applicable to the English Channel Islands, August 23, 1940 [1]

By virtue of the powers vested in me by the Führer and Supreme Commander of the Armed Forces, I hereby order as follows:

SECTION 1. The general orders issued or to be issued by the Supreme Commander of the Army for the area of the Chief Command of the Military Administration in France are applicable, by way of analogy, to the occupied English Channel Islands.

SECTION 2. This order shall take effect as of the day of publication.

On behalf of the Supreme Commander of the Army:

THE CHIEF OF THE MILITARY ADMINISTRATION IN FRANCE

[1] *Verordnungsblatt für die besetzten französischen Gebiete*, No. 6, August 27, 1940, p. 72.

FRANCE

I. ALSACE-LORRAINE

Regulation concerning Provisional Rearrangement of the Evangelical Church Organization in Lorraine, September 28, 1940 [1]

The Reformed and Lutheran Church congregations of Lorraine are consolidated with the Palatine Provincial Church (United Protestant Evangelical Christian Church of the Palatinate) in such wise that the powers of the Reformed Synod in Alsace-Lorraine and of the Directorium of the Church of the Augsburg Confession in Alsace-Lorraine pass to the Council of the Protestant Provincial Church of the Palatinate.

Saarbrücken, September 28, 1940.

BUERCKEL, *Gauleiter and Reich Governor*
Chief of the Civil Administration in Lorraine

Order in regard to Private Schools, December 6, 1940 [2]

In order to assure the uniform institution of National Socialist schooling for youth, as well as adaptation to the school system of the Reich, I issue, by virtue of the powers bestowed upon me by the Führer, the following order to become effective immediately:

1. All private schools and school camps shall be closed. The continuation, change of ownership, or opening of private teaching institutions, as well as the giving of any kind of private instruction (e.g., domestic science lessons, sewing lessons, etc.) shall be conditional upon permission of the school administration in Metz.

2. All buildings which have hitherto been used for schools shall be reserved for that purpose. Owners are forbidden to dispose of such quarters and buildings without the permission of the school administration in Metz.

3. Where religious bodies have hitherto exercised any sort of school supervision, such supervision shall cease. School supervision over all departments shall lie solely in the hands of the state school supervision authorities.

Saarbrücken, December 6, 1940.

Chief of the Civil Administration in Lorraine
By deputy: BARTH

[1] *Verordnungsblatt für Lothringen*, 1940, No. 88, p. 69.
[2] *Ibid.*, 1940, No. 273, p. 440.

Order concerning Compulsory Schooling in Lorraine (Compulsory Schooling Order), February 14, 1941 [3]

[EXCERPTS]

By virtue of the powers bestowed upon me by the Führer, I order:

SECTION I

1. *General Compulsory Schooling.* (1) There shall be general compulsory schooling in Lorraine. It will assure the training and instruction of youth in the spirit of National Socialism.

(2) The requirement as to compulsory schooling shall be discharged by attendance at a German school. Any exceptions that may be made shall be by decision of the school supervision authorities.

. . . . .

12. *Forced Attendance.* Children and youths who do not discharge the obligation to attend elementary and vocational schools shall be taken to school by compulsion. The help of the police may be enlisted for this purpose.

. . . . .

Saarbrücken, February 14, 1941.

BUERCKEL
Chief of the Civil Administration in Lorraine

Regulation for Implementation of the Order concerning Compulsory Schooling, February 14, 1941 [4]

[EXCERPT]

By virtue of paragraph 14 of the order concerning compulsory schooling of February 14, 1941 (*VBl.*, p. 100), I order:

1. *With respect to paragraph 1:*

(1) The requirement of compulsory schooling shall apply only to children and youths from families of German nationals and of the local population in Lorraine of German or related blood; foreigners and stateless persons shall not be subject to compulsory schooling, unless it has been otherwise agreed with respect to foreigners by international treaty. The admissibility of voluntary school attendance by foreigners and stateless persons is not hereby prejudiced. Foreigners or stateless persons are persons who are not Reich Germans and do not belong to the local population of Lorraine of German or

[3] *Verordnungsblatt*, 1941, No. 87, p. 100.
[4] *Ibid.*, 1941, No. 92, p. 107.

related blood (Lorrainers). Membership in the local Alsace or Luxemburg population is equivalent to membership in the population of Lorraine.

. . . .

Saarbrücken, February 14, 1941.

Chief of the Civil Administration in Lorraine
By deputy: BARTH

Order concerning the Elementary School System in Lorraine, February 14, 1941 [5]

[EXCERPTS]

By virtue of the powers bestowed upon me by the Führer, I order:

1. (1) The elementary schools in Lorraine are public.

(2) The obligation to attend an elementary school shall be regulated by the order concerning compulsory schooling of February 14, 1941 (*VBl.*, p. 100).

2. School fees shall not be charged in the public elementary schools.

3. The elementary schools are German community schools.

4. (1) Every city and town community shall be a school district.

(2) Several communities or parts thereof may be united in one school association, in so far as the interests of the schools may require. The association of schools shall be a legal entity of public law.

(3) Changes in or creation of new school districts and of school associations shall be within the jurisdiction of the Chief of Civil Administration.

. . . .

6. Every school shall have a Principal; the Superintendent's Office shall name the Principal's Deputy.

7. The Principal's Office shall order all measures which may be necessary for the functioning of the school and, the maintenance of order according to the regulations in force.

8. (1) The Chief of Civil Administration is the Superintendent of Schools.

(2) In the districts the supervision of the schools shall be entrusted to school offices (District School Office, City School Office). The District School Office shall consist of the District Chief and the Council for Schools.

: : : :

21. In regard to private schools, the order of December 6, 1940 (*VBl.*, p. 440), shall not be affected by this order.

. . . .

Saarbrücken, February 14, 1941.

BUERCKEL
Chief of the Civil Administration in Lorraine

[5] *Verordnungsblatt*, 1941, No. 88, p. 102.

Announcement for the Execution of the Order concerning the Elementary School System, February 14, 1941[6]

[EXCERPTS]

By virtue of paragraph 23 of the order concerning the elementary school system of February 14, 1941 (*VBl.*, p. 102), I order:

1. *With respect to paragraph 1:*

Private elementary and primary schools are closed by virtue of the order of December 6, 1940 (*VBl.*, p. 440). New private elementary and primary schools may not be opened. The extent to which exceptions may be made for individual students to receive private instruction in the subjects of the elementary schools will be determined in accordance with the order concerning compulsory schooling of February 14, 1941 (*VBl.*, p. 100), and the implementation regulation of the same date (*VBl.*, p. 107).

2. *With respect to paragraph 3:*

(1) The language of instruction is German.

(2) Clergymen are required to have my consent to give religious instruction. The consent will be withheld if the clergyman or his wife is not of German or related blood or if he is unsuitable as an educator. The consent may be revoked at any time if it later becomes apparent that the prerequisites for consent are not fulfilled.

3. *With respect to paragraph 4:*

The existing district divisions will be maintained except where changes have been authorized in particular cases.

4. (1) Only educationally suitable persons of German or related blood may be teachers in the public elementary schools.

(2) Cloistral teaching personnel will be eliminated.

(3) Teachers who are eliminated by virtue of subsection 1 or 2 may be granted by the Chief of the Civil Administration a retirement salary or other acceptable settlement with the waiver of legal action.

5. *With respect to paragraphs 6 and 7:*

(1) The objective of the school director is an educational fellowship of the teaching staff and students of the school molded to conform with the spirit of National Socialism. It is the task of the director to orient and conduct the school systematically according to National Socialist principles.

. . . . .

6. *With respect to paragraph 8:*

(1) The school supervision includes the state direction, promotion, and superintendence of the public elementary school system.

(2) School supervision is exclusively a state supervision; where supervision has been hitherto exercised by other authorities, particularly by representatives of religious creeds, such supervision shall cease. State

[6] *Verordnungsblatt*, 1941, No. 93, p. 109.

supervision extends also to religious instruction, regardless of whether it is given by clerical or lay teachers. The national political attitude of these teachers and their educational suitability in other respects are also to be watched. . . . . .

(4) The school supervision must be actuated by the spirit of National Socialism in all its work. It must in an even more comprehensive way than the directorship lead, promote, act as example, and feel responsible for, the continued general development of the elementary school system in its district. . . . . .

Saarbrücken, February 14, 1941.

Chief of the Civil Administration in Lorraine
By deputy: BARTH

II. OCCUPIED FRANCE[6a]

1. ADMINISTRATION

Announcement concerning General Orders Issued by the German Military Commanders, May 10, 1940[7]

Attention is called to the fact that, for the duration of the occupation. the Military Commanders may issue rules and general orders for their respective command areas which shall have the force of laws. Full familiarity with these rules and orders is therefore of the utmost importance for any resident of the country. They are issued in the *Verordnungsblatt für das besetzte Gebiet der französischen Departements Seine, Seine-et-Oise und Seine-et-Marne*, published by the Military Commander of Paris, and in part they are likewise issued in the form of posters. The rules and orders will also be discussed in the radio and press.

The general orders and regulations issued by the German Military Commanders take precedence over the law of the land. Local law not in conflict with these orders and regulations remains in force unless incompatible with the purposes of the occupation.

Failure to comply with the orders and regulations issued by the German Military Commanders cannot be justified by ignorance or conflicting local statutes.

[6a] As to Northern France; see also documents under Belgium.
[7] *Verordnungsblatt für das besetzte Gebiet der französischen Departements Seine, Seine-et-Oise und Seine-et-Marne*, No. 3, June 21, 1940, p. 13.

Order concerning the Withdrawal of French War Measures against German Property in France within the Jurisdiction of the German Military Governor of Paris [8]

For the area subject to my command, embracing the departments of Seine, Seine-et-Oise, and Seine-et-Marne, I hereby order:

ARTICLE 1. All French orders of seizure and any other extraordinary measures taken by French authorities against German property, rights, and interests (such as the decree of September 1, 1939, *Journal Officiel*, No. 309, September 4, 1939) are hereby withdrawn.

ARTICLE 2. The Chief of the Military Administration will safeguard all German interests affected by these measures. He will issue all rules and regulations necessary to attain this objective.

THE MILITARY COMMANDER OF PARIS

Order concerning the Preservation of Works of Art in the Occupied Territory of France, July 15, 1940 [9]

[EXCERPTS]

In order to protect works of art in the occupied territory of France against damage or theft I order, by virtue of the authority vested in me by the Führer and Supreme Commander of the Armed Forces, as follows:

SECTION 1. Movable works of art (chattels) may not be removed from their present situs or changed in any manner without the written authorization by a ranking officer of the Military Administration.

SECTION 2. Legal transactions involving the transfer or sale of movable works of art shall be invalid unless my consent is obtained; the same applies to orders of courts or other authorities involving the transfer of movable objects of art.

SECTION 3. [Owners or possessors of such objects of art worth more than 100,000 francs shall be required to register them with the field commander's office, giving all details about value, age, origin, etc.] [10]

SECTION 4. [The owners or possessors of works of art shall be under the duty of carefully preserving them.] [11]

. . . . .

On behalf of the Supreme Commander of the Army:

THE CHIEF OF THE MILITARY ADMINISTRATION IN FRANCE

[8] *Verordnungsblatt für das besetzte Gebiet der französischen Departements Seine, Seine-et-Oise und Seine-et-Marne*, No. 2, June 21, 1940, p. 9.

[9] *Verordnungsblatt für die besetzten französischen Gebiete*, No. 3, July 15, 1940, p. 49.

[10] Summary by the translator.

[11] Summary by the translator.

Rules and regulations of September 8, 1940, implementing Sections 4 and 5 of the above order, provide that the field commanders shall ascertain whether the works of art are kept

Order concerning the Prohibition of the Use of Certain French Textbooks, August 10, 1940 [12]

By virtue of the authority vested in me by the Führer and Supreme Commander of the Armed Forces, I hereby order as follows:

SECTION 1. The use of the school textbooks enumerated in the Appendix in any French school in the occupied territory is prohibited because they contain unjustifiable attacks on the German people and its armed forces.

SECTION 2. The unsold copies of these texts shall be seized and destroyed.

SECTION 3. This order shall take effect as of the day of publication.

SECTION 4. Any instructor who uses prohibited textbooks for purposes of instruction shall be liable to imprisonment for a period not exceeding one year and/or fines.

On behalf of the Supreme Commander of the Army:

THE CHIEF OF THE MILITARY ADMINISTRATION IN FRANCE

APPENDIX TO THE ORDER CONCERNING THE PROHIBITION OF THE USE OF FRENCH SCHOOL TEXTBOOKS, OF AUGUST 30, 1940

I. Brossolette: *Histoire de France.* Cours Moyen-Certificat d'Etudes. Paris, 1937, Librairie Delagrave, 15, rue Soufflot.

II. Guillemain et L'Abbé Le Ster: *Histoire de France.* Cours Préparatoire. Paris, 1936, Librairie "L'Ecole," 11, rue de Sèvres.

III. M. Guibaud: *Histoire de France.* Cours Préparatoire. Paris, 1934. J. de Gigord, Editeur, 15, rue Cassette.

IV. A. Lechevalier: *Précis historique de la Guerre de 1914.* Cours Moyen-Supérieur. Le Havre, Librairie Delahaye, 16, rue Thiers.

Order against Unauthorized Crossing of the Frontiers and Military Barriers of the Occupied French Territory and concerning Export, Import, and Transport of Goods, April 28, 1941 [13]

[EXCERPT]

By virtue of the powers conferred on me by the Führer and Supreme Commander of the Armed Forces, I order the following:

SECTION 1. (1) Punishment by imprisonment or hard labor will be imposed, except in so far as other regulations have provided for a more severe penalty, upon anyone:

---

safely and carefully preserved and whether the rooms in which they are kept are safely locked. Persons charged with inspection shall need no written authority for entering these rooms. *Verordnungsblatt für die besetzten französischen Gebiete,* No. 8, 1940, p. 88.

[12] *Verordnungsblatt für die besetzten französischen Gebiete,* No. 7, September 16, 1940, p. 79.

[13] *Verordnungsblatt des Militärbefehlshabers in Frankreich,* 1941, p. 260.

1. Who crosses without authority the frontiers of the occupied territory or the posted military barriers in this territory.
2. Who exports goods out of this territory or transports them through this territory without the permission of the military commander in France or an authority empowered by him to grant this permission.

(2) In cases of less gravity or of negligence a sentence of imprisonment up to six weeks or a fine may be imposed.

(3) The attempt to commit the acts specified shall likewise be punishable.

SECTION 2. (1) Exceptions to the necessity for permission, and permits outstanding at the time when this order becomes effective, shall not be affected thereby.

(2) The military commander in France reserves the right to issue further regulations concerning the export, import, and transport of goods.

SECTION 3. (1) The goods concerned in the criminal act defined in Section 1 and the transport equipment which the perpetrator has used in committing the act may be confiscated, even when they do not belong to the perpetrator or an accomplice.

(2) If the confiscation of the goods is not possible, the confiscation of an amount of equivalent value may be imposed (equivalent confiscation).

(3) If the punishment of any individual is not possible, confiscation of goods or equivalent confiscation may be independently imposed.

SECTION 4. (1) This order shall become effective upon its publication.

. . . . .

THE MILITARY COMMANDER IN FRANCE

Order for the Preservation of Labor Peace, November 6, 1941 [14]

[EXCERPTS]

By virtue of the powers conferred on me by the Führer and Supreme Commander of the Armed Forces, I order the following:

SECTION 1. Anyone who injures German interests connected with the occupation by the suspension of work without legal dissolution of the employment relationship, by locking out workmen, by influencing others to discontinue work or to lock out workmen, or by disturbing the labor peace in any other way, will be punished by hard labor, imprisonment, or fine. A fine may also be imposed in addition to hard labor or imprisonment.

In grave cases the death penalty may be imposed.

. . . . .

This order shall become effective upon its publication.

THE MILITARY COMMANDER IN FRANCE

[14] *Verordnungsblatt des Militärbefehlshabers in Frankreich*, 1941, p. 320.

Order concerning Medical Treatment for Members of the Armed Forces, February 5, 1942 [15]

By virtue of the powers conferred upon me by the Führer and Supreme Commander of the Armed Forces, I order the following:

SECTION 1. (1) Medical practitioners (physicians, dentists, nature-healers, male and female nurses, etc.) who are not in the service of the German armed forces are forbidden to give medical treatment to members of the German armed forces or to members of auxiliary services who are German nationals.

(2) The following are not forbidden: (*a*) the giving of medical first aid in emergencies; (*b*) treatment authorized by written permission from a German medical officer.

SECTION 2. Anyone who violates the prohibition of Section 1 shall be punished with imprisonment and fine, or with one of these penalties.

SECTION 3. This order shall become effective upon its publication.

THE MILITARY COMMANDER IN FRANCE

2. LAW AND COURTS

Order concerning the Administration of Justice in the Occupied Territory, July 23, 1940 [16]

By virtue of the authority vested in me by the Führer and Supreme Commander of the Armed Forces, I hereby order as follows:

SECTION 1. French public agencies charged with the prosecution of crimes are required to submit to the nearest German military court all reports, depositions, and records of every description involving:

a) Crimes committed against the German armed forces, their members, or persons affiliated with the armed forces.

b) Crimes committed in buildings, rooms, establishments, or ships in the service of the German armed forces.

c) Violations of orders and regulations enacted in the territory occupied by the German armed forces for the security of the German armed forces or for the achievement of the purposes of the occupation.

The military court may refer the matter back if the public interest does not warrant prosecution by the military court.

SECTION 2. French authorities charged with prosecution of crimes are re-

[15] *Verordnungsblatt des Militärbefehlshabers in Frankreich*, 1942, p. 343.
[16] *Verordnungsblatt für die besetzten französischen Gebiete*, No. 5, July 29, 1940, p. 59.

quired, on request by German military courts, to execute judgments carrying terms of imprisonment against persons other than German citizens.

For the Supreme Commander of the Army:

THE CHIEF OF MILITARY ADMINISTRATION

Order concerning the Authority of the District Commanders in the Occupied Territory of France to Exercise Summary Penal Jurisdiction, September 10, 1940 [17]

By virtue of the authority vested in me by the Führer and Supreme Commander of the Armed Forces, I hereby order as follows:

SECTION 1. District Commanders in the occupied territory of France may issue orders for summary punishment of persons not subject to the Military Penal Code.

In areas not under the command of a District Commander a field commander is vested with the authority mentioned in the preceding paragraph.

SECTION 2. Violations may be punished by orders for summary punishment provided that the facts are sufficiently ascertained and if, according to the degree of guilt of the perpetrator and the consequences of his act, this form of procedure seems sufficient.

SECTION 3. Any commander may issue such an order in whose command area the punishable act has been committed or the perpetrator is present or apprehended.

SECTION 4. By such order the following punishment may be imposed:

1. Imprisonment for a period not exceeding six weeks.
2. Fines not exceeding 30,000 Reichsmarks, and, if the fine cannot be levied, imprisonment in lieu of the fine for a period not exceeding six weeks.

SECTION 5. The written order of punishment shall specify:

1. The first and family names, occupation, and residence of the accused.
2. The criminal act.
3. The criminal law applicable.
4. The evidence.
5. Notice that the accused may lodge an appeal within twenty-four hours with the commander issuing the order.

SECTION 6. The summary order is to be issued immediately after a hearing, to be served on the accused, and to be executed at once.

SECTION 7. The issuance of a summary order for punishment does not preclude prosecution or trial for a serious crime or a felony. Where punish-

[17] *Verordnungsblatt für die besetzten französischen Gebiete*, No. 8, September 23, 1940, p. 86.

ment has already been imposed by the order, the subsequent sentence of a court shall be mitigated accordingly.

SECTION 8. The accused may lodge an appeal with the commander issuing the order within twenty-four hours after service on him of the order. Unless the commander considers the appeal well taken, the superior of the commander shall decide on the appeal.

SECTION 9. The superior officer authorized to pass on the appeal may:

1. Affirm the order for summary punishment.
2. Withdraw the order and issue instead another order for punishment from which no further appeal lies.
3. Withdraw the order and suspend the proceedings.

SECTION 10. The immediate execution of a summary order for punishment is not stayed by filing an appeal.

On behalf of the Supreme Commander of the Army:

THE CHIEF OF THE MILITARY ADMINISTRATION IN FRANCE

Order concerning Protection against Acts of Sabotage, October 10, 1940 [18]

By virtue of the authority vested in me by the Führer and Supreme Commander of the Armed Forces, I hereby order as follows:

SECTION 1. Any person who willfully fails to fufill or insufficiently fulfills an order to stand guard issued to him by the Chief of the Military Administration or by anyone authorized by him to issue such orders, shall be subject to the death penalty.

SECTION 2. Any person who hides or shelters prisoners of war who have escaped or prisoners of war who do not have a certificate of discharge or a pass for leave, shall be subject to the death penalty.

SECTION 3. In less serious violations of Sections 1 and 2 of this order, and in the case of negligent violations, the person found guilty shall be subject to hard labor or imprisonment.

SECTION 4. This order shall take effect as of the time of its broadcast by radio.[19]

On behalf of the Supreme Commander of the Army:

THE CHIEF OF THE MILITARY ADMINISTRATION IN FRANCE

[18] *Verordnungsblatt für die besetzten französischen Gebiete,* No. 11, October 17, 1940, p. 108.
[19] Note on page 108 of the official Gazette: The broadcast by radio took place on October 15, 1940, at 9:30 p.m.

3. ECONOMY AND FINANCE[19a]

Second Order concerning Provisional Regulation of Monetary Exchange between the Occupied French Territory and the Reich and Foreign Countries respectively (Second Provisional Foreign Exchange Order), August 14, 1940[20]

By virtue of the powers vested in me by the Führer and Supreme Commander of the Armed Forces, I hereby order as follows:

SECTION 1. Within the occupied territory it is forbidden:

1. To assign or otherwise transfer claims of residents abroad against residents of the occupied territory; or
2. To assign or otherwise transfer claims of residents of the occupied territory against residents abroad; or
3. To assign or otherwise transfer claims of one resident of the occupied territory against another on behalf or for the benefit of persons residing abroad; or
4. To acquire, transfer, mortgage, remit, or in any other manner convey to another person any currency or money other than French legal tender, which prohibition shall not apply to certificates and coins of the Reich Credit Institutes (*Reichskreditkassen*) and German small coins in the denominations of 1, 2, 5 and 10 Pfennig, Reichspfennig and Rentenpfennig; or
5. To deal in negotiable instruments, stocks, bonds, and similar documents, issued in a country other than France, the French Colonies, Protectorates, or African Mandates.

SECTION 2. The prohibitions contained in Section 1, numbers 1 and 2, shall not apply to:

a) Members of the German armed forces.
b) German citizens present in the occupied French territory under orders, or by permission, of the German authorities.

SECTION 3. The prohibitions contained in the order concerning the provisional regulation of monetary exchange between the occupied French territory and the Reich and foreign countries, respectively (Provisional Order concerning Foreign Exchange), of May 10, 1940, and the prohibitions in this order shall not apply to the Reich Credit Institutes.

SECTION 4. The provisions of Sections 3, 4, and 6 of the Provisional Order concerning Foreign Exchange of May 10, 1940, shall likewise be applicable to prohibitions contained in this order.

SECTION 5. The Offices of the Supreme Commander of the Army, the Reich Credit Institutes, and the Commando France for the Protection of Holdings of Foreign Exchange (*Devisenschutzkommando Frankreich*) may request from any person information and reports referring directly or indirectly to conditions, transactions, or acts pertaining to the regulation of

[19a] See also order concerning Reich Credit Institutes, above, p. 329.
[20] *Verordnungsblatt für die besetzten französischen Gebiete*, No. 6, August 27, 1940, p. 67.

foreign exchange which are made illegal by the Provisional Order concerning Foreign Exchange of May 10, 1940, by the order concerning sequestration in the occupied territories of the Netherlands, Belgium, Luxemburg, and France (Sequestration Order) of May 20, 1940,[21] and by this order. The production of books of account and other documents, as well as personal appearance of persons bound to give information, may be demanded.

SECTION 6. The Commando France for the Protection of Holdings of Foreign Exchange may take any and all action required to insure compliance with the Provisional Order concerning Foreign Exchange of May 10, 1940, with the Sequestration Order of May 20, 1940, and with this order.

SECTION 7. For action taken by virtue of the Provisional Order concerning Foreign Exchange of May 10, 1940, and of this order, and of rules and regulations implementing them, no indemnity shall be granted.

SECTION 8. Section 5 of the Provisional Order concerning Foreign Exchange of May 10, 1940, is hereby declared to be no longer in effect.

SECTION 9. (1) Violations of the Provisional Order concerning Foreign Exchange of May 10, 1940, and of this order are punishable by imprisonment or, in especially grave instances, by hard labor for a period not exceeding ten years. In addition, fines may be imposed and forfeiture of the exchange involved in the crime declared. Attempts to commit any of the acts thus made punishable are likewise punishable.

(2) Negligent violations are punishable by fines, and, if the fine is not paid, by imprisonment. The same shall apply to any person who violates or fails to comply in time or in full with any order issued by the offices of the Supreme Commander of the Army or the Commando France for the Protection of Holdings of Foreign Exchange issued by virtue of the Provisional Order concerning Foreign Exchange of May 10, 1940, of the Sequestration Order of May 20, 1940, or of this order.

(3) Section 1 shall apply to any person who intentionally invites or incites to, or offers himself for, the commission of any act made punishable by this order.

SECTION 10. (1) The foreign exchange involved in the crimes may be declared forfeited to the Military Administration, whether or not owned by the perpetrator or his accessories.

(2) If forfeiture of the foreign exchange is impossible, forfeiture of a corresponding amount of money may be declared (secondary forfeiture).

(3) If the perpetrator cannot be found or a definite person be prosecuted, forfeiture or secondary forfeiture may be declared without having an accused brought to trial.

SECTION 11. Persons accused of violating the Provisional Order concerning Foreign Exchange of May 10, 1940, and this order shall be tried by courts of the armed forces.

[21] See that order in the collection of documents on Belgium, above, p. 321.—ED.

SECTION 12. This order shall take effect as of the date of publication.

Paris, August 14, 1940.

On behalf of the Supreme Commander of the Army:

THE CHIEF OF THE MILITARY ADMINISTRATION IN FRANCE

Order concerning the Contribution of Goods and Services, January 31, 1942 [22]

By virtue of the powers conferred on me by the Führer and Supreme Commander of the Armed Forces, I order as follows:

SECTION 1. (1) Anyone who fails to make contributions of goods or services levied upon him by the Military Commander in France or by an authority empowered by the latter to make levies, or who complies in such a way as to vitiate or jeopardize the purpose of the contributions, shall be punished by hard labor, imprisonment, or fine. A fine may also be imposed in addition to hard labor or imprisonment.

(2) In grave cases the death penalty may be imposed.

SECTION 2. The same punishment shall be imposed upon anyone who interferes with another in the making of such contributions or in any other way vitiates or jeopardizes the contributions of another.

SECTION 3. This order shall become effective upon its publication.

THE MILITARY COMMANDER IN FRANCE

Order concerning the Suspension of Enterprises, February 25, 1942 [23]

By virtue of the powers conferred on me by the Führer and Supreme Commander of the Armed Forces, I order the following:

SECTION 1. If economic conditions, particularly the supply of raw materials and equipment, should so require, industrial enterprises and plants may be suspended in whole or in part.

SECTION 2. The suspension shall be announced by the field commander in a written instruction addressed to the enterprise or plant.

SECTION 3. Enterprises and plants may not receive deliveries of raw materials or equipment while they are thus suspended.

Concerning the disposition of raw materials and equipment on hand in enterprises and plants at the time of suspension, the decision shall be made by the director of the competent industrial products office.

[22] *Verordnungsblatt des Militärbefehlshabers in Frankreich,* 1942, p. 338.
[23] *Ibid.,* 1942, p. 348.

SECTION 4. Any loss resulting from the application of this order shall form no basis for a claim to compensation or settlement.

SECTION 5. Anyone who with intent or by negligence violates this order or regulations made on the basis of this order shall be punished by imprisonment and fine or by one of these penalties. In addition, the raw materials and equipment on hand in the enterprise or plant may be confiscated.

SECTION 6. This order shall become effective upon its publication.

THE MILITARY COMMANDER IN FRANCE

4. GENOCIDE LEGISLATION

Order concerning Measures against the Jews, September 27, 1940 [24]

By virtue of the authority vested in me by the Führer and Supreme Commander of the Armed Forces, I hereby order as follows:

SECTION 1. In the occupied territory any person will be considered a Jew who is or has been a member of the Jewish faith or who has more than two Jewish grandparents. Grandparents are to be considered as Jewish if they are or have been members of the Jewish faith.

SECTION 2. Jews who have fled from the occupied territory are forbidden to return to the same.[25]

SECTION 3. Not later than October 20, 1940, every Jew shall be required to apply to the Subprefect (*Sous-préfet*) of the district (*arrondissement*) in which he has his residence or usually lives, for registration in the Register of Jews. Application by the head of a family shall be considered sufficient for all members of the family.

SECTION 4. Any business, that is, any enterprise conducted for purposes of profit, whose owners or lessees are Jews, must be designated as a Jewish business in the German and French languages.

SECTION 5. The residents of the Jewish religious communities shall be required to submit, on request, to the French authorities, any evidentiary documents which may be material to the enforcement of this order.

SECTION 6. Violations of this order will be punishable by imprisonment and/or fine. In addition, forfeiture of the property of the violator may be ordered.

SECTION 7. This order shall take effect as of the day of publication.

On behalf of the Supreme Commander of the Army:

THE CHIEF OF THE MILITARY ADMINISTRATION IN FRANCE

[24] *Verordnungsblatt für die besetzten französischen Gebiete*, No. 9, September 30, 1940, p. 92.
[25] A similar prohibition of return was enacted for Belgian Jews.—ED.

Second Order concerning Measures against Jews, October 18, 1940[26]

By virtue of the authority vested in me by the Führer and Supreme Commander of the Armed Forces, I hereby order as follows:

SECTION 1. "Economic enterprise," as used in this order, means any enterprise conducted for the purpose of taking a direct part in the production, processing, exchange, distribution, or administration of goods, regardless of the legal form in which the business may be conducted and regardless of whether or not registration of the business is required. Included are banks, insurance companies, law offices, and offices of notaries public, official brokers in negotiable instruments, and real estate companies.

An enterprise is considered Jewish if the owners or lessees are:

a) Jewish, or
b) A partnership with one Jewish partner,
c) A limited partnership in which more than one third of the partners are Jewish or in which more than one-third of the shares are owned by Jewish partners, or in which the manager is a Jew or more than one third of the board of trustees are Jews, or
d) Corporations in which the president of the board of directors or managing officer is a Jew or in which more than one third of the board of directors are Jews.

An enterprise is also to be considered Jewish if the prefect having jurisdiction in that area serves notice on that enterprise that it is predominantly under Jewish control.

SECTION 2. Jewish economic enterprises or those economic enterprises which have been Jewish since May 23, 1940, are to be registered not later than October 31, 1940, with the subprefect having jurisdiction, or in Paris with the prefect of the police. Registration shall take place by the authority of the jurisdiction within which natural persons have their residence, and where corporations have their place of business. The same applies to Jewish economic enterprises which have their residence outside of the occupied territory for that part of the enterprise which is carried on within the occupied territory.

Enterprises designated as Jewish by virtue of subsection *c* of Section 1 are not subject to registration.

The application for registration must specify:

a) Name, seat, and owner or lessee of the enterprise. Facts must be stated by virtue of which the enterprise is, or since May 23, 1940, has been, Jewish.
b) In the case of enterprises which are no longer Jewish, the transactions by which the Jewish character has been ended.
c) The kind of enterprise according to the goods distributed, produced, or administered, stating the main article.

[26] *Verordnungsblatt für die besetzten französischen Gebiete*, No. 12, October 20, 1940, p. 112.

d) Branches, shops, and accessory plants.
e) The turnover according to the latest income tax report.
f) The value of the inventory, the raw material on hand, the real estate held, and the amount of cash on hand.

SECTION 3. All Jewish economic enterprises, all Jews and spouses of Jews, all corporations which are not engaged in economic activity and have more than one third Jews among their members or in the management, are required to register not later than October 31, 1940, with the subprefect, or in Paris with the police prefect:

a) Shares of stock or shares of partnership, "silent" participations in economic enterprises, and loans to economic enterprises which they hold either as owners or pledgees.
b) Their real estate holdings and their rights in real estate.

Application for registration must be filed with the authority in the district in which the enterprise is functioning, has its place of business, or where the realty held or mortgaged is situated.

SECTION 4. Legal transactions entered into at any time after May 23, 1940, and involving the property of persons designated in Section 3, may be declared void by the Chief of the Military Administration in France.

SECTION 5. An administrating trustee may be appointed for any Jewish economic enterprise. The provisions contained in the order concerning the administration of businesses of May 20, 1940 (*VBl.*, p. 31), are made applicable.

Section 1 of the order concerning the administration of businesses remains in force as to Jewish economic enterprises.

SECTION 6. Violations of Sections 2 and 3 are punishable with imprisonment and/or fine. In addition, the assets of enterprises which have not been registered and the rights and choses in action subject to registration according to Section 3 which have not been registered, may be declared forfeited.

SECTION 7. This order shall take effect as of the day of publication.

On behalf of the Supreme Commander of the Army:

THE CHIEF OF THE MILITARY ADMINISTRATION IN FRANCE

Sixth Order concerning Measures against Jews, February 7, 1942 [27]

By virtue of the powers conferred upon me by the Führer and Supreme Commander of the Armed Forces, I order the following:

SECTION 1. *Curfew Restriction.* Jews are forbidden to stay outside their dwellings between 8 p. m. and 6 a. m.

[27] *Verordnungsblatt des Militärbefehlshabers in Frankreich,* 1942, p. 340.

SECTION 2. *Prohibition on Moving.* Jews are forbidden to move from their present places of residence to other places.

SECTION 3. *Imposition of Penalties.* Anyone who violates the provisions of this order shall be punished by imprisonment and fine or by one of those penalties. In addition, assignment to a concentration camp may be imposed.

SECTION 4. *Effective Date.* This order shall become effective upon its publication.

THE MILITARY COMMANDER IN FRANCE

III. ITALIAN ZONE

Law concerning Provisions for the Administration of Justice in the Metropolitan Enemy Territories in the West Occupied by the Armed Forces and for the Extension of Customs Laws to Those Territories, December 5, 1940 [28]

[EXCERPTS]

Victor Emmanuel III, by the grace of God and by the will of the nation King of Italy and of Albania, Emperor of Ethiopia.

. . . . .

ARTICLE 1. Following the occupation of the metropolitan enemy territories in the west by the armed forces of the State, the military occupation authorities may provide that trials for offenses committed by inhabitants of the occupied territories be referred to the Court of Assizes in Turin, and that appeals from civil or criminal sentences pronounced by the judicial authorities of the occupied territories be referred to the Court of Appeals of Turin or to the Supreme Court of the Kingdom.

In such cases the Supreme Court of the Kingdom, the Court of Appeals of Turin, and the Court of Assizes of Turin are invested with the jurisdictional authority proper to the trial of such cases or appeals. The Italian rules for judicial proceedings are to be observed in regard to the form of processes before these judicial authorities of the Kingdom.

ARTICLE 2. The military occupation authorities may order the extension to the metropolitan enemy territories occupied by the State's armed forces of the legislative rules and regulations in force in the Kingdom in regard to customs, including those relative to import and export duties and to imposts which are in any way applicable upon goods imported into the Kingdom or exported from it.

[28] *Leggi e Decreti*, 1940, No. 1832, p. 7434. Published in the *Gazzetta ufficiale*, January 20, 1941, No. 15.

In this case the Minister of Finance is empowered to issue decrees regulating the tariffs to be levied on the movement of goods between the territory of the Kingdom and the metropolitan enemy territory occupied by the armed forces of the State, in conjunction with the regulations issued by the occupation authorities in regard to customs and the organization of the services concerned.

ARTICLE 3. This law shall become effective on the day of its publication in the *Gazzetta ufficiale* of the Kingdom.

We order that the present, after the seal of the state has been affixed, shall be inserted in the official collection (*Raccolta ufficiale*) of the Laws and Decrees of the Kingdom of Italy, and we require persons whom it may concern to observe it and to see that it is observed as a law of the State.

Given at Rome, December 5, 1940–XIX.

VICTOR EMMANUEL

MUSSOLINI—CIANO—GRANDI—
DI REVEL

Sealed, *Keeper of the Seal:* GRANDI

Proclamation of the Duce of Fascism, First Marshal of the Empire, Commander of the Operating Forces on all the Fronts, establishing Regulations in regard to the Issue of Academic Diplomas in the Occupied French Territory, May 22, 1941 [29]

The Duce, First Marshal of the Empire, Commander of the Forces Operating on all the Fronts;

Pursuant to the decree of the King of June 10, 1940–XVIII, No. 566, which orders the application of the law of war in the territories of the State;

Pursuant to Article 6 of the decree of the King of July 8, 1938–XVI, No. 1415, which approves the text of the law of war;

Pursuant to Articles 15, 16, 17, and 18 of the said law of war;

Orders:

ARTICLE 1. In the French territory occupied by the Italian armed forces, graduates who have completed the elementary course in schools operating in this territory according to French regulations may be issued diplomas which are equivalent for all purposes to the "Certificat d'Etudes Primaires Elémentaires."

This diploma will be issued by the competent civil commissioner.

ARTICLE 2. An order of the Supreme Command, in consultation with the Minister of National Education, will determine the conditions governing the

[29] *Gazzetta ufficiale,* 1941, No. 123, p. 2050.

issue of the diploma provided for in the preceding article and whatever else may be necessary for the implementation of that article.

ARTICLE 3. The present proclamation shall be published by insertion in the *Gazzetta ufficiale* of the Kingdom, and, in the occupied territory, through a public announcement by the civil commissioners.

It shall take effect as of the day of publication.

From the General Headquarters of the Armed Forces, May 22, 1941–XIX.

MUSSOLINI

Proclamation of the Duce of Fascism, First Marshal of the Empire, Commander of the Operating Forces on all the Fronts, establishing Regulations in regard to the Rate of Exchange between the Lira and the French Franc in the French Territory Occupied by the Italian Armed Forces, June 21, 1941 [30]

The Duce, First Marshal of the Empire, Commander of the Forces operating on all the Fronts.

Pursuant to the decree of the King of June 10, 1940–XVIII, No. 566, which orders the application of the law of war in the territories of the State;

Pursuant to Article 13 of the Proclamation of July 30, 1940–XVIII, concerning the administrative and judicial organization in the occupied territories;

Orders:

ARTICLE 1. From the effective date of this proclamation, the rate of exchange between the Italian lira and the French franc in the French territories occupied by the Italian armed forces is stabilized as follows:

100 French francs are equivalent to 38 Italian lire.

ARTICLE 2. This proclamation shall be made public by posting it in places where it may be seen by the public, near the offices of the civil commissioners of the French territory occupied by Italian armed forces.

The present shall take effect as of the date of its publication.

This proclamation shall, moreover, be inserted in the *Gazzetta ufficiale* of the Kingdom.

From the General Headquarters of the Armed Forces, June 21, 1941–XIX

MUSSOLINI

[30] *Gazzetta ufficiale,* No. 147, p. 2509.

IV. VICHY

1. CONSTITUTIONAL LAWS

Constitutional Law, July 10, 1940 [31]

The National Assembly has adopted,

The President of the Republic promulgates the following constitutional law:

SOLE ARTICLE. The National Assembly vests in Marshal Pétain all powers in the Government of the Republic in order that he may, by his authority and under his signature, promulgate a new constitution for the French State by one or several acts. This constitution shall guarantee the rights of labor, of the family, and of the fatherland.

It shall be ratified by the nation and applied by the assemblies which it shall create.

The present constitutional law, discussed and adopted by the National Assembly, shall be carried out as a law of the state.

Vichy, July 10, 1940.

ALBERT LEBRUN
President of the Republic

PH. PÉTAIN, *Marshal of France, President of the Council*

Constitutional Act No. 1, July 11, 1940 [32]

We, Philippe Pétain, Marshal of France,

In consideration of the Constitutional Law of July 10, 1940,

Declare that we have assumed the functions of Chief of the French State.

Therefore we decree:

Article 2 of the Constitutional Law of February 25, 1875, is abrogated.[33]

Vichy, July 11, 1940.

PH. PÉTAIN

[31] *Journal officiel de la République française*, 1940, No. 167. [32] *Ibid.*, No. 168.

[33] Article 2 of the constitutional law of February 25, 1875, reads: "The President of the Republic shall be chosen by an absolute majority of votes of the Senate and Chamber of Deputies united in National Assembly. He shall be elected for seven years. He shall be eligible for reelection."

Constitutional Act No. 2, Defining the Authority of the Chief of the French State, July 11, 1940 [34]

We, Marshal of France, Chief of the French State, in consideration of the Constitutional Law of July 10, 1940,

Decree:

ARTICLE 1. SECTION 1. The Chief of the French State shall have full governmental powers. He shall appoint and revoke the appointment of ministers and of state secretaries, who shall be responsible only to him.

SECTION 2. He shall exercise legislative power in the Council of Ministers:

1. Until the formation of the new Assemblies.
2. After this formation, in case of tension in foreign affairs, or of a serious internal crisis, on his own decision and in the same form. In the same circumstances, he may issue all regulations of a budgetary or fiscal nature.

SECTION 3. He shall promulgate laws and assure their execution.

SECTION 4. He shall make appointments to all civil and military posts for which the law does not provide any other method of appointment.

SECTION 5. He shall have full power over the armed forces.

SECTION 6. He shall have the right of granting pardon and amnesty.

SECTION 7. Envoys and ambassadors of foreign countries shall be accredited to him.

He shall negotiate and ratify treaties.

SECTION 8. He may declare a state of siege in one or more parts of the territories.

SECTION 9. He may not declare war without the previous consent of the Legislative Assemblies.

ARTICLE 2. All provisions of the constitutional laws of February 24, 1875, February 25, 1875, and July 16, 1875, which are incompatible with this act are hereby abrogated.

Vichy, July 11, 1940.

PH. PÉTAIN

Constitutional Act No. 7, January 27, 1941 [35]

We, Marshal of France, Chief of the French State, in consideration of the constitutional law of July 10, 1940,

Decree:

ARTICLE 1. The state secretaries, high dignitaries, and high officials of the state shall take oath before the Chief of the State. They shall swear al-

[34] *Journal officiel de la République française*, 1940, No. 168.
[35] *Journal officiel de l'Etat français*, 1941, No. 28.

legiance to his person and engage themselves to perform their duties for the welfare of the state in accordance with rules of honor and of probity.

ARTICLE 2. The state secretaries, high dignitaries, and high officials of the state shall be personally responsible to the Chief of State. This responsibility shall apply to their person and their property.

ARTICLE 3. In case any one of the above-mentioned group should prove unfaithful to his obligations, the Chief of State, after instituting an inquiry by means of a procedure upon which he shall decide, may require payment of reparation and fines, and may temporarily or definitively apply the following penalties: loss of political rights; surveillance of residence in France or in the Colonies; administrative internment; detention in a fortress.

ARTICLE 4. The imposition of penalties by virtue of the preceding article shall not prevent the prosecution, under normal judicial procedure, of crimes or offenses which may have been committed by the same persons.

ARTICLE 5. Articles 3 and 4 of the present act shall apply to former ministers, high dignitaries, and high officials who have exercised their duties within the past ten years.

Vichy, January 27, 1941.

PH. PÉTAIN

2. LABOR

Law concerning the Social Organization of Occupations, October 4, 1941 [36]

[EXCERPTS]

ARTICLE 1. Occupational activities shall be divided among a determined number of industrial or commercial "families" (*familles industrielles ou commerciales*).

These families and the occupations of which they are composed shall be organized in accordance with the general conditions provided by the present law, with a view both to joint administration of the occupational interests of their members of every category and to contribution to the support of the national economy in accordance with directions given by the public authorities.

. . . . .

ARTICLE 6. The organization provided for by the present law shall be both a social and occupational one; its activities shall consequently be subject to a double classification:

For matters of a social nature, industrial and commercial establishments shall be divided among a certain number of occupational families. A sepa-

[36] *Journal officiel de l'Etat français*, 1941, No. 293.

rate organization shall be established for each one of these families and, if necessary, for every industry and occupation within the framework of the family.

For occupational questions, each occupation shall be classed in one of the occupational families (*familles professionelles*), selected because of its particular competence in matters concerning that occupation; and this family shall be charged with the establishment of organizations qualified to treat the problems of the occupations covered.

. . . . .

ARTICLE 9. The members of occupations shall be grouped in occupational unions (*syndicats professionels*).

A single occupational union shall be formed in each area for each occupation, industry, or occupational family, and for each category of members.

The conditions under which new single unions shall be formed on the basis of existing organizations shall be fixed by decree.

ARTICLE 10. The occupational unions shall be composed of different categories of members. The following shall be considered as forming distinct categories:

1. Employers.
2. Workers.
3. Clerical staff.
4. Foremen and similar supervisory staff.
5. Engineers and administrative and commercial personnel.

. . . . .

ARTICLE 14. The functions of the occupational unions shall be:

The enlistment and representation of their members.
The transmission or execution of corporative decisions.
The study of occupational questions, with a view to presenting corporative suggestions.
The solving of problems affecting the members of their territorial unit.

Any activity of a political or religious nature shall be excluded.

. . . . .

ARTICLE 19. Occupational unions and federations shall be established for each occupation or group of occupations and each category.

The representatives of the councils of occupational unions (*syndicats professionels*) shall unite to form regional unions.

The representatives of the regional unions shall unite to form national federations (*fédérations*).

. . . . .

Social Committees for Enterprises

ARTICLE 23. In establishments with a staff of not less than one hundred workers or employees, collaboration between employers and employees shall be compulsorily organized by means of "works social committees" which shall be composed of the head of the enterprise and representatives of every category of personnel.

ARTICLE 24. The first object of the works social committees shall be to effect social and professional collaboration between the management and personnel.

In the exercise of their functions, they shall not have authority to interfere in the control and management of the enterprise or in matters outside the limits of the enterprise; subject to these reservations, they have the widest functions, particularly as regards:

Advising the management on all questions relative to the life and work of the staff.

Encouraging a mutual exchange of information on all problems relating to the social life of the staff and their families.

Effecting mutual aid measures within the limits of activities of the respective local social committees.

Their procedure shall be left to their own initiative.

They shall be placed under corporative authority and under control of the local social committee of the respective occupation.

. . . . .

Social Committees for Occupational Families or Occupations

ARTICLE 27. In each occupational family or occupation, and on every scale—local, regional, and national—there shall be created a corporative organization with social and occupational functions which shall be called, respectively, local social committee, regional social committee, and national social committee.

. . . . .

The Functions of the Social Committees

ARTICLE 31. The functions of the social committees shall be occupational and social. No political or religious activity shall be permitted.

In the occupational field, they shall include mainly:

Questions of salaries and collective agreements.

Questions of vocational training: apprenticeship, advanced training, reclassifying, personnel schools, and so on.

Drafting of regulations concerning engagement and dismissal.

Study and application of measures relating to industrial hygiene and safety.

Questions concerning appointments, salaries, and other matters affecting a particular category may be discussed jointly by representatives of the interested category and of employers.

. . . . .

Labor Jurisdiction

ARTICLE 60. All the occupational bodies of the different grades must endeavor to prevent and conciliate differences which may arise in connection with the application of the laws and social regulations relating to occupations.

ARTICLE 61. If, despite the intervention of the occupational bodies, it has not been possible to avoid disputes or to settle them by conciliation, they shall be:

Submitted to conciliation boards (*Conseils de prud'hommes*), or, if these do not exist, to justices of the peace, if individual disputes are involved.

Submitted to arbitration or to labor tribunals, if collective disputes are involved.

Offenses against such regulations as shall be established for the application of the present law shall also be referred to the labor tribunals.

Labor Tribunals

ARTICLE 63. Within the jurisdiction of every court of appeals there shall be established a regional labor tribunal, which shall be composed of the following:

Two judges, of whom one shall exercise the functions of the president, designated by order of the first president.

Three members of the regional social committee having jurisdiction, designated according to Article 28.

Appeals from decisions of regional labor tribunals shall be submitted to a national labor tribunal, which shall render final decision.

. . . . .

Vichy, October 4, 1941.

PH. PÉTAIN, *Marshal of France, Chief of the French State;* AL. DARLAN, *Admiral of the Fleet, Vice President of the Council, Minister of National Defense, Minister for Foreign Affairs and of the Navy;* HENRI MEYSSET, *Minister of State;* LUCIEN ROMIER, *Minister of State;* JOSEPH BARTHÉLEMY, *Keeper of the Seal, Minister of Justice;* GL. HUNTZIGER, *General of the Army, Minister of War;* PIERRE CAZIOT, *Minister of Agriculture;* PIERRE PUCHEU, *Minister of the Interior;* RENÉ BELIN, *Secretary of State for Labor;* YVES BOUTHILLIER, *Minister of National Economy and of Finance;* FRANÇOIS LEBIDEUX, *Secretary of State for Industrial Production;* TÉRÔURE CARCOPINO, *Secretary of State for National Education and Youth;* GL. BERGERET, *Secretary of State for Aviation;* PAUL CHARBIN, *Secretary of State for Food;* SERGE HUARD, *Secretary of State for the Family and Health;* JEAN BERTHELOT, *Secretary of State for Communications;* BENOIST-MECHIN, *Secretary to the Vice-presidency of the Council.*

Law No. 439 concerning the Institution of a "National Order of Labor," April 1, 1942 [37]

[EXCERPTS]

We, Marshal of France, Chief of the French State, after having heard the Council of Ministers,

Decree:

ARTICLE 1. A "National Order of Labor" shall be established for the purpose of conferring distinction upon persons who have displayed unusual technical ability in the exercise of their occupation, a high sense of responsibility to the community, or a particular and sustained devotion to the occupation and the nation.

ARTICLE 2. The National Order of Labor shall comprise the three following grades:

Commander (*Commandeur*)
Officer (*Officier*)
Knight (*Chevalier*)

ARTICLE 3. The awards and promotions shall be made by decrees issued upon the proposal of the Secretary of Labor, following the recommendation of the Council of the National Order of Labor, instituted in accordance with Article 8 below. They shall be published in the *Journal officiel de l'Etat français*.

ARTICLE 4. The awards and promotions shall take place on the occasion of the labor holiday on the 1st of May of each year.

. . . . .

ARTICLE 11. Special regulations issued by the public administration shall define the models of the emblems and insignia of the order and shall determine the conditions of the application of the present law.

. . . . .

ARTICLE 15. The present decree shall be published in the *Journal officiel* and shall be carried out as a law of the state.

Vichy, April 1, 1942.

PH. PÉTAIN, *Marshal of France, Chief of the French State;* DARLAN, *Admiral of the Fleet, Minister Vice President of the Council;* YVES BOUTHILLIER, *Minister of National Economy and Finance;* JOSEPH BARTHÉLEMY, *Keeper of the Seal, Minister of Justice;* RENÉ BELIN, *Secretary of State for Labor.*

[37] *Journal officiel de l'Etat français*, 1942, No. 104.

GREECE

I. ITALIAN OCCUPATION

Proclamation No. 2 of the High Commander of the Troops in Albania, October 28, 1940 [1]

[EXCERPT]

It is prohibited for persons who do not possess a special pass issued by the Supreme Command of the Royal "Carabinieri," to enter the occupied territory as well as the zones of operations indicated in a special order.

Violators shall be immediately apprehended and shall be punished, if the act does not involve a more serious offense, by arrest and imprisonment of from six months to two years.

The jurisdiction to try such an offense shall lie with the Military War Tribunal.

The present proclamation shall take effect on the day of its publication by means of posting in public places.

Zone of Operations, October 28, 1940-XVIII.

S. VISCONTI PRASCA, *Commanding General*

Proclamation No. 10 of the High Commander of the Troops in Albania, October 28, 1940 [2]

[EXCERPT]

ARTICLE 1. As of today the civil powers in the zone of operations are assumed by the High Commander of the Troops, who will exercise them through the agencies now constituted, with such exceptions as shall be established from time to time.

ARTICLE 2. There shall be a special "Office for Civil Affairs" established on the staff of the High Commander of the Troops, with the duty of coordinating civilian services and exercising the necessary control over them.

ARTICLE 3. All civilian authorities in the zone of operations shall carry out the orders which, for matters concerning their respective departments, shall be issued by the High Commander of the Troops and by the commanders of large units stationed in the respective districts in the zone of operations.

ARTICLE 4. All police services in the zone of operations shall be placed under the direction of the High Commander of the Royal "Carabinieri."

[1] *Fletorja Zyrtare*, November 26, 1940, No. 184, p. 1. [2] *Ibid.*, p. 8.

The present proclamation shall go into effect upon its publication by means of posting in public places, and it shall be printed in the *Gazzetta ufficiale* of the Kingdom of Albania.

From Headquarters, October 28, 1940–XVIII.

S. VISCONTI PRASCA, *Commanding General*

Proclamation No. 6 of the High Commander of the Troops in Albania, October 29, 1940 [3]

[EXCERPT]

ARTICLE 1. Any person who, knowing of the landing or crashing of enemy planes in occupied territory, fails to give immediate notice thereof to his superiors, if he is in the military service, or to the Royal "Carabinieri" of the locality, or to other authorities if the person in question does not belong to the armed forces of the state, shall be punished by imprisonment up to three years.

ARTICLE 2. Whoever removes, carries away, or retains parts, instruments, equipment, arms, or other accessories of enemy planes landed or shot down in occupied territory, or documents, papers, valuables, or other objects belonging to the members of the crews thereof, shall be punishable, if the act does not involve a more serious offense, by imprisonment of from three to ten years.

ARTICLE 3. The offenses covered by the preceding articles shall lie within the jurisdiction of military tribunals.

ARTICLE 4. The present proclamation shall take effect on the day of its publication by means of posting in public places.

From Headquarters, October 29, 1940–XIX.

S. VISCONTI PRASCA, *Commanding General*

Proclamation No. 7 of the High Commander of the Troops in Albania, October 30, 1940 [4]

[EXCERPT]

ARTICLE 1. Whoever shall possess by virtue of any title whatsoever grain and flour made therefrom, macaroni products, vegetables, barley, wheat and fodder, beef, poultry, goats, and pigs must make detailed report thereof to the nearest command of the Royal "Carabinieri" or to the Royal Finance Guards.

Failure to report or an incorrect report shall be punishable by arrest and

[3] *Fletorja Zyrtare*, November 26, 1940, No. 184, p. 4. [4] *Ibid.*, p. 5.

sentence of from six months to two years, and the unreported produce shall be sequestrated.

ARTICLE 2. Whoever destroys, damages or spoils food products, fodder, building or firewood, coal or peat, gasoline, lubricants, or other articles of prime necessity for the civilian population, or useful to the occupying army, shall be punishable by imprisonment of from three to fifteen years.

Where disruption in supplies to the population or to the occupying army has resulted from the act, imprisonment shall be from eight to twenty years.

ARTICLE 3. Whoever kills or renders unusable horses, mules, or donkeys without having received previous authorization from the responsible military authorities, shall be punished by imprisonment of from one to five years.

The same penalty shall apply to whoever, without necessity, shall kill or render unusable beef animals, poultry, goats, or pigs.

ARTICLE 4. Whoever destroys, damages, or spoils motor vehicles of any kind, or wagons or carts for animal traction, shall be punishable by imprisonment of from six months to three years.

ARTICLE 5. The trial of offenders covered by the present proclamation shall rest with the War Tribunal.

This proclamation shall take effect on the day of its publication by means of posters.

Zone of Operations, October 30, 1940–XIX.

S. VISCONTI PRASCA, *Commanding General*

Proclamation of the Duce of Fascism, First Marshal of the Empire, Commander of the Troops Operating on All Fronts, on Regulations concerning Monopoly Services in the Territories Occupied by the Italian Armed Forces, May 4, 1941 [5]

[EXCERPTS]

ARTICLE 1. The services for salt, tobacco, matches, cigarette boxes, automatic lighters, and flints in the territories previously belonging to the former Kingdom of Yugoslavia and to the Kingdom of Greece occupied by the Italian armed forces shall be provisionally taken over by the Administration of the State Monopolies, which shall provide them with separate and autonomous organizations according to the divisions of the civil commissariats into which the occupied territory is divided.

The regulations for these organizations shall be issued by the individual civil commissioners with the approval of the Minister of Finance.

. . . . .

General Headquarters of the Armed Forces, May 4, 1941–XIX.

MUSSOLINI

[5] *Gazzetta ufficiale*, 1941, No. 109, p. 1800.

Proclamation of the Duce of Fascism, First Marshal of the Empire, Commander of the Troops Operating on All Fronts, concerning Regulations with respect to the Rate of Exchange of the Italian Lira, the Albanian Franc, and the Drachma in the Greek Territory Occupied by the Italian Armed Forces, June 21, 1941 [6]

[EXCERPT]

ARTICLE 1. As of the effective date of this proclamation the rate of exchange of the Italian lira, the Albanian franc, and the drachma in the Greek territory occupied by the Italian armed forces is fixed as follows: 100 drachmae are equivalent to 12.50 lire; 100 drachmae are equivalent to 2 Albanian francs.

ARTICLE 2. The proclamation shall be published by means of posting in places visible to the public at the offices of the civil commissioners of the Greek territory occupied by the Italian armed forces. It shall become effective upon publication.

This proclamation shall moreover be printed in the *Gazzetta ufficiale* of the Kingdom of Italy and in that of the Kingdom of Albania.

General Headquarters of the Armed Forces, June 21, 1941–XIX.

MUSSOLINI

Proclamation of the Duce of Fascism, First Marshal of the Empire, Commander of the Troops Operating on All Fronts, on Measures regarding the Civil Administration of the Territory of the Greek Peninsula Occupied by Detachments of the High Command of the Armed Forces in Albania, July 2, 1941 [7]

[EXCERPT]

ARTICLE 1. In the territory of the Greek peninsula occupied by detachments of the High Command of the Armed Forces in Albania, civil authority, as defined in Articles 54 and 66 of the laws of war, shall be exercised by a High Commissioner.

The High Commissioner shall be appointed and recalled by order of the Supreme Command.

ARTICLE 2. The High Commissioner shall be responsible to the Supreme Command. The Supreme Command may provide that the High Commissioner in the exercise of particular functions or of all his functions shall be responsible to the High Command of the Armed Forces in Albania.

ARTICLE 3. In emergencies of a political or military nature, or affecting the public welfare, the High Commissioner may order the replacement of civil officials in the occupied territory who have been theretofore retained in

[6] *Gazzetta ufficiale*, 1941, No. 147, p. 2509. [7] *Ibid.*, No. 185, p. 3143.

office; and he may also appoint civil officials when vacancies occur in the various offices.

ARTICLE 4. The High Commissioner may issue orders regarding buildings, police, sanitation, supplies and consumption, and local finance in urgent cases affecting the public interest and concerning, in whole or in part, the territory under his jurisdiction.

Persons who violate the orders provided for in the preceding paragraph shall be punished, if the act does not constitute a heinous offense, by imprisonment of not more than six months or by fine up to 5,000 lire.

ARTICLE 5. This proclamation shall be published in the *Gazzetta ufficiale* of the Kingdom.

It shall also be posted in the municipal registers of the territory of the Greek peninsula occupied by detachments of the High Command of the Armed Forces in Albania.

General Headquarters of the Armed Forces, July 2, 1941–XIX.

MUSSOLINI

II. BULGARIAN OCCUPATION [7a]

Decree concerning Land Grants for Municipal Officials in the Villages of the Aegean Region, Approved by the 34th Decision of the Council of Ministers Taken at the Session of October 9, 1942, Protocol No. 131 [8]

[EXCERPTS]

The decree concerning land grants for municipal officials in the villages of the Aegean region is hereby approved.

ARTICLE 1. In accordance with the present decree, land shall be granted to the following municipal officials in the villages of the Aegean region, including villages annexed to the Kingdom in 1941 and comprised in the Plovdiv administrative district, as set forth in announcement No. 2624 of July 28, 1941, of the Minister of the Interior and Public Health (*Durjaven Vestnik*, No. 160, July 31, 1941):

a) Mayors of villages.
b) Municipal police and police sergeants.
c) Guards of the fields.
d) Municipal and school janitors.
e) Supervisors of breeding stations.

. . . .

ARTICLE 2. Land grants cover land as well as dwelling-houses. The land plot shall not be larger than that which the official's family is capable of cultivating and shall not exceed one half of a land plot of medium type

[7a] See also below, pp. 633–35.

[8] *Durjaven Vestnik*, No. 232, 1942, p. 2.

which is granted in the locality in question to colonists in the Aegean region, in accordance with the decree regarding agricultural economic colonization in the Aegean region (*Durjaven Vestnik*, No. 237, October 24, 1941) and the decree on granting land and dwelling-houses to colonists transferred to the Aegean region (*Durjaven Vestnik*, No. 138, June 27, 1942). Land shall not be granted to unmarried officials who do not live with their families at the place of their employment. Similarly, land shall not be granted to married officials whose families do not live at the place of their employment.

ARTICLE 3. Grants of land to the officials specified in Article 1 shall be either temporary or permanent. A temporary grant of land shall last throughout the completion of three years' uninterrupted service in the Aegean region. It shall become permanent after the official has completed three years of service.

ARTICLE 4. Application for temporary grants shall be made by the person involved by the filing of a petition with the regional director through the Committee for Land Grants established by the decree for the settlement and supply of dwelling-houses and lands to the colonists in the Aegean region (*Durjaven Vestnik*, No. 138, 1942). . . .

ARTICLE 5. The officials obtaining temporary grants of land in accordance with the present decree, shall not pay rent for the property. If they fail to receive permanent grants, the property shall be taken away from them by administrative order of the mayor. In such case the Committee for Land Grants shall determine the amount of rent due for the time the land was used.

ARTICLE 6. The permanent grant shall be established in accordance with a special procedure, which is provided for permanent grants of lands, as defined in the decree for settlement and granting of lands and dwelling-houses to colonists in the Aegean region (*Durjaven Vestnik*, No. 138, 1942).

. . . . .

G. K. SERAFIMOV
Secretary General of the Council of Ministers

Decree regarding the Construction, and Justification of Expenditures for the Construction, of Dwelling-houses for the Colonists in the Aegean Region, Approved by the 36th Decision of the Council of Ministers Taken at the Session of October 14, 1942, Protocol No. 133 [9]

[EXCERPTS]

The following decree regarding the construction, and justification of expenditures for the construction, of dwelling-houses for the colonists in the Aegean region, is hereby approved.

[9] *Durjaven Vestnik*, No. 233, 1942, pp. 1, 2.

ARTICLE 1. The audit of 12,000,000 leva, granted in accordance with the 53d decision of the Council of Ministers, which was taken at the session of August 26, 1942, Protocol No. 111 (Official Gazette [*Durjaven Vestnik*], No. 195, 1942), for the construction and repair of dwelling-houses for colonists in the Aegean region, shall be delegated to the Director of the Commissariat for the Construction of Dwelling-Houses in the Aegean Region—director at the Ministry of the Interior and Public Health—B. H. Bonchev, and to his assistant the technical commissioner, architect K. Drumev.

ARTICLE 2. At the Sofia branch of the Bulgarian Agrarian and Cooperative Bank a current account is established in the name of the Commissariat for the Construction of Dwelling-Houses in the Aegean Region, to which account the sum of 12,000,000 leva is credited. Withdrawal of amounts from the balance of this account shall be effected by means of checks issued against the Sofia branch of the bank, signed jointly by B. M. Bonchev and architect K. Drumev. The checks may be cashed in the following branches of the bank: Sofia, Xanti, Drama, Kawala, Seres, Sar-Shaban, Silachouo, Demir-Hisar, Sumurdgina, and Dede-Agach.

ARTICLE 3. The payments in connection with the construction of dwelling-houses for colonists in the Aegean region shall be made by checks in accordance with Article 2.

. . . . .

ARTICLE 5. The accounting for the amounts spent in accordance with this order shall be presented to the Council of Ministers through the Minister of Finance in the form of a written report, accompanied by the documents issued by the Director of the Commissariat for the Construction of Dwelling-Houses in the Aegean Region and by his technical assistant; before presenting the above-mentioned report to the Council of Ministers, the Minister of Finance shall appoint a counsellor of the General Accounting Office and a financial inspector to check it.

The Council of Ministers shall decide whether the expenditures have been made in accordance with the present decision.

ARTICLE 6. This order is issued by virtue of Article 1, paragraphs 2 and 16, of the law concerning the accelerated settlement of urgent matters in the liberated territories and shall be published in *Durjaven Vestnik*.

S. K. SERAFIMOV
Secretary General of the Council of Ministers

LUXEMBURG[1]

1. ADMINISTRATION

Order concerning Certain Changes of the Right to Vote, October 17, 1940 [1a]

In pursuance of the authority vested in the Chief of the Civil Administration in Luxemburg, the following order is issued for the area subject to his jurisdiction.

SECTION 1. The restrictions of the right to vote established by Luxemburg statutes concerning persons supported by a public institution for indigents or inmates of institutions for indigent persons are hereby abolished.

Luxemburg statutory provisions not in accordance with paragraph 1, especially Article 53, No. 3, of the Luxemburg Constitution of October 17, 1868, and Article 4, No. 9, of the Act of July 31, 1934, amending the Election Statute, shall be and hereby are repealed.

SECTION 2. This order shall take effect as of the date of its publication.

Luxemburg, October 17, 1940.

DR. MÜNZEL

Acting Chief of the Civil Administration in Luxemburg

Order concerning the Dissolution of the Chamber of Deputies and the Council of State in Luxemburg, October 22, 1940 [2]

In pursuance of the authority vested in the Chief of the Civil Administration in Luxemburg, the following order is issued for the area subject to his jurisdiction.

SECTION 1. The Chamber of Deputies and the Council of State established under the Constitution of Luxemburg of October 17, 1868, and pertinent Luxemburg statutes and other provisions, shall be and hereby are dissolved.

SECTION 2. This order shall take effect one day after the date of publication.

Luxemburg, October 22, 1940.

GUSTAV SIMON, *Gauleiter*

Chief of the Civil Administration in Luxemburg

[1] See also, under Belgium, order concerning sequestration of property, above, p. 321.
[1a] *Verordnungsblatt für Luxemburg*, No. 47, 1940, p. 254. [2] *Ibid.*, No. 52, 1940, p. 278.

Order concerning the Administration of Municipalities and other Subdivisions of Government in Luxemburg, November 14, 1940 [3]

In pursuance of the authority vested in the Chief of the Civil Administration in Luxemburg, the following order is issued for the territory subject to his jurisdiction.

SECTION 1. *Municipalities.* (1) The municipalities are corporations under public law; they govern themselves under their own responsibility. Their activities must accord with the laws and aims of the government of the state.

(2) The municipality shall be headed by the mayor. The associate councilmen shall be his deputies. Aldermen shall be appointed as his advisers. In addition to these provisions the provisions of the German Municipal Code of January 30, 1935 (*RGBl.* I, p. 49), shall be applicable.

(3) The municipalities shall be authorized to levy taxes and other contributions in accordance with pertinent statutes whenever other revenues shall be insufficient to defray the expenditures. They may also require the inhabitants to perform personal services.

SECTION 2. *Police.* The mayor shall establish the local police authority unless the functions of the police have been delegated to agencies of the state.

SECTION 3. *Public Corporations Formed for Specific Purposes.* Leagues of municipalities heretofore organized shall be administered as corporations formed for specific purposes in accordance with the act of June 7, 1939, concerning public corporations formed for specific purposes (*RGBl.* I, p. 979); they are required to amend their by-laws for the purpose of compliance with their new legal status not later than April 1, 1941.

SECTION 4. *Districts.* (1) The Chief of the Civil Administration in Luxemburg may organize municipalities into "districts." The district shall be headed by a district mayor. The associate district councilmen shall be his deputies. District aldermen shall be appointed as his advisers.

(2) Upon the establishment of district local police, authority over such police shall be vested in the district mayor.

SECTION 5. *County Districts.* (1) In lieu of the former county districts the following county districts are hereby established: Esch with its official seat in Esch on the Alzig, Diekirch with its official seat in Diekirch, Grevemacher with its official seat in Grevemacher. The county districts are subdivisions of the state administration and also corporations under public law.

(2) The county district shall be headed by the county chairman. The Chief of the Civil Administration in Luxemburg shall issue rules and regulations concerning the authority to act on the county chairman's behalf in matters of state administration and in matters of the county district in its

[3] *Verordnungsblatt*, No. 55, November 18, 1940, p. 290.

capacity as a self-governing corporation under public law. County councilmen shall be appointed as advisers of the county chairman.

(3) The county chairman shall be a supervising agent for the municipalities and districts which are members of the county district; he shall also be a supervising agent for the police administration in these municipalities and districts and he shall be the county police authority.

(4) The county district as a self-governing corporation under public law shall defray the expenditures not covered by taxes, levies, or other revenues by levying a contribution upon the municipalities which are members of the county districts.

(5) The Chief of the Civil Administration in Luxemburg shall be the supervising authority for the county districts.

SECTION 6. *Matters Affecting all Leagues of Public Corporations.* Matters affecting all leagues of public corporations shall be dealt with by the Chief of the Civil Administration in his capacity of administrator of matters affecting all leagues of public corporations.

SECTION 7. *Final and Transitional Provisions.* (1) This order shall take effect on December 1, 1940.

The Chief of the Civil Administration in Luxemburg shall issue rules and regulations necessary for the enforcement and implementation of this order.

(2) An official appointed to serve without compensation for the municipalities and districts, corporations organized for a specific purpose, and county districts may be dismissed by the supervising agency at any time before the lapse of his first year of office.

(3) For the organizational measures contemplated by this order or in any other provisions of law, Section 1 of the Second Order concerning Certain Changes in the Law of Public Officials of May 3, 1940 (*RGBl.* I, p. 732), shall apply.

Luxemburg, November 14, 1940.

GUSTAV SIMON, *Gauleiter*
Chief of the Civil Administration in Luxemburg

2. LAW AND COURTS

Order concerning the Preliminary Establishment of a German Criminal Court in Luxemburg, August 20, 1940 [4]

SECTION 1. A Special Court shall be established for the territory subject to the authority of the Chief of the Civil Administration in Luxemburg.

SECTION 2. The Special Court shall have jurisdiction over the following criminal proceedings:

[4] *Verordnungsblatt*, No. 1, September 1, 1940, p. 2.

a) Proceedings referred to in Section 4.
b) Proceedings removed to the Special Court by the Prosecuting Attorney's office.

SECTION 3. The Special Court and the Prosecuting Attorney shall apply German law.

SECTION 4. (1) It shall be unlawful:

a) To gather on streets, to produce and distribute pamphlets or leaflets unlawfully, to arrange unlawfully public assemblies and demonstrations or to participate therein, and generally to engage in any demonstration hostile to Germany or Germans.
b) To possess arms unlawfully.
c) To publish in newspapers or periodicals news inimical to the German Reich, or news barred from publication.
d) To spread radio news inimical to Germany or to Germans, or any other news inimical to Germany or to Germans.
e) To enter into unauthorized relations or contact with military or civil prisoners in the custody of the German armed forces or German authorities or officials.
f) To cease work in disregard of German interests, to lock out employees, or to incite to cessation of work or lockouts.

(2) Violations shall be punishable by imprisonment, in serious cases by hard labor or death, in less serious cases by fine.

SECTION 5. This order shall take effect as of August 14, 1940.

Luxemburg, August 20, 1940.

GUSTAV SIMON, *Gauleiter*
Chief of the Civil Administration in Luxemburg

Order concerning Transactions in Real Estate in Luxemburg, August 28, 1940[5]

[EXCERPTS]

SECTION 1. (1) Alienation (by purchase or exchange) of realty or the grant of an estate in realty shall be void unless a license of the authority having jurisdiction (Licensing Agency) has been obtained.

. . . . .

(3) A license may be granted subject to conditions.

(4) The provisions in subsections 1 to 3 shall apply to legal transactions entered into after May 10, 1940, even though the transaction shall have been completed.

SECTION 2. The Licensing Agency shall decide whether or not a license shall be required according to the provisions of this order. The decisions of the board shall not be subject to review by courts or administrative agencies.

[5] *Verordnungsblatt*, No. 2, September 24, 1940, p. 9.

SECTION 3. A license shall be denied if the transaction contemplated would be against the public interest.

SECTION 4. As Licensing Agency I hereby appoint the Administrative Commissioner for Luxemburg-City and the Administrative Commissioners for Luxemburg-County, Diekirch, and Grevenmacher, each for the territory subject to his jurisdiction.

SECTION 5. (1) Any person who 1) obtains or retains possession of realty or grants such possession to another or leaves him in possession thereof—*a*) notwithstanding a denial of a license required for the legal transaction involved, *b*) without having obtained the license required within a month of entering into a legal transaction subject to such license—or 2) does not comply with the conditions imposed when the license was granted, shall be liable to imprisonment, fine, or both.

(2) If the violation is committed through negligence the defendant shall be liable to fine.

SECTION 6. In lieu of criminal proceedings in a court, imprisonment or fine may be imposed by summary order of punishment issued by the police.

. . . . . .

Luxemburg, August 28, 1940.

GUSTAV SIMON, *Gauleiter*
Chief of the Civil Administration in Luxemburg

Order concerning the Provisional Organization of the Law Courts in Luxemburg, November 9, 1940[6]

In pursuance of the authority vested in me by the Chief of the Civil Administration in Luxemburg, the following order is issued for the territory subject to his jurisdiction.

SECTION 1. The Justice of the Peace Courts shall continue to operate under the designation of District Courts, and the County Courts shall continue to operate as Circuit Courts.

SECTION 2. In lieu of the State Supreme Court, chambers of the Provincial Court of Appeals shall be established in the number required. The chambers shall have their official seat in Luxemburg.

SECTION 3. (1) The courts of law, notaries public, and other law enforcement agencies shall retain the functions vested in them by the law heretofore in force. Whenever the law of the Reich is applicable in Luxemburg, they shall assume the functions which under the law of the Reich are entrusted to comparable German law enforcement agencies.

[6] *Verordnungsblatt*, No. 56, November 15, 1940, p. 297.

(2) The provisions of this order shall not be deemed to affect the jurisdiction of the Special Court in Luxemburg established by order of the Chief of the Civil Administration in Luxemburg of August 20, 1940.

SECTION 4. Any person qualified in accordance with the provisions of the law of the Reich to hold office in any law enforcement agency shall be deemed to have the qualifications required for a comparable public office in Luxemburg.

SECTION 5. (1) This order shall take effect as of the date of publication.

(2) The Chief of the Civil Administration in Luxemburg shall issue rules and regulations necessary for its enforcement and implementation and regulations for the purpose of resolving doubts arising from its interpretation.

Luxemburg, November 9, 1940.

DR. MÜNZEL
Acting Chief of the Civil Administration in Luxemburg

Order concerning Legal Education and Examination and Admission to the Bar, December 6, 1940 [7]

[EXCERPTS]

Pursuant to the authority vested in me by the Chief of the Civil Administration in Luxemburg, the following order is issued for the territory subject to his jurisdiction:

. . . . .

SECTION 6. Admission to the bar shall be subject in the future to the consent of the Chief of the Civil Administration.

. . . . .

SECTION 9. The Chief of the Civil Administration may, in individual instances, grant exemptions from the foregoing provisions whenever it is necessary to avoid substantial hardship caused as a result of the period of transition.

SECTION 10. This order shall take effect on the day after date of publication.

Luxemburg, December 6, 1940.

DR. MÜNZEL
Acting Chief of the Civil Administration in Luxemburg

[7] *Verordnungsblatt*, No. 65, December 9, 1940, p. 373.

Order concerning Insidious Attacks on the Party and the Movement, January 15, 1941 [8]

In pursuance of the authority vested in the Chief of the Civil Administration in Luxemburg, the following order is issued for the area subject to his jurisdiction:

SECTION 1. (1) Any person who makes or spreads an untrue or grossly misleading statement of facts which is of such a character as to injure the welfare of the Reich or the prestige of the Reich Government or the German Administration in Luxemburg, or of the National Socialist German Workers Party or its constituent organizations, or the prestige of the German National Movement in Luxemburg, shall be punishable by imprisonment for a period up to two years, unless in pursuance of other provisions a more severe penalty shall be incurred; if the statement is made or spread in public, the defendant shall be liable to imprisonment for a period of not less than three months.

(2) Any person committing an act punishable under subsection 1 through gross negligence shall be punishable by imprisonment for not less than three months or by fine.

(3) Prosecution of any act punishable under subsections 1 and 2 shall be subject to the consent of the Chief of the Civil Administration in Luxemburg.

SECTION 2. (1) Any person making in public utterances which are born of hatred, or are voiced for purposes of incitement, or are derogatory with respect to leading personalities of the German Reich or the N.S.D.A.P. (National Socialist German Workers Party) or of the German National Movement, its regulations, or the institutions established by them, shall be punishable by imprisonment if these utterances are of a character capable of undermining the confidence of the people in their political leaders.

(2) The same penalty shall apply to malicious utterances not made in public whenever the defendant realizes or should have realized that the utterance may be spread abroad.

(3) Prosecution of any act punishable under subsections 1 or 2 shall be instituted only upon order of the Chief of the Civil Administration.

SECTION 3. (1) Any person who, while committing or threatening to commit any criminal act, wears or carries on his person a uniform or an insignia of the N.S.D.A.P. or its constituent organizations, or an insignia of the German National Movement, without being a member of the N.S.D.A.P. or its constituent organizations, or without being a member in good standing of the German National Movement, shall be punishable by hard labor or, in less serious cases, by imprisonment for not less than six months.

(2) Any person committing an act punishable in accordance with subsection 1 with the intent to bring about a riot, or fright, or terror among the

[8] *Verordnungsblatt*, No. 6, January 17, 1941, p. 48.

population, or to create difficulties in the foreign relations of the German Reich, shall be punishable by hard labor for a period of from not less than three years to life. In especially serious cases the death penalty may be imposed.

SECTION 4. (1) Any person who for the purpose of gaining a personal advantage or for a political objective holds himself out as a member of the N.S.D.A.P. or its constituent organizations, or as a member of the German National Movement without in fact having such membership, shall be punishable by imprisonment for a period not exceeding one year or a fine or both.

(2) Prosecution shall be subject to the consent of the Chief of the Civil Administration.

SECTION 5. (1) Any person who has in his possession the official party uniform and insignia of the party, or insignia of the German National Movement without being entitled to such possession as a member of the N.S.D.A.P. or its constituent affiliated organizations, or as a member of the German National Movement, or without having the right to such possession for any other reason, shall be punishable by imprisonment for a period not exceeding one year; if the uniforms or insignia are worn on his person he shall be liable for imprisonment for a period of not less than one month.

(2) The same penalty shall apply to the wearing of uniforms, parts of uniforms, and insignia which are so similar to uniforms, parts of uniforms, and insignia of the party, or to insignia of the German National Movement that they may be mistaken for those of the latter.

(3) In addition to the penalty, confiscation of the uniform, parts of uniforms, cloth, flags, or insignia used in the commission of the criminal act shall be ordered. If no individual person can be prosecuted or brought to trial, confiscation may independently be ordered provided that such confiscation may otherwise be lawfully ordered.

(4) Prosecution shall be subject to the consent of the Chief of the Civil Administration.

SECTION 6. For the purpose of this order no person shall be considered a member of the N.S.D.A.P., or its constituent or affiliated organizations, or a member of the German National Movement, who has obtained membership by fraud or trick.

SECTION 7. This order shall take effect as of December 1, 1940.

Luxemburg, January 15, 1941.

GUSTAV SIMON, *Gauleiter*
Chief of the Civil Administration in Luxemburg

Order concerning the Establishment of a Special Honor Court for Attorneys in Luxemburg, February 12, 1941 [9]

In pursuance of the authority vested in the Chief of the Civil Administration in Luxemburg, the following order is issued for the territory subject to his jurisdiction:

SECTION 1. A Special Honor Court shall be established for attorneys admitted to practice in Luxemburg for the territory subject to the jurisdiction of the Chief of the Civil Administration. To the extent that articled clerks (*stagiaires*) are engaged in legal practice they shall be subject to the jurisdiction of the Honor Court.

SECTION 2. The Special Honor Court shall have jurisdiction to try acts which constitute a violation of the duties arising from the organization of a German administration in Luxemburg.

SECTION 3. The Honor Court may impose the following forms of punishment: warning, remonstration, fine not exceeding 5,000 Reichsmarks, disbarment.

Fine and remonstration may be combined in one sentence.

SECTION 4. The Chief of the Civil Administration in Luxemburg shall constitute the agent for initiating proceedings before the Special Honor Court.

SECTION 5. If an indictment has been presented against an attorney in a proceeding before the Special Honor Court, the Honor Court may issue an order restraining him from appearing on behalf of private parties if it is likely that his disbarment will be ordered by the judgment of the court.

SECTION 6. The Special Honor Court for attorneys shall be established within the offices of the Chief of the Civil Administration in Luxemburg. He shall appoint the members of the court. The court's decisions shall be made by three judges who shall be members of the bar; the judgment of the court shall not be subject to review.

SECTION 7. (1) The provisions of the German Lawyers' Code of November 1, 1936, and the rules and regulations issued for its enforcement and all amending orders shall be made applicable to the proceedings before the Special Honor Court unless incompatible with the provisions of this order and the purposes of the establishment of a German Civil Administration in Luxemburg.

(2) Luxemburg legal provisions in conflict with this order shall be and hereby are repealed.

SECTION 8. Rules and regulations for the enforcement of this order shall be issued by the Chief of the Civil Administration in Luxemburg.

SECTION 9. This order shall take effect on the day after publication.

Luxemburg, February 12, 1941. Dr. MÜNZEL

Acting Chief of the Civil Administration in Luxemburg

[9] *Verordnungsblatt*, No. 15, February 21, 1941, p. 104.

Order concerning Certain Changes of Family Law, March 22, 1941 [10]

[EXCERPTS]

In pursuance of the authority vested in the Chief of the Civil Administration in Luxemburg, the following order is issued for the territory subject to his jurisdiction:

PART I.—*Legal Status of Illegitimate Children*

SECTION 1. An illegitimate child shall, in relation to its mother and her relatives, have the legal status of a legitimate child.

SECTION 2. (1) An illegitimate child shall be given the family name of its mother.

(2) If the mother, because of her marriage, has assumed another name the child shall take the family name which the mother had before her marriage. The husband of the mother may by declaration to the proper authority, with the consent of the child and the mother, give his name to the child; the declaration of the husband and the consent of child and mother shall be given in notarized form.

SECTION 3. (1) The father of an illegitimate child shall be required to furnish the child, until the completion of the latter's sixteenth year of age, support in accordance with the mother's station in life. The support shall extend to all living expenses and shall include the cost of schooling and instruction and training for a profession.

(2) If the child, upon reaching sixteen years of age, is incapable of self-support as a result of physical or mental defects, the father shall be required to support the child beyond the period fixed in subsection 1. Such additional duty of support shall not be imposed if the father, with due regard to his other obligations, shall be unable to give such support without impairing the standard of living usual in his station of life.

. . .

SECTION 17. Article 908 of the Luxemburg Civil Code is repealed.

. . .

SECTION 19. This order shall take effect one day after the date of publication.

Luxemburg, March 22, 1941.

DR. MÜNZEL

Acting Chief of the Civil Administration in Luxemburg

[10] *Verordnungsblatt*, No. 24, March 25, 1941, p. 163.

3. ECONOMY

Order concerning the Appointment of a Commissioner for the Restriction and Control of Private Organization in Luxemburg, August 28, 1940 [11]

In pursuance of the authority vested in the Chief of the Civil Administration in Luxemburg, the following is ordered for the territory subject to his jurisdiction:

SECTION 1. The chief administrator (*Oberbereichsleiter*) Franz Schmidt is hereby appointed Commissioner for the Restriction and Control of Organizations within the jurisdiction of the Chief of the Civil Administration in Luxemburg.

SECTION 2. (1) All activities of all associations and organizations, whether or not incorporated, and of all leagues, foundations, and funds or groups similar to organized bodies constituting an organization of persons, and activities of all institutions and establishments connected with such organizations shall until further notice be unlawful unless authorized by license issued by the Commissioner.

(2) Any organizational, personal, or financial change in the present status of the organizations shall likewise be subject to this licensing requirement.

SECTION 3. The Commissioner for the Restriction and Control of Organizations shall, by the authority vested in him by order of the Civil Administration in Luxemburg, have exclusive authority to make all decisions concerning private organizations. Any organizational activities of other agencies shall be subject to his express approval.

SECTION 4. The Chief of the Civil Administration in Luxemburg reserves the power to entrust, in due course, to the Commissioner the task of reorganizing all private organizations.

SECTION 5. This order shall take effect one day after the date of publication.

Luxemburg, August 28, 1940.

GUSTAV SIMON, *Gauleiter*
Chief of the Civil Administration in Luxemburg

Order concerning the Establishment of Prices on and after October 1, 1940, September 30, 1940 [12]

[EXCERPTS]

In pursuance of the authority vested in the Chief of the Civil Administration in Luxemburg, the following order is issued for the territory subject to his jurisdiction:

[11] *Verordnungsblatt*, No. 2, September 24, 1940, p. 8.
[12] *Ibid.*, No. 4, October 11, 1940, p. 21.

SECTION 1. (1) On October 1, 1940, prices and remunerations for commodities and services of every description heretofore established may be adjusted to the level of prices and remunerations presently lawful for comparable commodities and services, subject to the limitations contained in the following provisions.

(2) Wherever in the Reich local differences in prices of identical commodities or services exist the prices within the areas of the city of Trier shall be considered the lawful prices for the area of the city of Luxemburg; the prices prevailing in the counties of the government district of Trier shall be the lawful prices for the area of the districts of Luxemburg.

. . . .

Luxemburg, September 30, 1940.

GUSTAV SIMON, *Gauleiter*
Chief of the Civil Administration in Luxemburg

Order concerning the Control of the Supply of Iron and Steel, October 31, 1940 [13]

[EXCERPTS]

In pursuance of the authority vested in the Chief of the Civil Administration, the following order is issued for the area subject to his jurisdiction.

SECTION 1. Orders for the supply of iron and steel products (products of rolling mills or foundries and manufactured commodities consisting wholly or partly of iron and steel) of a total weight exceeding one hundred kilograms (factory weight or shipping weight) (*Fertiggewicht oder Liefergewicht*) given by a customer resident in the German Reich, in Alsace-Lorraine, or the occupied territories, or by officials of a German authority in these territories, shall not be filled unless a permit of the Chamber of Industry and Commerce for Luxemburg has been obtained.

For the purpose of obtaining such permit the firms receiving these orders shall submit the original order or a copy, together with the check number tabulation obtained from the firm giving the order, to the Chamber of Industry and Commerce for Luxemburg. If the permit is granted the order marked with a clearing notation shall be returned to the firm receiving the order.

An order given by a firm resident in the Reich may not be filled after September 1, 1940, unless it has been cleared for shipment by the Chamber of Industry and Commerce for Luxemburg.

SECTION 2. Firms having their principal place of business in Luxemburg shall not give orders for the supply of iron and steel products from areas other

[13] *Verordnungsblatt*, No. 53, November 7, 1940, p. 281.

than Luxemburg unless a permit of the Chamber of Industry and Commerce for Luxemburg has been given. For the purpose of obtaining the permit the applicant shall submit the following statements:

a) Name and address of the firm which is to receive the order.
b) The product intended to be ordered (by trade-name).
c) The quantity of rolling mill and foundry products necessary for filling the order ("quota-weight").

If a permit is given, the Chamber of Industry and Commerce for Luxemburg shall issue a check number with the quota symbol "Lux." This check number shall be transmitted to the firm receiving the order when the order is given; the quantity for which it is valid shall be stated at this time.

SECTION 3. Firms having their place of business in Luxemburg shall not give orders for supplies of foundry and rolling mill products to iron producers situated in Luxemburg unless the consent of the Chamber of Industry and Commerce has been obtained. In such event, the Chamber of Industry and Commerce for Luxemburg shall likewise issue a check number with the quota symbol "Lux." For orders issued by Luxemburg firms to manufacturers processing iron or steel, or to commercial firms, the consent of the Chamber of Industry and Commerce or the issuance of a check number shall not be required.

. . . .

SECTION 5. Violations of the provisions of this order shall be punishable by fine or imprisonment or both.

SECTION 6. This order shall take effect on November 1, 1940.

Luxemburg, October 31, 1940.

GUSTAV SIMON, *Gauleiter*
Chief of the Civil Administration in Luxemburg

Order to Insure the Organic Structure of Economic Life in Luxemburg, November 12, 1940 [14]

In pursuance of the authority vested in the Chief of the Civil Administration in Luxemburg, the following order is issued for the territory subject to his jurisdiction:

SECTION 1. For the purpose of insuring an organic structure of economic life in Luxemburg the Chief of the Civil Administration may establish compulsory membership organizations for trade and industry, agriculture and forestry; all enterprises and establishments within any branch of economic life shall thereby be combined into organizations according to their activities.

[14] *Verordnungsblatt*, No. 56, November 15, 1940, p. 297.

These associations shall be incorporated membership associations as provided for in the German Civil Code.

SECTION 2. The Chief of the Civil Administration will determine for which branches of economic life specific organizations, according to their trades and occupations, shall be established. He will promulgate the by-laws of these organizations and will define their official objectives. He shall be authorized to dissolve the associations thus formed.

SECTION 3. Any person who negligently or intentionally violates any order issued by the Chief of the Civil Administration or his designees in pursuance of this order, or the rules or regulations issued for its enforcement or implementation, shall be liable to a summary order of punishment issued by the Chief of the Civil Administration.

SECTION 4. This order shall take effect one day after the date of publication.

Luxemburg, November 12, 1940.

SIEKMEIER
Acting Chief of the Civil Administration in Luxemburg

Order for the Protection of the Economy of Luxemburg, November 21, 1940 [15]

[EXCERPTS]

In pursuance of the authority vested in the Chief of the Civil Administration in Luxemburg, the following order is issued for the territory subject to his jurisdiction:

SECTION 1. (1) The following transactions shall be subject to licensing:

a. Transactions concerning the purchase or sale, or the granting or taking by lease, of industrial plants and establishments or parts thereof.
b. Transactions involving a transfer or other alienation of shares in industrial plants and enterprises in Luxemburg.
c. Transactions through which in any other fashion, directly or indirectly, decisive economic control for the grantee alone, or in conjunction with others, over industrial enterprises or establishments in Luxemburg is or is intended to be secured.
d. Transactions concerning a removal of industrial enterprises and establishments or of subsidiary plants of such plants or establishments from Luxemburg.

(2) A transfer without consideration or by way of execution of a judgment or by mortgage sale shall be deemed to constitute an alienation for the purposes of subsection 1.

[15] *Verordnungsblatt*, No. 61, November 28, 1940, p. 346.

(3) Agreements establishing an obligation to enter into a legal transaction of the kind referred to in subsection 1 shall likewise be subject to this licensing requirement.

(4) Transactions of the kind referred to in subsections 1 to 3 and entered into after May 9, 1940, shall likewise be subject to such licensing requirement.

SECTION 2. (1) The Chief of the Civil Administration shall issue licenses required in accordance with Section 1. License provisions arising under other provisions of law shall not be affected by this order.

(2) Licenses may be issued subject to conditions and other requirements.

SECTION 3. Any legal transaction which is subject to the licensing requirement in accordance with Section 1 shall be invalid unless a license has been issued.

. . . . . .

SECTION 7. The Chief of the Civil Administration shall issue rules and regulations necessary for the enforcement of this order.

SECTION 8. This order shall take effect one day after the date of publication.

Luxemburg, November 21, 1940.

DR. MÜNZEL
Acting Chief of the Civil Administration in Luxemburg

Order concerning Certain Measures Affecting Economic Life, February 21, 1941 [16]

In pursuance of the authority vested in the Chief of the Civil Administration, the following order is issued for the territory subject to his jurisdiction:

SECTION 1. (1) For enterprises of trade or industry whose management is unwilling to promote Germanism at all times, without any reservations, the Chief of the Civil Administration may issue orders which will insure the establishment of conditions in harmony with the fact of a German administration in Luxemburg.

(2) The same shall apply if the management of an enterprise in trade or industry shall violate its duties arising from the general principles of a National Socialist Labor Community or shall violate orders and instructions of the Chief of the Civil Administration or his designees.

The Chief of the Civil Administration may by order especially restrain managers of enterprises from exercising their authority and also by order define their legal position with regard to the enterprises and appoint in their

[16] *Verordnungsblatt*, No. 17, March 1, 1941, p. 119.

stead commissioners who will exercise authority as required. These orders shall not be subject to review by courts of general jurisdiction. The cost arising from the activity of such commissioners shall be borne by the enterprise.

SECTION 2. The Chief of the Civil Administration shall issue rules and regulations required for the enforcement of this order.

SECTION 3. This order shall take effect on the day after the date of publication.

Luxemburg, February 21, 1941.

SIEKMEIER
Acting Chief of the Civil Administration in Luxemburg

4. FINANCE[16a]

Order concerning the Designation of the Reichsmark as Legal Tender in Luxemburg, August 26, 1940[17]

SECTION 1. The Reichsmark shall be legal tender in Luxemburg in addition to the legal tender heretofore established by law.

SECTION 2. The rate of exchange shall be established as follows: 10 Luxemburg francs equal 1 Reichsmark.

SECTION 3. This order shall take effect as of August 26, 1940.

Luxemburg, August 25, 1940.

GUSTAV SIMON, *Gauleiter*
Chief of the Civil Administration in Luxemburg

Proclamation concerning the Calling in and Surrender of Foreign Exchange of September 13, 1940[18]

By virtue of my order concerning the statutes applicable to foreign exchange in Luxemburg of August 27, 1940, all individuals and incorporated associations resident in Luxemburg are required to sell their United States of America dollar notes, Swiss francs, Swedish crown notes (in denominations not exceeding fifty Swedish crowns), French franc notes, gold coins, gold, pure and alloyed (in unprocessed or in half-manufactured form), not later than September 15, 1940, to the International Bank or the General Bank, General Alsatian Bank, the Credit Institute for Alsace and Lorraine, or their branches. All other foreign legal tender not included in the above list

[16a] See also order concerning Reich Credit Institutes, above, p. 329.
[17] *Verordnungsblatt*, No. 2, September 24, 1940, p. 6. [18] *Ibid*., p. 13.

shall be registered not later than September 15, 1940, with the Reich Credit Institute in Luxemburg. In addition, claims in foreign and home currency against persons deemed to be aliens under the exchange regulations, and foreign and German securities as well as any other foreign exchange values are subject to such registration.

Violations of the duties of sale and registration are punishable by severe penalties. The duty of compliance with the aforementioned order is therefore called to the attention of every individual resident of Luxemburg for his own best interest. Special forms provided for the registration of national and foreign securities are available from the Reich Credit Institute or the other banks mentioned above. It may be added that the banks will give information on special questions.

Luxemburg, September 13, 1940.

Dr. Münzel
Acting Chief of the Civil Administration in Luxemburg

Order concerning the Calling in and Withdrawal from Circulation of Belgian and Luxemburg Francs and of Reich Credit Institute Notes in Luxemburg, January 29, 1941 [19]

[EXCERPTS]

In pursuance of the authority vested in the Chief of the Civil Administration in Luxemburg, the following order is issued for the territory subject to his jurisdiction:

Section 1. On the effective date of this order Belgian and Luxemburg francs and Reich Credit Institute notes shall cease to be legal tender within the territory subject to the jurisdiction of the Chief of the Civil Administration in Luxemburg.

The Reichsmark shall be exclusive legal tender.

Section 2. (1) The Public Treasury branch offices situated within the jurisdiction of the Chief of the Civil Administration, the Reichsbank in Luxemburg, and the banking institutions authorized by it will exchange not later than March 1, 1941, all Belgian and Luxemburg francs which were legal tender on the effective date of this order, and Reich Credit Institute notes against legal tender in Reichsmarks.

(2) The rate of exchange is established as follows: 1 Belgian franc equals 0.08 Reichsmark, 1 Luxemburg franc equals 0.10 Reichsmark.

(3) After the lapse of the period established for the exchange by subsection 1 the Belgian franc shall be considered as foreign exchange and be subject to the provisions of the order concerning foreign exchange regulations of August 27, 1940, applicable in Luxemburg (*Verordnungsblatt für Luxemburg*, p. 6).

[19] *Verordnungsblatt*, No. 9, February 4, 1941, p. 67.

SECTION 3. (1) Claims for Belgian and Luxemburg francs by residents, on other residents, as defined in Section 5, shall be changed into claims for Reichsmarks at the rate of exchange established in subsection 2 of Section 2 as if they had arisen on the effective date of this order.

(2) Such change of a claim shall not be prevented by a gold or gold value clause or by an agreement that performance shall be made in currency stipulated; such agreements shall be ineffective. This order shall not be deemed to affect, in any other manner, other rights and duties of the parties arising out of the obligation.

SECTION 4. (1) The same change in accordance with Section 3 shall be made in all mortgage or similar rights over vacant and improved lots of every description where the mortgage or other right is given to secure the performance of an obligation to pay money and to secure all usufructs and estates in land whether they were created under private or public law; to make such transformation effective as against third parties no special registration or rectification on the records of the land registry shall be required.

. . . . .

SECTION 5. For the purpose of this order all persons shall be considered as residents who have their domicile or usual residence, place of business, or of management within the territory of the German Reich, including the Protectorate of Bohemia and Moravia, or within the jurisdiction of the several Chiefs of the Civil Administrations in Alsace-Lorraine and Luxemburg. Branches of foreign enterprises situated within the territory referred to above and plants of an alien situated in that territory shall be considered as those of a resident for the purposes of this order regardless of the fact that they are branches and even though the place of management shall be situated abroad.

SECTION 6. The chief of the Civil Administration shall issue the necessary legal and administrative regulations for the implementation of this order.

SECTION 7. This order shall take effect on the day after publication.

Luxemburg, January 29, 1941.

SIEKMEIER

Acting Chief of the Civil Administration in Luxemburg

5. LABOR

Order concerning the Issuance of Work Books in Luxemburg, September 30, 1940 [20]

Pursuant to the authority vested in the Chief of the Civil Administration in Luxemburg, the following order is issued for the territory subject to his jurisdiction.

[20] *Verordnungsblatt*, No. 5, October 12, 1940, p. 24.

SECTION 1. (1) For the purpose of assuring a suitable distribution of manpower in the Luxemburg economy, work books shall be issued.

(2) The work books heretofore legally issued for Luxemburg shall, on issuance of the new books, be called in and shall thereupon become invalid.

SECTION 2. The work books shall be issued by the Labor Office in Luxemburg. No other agency may issue work books or similar documents intended as a prerequisite for hiring as worker or employee, or for a preferred status for such hiring, unless special regulations shall otherwise provide.

SECTION 3. Any person issuing work books or similar documents in intentional violation of the provisions of Section 2 shall be punishable by imprisonment or fine, or both. The same penalty shall apply to any person violating the provisions contained in subsection 2 of Section 1.

SECTION 4. For the enforcement and implementation of this order the following provisions shall apply:

1. The order of the Reich Labor Minister concerning the work book of April 22, 1939 (*RGBl.* I, p. 834).

2. The proclamation of the Reich Labor Minister concerning the combination of reports to be made on the work book and to the Public Health Insurance Office, of February 8, 1938 (*Deutscher Reichsanzeiger*, No. 34).

SECTION 5. The Chief of the Civil Administration in Luxemburg shall issue all rules and regulations he may deem necessary for the enforcement of this order.

SECTION 6. This order shall take effect as of October 1, 1940.

Luxemburg, September 30, 1940.

GUSTAV SIMON
Chief of the Civil Administration in Luxemburg

Proclamation concerning Entry into the Reich Labor Service, February 12, 1941 [21]

Single men and women born in the years 1919 to 1922 shall register immediately, and in no event later than February 20, 1941, for entry into the Reich Labor Service. Registration shall take place with the county police authority having jurisdiction in the domicile of the registrant, i.e., in the County Districts of Esch, Diekirch, Grevenmacher, at the office of the County Chairman; in the city of Luxemburg, at the office of the President of the Police. The written application for registration shall contain first and family names, full address, occupation, and nationality. Examination of the registrants shall take place on and after February 24, 1941. Further announcements as to the exact date and place for the several counties will be

[21] *Verordnungsblatt*, No. 13, February 14, 1941, p. 98.

established. The registrant shall be reimbursed for traveling expenses to the place of the examination.

Prerequisites for entry into the Reich Labor Service are the following: The applicants must be of German or of kindred blood; they must possess Luxemburg nationality and have their domicile within the territory of the jurisdiction of the Chief of the Civil Administration. Applicants will be preferred for induction who are candidates for a career of leadership (men and women leaders) in the Reich Labor Service.

Induction into a six months' term of labor service for men is expected to take place on March 15, 1941, and those inducted will be formed, if possible, into detachments of the Reich Labor Service garrisoned within the district of the Moselland. Induction into the labor service for women is expected to take place on April 2, 1941.

Labor service performed now on a voluntary basis will, upon later establishment of compulsory service in the Reich Labor Service for Luxemburg, be fully credited toward the term of compulsory service.

Luxemburg, February 12, 1941.

GUSTAV SIMON, *Gauleiter*
Chief of the Civil Administration in Luxemburg

6. RELIGION

Order concerning Withdrawal from Religious Congregations, December 9, 1940 [22]

In pursuance of the authority vested in the Chief of the Civil Administration in Luxemburg, the following order is issued for the territory subject to his jurisdiction:

SECTION 1. Persons who have completed their fourteenth year of life may declare their resignation from a religious body. On behalf of children under fourteen years of age a declaration of resignation may be made by his or her guardian. Such resignation cannot be declared by way of proxy.

SECTION 2. (1) The resignation shall be declared before the Registrar of Vital Statistics at the domicile or usual residence of the declarant. Persons in active military service, members of the armed units of the S.S., of Police Units mobilized for Special Purposes, of the Reich Labor Service, and of the Todt Organization may make such declaration also before the Registrar of Vital Statistics of the locality where they are at the time of their declaration.

(2) The declaration of resignation may be made orally and recorded by the Registrar, or submitted in writing. An official form shall preferably be used for a written declaration.

[22] *Verordnungsblatt*, No. 66, December 11, 1940, p. 377.

(3) Spouses, parents, and children may make their declaration in a single instrument.

SECTION 3. The resignation shall take effect upon the recording of an oral declaration or the receipt of a written declaration by the Registrar.

SECTION 4. The Registrar shall issue a Certificate of Resignation to the declarant and immediately inform the secretary of the religious group within whose parish the resident is situated, of such resignation.

SECTION 5. The declaration of resignation and the Certificate of Resignation shall be exempt from all cost, fees, and excises.

SECTION 6. The Chief of the Civil Administration in Luxemburg shall issue rules and regulations necessary for the enforcement of this order.

SECTION 7. This order shall take effect as of January 1, 1941. All provisions of law not in accordance with this order shall be repealed as of that date.

Luxemburg, December 9, 1940.

GUSTAV SIMON, *Gauleiter*
Chief of the Civil Administration in Luxemburg

Order for the Preservation of Freedom of Religious Belief, December 9, 1940 [23]

Pursuant to the authority vested in the Chief of the Civil Administration in Luxemburg, the following order is issued for the territory subject to his jurisdiction:

SECTION 1. (1) Any publication of names of persons who have resigned from a religious congregation or intend to do so, or who do not participate in activities of a religious character or do not intend to do so, shall be unlawful. The same applies to a public announcement made under such circumstances that the individual involved can be identified in any other way.

(2) Any other announcement shall likewise be unlawful unless it is neither intended to be nor is of such a kind as to restrict the freedom of religious belief in any manner, or to prejudice the person involved or third persons in any manner whatsoever.

SECTION 2. Violations shall be punishable by imprisonment for not less than one month or by fines of not less than 150 and not more than 15,000 Reichsmarks.

SECTION 3. This order shall take effect one week after the date of publication.

Luxemburg, December 9, 1940.

GUSTAV SIMON, *Gauleiter*
Chief of the Civil Administration in Luxemburg

[23] *Verordnungsblatt*, No. 66, December 11, 1940, p. 378.

7. GENOCIDE LEGISLATION

Order concerning the Use of the German Language in Luxemburg, August 6, 1940 [24]

The language of Luxemburg and of its inhabitants is, and always has been, German. Pursuant to the authority vested in me as the Chief of the Civil Administration of Luxemburg, I hereby order for the entire territory of Luxemburg as follows:

SECTION 1. The German language shall be the exclusive official language. The language used in judicial proceedings shall be exclusively German.

SECTION 2. The language of instruction in all schools shall be exclusively German. In primary schools the French language shall no longer be taught as a subject of instruction; in secondary schools courses in the French language shall continue to be given.

SECTION 3. Daily papers, weekly publications, and all other periodicals, including any private advertising they may contain, shall be published in the German language only. Likewise, the German language shall be the only one permissible in all other printed matter.

It shall be unlawful to display advertisements printed in the French language, in show cases or in any other offerings to the public.

SECTION 4. In the economic life of the country throughout all its occupations, the German language shall be used exclusively; this applies especially to written communications and advertisements of every description.

SECTION 5. Commercial signs and inscriptions on buildings shall be permissible only in the German language.

SECTION 6. For traffic, street, and road signs, only inscriptions in the German language and with the German versions of local names shall be permissible.

SECTION 7. The term "German language" for the purpose of this order shall be deemed to refer to "High German" (*Hochdeutsch*).

SECTION 8. Violations of this order shall be punishable by imprisonment or fine; in lieu of a sentence imposed by a court, punishment by imprisonment or fine may be imposed by summary order of the police.

SECTION 9. This order shall take effect as of the date of publication. Likewise, changes necessary in commercial signs, inscriptions on buildings, traffic, street, and road signs shall immediately be made and completed not later than September 30, 1940.

SECTION 10. The administrative agencies in Luxemburg shall be responsible for the enforcement of this order.

Luxemburg, August 6, 1940.

GUSTAV SIMON, *Gauleiter*
Chief of the Civil Administration in Luxemburg

[24] *Verordnungsblatt*, No. 1, September 1, 1940, p. 1.

Proclamation in connection with the Order concerning the Use of the German Language, September 14, 1940 [25]

In connection with the order concerning the use of the German language in Luxemburg of August 6, 1940 (*Verordnungsblatt für Luxemburg*, p. 1), it is pointed out as follows:

In legal transactions, in communications to authorities, in business, and in advertising of every description, Luxemburg nationals may use their Christian names in the German version only.

Luxemburg, September 14, 1940.

GUSTAV SIMON, *Gauleiter*
Chief of the Civil Administration in Luxemburg

Order concerning the Change of First and Family Names in Luxemburg, January 31, 1941 [26]

Pursuant to the authority vested in the Chief of the Civil Administration in Luxemburg the following order is issued for the territory subject to his jurisdiction.

SECTION 1. (1) Nationals of Luxemburg and persons without nationality having their domicile or usual residence within the territory of the Chief of the Civil Administration in Luxemburg, who have a foreign or non-German first name, are required to assume, in lieu of such name, the corresponding German first name or, if that is impossible, to select a German first name.

(2) Nationals of Luxemburg and persons without nationality referred to in subsection 1, who have a family name of German origin which later has been given a foreign or non-German form, are required to resume the original German form.

(3) Applications for the change shall be made not later than February 15, 1941, to the County Chairman having jurisdiction, and in the City of Luxemburg, to the Chief Mayor.

(4) If application for the change is not made in suitable form, the authority receiving the application shall determine the name after a hearing granted the applicant.

(5) Persons who do not apply within the period established for a change of their names, may, after lapse of the period, be ordered *ex officio* by the authorities to make such application for change of their name, and in the event of delay, a penalty may be established in the order. A person disregarding the official order to submit an application may be adjudged liable for the penalty forfeited. In addition, a German first name may be given to a

[25] *Verordnungsblatt*, No. 2, September 24, 1940, p. 15.
[26] *Ibid.*, No. 21, March 14, 1941, p. 146.

defaulting applicant and, in the case of subsection 1 or in the case of subsection 2, the required change of the family name may be ordered without a hearing.

SECTION 2. (1) It is recommended that Luxemburg nationals and persons without nationality referred to in subsection 1 of Section 1, who have a foreign or non-German family name which is not, as in the case of subsection 2 of Section 1, of German origin shall apply for a suitable change of their family name as an expression of their adherence to Germanism.

(2) Application shall be made to the County Chairman having jurisdiction, and in the city of Luxemburg, to the Chief Mayor.

(3) Members of a clan[27] shall assume an identical name. If their applications disagree, a decision will be made *ex officio* by the authorities and promptly communicated to all members of the clan.

SECTION 3. (1) A husband shall make an application on behalf of his wife.

(2) A legal guardian shall apply on behalf of a ward whose legal capacity is limited or who is incompetent.

(3) A change of family name shall be deemed to operate as a change of the name of the wife and the children of the applicant who are in his custody. The same applies to an application of a woman with regard to her illegitimate children.

(4) After the change of name the authority concerned shall cause an annotation to be entered indicating the change of name in the Register of Births and Families, and shall report the change to the Registrar of Prior Convictions and to the local police authority of the domicile or residence of the person whose name has been changed.

(5) The change of foreign or non-German names shall be made free of charge.

SECTION 4. The Chief of the Civil Administration shall prescribe rules and regulations necessary for the enforcement of this order.

SECTION 5. This order shall take effect on the day after the date of publication.

Luxemburg, January 31, 1941.

GUSTAV SIMON, *Gauleiter*
Chief of the Civil Administration in Luxemburg

Duty of Registration for All Persons Engaged in Creating or Transmitting Cultural Values in Luxemburg[28]

In order to complete the cultural organization it is useful and necessary to organize all forces engaged in the creation and transmission, or in activi-

[27] Clan means "family group."—ED.
[28] *Verordnungsblatt*, No. 15, February 21, 1941, p. 109.

ties in connection with the communication to the public, of cultural values in the fields of painting, drawing, sculpture, music, writing, or the theatre.

For this reason all persons engaged in any of the pursuits of art hereinafter mentioned are hereby required, whether or not they engage in these activities on a full- or part-time basis, to apply in writing to the Public Relations Section of the Reich Propaganda Office in the Division of the Chief of the Civil Administration in Luxemburg (Luxemburg, Krautmarkt); the application must be in writing and contain a statement of the name, the activity engaged in on a full- or part-time basis, and a short statement of the most important artistic creations and public successes of the applicant. Application shall be made not later than January 20, 1941; the lower left corner of the envelope must carry the notation "Culture."

Any person who fails to register and who engages in any artistic activity after January 20, 1941, will run the risk of being forbidden to engage in any further activity of this kind.

All persons engaged in any of the pursuits of art mentioned hereinafter are required to apply for registration not later than January 20, 1941.

Painting, Architecture, Designing, Drawing, etc.

Architects
Interior Decorators
Landscape Architects
Sculptors
Painters
Etchers
Commercial Artists
Designers
Artistic Craftsmen
Copyists
Restorers of art objects
Art and Antique Dealers
Art Publishers
Dealers in Reproductions of Paintings

Music

Composers
Soloists
Orchestra Musicians
Music Teachers
Music Schools
Choir Directors
Glee Clubs (men only)
Glee Clubs (mixed)
Concert Agents

Literature

Writers
Publishers
Book Dealers

Theatre

Actors
Radio Announcers
Circus Performers
Dancers
Exhibitors

Dr. PERIZONIUS, Director of the Public Relations Branch Section of the Reich Propaganda Office established as a division of the Civil Administration in Luxemburg.

MEMEL TERRITORY

Law concerning the Reunion of the Memelland with the German Reich, March 23, 1939 [1]

The Government of the Reich has decided upon the following law, which is hereby promulgated.

SECTION 1. Memel Territory is again a part of the German Reich.

SECTION 2. (1) The Memelland is hereby incorporated into the land of Prussia and into the province of East Prussia. It shall be attached to the district Gumbinnen.

(2) The Reich Minister of the Interior shall decide as to the division of the Memelland into town and rural counties or the incorporation of the Memelland into existing town or rural counties.

SECTION 3. Inhabitants of the Memelland, who lost German citizenship on July 30, 1924, because of the separation of the Memelland, shall again become German citizens, if on March 22, 1939, they had their domicile in the Memelland or in the German Reich. The same shall apply to persons who derive their citizenship from such an inhabitant of the Memelland.

SECTION 4. (1) In the Memelland the whole body of German law shall go into effect on May 1, 1939.

(2) The proper Minister of the Reich may decide, in cooperation with the Reich Minister of the Interior, whether the law of the Reich shall or shall not go into effect at a later date or with special limitations. Such regulations shall be published in the *Reichsgesetzblatt*.

SECTION 5. (1) In the Memelland all Prussian law (*Landesrecht*) shall go into effect on May 1, 1939.

(2) The Prussian Provincial Government (*Landesregierung*) may decide that the Prussian law shall not apply in the Memelland or shall apply at a later date or with special limitations in the Memelland. Such regulations shall be promulgated in the Prussian Law Collection.

SECTION 6. (1) The central office (*Zentralstelle*) for the reunion of the Memelland with the German Reich shall be under the Reich Minister of the Interior.

(2) The chief president (*Oberpräsident*) of the province of Eastern Prussia shall serve as commissioner for the transitional period. The leader of the Germans of Memel shall serve as his deputy.

(3) The Reich Minister of the Interior shall be authorized to issue decrees and administrative regulations necessary for the implementation and completion of this law.

[1] *Reichsgesetzblatt*, 1939, No. 54.

SECTION 7. This law shall go into effect as of March 22, 1939.

On the deck of the battleship *Deutschland*, March 23, 1939.

ADOLF HITLER, *Führer and Reich Chancellor;* FRICK, *Reich Minister of the Interior;* GÖRING, *Commissioner for the Four-Year Plan, General Field Marshal, Minister-President of Prussia;* VON RIBBENTROP, *Reich Minister for Foreign Affairs;* DR. LAMMERS, *Reich Minister and Chief of the Reich Chancellery.*

Decree concerning the Introduction of German Currency in the Territory of Memel, March 23, 1939 [2]

Pursuant to the decree of the Führer and Reich Chancellor on the implementation of the Four-Year Plan, of October 18, 1936 (*RGBl.* I, p. 887), the following is ordered:

SECTION 1. Legal tender for the Memel Territory is the Reichsmark. The exchange rate is one lit to 40 Reichspfennigs.

SECTION 2. The Reich Minister of Economy shall issue, in agreement with the Reich Minister of Finance, the regulations necessary for the completion and implementation of this decree.

SECTION 3. This decree shall take effect as of March 23, 1939.

Berlin, March 23, 1939.

The Commissioner for the Four-Year Plan
By deputy: KÖRNER
The Reich Minister of Finance
Count SCHWERIN VON KROSIGK
The Reich Minister of Economy
By deputy: DR. LANDFRIED
The Reich Minister of the Interior
By deputy: PFUNDTNER

[2] *Reichsgesetzblatt*, 1939, No. 56.

NETHERLANDS

1. ADMINISTRATION

Decree of the Führer concerning the Exercise of Governmental Authority in the Netherlands, May 18, 1940 [1]

In order to safeguard public order and public life within the Netherlands territories now under the protection of the German Army, I hereby decree:

SECTION 1. The occupied Netherlands territories shall be administered by the "Reich Commissioner for the Occupied Netherlands Territories." His official residence shall be in The Hague. The Reich Commissioner is guardian of the interests of the Reich and is vested with supreme civil authority. He shall be directly responsible to me and shall be subject to my instructions as to general policies and to my orders.

SECTION 2. The German Supreme Commander in the Netherlands is vested with supreme military authority; his orders in so far as they relate to the civil domain shall be enforced by the Reich Commissioner. He is authorized to order any and all measures necessary for the execution of his military orders and for military security. The same authority is vested in the Chief Commanders of the several branches of the German armed forces.

SECTION 3. The Reich Commissioner may employ members of the German police forces for the execution of his orders. These German police forces shall be subject to the orders of the German Supreme Commander in the Netherlands in accordance with military requirements and with due regard to the duties of the Reich Commissioner.

SECTION 4. The Reich Commissioner may call on the Netherlands authorities for the enforcement of regulations and for aid in connection with the exercise by him of his administrative functions.

SECTION 5. The law, heretofore in force, shall remain in effect in so far as compatible with the purposes of the occupation.

The Reich Commissioner may, by order, promulgate laws. His orders shall be published in the *Verordnungsblatt für die besetzten niederländischen Gebiete.*[2]

SECTION 6. Dr. Arthur Seyss-Inquart is hereby appointed Reich Commissioner for the occupied Netherlands territories.

SECTION 7. Rules and regulations for the enforcement and implementation of this order shall be issued (in accordance with my instructions) by

[1] *Verordnungsblatt für die besetzten niederländischen Gebiete*, No. 1, June 5, 1940, p. 2; and *Reichsgesetzblatt*, 1940, I, p. 778.

[2] Official designation of the legal gazette for the occupied Netherlands territories, published by the German occupying authorities in Holland.—ED.

the Reich Minister and Chief of the Reich Chancellery for the civil domain, and by the Chief of the Supreme Command of the German armed forces for the military domain.

SECTION 8. This order shall be operative as soon as and in so far as I shall withdraw the order for the exercise of full executive powers by the Chief Commander of the Army.

Headquarters of the Führer, May 18, 1940.

ADOLF HITLER, *Führer;* GÖRING, *General Field Marshal, President of the Council of Ministers for the Defense of the Reich;* DR. LAMMERS, *Reich Minister and Chief of the Reich Chancellery;* KEITEL, *Chief of the Supreme Command of the Wehrmacht;* VON RIBBENTROP, *Reich Minister of Foreign Affairs;* FRICK, *Reich Minister of the Interior.*

Proclamation of the Reich Commissioner for the Occupied Netherlands Territories to the Netherlands Population, May 25, 1940 [3]

On this day I have assumed supreme governmental authority within the civil domain in the Netherlands.

It is due to the magnanimity of the Führer and the power of the German armed forces that within a few days after the catastrophe brought about by the former leadership of the Netherlands, an order of public life is restored which will interfere with the usual and prevailing state of affairs only to the extent demanded by the special conditions.

As Reich Commissioner I hold supreme governmental authority in the civil domain in the Netherlands territories placed under the protection of German troops, for the purpose of safeguarding public order and public life. I shall take all measures, including those of a legislative nature, which are necessary for the fulfillment of this task. It is my will to leave unimpaired, as far as this is possible, the Netherlands law as heretofore in force, to avail myself of the Netherlands authorities for the fulfillment of administrative tasks, and to preserve the independence of the judiciary. I expect, however, that all Netherlands judges, officials, and employees presently active in public service will conscientiously comply with my orders directed toward that objective, and that the Netherlands nation will follow this leadership with understanding and self-discipline.

The Netherlands soldiers have fought well in battle. The Netherlands civil population has adopted a satisfactory attitude toward the fighting troops. There is nothing which should prevent us from meeting each other on a plane of mutual respect.

[3] *Verordnungsblatt,* No. 1, June 5, 1940, p. 6.

Under their Führer the German people are fighting a decisive battle for their survival or destruction, a struggle which the hatred and envy of their enemies have forced upon them. This struggle compels the German nation to exert all its strength and gives it the right to avail itself of all means within its reach. This compulsion and privilege will also necessarily affect the life of the Netherlands nation and its economy. It will, however, be my concern that the Netherlands nation, akin in blood to the German nation, shall not be subject to living conditions less favorable than those necessitated by the community of fate and the destructive intentions of our enemies at this time.

As Reich Commissioner I have to safeguard the interests of the Reich in the Netherlands territories placed under the protection of the German troops and I shall safeguard them. The Netherlands nation, in fulfilling the duties resulting from the common task, will be able to secure its country and its liberty for the future.

Headquarters of the Führer, May 25, 1940.

SEYSS-INQUART
Reich Commissioner for the Occupied Netherlands Territories

Order of the Reich Commissioner for the Occupied Netherlands Territories concerning the Exercise of Governmental Authority in the Netherlands, May 29, 1940 [4]

By virtue of Section 5 of the decree of the Führer concerning the exercise of governmental authority in the Netherlands of May 18, 1940 (*RGBl.* I, p. 778), I hereby issue the following order, which shall remain in force for the duration of the occupation of the Netherlands territories by the German armed forces.

SECTION 1. (1) To the extent required for the fulfillment of his duties, the Reich Commissioner for the occupied Netherlands territories assumes all powers, privileges, and rights heretofore vested in the King and the government in accordance with the Constitution and the laws of the Netherlands.

(2) Should the interests of the Greater German Reich or the safeguarding of public order or life in the Netherlands so require, the Reich Commissioner may take appropriate measures, including the issuance of general orders. These orders of the Reich Commissioner shall have the force of laws.

SECTION 2. (1) The Netherlands law heretofore in force shall remain in force in so far as it is compatible with the occupation and not contrary to the provisions of the decree of the Führer concerning the exercise of governmen-

[4] *Verordnungsblatt*, 1940, No. 1, p. 8.

tal functions in the Netherlands. The general orders of the Commander in Chief of the Army issued for the occupied Netherlands territories shall remain in force until further notice.

(2) All rules and regulations shall be submitted to the Reich Commissioner before publication. Publication shall not take place if the Reich Comissioner so requests.

(3) The Reich Commissioner hereby reserves the right of delegating the power vested in him by virtue of subsection 2 to the German authorities which are subject to his orders.

SECTION 3. (1) The Reich Commissioner will enforce his orders through the Netherlands authorities unless the German authorities which are subject to this order take direct action themselves.

(2) The Secretaries General of the Netherlands ministries shall, within their respective jurisdictions, be responsible to the Reich Commissioner for the orderly supervision and administration of official business. They may, in compliance with subsections 2 and 3 of Section 2, issue rules and regulations implementing Netherlands statutes and orders of the Reich Commissioner.

SECTION 4. (1) The Reich Commissioner will exercise his authority through general commissioners, who will operate as members of his staff.

(2) The Reich Commissioner will further appoint commissioners for the several provinces. He will also appoint special commissioners for specified areas or purposes as the need may arise.

SECTION 5. (1) The maintenance of public peace, safety, and order shall be entrusted to the Netherlands police force unless the Reich Commissioner calls on German S.S. or police forces for the enforcement of his orders. The Netherlands police forces shall be subject to the supervision of the German police force and shall be required to comply with its orders.

(2) The investigation and combating of all activities hostile to the Reich and Germanism shall be the concern of the German police force.

SECTION 6. (1) The judiciary shall be independent.

(2) Judgments shall be entered in the name of the law.

(3) The Reich Commissioner will determine which judgments are to be submitted for his confirmation before execution may be issued.

(4) The Reich Commissioner will designate by general order the crimes to be tried by special courts and the conditions under which Netherlands citizens are subject to the criminal jurisdiction of the German Army or the German police force, respectively.

SECTION 7. Within such period as shall be determined by the Reich Commissioner, judges, officials, and employees who hold public office, as well as persons engaged in full-time or part-time teaching in public or private schools and universities, shall make a declaration in lieu of an oath that they will comply conscientiously with the general and other orders of the Reich

Commissioner and the German authorities subordinate to him and that they will refrain from any action directed against the German Reich or the German armed forces.

SECTION 8. All German authorities, agencies, and officials, with the exception of those of the armed forces, shall be subject to the orders of the Reich Commissioner.

SECTION 9. General orders will be published in the *Verordnungsblatt für die besetzten niederländischen Gebiete*, which will be issued in the German and Dutch languages. The German text will be authoritative.

SECTION 10. This order shall take effect as of the date of publication.

The Hague, May 29, 1940.

SEYSS-INQUART

Reich Commissioner for the Occupied Netherlands Territories

Decree of the Reich Commissioner for the Occupied Netherlands Territories concerning the Organization and Establishment of the Office of the Reich Commissioner, June 3, 1940 [5]

[EXCERPTS]

By virtue of Section 5 of the decree of the Führer concerning the exercise of governmental authority in the Netherlands of May 18, 1940 (*RGBl.* I, p. 778), I hereby decree:

SECTION 1. (1) For the fulfillment of his official duties the Reich Commissioner for the occupied Netherlands territories will act through general commissioners, who are members of his staff and who will head the following sections:

1. General Administration and Judiciary.
2. Public Safety (Superior S.S. and Police Chief).
3. Finance and Commerce (Economics).
4. Special Matters.

(2) The representative of the Foreign Office and the Custodian for the Netherlands Bank shall be directly subject to the orders of the Reich Commissioner.

(3) The Reich Commissioner will appoint commissioners for the several provinces. He will appoint a special commissioner for specific localities or purposes as the need may arise.

. . . .

SECTION 3. (1) The general commissioners shall be authorized (within the scope of their official duties) to require information of all and every

[5] *Verordnungsblatt*, 1940, No. 1, p. 11.

description from all Netherlands authorities, agencies, and establishments of a public or private character and to give them the necessary instructions for that purpose.

. . . . .

SECTION 4. The official duties of the Commissioner General for Administration and the Judiciary shall embrace all matters relating to:

1. General orders and legislation, constitutional law, and the *Verordnungsblatt für die besetzten niederländischen Gebiete.*
2. Planning.
3. Civil administration, especially the supervision of municipalities with the exception of municipal police forces.
4. The administration of justice with the exception of the Reich police forces.
5. The furtherance of culture (art, protection of public monuments, science, public education, etc.) as well as matters relating to schools and churches.
6. Public health, and the cultural and social welfare of juveniles.

SECTION 5. The Superior S.S. and Police Chief shall command the units of the military S.S. and the German police forces transferred to the occupied Netherlands territories, supervise the Netherlands central and municipal police forces, and issue to them the necessary orders.

SECTION 6. The official duties of the Commissioner General of Finance and Commerce shall embrace all matters relating to:

1. The Ministry of Finance.
2. The Ministry of Economics (Commerce).
3. The Ministry of Waterways.
4. The Postal Administration.
5. The Ministry of Public Welfare, with the exception of the matters enumerated in Section 4 (6).

SECTION 7. The official duties of the Commissioner General for Special Matters shall embrace all issues relating to:

1. The molding of public opinion, and to associations formed for purposes other than private gain.
2. Such duties as may devolve upon him by virtue of special orders of the Reich Commissioner.

SECTION 8. (1) The official duties of the commissioners for the several provinces, appointed by the Reich Commissioner, shall embrace—with the exception of the maintenance of public safety—all matters pertaining to public administration, economic welfare, and the molding of public opinion within the areas to which they are appointed. They may call, for the fulfillment of their duties, on members of the German police force, in accordance with general rules and regulations issued by the Superior S.S. and Police Chief.

(2) The Netherlands authorities, agencies, institutions, and establishments of a public and private character, and their officers and agents, shall be required, by virtue of a special order, to report to the commissioners appointed by the Reich Commissioner concerning certain matters without being requested to do so in every instance and to inform them about impending administrative action. Such action shall be suspended on request of the commissioner concerned.

SECTION 9. The authority of special commissioners appointed for specified areas or purposes shall be determined by the duties assigned to them.

SECTION 10. (1) The commissioners appointed for the several provinces by the Reich Commissioner shall have the same official residence as the commissioners appointed under Article 141 of the Constitution.

(2) The official residence of the special commissioners will be designated by the Reich Commissioner.

SECTION 11. The Reich Commissioner alone will establish or abolish German governmental agencies for civil administration and determine their official duties and jurisdiction.

SECTION 12. This decree shall take effect as of the date of publication.

The Hague, June 3, 1940.

SEYSS-INQUART
Reich Commissioner for the Occupied Netherlands Territories

Order of the Reich Commissioner for the Occupied Netherlands Territories concerning the Entry and Departure of Persons into and from the Netherlands Territories, June 6, 1940 [6]

[EXCERPTS]

By virtue of Section 5 of the decree of the Führer concerning the exercise of governmental authority in the Netherlands of May 18, 1940 (*RGBl.* I, p. 778), I hereby order as follows:

SECTION 1. No person shall be permitted to enter into, or depart from, the occupied Netherlands territory.

SECTION 2. If the existence of exceptional circumstances can be proven, permission to enter or leave the territories will be granted by the Commissioner.

. . . . .

The Hague, June 6, 1940.

SEYSS-INQUART
Reich Commissioner for the Occupied Netherlands Territories

[6] *Verordnungsblatt*, No. 2, June 7, 1942, p. 19.

Order of Reich Commissioner for the Occupied Netherlands Territories concerning the Authority of the Secretaries General of the Several Netherlands Ministries, June 21, 1940 [7]

Pursuant to Section 5 of the decree of the Führer concerning the exercise of governmental authority in the Netherlands of May 18, 1940 (*RGBl.*, p. 778), I hereby order as follows:

SECTION 1. (1) The Secretaries General of the several Netherlands ministries shall be authorized, within the general jurisdiction of their respective departments, to take all measures necessary for the maintenance of public order and preservation of public life. These measures may in particular include the promulgation of general rules and regulations and the issuance of instructions to authorities, agencies, offices, institutions, establishments, and organizations, private or public, and their agents, which are subject to their authority or supervision.

(2) Rules and regulations issued in accordance with subsection 1 may include criminal provisions for cases of violations.

SECTION 2. The Reich Commissioner for the occupied Netherlands territories reserves the power to limit or revoke, in specific instances, the authority conferred by virtue of Section 1.

SECTION 3. This order shall take effect as of the day of publication.

The Hague, June 21, 1940.

SEYSS-INQUART
Reich Commissioner for the Occupied Netherlands Territories

Order of the Reich Commissioner for the Occupied Netherlands Territories concerning the Functions of the Council of State and Several Representative Agencies of Public Law, June 21, 1940 [8]

Pursuant to Section 5 of the decree of the Führer concerning the exercise of governmental authority in the Netherlands of May 18, 1940 (*RGBl.* I, p. 778), I hereby order as follows:

SECTION 1. All activities of the two chambers of the States-General (*Generalstaaten*) shall be suspended until further notice.

SECTION 2. The functions of the councilors of state in accordance with Article 19, Section 2, of Article 38, Articles 39, 46, 77, and Section 3 of Article 136 of the Constitution, and in accordance with Sections 21, 22, 24, 25, and 26 of the Act concerning the Council of State of December 21, 1861 (*Staatsblad*, No. 129), shall be suspended until further notice.

SECTION 3. (1) Elections for the Chambers of the States-General shall be suspended until further notice.

[7] *Verordnungsblatt*, No. 5, June 22, 1940, p. 54. [8] *Ibid.*

(2) The Reich Commissioner for the occupied Netherlands territories shall determine the elections, if any, which shall take place for the Provincial States (*Provinzialstaaten*), the Municipal Councils, or other representative bodies.

(3) The Reich Commissioner shall determine what new appointments of members of Provincial or Municipal Councils are to be made, if any. If the need arises, he shall also decide on the appointemnt of other public officials.

SECTION 4. (1) Where elections come due but may not be held in accordance with the provisions contained in Section 3, the mandate of the persons previously elected shall be considered extended until further notice.

(2) If such a situation should arise, the Reich Commissioner shall take all measures necessary to assure the existence of a quorum of a representative body of public law.

SECTION 5. This order shall take effect as of the date of publication.

The Hague, June 21, 1940.

SEYSS-INQUART
Reich Commissioner for the Occupied Netherlands Territories

Order of the Secretary General of the Ministry of Justice for the Safeguarding of the Economic Independence of the Press, August 17, 1940 [9]

By virtue of the powers granted by Section 1 of Order No. 23/1940, and in accordance with Sections 2 and 3 of Order No. 3/1940 of the Reich Commissioner for the occupied Netherlands territories, it is hereby decreed:

SECTION 1. (1) The editors of daily or weekly papers, illustrated journals, periodicals, newsletters, or any other periodical press publication, as well as the owners or managers of a business engaged fully or mainly in the production or distribution of such press publications, are hereby ordered to submit, not later than September 25, 1940, a completed questionnaire to the director of police or the public prosecutor having jurisdiction in their district.

(2) A person thus subject to the duty of answering such a questionnaire shall be required, not later than September 10, 1940, to apply to the officer mentioned in subsection 1 for a questionnaire. The application must fully state the kind of enterprise involved.

(3) The provisions of subsections 1 and 2 shall apply to businesses carried on by individuals or partnerships, associations, corporations, or endowments.

(4) The directors of police or public prosecutors shall be authorized to check the correctness of the statements made.

[9] *Verordnungsblatt*, No. 20, August 19, 1940, p. 327.

SECTION 2. (1) Before complete or partial assignments, transfers, or hypothecations are made, the consent of the Secretary General must be obtained in the case of:

1. Publishing or distributing firms as described in Section 1.
2. Individual publications, especially as regards authors' rights.
3. Such real estate and plants as are essential for the operation of the business and the printing of publications.

(2) Subsection 1 shall likewise apply to contracts to assign, transfer, or hypothecate.

SECTION 3. A person found guilty of a violation of the provisions of this order may, by order of the Secretary General in the Ministry of Justice, be barred, permanently or for a definite period, from engaging in any of the activities described in Section 1.

SECTION 4. A person who wilfully violates a barring order issued under Section 3 is liable to imprisonment for not longer than one year or a fine not exceeding one thousand guilders.

Violations punishable under the preceding paragraph shall be considered misdemeanors.

SECTION 5. Legal transactions of the kind mentioned in Section 2, entered into after May 10, 1940, and before the effective date of this order, shall be registered not later than September 25, 1940, with the director of police or public prosecutor having jurisdiction in that area.

SECTION 6. This order shall take effect as of the day of publication.

J. C. TENKINK
Secretary General of the Ministry of Justice

Fourth Order of the Reich Commissioner for the Occupied Netherlands Territories concerning Certain Administrative Measures, August 20, 1940 [10]

By virtue of Section 5 of the decree of the Führer concerning the exercise of governmental authority in the Netherlands of May 18, 1940 (*RGBl.* I, p. 778), I hereby decree:

SECTION 1. The Reich Commissioner for the occupied Netherlands territories appoints and dismisses the officials and employees hereinafter mentioned:

1. The Secretaries General in the ministries.
2. The Vice-president and the members of the Council of State.
3. The President, Vice-president, Attorney General, Solicitors General, and the members of the Supreme Court.

[10] *Verordnungsblatt*, No. 22, August 24, 1940.

4. The Presidents and the District Attorneys of the courts.
5. The Inspector of the Ryksveldwacht and the Inspector of the Netherlands Marechaussee.
6. The Chief Police Commissioners.
7. The Commissioners for the provinces.
8. The Mayors of the capitals of the provinces and of municipalities of more than 50,000 inhabitants.
9. The President of the Netherlands Bank.
10. The President of the Board of Directors of the Netherlands Railways, Inc.
11. The Inspector General of the office for pilotage.
12. The directors of the government arms works and the government shipyards.
13. The Labor Commandant of the Netherlands Reconstruction Service.

SECTION 2. (1) Officials and employees, not mentioned in Section 1, who heretofore could be appointed or dismissed by the King, are now appointed or dismissed by the Secretaries General of the ministries concerned. Powers of appointment or dismissal held by other Netherlands authorities or public agencies shall not be affected by this order.

(2) Subsection 1 shall likewise apply to the appointment and dismissal of the president and the members of commissions formed for purposes of administration, examination, or investigation, and furthermore to all committees, councils, or advisory committees as, if, and when the Reich Commissioner orders them to suspend their activities.

SECTION 3. The Reich Commissioner reserves the right to exercise the powers of appointment or dismissal of persons mentioned in Section 2 if he sees fit so to do.

SECTION 4. In the case of a dismissal by virtue of Article 97*b* of the General Code for Government Officials the commission mentioned in that article need not be heard.

SECTION 5. This order shall take effect as of the day of publication.

The Hague, August 20, 1940.

SEYSS-INQUART
Reich Commissioner for the Occupied Netherlands Territories

Order of the Secretaries General of the Ministries of the Interior and Justice concerning the Duty of Identification, September 6, 1940 [11]

[EXCERPT]

By virtue of the powers granted by Section 1 of Order No. 13/1940, and in accordance with Sections 2 and 3 of Order No. 3/1940, of the Reich Commissioner for the occupied Netherlands territories, it is hereby ordered:

[11] *Verordnungsblatt*, No. 25, September 9, 1940, p. 408.

SECTION 1. Until such time as a uniform identification card is introduced in the occupied Netherlands territories, any Netherlands citizen of the age of fifteen years and above who is a permanent or temporary resident in the occupied Netherlands territories shall be required to carry with him, at all times, an official identification card with a photo attached enabling him at all times to prove his identity in a satisfactory manner.

. . . . .

K. J. FREDERIKS, *Secretary General of the Ministry of the Interior*
J. C. TENKINK, *Secretary General of the Ministry of Justice*

Order of the Secretaries General of the Ministries of Social Welfare and the Interior, Establishing an Insurance Fund for Accidents Arising out of Air Raid Defense Activities, January 3, 1941 [12]

[EXCERPTS]

In pursuance of Section 1 of Order No. 23/1940, and in accordance with Sections 2 and 3 of Order No. 3/1940 of the Reich Commissioner for the occupied Netherlands territories, it is hereby ordered as follows:

SECTION 1. (1) Persons who are engaged in activities of the Air Raid Defense Service, or who, in accordance with Article 12 of the Air Raid Defense Act, have been called for such service, shall be insured against accidents suffered in connection with such service unless they are covered by insurance in accordance with the provisions of the Accidents Insurance Act of 1921 or the Agricultural Accident Act of 1922, regardless of whether such service shall be compensated or not.

(2) The provisions of the Accidents Insurance Act of 1931 and of the Appeals Act (*Beroepswet*) and of the royal orders and orders of the several ministers issued in pursuance of these acts shall apply to the insurance established in accordance with subsection 1 unless the provisions contained hereinafter shall otherwise provide.

. . . . .

The Hague, January 3, 1941.

R. A. BERWEI, *Acting Secretary General of the Ministry of Social Welfare*
K. J. FREDERIKS, *Secretary General of the Ministry of the Interior*

[12] *Verordnungsblatt*, No. 2, January 13, 1941, p. 46.

Order of the Reich Commissioner for the Occupied Netherlands Territories concerning the Personal Status of German Nationals in the Occupied Netherlands Territories, February 28, 1941 [13]

[EXCERPTS]

Pursuant to Section 5 of the decree of the Führer concerning the exercise of governmental authority in the Netherlands of May 18, 1940 (*RGBl.* I, p. 778), I hereby order as follows:

. . . . .

SECTION 1. (1) German vital statistics officers (Registrars) shall be appointed in the occupied Netherlands territories.

. . . . .

SECTION 2. The German Registrars shall have exclusive jurisdiction of the Netherlands registrar officers in the following matters:

First, as regards registering the birth or death of German nationals.

Secondly, as regards officiating in marriage ceremonies where the bridegroom is a German national, unless such persons are Jews or are deemed to be Jews in accordance with Section 5 of the First Order implementing the Reich Citizens Act of November 14, 1935 (*RGBl.* I, p. 1333).

. . . . .

The Hague, February 28, 1941.

SEYSS-INQUART
Reich Commissioner for the Occupied Netherlands Territories

First Order of the Reich Commissioner for the Occupied Netherlands Territories concerning Extraordinary Measures of a Constitutional and Administrative Nature, March 1, 1941 [14]

Pursuant to Section 5 of the decree of the Führer concerning the exercise of governmental authority in the Netherlands of May 18, 1940 (*RGBl.* I, p. 778), I hereby order as follows:

SECTION 1. The following provisions shall apply to the administration of those communities for which the Reich Commissioner for the occupied Netherlands territories shall deem their application necessary.

SECTION 2. (1) The Municipal Councils, the Joint Boards of the Mayors and Aldermen, and all other municipal boards or commissions shall be and hereby are dissolved.

(2) The powers, provisions, and duties vested in or imposed upon the agencies dissolved in accordance with subsection 1 by virtue of statute or

[13] *Verordnungsblatt*, No. 8, March 3, 1941, p. 143. [14] *Ibid.*, p. 137.

contractual provisions and the official powers and duties of the mayor shall be vested in a Government Commissioner.

(3) The dissolution of the Joint Boards of the Mayor and Aldermen shall not affect the remaining activities of the aldermen within the municipal administration unless it shall be otherwise provided in a specific instance.

SECTION 3. The Government Commissioner shall, with regard to his official duties, be subject to the supervision of the Provincial Commission and the Secretary General in the Ministry of the Interior who may issue instructions binding on him.

SECTION 4. (1) Section 1, No. 8, subsection 1 of Section 2, and Section 3 of Order No. 108/1940 (Fourth Order concerning certain Administrative Measures) shall be made applicable to the appointment and dismissal of the Government Commissioner.

(2) The Government Commissioner, at his free discretion, shall appoint and dismiss the aldermen. In provincial capitals and in communities with more than 50,000 inhabitants the appointment and dismissal by the Government Commissioner shall be subject to the consent of the Secretary General in the Ministry of the Interior.

SECTION 5. The Government Commissioner shall appoint no less than four and no more than eight persons from among the inhabitants, who shall advise him in the fulfillment of his official duties. They shall be designated as "Advisers of the Government Commissioner."

SECTION 6. (1) The Reich Commissioner for the occupied Netherlands territories will, by order, determine the municipalities to which the provisions of this order shall apply.

(2) Such order shall be published in the *Verordnungsblatt für die besetzten niederländischen Gebiete.*

SECTION 7. Rules and regulations necessary for the enforcement of this order may be issued in the form of an administrative order.

SECTION 8. This order shall take effect as of the date of publication.

The Hague, March 1, 1941.

SEYSS-INQUART

Reich Commissioner for the Occupied Netherlands Territories

Order of the Reich Commissioner for the Occupied Netherlands Territories concerning the Dissolution of Parliamentary Parties, July 4, 1941 [15]

Pursuant to Section 5 of the decree of the Führer concerning the exercise of governmental authority in the Netherlands of May 18, 1940 (*RGBl.* I, p. 778), I hereby order as follows:

[15] *Verordnungsblatt,* No. 27, July 5, 1941, p. 513.

SECTION 1. The following associations and institutions shall be, and hereby are, dissolved:

1. Roman Catholic State Party (Roomsch-Katholieke Staats-Partij).
2. Social Democratic Labor Party (Sociaal Democratische Arbeiders Partij).
3. Anti-Revolutionary Party (Anti-Revolutionaire Partij).
4. Christian Historical Union (Christelyk-Historische Unie).
5. Liberal Democratic Association (Vryzinnig-Democratische Bond).
6. Liberal State Party (Liberale Staats Partij).
7. Christian Democratic Union (Christelyk-Democratische Unie).
8. Political Reform Party (Staatkundig Gereformeerde Partij).

SECTION 2. The Commissioner for non-profit associations and institutions shall liquidate such associations and institutions in accordance with the provisions of Order No. 41/1941 concerning the new order in the field of non-profit associations and institutions.

SECTION 3. This order shall take effect as of the date of publication.

The Hague, July 4, 1941.

SEYSS-INQUART
Reich Commissioner for the Occupied Netherlands Territories

Third Order of the Reich Commissioner for the Occupied Netherlands Territories concerning Certain Provisions in Connection with Netherlands Nationality, August 8, 1941 [16]

[EXCERPTS]

Pursuant to Section 5 of the decree of the Führer concerning the exercise of governmental authority in the Netherlands of May 18, 1940 (*RGBl.* I, p. 778), I hereby order as follows:

SECTION 1. (1) A Netherlands national acquiring German nationality shall not be deemed to have lost Netherlands nationality unless he in person, or, if a minor, his legal representative acting on his behalf, shall renounce by declaration Netherlands nationality within one year after acquisition of German nationality.

. . . . .

SECTION 2. A declaration made in accordance with subsection 1 of Section 1 shall take effect as of the date on which the declarant shall have obtained German nationality.

SECTION 3. This order shall take effect as of the date of publication.

The Hague, August 8, 1941.

SEYSS-INQUART
Reich Commissioner for the Occupied Netherlands Territories

[16] *Verordnungsblatt*, No. 32, August 9, 1941, p. 622.

Eighth Order of the Reich Commissioner for the Occupied Netherlands Territories concerning Special Measures Affecting Administrative Organization, August 11, 1941 [17]

[EXCERPTS]

Pursuant to Section 5 of the decree of the Führer concerning the exercise of governmental authority in the Netherlands of May 18, 1940 (*RGBl.* I, p. 778), I hereby order as follows:

CHAPTER I.—*Provisions concerning the Function of Representative Bodies and Agencies of Public Law*

SECTION 1. (1) All functions of the Municipal Councils and Provincial States (*Provinzialstaaten*) shall be suspended; elections to these representative bodies shall not take place.

(2) The functions of the following bodies shall likewise be suspended:

1. The Joint Councils of Mayors and Aldermen.
2. The Provincial Councils.
3. The Council of the States-General.
4. The Election Boards (Articles 32, 33, and 58 of the Election Statute).

(3) The functions of the Municipal Council shall be suspended, as determined by the mayor; those of the Provincial Councils, as determined by the commissioner of the province.

. . . . . .

CHAPTER II.—*Provisions concerning Local Administration*

SECTION 3. The powers and duties of the Municipal Council and the Joint Council of the Mayor and Aldermen shall be assumed by the mayor. The same applies to the powers and duties of those municipal boards which shall be suspended in pursuance of an order made in accordance with subsection 3, sentence 1, of Section 1.

SECTION 4. (1) The mayor shall appoint, for a term of six years, no less than two but no more than six aldermen as his representatives and agents in the administration of municipal affairs.

. . . . . .

SECTION 5. (1) The appointment of an alderman shall be subject to ratification by the supervising authority.

(2) With the consent of the supervising authority the mayor shall be authorized to dismiss an alderman without notice. At the request of the supervising authority the mayor shall dismiss any alderman without notice.

. . . . . .

SECTION 7. (1) The mayor shall appoint councilmen from among the Netherlands nationals domiciled in the community.

[17] *Verordnungsblatt*, No. 33, August 12, 1941, p. 637.

(2) The number of councilmen shall be determined in accordance with Section 5 of the Municipalities Act, subject, however, to a reduction by half of the number prescribed there and diminished by one.

. . . . .

SECTION 9. (1) The mayor shall report immediately to the supervising authority any appointment of a councilman that he may make.

(2) At the request of the supervising authority, the mayor shall without delay dismiss any councilman.

SECTION 10. (1) It shall be the duty of the councilmen:

1. To advise the mayor and to submit to him suggestions on the administration of municipal affairs.
2. To promote understanding of his measures among the citizenry.

(2) The councilmen shall not receive any compensation for their activities.

. . . . .

SECTION 12. (1) The term of a councilman shall be four years.

(2) It shall terminate before that time: first, if the councilman removes his domicile from the community; secondly, if he is removed from office.

SECTION 13. (1) The mayor shall call a general meeting of councilmen in every instance in which, in accordance with the provisions of the Municipalities Act, a resolution of the Municipal Council is necessary.

(2) The mayor shall determine the agenda. The general meetings shall be public whenever the mayor so orders. Such order shall be made public.

(3) The several items of the agenda shall be discussed in the general meetings; no vote shall be taken nor any resolution adopted. The councilmen shall be required to state their opinion if it varies from that of the mayor; such statement shall be made part of the record.

. . . . .

SECTION 14. (1) The supervising authority shall see to it that the administration of the mayor conforms to law and furthers the public interest.

(2) The supervising authority may issue instructions to the mayor. The mayor shall be bound to follow these instructions.

(3) The Secretary General of the Ministry of the Interior shall also be authorized to issue instructions in accordance with subsection 2 to mayors of communities mentioned in subsection 1, No. 2, of Section 15, except in matters relating to the Waterstaat;[17a] the Secretary General of the Ministry of Waterstaat shall exercise this authority in regard to all matters relating to Waterstaat.

[17a] The Ministry of "Waterstaat" supervises the waterways and waterworks, the ports, and generally all communications.

A special Engineer Corps functions within this ministry to carry out the technical tasks of this office. There has never been a special Ministry for Communications in the Netherlands.—ED.

SECTION 15. (1) The supervising power shall be exercised in all matters except those of the Waterstaat:

1. For the communities of The Hague, Amsterdam, and Rotterdam, by the Secretary General of the Ministry of the Interior.
2. For all other communities, by the commissioner of the province notwithstanding the authority of the Secretary General of the Ministry of the Interior vested in him by virtue of other provisions of law.

(2) The supervising power in matters of the Waterstaat shall be exercised in all communities by the commissioner of the province notwithstanding the authority of the Secretary General of the Ministry of Waterstaat vested in him in pursuance of the law.

CHAPTER III.—*Provisions relating to Provincial Administration*

SECTION 16. (1) The powers and duties of the Provincial States shall be assumed by the commissioner of the province.

. . . . .

SECTION 18. (1) The commissioner of the province shall be authorized to request information from, to submit suggestions and, in cases of emergency, to issue instructions to, all public authorities or agencies in the province unless the authority of such agencies shall extend beyond the limits of the province; the authority to issue such instructions, in case of emergency, shall exist notwithstanding the power of the central authorities concerned to issue such instructions.

Secondly, he shall be authorized to require information from, and to submit suggestions to, all agencies whose powers shall extend beyond the limits of the province unless they constitute central authorities.

(2) The commissioner of the province shall have power to issue the instructions mentioned in subsection 1, No. 1, to officials of the Netherlands police force only if the commissioner takes measures within the usual scope of his official duties which these police officials are required to carry out. The commissioner of the province and the director general of the police shall provide each other with such information as they may require for the fulfillment of their official duties. They may submit suggestions to each other.

. . . . .

SECTION 19. (1) The commissioner of the province shall appoint, for a term of six years, no less than two but no more than six provincial administrators as his agents and representatives in the administration of provincial affairs.

. . . . .

The Hague, August 11, 1941.

SEYSS-INQUART

Reich Commissioner for the Occupied Netherlands Territories

Order of the Secretaries General of the Ministries of Justice and Social Welfare concerning the Control of Prostitutes, September 15, 1941 [18]

Pursuant to Section 1 of Order No. 23/1940, and in accordance with subsections 2 and 3 of Order No. 3/1940 of the Reich Commissioner for the occupied Netherlands territories, it is hereby ordered as follows:

SECTION 1. As used in this order the term "local police authority" shall be deemed to refer to the Chief Commissioner of Police in all communities in which such commissioner shall have his official residence; in all other communities it shall be deemed to refer to the mayor. The term "prostitute" shall be deemed to refer to a woman professionally or habitually engaging in fornication.

The term "domicile" shall be deemed to refer to the community in the record of the inhabitants of which such prostitute shall have been entered, or if such a community cannot be established, to the community of her actual residence.

SECTION 2. (1) A prostitute shall be obliged to carry on her person at all times a valid certificate of identification issued by the local police authority of her domicile, or by the designees of such authority, and containing the prescribed entries.

(2) Upon request, she shall be required to exhibit this certificate promptly to a plain-clothes officer.

(3) She shall not transfer or damage this certificate of identification.

SECTION 3. A prostitute shall be required upon request issued by the local police authority or its designees;

First, to appear at the place and time stated;
Second, to produce and deliver her certificate of identification for the purpose of making therein the required entries;
Third, to submit to a medical examination by a physician named in the request at the times stated therein.

SECTION 4. (1) Any prostitute violating the provisions contained in Sections 2 and 3 shall be liable to imprisonment for a period not exceeding six weeks or a fine not exceeding 500 gulden.

(2) Violations punishable in accordance with subsection 1 shall constitute misdemeanors.

(3) In addition to the officials designated in Article 141 of the Code of Criminal Procedure (*Wetboek van Strafvordering*), the officers of the national and municipal police forces shall exercise police control over prostitutes.

SECTION 5. (1) The Secretary General of the Ministry of Justice shall be authorized to issue all rules and regulations required for the implementation of this order.

[18] *Verordnungsblatt*, No. 39, September 20, 1941, p. 791.

(2) Rules and regulations which contain provisions having the force and effect of rules of law shall be published in the *Nederlandsche Staatscourant*.

SECTION 6. This order shall take effect within one month after the date of publication.

The Hague, September 15, 1941.

SCHRIEKE, *Secretary General of the Ministry of Justice*

BERWEI, *Acting Secretary General of the Ministry of Social Welfare*

2. LAW, COURTS, AND LAWYERS

Order of the Reich Commissioner for the Occupied Netherlands Territories concerning the Jurisdiction of Courts of the German Armed Forces, June 8, 1940 [19]

By virtue of Section 5 of the decree of the Führer concerning the exercise of governmental authority in the Netherlands of May 18, 1940 (*RGBl.* I, p. 778), I hereby order as follows:

SECTION 1. Civilians of other than German nationality shall be subject to the jurisdiction of the courts of the German armed forces for punishable acts which:

1. Are directed against the German armed forces, their members, or auxiliary organizations; or
2. Have been committed in buildings, rooms, or installations used by or serving the purposes of the German armed forces.

SECTION 2. If the commanding officer in charge of the court of the German armed forces declares that he yields the powers conferred on him by virtue of Section 1 of this order, jurisdiction to prosecute and adjudge shall revest in the officials who have general jurisdiction over the prosecution and trial of crimes.

SECTION 3. This order shall take effect as of the day of publication.

The Hague, June 8, 1940.

SEYSS-INQUART

Reich Commissioner for the Occupied Netherlands Territories

[19] *Verordnungsblatt*, No. 3, June 13, 1940, p. 26.

Order of the Reich Commissioner for the Occupied Netherlands Territories concerning the Jurisdiction of German Courts in Criminal Proceedings, July 17, 1940 [20]

By virtue of Section 5 of the decree of the Führer concerning the exercise of governmental authority in the Netherlands of May 18, 1940 (*RGBl.* I, p. 778), I hereby order as follows:

TITLE I.—*General Provisions*

SECTION 1. (1) For the occupied Netherlands territories German jurisdiction in criminal proceedings shall be, and hereby is, established. This jurisdiction shall be exercised by the German Circuit Court (*Landesgericht*) and the German Superior Court (*Obergericht*) for the occupied Netherlands territories, and the Prosecuting Attorneys jointly attached to both these courts.

(2) This order shall not affect in any manner the provisions concerning the jurisdiction of the courts of the German armed forces, and the special jurisdiction in criminal proceedings against members of the S.S. and of the police units mobilized for special tasks.

TITLE II.—*Jurisdiction*

SECTION 2. (1) The German Courts shall have jurisdiction for the prosecution and trial of crimes committed by German nationals or former German nationals or by nationals of the Protectorate of Bohemia and Moravia. This jurisdiction shall be exclusive of the Netherlands Courts.

(2) The provisions of subsection 1 shall apply regardless of the nationality of the principal of, or accessory to, the crime:

1. If it is directed against the Greater German Reich, the German nation, the National Socialist German Workers Party (N.S.D.A.P.), or its organizations and affiliated groups.
2. If it is directed against a German national or a person in the service of the Greater German Reich, the National Socialist German Workers Party (N.S.D.A.P.), or its organizations and affiliated units, and if the crime is committed during the performance of such service or in connection therewith;
3. If it is committed during service for the German authorities or in connection with such service or on German territory or in buildings, rooms, or installations used for purposes of the Greater German Reich, the National Socialist German Workers Party (N.S.D.A.P.), or its organizations and affiliated units.
4. If it constitutes an act of pillage in the freed area or in buildings or rooms voluntarily evacuated, or if it constitutes a felony or crime against life or property committed in taking advantage of civil defense measures against air attacks, or if it constitutes a crime endangering the community, especially its food supply.

[20] *Verordnungsblatt*, No. 12, July 20, 1940, p. 181.

TITLE III.—*Organization and Procedure*

SECTION 3. (1) The provisions in force in the Old Reich (*Alt-Reich*) [21] on the effective date of this order shall apply to the organization of the German Courts and the offices of the Prosecuting Attorneys unless otherwise provided hereinafter.

(2) The term District Court (*Amtsgericht*) shall be deemed to refer to the Circuit Court (*Landesgericht*). The term Circuit Court (*Landesgericht*) shall be deemed to refer to the Superior Court (*Obergericht*).

SECTION 4. The German Courts in the occupied Netherlands territories shall have their official seat in The Hague.

SECTION 5. The Reich Commissioner for the occupied Netherlands territories will appoint and dismiss the judges of the German Courts in the occupied Netherlands territories.

SECTION 6. The German Courts shall be authorized to perform official acts in any locality within the occupied Netherlands territories.

SECTION 7. (1) The Circuit Judge shall constitute the Circuit Court (one-judge court).

(2) The Circuit Judge shall be authorized to sentence a defendant to hard labor not exceeding five years, imprisonment, confinement in a fortress, or confinement and fine either separately or in connection with penalties imposed in lieu of others; in addition, he may order all measures of correction and isolation.

(3) Appeal may be made from the judgments of the Circuit Court; all other orders of the court are subject to motions to set them aside in accordance with German criminal procedure. An appeal must be lodged within two weeks; the same applies to motions in accordance with Section 311 of the Reich Code of Criminal Procedure.

SECTION 8. (1) The Superior Court shall be composed of three justices.

(2) The justices of the German Superior Court in the occupied Netherlands territories may hold office as judges of a court in the German Reich. One of its justices shall have his official residence in The Hague.

SECTION 9. (1) The Superior Court shall be authorized to sentence a person found guilty to any form of punishment according to law.

(2) It shall decide motions made regarding, and appeals filed from, orders and judgments of the Circuit Judge.

(3) A justice of the Superior Court shall be authorized, if an urgent need arises, to issue orders for the advancement of the proceedings. The Prosecuting Attorney in all cases, the accused only when aggrieved, shall have the right to appeal from the decisions of the single justice to the full court. Unless the single justice considers a motion to set an order aside well taken he shall be authorized, in the same manner as the full court, to issue tem-

[21] By "Alt-Reich" (Old Reich) is meant Germany before the incorporation of the Sudeten, Austria, Memel, and all the other territories annexed by Germany in the present war.—ED.

porary orders amending his original order; he may in particular suspend its execution or limit its scope. The single justice whose order has been attacked by a motion to set it aside shall not be disqualified from sitting with the full court in deciding on such motion.

(4) A judgment of the German Superior Court shall not be subject to review.

SECTION 10. (1) No preliminary judicial investigation shall take place.

(2) Whenever, according to the provisions in force in the Old Reich, the Special Court would have jurisdiction, the Prosecuting Attorney, instead of moving for initiation of the main proceeding, may move to have the main trial conducted before the Superior Court according to the rules of procedure applicable to a trial before a Special Court. In such event, the rules of procedure applicable in the Special Courts shall apply to the ensuing proceedings.

SECTION 11. The Reich Commissioner for the occupied Netherlands territories shall be authorized, within his discretion, to refer any criminal procedure, for prosecution and trial, to the Special Criminal Courts established for members of the S.S. and for members of the police units mobilized for special duty, if the crime has been committed against the German S.S. and police, or its members or auxiliary organizations while they act in their official capacity or in connection therewith.

SECTION 12. Subsections 1 and 2 of Section 153*a* of the Reich Code of Criminal Procedure shall not apply.

SECTION 13. (1) If the crime for the trial of which the German Courts have jurisdiction is of minor importance and the accused is neither a German national nor a national of the Protectorate of Bohemia and Moravia, the proceedings may be transferred to the Netherlands authorities for prosecution and trial in accordance with Netherlands law.

(2) For such transfer the consent of the court shall be required until the date for the main trial has been set. Thereafter, the consent of the Prosecuting Attorney shall be required for such transfer.

SECTION 14. (1) If sentences of both the German and Netherlands courts have been passed, the German Courts shall be authorized to consolidate such sentences.

(2) As regards sentences passed by different German Courts, or Netherlands Courts and different German Courts, the German Superior Court shall have jurisdiction to consolidate the same.

SECTION 15. The officer in charge of the offices of the Prosecuting Attorney attached to the Circuit Court and Superior Court shall be designated as "German Attorney General in the Occupied Netherlands Territories."

SECTION 16. The following persons shall be admitted to appear as defense counsel before the German Courts in the occupied Netherlands territories:

1. Any person admitted as defense counsel before a General Court in the German Reich.

2. Any member of the bar registered with a Netherlands Court who has been specially admitted to these courts by the Reich Commissioner for the occupied Netherlands territories.

TITLE IV.—*Substantive Law*

SECTION 17. (1) The German authorities charged with the prosecution and trial of crimes shall apply:

1. Substantive provisions promulgated or to be promulgated by the Reich Commissioner for the occupied Netherlands territories or by German authorities authorized by him; and such provisions issued by German military authorities up to and including May 28, 1940.
2. The criminal law now or hereafter enforced in the Old Reich.
3. The Netherlands Criminal Law now in force in the Netherlands including all substantive provisions promulgated or to be promulgated by the Secretaries General in the Netherlands ministries after May 28, 1940, in pursuance of authority vested in them by the Reich Commissioner for the occupied Netherlands territories.

(2) The substantive law referred to in number 1 of subsection 1, and the substantive law promulgated by the Secretaries General in the Netherlands ministries shall take precedence in the case of conflict. If the act is not punishable according to any provisions promulgated by the Reich Commissioner or his designees or by the Secretaries General in the Netherlands ministries, the provisions of substantive law referred to in either paragraphs 2 or 3 of subsection 1, whichever shall admit of a more severe punishment, shall apply. The sentence passed, however, shall not be less than the minimum penalty established by the substantive law provisions excluded from application in accordance with the preceding sentence.

(3) Whenever the application of a provision of substantive law prescribed in accordance with subsection 2 would result in an unjustifiably harsh sentence, the substantive law which would be excluded according to subsection 2 shall take its place.

SECTION 18. Wherever the prosecution of a criminal act is subject to the consent or to the order of a public authority, the Reich Commissioner for the occupied Netherlands territories shall be vested with the authority to give such consent or order.

SECTION 19. If the court decides that the crime is punishable by death, the defendant shall be sentenced to death only once even though he shall have committed several crimes punishable by death. No person shall be sentenced to hard labor or imprisonment in addition to a death penalty. In such event no sentence of imprisonment shall be entered.

SECTION 20. The following penalties of the Netherlands law shall be considered the equivalent of the following penalties of the German law: life imprisonment shall correspond to hard labor for life; imprisonment exceeding a period of five years shall correspond to hard labor for a period equivalent to two thirds of the term of imprisonment; imprisonment not exceeding five years confinement shall correspond to confinement; and amends shall correspond to fine.

TITLE V.—*Petition to Have the Judgment Set Aside and Cancelled by the Reich Commissioner*

SECTION 21. (1) The German Attorney General in the occupied Netherlands territories shall be authorized to file, within one year after a judgment of a German Circuit Court and the German Superior Court shall have become final, a petition with the Reich Commissioner for the occupied Netherlands territories to have such judgment declared void.

(2) Such petition shall only be brought for the reason that the judgment is unjust because of a mistake in applying the law to the facts established.

(3) If the Reich Commissioner sets aside the judgment, the German Superior Court shall make a new decision after a trial *de novo*. The court shall be bound to follow the mandate as to the applicable law contained in the reasons given for setting aside the original judgment.

TITLE VI.—*General Provisions concerning the Procedure before the German and Netherlands Courts*

SECTION 22. (1) If in accordance with the provisions of this order the German or Netherlands court is without jurisdiction the proceedings shall be transferred to the court having jurisdiction.

(2) If both the German and Netherlands courts deem themselves to have jurisdiction or to have no jurisdiction, the Reich Commissioner for the occupied Netherlands territories shall decide which court shall take jurisdicton.

(3) A proceeding shall be considered as a continuous one even though it has been transferred to another court for lack of jurisdiction. This shall apply especially to periods of time prescribed by the court and to expenditures, costs, fees, and reimbursements.

SECTION 23. In cases of emergency, courts and prosecuting attorneys, although not having jurisdiction, shall perform all official acts in accordance with the provisions applicable to proceedings before them even though such acts shall be within the authority of courts having jurisdiction. The court having jurisdiction shall act expeditiously; and the official files and records shall be promptly delivered to it.

TITLE VII.—*Final Provisions*

SECTION 24. The Reich Commissioner for the occupied Netherlands territories may, by administrative order, delegate wholly or in part the authority vested in him by this order.

SECTION 25. This order shall take effect as of the day of publication.

The Hague, July 17, 1940.

SEYSS-INQUART
Reich Commissioner for the Occupied Netherlands Territories

First Order of the Reich Commissioner for the Occupied Netherlands Territories concerning Certain Measures relating to Civil Claims, December 19, 1940 [22]

Pursuant to Section 5 of the decree of the Führer concerning the exercise of governmental authority in the Netherlands of May 18, 1940 (*RGBl.* I, p. 778), I hereby order as follows:

SECTION 1. The Reich Commissioner or his designee shall decide disputes over civil claims which are advanced in immediate connection with orders of the Reich Commissioner for the occupied Netherlands territories or his designees by persons aggrieved by such orders or by their successors. The jurisdiction of the Reich Commissioner or his designee shall exclude any jurisdiction of the courts of general jurisdiction over these claims.

SECTION 2. Until further notice suit on civil claims, if the cause of action has arisen directly or indirectly as a result of the events of war, shall not be brought in Netherlands Courts against German nationals having their domicile or usual residence within the territory of the Greater German Reich, or against corporations, associations, institutions, foundations, trusts, etc., which have their place of business or official seat within the territory of the Greater German Reich.

SECTION 3. (1) Court proceedings in which, in accordance with Section 1, the courts no longer have jurisdiction shall be abated on the courts' own motions. Costs and fees shall not be charged; if they have been paid no refund shall be made. All other expenses shall be borne by the parties who have incurred them.

(2) Pending proceedings in which claims referrred to in Section 2 are asserted shall be abated on the courts' own motions.

(3) In the case of abatements in accordance with subsections 1 and 2, all preliminary orders or writs for the protection of a judgment creditor, especially attachments, shall be set aside.

SECTION 4. The Reich Commissioner shall have the right to provide, in individual cases, a disposition of the claim at variance with the provisions contained in Sections 1 and 2.

SECTION 5. This order shall take effect as of the date of publication.

The Hague, December 19, 1940.

SEYSS-INQUART
Reich Commissioner for the Occupied Netherlands Territories

[22] *Verordnungsblatt*, No. 42, December 27, 1940, p. 699.

Decree of the Führer concerning the Grant of Pardons in the Occupied Netherlands Territories, December 20, 1940 [23]

I hereby delegate to the Reich Commissioner for the occupied Netherlands territories the right to order the abatement of criminal proceedings and the right to grant or refuse pardons in the occupied Netherlands territories. The Reich Commissioner shall be authorized to delegate the authority conferred on him by the preceding sentence. I reserve the right to decide personally in individual cases.

This decree shall not be deemed to affect Section 114 of the order concerning criminal proceedings in military courts in wartime and in time of mobilization for special purposes of August 17, 1938 (*RGBl.* 1939, I, p. 1457), as amended by Article V of the seventh order implementing and supplementing the order concerning criminal proceedings in military courts in wartime and in time of mobilization for special purposes of May 18, 1940 (*RGBl.* I, p. 787). Nor shall this decree be deemed to affect the provisions governing the right of granting pardon in criminal proceedings subject to the jurisdiction of the S.S. and police courts.

Berlin, December 20, 1940.

ADOLF HITLER, *Führer*
DR. LAMMERS, *Reich Minister and Chief of the Reich Chancellery*

Order of the Reich Commissioner for the Occupied Netherlands Territories concerning the Right of Pardon, January 6, 1941 [24]

Pursuant to the decree of the Führer concerning the exercise of the right of pardon in the occupied Netherlands territories of December 20, 1940 (*RGBl.* I, p. 1644), I hereby order as follows:

SECTION 1. (1) I reserve the right to grant pardons in all matters:

1. Within the jurisdiction of the German Circuit Court or the German Superior Court in the occupied Netherlands territories.
2. In which, before the effective date of Order No. 52/1940 concerning German jurisdiction in criminal proceedings, the Netherlands Courts have entered sentence for the commission of a crime which, after the effective date of this order, would be, in accordance with Section 2 of that order, within the jurisdiction of German Courts.
3. In which Netherlands Courts have entered sentence of imprisonment for a period exceeding three months either as the main penalty or as the penalty for non-payment of a fine, or have imposed a fine in an amount exceeding 1,000 gulden.

[23] *Reichsgesetzblatt*, 1940, I, p. 1644. *Verordnungsblatt*, No. 1, January 7, 1941, p. 2.
[24] *Verordnungsblatt*, No. 1, January 7, 1941, p. 4.

(2) The same shall apply to the right to abate pending criminal proceedings.

SECTION 2. In all other cases I delegate the right of pardon in criminal proceedings within the jurisdiction of the Netherlands Courts to the Secretary General of the Ministry of Justice, subject, however, to my right of decision on petitions for pardons in individual cases.

SECTION 3. All provisions conflicting with this order, especially Articles 14a–17 of the Netherlands Criminal Code (*Wetboek van Strafrecht*) and Articles 559 and 560 of the Netherlands Code of Criminal Procedure (*Wetboek van Strafvordering*), shall be inapplicable.

SECTION 4. Rules and regulations implementing this order shall be issued by administrative order.

SECTION 5. This order shall take effect as of the date of publication.

The Hague, January 6, 1941.

SEYSS-INQUART
Reich Commissioner for the Occupied Netherlands Territories

Order of the Reich Commissioner for the Occupied Netherlands Territories concerning the Indemnification of German Nationals for Damages to Property Suffered as a Result of the War, February 7, 1941 [25]

Pursuant to Section 5 of the decree of the Führer concerning the exercise of governmental authority in the Netherlands of May 18, 1940 (*RGBl.* I, p. 778), I hereby order as follows:

SECTION 1. (1) German nationals shall be indemnified for damages to property which they have suffered or may suffer in the occupied Netherlands territories as a result of the war. The provisions concerning indemnification for like damage applicable in the German Reich shall apply to such indemnification.

(2) For the purposes of this order, nationals of other states may be assimilated with German nationals by order of the Reich Commissioner for the occupied Netherlands territories (through the Commissioner General of Finance and Economic Affairs). Such order may provide for individual cases or a group of cases.

SECTION 2. (1) The Aid Committee for the Germans in the Netherlands shall ascertain the extent of the damage and determine and pay the amount of indemnification. The Aid Committee shall, for the purposes of this order, operate under the supervision and in accordance with instructions issued by the Reich Commissioner for the occupied Netherlands territories (through

[25] *Verordnungsblatt*, No. 5, February 10, 1941, p. 83.

the Commissioner General of Finance and Economic Affairs); in addition, the Commissioner shall audit the books of the committee.

(2) The cost of indemnification and of the proceedings directed thereto shall be borne by the Reconstruction Fund, 1940 (Order No. 21/1940).

SECTION 3. This order shall take effect as of the date of publication.

The Hague, February 7, 1941.

SEYSS-INQUART

Reich Commissioner for the Occupied Netherlands Territories

Order of the Reich Commissioner for the Occupied Netherlands Territories concerning Marriages of Male Persons of German Nationality in the Occupied Netherlands Territories, and Related Matters, February 28, 1941 [26]

[EXCERPTS]

In pursuance of Section 5 of the decree of the Führer concerning the exercise of governmental authority in the Netherlands of May 18, 1940 (*RGBl.* I, p. 778), I hereby order as follows:

SECTION 1. (1) The marriage of a male person of German nationality shall have validity only if the marriage ceremony is performed by a German official.

. . . . .

SECTION 4. (1) Upon the application of a female person of Netherlands nationality intending to marry a German and requiring for such marriage, in accordance with Articles 92–98 of the Netherlands Civil Code, the consent of her parents, grandparents, guardian, or guardians, the approval of the Reich Commissioner for the occupied Netherlands territories (through the Commissioner General for Administration of Justice) may be substituted for such consent.

SECTION 5. On application of a female person of Netherlands nationality intending to marry a German national, the Reich Commissioner for the occupied Netherlands territories (through the Commissioner General for the Administration of Justice) may grant dispensation from the observance of the waiting period required in accordance with Articles 91 and 103 of the Netherlands Civil Code.

. . . . .

The Hague, February 28, 1941.

SEYSS-INQUART

Reich Commissioner for the Occupied Netherlands Territories

[26] *Verordnungsblatt*, No. 8, March 3, 1941, p. 139.

Order of the Reich Commissioner for the Occupied Netherlands Territories concerning the Establishment of Administrative Courts Martial, March 19, 1941 [27]

[EXCERPTS]

Pursuant to Section 5 of the decree of the Führer concerning the exercise of governmental authority in the Netherlands of May 18, 1940 (*RGBl.* I, p. 778), I hereby order as follows:

SECTION 1. (1) The Reich Commissioner for the occupied Netherlands territories may, if he shall deem it necessary for the maintenance or restoration of public order and safety of public life, establish administrative courts martial for these territories or for certain areas within these territories.

. . . . . .

SECTION 3. (1) The Superior S.S. and Police Chief shall take all measures deemed necessary by him for the maintenance or restoration of public order and safety of public life.

(2) He may promulgate rules and regulations, having the force and effect of laws, which are necessary for the fulfillment of his duties. Notwithstanding the provisions contained in Section 7, such rules and regulations may contain penal provisions subjecting a defendant to fines of unlimited amount, imprisonment, or jail, and shall be published in accordance with the provisions contained in the second sentence of subsection 2 of Section 1.

(3) In the fulfillment of his duties the Superior S.S. and Police Chief may deviate from existing regulations.

SECTION 4. (1) The Reich Commissioner shall appoint a Special Agent for the entire area for which an administrative court martial has been decreed.

(2) The Special Agent shall be the head of the entire public administration and may even exclude the police administration therefrom unless the Superior S.S. and Police Chief assumes administrative tasks in accordance with subsection 1 of Section 3.

(3) The Special Agent shall promulgate rules and regulations necessary for the fulfillment of his duty. Notwithstanding the provisions contained in Section 7, they may contain penal provisions subjecting a defendant to fines of unlimited amount, imprisonment, or jail, and shall be published in accordance with the provisions contained in the second sentence of subsection 2 of Section 1.

(4) In the fulfillment of his duties the Special Agent shall not be bound by law.

(5) The Reich Commissioner shall have the right to appoint Special Agents also for certain parts of the area for which administrative courts martial has been ordered.

. . . . . .

[27] *Verordnungsblatt*, No. 11, March 20, 1941, p. 190.

SECTION 7. Any person shall be subject to court martial who, after the establishment of an administrative court martial, shall intentionally participate in activities likely to disturb or to endanger public order and the safety of public life, or who intentionally violates special orders of the Reich Commissioner issued in accordance with subsection 3 of Section 1. Such person shall be punishable by death, or, in less serious cases, by hard labor either for life or for a period of not less than ten years.

SECTION 8. (1) The German Superior Court shall operate as a Court Martial in accordance with the procedure established in the Old Reich [28] for proceedings before Special Courts.

. . . . .

(3) The judges of the Court Martial shall be appointed by the Reich Commissioner. The Court Martial shall be considered lawfully constituted even if only one judge has the educational qualifications required for judicial tenure.

(4) Death sentences shall be executed by shooting.

. . . . .

The Hague, March 19, 1941.

SEYSS-INQUART

Reich Commissioner for the Occupied Netherlands Territories

Order of the Reich Commissioner for the Occupied Netherlands Territories concerning the Sale of Enterprises and Factories to Aliens, March 24, 1941 [29]

[EXCERPTS]

Pursuant to Section 5 of the decree of the Führer concerning the exercise of governmental authority in the Netherlands of May 18, 1940 (*RGBl* I, p. 778), I hereby order as follows:

SECTION 1. (1) It shall be unlawful for persons or corporations having their domicile or their principal place of business in the occupied Netherlands territories to sell enterprises or factories engaged in manufacturing, developing, or processing of materials (industrial enterprises), or commercial enterprises to persons or corporations having their domicile or principal place of business outside the occupied Netherlands territories unless permission to do so shall have been obtained.

(2) The transfer of partnership or similar interests in enterprises or factories referred to in subsection 1 shall be subject to the same provisions.

. . . . .

SECTION 2. (1) Section 1 shall apply only if the sales price exceeds 100,000 gulden.

[28] See note above, p. 467.—ED.

[29] *Verordnungsblatt*, No. 12, March 25, 1941, p. 204.

(2) The Reich Commissioner for the occupied Netherlands territories (through the Commissioner General of Finance and Economic Affairs) may designate a different amount either generally or for certain groups of enterprises or factories.

SECTION 3. The Reich Commissioner for the occupied Netherlands territories (through the Commissioner General of Finance and Economic Affairs) shall be authorized to grant or refuse the permission required in accordance with Section 1.

. . . . .

The Hague, March 24, 1941.

SEYSS-INQUART
Reich Commissioner for the Occupied Netherlands Territories

Order of the Reich Commissioner for the Occupied Netherlands Territories concerning Defense Against Acts of Sabotage, October 16, 1941 [30]

[EXCERPTS]

On behalf of Europe's future, Germany is engaged in a fight against the enemy powers. This fight requires the ruthless elimination of all attempts at interference. By virtue of Section 5 of the decree of the Führer concerning the exercise of governmental authority in the Netherlands of May 18, 1940 (*RGBl.* I, p. 778), I therefore order as follows:

SECTION 1. (1) Any person wilfully perpetrating an act punishable under existing statutes and intended or liable to endanger public order or security of public life in the occupied Netherlands territories, shall as a saboteur be punishable by death.

(2) A person attempting to commit an act described in subsection 1, and any accessory thereto, shall be punishable as if the act had been completed.

(3) If the death penalty, in exceptional cases where extenuating personal circumstances are present, should not be appropriate, punishment shall consist of hard labor for life or for a period of not less than ten years.

(4) The court shall determine the manner of execution of the defendant.

SECTION 2. (1) In cases arising under Section 1 the German Superior Court (*Obergericht*) shall, as a special court, have exclusive jurisdiction.

(2) The date of trial shall be set without the usual restriction as to the time within which such date may be set.

(3) The indictment may be preferred orally. Its essential contents must be made part of the record of trial.

. . . . .

[30] *Verordnungsblatt*, No. 43, October 17, 1941, p. 835.

SECTION 3. If it is shown during the trial that the facts are not such as are specified in Section 1, the court shall refer the case to the courts of general jurisdiction.

SECTION 4. This order shall take effect as of the date of publication.

The Hague, October 16, 1941.

SEYSS-INQUART
Reich Commissioner for the Occupied Netherlands Territories

3. PROPERTY[30a]

General Order of the Reich Commissioner for the Occupied Netherlands Territories concerning the Confiscation of Property, July 4, 1940 [31]

[EXCERPT]

By virtue of Section 5 of the decree of the Führer concerning the exercise of governmental authority in the Netherlands of May 18, 1940 (*RGBl.* I, p. 778), I decree:

SECTION 1. (1) The property of persons or associations which have furthered activities hostile to the German Reich or Germanism, or of whom it must be assumed that they will further such activities in the future, may be confiscated in whole or in part.

(2) The same applies to property and rights which have been used for the furtherance of the activities described in subsection 1, or which are capable of being thus used.

. . . . .

SEYSS-INQUART
Reich Commissioner for the Occupied Netherlands Territories

Order of the Reich Commissioner for the Occupied Netherlands Territories concerning the Alienation of Real Property Owned by the State and the Conclusion of Settlements of Disputes Involving Real Property Owned by the State, October 4, 1940 [32]

Pursuant to Section 5 of the decree of the Führer concerning the exercise of governmental authority in the Netherlands of May 18, 1940 (*RGBl.* I, p. 778), I hereby order as follows:

SECTION 1. (1) Notwithstanding the provisions contained in subsections 2, 3, and 4 of Article 1 of the Act of August 29, 1848 (*Staatsblad*, No. 39), as

[30a] See also order concerning sequestration, above, p. 321.
[31] *Verordnungsblatt*, 1940, No. 9, p. 128. [32] *Ibid.*, No. 30, p. 483.

revised by the Act of April 8, 1937 (*Staatsblad*, No. 403), real property owned by the state, referred to in the said subsections, may be freely alienated by the Secretary General of the Ministry of Finance, subject to conditions to be determined by him.

(2) Notwithstanding the provisions contained in Article 1 of the Act of December 22, 1850 (*Staatsblad*, No. 99), as revised by the Act of July 21, 1927 (*Staatsblad*, No. 259), the Secretary General of the Ministry of Finance shall be authorized to enter into settlements involving rights in real property in which the government has a legal interest.

(3) If the value of the subject-matter of alienation or litigation exceeds 50,000 gulden, such sale or settlement shall be subject to the consent of the Reich Commissioner for the occupied Netherlands territories.

SECTION 2. Sales or settlements referred to in Section 1 which have been entered into subject to the above-mentioned consent, but which have not yet been ratified by such consent, may be ratified in accordance with the provisions of Section 1 by the Reich Commissioner for the occupied Netherlands territories or the Secretary General of the Ministry of Finance. Such ratification shall take the place of the consent required for the validity of the transaction.

SECTION 3. This order shall take effect as of the date of publication.

The Hague, October 4, 1940.

SEYSS-INQUART
Reich Commissioner for the Occupied Netherlands Territories

4. ECONOMY

First Order of the Secretary General of the Ministry of Social Welfare, Implementing Order No. 8/1940 of the Reich Commissioner for the Occupied Netherlands Territories concerning Restriction of Industrial Operations, June 11, 1940 [33]

[EXCERPTS]

By virtue of Section 1 of Order No. 8/1940 of the Reich Commissioner for the occupied Netherlands territories concerning restrictions of industrial operations, and in accordance with Sections 2 and 3 of the order of the Reich Commissioner No. 3/1940 concerning the exercise of governmental authority in the Netherlands, I hereby order as follows:

SECTION 1. Managers of industrial enterprises or their agents shall not:

1. Suspend operations in plants for a limited or indefinite period.
2. Shorten working hours in plants to a period of less than thirty-six hours per week.

[33] *Verordnungsblatt*, No. 3, June 13, 1940, p. 23.

3. Dismiss workers or employees except in cases to which Article 1639 of the Civil Code shall be applicable. Dismissals made after May 9 shall be immediately revoked unless they have been specially ratified by the Director General of Labor.

. . . . .

The Hague, June 11, 1940.

SCHOLTENS
Secretary General of the Ministry of Social Welfare

Order of the Reich Commissioner for the Occupied Netherlands Territories concerning the Transportation of Persons and Goods, June 17, 1940 [34]

[EXCERPTS]

By virtue of Section 5 of the decree of the Führer concerning the exercise of governmental authority in the Netherlands of May 18, 1940 (*RGBl.* I, p. 778), I hereby order as follows:

SECTION 1. (1) The Secretary General of the Ministry of Waterstaat shall be authorized to issue rules and regulations concerning the transportation of persons and goods and to take all measures necessary in connection therewith.

(2) The rules and regulations issued by virtue of subsection 1 may contain penal sanctions for their violation.

. . . . .

The Hague, June 17, 1940.

SEYSS-INQUART
Reich Commissioner for the Occupied Netherlands Territories

Order of the Secretary General of the Ministry of Trade, Industry, and Shipping concerning the Rationing of Special Gasoline, June 17, 1940 [35]

[EXCERPTS]

Pursuant to Sections 4 and 5 of the Act of June 24, 1939 (*Staatsblatt*, No. 633), concerning the distribution of goods, and in pursuance of the order concerning benzine and benzol, 1939 No. 1, and in accordance with Sections 2 and 3 of Order No. 3/1940 of the Reich Commissioner for the occupied Netherlands territories, it is hereby ordered as follows:

. . . .

[34] *Verordnungsblatt*, No. 4, June 20, 1940, p. 34.
[35] *Ibid.*, No. 8, June 28, 1940, p. 121.

SECTION 2. (1) Producers or importers shall not be permitted to sell or deliver special benzine without written permit issued by the Director or his designees. The permit may be issued subject to conditions and limitations.

(2) Rules and regulations concerning the issuance of permits in accordance with subsection 1 shall be issued by the Secretary General.

. . .

The Hague, June 17, 1940.

H. M. HIRSCHFELD

Secretary General of the Ministry of Trade, Industry, and Shipping

First Order of the Secretary General of the Ministry of Waterstaat Implementing Order No. 15/1940 of the Reich Commissioner for the Occupied Netherlands Territories concerning the Transportation of Persons and Goods, June 18, 1940 [36]

[EXCERPTS]

By virtue of Section 1 of Order No. 15/1940, and in accordance with Sections 2 and 3 of Order No. 3/1940 of the Reich Commissioner for the occupied Netherlands territories, I hereby order as follows:

SECTION 1. In order to assure the most drastic restriction on the use of gasoline, the use of a motorcycle or any motor vehicle adapted for the transportation of persons, with the exception of motor busses as defined by the Act concerning Transportation of Persons by Motor Vehicles, shall be unlawful unless the owner of the vehicle has obtained permission for such use from the Inspector General of Traffic.

. . .

The Hague, June 18, 1940.

D. G. W. SPITZEN

Secretary General of the Ministry of Waterstaat

Second Order of the Secretary General of the Ministry of Waterstaat Implementing Order No. 15/1940 of the Reich Commissioner for the Occupied Netherlands Territories concerning the Transportation of Persons and Goods, June 18, 1940 [37]

[EXCERPTS]

In pursuance of Section 1 of Order No. 15/1940, and in accordance with Sections 2 and 3 of Order No. 3/1940 of the Reich Commissioner for the occupied Netherlands territories, I hereby order as follows:

[36] *Verordnungsblatt*, No. 4, June 20, 1940, p 35. [37] *Ibid.*, p. 38.

SECTION 1. (1) The transportation of goods on public highways for personal requirements shall be unlawful unless the person transporting such goods shall have obtained from the Inspector General of Traffic a permit for the use of a vehicle for such purpose.

(2) The term "personal requirements" as used in this order shall be deemed to refer to the transportation of goods owned and transported in vehicles owned by the person so transporting. If another person assists in such transport, he must do so by virtue of agreement of employment entered into directly with the person so transporting.

(3) In cases not subject to the provisions of the preceding subsection, the Inspector General of Traffic may nevertheless require application for a permit if, in his judgment, the transportation is economically equivalent to transportation for personal requirements.

. . . . .

SECTION 8. To the extent deemed necessary by the German armed forces for military reasons or for the purposes of defense against enemy air attacks, transportation shall take place according to rules and regulations established by the armed forces. These rules and regulations may vary from the provisions contained in this order.

. . . . .

The Hague, June 18, 1940.

D. G. W. SPITZEN
Secretary General of the Ministry of Waterstaat

Third Order of the Secretary General of the Ministry of Waterstaat Implementing Order No. 15/1940 of the Reich Commissioner for the Occupied Netherlands Territories concerning the Transportation of Persons and Goods, June 18, 1940 [38]

[EXCERPTS]

Pursuant to Section 1 of Order No. 15/1940, and in accordance with Sections 2 and 3 of Order No. 3/1940 of the Reich Commissioner for the occupied Netherlands territories, I hereby order as follows:

SECTION 1. (1) The transportation of goods on public highways on behalf of third parties is unlawful unless the person transporting such goods shall have obtained from the Inspector General of Traffic a permit for the use of the vehicle employed.

. . . . .

SECTION 10. To the extent deemed necessary by the German armed forces for military reasons or for the purposes of defense against air attacks,

[38] *Verordnungsblatt*, No. 4, June 20, 1940, p. 41.

transportation shall take place according to rules and regulations issued by the armed forces. Such rules and regulations may differ from the provisions contained in this order.

. . . . .

The Hague, June 18, 1940.

D. G. W. SPITZEN
Secretary General of the Ministry of Waterstaat

Order of the Secretary General of the Ministries of Trade, Industry, and Shipping, and Agriculture and Fisheries, concerning Prohibition of Price Increases (Price Fixing Order 1940, No. 1), July 11, 1940 [39]

[EXCERPTS]

Pursuant to Articles 1, 3, and 4 of the Act of 1939 to prevent unjustified raising of prices and hoarding, and in accordance with Sections 2 and 3 of Order No. 3/1940 of the Reich Commissioner for the occupied Netherlands territories, it is hereby ordered as follows:

SECTION 1. (1) It shall be unlawful to sell or offer for sale goods at prices higher than those usually obtained for goods of identical description, quantity, and quality on May 9, 1940.

(2) A person selling or offering for sale goods of identical description but of different quality and quantity than those sold or offered for sale on May 9, 1940, shall not demand or charge a price higher than that obtainable for such goods on May 9, 1940.

SECTION 2. (1) A person who, on May 9, 1940, did not sell or offer for sale goods referred to in Section 1, or who on that day received a price for them which must be considered exceptional, shall not demand or charge a price for such goods higher than that obtained in the majority of sales made of goods of identical description, quantity, and quality during the period of April 9 to May 9, 1940, inclusive.

(2) The provisions contained in Section 1, subsection 2, shall apply to sales referred to in subsection 1 of Section 2.

(3) A person who made no sales of the type referred to in subsection 1 in the period from April 9 to May 9, 1940, shall not demand or charge a price higher than the price usual and customary for such sales.

. . . . .

SECTION 6. The Secretary General of the Ministries of Trade, Industry, and Shipping, and Agriculture and Fisheries, may exempt certain goods from the provisions of this order, or may establish prices varying from the prices established by this order.

[39] *Verordnungsblatt*, No. 14, July 27, 1940, p. 211.

SECTION 7. The provisions of this order shall not apply:

1. Whenever the Secretary General in the Ministry of Agriculture and Fisheries (or his designees) establishes or authorizes, or shall establish or authorize, prices varying from those established by Sections 1 to 3 in pursuance of the Agricultural Emergency Act of May 5, 1933 (*Staatsblad*, No. 261).
2. To tariffs or prices for the transportation of persons or goods.
3. To labor wages.
4. To goods imported from abroad unless title has been vested in the Netherlands recipients of such goods.

. . . . .

The Hague, July 11, 1940.

H. M. HIRSCHFELD
Secretary General of the Ministries of Trade, Industry, and Shipping, and Agriculture and Fisheries

Order of the Secretary General of the Ministry of Agriculture and Fisheries concerning the Authority of the Director General for the Food Supply and the Establishment of a Commission to Secure the Food Supply, September 10, 1940 [40]

Pursuant to Section 1 of Order No. 23/1940, and in accordance with Sections 2 and 3 of Order No. 3/1940 of the Reich Commissioner for the occupied Netherlands territories, it is hereby ordered as follows:

SECTION 1. The powers vested in, and duties imposed upon a Government Commissioner in valid statutory provisions, stipulations, documents, charters, and by-laws in accordance with Article 26*a* of the Agricultural Emergency Act of 1933 (*Staatsblad*, No. 261) shall be exercised and assumed by the Director General for the Food Supply or his designee.

SECTION 2. (1) There shall be established a Commission for Securing the Food Supply. It shall be the duty of such commission to advise the Secretary General of the Ministry of Agriculture and Fisheries as to the enforcement of the Agricultural Emergency Act of 1933, the Act of September 30, 1938 (*Staatsblad*, No. 639 C), and any other act dealing with the food supply.

(2) The commission mentioned in the preceding subsection shall take the place of the Board of Government Commissioners established in accordance with Article 26*a* of the Agricultural Emergency Act of 1933.

SECTION 3. The personnel of the Commission for Securing the Food Supply shall be appointed by the Secretary General of the Ministry of

[40] *Verordnungsblatt*, No. 26, September 14, 1940, p. 430.

Agriculture and Fisheries; the names of the members shall be published in the *Nederlandsche Staatscourant.*

SECTION 4. This order shall take effect as of the date of publication.

The Hague, September 10, 1940.

H. M. HIRSCHFELD
Secretary General of the Ministry of Agriculture and Fisheries

Order of the Secretaries General in the Ministries of Trade, Industry and Shipping, Agriculture and Fisheries, Waterstaat, the Interior, Finance, Social Welfare, and Justice, concerning the Appointment of a Price Commissioner, November 11, 1940 [41]

Pursuant to Section 1 of Order No. 23/1940, and in accordance with Sections 2 and 3 of Order No. 3/1940 of the Reich Commissioner for the occupied Netherlands territories, it is hereby ordered as follows:

SECTION 1. For the establishment of prices and other remuneration for goods and services of every description, and for the supervision of such prices and remuneration, the office of a Price Commissioner (hereinafter designated as "Commissioner") shall be established. The Commissioner shall be appointed, and subject to removal, by the Secretary General of the Ministry of Trade, Industry, and Shipping. His authority shall extend especially to prices for all articles of everyday need, to rentals for chattels and real property, and to tariffs for transportation, gas, and electricity, and to interest rates.

SECTION 2. General orders establishing prices shall be issued by the Secretary General of Trade, Industry, and Shipping after consultation with the Commissioner.

SECTION 3. The Commissioner shall assure the maintenance of prices which conform to the public welfare. For that purpose, he may, among other things, issue general directives for the enforcement of prices established. He may issue instructions to officers appointed by the Secretaries General for the administration of price-fixing matters.

SECTION 4. It shall be the duty of the Commissioner to supervise compliance with price-fixing orders. He may issue to officials charged with the prosecution of violations, instructions which he deems necessary for the purpose of enforcing such orders.

SECTION 5. In the fulfillment of his official duties the Commissioner shall be assisted by a board to be appointed by the Secretary General in the Ministry of Trade, Industry, and Shipping. On this board the Ministries of

[41] *Verordnungsblatt,* No. 39, November 30, 1940, p. 631.

Trade, Industry, and Shipping, of Agriculture and Fisheries, of Waterstaat, of the Interior, of Finance, of Justice, and of Social Welfare shall be represented.

SECTION 6. This order shall take effect as of the date of publication.

The Hague, November 11, 1940.

H. M. HIRSCHFELD, *Secretary General of the Ministry of Trade, Industry, and Shipping;* H. M. HIRSCHFELD, *Secretary General of the Ministry of Agriculture and Fisheries;* D. G. W. SPITZEN, *Secretary General of the Ministry of Waterstaat;* K. J. FREDERIKS, *Secretary General of the Ministry of the Interior;* L. J. A. TRIP, *Secretary General of the Ministry of Finance;* R. A. BERWEI, *Acting Secretary General of the Ministry of Social Welfare;* J. C. TENKINK, *Secretary General of the Ministry of Justice.*

Order of the Secretaries General in the Ministries of Finance, and Trade, Industry, and Shipping concerning the Levy of Customs Duties on the Importation of German Goods, December 16, 1940 [42]

[EXCERPT]

Pursuant to Section 1 of Order No. 127/1940 and of Section 1 of Order No. 23/1940, and in accordance with Sections 2 and 3 of Order No. 3/1940 of the Reich Commissioner for the occupied Netherlands territories, it is hereby ordered as follows:

SECTION 1. German goods which are registered as such for importation shall be exempt from the customs duty payable in accordance with subsection 1 of Article 1 of the Customs Duties Act of 1934 (*Tariefwet* 1934). If such goods are subject to a specific levy in connection with the excises on distilled spirits, grain alcohol, sugar, beer, salt, and the slaughter of animals, such amount shall be payable as is determined by the Secretary General of the Ministry of Finance, and it shall be an equivalent for the tax on consumption.

. . . . .

The Hague, December 16, 1940.

L. G. A. TRIP, *Secretary General of the Ministry of Finance*

H. M. HIRSCHFELD, *Secretary General of the Ministry of Trade, Industry and Shipping*

[42] *Verordnungsblatt,* No. 42, December 27, 1940, p. 722.

5. FINANCE[42a]

Order of the Reich Commissioner for the Occupied Netherlands Territories concerning the Establishment of a Reconstruction Fund, June 21, 1940[43]

Pursuant to Section 5 of the decree of the Führer concerning the exercise of governmental authority in the Netherlands of May 18, 1940 (*RGBl.*, p. 778), I hereby order as follows:

SECTION 1. For the purpose of financing the expenditures which the government may incur by reason of the damage caused by the war, a fund shall be established which shall be designated as "Reconstruction Fund, 1940."

SECTION 2. The term "expenditures" as used in Section 1 shall be deemed to refer to:

1. Payments which the government makes available as a contribution to the damage caused by the war.
2. The costs of the restoration of governmental property and contributions of the government for the restoration of property owned by other corporations of public law;
3. Other expenses, which, because of their connection with the purposes of the fund, shall, within the discretion of the Secretary General of the Ministry of Finance, likewise be defrayed from this fund.

SECTION 3. (1) The procedure by which payments in accordance with Section 2, Number 1, are to be made, and the several amounts of such payments, shall be established by rules and regulations.

(2) The expenditures mentioned in Section 2, number 2, shall be governed by regulations issued by the Secretary General of the Ministry of Finance.

SECTION 4. The expenditures mentioned in Section 2 shall be financed as follows:

1. Through transfer of budget appropriations, especially those which, because of the changed political and constitutional conditions, can no longer be used for the purpose contemplated.
2. From the surplus arising from the Currency Stabilization Fund.
3. Through short-term and long-term loans.

SECTION 5. The Secretary General of the Ministry of Finance shall be authorized to issue regulations concerning the appropriation of funds required for interest and amortization payments on loans obtained in accordance with Section 4, number 3.

SECTION 6. (1) The Reconstruction Fund, 1940, shall be administered by the Ministry of Finance in accordance with general regulations issued by the Secretary General of the said Ministry.

[42a] See also order concerning Reich Credit Institutes, above, p. 329.
[43] *Verordnungsblatt*, No. 5, June 22, 1940, p. 52.

(2) The income and expenditure of this fund shall be established by an annual budget.

SECTION 7. This order shall take effect as of the date of publication.

The Hague, June 21, 1940.

SEYSS-INQUART
Reich Commissioner for the Occupied Netherlands Territories

Order of the Reich Commissioner for the Occupied Netherlands Territories Changing the Rate of Exchange of the Reich Credit Institute Notes and the Gulden, July 16, 1940 [44]

Pursuant to Section 5 of the decree of the Führer concerning the exercise of governmental authority in the Netherlands of May 18, 1940 (*RGBl.* I, p. 778), I hereby order as follows:

SECTION 1. The rate of exchange of the Reich Credit Institute Notes and the gulden shall be established as follows: 1 gulden equals 133 Reichspfennigs.

SECTION 2. Section 2 of Order No. 8 of the Commander in Chief of the Army concerning legal tender in the occupied Netherlands territories, shall be and hereby is repealed.

SECTION 3. This order shall take effect as of the day of publication.

The Hague, July 16, 1940.

SEYSS-INQUART
Reich Commissioner for the Occupied Netherlands Territories

Order of the Secretary General of the Ministry of Finance concerning the Registration of Foreign Exchange, September 18, 1940 [45]

By virtue of Article 10 of the order concerning foreign exchange of 1940, and in accordance with Sections 2 and 3 of Order No. 3/1940 of the Reich Commissioner for the occupied Netherlands territories, it is hereby ordered:

SECTION 1. All Netherlands residents are required within one month of the effective date of this order to register foreign exchange owned by them, at the time this order goes into effect, with the "Vereeniging voor den Effectenhandel" at Amsterdam.

The Bureau for Foreign Exchange may determine by special rules that foreign exchange which for other reasons has been filed for registration or has been registered or which is of little value, shall be exempt from registration. These rules shall be published in the *Nederlandsche Staatscourant*.

SECTION 2. (1) All Netherlands residents are required to register foreign

[44] *Verordnungsblatt*, No. 11, July 17, 1940, p. 156. [45] *Ibid.*, September 26, 1940.

exchange acquired after the effective date of this order within three days after acquisition, in accordance with the provisions of Section 1. The registrant shall state the name of his predecessor in title.

(2) No registration under subsection 1 need be made if the foreign exchange has been registered with the "Vereeniging voor den Effectenhandel" provided that its number has been indicated upon registration, and provided further that a chain registration statement has been attached to it and that the exchange is acquired in the ordinary course of trade on the Exchange.

(3) The phrase "acquired in the ordinary course of trade on the Exchange" shall be considered as applying to any acquisition, made in compliance with the exchange regulations of 1940 (see *Nederlandsche Staatscourant*, 1940, No. 1927) and the rules and regulations of the "Vereeniging voor den Effectenhandel," Amsterdam, of the "Bond voor den Gelden Effectenhandel in de Provincie," The Hague, and the "Vereeniging van Effectenhandelaren te Rotterdam," provided that such acquisition is made by members of the above-mentioned associations acting for themselves or on behalf of others.

SECTION 3. Persons who become Netherlands residents are required to register within ten days foreign exchange owned by them at the time when they became Netherlands residents, in accordance with the provisions of Section 1.

SECTION 4. Foreign exchange for which within the occupied Netherlands territories certificates, fractional certificates of deposit, or other similar bearer documents were issued must be registered by the Netherlands resident who has issued these certificates.

SECTION 5. This order shall take effect as of the day of publication.

The Hague, September 18, 1940.

L. J. A. TRIP
Secretary General of the Ministry of Finance

Order of the Secretaries General of the Ministries of Trade, Industry and Shipping, and Finance, concerning Aid to Firms Experiencing Difficulties in Maintaining Their Liquidity, October 10, 1940 [46]

In pursuance of Section 1 of Order No. 23/1940, and in accordance with Sections 2 and 3 of Order No. 3/1940 of the Reich Commissioner for the occupied Netherlands territories, it is hereby ordered as follows:

SECTION 1. (1) In the interest of the maintenance of economic life financial aid, through the execution of guarantees for loans or otherwise, may be extended to enterprises which find themselves financially embarrassed through their inability to enforce claims arising out of shipments abroad,

[46] *Verordnungsblatt*, No. 31, October 14, 1940, p. 512.

as a result of the extraordinary circumstances prevailing or of orders freezing accounts abroad as a result of these conditions.

(2) Aid in accordance with subsection 1 shall, however, be extended only if the profitableness of the enterprise under the prevailing conditions appears to be sufficiently assured or if the continued operation of such enterprise in the future will be in the public interest.

SECTION 2. This order shall take effect as of the date of publication.

The Hague, October 10, 1940.

H. M. HIRSCHFELD, *Secretary General of the Ministry of Trade, Industry, and Shipping*
L. J. A. TRIP, *Secretary General of the Ministry of Finance*

Order of the Secretaries General in the Ministries of Finance, Justice, Trade, Industry and Shipping, Agriculture and Fisheries, and the Colonies, concerning Foreign Exchange Control (Foreign Exchange Order 1941), March 26, 1941 [47]

[EXCERPTS]

Pursuant to Section 1 of Order No. 23/1940, and in accordance with Order No. 3/1940 of the Reich Commissioner for the occupied Netherlands territories, it is hereby ordered as follows:

. . . .

SECTION 50. (1) It shall be unlawful to pay or extinguish in any other manner an obligation which is payable by deposit with the Netherlands Clearing Institute unless permission to do so shall have been obtained.

(2) If an obligation payable by deposit with the Netherlands Clearing Institute shall have been paid or extinguished without such permission in any other manner, the Netherlands Clearing Institute may require the person who had owed such debt or any person participating in the unlawful payment or extinction of the debt to deposit the amount of the debt with the Institute.

. .

SECTION 52. It shall be unlawful to accept drafts or to sign notes or checks in connection with debts which are payable by deposit with the Netherlands Clearing Institute unless the bill, note, or check thus signed contains a notice indicating that the obligation is payable by deposit with the Netherlands Clearing Institute.

III. AGREEMENTS TO PAY FOR GOODS OR SERVICES

SECTION 53. (1) Unless permission shall have been obtained it shall be unlawful for Netherlands nationals:

[47] *Verordnungsblatt*, No. 13, March 29, 1941, p. 220.

a) To acquire or accept chattels or real property, or choses in action and services which are payable by deposit with the Netherlands Clearing Institute if such acquisition or acceptance takes place under conditions or circumstances which may indicate that the entire consideration will not be paid at all or only in part, or will be paid later than usual in transactions of such kind.

b) To supply or furnish goods and services which are payable by way of clearing if they are furnished or supplied under circumstances or conditions which may indicate that more than their usual value will have to be paid for them.

(2) Whenever personalty or realty, or incorporeal rights or services which are payable by deposit with the Netherlands Clearing Institute, shall have been acquired or accepted by a Netherlands national and its full consideration shall not have been deposited within the usual time for such transactions with the Netherlands Clearing Institute, the Institute may require the person who has thus acquired or accepted goods or services, etc., to deposit the full consideration.

IV. Advance Deposit or Guarantees in the Case of Imports

Section 54. The Netherlands Clearing Institute may determine that in instances to be designated by it, it shall be unlawful to import goods payable through deposit with the Netherlands Clearing Institute unless an advance deposit has been made or certain guarantees given.

. . . . .

VI. Official Order of Payment

Section 58. The Netherlands Clearing Institute may by registered letter require a person owing an obligation due and payable by deposit with the Netherlands Clearing Institute, or the persons required to make a deposit in accordance with subsection 2 of Section 50 or subsection 2 of Section 53, to deposit the amount due within a period of not less than ten days. The order shall contain a notice that, in the case of non-payment, execution may take place in accordance with the provisions of Section 59.

Section 59. (1) If such order is not complied with, the amount due may be demanded by a summary order of payment which shall be enforceable against the assets of the debtor with the force and effect of an execution issued upon a judgment.

(2) Execution may issue upon such order for the amount of principal as well as for the cost of the demand and execution.

. . . . .

The Hague, March 26, 1941.

B. J. Deleeuw
Acting Secretary General of the Ministry of Finance

Order of the Reich Commissioner for the Occupied Netherlands Territories Amending Order No. 48/1940 concerning the Change of Rate of Exchange of Reich Credit Institute Notes and the Gulden, April 23, 1941 [48]

Pursuant to Section 5 of the decree of the Führer concerning the exercise of governmental authority in the Netherlands of May 18, 1940 (*RGBl.* I, p. 778), I hereby order as follows:

SECTION 1. In Section 1 of Order No. 48/1940 concerning the change of the rate of exchange of Reich Credit Institute notes and the gulden, the figure "133" shall be changed to the figure "132.70."

SECTION 2. This order shall take effect as of the date of publication.

The Hague, April 23, 1941.

SEYSS-INQUART
Reich Commissioner for the Occupied Netherlands Territories

Order of the Reich Commissioner for the Occupied Netherlands Territories concerning the Registration of Assets of the United States, its Citizens and Certain Other Persons, September 11, 1941 [49]

[EXCERPTS]

By virtue of Section 5 of the decree of the Führer concerning the exercise of governmental authority in the Netherlands of May 18, 1940 (*RGBl.* I, p. 778), I hereby order as follows:

SECTION 1. Real and personal properties situated in the occupied Netherlands which are legally owned or controlled by:

1. The United States of America (United States) or its possessions, or its political subdivisions, and other public corporations;
2. Persons who are citizens of the United States or have their domicile or temporary residence in the United States or its possessions;
3. Corporations, private associations, foundations, endowments, trusts, or other forms of organizations, which have their seat or principal place of business in the territory of the United States or its possessions or which have been incorporated under the laws of the United States;
4. Persons other than those designated in numbers 2 or 3, by virtue of branches, etc., which they have in the United States;

shall be registered as they appeared on September 30, 1940, and on June 30, 1941, and if they were acquired at a later date, as they appeared on the day of acquisition.

SECTION 2. The following shall be considered as situated in the occupied Netherlands territories:

[48] *Verordnungsblatt*, No. 16, April 24, 1941, p. 309. [49] *Ibid.*, No. 38, p. 768.

I

1. Realty and rights assimilated to realty and chattels, situated in the occupied Netherlands territories.
2. Securities, shares, and participation certificates of every description, found in the occupied Netherlands territories; bonds of the German Reich, of the Kingdom of the Netherlands, and of other debtors who have their seat or principal place of business in the occupied Netherlands territories even if the documents are not found in the Netherlands territories.
3. Currency found in the occupied Netherlands territories.
4. Rights of participation, and options for such participation rights, in enterprises which have either their seat or principal place of business in the occupied Netherlands territories or which have been incorporated under Netherlands law regardless of whether these rights of participation are embodied in securities or not.
5. Claims against debtors who have their domicile or permanent residence in the occupied Netherlands territories, and claims which have arisen in connection with a branch of the debtor situated in the occupied Netherlands territories.
6. Rights and claims which are entered in a Netherlands public record or register.
7. Trade or business licenses and permits granted in the occupied Netherlands territories.
8. Patents, authors', and other protective rights which have obtained protection in the occupied Netherlands territories.
9. All other assets, not included in numbers 1–8, which are used in connection with the operation of a branch establishment or the practice of any occupation in the occupied Netherlands territories.

II

1. Rights in or to assets described in I.
2. Rights under contracts to convey or transfer assets described in I.

. . . . .

SECTION 10. (1) The Reich commissioner for the occupied Netherlands territories (through the Commissioner General for Finance and Economic Affairs) shall take all measures necessary for the enforcement of this order. He may delegate his authority to others.

. . . . .

SECTION 11. This order shall take effect as of the date of publication.
The Hague, September 11, 1941.

SEYSS-INQUART
Reich Commissioner for the Occupied Netherlands Territories

6. LABOR

Order of the Reich Commissioner for the Occupied Netherlands Territories concerning the Netherlands Reconstruction Service, July 30, 1940 [50]

By virtue of the powers vested in me by Section 5 of the decree of the Führer concerning the exercise of governmental authority in the Netherlands of May 18, 1940 (*RGBl.* I, p. 778), I hereby decree:

SECTION 1. (1) A Netherlands Reconstruction Service (abbreviation "Reconstruction Service") is hereby established.

(2) It is the objective of the Reconstruction Service to afford members of the erstwhile Netherlands armed forces the opportunity of engaging in activities useful for the Netherlands national community.

(3) The Reconstruction Service is a service of honor on behalf of the nation and the fatherland.

SECTION 2. (1) The Reconstruction Service will be headed by (1) the Labor Commandant, (2) the Administrative Director.

(2) The Labor Commandant and the Administrative Director shall be appointed and dismissed by the Reich Commissioner for the occupied Netherlands territories. They shall be subject to the orders of the Secretary General of the Ministry for General Affairs.

SECTION 3. The annual budget of the Reconstruction Service shall be established on the basis of a joint proposal of the Labor Commandant and the Administrative Director by the Secretary General of the Ministry for General Affairs with the assent of the Secretary General of the Finance Ministry. It shall be subject to approval by the Reich Commissioner for the occupied Netherlands territories.

SECTION 4. The Secretary General of the Ministry for General Affairs shall issue rules and regulations necessary for the enforcement of this order. They shall be published in the Netherlands Official Gazette.

SECTION 5. This order shall take effect as of the day of its promulgation, with retroactive force, however, as of July 15, 1940.

The Hague, July 30, 1940.

SEYSS-INQUART
Reich Commissioner for the Occupied Netherlands Territories

[50] *Verordnungsblatt*, No. 15, August 1, 1940, p. 232.

Order of the Reich Commissioner for the Occupied Netherlands Territories Prohibiting Reduction in Wages and Salaries, August 27, 1940 [51]

[EXCERPTS]

Pursuant to Section 5 of the decree of the Führer concerning the exercise of governmental authority in the Netherlands of May 18, 1940 (*RGBl.* I, p. 778), I hereby order as follows:

SECTION 1. (1) It shall be unlawful to reduce prevailing wage and salary rates for employment contracts in agricultural, industrial, and commercial enterprises or for professional and similar services unless such reduction shall have been authorized.

(2) No such authorization shall be required if, in the case of a collective labor agreement, the parties to such an agreement or, in the case of an individual employment contract, the parties to such contract, shall agree on such reduction.

. . . . .

The Hague, August 27, 1940.

SEYSS-INQUART
Reich Commissioner for the Occupied Netherlands Territories

Order of the Secretary General of the Ministry of Social Welfare concerning Employment Service, September 24, 1940 [52]

[EXCERPTS]

By virtue of Section 1 of Order No. 23/1940, and in accordance with Sections 2 and 3 of Order No. 3/1940 of the Reich Commissioner for the occupied Netherlands territories, it is hereby ordered:

SECTION 1. (1) The State Labor Office shall be the official agency charged with the administration of the public employment service.

(2) The State Labor Office is a division in the Ministry of Social Welfare and is headed by a General Director.

(3) The State Labor Office shall succeed to all rights and duties of the State Bureau for Unemployment Insurance and Employment Service.

(4) The activities of the State Labor Office shall extend also to public occupational guidance and apprenticeship placement service.

. . . . .

SECTION 6. (1) Employment agencies for occupations other than those in trade and industry shall require approval by the Secretary General of the Ministry of Social Welfare. The approval may be subject to conditions.

[51] *Verordnungsblatt*, No. 23, August 29, 1940, p. 359.
[52] *Ibid.*, No. 30, October 5, 1940, p. 500.

(2) The Secretary General of the Ministry of Social Welfare may, notwithstanding the provisions of subsection 1, Article 55, of the Employment Service Act of 1930, withdraw a license granted to a person operating a private employment agency for trade and/or industry. In that event, the licensee must be paid an indemnity to be fixed by the Secretary General.

(3) A person operating a private employment agency for occupations other than those in trade and industry without first obtaining a license shall be punishable by imprisonment for not more than six months or by a fine not exceeding one thousand guilders. The same penalties shall apply to any member of the board of directors of a corporation or other incorporated association or endowment who acts in such a manner, or who fails to prevent the corporation or other incorporated association or endowment from engaging in such employment service without having first obtained a license. Articles 59, 60, and 61 of the Employment Service Act of 1930 shall be applicable.

(4) The acts punishable according to subsection 3 shall be considered misdemeanors.

R. A. Berwei
Acting Secretary General in the Ministry of Social Welfare

Order of the Reich Commissioner for the Occupied Netherlands Territories to Insure Labor Peace, May 19, 1941 [53]

Pursuant to Section 5 of the decree of the Führer concerning the exercise of governmental authority in the Netherlands of May 18, 1940 (*RGBl.* I, p. 778), I hereby order as follows:

Section 1. (1) Any person participating in a strike or locking out laborers or employees shall be liable to imprisonment of not less than one year, and in more serious cases to hard labor.

(2) The same penalties shall apply to any person who in the capacity of an employer shall, acting in agreement with the persons employed by him, wholly or partly suspend operations unless such suspension of operations is caused by the pursuit of justifiable interests of the enterprise itself.

(3) The attempt to commit any of the acts made punishable in accordance with subsections 1 and 2 shall likewise be punishable.

Section 2. Any person who incites others to commit an act declared punishable by Section 1 or who undertakes to prevent others from the resumption of work shall be punishable by hard labor.

Section 3. In the case of an especially serious violation of Sections 1 and 2 the penalty shall be death or hard labor for life.

[53] *Verordnungsblatt*, No. 22, May 20, 1941, p. 364.

SECTION 4. Acts punishable in accordance with Sections 1 to 3 shall be considered crimes in accordance with subsection 2, Section 2, of Order No. 52/1940 concerning the jurisdiction of German courts in criminal proceedings.

SECTION 5. This order shall take effect as of the date of publication.

The Hague, May 19, 1941.

SEYSS-INQUART

Reich Commissioner for the Occupied Netherlands Territories

NORWAY

1. ADMINISTRATION

Decree of the Führer concerning the Exercise of Governmental Authority in Norway, April 24, 1940 [1]

In order to safeguard public order and public life in the Norwegian territories placed under the protection of the German armed forces, I hereby decree:

SECTION 1. The Reich Commissioner for the occupied Norwegian territories shall administer these territories. His official residence shall be at Oslo. The Reich Commissioner shall be guardian of the interests of the German Reich and, within the domain of civil administration, shall be vested with supreme governmental authority.

SECTION 2. The Reich Commissioner may, for the enforcement of his orders and the exercise of his administrative functions, call on the Norwegian Administrative Council and the Norwegian civil authorities.

SECTION 3. The laws and statutes heretofore in force shall continue in effect in so far as is compatible with the fact of occupation.

The Reich Commissioner may issue laws in the form of orders. These orders shall be published in the *Verordnungsblatt für die besetzten norwegischen Gebiete.*

SECTION 4. The Commander of the German Forces in Norway shall be vested with supreme military authority; his orders, in so far as they relate to the domain of civil administration, shall be enforced by the Reich Commissioner exclusively. In so far as, and as long as, military considerations demand, he shall be authorized to take all measures necessary for the execution of his military orders and for the military security of Norway.

SECTION 5. The Reich Commissioner may employ members of the German police forces for the execution of his orders. The German police forces shall be subject to the orders of the Commander of the German Forces in Norway in accordance with military requirements and with due regard to the duties of the Reich Commissioner.

SECTION 6. The Reich Commissioner shall be directly responsible to me and shall be subject to my instructions as to general policies, and to my orders.

SECTION 7. I hereby appoint President Terboven Reich Commissioner for the occupied Norwegian territories.

SECTION 8. In accordance with my instructions, rules and regulations for the enforcement and implementation of this order shall be issued for the

[1] *Verordnungsblatt für die besetzten norwegischen Gebiete*, No. 1, May 6, 1940, p. 1.

domain of civil administration by the Reich Minister and Chief of the Reich Chancellery, and for the military domain by the Chief of the Supreme Command of the German Armed Forces.

ADOLF HITLER, *Führer*
DR. LAMMERS, *Reich Minister and Chief of the Reich Chancellery*
KEITEL, *Chief of the Supreme Command of the Armed Forces*
FRICK, *Reich Minister of the Interior*

Order Prohibiting Political Parties in Norway, September 25, 1940 [2]

By virtue of subsection 2 of Section 3 of the decree of the Führer concerning the exercise of governmental authority in Norway of April 24, 1940, the following is hereby ordered:

SECTION 1. (1) All political parties and any other political organizations in Norway are hereby declared dissolved. The order of dissolution shall apply also to subsidiary organizations, and affiliated groups and associations.

(2) This order shall not apply to the Nasjonal Samling [3] and its subsidiary organizations.

SECTION 2. In cases of doubt whether or not an organization is to be considered political, the Reich Commissioner's decision shall be final.

SECTION 3. The Reich Commissioner shall appoint trustees for the liquidation of the affairs of organizations dissolved in accordance with Section 1.

TERBOVEN
Reich Commissioner for the Occupied Norwegian Territories

Order concerning the Dismissal and Transfer of Officials, October 7, 1940 [4]

For the purpose of facilitating the task of the Commissioners of State (*kommissarische Staatsräte*) in establishing a new political order, and by virtue of subsection 2 of Section 3 of the decree of the Führer concerning the exercise of governmental authority in Norway of April 24, 1940, the following is hereby ordered.

[2] *Verordnungsblatt*, No. 5, September 26, 1940, p. 19.
[3] "Nasjonal Samling" is the official designation of the Norwegian Quisling party.—ED.
[4] *Verordnungsblatt*, No. 7, October 9, 1940, p. 24.

SECTION 1. (1) Officials whose political attitude does not warrant the assumption that they will cooperate wholeheartedly in the establishment of a new political order, may be dismissed from office.

(2) Dismissals in accordance with subsection 1 may only be ordered within six months after the effective date of this order.

SECTION 2. (1) If the establishment of the new political order so requires, officials may, in the interests of better public service, be transferred to another office or another locality. In such event, the position to which the official is transferred must correspond in its character and salary to the previous position of the official.

(2) If the requirements outlined in subsection 1 are present, officials may also be placed on the waiting list.

(3) Dismissals in accordance with Section 1, subsection 1, and transfers of officials to the waiting list in accordance with Section 2, subsection 2, may be ordered not later than six months after the effective date of this order.

SECTION 3. Orders issued by virtue of this order shall not be subject to judicial review.

TERBOVEN
Reich Commissioner for the Occupied Norwegian Territories

Order concerning the Prohibition of Activities on Behalf of the Royal House of Norway, October 7, 1940 [5]

By virtue of subsection 2 of Section 3 of the decree of the Führer concerning the exercise of governmental authority in Norway of April 24, 1940, the following is hereby decreed:

SECTION 1. Any propaganda on behalf of the Royal House of Norway or of any of its members shall be forbidden.

SECTION 2. (1) Whoever takes any step to make propaganda on behalf of the Royal House of Norway by word of mouth, picture, printing, or in any other manner shall be punishable by forced labor for not longer than three years or by imprisonment; in addition, a fine may be imposed.

(2) For the trial of crimes described in subsection 1 special courts are hereby established.

SECTION 3. This order shall take effect as of the day of publication.

Oslo, October 7, 1940.

TERBOVEN
Reich Commissioner for the Occupied Norwegian Territories

[5] *Verordnungsblatt*, No. 8, October 25, 1940, p. 27.

2. LAW AND COURTS

Order concerning Procedure before the German Court, August 27, 1940 [6]

By virtue of Section 3 of the decree of the Führer concerning the exercise of governmental authority in Norway of April 24, 1940, the following order establishing the procedure before the German Court is hereby issued:

SECTION 1. (1) The official seat of the German Court shall be in Oslo. If the need arises, its president may designate any other locality as a proper place for sessions of the court.

(2) The German Court may transact official business in any locality within the occupied Norwegian territories.

SECTION 2. The president and the members of the German Court shall be directly subject as to their official duties to the supervision of the Reich Commissioner.

SECTION 3. (1) The German Court shall have jurisdiction over such crimes as are designated by express orders of the Reich Commissioner. The German Court shall exercise jurisdiction without respect to the jurisdiction of the Norwegian criminal courts.

(2) Any criminal act within the jurisdiction of the German Court which also constitutes a crime punishable according to Norwegian law shall be subject, in so far as Norwegian law applies, to the jurisdiction of Norwegian courts. In such event, however, the proceedings before the German Court shall take precedence.

SECTION 4. Nothing contained in this order shall be construed to affect the jurisdiction of the courts of the German armed forces and the S.S. and police courts.

SECTION 5. (1) The German Court shall apply the general principles of German criminal law.

(2) If, in the course of a proceeding, issues of law should arise to be determined according to Norwegian law, the president or, after the trial has begun, the court may request an advisory opinion from the Legal Division of the Ministry of Justice and Police.

SECTION 6. The rules of procedure in force in the German Reich shall be made applicable as nearly as may be to the procedure before the German Court, subject to such modifications as are provided for in this order or as may be provided for the particular proceeding by decision of the court.

SECTION 7. Motions to have a trial held before another judge shall be decided by the German Court. In passing on such motion the place of the judge against whom such motion is directed shall be taken by a substitute judge. No such motion against the substitute is permissible.

[6] *Verordnungsblatt*, No. 3, August 31, 1940, p. 11.

SECTION 8. (1) No preliminary investigation by the court shall take place.

(2) The date of trial shall be set by the president after the indictment has been filed and if he deems the prerequisites for such trial to be present.

(3) Notice and summons may be issued twenty-four hours before the trial.

SECTION 9. (1) No appeal may be made from the decisions of the German Court.

(2) From a decision of the presiding judge the prosecuting attorney may appeal to the full court.

SECTION 10. (1) Attorneys who are admitted to practice in Germany or in Norway may appear before the German Court.

(2) Other persons may be admitted as defense counsel by the presiding judge, provided that their character is such as to assure adequate fulfillment of the duties of a defense counsel.

(3) The court may reject any defense counsel for special reasons.

SECTION 11. The presiding judge of the German Court may appoint a defense counsel if such appointment appears necessary to assure a suitable defense of the accused.

SECTION 12. In cases in which goods may be seized and declared forfeited without a proceeding against an individual, the court may decide without oral trial.

SECTION 13. Goods which are declared forfeited shall become the property of the German Reich.

SECTION 14. (1) The Norwegian prosecuting attorneys and their agents, as well as the Norwegian courts, shall be required to comply with requests of the German Court or of the German prosecuting attorney to lend their assistance in aid of proceedings instituted.

(2) The Norwegian prosecuting attorneys and their agents shall be required, in case of urgent need, to take all measures, in accordance with the provisions applicable to proceedings originally before them, which may aid in ascertaining the facts, in apprehending the perpetrator, or in safeguarding the evidence.

SECTION 15. This order shall take effect as of the date of publication.

Oslo, August 27, 1940.

TERBOVEN

Reich Commissioner for the Occupied Norwegian Territories

Order concerning the Establishment of a Norwegian Special Court, October 25, 1940 [7]

By virtue of subsection 2 of Section 3 of the decree of the Führer concerning the exercise of governmental authority in Norway of April 24, 1940, the following is hereby ordered:

SECTION 1. For the institution of criminal proceedings brought under the order concerning the prohibition of political parties in Norway of September 25, 1940 (*VBl.*, p. 19), and under the order concerning the prohibition of activities on behalf of the Royal House of Norway of October 7, 1940 (*VBl.*, p. 27), a Norwegian Special Court, with its official seat in Oslo, is hereby established.

SECTION 2. (1) The Special Court shall be composed of a presiding judge and two associate judges. The presiding judge must be eligible for the office of a judge of the Supreme Court.

(2) The presiding judge and the associate judges shall be appointed by the Commissioner of State for the Department of Justice.

SECTION 3. No appeal lies from the decisions of the Special Court.

SECTION 4. The Commissioner of State for the Department of Justice is hereby authorized to issue all necessary rules and regulations, especially for the procedure before the Special Court.

SECTION 5. This order shall take effect as of the day of publication.

Oslo, October 25, 1940.

TERBOVEN
Reich Commissioner for the Occupied Norwegian Territories

Law concerning Postponement of Foreclosure Sales in respect to Volunteers for War Service, February 26, 1942 [8]

SECTION 1. Should an executor's forced sale or any other prosecutions for payment, as well as for surrender of goods in accordance with the law concerning purchase on the installment system of July 21, 1916, be applied for in respect to a claim against defendants who are serving as volunteers in the Norwegian Legion, the Regiment Nordland, or otherwise in the German forces, the competent authorities may postpone the prosecution for payment for six months if the non-payment of the defendant's debts is caused by his service.

On the same terms the prosecution for payment shall be postponed when the claim applies to amounts of Kr. 500, or more. The same rules shall

[7] *Verordnungsblatt*, No. 9, November 5, 1940, p. 29.
[8] *Norsk Lovtidend*, No. 16, March 13, 1942.

apply to cases where the claim is made for state or municipality taxes of property and income, for old-age pension fees, extraordinary property taxes, special state taxes on increase of income, or taxes on motorcars.

A postponement may be made with a proviso that the legal expenses or interest due be paid. This does not apply, however, to claims for taxes as mentioned in the preceding paragraph.

The regulations in the first and second paragraphs shall be applied in corresponding measure when a postponed payment prosecution is resumed.

The regulations in the first to the third paragraphs shall apply in corresponding measure when attempts to collect a claim in accordance with a special regulation are being made through a deduction from wages, etc.

Before the authority dealing with the seizure makes a decision in conformity with this section, the said authority must give the prosecutor an opportunity to express his views.

The regulations in this section do not apply to prosecutions for payment in respect to claims for family maintenance allowance for spouse or children.

SECTION 2. As long as the volunteer serves as mentioned in Section 1, his estate cannot be declared bankrupt at the request of any creditor. The time-limits stipulated in the Bankruptcy Act of June 6, 1863, paragraphs 42–46, shall not apply during the period of service.

Oslo, February 26, 1942.

QUISLING, *Minister President*

SVERRE RIISNAES R. J. FUGLESANG

3. GENOCIDE LEGISLATION

Order concerning the Subsidizing of Children Begotten by Members of the German Armed Forces in Occupied Territories, July 28, 1942 [9]

[EXCERPTS]

SECTION 1. To maintain and promote a racially valuable German heritage, children begotten by members of the German armed forces in the occupied Norwegian and Netherlands territories and born of Norwegian or Dutch women shall upon the application of the mother be granted a special subsidy and benefit through the offices of the Reich Commissioners for the occupied Norwegian and Dutch territories.

SECTION 2. (1) The benefit shall include the costs of delivery of such children, the payment to the mothers of maintenance benefits for the time before and after delivery, the payment of maintenance benefits for the children, the sheltering of mothers in clinics or homes, with the consent of

[9] *Reichsgesetzblatt*, 1942, I, p. 488.

the mothers, as well as the sheltering of the children in homes, and similar care.

(2) Details shall be arranged by the Reich Commissioners for the occupied Norwegian and Dutch territories.

SECTION 3. (1) The subsidizing of the mothers and children shall have the effect of removing any disadvantage from the mothers and promoting the development of the children.

(2) If she desires, the mother shall be given suitable employment.

. . . . .

SECTION 7. (2) The Chief of the High Command of the Armed Forces, in consultation with the Reich Minister and Chief of the Reich Chancellery, may extend the sphere of validity of this order in part or in its entirety to other occupied territories.

Headquarters of the Führer, July 28, 1942.

ADOLF HITLER, *Führer*
KEITEL, *Chief of the Supreme Command of the Armed Forces*
DR. LAMMERS, *Reich Minister and Chief of the Reich Chancellery*

POLAND[1]

INCORPORATED TERRITORIES

1. ADMINISTRATION

Decree of the Führer and Reich Chancellor concerning the Organization and Administration of the Eastern Territories, October 8, 1939 [1a]

[EXCERPTS]

SECTION 1. (1) In the process of reorganization of the Eastern Territories the Reich Districts (*Gaue*) of Western Prussia and Posen shall be incorporated as parts of the German Reich.

(2) The Reich District shall be administered by a Reich Governor (*Statthalter*).

(3) The Reich Governor in Western Prussia shall have his official residence in Danzig; the Reich Governor in Posen shall have his official residence in Posen.

SECTION 2. (1) The Reich District of Western Prussia shall be subdivided into the government districts of Danzig, Marienwerder, and Bromberg.

(2) The Reich District Posen shall be subdivided into the government districts of Hohensalza, Posen, and Kalisch.

SECTION 3. (1) For the organization of the administration in the Reich districts, the statute concerning the organization of the administration in the Reich District of the Sudetenland [2] (short title "Sudeten Statute") of April 14, 1939 (*RGBl.* I, p. 780), shall apply unless modified by this decree.

(2) All branches of the administration shall be subject to the jurisdiction of the Reich Governor. The Reich Minister of the Interior shall decide, in agreement with the Reich minister concerned, upon the transfer of special branches of the administration to the existing Reich administrative agencies. Special agencies for counties shall be subject to the jurisdiction of county commissioners (*Landräte*) until further notice.

. . . . .

SECTION 6. (1) Residents of German blood or of racially related blood shall become German nationals in accordance with further provisions to be issued.

[1] Acknowledgment is hereby made to the Ministry of Foreign Affairs of the Republic of Poland, whose Note Addressed to the Allied and Neutral Powers, of May 3, 1941, published in *German Occupation of Poland* (Polish White Book), has largely helped the author in the preparation of this section of the volume.

Translations of some of the documents included in this section, together with additional documents relating to Poland, may likewise be found in the appendices to the Polish White Book and *The Black Book of Poland*, previously cited.

[1a] *Reichsgesetzblatt*, 1939, I, p. 2042.

[2] See this statute under Czechoslovakia (Sudetenland), above, p. 341.—ED.

(2) Residents of German origin in these territories shall become German citizens in accordance with the Reich Nationality Code.

SECTION 7. The law heretofore in force shall continue in effect unless incompatible with the fact of incorporation in the German Reich.

SECTION 8. The Reich Minister of the Interior may, by means of general orders, and in agreement with the Reich minister concerned, introduce Reich law and Prussian law.

. . .

SECTION 12. (1) The Reich Minister of the Interior shall be the official chiefly responsible for the reorganization of the Eastern Territories.

(2) He shall issue the general rules and regulations required for the enforcement and execution of this decree.

SECTION 13. (1) This decree shall take effect as of November 1, 1939.

(2) The Reich Minister of the Interior may, for specified areas, declare the provisions of this decree to be in effect at an earlier date.

Berlin, October 8, 1939.

ADOLF HITLER, *Führer and Reich Chancellor*
GÖRING, *General Field Marshal, President of the Council of Ministers for the Defense of the Reich*
FRICK, *Reich Minister of the Interior*
R. HESS, *Representative of the Führer*
DR. LAMMERS, *Reich Minister and Chief of the Reich Chancellery*

Second Order for the Enforcement of the Decree of the Führer and Reich Chancellor concerning the Organization and Administration of the Eastern Territories, November 2, 1939 [3]

[EXCERPT]

By virtue of subsection 2 of Section 12 of the decree of the Führer and Reich Chancellor concerning the organization and administration of the Eastern Territories of October 8, 1939 (*RGBl.* I, p. 2042), the following is hereby ordered:

SECTION 1. The office of the Reich Governor (*Reichstatthalter*) shall be headed by the Governmental President (*Regierungspräsident*) and divided into the following sections:

1. General, Financial and Organizational Matters.
2. Public Health and Hygiene.
3. Education, Instruction, Furtherance of Cultural and Communal Life.

[3] *Reichsgesetzblatt*, 1939, I, p. 2133.

4. Agriculture, Settlement, Reallocation of Realty and Waterways.
5. Economics and Labor.
6. Forestry and Hunting.
7. Private and Public Construction.

SECTION 2. (1) A ranking S.S. and Police Chief shall be attached to the office of the Reich Governor and shall be personally subject to the direct orders of the Reich Governor. He shall at the same time serve as the agent of the Reich Commissioner for the Strengthening of Germanism.

(2) The Governmental President, as the general representative of the Reich Governor, shall act on his behalf provided the latter is not merely temporarily unable to attend to his duties.

. . . . .

FRICK
Reich Minister of the Interior

Decree concerning the Introduction of Military Law in the Incorporated Eastern Territories, April 30, 1940 [4]

[EXCERPTS]

SECTION 1. The following legal and administrative provisions shall apply in the incorporated Eastern Territories as from March 1, 1940, in so far as they were not already in force in individual parts of these territories before that date, in accordance with the special provisions contained in Sections 2 to 5:

(1) The military law of May 21, 1935 (*RGBl.* I, p. 609), as revised on June 26, 1936 (*RGBl.* I, p. 518).

. . . . .

(4) Decree of the Führer and Reich Chancellor concerning the duration of military service, of August 24, 1936 (*RGBl.* I, p. 706).

SECTION 2. The military law shall be applied with the following provisos:

(1) As to Section 7. When recruits are called up for their active military service, allowance may be made for the period served in the army of the former Polish Republic.

. . . . .

Berlin, April 30, 1940.

KEITEL, *Supreme Commander of the Forces*
DR. STUCKART, *On behalf of the Reich Minister of the Interior*

[4] *Reichsgesetzblatt*, 1940, I, p. 707.

Order concerning the Organization and Administration of the Eastern Territories, May 31, 1941 [5]

[EXCERPTS]

By virtue of Section 8 of the decree of the Führer and Reich Chancellor (*RGBl.* I, p. 2042), of October 8, 1939, it is hereby ordered:

SECTION 1. In the annexed Eastern Territories the following are applicable:

(1) The Reich Nationality Code of September 15, 1935 (*RGBl.* I, p. 1146).

(2) Subsection 2 of Section 2, subsections 1 and 3 of Section 4, Section 5, subsection 1 of Section 6, and Section 7 of the First Order implementing the Reich Nationality Code of November 14, 1935 (*RGBl.* I, p. 1333).

. . . . .

SECTION 3. In the annexed Eastern Territories the Act for the Protection of German Blood and German Honor of September 15, 1935 (*RGBl.* I, p. 1146), and the First Order implementing that act of November 14, 1935 (*RGBl.* I, p. 1334), as well as the order implementing the First Order for the enforcement of the Act for the Protection of German Blood of February 16, 1940 (*RGBl.* I, p. 394) shall be applicable.

SECTION 4. (1) This order shall take effect one week after publication.

(2) Article 1, Section 7, of the order concerning the introduction of the German Criminal Law in the annexed Eastern Territories of June 6, 1940 (*RGBl.* I, p. 844), shall be applied to violations of the provisions for the protection of German blood and German honor.

Berlin, May 31, 1941.

Dr. STUCKART, *Acting Reich Minister of the Interior*
M. BORMANN, *Chief of the Party Chancellery*
Dr. SCHLEGELBERGER, *Acting Reich Minister of Justice*

Second Order Implementing the Act for the Protection of German Blood and German Honor, May 31, 1941 [6]

By virtue of Section 6 of the Act for the Protection of German Blood and German Honor of September 15, 1935 (*RGBl.* I, p. 1146), the following is hereby decreed:

SECTION 1. The protection afforded to German blood or to blood racially related to German blood by the Act for the Protection of German Blood and German Honor of September 15, 1935 (*RGBl.* I, p. 1146), and the First Order implementing that act of November 14, 1935 (*RGBl.*, I, p. 1334), as amended by the implementing order of February 16, 1940 (*RGBl.* I, p. 394),

[5] *Reichsgesetzblatt*, No. 60, June 4, 1941, p. 297. [6] *Ibid.*

shall not extend to former Polish nationals, unless they have acquired German nationality or have been entered in the roll of German nationals by virtue of the decree of the Führer and Reich Chancellor concerning the organization and administration of the Eastern Territories of October 8, 1939 (*RGBl.* I, p. 2042).

SECTION 2. (1) This order shall be applicable also in the annexed Eastern Territories.

(2) It shall take effect one day after publication.

Berlin, May 31, 1941.

Dr. STUCKART, *Acting Reich Minister of the Interior*
M. BORMANN, *Chief of the Party Chancellery*
Dr. SCHLEGELBERGER, *Acting Reich Minister of Justice*

2. LAW AND COURTS

Order concerning Organization of Courts in the Incorporated Eastern Territories, June 13, 1940[7]

By virtue of the decree of the Führer concerning organization and administration of the Eastern Territories of October 8, 1939 (*RGBl.* I, p. 2042), the following is hereby ordered:

SECTION 1. The courts in the incorporated Eastern Territories shall render judgments in the name of the German people.

SECTION 2. The following statutes shall take effect in the incorporated territories:

1. The German law on the organization of courts.

2. The law on the jurisdiction of courts, with respect to changes in the division of courts, of December 6, 1933 (*RGBl.* I, p. 1037).

3. The decree concerning a uniform organization of courts, of March 20, 1935 (*Bl.* I, p. 403).

4. The law concerning the distribution of functions in the courts, of November 24, 1937 (*Bl.* I, p. 1286).

5. The decree concerning qualifications for the offices of a judge, prosecuting attorney, notary, and attorney, of January 4, 1939 (*Bl.* I, p. 5).

6. Decree concerning preparation for the offices of a judge and a prosecuting attorney, of May 16, 1939 (*Bl.* I, p. 917).

7. Decree concerning certain measures in the organization of courts and the administration of justice, of September 1, 1939 (*Bl.* I, p. 1658), and the implementing orders issued hitherto on September 8 and October 4, 1939 (*Bl.* I, pp. 1703, 1994).

[7] *Reichsgesetzblatt*, 1940, p. 907.

8. Decree concerning simplification of the legal examinations of September 2, 1939 (*Bl.* I, p. 1606).

SECTION 3. This decree shall take effect as of June 15, 1940.

Berlin, June 13, 1940.

DR. GÜRTNER, *Reich Minister of Justice*
FRICK, *Reich Minister of Interior*

3. PROPERTY

Decree concerning the Treatment of the Property of Citizens of the Former Polish State, September 17, 1940 [8]

[EXCERPT]

By virtue of the decree concerning the execution of the Four-Year Plan of October 18, 1936 (*RGBl.* I, p. 887), and the decree relating to the introduction of the Four-Year Plan in the Eastern Territories of October 30, 1939 (*RGBl.* I, p. 2125), it is decreed as follows for the territory of the Greater German Reich, including the incorporated Eastern Territories:

SECTION 1. (1) The property of citizens of the former Polish State within the territory of the Greater German Reich, including the incorporated Eastern Territories, shall be subject to sequestration, trustee administration, and confiscation in accordance with the following provisions.

(2) Subsection 1 shall not apply to the property of persons who, in accordance with Section 6 of the decree of the Führer and Reich Chancellor relating to the organization and administration of the Eastern Territories of October 8, 1939 (*RGBl.* I, p. 2042), have acquired German nationality. The agency having jurisdiction in accordance with Section 12 may allow further exemptions.

(3) Citizens of Polish origin of the former Free City of Danzig shall have the status of citizens of the former Polish State.

SECTION 2. (1) Sequestration shall be ordered in connection with the property of:

a) Jews.
b) Persons who have fled or are not merely temporarily absent.

(2) Sequestration may be ordered:

a) If the property is required for the public welfare, particularly in the interests of Reich defense or the strengthening of Germanism.
b) If the owners or other title holders immigrated into the territory of the German Reich as it was then delimited, after October 1, 1918.

[8] *Reichsgesetzblatt*, 1940, I, p. 1270.

(3) Sequestration may be confined to individual items of property.

(4) The following shall as a general rule be exempted from sequestration:

a) Movable objects serving exclusively for personal needs.
b) Cash, bank, and savings-bank deposits and securities not exceeding in total one thousand Reichsmarks.

SECTION 3. For the purposes of this order, property shall be deemed to include: immovable and movable objects (together with all accessories), claims, shares, rights, and interests of all kinds.

SECTION 4. (1) By the order of sequestration, those previously entitled to the sequestrated property shall lose the right of disposal over it. The rights of the Administrator General under the decree relating to public administration of agricultural and forestry establishments and enterprises and land in the incorporated Eastern Territories of February 12, 1940 (*RGBl.* I, p. 355) shall not be affected.

(2) Owners or trustees of sequestrated property shall hold and administer it until further notice. Changes in, or dispositions relating to, the property or the proceeds thereof shall be admissible only within the limits of orderly administration. All other transactions, particularly transfer of real estate, shall require the permission of the agency having jurisdiction in accordance with Section 12.

SECTION 5. (1) Trustee administration may be ordered in respect of property subject to sequestration if orderly administration requires it.

(2) The imposition of trustee administration shall be considered as equivalent to sequestration.

SECTION 6. (1) The trustee administrator shall be appointed by the agency having jurisdiction under Section 12. He shall receive written notice of appointment. He shall be subject to dismissal.

(2) In his administration he shall exercise the same care as a prudent businessman or manager and shall be responsible for any losses arising from his failure to fulfill these obligations. He shall at all times supply to the agency vested with jurisdiction in accordance with Section 12 any information required by it, and shall, unless otherwise ordered, also report to it on his management without special request.

(3) The trustee administrator may be held to his obligations by the competent agency (Section 12)—without prejudice to his responsibility under the criminal law—by means of disciplinary fines up to ten thousand Reichsmarks.

SECTION 7. (1) The trustee administrator shall be authorized to enter into any legal or other transactions involved in the administration of the property within the ordinary course of business.

(2) The administrator shall not, without previous express authorization from the competent agency (Section 12):

a) Dispose of or contract a charge upon land.
b) Alter the purpose or legal form of an enterprise.
c) Engage in any legal transaction resulting in the disposal or liquidation of an enterprise or concern or in the disposal of the administered stock of goods or any other part of the property in its entirety.
d) Lease industrial, agricultural, and forestry concerns and agricultural and forest land of more than ten hectares in extent.
e) Engage in any legal transaction whose conclusion has been made dependent on previous express authorization from the competent agency (Section 12) through the publication of such authorization in the *Deutscher Reichsanzeiger* and *Preussischer Staatsanzeiger*.

(3) Legal transactions carried out without the authorization required under subsection 2 shall be void.

SECTION 8. (1) The administrator shall receive for his work remuneration to be fixed by the competent agency (Section 12).

(2) The cost of trustee administration, including the trustee's compensation, shall be borne by the undertaking, property, or portion of property administered.

SECTION 9. (1) Sequestrated property may be confiscated by the competent agency (Section 12) for the benefit of the German Reich if the public welfare, particularly the defense of the Reich, or the strengthening of Germanism, so requires.

(2) Before confiscation the sequestrated property shall be defined in accordance with detailed directions from the competent agency (Section 12).

(3) The Reich shall be liable for claims against the confiscated property to an amount not exceeding the market value of the confiscated property. The order of confiscation shall not be deemed to affect liens on the confiscated property.

(4) The agencies entitled to effect confiscation (Section 12) shall be entitled to transfer or otherwise dispose of confiscated property. For any transfer or other disposition of agricultural property, agreement shall be required between the Reich Commissioner for Strengthening Germanism and the Reich Minister of Food and Agriculture.

(5) Regulations concerning the manner and amount of compensation to be granted for loss of property involved in the execution of the present decree will be issued. No compensation shall be granted in connection with measures taken by the competent agency (Section 12) under Sections 16 and 17.

SECTION 10. (1) Trustee administration may further be ordered for the property of corporations, companies, societies, and other personal associations in whose capital citizens of the former Polish State still held a controlling share in the year 1939 or whose administration had been materially influenced by citizens of the former Polish State.

(2) Throughout the duration of the trustee administration the authority of the heads or other persons entitled to act as representatives or managers,

shall be suspended; the same shall apply to the rights of all other persons to act for, or on behalf of, these associations.

(3) With respect to these measures only the shares and other evidences of participation of citizens of the former Polish State shall be subject to confiscation.

SECTION 11. (1) The order of sequestration or imposition of trustee administration shall, upon the request of the competent agency (Section 12), be entered upon the records of the land register or other suitable public register. Registration of the name of the trustee administrator may also be requested.

(2) If the entries on the records of the land register or other suitable public register no longer agree with the facts as a result of action based on the present decree, they shall be corrected on the instructions of the competent agency (Section 12). Paragraphs 3 to 5 of Section 1 of the second decree relating to the execution and implementation of the law on the granting of compensation in connection with the confiscation or transfer of property of March 18, 1938 (*RGBl.* I, p. 317), shall forthwith be applicable.

SECTION 12. (1) As regards measures and decisions on the basis of the present decree the Commissioner for the Four-Year Plan within the Chief Trustee Administration for the East (*Haupttreuhandstelle Ost*) shall be competent; as regards agriculture, including enterprises processing agricultural produce for marketing, the Reich Commissioner for Strengthening Germanism.

(2) The agencies vested with jurisdiction in accordance with subsection 1, may delegate this authority, either wholly or in part, to other agencies. Appeals against the decisions of the latter shall be addressed to the agency competent according to subsection 1. An appeal shall not stay the proceedings against which it is directed. An appeal shall not be admissible if more than a year has passed since the issue of the decision appealed from.

SECTION 13. If anyone opposes sequestration or the imposition of trustee administration on the ground that he is a German national, then the proceeding shall be suspended. The competent agency (Section 12) shall request the President of the Government Board to decide the matter of German nationality. The interested party shall also be entitled to make such request. Appeal against the decision of the President of the Government Board to the Reich Minister of the Interior shall be admissible. The decision relating to German nationality shall be binding on the competent agency (Section 12) as regards any proceedings under the present decree.

SECTION 14. Orders issued in accordance with Sections 2, 5 and 10 shall be made in writing and served upon the party in interest. In lieu of such notice, service may be made by public notice, poster, or publication.

SECTION 15. (1) Dispositions with respect to land and land title of citizens of the former Polish State which do not come under the exemption laid down in subsection 2 of Section 1, shall not become effective until confirmed by the competent agency (Section 12). This provision is not applicable, however, to the disposition concerning the claim to interest and other recurrent payments.

(2) Whether or not confirmation according to subsection 1 is necessary shall be decided by the competent agency (Section 12). The decision shall be binding upon courts and administrative authorities. In case of a decision in the negative, the competent agency (Section 12) shall, upon request, issue a certificate that confirmation is not necessary.

SECTION 16. (1) No distraint of any kind on objects which are subject to sequestration under this present decree shall be commenced without the consent of the competent agency (Section 12). If one of the agencies having jurisdiction according to Section 12 has given its consent, the fact that it was wrong in its assumption of competence shall not affect further procedure in the case.

(2) If it is believed that the debtor may evade execution, or if for any other reason immediate action is indicated, then, by the order of the court issuing the warrant of execution, that execution may be begun before the issue of the consent required under subsection 1. In such case execution shall be limited to the measures permissible with respect to the execution of an attachment, and shall only be pursued further when consent has been granted. Upon the proposal of the competent agency (Section 12) the court issuing the warrant shall order that the provisional measures of execution be suspended.

SECTION 17. (1) If, in the incorporated Eastern Territories, bankruptcy proceedings are instituted against the estate of an insolvent debtor, the provisions of Section 16 shall apply to the disposal of the property constituting the estate.

(2) If the institution or suspension of bankruptcy proceedings in the incorporated Eastern Territories depends upon the existence of an estate equal in value to the cost of the proceedings, objects that are subject to sequestration by reason of this decree shall be regarded as forming part of the estate only if the competent agency (Section 12) has consented to their disposal in the bankruptcy proceedings.

SECTION 18. Property subject to sequestration may be ordered to be registered by public announcement. The order concerning agricultural property shall be issued by agreement with the Reich Minister of Food and Agriculture.

SECTION 19. The competent agency (Section 12) shall be authorized for the purpose of its tasks to request information from anyone. Administrative authorities and courts shall render it official aid, and in particular examine witnesses and experts upon its request.

SECTION 20. (1) A fine and imprisonment or either of these penalties shall be imposed on anyone who, seeking to obtain material advantage for himself or others, attempts to withhold a sequestrated item of property from the agencies indicated in Section 12 or from their representatives, or to prevent, circumvent, or impede in any manner whatsoever the carrying out of the sequestration.

(2) In serious cases the penalty shall be imprisonment. If the culprit acts from opposition to the new political order, or if the case is particularly serious for some other reason, then the death penalty shall be imposed.

SECTION 21. (1) Imprisonment and a fine or either of these penalties shall be imposed on anyone who, intentionally or through negligence, fails to carry out, or carries out incorrectly or incompletely, the obligation imposed by the present decree, an executive order issued in connection therewith, or an order, under Sections 18 and 19, to register property or give information.

(2) Prosecution shall be instituted only upon the proposal of the agency vested with jurisdiction under Section 12.

. . . .

Berlin, September 17, 1940.

GÖRING, *Reich Marshal*
Chairman of the Council of Ministers for the Defense of the Reich, Commissioner for the Four-Year Plan

4. TAXATION

Order concerning Tax Abatement for the Benefit of the Incorporated Eastern Territories (Eastern Tax Abatement Order), December 9, 1940 [9]

[EXCERPTS]

In the effort to establish and promote Germanism (*Deutschtum*) in the incorporated Eastern Territories through taxation measures, as well as by other means, we order by virtue of Section 13 of the Reich tax ordinance:

SECTION I. ABATEMENT OF TAXES FOR INDIVIDUALS

PARAGRAPH 1. *Exemption for Income Tax.* German nationals and persons of German origin (*Volkszugehörige*) in the incorporated Eastern Territories shall be entitled to an exemption of 3,000 Reichsmarks from their income provided that the income does not exceed 25,000 Reichsmarks. The exemption of 3,000 Reichsmarks shall be increased by 300 Reichsmarks for each minor child belonging to the household.

PARAGRAPH 2. *Release from the War Supplement* (Zuschlag) *to the Income*

[9] *Reichsgesetzblatt*, 1940, I, p. 1565.

Tax. The war supplement to the income tax shall not be imposed in the incorporated Eastern Territories.

PARAGRAPH 3. *Release from the Defense Tax*. The defense tax shall not be imposed for the present in the incorporated Eastern Territories.

PARAGRAPH 4. *Triple Exemption for Property Tax*. The exemptions of Section 5 of the property tax law shall be tripled in the assessment of German nationals and persons of German origin in the incorporated Eastern Territories.

PARAGRAPH 5. *Release from Real Estate Acquisition* (Grunderwerb) *Tax*. The following shall be released from the real estate acquisition tax:

1. The acquisition of real estate situated in the incorporated Eastern Territories by a German national or a person of German origin in the incorporated Eastern Territories, provided that the acquisition was not made through means accruing from the sale of real estate acquired in the incorporated Eastern Territories while this regulation was in force.
2. An acquisition of real estate which contributes to the restoration of an economic unit divided by the former demarcation or to the rectification of errors in demarcation.

PARAGRAPH 6. *Release from Sales* (Umsatz) *Tax*. The following shall be released from the sales tax:

1. The transfer of the stock (*Lieferung des Inventars*) belonging to a piece of real estate the acquisition of which is released from the real estate acquisition tax.
2. Transactions which contribute to the restoration of an economic unit divided by the former demarcation or to the rectification of errors in demarcation.
3. The sale of an enterprise as a whole (paragraph 81 of the implementation provisions of the sales tax law), or of a division of an enterprise conducted as a separate business, to a German national or to a person of German origin in the incorporated Eastern Territories, provided that it is the first time while this regulation has been in force that this German national or person of German origin has acquired in the incorporated Eastern Territories an enterprise as a whole or a division of an enterprise conducted as a separate business.

PARAGRAPH 7. *Release from Inheritance Tax*. The inheritance tax and gift tax shall not be imposed upon acquisition by reason of death or by gifts from living persons if the following conditions prevail:

1. The acquisitor must at the time of incurring the tax obligation be a German national or a person of German origin resident in the incorporated Eastern Territories.
2. The bequeather or donor must, at least during the period from September 1, 1939, to the time of the incurrence of the tax obligation, have had his exclusive residence or his normal dwelling outside the incorporated eastern areas.

3. The acquisition must consist of property which is moved from other Reich territory or from abroad into the incorporated Eastern Territories for the purpose of establishing an independent position (*Lebensstellung*) or for the establishment or improvement of the business or household of the acquisitor.

Section II. Abatement for Business Management

Paragraph 8. *Depreciation Exemption* (Bewertungsfreiheit). (1) German nationals, persons of German origin, and German enterprises in the incorporated Eastern Territories shall have depreciation exemption for depreciable (*abnutzbare*) business property equipment (*Anlagegueter*) procured or installed in the calendar or fiscal years 1940 to 1950. The provisions concerning deductions for regular business depreciation in Section 7 of the income tax law shall not thereby be affected.

(2) Depreciation exemption may be invoked for construction equipment only to a total of 20 per cent of the cost of procurement or installation.

Paragraph 9. *Construction Reserve* (Aufbauruecklage). (1) German nationals, persons of German origin, and German enterprises in the incorporated Eastern Territories whose profit is computed from a statement of assets and liabilities (*Betriebsvermögensvergleich*) by a regular system of bookkeeping, may form a tax-exempt reserve (construction reserve) in the calendar or fiscal years 1940 to 1944 to the amount of the estimated cost of procurement of depreciable business property equipment which may be ordered during a fiscal year and not delivered by the end of that fiscal year.

(2) Allotments to the construction reserve in a single calendar or fiscal year may not exceed 25 per cent of the profit. Profit in this sense is that part of the profit remaining after subtraction of the amount which is claimed as income-tax-exempt under Paragraph 10, subsection 1, of this order.

(3) The allotment of a percentage of the profit to a construction reserve entails as a condition that the taxable person or enterprise cannot carry out the renovation or improvement of his business equipment out of his own means without a tax abatement.

. . . . .

Paragraph 10. *Special Benefit for Retailers and Partnerships* (Personengesellschaften). (1) German nationals and persons of German origin in the incorporated Eastern Territories who are retailers maintaining books, or who are members of partnerships, may upon application be exempted in the calendar years 1940 to 1950 from income tax on an amount not to exceed 50 per cent of the net profit or 20 per cent of the gross profit of the enterprise. The taxable person may, if it is more advantageous to him, claim as income-tax-exempt the amount of 40,000 Reichsmarks instead of 20 per cent of gross profit.

. . . . .

PARAGRAPH 11. *Special Benefit for Corporations.* (1) The corporations tax for German enterprises in the incorporated Eastern Territories for the calendar years 1940 to 1943 amounts:

1. To 20 per cent of an income not exceeding 300,000 Reichsmarks.
2. To 30 per cent of an income exceeding 300,000 Reichsmarks.

(2) The corporations tax ratios of subsection 1 are increased for the calendar year 1944 and for every second calendar year thereafter by 2 per cent until the tax ratio generally in force in the Reich is reached.

(3) In cases in which one half the tax ratio is to be applied according to prevailing law, one half the tax ratios of subsections 1 and 2 shall be used.

PARAGRAPH 12. *Credit Associations.* Credit associations and association credit offices (*genossenschaftliche Zentralkassen*) which extend credits to German nationals, to persons of German origin, or to German enterprises in the incorporated Eastern Territories shall not lose the benefits allowed them on the corporation tax, property tax, and business tax when the accredited are not members of the crediting association, provided that:

1. The credits are extended in the period preceding January 1, 1943, and
2. The German central credit association office (*Zentralgenossenschaftskasse*) has approved the credits. This approval is not necessary for credits extended before the effective date of this order.

PARAGRAPH 13. *Tax Exemption for Profit from Sale.* (1) Profits from sales in the sense of Sections 14, 16, 17, and 18, subsection 3, of the income tax law which have been or shall be realized in the calendar years 1940 to 1946 outside the incorporated Eastern Territories shall be tax-exempt if the proceeds of the sales are applied within one year after the realization of the profit to the acquisition or creation of an enterprise in the incorporated Eastern Territories. The same provision shall be valid if the proceeds of a sale are used for the acquisition of shares in a civil law or commercial law company whose business is situated in the incorporated Eastern Territories.

. . . .

PARAGRAPH 14. *Exemption from Real Estate Acquisition* (Grunderwerb) *Tax and Sales* (Umsatz) *Tax.* (1) If from the proceeds of a sale as specified in Paragraph 13, subsection 1, real estate in the incorporated Eastern Territories is acquired within one year after the realization of the profit from the sale, this acquisition is exempt from the real estate acquisition tax, provided that the real estate is used by a business which is situated or is being established in the incorporated eastern areas.

(2) The transfer of the stock (*Lieferung des Inventars*) belonging to a piece of real estate the acquisition of which is released from the real estate acquisition tax (subsection 1) is exempt from the sales tax.

PARAGRAPH 15. *Partial Tax Exemption of Property from the Property Tax.* Property of German nationals, of persons of German origin, and of

German enterprises which constitute a farm and lumber business, or an industrial enterprise or plant (*Betriebsstaette*) in the incorporated Eastern Territories, shall be taken into account in the assessment for property tax only in so far as its value exceeds 250,000 Reichsmarks.

. . .

SECTION III. MUNICIPAL TAXES

PARAGRAPH 19. *Amount of Realty Taxes.* (1) Municipalities in the incorporated Eastern Territories shall impose upon German nationals and persons of German origin and upon German enterprises land taxes (*Grundsteuer*), real estate taxes (*Grundstuecksteuer*), and industrial taxes only to the amount of 50 per cent of the tax ratio. This shall be valid as concerns land and real estate taxes even for real property which is under trustee administration for the Reich.

(2) The provisions of subsection 1 shall also be valid for municipal taxes which are levied in place of the designated taxes.

. . . . .

PARAGRAPH 21. *Exemption from the Industrial Tax on Industrial Capital for the Fiscal* (Rechnungs) *Years 1940 to 1943.* In determining the industrial capital of businesses of German nationals, persons of German origin, and German enterprises in the incorporated Eastern Territories, a sum of 250,000 Reichsmarks may be omitted from the computation.

SECTION IV. GENERAL PROVISIONS

PARAGRAPH 22. *Territorial Validity.* (1) The provisions of this order shall be valid under the restriction of subsection 2 for the Reich Districts Wartheland and Danzig-West Prussia (with exception of the former East Prussian district) and for the Eastern Territories incorporated into the provinces of East Prussia and Silesia.

(2) For the district of the former Free State of Danzig, only the provisions of Section II (Abatement for Business Management) and the provisions of Section IV (General Provisions), in so far as applicable to Section II, shall be valid.

. . . . .

Berlin, December 9, 1940.

The Reich Minister of Finance
By deputy: REINHARDT
The Reich Minister of the Interior
By deputy: PFUNDTNER

5. ECONOMY AND FINANCE

Order concerning the Introduction of the Four-Year Plan in the Eastern Territories, October 30, 1939 [10]

By virtue of Section 8 of the decree of the Führer and Reich Chancellor concerning the organization and administration of the Eastern Territories of October 8, 1939 (*RGBl.* I, p. 2042), it is hereby ordered:

SECTION 1. (1) In the Reich District (*Reichsgau*) of Western Prussia with the exception of the government district of Marienwerder with its present area, in the Reich District of Posen, and in the government districts of Zichenau (Ciechanów) and Kattowitz (Katowice), the order concerning the execution of the Four-Year Plan of October 18, 1936 (*RGBl.* I, p. 887), shall apply.

(2) For the government district of Marienwerder with its present area the existing provisions concerning the application of the Four-Year Plan shall continue to apply without modification.

SECTION 2. This order shall take effect as of the day of publication.

Berlin, October 30, 1939.

GÖRING, *General Field Marshal, Commissioner for the Four-Year Plan*

PFUNDTNER, *Acting Reich Minister of the Interior*

Order concerning the Introduction of Reichsmark Currency in the Incorporated Eastern Territories, November 22, 1939 [11]

[EXCERPTS]

By virtue of the decree of the Führer and Reich Chancellor concerning the organization and administration of the Eastern Territories of October 8, 1939 (*RGBl.* I, p. 2042), as amended by decree of November 2, 1939 (*RGBl.* I, p. 2135), it is hereby ordered as follows:

SECTION 1. (1) In the Eastern Territories incorporated in the German Reich the zloty shall cease to be legal tender on November 27, 1939. The Reichsmark shall be sole legal tender.

(2) The branch offices of the German Treasury and Reichsbank established in these territories, and other agencies authorized by the Reichsbank for that purpose shall exchange, not later than December 9, 1939, with reference to all residents of these territories, the notes of the Bank Polski of the denominations of 500, 100, 50, 20, 10, 5, and 2 zlotys, the Polish Government notes of the denomination of 1 zloty, and the Polish Government coins

[10] *Reichsgesetzblatt*, 1939, I, p. 2125. [11] *Ibid.*, p. 2291.

in the denominations of 10, 5 and 2 zlotys, for German Reichsmark tender at a rate of exchange of 2 zlotys for 1 Reichsmark.

. . . . .

SECTION 4. The Reich Minister of Economic Affairs shall be authorized to promulgate, in agreement with the Reich Minister of Finance, rules and regulations necessary for the implementation and execution of this order.

Berlin, November 22, 1939.

DR. LANDFRIED, *Acting Reich Minister of Economic Affairs*
REINHARDT, *Acting Reich Minister of Finance*
DR. STUCKART, *Acting Reich Minister of the Interior*

Second Order for the Introduction of the Four-Year Plan in the Annexed Eastern Territories, July 9, 1940 [12]

By virtue of the order concerning the introduction of the Four-Year Plan in the Eastern Territories of October 30, 1939 (*RGBl.* I, p. 2125), it is hereby ordered:

In the Reich District (*Reichsgau*) Danzig-Western Prussia, with the exception of the government district of Marienwerder in its previous area, in the Reich District of Wartheland, and in the government districts of Zichenau (Ciechanów) and Kattowitz (Katowice), the Second Order for the realization of the Four-Year Plan of November 5, 1936 (*RGBl.* I, p. 936), shall be applicable as of November 1, 1939.

Berlin, July 9, 1940.

KÖRNER
Acting Commissioner for the Four-Year Plan

GOVERNMENT GENERAL

1. ADMINISTRATION

Decree of the Führer and Reich Chancellor concerning the Administration of the Occupied Polish Territories, October 12, 1939 [13]

In order to restore and maintain public order and public life in the occupied Polish territories, I decree:

[12] *Reichsgesetzblatt*, I, No. 123, July 12, 1940, p. 956. [13] *Ibid.*, 1939, I, p. 2077.

SECTION 1. The territories occupied by German troops shall be subject to the authority of the Governor General of the occupied Polish territories, except in so far as they are incorporated within the German Reich.

SECTION 2. (1) I appoint Reich Minister Dr. Frank as Governor General of the occupied Polish territories.

(2) As Deputy Governor General I appoint Reich Minister Dr. Seyss-Inquart.

SECTION 3. (1) The Governor General shall be directly responsible to me.

(2) All branches of the administration shall be directed by the Governor General.

SECTION 4. The laws at present in force shall remain in force, except in so far as they are in conflict with the taking over of the administration by the German Reich.

SECTION 5. (1) The Cabinet Council for Reich Defense, the Commissioner for the Four-Year Plan, and the Governor General may legislate by decree.

(2) The decrees shall be promulgated in the *Verordnungsblatt für die besetzten polnischen Gebiete*.

SECTION 6. The Chairman of the Cabinet Council for Reich Defense and Commissioner for the Four-Year Plan, and also the supreme Reich authorities, may make the arrangements required for the planning of German life and the German economic sphere with respect to the territories subject to the authority of the Governor General.

SECTION 7. (1) The cost of administration shall be borne by the occupied territory.

(2) The Governor General shall draft a budget. The budget shall require the approval of the Reich Minister of Finance.

SECTION 8. (1) The central authority for the occupied Polish territories shall be the Reich Minister of the Interior.

(2) The administrative decrees required for the implementing and supplementing of the present decree shall be issued by the Reich Minister of the Interior.

SECTION 9. (1) The present decree shall come into force as soon as and to the extent to which I withdraw the order given to the Commander in Chief of the Army for the exercise of military administration.

(2) Authority for the exercise of executive power shall be the subject of special provisions.

Berlin, October 12, 1939.

ADOLF HITLER
Führer and Reich Chancellor

Proclamation of the Governor General, October 26, 1939[14]

The Führer and Chancellor of the German Reich, Adolf Hitler, by decree of October 12, 1939, effective on October 26, 1939, has vested in me governmental authority over the Government General in the occupied Polish territories. With the establishment of the Government General, the Polish territories having been brought safely within the German sphere of interest by military action, a historical episode has been concluded the responsibility for which must be borne equally by the misguided government clique of the former Poland and the hypocritical warmongers in Britain. The advance of the German troops has restored order in the Polish territories; the threat to European peace through the unjustified demands of a political structure that had been built upon the dictated peace of Versailles and will never be restored, has thus been removed once and for all.

Polish men and women! I have been instructed by the Führer, in my capacity as Governor General of the occupied Polish territories, to take decisive steps in order to ensure that there shall be peace in this country forever, and that the relations of the Poles with the mighty world empire of the German nation shall develop normally. You shall live your life in accordance with the customs observed by you for a long period; you shall be permitted to retain your Polish character in all the manifestations of community life. But the country, which has been completely destroyed through the criminal fault of your former rulers, requires the most decisive, organized employment of your collective labor. Freed from the compulsion of the adventurous policy of your intellectual governing class, you will, under the strong protection of the Greater German Reich, do your best in the performance of a universal obligation to work. Under a just rule everyone will earn his bread by work. On the other hand, there will be no room for political agitators, shady dealers, and Jewish exploiters in a territory that is under German sovereignty.

Any attempt at recalcitrance against the decrees issued and against peace and order in the Polish territories will be crushed with the strong weapons of the Greater German Reich and with the most ruthless severity. But those who comply with the just orders of our Reich, which will be in absolute accord with your mode of life, shall be allowed to work in safety. These orders will free you of many abominable conditions which you still have to bear today in consequence of incredibly bad management on the part of your former rulers.

FRANK

Governor General of the Occupied Polish Territories

[14] *Verordnungsblatt des Generalgouverneurs*, etc., No. 1, October 26, 1939, p. 1.

2. LAW AND COURTS

Decree concerning German Jurisdiction in the Government General, February 19, 1940 [15]

[EXCERPTS]

In pursuance of subsection 1 of Section 5 of the decree of the Führer and Reich Chancellor concerning the administration of the occupied Polish territories of October 12, 1939 (*RGBl.* I, p. 2077), I hereby order as follows:

TITLE I.—*General Provisions*

SECTION 1. (1) For the exercise of German jurisdiction under the Government General, and in addition to the Special Courts, "German Courts" and "German Superior Courts" shall be established.

(2) The decree relating to special courts in the Government General of November 15, 1939 (*VBl.GG.BG.*, 1939, p. 34), shall not be affected by this decree.

(3) This decree shall not be deemed to affect the jurisdiction of any court martial based on the provisions of law.

SECTION 2. (1) German Superior Courts shall be established for each district at the official seat of the District Chief; unless otherwise provided their decisions shall be given by a court of three judges.

(2) German Courts shall be established in Cracow, Rzeszow, Lublin, Chelm, Radom, Petrikau,[16] Warsaw, and Zyrardow; their decisions shall be given by a court of one judge. The District Chief shall define the limits of their circuit within the district; he may also order the holding of sessions of court outside the locality which is the seat of the court.

(3) The commencement of the judicial functions of the individual courts shall be announced locally.

. . . . .

SECTION 4. (1) Attorneys admitted to the bar of the German Reich and attorneys admitted to the bar of the Government General who are of German origin may plead before the German Courts.

(2) In addition, persons who have professional qualifications required for an appointment to a judicial position in the Reich, and other German citizens or persons of German origin whose qualifications are such as to assure orderly fulfillment of the duties of defense counsel, may be admitted or appointed as defense counsel in individual criminal proceedings; the presiding judge shall also determine the amount of fees to be paid according to his reasonable discretion.

. . . . .

[15] *Verordnungsblatt des Generalgouverneurs*, etc., No. 13, February 24, 1940, p. 57.

[16] German name for the Polish town of Piotrków.—ED.

TITLE II.—*Criminal Jurisdiction*

SECTION 7. (1) German citizens and persons of German origin shall be subject to German criminal jurisdiction.

(2) Other persons, to the extent that they are not already subject to German criminal jurisdiction under Section 2 of the decree concerning special courts in the Government General of November 15, 1939 (*VBl.GG.-BG.*, 1939, p. 34), shall always be subject to such jurisdiction for criminal acts which:

1. Are directed against the security and authority of the German Reich and people, against their interests, and against the life, health, honor, and property of German citizens and persons of German origin.
2. Have been made punishable by orders of the Governor General or his designees.
3. Have been committed in a building, room, or plant used for the purposes of a German authority or agency.
4. Have been committed in the service of the German administration or in connection with such service.

(3) If several persons are involved in a criminal act as principals, accomplices, accessories after the fact, or receivers of stolen goods, they shall all be subject to German criminal jurisdiction, provided any one of them shall be subject to such jurisdiction in accordance with subsection 1. If a person is indicted for several criminal acts, and is subject, with regard to one of these acts, to German criminal jurisdiction, this jurisdiction shall also extend to the other acts set forth in the indictment.

SECTION 8. German Courts shall decide in accordance with German law.

SECTION 9. Unless otherwise provided, the provisions governing procedure in the Old Reich (*Alt-Reich*) [17] shall apply to the proceedings before the German Court.

SECTION 10. (1) The German Court shall sit as a court of first instance; appeal shall lie from its judgments.

(2) The German Superior Court shall decide upon appeals and objections against decisions of the German Court. Upon motion of the prosecuting attorney, the decision may be given by one judge. The decisions of the German Superior Court shall be final.

SECTION 11. Whenever, in accordance with pertinent statutes of the Reich, criminal prosecution is made subject to consent or order, the Governor General of the occupied Polish territories shall be considered to be the competent agency authorized to give such consent or order.

SECTION 12. (1) At the trial before the German Court, attendance by a representative of the prosecuting attorney shall not be required.

[17] See note 21, above, p. 467.—ED.

(2) A defense counsel shall be appointed only if it appears expedient.

SECTION 13. The time-limit for the lodging of an appeal and complaint shall be two weeks.

SECTION 14. In the process relating to the retrial of a criminal case concluded before the Special Court, it is the Special Court, not the German Court, that shall decide.

SECTION 15. Prosecution by private parties shall not be permitted.

SECTION 16. Confiscations and forfeitures shall be effected for the benefit of the Government General; fines shall be remitted to the Treasury of the Government General.

SECTION 17. The Polish prosecuting attorney and criminal courts of the Government General shall, if prompt action be necessary, take all steps in accordance with the provisions generally applicable to their proceedings which may lead to the ascertainment of facts, the arrest of the accused, or the seizure of chattels used or intended to be used for the commission of criminal acts. They shall be required to report immediately any such steps taken to the German state attorney having jurisdiction.

SECTION 18. The Polish law enforcement agencies named in Section 17 shall not be permitted to take official action in a building, room, or installation used for the purposes of a German authority unless prior consent thereto has been obtained from that authority.

TITLE III.—*Civil Jurisdiction*

SECTION 19. (1) German citizens and persons of German origin shall be subject to German jurisdiction in civil matters. It shall extend to:

1. Civil litigation (including *ex parte* injunctions) if one of the parties or third-party intervenors shall be a German citizen or a person of German origin.
2. To attachment and execution proceedings if the judgment debtor is a German citizen or a person of German origin, or if execution is had on an instrument issued by a German court or signed before a German notary public.
3. Matters in bankruptcy and composition, if the bankrupt debtor or the debtor who has applied for a composition proceeding shall be a German citizen or a person of German origin.
4. Non-litigious proceedings before surrogates or other courts if, in accordance with provisions applicable in the Old Reich, the citizenship of a person involved shall determine the law applicable and that person shall be a German citizen or person of German origin.
5. The keeping of the German commercial register.

(2) Whenever in cases mentioned in subsections 2, 3, and 4 of Section 1 the proceedings brought against several persons shall not be separable, German jurisdiction shall be established if one of the persons involved shall be a German citizen or a person of German origin.

(3) The question of whether or not a particular proceeding shall constitute one of the proceedings referred to in Section 1 shall be determined in accordance with the law applicable in the Old Reich.

SECTION 20. (1) The following organizations shall be considered as German citizens for the purposes of this order: partnerships, mutual insurance associations, commercial and agricultural cooperatives, mining corporations, other corporations under private or public law, foundations, and incorporated endowments having their seat or principal place of business in the German Reich or having been incorporated in the Government General in accordance with German law.

. . . . .

SECTION 21. If a German citizen or a person of German origin has been appointed as trustee administrator of the property of another person and if, in such capacity, he becomes involved in a civil action, either as plaintiff or defendant, German jurisdiction shall be established by the fact of his citizenship or German origin; the nationality of the owner of the property shall be immaterial.

. . . . .

SECTION 26. (1) The German Court shall decide as a court of first instance.

(2) The German Superior Court shall decide on appeals and objections from or against decisions of the German Court. The decisions of the German Superior Court shall be final.

SECTION 27. In proceedings before the German Courts the parties may plead without being represented by counsel.

. . . . .

SECTION 30. (1) A German Commercial Register shall be kept by the German Court.

(2) Firms of German citizenship or nationality and trading companies established in accordance with German law shall be entered in the Commercial Register.

(3) No registration shall be required in the case of trading companies permitted by virtue of the decree relating to the establishment of trading companies in the Government General of November 15, 1939 (*VBl.GG.BG.*, p. 38).

. . . . .

SECTION 31. (1) The land and mortgage records kept heretofore shall be continued under Polish jurisdiction.

(2) Decisions of the Polish Courts of second instance may within two months be appealed from to the German Superior Court by German citizens or persons of German origin aggrieved by the decision; the German Superior Court shall determine its proceeding according to its discretion with due regard to the circumstances of the individual case.

TITLE IV.—*Extraordinary Bill to Set Aside a Judgment*

SECTION 32. (1) The chief of the Law Enforcement Section within the office of the Government General may bring suit to set aside final judgments of the German Courts within six months after such judgments have become final if he considers a trial and a decision *de novo* necessary because of grave doubts concerning the justice of the decision.

(2) If a bill to set aside is brought, the Special Court shall decide in criminal and the Superior Court in civil matters; the Chief of the Law Enforcement Section within the offices of the Government General shall for each individual case designate the Superior Court before which the trial *de novo* will be held. The decisions of these courts shall be final.

. . . . . .

SECTION 34. This order shall take effect as of the date of publication.

Cracow, February 19, 1940.

FRANK
Governor General of the Occupied Polish Territories

Order concerning Polish Jurisdiction in the Government General, February 19, 1940 [18]

[EXCERPTS]

In pursuance of subsection 1 of Section 5 of the decree of the Führer and Reich Chancellor concerning the administration of the occupied Polish territories of October 12, 1939 (*RGBl.* I, p. 2077), I hereby order as follows:

TITLE I.—*Scope of Jurisdiction*

SECTION 1. (1) Polish Courts shall have jurisdiction unless jurisdiction of a German Court shall be established.

(2) A Polish Court shall not have jurisdiction in criminal matters unless the proceedings have been referred by a German prosecuting attorney to a Polish prosecuting attorney.

(3) If other nationalities living in separate settlements within the Government General shall require courts of their own, special provisions may be issued.

SECTION 2. If a case is pending before a Polish Court in the Goverment General which has arisen in an area not included within the Government General, the jurisdiction of the courts in the Government General shall abate.

SECTION 3. The provisions of Polish law authorizing Polish judicial authorities to defer the execution of penalties involving loss of liberty or fines or to exercise mercy in any other way, shall be invalid.

[18] *Verordnungsblatt des Generalgouverneurs*, etc., No. 13, February 24, 1940, p. 64.

TITLE II.—*Organization and Proceedings of Courts*

SECTION 4. Polish laws and Polish acts and general orders shall apply to the exercise of jurisdiction by the Polish Courts unless the Governor General shall order otherwise.

SECTION 5. (1) Jurisdiction by Polish Courts shall be exercised by local courts, district courts, and courts of appeal.

(2) The Supreme Court shall until further notice not resume its judicial functions.

. . . . .

SECTION 7. Labor courts shall be abolished. Suits pending before these courts shall be referred to local courts.

SECTION 8. (1) Polish Courts shall be under the direct supervision of the District Governor.

(2) Former Polish officials who have been reemployed and other employees shall declare in writing that they will faithfully and conscientiously perform their duties as law enforcement officers, in obedience to the German administration.

. . . . .

SECTION 10. The courts shall decide by a quorum of judges as determined by Polish law. Lay judges shall no longer sit; in lieu of the provisions requiring the participation of lay judges the general provisions concerning the organization of the courts shall reply.

TITLE V.—*Right of Revision*

SECTION 16. Final decisions of Polish Courts may be reexamined whenever the public interest so requires.

SECTION 17. (1) The head of the Law Enforcement Section within the offices of the District Governor shall alone be authorized to apply for reexamination. The application and the reasons therefor shall be filed with the German Superior Court within six months after the judgment has become final.

(2) The German Superior Court may affirm the decision or set it aside and decide itself, or refer the matter for decision to a German Court. If the case under examination has been settled by a formal judgment, then the German Superior Court, after an oral trial, shall also give its decision as a formal judgment; otherwise the case shall be settled by means of an order. The German Superior Court, subject to the provisions mentioned hereinabove, shall determine its proceedings according to its discretion with due regard to the circumstances of the individual case.

(3) If the matter is referred to a German Court, the German Court having local jurisdiction, and in criminal matters the Special Court, shall decide the case.

SECTION 18. (1) If the decision of a Polish Court shall have become final on the effective date of this order, the period for application for reexamination shall run from the effective date of this order. This shall apply only to decisions which have become final after July 31, 1938.

(2) In especially important cases, in which the interests of the German people are affected by the decision, decisions which have become final prior to July 31, 1938, may be reexamined by order of the head of the Law Enforcement Section within the offices of the Government General.

SECTION 20. This order shall take effect as of the date of publication.

Cracow, February 19, 1940.

FRANK

Governor General of the Occupied Polish Territories

Decree concerning German Advocates in the Government General, September 13, 1940 [19]

The head of the Department of Justice in the office of the Governor General may give permission, subject to its revocation, to advocates admitted to practice in the German Reich to establish offices in the Government General. The permission may be conditioned upon the provision that they shall appear only before certain German courts of the Government General.

Cracow, September 13, 1940.

FRANK

Governor General of the Occupied Polish Territories

3. PROPERTY

Decree concerning Sequestration of Private Property in the Government General, January 24, 1940. [20]

In pursuance of subsection 1 of Section 5 of the decree of the Führer and Reich Chancellor concerning the administration of the occupied Polish territories of October 12, 1939 (*RGBl.* I, p. 2077), I hereby order as follows:

SECTION 1. *Purpose of the Sequestration.* Sequestrations may be ordered and carried out only in connection with the performance of tasks serving

[19] *Verordnungsblatt für das Generalgouvernement*, 1940, No. 56, p. 297.

[20] *Verordnungsblatt des Generalgouverneurs*, etc., No. 6, January 27, 1940, p. 23.

the public interest. They shall be effective only if the following provisions have been observed.

SECTION 2. *Sequestration Agencies.* (1) The right of sequestration shall be vested exclusively in the Governor General of the occupied Polish territories. It shall be exercised, in his name and in accordance with his directions, by the Director of the office of the Governor General and the district chiefs or other agencies designated by the Governor General.

(2) The right to sequestrate agricultural and forest property shall be exercised by the Director of the Trustee Administration for the Government General in agreement with the Director of the Department of Food and Agriculture or the Director of the Forestry Department.

(3) The right of the Director of the office of the Commissioner for the Four-Year Plan in the Government General to sequestrate raw materials of all kinds, and also manufactured and semi-manufactured products, shall not be affected by the provisions of the present decree.

(4) The seizure, administration, and exploitation of the sequestrated property shall be entrusted to the Director of the Trustee Administration of the Government General.

SECTION 3. *Order of Sequestration.* (1) Sequestration orders shall be issued in writing by the agency carrying out the sequestration in agreement with the Director of the Trustee Administration of the Government General. Sequestration shall take effect upon service of the order for sequestration.

(2) Service by poster or public announcement may be substituted for written notification to the owner of the property.

SECTION 4. *Effect of Sequestration.* (1) Sequestration implies a legal prohibition against alienation of the property. Legal transactions of any kind in connection with the sequestrated property and changes therein shall be null and void without the previous consent of the Director of the Trustee Administration of the Government General or of the agency designated by him.

(2) The same shall apply to any transfers or other rights obtained by way of execution of a judgment, attachment, or injunction.

(3) Rights of third parties in the property sequestrated, including those vesting title in a third party for the purpose of securing obligations owed, shall be held in abeyance.

SECTION 5. *Entry of Notice of the Order of Sequestration in the Land Register.* Upon sequestration of realty and other rights in realty subject to registration in the public records, notice of the sequestration shall be entered upon the records. Application for entry of such notice shall be made by the authority decreeing the sequestration; or, where a trustee has been appointed, by the trustee.

SECTION 6. *Exemptions from Sequestration.* Movable objects which at the time of the entry into force of the present decree serve exclusively for the personal use of the person affected by the sequestration shall be exempt therefrom provided they are not objects of luxury and do not exceed the requirements of bare living.

SECTION 7. *Duty of Registration.* Property liable to sequestration may be made the subject of compulsory registration by decree of the Governor General.

SECTION 8. *Seizure of Abandoned Property.* (1) Abandoned property shall be seized by the District Chief or Town Prefect and handed over for administration to the Director of the Trustee Administration of the Government General. Such seizure shall be ordered in writing.

(2) The rights of third parties in the seized property, including legal title transferred or reserved for the purpose of securing the payment of obligations, shall abate upon seizure. The Director of the Trustee Administration of the Government General may grant exemptions from such abatement.

SECTION 9. *Appointment of Trustees.* Upon the issuance of the order of sequestration or seizure of abandoned property the agency issuing the order may appoint a trustee. The appointment shall be subject to confirmation by the Director of the Trustee Administration of the Government General.

SECTION 10. *Status of the Trustee.* (1) The trustee shall be authorized to enter into any and all transactions, judicial and otherwise, which are required for the administration of the sequestrated property. His authority in this connection shall be equivalent to any power of attorney required by law.

(2) The trustee shall submit to the Director of the Trustee Administration of the Government General proposals concerning any disposal or liquidation, particularly of anti-social or financially unremunerative concerns. The decision concerning alienation or liquidation of the concern shall be made by the Director of the Trustee Administration of the Government General.

(3) The trustee shall be subject to supervision by the district officer of the field office of the Trustee Administration (*Treuhand-Aussenstelle*) and to the further supervision of the Director of the Trustee Administration of the Government General.

(4) The trustee in his conduct of affairs shall act with the care of a prudent businessman. He shall be responsible to the appointing agency for any loss arising from infraction of his duties. He shall supply to such agency any required information at any time. He shall, unless otherwise instructed, present a report of his conduct of affairs, without being called upon to do so, at the end of each month after his appointment.

(5) The trustee shall be subject to dismissal without notice.

(6) The cost of trustee administration shall be charged to the property administered.

SECTION 11. *Sequestration by Military Authorities.* (1) Sequestrations already ordered or which may be ordered in the future by the Commander in Chief in the East shall not be subject to the restrictions imposed by the present decree if they are effected in the interests of Reich defense and the increase of armaments. Such sequestrations shall be certified to the Director of the Trustee Administration of the Government General.

(2) The Director of the Trustee Administration of the Government General shall be authorized to review orders of sequestration issued and enforced by the military authorities with a view to determining whether they are required for the purposes referred to in subsection 1.

(3) Appointment of all trustees shall be subject to confirmation by the Director of the Trustee Administration of the Government General.

SECTION 12. *Sequestration by the Armed S.S. and Police.* (1) The Superior S.S. and Police Chief may, in exceptional cases, order sequestrations with the object of increasing the striking power of the units of the uniformed police and armed S.S. Such sequestrations shall not be subject to the limitations imposed by the present decree; notification of orders of sequestration shall be made to the Director of the Trustee Administration of the Government General.

(2) Subsections 2 and 3 of Section 11 shall be made applicable to the sequestration referred to in subsection 1.

SECTION 13. *Orders of Sequestration Issued by the Uniformed Police Forces* (*Sicherheitspolizei*). (1) Sequestrations ordered by officers of the uniformed police shall not be subject to the limitations of the present decree, provided they relate to objects directly connected with punishable acts. The Director of the Trustee Administration of the Government General shall be notified of such sequestrations.

(2) Subsections 2 and 3 of Section 11 shall be made applicable to the sequestrations referred to in subsection 1.

SECTION 14. *Notice of Sequestration Orders Issued before the Effective Date of this Order.* (1) Notice of sequestrations ordered and executed before the coming into force of the present decree shall be given to the Director of the Trustee Administration of the Government General.

(2) Whenever a trustee has been appointed, confirmation of such appointment shall be obtained from the Director of the Trustee Administration of the Government General not later than April 1, 1940. To appointments of trustees made before November 20, 1939, Section 3 of the order concerning the establishment of an Office of Trustee Administration of the Government General of November 15, 1939 (*VBl.GGP.*, p. 36) shall remain applicable.

SECTION 15. *Compensation.* (1) Compensation may be granted for losses arising from the enforcement of the present decree; courts of law shall have no jurisdiction to entertain suits for payment of such compensation.

(2) The Director of the Trustee Administration of the Government

General shall by order establish the amount of compensation after hearing the agency which has ordered the sequestration. His order shall be final.

SECTION 16. *Restrictions on Property Rights heretofore Imposed.* (1) Order No. 4 of the head of the Foreign Exchange Section of the office of the Governor General of November 20, 1939 (*VBl.GGP.*, p. 57) shall not be affected by the provisions of this order.

(2) Debtors in respect of obligations owed to a Jew which are subject to an order of sequestration may terminate their obligation by paying the amount due into a blocked bank account of such Jewish creditor.

SECTION 17. *Penalties.* (1) Violations of the present decree and of the rules and regulations implementing and supplementing it shall be punishable by imprisonment and fine of unlimited amount or by either of these penalties, and in especially serious cases by hard labor.

(2) The Special Court shall have jurisdiction to try violations referred to in subsection 1.

SECTION 18. *Final Provisions.* (1) The order concerning housing of public authorities of November 1, 1939 (*VBl.GGP.*, p. 27) shall be repealed on the effective date of this decree.

(2) The following shall not be affected by this decree:

a) The decree relating to the sequestration of the property of the former Polish State within the Government General of November 15, 1939 (*VBl.GGP.*, p. 37).

b) The decree relating to mining rights and mining shares in the Government General of December 14, 1939 (*VBl.GGP.*, p. 235).

c) The decree relating to the sequestration and surrender of wireless apparatus of December 15, 1939 (*VBl.GGP.*, p. 225).

d) The decree relating to the sequestration of objects of art in the Government General of December 16, 1939 (*VBl.GGP.*, p. 209).

e) The decree relating to the sequestration of installations and equipment of the mineral oil industry in the Government General of January 23, 1940 (*VBl.GGP.*, p. 21).

Cracow, January 24, 1940.

FRANK

Governor General of the Occupied Polish Territories

4. ECONOMY

Order Establishing a Planning Board for Chemical Products within the Government General, April 9, 1941 [21]

By virtue of subsection 1, Section 5, of the decree of the Führer and Reich Chancellor of October 12, 1939 (*RGBl.* I, p. 2077), I hereby order as follows:

[21] *Verordnungsblatt für das Generalgouvernement*, 1941, p. 198.

SECTION 1. *Jurisdiction.* For the regulation and supervision of dealings in chemical products, in products needed for the supply of industrial fats, in rubber, asbestos, and mineral products—notwithstanding the provisions contained in subsection 1, numbers 1 and 2, and subsection 2 of Section 4—with the exception of goods controlled by government monopoly, a "Planning Board for Chemical Products within the Government General" with its official seat in Cracow is hereby established. The board shall be subject to the orders of the office of the Government General (Main Section: Economics).

SECTION 2. *Official Duties.* The Planning Board for Chemical Products within the Government General shall undertake, subject to the approval by the office of the Government General:

1. To determine the kind of products to be subject to planning.
2. To issue orders to individual shops or plants or to groups of shops or plants concerning the production, distribution, sale, and consumption of the products subject to planning.
3. To determine the import requirements, notwithstanding the provisions contained in subsection 2, Section 4, and to regulate the distribution of and to distribute the products imported, and to regulate exports.
4. To discontinue temporarily or permanently the operation of plants of producers or of wholesale or retail firms in the event of violations of orders by the owners or managers and to order the delivery of the stocks on hand to a place to be designated by the board.
5. To require plants described in number 4 to continue in operation subject to approval by the board.
6. To request information from shops or enterprises concerning economic data, especially prices and stocks on hand, output, and capacity, to inspect business correspondence, books of account and other documents, to inspect plant installations and business or factory rooms, and to make an audit or order an audit to be made at the expense of the enterprise.

SECTION 3. *Duty of Secrecy.* The agents of the Planning Board for Chemical Products shall be required to observe secrecy concerning the installations and business data which they learn in the course of their duties, and to refrain from communicating or utilizing business or technical secrets thus learned.

. . . . .

This order shall take effect as of May 1, 1941.
Cracow, April 9, 1941.

FRANK
Governor General of the Occupied Polish Territories

5. FINANCE

Decree concerning the Bank of Issue in Poland, December 15, 1939 [22]

[EXCERPTS]

By virtue of subsection 1 of Section 5 of the order of the Führer and Reich Chancellor concerning the administration of the occupied Polish territories of October 12, 1939 (*RGBl.* I, p. 2077), I hereby order as follows:

I. ORGANIZATION

SECTION 1. (1) In order to maintain monetary, financial, and credit business in the occupied Polish territories, the Bank of Issue in Poland (*Bank Emisyjny w Polsce*) shall be established.

(2) The bank shall be a legal entity with its principal office in Cracow. The Governor General of the occupied Polish territories may order the transfer of the principal office to another locality.

(3) The bank shall be authorized to maintain branch offices within the territory of the Government General.

SECTION 2. (1) The bank shall be directed and managed by a president and one or two deputies. If required, additional permanent or temporary deputies may be appointed.

(2) The president and his deputies shall be appointed by the Governor General of the occupied Polish territories, who shall also confirm their contracts of employment with the bank, particularly as regards their remuneration.

(3) The president and his deputies shall be subject to dismissal without notice.

SECTION 3. (1) A governor of the Bank of Issue in Poland shall be appointed. He shall be directly subordinated to the Governor General of the occupied Polish territories, by whom he shall be appointed and discharged. The Governor General shall exercise supervision over the bank through the bank governor. The governor shall be currently kept informed concerning the policies of the bank; he may require information concerning all transactions of the bank. At the end of each calendar month a statement concerning the bank notes issued and the available cover shall be submitted to him.

(2) The president, his deputies, and any other persons in executive positions shall obtain the approval of the bank governor on all important measures. This shall apply in particular to the extension of credit and the fixing of the rates of interest in the business of the bank. The bank governor may give general consent for certain kinds of transactions; such consent may be revoked.

[22] *Verordnungsblatt des Generalgouverneurs*, No. 14, December 23, 1939, p. 238.

(3) The staff, offices, and equipment required by the bank governor for the execution of his tasks shall be placed at his disposal free of charge.

SECTION 4. (1) An administrative board may be established for the bank. It shall be the function of this board to assist the president in an advisory capacity. The president may request the advice of the board. The president, at the end of each fiscal year, shall submit a report concerning that year to the administrative board.

(2) The members of the administrative board shall be appointed and discharged by the Governor General.

SECTION 5. (1) The branch offices of the bank shall be directed and managed by managers and the required number of deputies as ordered by the president of the bank.

(2) The managers of the branches and their deputies shall be appointed by the president in agreement with the bank governor.

SECTION 6. (1) Commitments shall be binding upon the bank if made by the president and one of his deputies or by two deputies.

(2) For purposes of the current business of the head office of the bank the president shall give authority to special agents. Their commitments shall be binding upon the bank if made by two authorized agents within their scope of activity.

. . . . .

(6) Legal actions against the bank can be instituted only before the competent German court where the head office is situated.

SECTION 7. (1) The president of the bank, in agreement with the governor of the bank and the chief of the Economics Section of the office of the Governor General, shall determine the employment conditions, especially the salaries, of the employees of the bank.

(2) The president, his deputies, and all persons in the service of the bank shall be required to treat as confidential all matters and arrangements of the bank, especially the extent of its credit business of which they may learn in the course of their employment. This duty shall continue beyond the termination of their employment.

II. OPERATIONS OF THE BANK

SECTION 8. The bank shall be authorized to engage in the following operations:

1. Discounting bills, notes, and checks guaranteed as a rule by three, but by at least two guarantors known to be solvent; the bills shall mature within six months from the date of discounting.
2. Granting interest-bearing loans against suitable security, as a rule for not longer than six months.
3. Accepting non-interest-bearing payments in deposit and current accounts; from the staff of the bank deposits at interest may also be accepted.

4. Effecting all kinds of banking operations, particularly collecting notes and other documents.
5. Accepting into its custody and management valuables and particularly securities.

. . . . .

SECTION 11. Transactions other than those permitted by this order may not be entered into unless express consent of the governor of the bank has been obtained. The bank shall not be authorized to accept drafts.

SECTION 12. The bank shall be required to undertake all banking and financial business on behalf of the administration of the Government General and to act as clearing agent for the branch offices of the Public Treasury within the occupied Polish territories. Charges made for such services shall not exceed actual expenditures made.

III. ISSUE AND COVERAGE OF NOTES

SECTION 13. (1) The bank shall be authorized to issue zloty notes.

(2) The notes of the bank shall constitute the sole unqualified legal tender in the occupied Polish territories.

. . . . .

SECTION 16. (1) The following shall be admitted as coverage for the notes issued by the bank and for the balances kept by it:

1. Claims arising from discount and credit business according to Section 8, paragraphs 1 and 2.
2. German legal tender and accounts maintained with the German Reichsbank or the German Clearing Office.

(2) As further coverage for the obligations mentioned in subsection 1 above, a first mortgage on all real estate situated in the occupied Polish territories to a maximum amount of three billion zlotys, free of all taxes and other charges, shall be established in favor of the bank. This mortgage shall take precedence over all tax claims and other encumbrances. The mortgage shall not require, for its establishment, registration in the Land Register. Further details concerning this mortgage shall be issued in the form of decrees.

. . . . .

Cracow, December 15, 1939.

FRANK
Governor General of the Occupied Polish Territories

Decree concerning Industrial Tax (Registration Fee), February 14, 1940 [23]

[EXCERPTS]

SECTION 3. *Rate of Tax.* The tax shall be levied in the amount of 200 per cent of the rates of Appendix I to Article 7 of the Polish Law of April 25, 1938 (*Law Journal of the Polish Republic*, 1938, No. 14, item 293).

. . .

SECTION 5. *Appeals.* The provisions relating to appeals shall not apply.

Cracow, February 14, 1940.

FRANK

Governor General of the Occupied Polish Territories

Decree concerning the Increase of Property Tax for the Fiscal Year 1940, March 16, 1940 [24]

[EXCERPT]

SECTION 1. The Polish property tax for the fiscal year 1940 shall be increased by 50 per cent.

. . . . .

Cracow, March 16, 1940.

FRANK

Governor General of the Occupied Polish Territories

Decree concerning the Imposition of a Head Tax, June 27, 1940 [25]

[EXCERPTS]

SECTION 1. Communes and amalgamated communes may and must collect a tax per head of the inhabitants in conformity with the provisions of the present decree.

. . . . .

SECTION 3. The tax shall be calculated as a percentage of a basic value.

Cracow, June 27, 1940.

FRANK

Governor General of the Occupied Polish Territories

[23] *Verordnungsblatt des Generalgouverneurs*, etc., 1940, p. 51.
[24] *Ibid.*, 1940, p. 109. [25] *Ibid.*, 1940, p. 211.

Order concerning the Establishment of the Budget of the Government General for the Fiscal Year 1940, March 3, 1941 [26]

By virtue of subsection 1 of Section 5 of the decree of the Führer and Reich Chancellor of October 12, 1939 (*RGBl.* I, p. 2077), I hereby decree as follows:

SECTION 1. The Budget of the Government General, attached to this order as Appendix is hereby established for the fiscal year 1940:

Ordinary Budget:	Income	974,004,400 zlotys
	Expenditure	1,004,004,400 zlotys
Extraordinary Budget:	Income	278,100,000 zlotys
	Expenditure	278,100,000 zlotys

[APPENDIX]

TABULATION OF THE BUDGET OF THE GOVERNMENT GENERAL FOR THE FISCAL YEAR 1940 [27]

A.—*Ordinary Budget*

		Income	Expenditure
I.	Governor General and Chiefs of the Districts	3,526,300	92,010,200
II.	Financial Administration	4,645,350	25,976,300
III.	Internal Administration	7,700,650	64,594,300
IV.	Police Administration		61,932,850
V.	Public Health Administration	7,821,150	12,973,350
VI.	Administration of Justice	8,306,200	36,001,300
VII.	Sciences, Education and Adult Education	554,200	94,185,150
VIII.	Food Supply and Agriculture	11,503,800	62,560,300
IX.	Forests	85,745,450	63,732,100
X.	Economics	7,487,100	8,167,700
XI.	Labor	26,490,700	95,559,650
XII.	Construction	384,100	44,699,250
XIII.	Traffic		
XIV.	Propaganda	278,400	7,337,100
XV.	General Financial Administration	809,561,000	329,629,500
	Sum Total, Ordinary Budget	974,004,400	1,004,004,400

B.—*Extraordinary Budget*

Income	278,100,000 zlotys
Expenditure	278,100,000 zlotys

. . . .

[26] *Verordnungsblatt für das Generalgouvernement*, 1941, p. 83.
[27] Tabulation somewhat abbreviated by the translator.—ED.

SECTION 4. (1) This order shall take effect as of April 1, 1940.

(2) The office of the Government General (Section on Finances) shall enforce this order.

Berlin, March 3, 1941.

FRANK

Governor General of the Occupied Polish Territories

6. LABOR

Decree concerning the Introduction of Compulsory Labor for the Polish Population of the Government General, October 28, 1939 [28]

By virtue of subsection 1, Section 5, of the decree of the Führer and Reich Chancellor concerning the administration of the occupied Polish territories issued October 12, 1939 (*RGBl.* I, p. 2077), I hereby order:

SECTION 1. (1) Effective immediately, all Polish inhabitants of the Government General between the ages of 18 and 60 years shall be subject to compulsory public labor.

(2) A special decree will be issued with regard to Jews.

SECTION 2. Persons who can prove permanent employment useful to the commonwealth shall not be called for the performance of public work service.

SECTION 3. Compulsory public labor shall comprise, in particular, work in agricultural undertakings, the construction and maintenance of public buildings, the construction of roads, waterways, and railways, the regulation of rivers, and work on land improvements.

SECTION 4. (1) The payment of persons subject to compulsory labor shall be effected at equitable rates.

(2) The welfare of persons subject to compulsory labor and their families shall be protected as far as possible.

SECTION 5. The regulations required for the execution of the present decree shall be issued by the Director of the Department of Labor in the office of the Government General.

Warsaw, October 28, 1939.

FRANK

Governor General of the Occupied Polish Territories

[28] *Verordnungsblatt des Generalgouverneurs*, etc., 1939, p. 6.

Order concerning the Determination of Working Conditions and the Protection of Labor in the Government General, October 31, 1939 [29]

[EXCERPT]

By virtue of subsection 1, Section 5, of the decree of the Führer and Reich Chancellor concerning the administration of the occupied Polish territories issued October 12, 1939 (*RGBl.* I, p. 2077), I hereby order:

SECTION 1. For the regulation of working conditions and the protection of labor the regulations in force at present shall remain in force in so far as it is not hereinafter otherwise provided.

SECTION 2. (1) The contracts in force on August 30, 1939, for workers and salaried employees shall continue in force at present and shall be legally binding on all parties. Variations from the prescribed wages and salaries and other working conditions shall not be permitted without the written consent of the District Governor. Where changes had already taken place before this order became effective, they shall be revoked unless consent is obtained subsequently.

(2) Where there were no contracts in effect on August 30, 1939, the actual wages and salaries paid on that date shall be continued. Exceptions shall be permissible only with the written consent of the District Governor.

. . . . .

Warsaw, October 31, 1939.

FRANK

Governor General of the Occupied Polish Territories

Order concerning the Introduction of Wage Scales for Craftsmen in the Public Service, November 23, 1939 [30]

[EXCERPTS]

By virtue of subsection 1, Section 5, of the decree of the Führer and Reich Chancellor concerning the administration of the occupied Polish territories of October 12, 1939 (*RGBl.* I, p. 2077), I hereby order as follows:

SECTION 1. Effective October 1, 1939, the following wage scales shall be applied in the territory of the Government General:

1. General Wage Scale for Craftsmen in the Public Service (ATO), *Reichshaushalts- und Besoldungsblatt* 1939, Nr. 17.
2. Wage Scale A for Craftsmen in the Public Service (TO A), *ibid.*, 1939, Nr. 18.
3. Wage Scale B for Craftsmen in the Public Service (TO B), *ibid.*, 1939, Nr. 19.

[29] *Verordnungsblatt des Generalgouverneurs*, etc., 1939, p. 12.

[30] *Ibid.*, No. 8, p. 62.

SECTION 2. (1) The provisions of Section 1 shall apply only to Reich German workers and salaried employees employed in the Government General on the order of the German authorities. They shall not apply to workers and salaried employees of Polish nationality taken over by former Polish authorities.

(2) For German workers and salaried employees special regulations shall be issued.

. . . . .

Cracow, November 23, 1939.

FRANK

Governor General of the Occupied Polish Territories

Second Order Implementing the Order of October 26, 1939: concerning the Introduction of Forced Labor for the Jewish Population of the Government General, December 12, 1939 [31]

[EXCERPTS]

By virtue of the order of October 26, 1939, subsection 2 of Section 1, concerning the introduction of forced labor for the Jewish population of the Government General (*VBl.GGP.*, p. 6), I hereby order:

SECTION 1. All Jewish inhabitants of the territory of the Government General from 14 to 60 years of age shall be subject to forced labor. The duration of this forced labor shall amount normally to two years; it shall be lengthened if the educational purpose of such forced labor should not be attained within that period.

SECTION 2. For the utilization of their working capacity as far as possible according to skilled trades which they may have, those subject to forced labor shall be put to work in labor camps. Those not fully capable of work shall be assigned activities corresponding to their capacities.

SECTION 3. The regulations for registration of those subject to forced labor shall be applied for the present to male Jews from 12 to 60 years of age. These shall be required, upon public summons by the burgomasters in accordance with special directions which the county and city chiefs will issue, to report to their appropriate Jewish Councils for entry on the registration roll. The burgomasters, along with the Jewish Councils, shall be responsible for complete and correct registration.

SECTION 4. Induction into labor shall follow upon special summons from the German authorities.

[31] *Verordnungsblatt des Generalgouverneurs*, etc., 1939, p. 246.

SECTION 5. After being entered on the registration roll, Jews who are summoned to forced labor shall appear punctually at the appointed hour at the designated place of assembly. They shall bring with them provisions for two days and two clean blankets. Craftsmen, especially owners of shops, shall deliver their entire equipment at the place of assembly. They must be notified by the Jewish Council to deliver their equipment promptly. Handicraft tools and accessories of those subject to forced labor shall, after induction, be at the disposal of the Forced Labor Service.

SECTION 6. (1) Effective immediately, all Jews subject to forced labor shall be forbidden to sell, pawn, or otherwise dispose of professional craftsman's equipment, including tools and accessories, at present in their possession, without the written consent of their appropriate county or city chief. Further, any removal or concealment of this equipment shall be forbidden.

. . . . .

SECTION 7. [Ten years at hard labor shall be the penalty for (*a*) Jews who fail to appear promptly for registration, fail to tell the whole truth about themselves, pretend disability, dispose of tools, or fail to bring them when called for induction, or otherwise attempt to escape service; (*b*) members of the Jewish Council who fail to register Jews properly or who help a Jew to escape service; and (*c*) any person who impedes the execution of this program or buys or accepts tools from Jews subject to service. Confiscation of all property may accompany such sentence.] [32]

. . . . .

SECTION 10. (1) This implementing order shall become effective immediately.

. . . . .

Cracow, December 12, 1939.

KRUEGER, *Chief S.S. Group Leader*
Chief Director of S.S. and Police in the Government General for the Occupied Polish Territories

Decree concerning the Extension of Compulsory Labor for the Population of the Government General, December 14, 1939 [33]

By virtue of subsection 1, Section 5, of the decree of the Führer and Reich Chancellor concerning the administration of the occupied Polish territories issued October 26, 1939 (*RGBl.* I, p. 2077), I hereby order as follows:

SECTION 1. The District Governors shall be authorized to extend the compulsory labor requirement for the Polish inhabitants of the Government

[32] Summary by the translator.
[33] *Verordnungsblatt des Generalgouverneurs*, etc., 1939, I, p. 224

General to juveniles between the ages of 14 and 18 years. Juveniles shall be required to work according to their capacity.

SECTION 2. For the classes of persons included in Section 1 of this order, Sections 1 to 4 of the order concerning work service for the Polish population of the Government General issued October 26, 1939 (*VBl.GGP.*, p. 6), shall be effective.

SECTION 3. This order shall become effective immediately.

Cracow, December 14, 1939.

FRANK
Governor General of the Occupied Territories

Order concerning the Payment of Unemployment Relief, December 16, 1939 [34]

[EXCERPTS]

By virtue of subsection 1, Section 5, of the decree of the Führer and Reich Chancellor concerning the administration of the occupied Polish territories of October 12, 1939 (*RGBl.* I, p. 2077), I hereby order as follows:

SECTION 1. (1) Persons capable of work who are involuntarily unemployed and are available for employment may receive unemployment relief from the Labor Office for the duration of their unemployment, in so far as they are in need.

(2) No legal claim may be made for unemployment relief.

SECTION 2. (1) [Agricultural workers and persons under 18 years or over 60 years of age may receive relief payments only if they are performing labor service; but under special conditions the District Governor may permit agricultural workers to receive relief payments.] [35]

(2) Jews shall be excluded from unemployment relief and shall in case of need be referred to the Jewish relief organizations.

SECTION 3. The payment of unemployment relief may be made conditional upon the performance of labor service.

. . .

SECTION 5. The maximum weekly basic payment is Zl. 9.00; the maximum weekly family increment for the first dependent, Zl. 4.20; and the weekly maximum for each additional dependent, Zl. 2.40. The unemployment relief may be paid wholly or in part in goods.

. . .

SECTION 6. Unemployment relief may be paid also to part-time workers. It shall in this case be reduced proportionately.

SECTION 7. Any additional income of the recipient of the basic relief pay-

[34] *Verordnungsblatt des Generalgouverneurs*, 1940, I, No. 64, p. 239.
[35] Summary by the translator.

ment and of dependents entitled to allowances shall be taken into account proportionately in the relief payment.

. . . .

SECTION 9. [Within the limits of this regulation, the District Governor may issue regulations governing the payment of relief, including the exclusion of persons or groups from benefits.] [36]

Cracow, December 16, 1939.

FRANK

Governor General of the Occupied Polish Territories

Order concerning the Restriction of the Right to Change Employment, February 22, 1940 [37]

By virtue of subsection 1, Section 5, of the decree of the Führer and Reich Chancellor concerning the administration of the occupied Polish territories of October 12, 1939 (*RGBl.* I, p. 2077), I hereby order as follows:

SECTION 1. The managers of private and public enterprises and administrations of every description, heads of households, workers, and employees may not give notice unless the Labor Office has consented to the termination of the employment contract.

SECTION 2. The managers of enterprises and the heads of households shall not employ workers and employees unless the consent of the Labor Office has been obtained.

SECTION 3. Sections 1 and 2 shall be applicable to members of the family who regularly aid in enterprises and households of spouses, parents, grandparents, brothers, or sisters even though they are not employed as workers or employees.

SECTION 4. (1) In deciding on applications for the termination or the conclusion of employment contracts, the Labor Office shall take into account political and social considerations as well as the general instructions with regard both to the channelling of labor forces and to wage policies.

(2) The application may be granted subject to conditions.

SECTION 5. The grant of consent

a) for a termination of employment shall fall under the jurisdiction of the Labor Office within whose province the last place of work is situated;

b) for employment shall fall under the jurisdiction of the Labor Office within whose province the enterprise which intends to employ is situated.

SECTION 6. (1) The application for consent under Section 1 shall be made to the appropriate Labor Office by the contracting party which seeks the dissolution of the employment relationship.

[36] Summary by the translator.

[37] *Verordnungsblatt des Generalgouverneurs*, etc., 1940, I, No. 15, p. 80.

(2) The application for consent under Section 2 shall be made to the appropriate Labor Office by the prospective employer.

SECTION 7. The Director of the Department of Labor in the office of the Governor General shall be empowered to except types of industries, enterprises, households, and persons from the provisions of Sections 1 to 3. He may delegate this power to the directors of the Department of Labor in the offices of the District Governors.

SECTION 8. Any person who violates or evades this order or discontinues his work before the lawful termination of the employment contract shall be, on motion of the director of the Labor Office, subject to imprisonment and/or fine.

SECTION 9. This order shall take effect as of March 15, 1940.

Cracow, February 22, 1940.

FRANK
Governor General of the Occupied Polish Territories

Second Order concerning Social Security in the Government General (Benefits and Procedure), March 7, 1940 [38]

[EXCERPTS]

By virtue of subsection 1, Section 5, of the decree of the Führer and Reich Chancellor concerning the administration of the occupied Polish territories of October 12, 1939 (*RGBl.* I, p. 2077), I hereby order as follows:

SECTION 1. Claims for payments under the Polish social security law are nullified. They shall be replaced, beginning March 1, 1940, by benefits for which no legal claim may be made. This provision shall be effective without regard to the date of the social security case.

. . . . .

Cracow, March 7, 1940.

FRANK
Governor General of the Occupied Polish Territories

Order Changing Regulations for the Protection of Labor, June 13, 1940 [39]

[EXCERPTS]

By virtue of subsection 1, Section 5, of the decree of the Führer and Reich Chancellor concerning the administration of the occupied Polish territory of October 12, 1939 (*RGBl.* I, p. 2077), I hereby order:

[38] *Verordnungsblatt des Generalgouverneurs*, etc., 1940, I, No. 18, p. 92. [39] *Ibid.*, p. 200.

SECTION 1. The management of enterprises may order an extension of daily working time to ten hours where a ten-hour or longer working day is not already permitted under the existing regulations.

SECTION 2. By wage scale or service regulation the regular working time may be lengthened to ten hours daily, and, in the case of time on call, to still longer hours.

SECTION 3. (1) The Labor Office as the authority for business supervision, may, upon proof of urgent need, permit more extensive temporary exceptions from the regulations in force regarding working time.

(2) [Jurisdiction of authorities for permitting exceptions of more than local application.] [40]

(3) When work on Sundays or holidays in cases of necessity or in the public interest must be undertaken without delay, it shall not be necessary to obtain permission of the authorities in advance; but a subsequent report shall be made to the Labor Office, as the authority for business supervision.

SECTION 4. The provisions of Sections 1 to 3 shall be valid also for the employment of female labor.

. . . . .

SECTION 6. The Director of the Department of Labor in the office of the Governor General may permit more extensive exceptions than are provided in other regulations for the protection of labor if such exceptions become urgently necessary in the public interest.

SECTION 7. This order shall become effective on the day of its promulgation.

Cracow, June 13, 1940.

FRANK
Governor General of the Occupied Polish Territories

Order concerning the Introduction of a Work Card in the Government General, December 20, 1940 [41]

[EXCERPTS]

By virtue of subsection 1, Section 5, of the decree of the Führer and Reich Chancellor of October 12, 1939 (*RGBl.* I, p. 2077), I hereby order:

SECTION 1. (1) In order to insure a proper distribution of labor in the Government General, a work card shall be introduced.

(2) Implementing regulations shall determine what classes of persons must be holders of work cards and the details of form and procedure for work cards, with particular regard to the duties required of employers and employees in connection therewith.

[40] Summary by the translator.
[41] *Verordnungsblatt für das Generalgouvernement*, 1940, I, No. 73, p. 377.

SECTION 2. (1) Workers and salaried employees who are required to hold work cards may be continued in employment and may accept employment only if they have work cards properly made out.

. . . .

SECTION 3. [The right to issue work cards shall rest exclusively with the Labor Office.] [42]

. . . .

SECTION 5. This order shall be effective as of January 15, 1941.

Cracow, December 20, 1940.

FRANK
Governor General

Wage Scale for Male and Female Workers in Forest Industry (Wage Scale Register No. 12/1), February 7, 1941 [43]

[EXCERPTS]

By virtue of subsection 1, Section 5, of the decree of the Führer and Reich Chancellor concerning the administration of the occupied Polish territories of October 12, 1939 (*RGBl.* I, p. 2077), I hereby order as follows:

SECTION 1. *Scope of Validity.* (1) This wage scale shall be valid for male and female workers employed in enterprises of state, community, and private forest industry in the Government General. It shall not be applicable to Germans newly employed from the Reich.

SECTION 2. *Hourly Wage Rates.* (1) The following hourly rates shall be paid:

1. Male	
21 years or older	0.50 zloty
17 years or older	0.40 zloty
less than 17 years old	0.26 zloty
2. Female	
18 years or older	0.36 zloty
16 years or older	0.26 zloty
less than 16 years old	0.22 zloty

(2) These rates include compensation for the use of such tools in good condition as are ordinarily used for cutting timber and clearing ground.

(3) Foremen shall receive an additional 10 per cent.

(4) The District Governor may permit variations for individual enterprises or well-defined branch enterprises and for special work.

SECTION 3. *Piece-Work Rates.* (1) For cutting timber the following piece-work rates shall be applied. Where types of timber are not named or

[42] Summary by the translator.

[43] *Verordnungsblatt für das Generalgouvernement*, 1941, No. 10, p. 46.

where other work is carried out on a piece-work basis, the rates shall be so adjusted that a worker with normal production can earn 120 per cent of the hourly wage of a 21-year-old worker.

. . . . .

SECTION 4. *Working Time.* (1) The regular daily working time, exclusive of rest periods and a reasonable time for walking to and from work, shall be eight hours daily or 96 hours in the double week, except where it must be shortened on account of daylight and weather conditions. In reforestation the working time shall be ten hours daily or 120 hours in the double week.

(2) If the time required for walking from home to the place of work and back amounts in all to more than three and one-half hours daily, compensation shall be paid for the time in excess of this amount at the rate of the hourly wage for each hour or fraction thereof.

SECTION 5. *Annual Leave.* [Workers who have been in the employ of the same enterprise at least six months of each year for three consecutive years shall be granted a paid annual leave of six working days. Those particularly in need of rest may, with the consent of the Labor Office, be given an additional leave not to exceed three, or, in the case of workers over forty years of age, six days. Pay while on leave shall be at the corresponding rate for eight hours daily, in reforestation for ten hours daily, and may be paid one half at the beginning and one half at the end of the leave period. Gainful employment while on leave is forbidden.] [44]

SECTION 6. *Effective Date.* This wage scale shall become effective March 1, 1941.

Cracow, February 7, 1941.

Dr. FRAUENDORFER
Director of the Department of Labor in the Administration of the Government General

Order concerning the Distribution of Labor Forces, Employment Service, Occupation Guidance, and Apprenticeship Placement Service, February 20, 1941 [45]

By virtue of subsection 1, Section 5, of the decree of the Führer and Reich Chancellor of October 12, 1939 (*RGBl.* I, p. 2077), I hereby order:

SECTION 1. The channelling of labor forces, especially their distribution and exchange, the employment service, and the apprenticeship placement service shall be governed exclusively by orders of the Government General (Labor Section).

[44] Summary by the translator.
[45] *Verordnungsblatt für das Generalgouvernement*, 1941, p. 53.

SECTION 2. The employment service, occupational guidance, and the apprenticeship placement service shall be administered exclusively by the County Chief (*Kreishauptmann*) or Town Chief (*Stadthauptmann*) through the Labor Office.

SECTION 3. (1) Upon application being made thereto, the office of the Government General may delegate the administration of public employment services, occupational guidance, and apprenticeship placement services to agencies not connected with the administrative offices of the County Chief or Town Chief.

(2) The office of the Government General (Labor Section) may by order license private employment agencies for specified occupations. The several private agencies shall be licensed by the District Director having jurisdiction over the district wherein they have their place of business.

(3) The establishments and enterprises which under subsections 1 and 2 are commissioned for employment service, vocational guidance, and apprenticeship placement service, or are given permits for employment service, shall be subject to the supervision of the County Chief.

SECTION 4. [Penalties for violations.]

SECTION 5. (1) This order shall take effect as of the day of publication.

(2) [Invalidation of previous ordinances.]

Dresden, February 20, 1941.

FRANK
Governor General of the Occupied Polish Territories

7. GENOCIDE LEGISLATION

Order concerning the Introduction of a Certificate for Persons of German Origin in the Government General, October 29, 1941 [46]

[EXCERPTS]

By virtue of Section 5, subsection 1, of the decree of the Führer of October 12, 1939 (*RGBl.* I, p. 2077), I order:

SECTION 1. (1) A person of German origin, upon his own application or that of a German authority, may obtain through the county (or city) chief within whose jurisdiction he resides a certificate which establishes his German origin.

(2) Documentary proofs shall be submitted as to the facts stated in support of the application.

(3) The issuing authorities shall make the final decision after examination of the application and of the documents submitted.

[46] *Verordnungsblatt für das Generalgouvernement*, 1941, No. 104, p. 622.

SECTION 2. A person of German origin within the meaning of this order is one who has German antecedents but does not possess German nationality (*Staatsangehörigkeit*) or the identification card for Germans (*Volkszugehörige*) (Order concerning the introduction of an identification card for Germans in the Government General of January 26, 1940; *VBl.GG.* I, p. 36).

SECTION 3. A non-German who is married to a German may also obtain upon his own application a certificate as specified in Section 1, if the marriage has not been terminated and if it has produced children who are still alive.

SECTION 4. (1) Any person who falsely obtains a certificate as specified in Section 1 shall be punished by penal servitude.

. . . . .

SECTION 5. The administration of the Government General (Major Division of Interior Administration) shall make regulations to determine under what conditions persons who possess a certificate by virtue of this order may obtain the identification card for Germans in accordance with the order concerning the introduction of an identification card for Germans in the Government General of January 26, 1940 (*VBl.GG.* I, p. 36).

SECTION 6. The administration of the Government General (Major Division of Interior Administration) shall be empowered to issue administrative regulations for the enforcement of this order.

SECTION 7. This order shall become effective November 15, 1941.

Cracow, October 29, 1941.

FRANK
Governor General

Order concerning the Granting of Child Subsidies to Germans in the Government General, March 10, 1942 [47]

[EXCERPTS]

By virtue of Section 5, subsection 1, of the decree of the Führer of October 12, 1939 (*RGBl.* I, p. 2077), I order:

SECTION 1. *The Purpose of Child Subsidies.* For the relief of family expenses, child subsidies shall be granted to healthy and socially responsible German families in the Government General.

SECTION 2. *The Amount of the Child Subsidy.* The child subsidy shall amount to twenty zlotys per month for each child qualified for a subsidy.

SECTION 3. *Persons Entitled to Subsidies.* (1) The head of the household shall be entitled to receive the subsidy.

[47] *Verordnungsblatt für das Generalgouvernement,* 1942, No. 23, p. 125. Text in part abbreviated by the translator.

(2) The child subsidy must be granted if:

1. The head of the household is a German national (*Staatsangerhöriger*) or a person of German origin (*Volkszugehöriger*).
2. The household comprises at least three minor children.
3. The head of the household has his residence or usual dwelling-place in the Government General. If the head of the household also has a residence or usual dwelling in the German Reich (including the Protectorate of Bohemia and Moravia), he is entitled to subsidies in the Government General only if the center of the actual household administration lies in the Government General.

(3) [Conditions under which subsidies may be granted for fewer than three children.]

(4) Child subsidies may also be granted to the head of a household who possesses a certificate of German origin under the order concerning the introduction of a certificate for persons of German origin in the Government General of October 29, 1941 (*VBl.GG.*, p. 622), if the German upbringing of all children is guaranteed and the conditions of subsection 2, Nos. 2 and 3, or of subsection 3 are fulfilled.

. . . . .

SECTION 4. *Children Qualified for Subsidies.* (1) The following shall be qualified for subsidies:

1. In general, the third and each additional minor child which is a member of the household.
2. In the cases of Section 3, subsection 3, numbers 1 and 2, the first and each additional minor child which is a member of the household.
3. In the cases of Section 3, subsection 3, number 3, the minor children adopted into the household.

(2) Children in the sense of this order are the issue of the head of the household, his stepchildren, his adopted children, his foster-children, and the issue of these persons, if they are of German or related blood.

SECTION 5. *Household Membership.* [Definitions and conditions.]

SECTION 6. *Authority.* [Decisions rest with the county or city chiefs.]

SECTION 7. *Payment of Child Subsidies.* [Payment is quarterly.]

SECTION 8. *Revocation.* [County and city chiefs may revoke the subsidy.]

SECTION 9. *Objection.* [Authorities of the National Socialist German Workers Party (N.S.D.A.P.) may register objections, upon which the county or city chief must act positively.]

SECTION 10. *Complaints.* [Procedure for complaints against refusal, revocation, or suspension.]

SECTION 11. *Reclamation.* [Procedure for recovery of subsidies improperly paid.]

SECTION 12. *Child Subsidy List.* [Only N.S.D.A.P. authorities may see the list of recipients.]

SECTION 13. [The claim to a subsidy shall not be negotiable, but may be applied to obligations to the Government General.]

SECTION 14. [Subsidies shall not be counted as public grants.]

SECTION 15. [Heads of households must report changes in their situation as regards subsidies.]

SECTION 16. [First subsidies shall be paid for January, 1942.]

SECTION 17. [The administration of the Government General, with N.S.D.A.P. authorities, may make further regulations.]

Cracow, March 10, 1942.

FRANK
Governor General

8. MISCELLANEOUS

Order concerning Prohibition of Dancing in the Government General, April 9, 1941 [48]

By virtue of the authority vested in me by the Governor General, I hereby order, effective as of today, a general prohibition of dancing in the territory of the Government General. This prohibition likewise applies to private parties. It does not apply to dance performances licensed by the authorities.

Cracow, April 9, 1941.

KUNDT
Acting First Secretary
Assistant First Secretary

[48] *Amtlicher Anzeiger für das Generalgouvernement*, 1941, No. 17.

UNION OF SOVIET SOCIALIST REPUBLICS [1]

Proclamation, November 15, 1941 [2]

In the interest of the safety of the country and the security of the property of the inhabitants, the combatting of terroristic bands and groups will be carried out by the authorities with all intensity.

The people are urged to give their active cooperation to this effort.

1. Anyone who observes suspicious elements, particularly parachute jumpers, escaped Soviet Russian officers or soldiers, spies or saboteurs, Soviet Russian officials, etc., or members of their families, or who has or obtains knowledge of their appearance or places to which they resort, must report this information immediately to the nearest German or non-German public agency.

2. Anyone who fails to make such a report or gives these enemies any kind of aid (maintenance, care, or any other assistance) will be shot.

3. Any member of a non-German public agency who does not immediately transmit a report made to him to the nearest German officer will be shot.

4. For information leading to the prevention of disruptions of public security and order, or to the apprehension of the offender, a reward to the amount of 5,000 rubles may be granted by the District Commissioner. Informers shall be assured that if they wish their names will be kept secret.

5. The residents of communities shall be collectively responsible for the security of communication lines passing in their vicinity—roads, railways, wires, and all other German installations. For neglect of this responsibility drastic proceedings will be taken against the residents, particularly against the responsible elders of communities, counties, and districts.

Riga, November 15, 1941.

LOHSE
Reich Commissioner for the Ostland

Decree concerning the Conditions of Employment of Eastern Workers, June 30, 1942 [3]

The Ministerial Council for Defense of the Reich orders with force of law:

SECTION I. DEFINITION OF EASTERN WORKER

PARAGRAPH 1. Eastern workers are those laborers of non-German national origin who inhabited the Reich Commissariat for the Ukraine, the

[1] For additional documents relating to the U.S.S.R., see also documents under the Baltic States, above, pp. 300–12.

[2] *Verkündungsblatt für das Ostland*, 1941, p. 61.

[3] *Reichsgesetzblatt*, 1942, No. 71, p. 419.

General Commissariat for White Russia, or territories bordering on these territories to the east or on the former free states of Lithuania and Estonia, and who were brought into the German Reich, including the Protectorate of Bohemia and Moravia, and employed there after the occupation by the German armed forces.

SECTION II. CONDITIONS OF EMPLOYMENT

PARAGRAPH 2. *General Conditions.* The eastern workers employed in the Reich have an employment relationship of a special type. German labor code and labor protection provisions shall be applicable to them only in so far as specifically stated.

PARAGRAPH 3. *Compensation.* (1) The eastern workers employed in the Reich shall receive compensation graded according to their work.

(2) The amount of this compensation shall be determined from the tables which are attached as an appendix to this decree.

(3) In determining the compensation which is to be paid individual eastern workers under the appended tables, the point of departure (the reference wage [4]) shall be the wage-rate (hourly, piece, and premium wage-rates) of comparable German workers.

If a part of the reference wage consists of payment in goods, such payment shall be considered equivalent, in determining this wage, to the rate calculated for it for German workers in the enterprise in event of payment in cash.

Social security deductions and payments of all kinds to which the German workers are subject shall not be included in the determination of the reference wage.

With respect to incentive payments, these shall be computed, in determining the reference wage, at the same rate at which they are made to German workers in the enterprise for the same work. If the eastern worker's production falls behind the average production of a German worker, a correspondingly reduced reference wage will be the point of departure in determining the compensation to be paid him.

Extra pay for difficult work, dirty work, etc. shall be included in determining the proper reference wage for calculating the individual eastern worker's compensation.

(4) The eastern worker shall receive compensation only for work actually performed; but the regulations on idleness resulting from bad weather may be applied in his case.

(5) Higher compensation than that determined under these provisions may not be paid to eastern workers.

PARAGRAPH 4. *Extra Rates and Other Payments.* Except as otherwise provided by the General Manpower Authority, eastern workers shall have no claim to extra compensation for overtime or Sunday, holiday, and night

[4] That is, the rate used as a basis in the wage computations for eastern workers.—ED.

work. Per diem and maintenance payments, as well as travel and board expense payments, may not be made.

PARAGRAPH 5. *Payment in Goods.* (1) The compensation due the individual eastern worker according to the tables appended to this decree shall be paid in cash at the end of the regular pay period for the enterprise after deduction of the equivalent of payments made in goods. The board and room furnished by the employer shall be computed according to the rates specified by the tables appended to this decree. Other payment in goods, such as clothing, shoes, etc., shall be computed at proportionate prices.

(2) Employers may cover the commutation cost of eastern workers to and from the place of work for the entirety of eastern workers employed by them and make deductions for this expense from the amounts to be paid in cash according to the tables.

PARAGRAPH 6. *Compensation in Case of Illness.* For days on which the eastern worker is unable to work on account of sickness or accident, free board and room only shall be furnished by the employer, unless hospital care is given. In other respects the sick care of these workers shall be regulated by prescriptions issued by the Reich Minister of Labor.

PARAGRAPH 7. *Leave and Family Visits.* Leave and family visits will not be granted for the present. Detailed regulations concerning the institution of leave and family visits will be issued by the General Manpower Authority.

PARAGRAPH 8. *Pay Invoices.* Pay invoices shall not be issued to eastern workers.

PARAGRAPH 9. *Exceptions.* The Reich Trustee or Special Trustee of Labor may permit exceptions from the provisions of this decree in regard to the calculation of compensation.

SECTION III. EASTERN WORKERS TAX

PARAGRAPH 10. *Tax Obligation.* (1) Employers who use eastern workers within the German Reich, including the Protectorate of Bohemia and Moravia, are subject to a tax in amounts specified by the tables appended to this decree (Eastern Workers Tax).

(2) Agricultural employers must pay only one half of this tax.

PARAGRAPH 11. *Accruement of the Tax.* The Eastern Workers Tax accrues exclusively to the German Reich.

PARAGRAPH 12. *Tax Exemption of Eastern Workers.* Eastern workers must pay no wage tax nor citizen tax during their employment in the German Reich.

SECTION IV. SAVINGS

PARAGRAPH 13. Eastern workers may lay up their compensation in whole or in part as savings with interest: the sum saved is transferred to the saver's homeland, and is there available to him or to members of his family according to detailed regulations issued by the Reich Minister for the Occupied Eastern Territories or by the Commander in Chief of the Armed Forces.

SECTION V. GRANT OF POWERS

PARAGRAPH 14. (1) The General Manpower Authority shall be empowered to issue, in consultation with the interested Reich ministers, regulations for the execution, implementation, and revision of Sections I and II of this decree.

(2) The Reich Minister of Finance shall be empowered to issue, in consultation with the General Manpower Authority, the Reich Minister of the Interior, the Reich Minister for the Occupied Eastern Territories and, in so far as eastern workers employed in agriculture are in question, with the Reich Minister for Food and Agriculture, regulations for the execution, implementation, and revision of Section III of this decree.

(3) The Reich Minister of Finance, in consultation with the General Manpower Authority, may change by executive order the amounts of the Eastern Workers Tax as specified in the appended tables.

(4) The Reich Minister of Economic Affairs, the Reich Minister for the Occupied Eastern Territories, and the Commander in Chief of the Armed Forces shall be empowered to issue, in consultation with the General Manpower Authority, regulations for the execution and implementation of Section IV of this decree.

SECTION VI. EFFECTIVE DATE, SPHERE OF VALIDITY

PARAGRAPH 15. (1) This decree shall become effective June 15, 1942. The provisions of Sections II and III shall be first applicable to compensation paid after June 15, 1942.

(2) Sections 1 to 5 and Section 7, subsection 1, of the decree concerning taxing and treatment under the labor code for workers from the newly occupied eastern territories (StVAOst) of January 20, 1942 (*RGBl.* I, p. 41), as well as the regulation of the Reich Minister of Labor concerning treatment under the labor code for workers from the newly occupied eastern territories of February 9, 1942 (*Deutscher Reichsanz.* No. 37, of February 13, 1942), shall become invalid on the effective date of this decree.

(3) This decree shall be valid also in the Protectorate of Bohemia and Moravia and in the incorporated Eastern Territories.

Berlin, June 30, 1942.

The Chairman of the Ministerial Council for Defense of the Reich and Commissioner for the Four-Year Plan
GÖRING, *Reich Marshal*

The General Manpower Authority
By deputy: Dr. STUCKART

The Reich Minister and Chief of the Reich Chancellery
Dr. LAMMERS

APPENDIX

(To Paragraphs 3 and 10 of the Decree concerning Conditions of Employment for Eastern Workers)

TABLE OF COMPENSATION FOR EASTERN WORKERS

A.—Compensation Table at Day Rates

Gross wage of comparable German worker (Hourly wage, piece wage, premium wage) per day more than—to	Compensation of Eastern Workers			Eastern Workers Tax (Par. 10)
	Total per day (Sec. 2, Par. 3)	To be subtracted for free board and room	Amount to be paid	
in Reichsmarks	in Reichsmarks	in Reichsmarks	in Reichsmarks	in Reichsmarks
to 1.40	1.60	1.50	0.10	—
1.40— 1.45	1.62	1.50	0.12	—
1.45— 1.50	1.65	1.50	0.15	—
1.50— 1.60	1.67	1.50	0.17	—
1.60— 1.70	1.70	1.50	0.20	—
1.70— 1.80	1.72	1.50	0.22	—
1.80— 1.90	1.75	1.50	0.25	0.10
1.90— 2.00	1.80	1.50	0.30	0.15
2.00— 2.15	1.85	1.50	0.35	0.20
2.15— 2.30	1.90	1.50	0.40	0.30
2.30— 2.45	1.95	1.50	0.45	0.40
2.45— 2.60	2.00	1.50	0.50	0.50
2.60— 2.75	2.05	1.50	0.55	0.60
2.75— 2.90	2.10	1.50	0.60	0.70
2.90— 3.05	2.15	1.50	0.65	0.80
3.05— 3.20	2.20	1.50	0.70	0.90
3.20— 3.35	2.25	1.50	0.75	1.00
3.35— 3.50	2.30	1.50	0.80	1.10
3.50— 3.65	2.35	1.50	0.85	1.20
3.65— 3.80	2.40	1.50	0.90	1.30
3.80— 3.95	2.45	1.50	0.95	1.40
3.95— 4.10	2.50	1.50	1.00	1.50
4.10— 4.25	2.55	1.50	1.05	1.60
4.25— 4.40	2.60	1.50	1.10	1.70
4.40— 4.60	2.65	1.50	1.15	1.80
4.60— 4.80	2.70	1.50	1.20	1.95
4.80— 5.00	2.75	1.50	1.25	2.10
5.00— 5.20	2.80	1.50	1.30	2.25
5.20— 5.40	2.85	1.50	1.35	2.40
5.40— 5.60	2.90	1.50	1.40	2.55
5.60— 5.80	2.95	1.50	1.45	2.70
5.80— 6.00	3.00	1.50	1.50	2.85
6.00— 6.20	3.05	1.50	1.55	3.00
6.20— 6.40	3.10	1.50	1.60	3.15
6.40— 6.60	3.15	1.50	1.65	3.30
6.60— 6.80	3.20	1.50	1.70	3.45
6.80— 7.00	3.25	1.50	1.75	3.60
7.00— 7.25	3.30	1.50	1.80	3.75
7.25— 7.50	3.35	1.50	1.85	3.90
7.50— 7.75	3.40	1.50	1.90	4.05
7.75— 8.00	3.45	1.50	1.95	4.25
8.00— 8.25	3.50	1.50	2.00	4.45
8.25— 8.50	3.55	1.50	2.05	4.65
8.50— 8.75	3.60	1.50	2.10	4.85
8.75— 9.00	3.65	1.50	2.15	5.05
9.00— 9.25	3.70	1.50	2.20	5.25
9.25— 9.50	3.75	1.50	2.25	5.45
9.50— 9.75	3.80	1.50	2.30	5.65
9.75—10.00	3.85	1.50	2.35	5.85
10.00—10.25	3.90	1.50	2.40	6.05
10.25—10.50	3.95	1.50	2.45	6.25
10.50—10.75	4.00	1.50	2.50	6.45
10.75—11.00	4.05	1.50	2.55	6.65
11.00—11.25	4.10	1.50	2.60	6.85
11.25—11.50	4.15	1.50	2.65	7.05
11.50—11.75	4.20	1.50	2.70	7.25
11.75—12.00	4.25	1.50	2.75	7.45
12.00—12.25	4.30	1.50	2.80	7.65
12.25—12.50	4.35	1.50	2.85	7.85
12.50—12.75	4.40	1.50	2.90	8.05
12.75—13.00	4.45	1.50	2.95	8.25

For each additional 25 Reichspfennigs the total compensation and the amount to be paid shall each be increased by 0.05 Reichsmark and the Eastern Workers Tax by 0.20 Reichsmark.

B.—Compensation Table at Weekly Rates

Gross wage of comparable German worker (Hourly wage, piece wage, premium wage) per week more than—to	Compensation of Eastern Workers			Eastern Workers Tax (Par. 10)
	Total per week (Sec. 2, Par. 3)	To be subtracted for free board and room	Amount to be paid	
in Reichsmarks	in Reichsmarks	in Reichsmarks	in Reichsmarks	in Reichsmarks
to— 9.80	11.20	10.50	0.70	—
9.80—10.15	11.34	10.50	0.84	—
10.15—10.50	11.55	10.50	1.05	—
10.50—11.20	11.69	10.50	1.19	—
11.20—11.90	11.90	10.50	1.40	—
11.90—12.60	12.04	10.50	1.54	—
12.60—13.30	12.25	10.50	1.75	0.70
13.30—14.00	12.60	10.50	2.10	1.05
14.00—15.05	12.95	10.50	2.45	1.40
15.05—16.10	13.30	10.50	2.80	2.10
16.10—17.15	13.65	10.50	3.15	2.80
17.15—18.20	14.00	10.50	3.50	3.50
18.20—19.25	14.35	10.50	3.85	4.20
19.25—20.30	14.70	10.50	4.20	4.90
20.30—21.35	15.05	10.50	4.55	5.60
21.35—22.40	15.40	10.50	4.90	6.30
22.40—23.45	15.75	10.50	5.25	7.00
23.45—24.50	16.10	10.50	5.60	7.70
24.50—25.55	16.45	10.50	5.95	8.40
25.55—26.60	16.80	10.50	6.30	9.10
26.60—27.65	17.15	10.50	6.65	9.80
27.65—28.70	17.50	10.50	7.00	10.50
28.70—29.75	17.85	10.50	7.35	11.20
29.75—30.80	18.20	10.50	7.70	11.90
30.80—32.20	18.55	10.50	8.05	12.60
32.20—33.60	18.90	10.50	8.40	13.65
33.60—35.00	19.25	10.50	8.75	14.70
35.00—36.40	19.60	10.50	9.10	15.75
36.40—37.80	19.95	10.50	9.45	16.80
37.80—39.20	20.30	10.50	9.80	17.85
39.20—40.60	20.65	10.50	10.15	18.90
40.60—42.00	21.00	10.50	10.50	19.95
42.00—43.40	21.35	10.50	10.85	21.00
43.40—44.80	21.70	10.50	11.20	22.05
44.80—46.20	22.05	10.50	11.55	23.10
46.20—47.60	22.40	10.50	11.90	24.15
47.60—49.00	22.75	10.50	12.25	25.20
49.00—50.75	23.10	10.50	12.60	26.25
50.75—52.50	23.45	10.50	12.95	27.30
52.50—54.25	23.80	10.50	13.30	28.35
54.25—56.00	24.15	10.50	13.65	29.75
56.00—57.75	24.50	10.50	14.00	31.15
57.75—59.50	24.85	10.50	14.35	32.55
59.50—61.25	25.20	10.50	14.70	33.95
61.25—63.00	25.55	10.50	15.05	35.35
63.00—64.75	25.90	10.50	15.40	36.75
64.75—66.50	26.25	10.50	15.75	38.15
66.50—68.25	26.60	10.50	16.10	39.55
68.25—70.00	26.95	10.50	16.45	40.95
70.00—71.75	27.30	10.50	16.80	42.35
71.75—73.50	27.65	10.50	17.15	43.75
73.50—75.25	28.00	10.50	17.50	45.15
75.25—77.00	28.35	10.50	17.85	46.55
77.00—78.75	28.70	10.50	18.20	47.95
78.75—80.50	29.05	10.50	18.55	49.35
80.50—82.25	29.40	10.50	18.90	50.75
82.25—84.00	29.75	10.50	19.25	52.15
84.00—85.75	30.10	10.50	19.60	53.55
85.75—87.50	30.45	10.50	19.95	54.95
87.50—89.25	30.80	10.50	20.30	56.35
89.25—91.00	31.15	10.50	20.65	57.75

For each additional 1.75 Reichsmarks the total compensation and the amount to be paid shall be increased by 0.35 Reichsmark and the Eastern Workers Tax by 1.40 Reichsmarks.

C.—Compensation Table at Monthly Rates

Gross Wage of comparable German worker (Hourly wage, piece wage premium wage) per month more than—to in Reichsmarks	Compensation of Eastern Workers			Eastern Workers Tax (Par. 10) in Reichsmarks
	Total per month (Sec. 2, Par. 3) in Reichsmarks	To be subtracted for free board and room in Reichsmarks	Amount to be paid in Reichsmarks	
to 42.00	48.00	45.00	3.00	—
42.00— 43.50	48.60	45.00	3.60	—
43.50— 45.00	49.50	45.00	4.50	—
45.00— 48.00	50.10	45.00	5.10	—
48.00— 51.00	51.00	45.00	6.00	—
51.00— 54.00	51.60	45.00	6.60	—
54.00— 57.00	52.50	45.00	7.50	3.00
57.00— 60.00	54.00	45.00	9.00	4.50
60.00— 64.50	55.50	45.00	10.50	6.00
64.50— 69.00	57.00	45.00	12.00	9.00
69.00— 73.50	58.50	45.00	13.50	12.00
73.50— 78.00	60.00	45.00	15.00	15.00
78.50— 82.50	61.50	45.00	16.50	18.00
82.50— 87.00	63.00	45.00	18.00	21.00
87.00— 91.50	64.50	45.00	19.50	24.00
91.50— 96.00	66.00	45.00	21.00	27.00
96.00—100.50	67.50	45.00	22.50	30.00
100.50—105.00	69.00	45.00	24.00	33.00
105.00—109.50	70.50	45.00	25.50	36.00
109.50—114.00	72.00	45.00	27.00	39.00
114.00—118.50	73.50	45.00	28.50	42.00
118.50—123.00	75.00	45.00	30.00	45.00
123.00—127.50	76.50	45.00	31.50	48.00
127.50—132.00	78.00	45.00	33.00	51.00
132.00—138.00	79.50	45.00	34.50	54.00
138.00—144.00	81.00	45.00	36.00	58.50
144.00—150.00	82.50	45.00	37.50	63.00
150.00—156.00	84.00	45.00	39.00	67.50
156.00—162.00	85.50	45.00	40.50	72.00
162.00—168.00	87.00	45.00	42.00	76.50
168.00—174.00	88.50	45.00	43.50	81.00
174.00—180.00	90.00	45.00	45.00	85.50
180.00—186.00	91.50	45.00	46.50	90.00
186.00—192.00	93.00	45.00	48.00	94.50
192.00—198.00	94.50	45.00	49.50	99.00
198.00—204.00	96.00	45.00	51.00	103.50
204.00—210.00	97.50	45.00	52.50	108.00
210.00—217.50	99.00	45.00	54.00	112.50
217.50—225.00	100.50	45.00	55.50	117.00
225.00—232.50	102.00	45.00	57.00	121.50
232.50—240.00	103.50	45.00	58.50	127.50
240.00—247.50	105.00	45.00	60.00	133.50
247.50—255.00	106.50	45.00	61.50	139.50
255.00—262.50	108.00	45.00	63.00	145.50
262.50—270.00	109.50	45.00	64.50	151.50
270.00—277.50	111.00	45.00	66.00	157.50
277.50—285.00	112.50	45.00	67.50	163.50
285.00—292.50	114.00	45.00	69.00	169.50
292.50—300.00	115.50	45.00	70.50	175.50
300.00—307.50	117.00	45.00	72.00	181.50
307.50—315.00	118.50	45.00	73.50	187.50
315.00—322.50	120.00	45.00	75.00	193.50
322.50—330.00	121.50	45.00	76.50	199.50
330.00—337.50	123.00	45.00	78.00	205.50
337.50—345.00	124.50	45.00	79.50	211.50
345.00—352.50	126.00	45.00	81.00	217.50
352.50—360.00	127.50	45.00	82.50	223.50
360.00—367.50	129.00	45.00	84.00	229.50
367.50—375.00	130.50	45.00	85.50	235.50
375.00—382.50	132.00	45.00	87.00	241.50
382.50—390.00	133.50	45.00	88.50	247.50

For each additional 7.50 Reichsmarks the total compensation and the amount to be paid shall be increased by 1.50 Reichsmarks and the Eastern Workers Tax by 6.00 Reichsmarks.

For a one-day pay period use Table A
For a 10-day pay period use Table A with a factor of 10
For a weekly pay period use Table B
For a bi-weekly pay period use Table B with a factor of 2
For a 4-week pay period use Table B with a factor of 4
For a monthly pay period use Table C

BESSARABIA AND BUKOVINA

Decree-Law for the Creation of a National Center for Rumanianization, May 2, 1941[1]

[EXCERPTS]

ARTICLE 1. Attached to the presidency of the Council of Ministers, in the Undersecretariat of State for Rumanianization, Colonization, and Inventorization, there shall be created, as of the date of the present decree, a National Center for Rumanianization, which shall be a legal entity and shall have as its purpose the Rumanianization of properties incorporated into the domain of the state and also the Rumanianization of economic life.

ARTICLE 2. The property which is to be under the control and administration of the National Center for Rumanianization shall consist of all properties which shall have been taken over by the state on the basis of the decree-laws of October 5, 1940, November 17, 1940, December 4, 1940, March 28, 1941, March 29, 1941, the treaty with Germany of October 22, 1940, and the treaty with Bulgaria of September 7, 1940, all property belonging to it as of the date of the present decree-law, as well as all other properties which may come into its possession in the future.

ARTICLE 3. The National Center for Rumanianization shall carry out the following functions:

a) It shall organize, direct, and supervise the taking into possession of properties which have been taken over by the state.

For this purpose the National Center for Rumanianization shall be authorized to make such inquiries as it may deem necessary for locating properties which were not declared by Jews. It may for this purpose request the cooperation of all authorities.

b) It shall temporarily administer the property, and it shall keep files and accounts.

c) It shall apportion and liquidate the properties in accordance with regulations established by the present decree-law.

d) It shall issue bonds for the payment of indemnities to former Jewish owners and to creditors.

e) It shall pay the coupons of such bonds.

f) It shall amortize the revenue due to creditors who are not Jews.

g) It shall supervise and amortize the revenue which shall be due to Jews.

h) It shall assist in Rumanianizing economic, commercial, and industrial life.

ARTICLE 4. The organs which administer the National Center for Rumanianization shall be the following:

a) The Interministerial Committee.

b) The Advisory Commission; the legal bodies; the Central Judiciary Board.

[1] *Monitorul oficial*, No. 102, May 3, 1941.

The executive organs are:

a) The Administrative Council.
b) The Board of Directors.

The organ of control is the Board of Control.

. . . . .

ARTICLE 43. The properties taken over by the state can be sold, leased, or used only by persons of Rumanian ethnic origin, by partnerships or limited companies of which the members are Rumanian by origin, or by stock companies or limited joint-stock companies of which the major part of the capital belongs to persons of Rumanian ethnic origin.

. . . . .

ARTICLE 46. Personal property shall be sold by the National Center for Rumanianization at its discretion. If the value of the properties exceeds 500,000 lei, the sale may be made only by authorization of the Interministerial Committee.

. . . . .

ARTICLE 53. For properties taken over by the state in accordance with the decrees of October 5, 1940, November 17, 1940, December 4, 1940, and March 28, 1941, indemnity shall be paid to the former Jewish owners in the form of 3 per cent bonds.

ARTICLE 54. The indemnity paid to former Jewish owners shall be equal to eight times the gross income from such property as fixed for taxation purposes at the date when the properties were taken over by the state, or at a reduced value in accordance with Article 13 of the decree of March 28, 1941, relating to urban properties taken over by the state.

. . . . .

ARTICLE 56. . . . Mortgagees who are not Jews shall be paid in cash. They have no right to receive more than the price obtained through sale of the properties by the Undersecretariat for Rumanianization, Colonization, and Inventorization through the office of the National Center for Rumanianization.

Mortgagees shall be paid the difference up to the total amount of the debt secured by the mortgage, in the same way that non-Jewish creditors are paid.

ARTICLE 57. The National Center for Rumanianization shall be authorized to issue bonds in value equal to the indemnity due to former owners, in accordance with a decision by the Judiciary Board.

The bonds which are due to Jews shall be perpetual.

. . . . .

Given in Bucharest, May 2, 1941.

General ION ANTONESCU, *Leader of the State of Rumania and President of the Council of Ministers*
MIHAI A. ANTONESCU, *Minister of State*
CONST. STOICESCU, *Minister of Justice*
Brigadier General, N. STOENESCU, *Minister of Finance*

Proclamation by the Presidency of the Council of Ministers concerning the Return of Refugees and Entry on the Territory of Bessarabia and Bukovina, July 25, 1941 [2]

As from today, the 25th of July, 1941, entry into Bessarabia and Bukovina shall be permitted.

Persons belonging to Rumanian or German ethnic groups who are landowners, business men, or industrialists, and who desire to return to Bessarabia and to Bukovina shall file applications with the Civil-Military Cabinet for Administration of Bessarabia and Bukovina established at the presidency of the Council of Ministers.

Landowners shall present their petitions endorsed with the visa of the Ministry of Agriculture and Domains.

As to business men and industrialists, the petition shall bear the visa of the Minister of National Economy.

Refugees from Bessarabia and Bukovina who have received parcels of land for cultivation from the Undersecretariat of State for Rumanianization, Colonization, and Inventorization (*Subsecretariatul de Stat al Românizării, Colonizării și Inventarului*) must be provided with a visa from the ministries of Agriculture and National Economy only if they have first obtained authorization from the Ministerial Committee of the Undersecretariat of State for Rumanianization, Colonization, and Inventorization.

Until communications have been completely organized and traffic with Bessarabia and Bukovina has been freely established, persons who have received authorization to enter the territory of these provinces cannot return unless they receive an authorization from local authorities.

The public officials in charge of various functions in the territories of Bessarabia and Bukovina may enter these provinces without any other formality than an entry authorization issued by the ministry which has appointed them, and on the responsibility of the office concerned.

Bucharest, July 25, 1941, No. 258.

TRANSNISTRIA

Decree-Law concerning Ownership of Goods Left by the Retreating Enemy, and concerning Introduction of Capital Punishment for Certain Offenses Committed behind the Lines or on the Territory Reoccupied by the Armies on the Rumanian-Russian Front, July 9, 1941 [3]

General Ion Antonescu, Leader of the Rumanian State and President of the Council of Ministers.

[2] *Monitorul oficial*, No. 175, July 26, 1941. [3] *Ibid.*, No. 161, July 10, 1941.

By virtue of decree-laws 3,052 of September 5 and 3,072 of September 7, 1940,

We have decreed and we decree:

[Title of the decree-law.]

ARTICLE I. Stocks and materials of every kind left in the course of the retreat of the enemy are declared the property of the state of Rumania.

The military and administrative authorities may make use thereof for the needs of the population.

Every person who has knowledge of or is in possession of such goods and stocks must surrender them to the Rumanian authorities, or divulge the name of the possessor thereof within twenty-four hours after the publication of the decree-law.

ARTICLE II. Arms of every kind, or material left by the enemy, which the military authorities have not yet taken over must be surrendered or declared within twenty-four hours from the publication of this decree-law.

ARTICLE III. Persons who violate the above regulations, as well as persons who attack German or Rumanian soldiers or the civilian population, or those who destroy or injure stocks or goods, or attempt to commit acts of espionage or of sabotage behind the armies or in the territories occupied by them, shall be punished by death.

The trial and execution shall take place within twenty-four hours.

In case of *flagrante delicto*, the culprit shall be executed on the spot.

Given in headquarters, July 9, 1941.

General ION ANTONESCU

Leader of the Rumanian State and President of the Council of Ministers

Decree-Law No. 252 concerning the Prohibition of Use of Secret Mail in Transnistria, March 28, 1942 [4]

Antonescu, Marshal of Rumania and Leader of State.

Pursuant to Decree-Laws No. 3052 of September 5 and No. 3072 of September 7, 1940; and in accordance with report No. 43,194 of 1942 of the ministers of Public Works, Communications, and Justice,

We have decreed and we decree:

[Title of the decree-law.]

ARTICLE 1. Whoever shall receive with intent to transport and to distribute, or whoever transports or distributes, objects of correspondence, money, or valuables, or packages which are comprised within the postal

[4] *Monitorul oficial*, No. 76, March 30, 1942.

monopoly of the state, if their destination is to the inhabitants of the other side of the Dniester River or to persons on this side of the Dniester River, if the expedition is made from Transnistria, shall be punished by a term of imprisonment of from three to five years.

The same penalty shall apply to accomplices and accessories before and after the fact.

Correspondence, objects, packages, money, or valuables which are sent through secret mail shall be confiscated.

ARTICLE 2. If the culprit is a public official or a member of the armed forces, the penalty provided for in Article 1 shall be doubled.

ARTICLE 3. The investigation and the trial of offenses provided for in this law shall be carried out in accordance with regulations provided for the trial of *flagrante delicto*.

Given in Bucharest, March 28, 1942.

ANTONESCU, *Marshal of Rumania and Leader of the State*
CONSTANTIN D. BUȘILĂ, *Minister of Public Works and Communications*
CONSTANTIN C. STOICESCU, *Minister of Justice*

Decree-Law No. 698 for the Institution of the Death Penalty for Jews Who Were Sent to Transnistria and Who Have Returned Fraudulently to this Country, September 19, 1942[5]

Antonescu, Marshal of Rumania and Leader of the State.

After having seen the report of the ministers of National Defense and Justice, No. 2400 of September 19, 1942,

Pursuant to Decree-Law No. 3052 of September 5, and No. 3072 of September 7, 1940,

We have decreed and we decree:

[Title of the decree-law.]

ARTICLE 1. Jews of both sexes, above fifteen years of age, deported to Transnistria shall be punished by death if they return fraudulently to this country.

ARTICLE 2. Whoever facilitates the fraudulent return of Jews into this country shall be punished by a term of forced labor of from five to twenty-five years.

The same penalty shall be applied to accomplices and accessories before and after the fact.

ARTICLE 3. The trial of offenses provided for by the present decree-law lies within the jurisdiction of military courts.

[5] *Monitorul oficial*, No. 221, September 22, 1942.

ARTICLE 4. All other regulations contrary to this decree-law are abrogated.

Given in Bucharest, September 19, 1942.

ANTONESCU, *Marshal of Rumania and Leader of State*
CONSTANTIN PANTAZI, *Minister of National Defense, Division General*
JON C. MARINESCU, *Minister of Justice*

YUGOSLAVIA

I. ITALIAN LAWS OF OCCUPATION BEFORE THE DIVISION OF YUGOSLAVIA

1. ADMINISTRATION AND JUDICIARY

Proclamation of the Duce on Measures concerning the Administration of Justice in the Territories Formerly Forming Part of the Yugoslav State and Occupied by the Italian Armed Forces, April 24, 1941 [1]

[EXCERPT]

ARTICLE 1. The legislation in force in the territories of the former Kingdom of Yugoslavia occupied by the Italian armed forces in matters of civil, commercial, exchange, and penal law shall continue in effect, except as may be otherwise established by special regulations issued by the Italian authorities.

. . . . .

MUSSOLINI

Proclamation of the Duce on Authority to Appoint Extraordinary Commissioners for the Navigation Associations in the Territories of the Former Kingdom of Yugoslavia Occupied by the Italian Armed Forces, May 6, 1941 [2]

[EXCERPTS]

ARTICLE 1. For the navigation associations having seats in the territories of the former Kingdom of Yugoslavia occupied by the Italian armed forces, extraordinary commissioners may be appointed by order of the Supreme Command on the nomination of the Minister of Communications.

The extraordinary commissioners shall have the powers conferred upon the ordinary administrative officers of the associations.

ARTICLE 2. The regulations established by local legislation for the publication and registration of the constitutional documents of commercial associations shall also be observed, in so far as they are applicable, by the competent civil commissioner with respect to the appointment of the extraordinary commissioners.

ARTICLE 3. Upon taking up their duties, the extraordinary commissioners shall make an inventory of the activities in progress. The inventory shall be prepared with the assistance of an officer delegated by the local commander of the Italian armed forces of occupation and of the present legal

[1] *Gazzetta ufficiale,* 1941, No. 99, p. 1630. [2] *Ibid.*, No. 111, p. 1844.

representative of the association or, in the absence of such legal representative, of two witnesses.

ARTICLE 4. The extraordinary commissioners shall make a quarterly report of their activities to the competent civil commissioner, within whose jurisdiction lies the authorization of acts which go beyond the regular administrative routine.

. . . . .

General Headquarters of the Armed Forces, May 6, 1941–XIX.

MUSSOLINI

Proclamation of the Duce on Administrative and Judiciary Organization in the Territory of the Former Kingdom of Yugoslavia Occupied by the Italian Armed Forces, May 17, 1941 [3]

[EXCERPT]

PART I. ADMINISTRATIVE ORGANIZATION

ARTICLE 1. *Exercise of Civil Authority. Appointment of Civil Commissioners.* In the territory of the former Kingdom of Yugoslavia occupied by the Italian armed forces, the civil authority in the sense of Articles 16 and 54 to 66 of the war laws shall be exercised by civil commissioners.

Provision for the appointment and if necessary the recall of civil commissioners shall be made by an order of the Supreme Command.

The order which appoints a civil commissioner shall determine the territory in which he is to exercise the authority granted him.

ARTICLE 2. *Responsibility of Civil Commissioners.* The civil commissioners are responsible to the Supreme Command. However, the Supreme Command may provide that a civil commissioner be responsible in the exercise of some or all of his powers to the local commander of a major unit of the armed forces of occupation.

In any case the civil commissioners shall be required to observe the instructions given by the commanders of the aforesaid major units in all matters concerning public order, as well as the security and activities of the armed forces of occupation.

ARTICLE 3. *Powers of the Civil Commissioner.* The civil commissioner shall exercise the powers formerly attributed by local ordinances to the highest regional governing authority.

In particular, he shall take measures to ensure public order and safety and he shall see that family honor and rights, individual life, and private property, as well as religious faiths and the performance of acts of worship are respected.

[3] *Gazzetta ufficiale,* 1941, No. 116, p. 1912.

ARTICLE 4. *Civil Officials of the Occupied Territory.* The authorities and civil officials of the occupied territory shall be retained in the performance of their duties in accordance with the ordinances there in force; but the civil commissioner may, for the sake of public order or political or military requirements, provide for their replacement.

The civil commissioner shall in addition have the power to provide for the appointment of civil officials in case of vacancy in the respective offices.

When the civil commissioner exercises the power of appointment or replacement in respect to elective offices of local administration, the duties pertaining to such offices shall be entrusted to an extraordinary commissioner, preferably chosen from among the inhabitants of the territory.

ARTICLE 5. *Effectiveness of the Provisions of the Administrative Authorities.* The decisions and provisions of the administrative authorities of the occupied territory, which under the local laws are subject to approval, ratification, or review by a higher authority, shall not be effective unless they have also been reviewed by the civil commissioner, who shall be empowered to withhold approval when he considers that the decision or the provision is not in order or is inconsistent with the needs of the civilian population or of the armed forces of occupation. Such review shall supplant the approval, ratification, or review by a superior authority which does not have its seat in the territory occupied by the Italian armed forces.

In any case, provisions designed to regulate matters affecting the general public, shall be subject to the review provided in the foregoing paragraph.

The civil commissioner shall have the power to demand at any time that any decision or provision of the aforementioned administrative authorities be communicated to him, and to countermand or suspend its execution.

ARTICLE 6. *Power of the Civil Commissioner to Issue Ordinances.* The civil commissioner may issue ordinances in regard to public works, police matters, hygiene, supplies and consumption, or local finance for urgent reasons affecting the public interest and relating, in whole or in part, to the territory under his jurisdiction.

Violators of the ordinances authorized in the foregoing paragraph shall be punished, unless the deed constitutes a more serious offense, by imprisonment up to six months or by fine up to 5,000 lire.

ARTICLE 7. *Safe-Conduct for Return into Occupied Territory.* Inhabitants of the territory occupied by the Italian armed forces who, after having moved away, wish to return, must provide themselves with a special safe-conduct issued by the military authorities and approved by the civil commissioner.

PART II. JUDICIAL ORGANIZATION

ARTICLE 8. *Judicial Institutions.* In the territory of the former Kingdom of Yugoslavia occupied by the Italian armed forces justice shall continue to be administered in civil, commercial, and criminal cases by the competent justices, tribunals, and courts of appeal as determined by the judicial regulations in force there.

The territorial jurisdictions of individual judiciary authorities shall remain unchanged except as prescribed in the following article.

ARTICLE 9. *Territorial Jurisdiction.* The portions of the territory which are included in the jurisdictions of justices, tribunals, or courts of appeal which have their seats outside of this territory shall be attached by provision of the commander of the occupation troops to the respective jurisdictions of justices, tribunals, and courts of appeal established in the occupied territory.

The aforesaid commander shall make provision therefor in consultation with the competent civil commissioners. The ordinances issued for such purposes shall be published by posting in the public registers.

ARTICLE 10. *Use of the Italian Language.* In the jurisdictions of the tribunals of Sussak, Sebenico, Spalato, Ragusa, and Cattaro the Italian language shall be used:

1. In civil cases, for the decision of the judge when that language has been used in the action which introduced the suit or in the charges.
2. In criminal processes, for the argument of the case and for the decision of the judge when the plaintiff requests it.

In any case, the parties and their counsels shall be permitted to use the Italian language in the proceedings.

ARTICLE 11. *Jurisdiction of Military Tribunals.* The jurisdiction of the Italian military tribunals in the sense of Article 4 of the proclamation of April 24, 1941–XIX, shall remain unchanged.

To these military tribunals shall be assigned the trial of offenses defined by proclamations issued in the occupied territory.

ARTICLE 12. *Execution of Fines.* A sentence of fine pronounced by military tribunals in the territory of the former Kingdom of Yugoslavia occupied by the Italian armed forces may be executed by payment in dinari according to the rate of exchange established between Italian money and that which is legally current in this territory.

ARTICLE 13. *Appeals to the Supreme Court.* With respect to the territory specified in the preceding article, the jurisdiction pertaining under the terms of local laws to the Supreme Court shall be transferred to the Appellate Courts of Spalato and of Podgorica for the appeals from decisions handed down by the tribunals of the respective districts and to the Italian Supreme Court (*Corte di Cassazione*) for appeals from decisions of those courts.

PART III. MISCELLANEOUS PROVISIONS

ARTICLE 14. *Validation of Terms and Prescriptions.* Effective June 10, 1941–XIX, the legal or conventional terms and prescriptions whose suspension was ordered by Article 3 of the proclamation of April 24, 1941–XIX, shall again be valid.

ARTICLE 15. *Prohibition of Exportation.* Without authorization in advance by the competent civil commissioner it is forbidden to export from the territory of the former Kingdom of Yugoslavia occupied by the Italian armed forces, any object which is of artistic, historical, archeological, or paleoethnological interest.

ARTICLE 16. *Publication.* The present proclamation shall be promulgated by insertion in the *Gazzetta ufficiale* of the Kingdom. It shall be posted in the record books of the communities within the territory of the former Kingdom of Yugoslavia occupied by Italian armed forces.

General Headquarters of the Armed Forces, May 17, 1941–XIX.

MUSSOLINI

2. CUSTOMS

Proclamation of the Duce on Regulations in regard to Customs in the Territories of the Former Kingdom of Yugoslavia Occupied by the Italian Armed Forces, April 29, 1941 [4]

[EXCERPTS]

ARTICLE 1. In the territories of the former Kingdom of Yugoslavia occupied by the Italian armed forces the validity of the tariffs and other customs laws and regulations formerly in effect in the territories of the former Kingdom of Yugoslavia shall remain unchanged.

Likewise shall the regulations previously in effect in the former Kingdom of Yugoslavia in regard to fiscal monopolies and domestic manufacturing, sales, and consumption taxes, remain unchanged in so far as they apply to goods imported and exported.

ARTICLE 2. Goods shipped from any territory other than that of the Italo-Albanian Customs Union shall be subject, upon entrance into the territories of the former Kingdom of Yugoslavia occupied by the Italian armed forces, to the payment of the import duties provided by the tariffs and by the regulations cited in Article 1 under the conditions laid down by these regulations.

The same treatment shall be accorded goods shipped from customs warehouses, from free warehouses and free points (*Punti franchi*) and from the free zones of the Kingdom of Italy, in so far as their national origin is not certified and they have been granted abatement or refund of duties or are being reexported after a temporary importation.

[4] *Gazzetta ufficiale*, 1941, No. 105, p. 1727.

ARTICLE 3. Goods consigned to any territory other than that of the Italo-Albanian Customs Union or to the free points of Trieste and Fiume shall be subject, upon export from the territories occupied by the Italian armed forces, to the payment of the export duties provided by the tariffs and by the regulations cited in Article 1 under the conditions laid down by these regulations and those of Article 3 of the proclamation of April 24, 1941–XIX.

ARTICLE 4. Goods originating in and shipped from the territories of the Italo-Albanian Customs Union, as well as those nationalized in Italy or in Albania, shall be admitted for importation into the territories of the former Kingdom of Yugoslavia occupied by the Italian armed forces with exemption from import duties provided by the customs tariffs of the former Kingdom of Yugoslavia.

When monopoly duties or domestic manufacturing or consumption taxes have been paid on such goods, in the territory of the Italo-Albanian Customs Union, but in lesser amount than that applicable, under the provisions of Article 1, in the territories occupied by the Italian armed forces, the goods shall be admitted for importation into these territories upon payment of the difference.

ARTICLE 5. Goods consigned to the territory of the Italo-Albanian Customs Union and to the free zones of Carnaro and of Zara shall be exempted, upon egress from the territories occupied by the Italian armed forces, from the payment of the duties provided by the tariffs and by the regulations cited in Article 1.

These goods shall not be granted a refund of the duties originally paid upon the raw materials used in their manufacture.

ARTICLE 6. The civil commissioners, in consultation with the military and customs authorities, shall have the power to regulate by ordinance, on the basis of exemption from frontier duties, the local retail trade with the territories of the former Kingdom of Yugoslavia adjoining those occupied by the Italian armed forces and included within a radius of fifteen kilometers from the borderline of occupation.

ARTICLE 7. The fiscal district of the city of Fiume shall be extended integrally to the town of Sussak.

The definition of the territory which will thus be included within the free zone of Carnaro shall be made by a commission appointed for this purpose by the prefect of Fiume and including, among others, the civil commissioner of Sussak and the representatives of the Italian Customs and Royal Finance Guards.

. . . . .

ARTICLE 8. The regulations which governed frontier trade prior to the outbreak of hostilities with the former Kingdom of Yugoslavia shall again be in effect with respect to the free zones of Carnaro and of Zara.

ARTICLE 9. The civil commissioner shall be authorized to make whatever provisions are necessary for the implementation of this proclamation, and in particular for the reactivation and the establishment of the customs offices. For this purpose the customs personnel of the former Kingdom of Yugoslavia recalled or reconfirmed in service may also be employed.

In every case officials of the Italian Royal Customs shall be delegated to every office with mandatory powers to safeguard the interests of the Italian administration.

The customs offices shall operate and make collections in the name of the Supreme Command.

The duties of vigilance and interception will be entrusted to the Italian Royal Finance Guards. Nevertheless, within the limits of the duties allotted to them and in accordance with the powers conferred upon them, the officials of the aforementioned offices shall also have jurisdiction to prosecute violations of the provisions of laws cited by this proclamation.

. . . . .

Headquarters of the Armed Forces, April 29, 1941–XIX.

MUSSOLINI

Royal Decree-Law No. 290 concerning Provisions in regard to Customs for Shipments of Goods between the Territories of the Italo-Albanian Customs Union and Those of the Former Kingdom of Yugoslavia Occupied by the Italian Armed Forces, April 30, 1941[5]

[EXCERPTS]

ARTICLE 1. Goods produced in the territories of the former Kingdom of Yugoslavia occupied by the Italian armed forces and those of any other origin which at the date of occupation were in circulation in those territories or stored in warehouses not connected with the customs office shall be regarded as nationalized by virtue of the occupation and shall be admitted for importation into the territory of the Italo-Albanian Customs Union with exemption from duties and from any other customs imposts in force.

Excepted from this rule are the classes of goods under state monopoly and goods subject to domestic manufacturing, consumption, or general taxes upon entrance, for which the application of regulations and of duties in force in Italy and in Albania, respectively, shall remain unaffected.

ARTICLE 2. Goods produced in the territories of the former Kingdom of Yugoslavia occupied by the Italian armed forces and those originating in any other territory not that of the Italo-Albanian Customs Union which have been discounted in the occupied territories in accordance with the regulations in force in the former Kingdom of Yugoslavia in payment of

[5] *Gazzetta ufficiale*, 1941, No. 105, p. 1724.

monopoly or tax duties or domestic manufacturing, sales, or consumption imposts or of duties or other frontier taxes of lesser amount than those provided by analogous regulations in force in the territory of the Italo-Albanian Customs Union, shall be admitted for importation into the territories of the Union upon payment of the difference.

ARTICLE 3. Goods coming from the territories of the Italo-Albanian Customs Union exported to the territories of the former Kingdom of Yugoslavia occupied by the Italian armed forces shall be regarded as appurtenant to the occupation forces and shall be passed with exemption from duties and other imposts of egress provided by the regulations in force in the Customs Union.

The abatement of duties upon these goods shall not affect the continued validity of the domestic imposts provided by the prevailing laws.

. . . .

Rome, April 30, 1941–XIX.

VICTOR EMMANUEL

MUSSOLINI—CIANO—DI REVEL—
TASSINARI—AMICUCCI—RICCARDI

Proclamation of the Duce on Regulations concerning the Control of Imports into the Territories of the Former Kingdom of Yugoslavia Occupied by the Italian Armed Forces, May 17, 1941 [6]

[EXCERPTS]

ARTICLE 1. The importation of goods into the territories of the former Kingdom of Yugoslavia occupied by the Italian armed forces from territories other than those of the Italian State and of the Kingdom of Albania shall be permitted only under authorization by the competent civil commissioner.

Permits issued under the foregoing paragraph shall prescribe the form and manner of payment for the goods imported, including deviations, when necessary, from the regulations in effect concerning the export of notes the face value of which is expressed in Yugoslav currency.

ARTICLE 2. The civil commissioners, even in other cases than those specified by Article 6 of the proclamation of April 29, 1941–XIX, published in *Gazzetta ufficiale* No. 105 of May 3, 1941–XIX, shall have the power to admit for importation from the territories of the former Kingdom of Yugoslavia not occupied by the Italian armed forces and from the Free Zones of Carnaro and Zara the types of consumers' goods necessary for the life of the civilian population and for the needs of the occupation troops, with exemption from tariffs and other customs duties.

[6] *Gazzetta ufficiale*, 1941, No. 119, p. 1956.

Exemption cannot be granted from domestic manufacturing, sales, and consumption imposts, for which the regulations in effect shall remain unchanged.

ARTICLE 3. In regard to the export of goods and other objects from the territories of the former Kingdom of Yugoslavia occupied by the Italian armed forces, the regulations of Article 3 of the proclamation of April 24, 1941-XIX, published in the *Gazzetta ufficiale* of the 25th of that month, shall remain unchanged.

. . . . .

General Headquarters of the Armed Forces, May 17, 1941-XIX.

MUSSOLINI

3. FINANCE

Proclamation of the Duce on Regulations concerning Payments to be Made in the Occupied Yugoslav Territory, April 16, 1941 [7]

[EXCERPTS]

ARTICLE 1. From the effective date of this decree, in the Yugoslav territory adjacent to the territory of the Kingdom of Italy occupied by the Italian armed forces, payments of any nature by the commands, units, and services of the occupation forces, as well as by persons attached to these forces or to their supplementary services, may be made in Italian lire.

ARTICLE 2. The exchange in the territory specified in the preceding article is fixed at the following rate: 100 dinari are equivalent to 30 Italian lire.

. . . . .

General Headquarters of the Armed Forces, April 16, 1941-XIX.

MUSSOLINI

Proclamation of the Duce on Regulations concerning Exchange and Currency in the Territories of the Former Kingdom of Yugoslavia Occupied by the Italian Armed Forces, April 24, 1941 [8]

[EXCERPTS]

ARTICLE 1. *Authorization of Payments in Italian Lire and Albanian Francs.* In the territory of the former Kingdom of Yugoslavia occupied by the Italian armed forces it is made mandatory to receive payments in Italian and Albanian currency, as well as in the local currency.

[7] *Gazzetta ufficiale*, 1941, No. 92, p. 1450. [8] *Ibid.*, No. 98, p. 1621.

Within the territorial limits specified in the preceding paragraph the rate of exchange is fixed as follows: 30 lire = 100 dinari (333.33 dinari = 100 lire); 4.80 Albanian francs = 100 dinari (2083.33 dinari = 100 Albanian francs).

Any negotiation which applies to the above-mentioned currencies a rate of exchange different from that established in the preceding paragraph is prohibited.

ARTICLE 2. *Negotiation of Foreign Currencies.* Any form of commerce in currencies other than the Italian, Albanian, or Yugoslav, as well as in stocks, bonds, and securities the face value of which is expressed in currencies other than the Italian, Albanian, or Yugoslav, shall be reserved exclusively to the National Institute for Foreign Exchange operating through the Bank of Italy, the National Bank of Albania, and the credit organizations authorized by the Supreme Command in consultation with the Minister of Currency and Exchange.

ARTICLE 3. *Prohibition concerning the Export of Merchandise and Other Items.* The export of merchandise or of any other item to territories other than those of the Italian State or of the Kingdom of Albania shall be permissible only with authorization in advance from the competent civil commissioner, who will determine for each case the conditions of the authorization, including matters in regard to the form and manner of payment. Authorization may not be granted for objects of artistic, archeological, or historical interest.

ARTICLE 4. *Introduction and Export of Notes of the State and of Italian, Albanian, and Yugoslav Banks.* Except as otherwise provided in the following paragraphs, it is prohibited:

1. To introduce from any territory other than those of the Italian State and of the Kingdom of Albania notes of the state and of Italian, Albanian, and Yugoslav banks.
2. To export to territories other than those of the Italian State or of the Kingdom of Albania notes of the state or of the banks specified in the foregoing item.

Persons who go from the territories of the former Kingdom of Yugoslavia occupied by the Italian armed forces into any territory other than that of the Italian State or of the Kingdom of Albania shall be permitted to carry with them Italian currency to the amount of 250 Italian lire or Albanian currency to the amount of 60 Albanian francs, or Yugoslav currency to the amount of 2,000 dinari.

Persons who go from any territory other than that of the Italian State or of the Kingdom of Albania into territories of the former Yugoslav Kingdom occupied by the Italian armed forces shall be permitted to carry with them Italian currency to the amount of 250 lire or Albanian currency to the amount of 60 Albanian francs.

Inhabitants of the territories of the former Kingdom of Yugoslavia occupied by the Italian armed forces who are returning permanently to these territories after having left them shall be permitted to carry with them Yugoslav currency to the amount of 2,000 dinari.

ARTICLE 5. *Introduction and Export of Checks, Promissory Notes, etc., Expressed in Italian, Albanian, or Yugoslav Currency.* Without authorization in advance from the competent civil commissioner, it is forbidden to introduce or to export from or into territories other than those of the Italian State or of the Kingdom of Albania checks, promissory notes, or any other kind of credits expressed in Italian, Albanian, or Yugoslav currency, except as specified in Articles 7 and 8 below.

ARTICLE 6. *Export of Foreign Currencies and of Other Foreign Media of Exchange.* Without authorization in advance from the competent civil commissioner, it is forbidden to export into territories other than those of the Italian State or of the Kingdom of Albania government notes or banknotes, promissory notes, checks, or any other sort of securities the face value of which is expressed in a currency other than the Italian, Albanian, or Yugoslav.

This prohibition shall not apply to persons who have obtained a certificate issued by the competent Italian or Albanian customs authority attesting the previous introduction of the notes and securities in question into territories of the Italian State or of the Kingdom of Albania or into territories of the former Kingdom of Yugoslavia.

ARTICLE 7. *Introduction of Government Securities and Stocks and Bonds.* The introduction from any territory other than that of the Italian State or of the Kingdom of Albania of government securities or stocks and bonds of any kind, the face value of which is expressed in any currency whatever, and of the corresponding dividend or interest vouchers, shall be permitted only through dispatch by mail to one of the banks or credit organizations specified in Article 2 and for the purposes stipulated in the following paragraph.

The banks or credit organizations above mentioned which receive by mail from territory other than that of the Italian State or of the Kingdom of Albania the aforementioned stocks, bonds, or securities may make deposits of them with the authorization of the competent civil commissioner if the deposit is to be made in favor of persons resident in the territories of the former Kingdom of Yugoslavia occupied by the Italian armed forces, or without necessity of authorization if it is to be made in favor of persons resident in territories other than those of the Italian State, of the Kingdom of Albania, or of the former Kingdom of Yugoslavia occupied by the Italian armed forces.

ARTICLE 8. *Export of Government Securities and Stocks and Bonds.* The export into territories other than those of the Italian State or of the Kingdom of Albania of government securities and stocks and bonds of any kind, the face value of which is expressed in any currency whatever, and of the corresponding dividend or interest vouchers, may take place only after authorization in advance by the competent civil commissioner.

ARTICLE 9. *Investments and Payments in Dinari.* It is prohibited, without authorization in advance from the competent civil commissioner:

1. To make investments and payments of sums in dinari on any security and in any manner involving the utilization of holdings in any currency whatever which are outstanding in territory other than that of the Italian State, the Kingdom of Albania, or territories of the former Kingdom of Yugoslavia occupied by the Italian armed forces.
2. To make such investments and payments involving the utilization of holdings in any currency whatever which are outstanding in the territory of the Italian State or of the Kingdom of Albania, or in the territories of the former Kingdom of Yugoslavia occupied by the Italian armed forces, in connection with persons resident outside of these territories.

ARTICLE 10. *Operations in Stocks, Bonds, and Securities.* It is prohibited, without authorization in advance from the competent civil commissioner:

1. To make any disposition, in favor of persons resident outside the territory of the Italian State, of the Kingdom of Albania, and of the territory of the former Kingdom of Yugoslavia occupied by the Italian armed forces, of government securities and stocks and bonds the face value of which is expressed in any currency whatever and which are outstanding in the territories of the former Kingdom of Yugoslavia occupied by the Italian armed forces or are placed on deposit there.
2. To make any disposition, in favor of persons resident in the territories of the Italian State, of the Kingdom of Albania, or the territories of the former Kingdom of Yugoslavia occupied by the Italian armed forces, of the stocks, bonds, and securities specified in the preceding paragraph in connection with persons resident outside the territory of the Italian State or the Kingdom of Albania, and of the territories of the former Kingdom of Yugoslavia occupied by the Italian armed forces.

ARTICLE 11. *Regulation of Local Retail Trade.* The civil commissioners shall be empowered to issue orders in consultation with the military and customs authorities regulating local retail trade with adjacent territories in deviation from the provisions of the preceding articles.

ARTICLE 12. *Violation of the Provisions of this Proclamation.* Jurisdiction to prosecute violations of the provisions of this proclamation shall lie with all persons in the territories of the former Kingdom of Yugoslavia occupied by the Italian armed forces who are vested with the functions of police magistrate, as well as with the officers of the Royal Customs and the postal officials within the limits of the services in which they are employed and according to the authority conferred upon them.

On the basis of the indictment a verbal process shall be drawn up, a copy of which shall be sent as notice to the violator.

The violations referred to in the first paragraph shall be punished, except as otherwise provided in the following article, in accordance with the provisions of Articles 2, 3, 4, 5, 6, 7, and 8 of the royal decree-law of December 5, 1938–XVII, No. 1928, converted into law of June 2, 1939–XVII, No. 739.

The competence granted by these articles to the Minister of Currency and Exchange shall rest, in the territories of the former Kingdom of Yugoslavia occupied by the Italian armed forces, with the Supreme Command or with the command of the forces of occupation as delegated by the Supreme Command.

ARTICLE 13. *Penal Measures in Matters of Currency and Exchange.* In the territories of the former Kingdom of Yugoslavia occupied by the Italian armed forces, the provisions of the law of July 28, 1939–XVII, No. 1097, shall be observed in so far as they are pertinent.

. . . . .

General Headquarters of the Armed Forces, April 24, 1941–XIX.

MUSSOLINI

Ministerial Decree concerning Regulations for Monetary Relations between the Territory of the Italian State and the Territories of the Former Kingdom of Yugoslavia Occupied by the Italian Armed Forces, as well as for the Introduction into Italy of Stocks, Bonds, and Securities, April 25, 1941 [9]

ARTICLE 1. It is prohibited to introduce into the territory of the Italian State Yugoslav or Greek government notes or bank notes, as well as money orders, checks, or any other kind of security, except stocks, the face value of which is expressed in terms of Yugoslav or Greek currency.

ARTICLE 2. The prevailing duties upon the exportation from the territory of the Italian State or upon the introduction into this territory of Italian government notes or bank notes or of money orders, checks, or any other kind of security the face value of which is expressed in Italian lire, shall not be applicable to the export and import of such notes and securities between the territory of the Italian State and the territories of the former Kingdom of Yugoslavia occupied by the Italian armed forces.

ARTICLE 3. The introduction into the territory of the Italian State of government securities and stocks and bonds of any sort, even though they be expressed in currency other than Italian, and of the corresponding coupons shall be permitted only if they are consigned by mail to the Bank of Italy or to one of the banks authorized to act as agent for the Bank of Italy, in the meaning of Article 10 of the ministerial decree of December 8, 1934–XIII.

It is prohibited to introduce in any other manner into the territory of the Italian State the securities specified in the preceding paragraph.

The banks indicated in the first paragraph of this article which receive by mail from abroad the aforementioned stocks, bonds, and securities may accept them for deposit or deposit them with any other bank in the territory

[9] *Gazzetta ufficiale*, 1941, No. 99, p. 1632.

of the Italian State designated by the person entitled to do so, without necessity for authorization from the National Institute for Foreign Exchange, provided that the deposit is to be made in favor of persons resident abroad. Any further movement of such deposits, and any movement of the stocks, bonds, and securities cited in the first paragraph with ownership abroad (even if they have entered the territory of the Italian State before the effective date of this decree) shall be conditional upon authorization in advance by the National Institute for Foreign Exchange.

ARTICLE 4. This decree shall become effective on the day of its publication in the *Gazzetta ufficiale* of the Kingdom.

Rome, April 25, 1941–XIX.

By the Minister: GATTI

II. LOWER STYRIA, CARINTHIA, AND CARNIOLA

(German Occupation)

Order concerning Money and Credit Institutions in Lower Styria, May 19, 1941 [10]

[EXCERPTS]

In order to organize the money and credit matters of the population in Lower Styria in accordance with its needs, I ordain, by virtue of the powers vested in me, as follows:

SECTION 1. The following banks shall be allowed to carry on banking business: the Creditanstalt-Bankverein A. G., Wien, to establish branches in Marburg and Celje; the Länderbank, to establish a bank in Marburg.

SECTION 2. County savings banks shall be established in Marburg, Celje, Pettan, and Rann.

. . . .

SECTION 5. The establishment of other money and credit institutions, including cooperatives and all preparatory measures, shall depend on my permission.

. . . .

SECTION 6. All other banks or branches thereof, savings banks, and agricultural cooperatives remaining in Lower Styria (*Untersteiermark*) shall wind up their business in accordance with special instructions of my plenipotentiary for banking and credit institutions. He shall appoint managers, who shall follow his instructions.

Marburg on the Drava, May 19, 1941.

UIBERREITHER

[10] *Verordnungs-und Amtsblatt*, 1941, No. 15, p. 106.

First Implementary Order to the Order concerning Money and Credit Institutions in Lower Styria, June 5, 1941

[EXCERPTS]

SECTION 2. The new savings banks shall be administered by a Board of Managers. This board shall consist of a political commissioner and the manager of the savings bank. The political commissioner may appoint for himself a deputy. He is also authorized to decide whether the manager shall have a deputy from among the officials and clerks of the savings bank. The Board of Managers shall appoint the officials and clerks of the savings bank. The manager shall be appointed by the Chief of Civil Administration.

The manager is the superior of all other officials of the savings bank and shall be responsible to the political commissioner as to the course of business and accountability.

. . . . .

Payments out of previous deposits may be made within the limits established by the Board of Managers of the savings banks, provided the Chief of Civil Administration has issued detailed orders thereon.

. . . . .

SECTION 8. The former savings banks or their branches in the headquarters of the new savings banks shall furnish for an adequate consideration, as far as may be necessary, premises, business equipment, and personnel.

Marburg on the Drava, June 5, 1941.

By proxy: DR. MÜLLER—HACCIUS

20th Decree regarding the Introduction of Reichsmark Currency and the Withdrawal from Circulation of the Dinar and the "Reichskreditkassenscheine" in the Occupied Territories of Carinthia and Carniola, May 23, 1941 [11]

[EXCERPTS]

By virtue of the special powers conferred upon me, I hereby decree:

SECTION 1. (1) The Reichsmark shall be legal tender in the occupied territories of Carinthia and Carniola. (2) After June 15, 1941, the dinar and the *Reichskreditkassenscheine* shall no longer be legal tender in the occupied territories of Carinthia and Carniola.

[11] *Verordnungsblatt des Chefs der Zivilverwaltung in den besetzten Gebieten von Kärnten und Carniola*, May 24, 1941.

SECTION 2. . . . The rate of conversion shall be as follows: 1 dinar equals 0.05 Reichsmark.

. . . . .

SECTION 5. This decree shall become effective on June 1, 1941.
Veldes, May 23, 1941.

KUTSCHERA
Chief of Civil Administration

III. LJUBLJANA

(Italian Occupation)

Royal Decree-Law No. 291 concerning Establishment of the Province of Ljubljana, May 3, 1941 [13]

[EXCERPTS]

ARTICLE 1. The Slovene territories the boundaries of which are specified on the attached map [14] drawn up at my order by the Duce of Fascism, Head of the Government, form an integral part of the Kingdom of Italy and constitute the Province of Ljubljana.

ARTICLE 2. Royal decrees to be issued on the motion of the Duce of Fascism, Head of the Government and Minister of the Interior, will establish the ordinances of the Province of Ljubljana, which, having a uniformly Slovene population, shall have an autonomous form of organization with due consideration for the racial characteristics of the population, the geographical position of the territory, and its special local needs.

ARTICLE 3. The powers of government shall be exercised by a High Commissioner, appointed by royal decree on the motion of the Duce of Fascism, Head of the Government and Minister of the Interior.

ARTICLE 4. The High Commissioner shall be assisted by a Council consisting of fourteen representatives chosen from among the productive classes of the Slovene population.

ARTICLE 5. Military service shall not be obligatory for the Slovene population of the Province of Ljubljana.

ARTICLE 6. In the elementary schools the Slovene language shall be obligatory. In secondary and higher education instruction in the Italian language shall be optional.

All official documents shall be printed in both languages.

ARTICLE 7. The Government of the King is authorized to publish in the territory of the Province of Ljubljana the constitution and other laws of the

[13] *Gazzetta ufficiale*, 1941, No. 105, p. 1725.
[14] The map is not printed in this publication.—ED.

Kingdom and to issue the necessary regulations for coordinating them with the legislation in force there and with the ordinances which are to be established under the provisions of Article 2.

ARTICLE 8. The present decree shall come into force from the date of its publication in the *Gazzetta ufficiale* of the Kingdom, and shall be submitted to the Legislative Assembly for conversion into law.

The Duce of Fascism, Head of the Government, shall be authorized to submit the draft of the corresponding law.

. . . . .

Rome, May 3, 1941–XIX.

VICTOR EMMANUEL
MUSSOLINI

Royal Decree-Law No. 415 concerning Establishment of Monopoly Services in the Province of Ljubljana, May 19, 1941 [15]

[EXCERPTS]

Victor Emmanuel III, by the grace of God and by the will of the nation King of Italy and of Albania, Emperor of Ethiopia,

By virtue of Article 18 of the law of January 19, 1939–XVII, no. 129;

By virtue of the Royal decree-law of May 3, 1941–XIX, no. 291;

In view of the urgent and absolute necessity, on account of the war, of authorizing the administration of state monopolies to assume in the Province of Ljubljana the services which relate to salts, tobaccos, matches, packages for cigarettes, automatic lighters, and flints in the pending organization of these services under the Royal decree-law cited above;

Having consulted the Council of Ministers;

On the motion of Our Minister, the State Secretary of Finance;

We have decreed and we decree:

ARTICLE 1. The administration of state monopolies is authorized to take over provisionally in the Province of Ljubljana the services which relate to salts, tobaccos, matches, packages for cigarettes, automatic lighters, and flints pending the definitive organization of such services under royal decree-law of May 3, 1941–XIX, No. 291.

ARTICLE 2. The services specified in the preceding article shall be regulated by local administration in accordance with general directives to be issued by the Minister of Finance.

ARTICLE 3. This decree shall come into force on the day following that of its publication in the *Gazzetta ufficiale* of the Kingdom, and shall be submitted to the Legislative Assembly for conversion into law.

[15] *Gazzetta ufficiale*, 1941, No. 127, p. 2131.

The minister proposing it shall be authorized to submit the draft of the corresponding law.

. . . . .

Rome, May 19, 1941–XIX.

VICTOR EMMANUEL
MUSSOLINI—DI REVEL

Proclamation of the Duce of Fascism, First Marshal of the Empire, Commander of the Armed Forces Operating on All Fronts, concerning Jurisdiction within the Territory of the Former Kingdom of Yugoslavia Occupied by the Italian Armed Forces, June 2, 1941 [16]

[EXCERPT]

ARTICLE 1. As to the territory of the former Kingdom of Yugoslavia which is occupied by the Italian armed forces and which is within the provinces of Fiume and Ljubljana, jurisdiction in penal, civil, and commercial matters which previously belonged to the Court of Appeals in Zagreb according to laws there in force is hereby transferred to a branch of the Court of Appeals in Fiume.

ARTICLE 2. In such branch of the court three judges, including the president, shall try the cases provided for in the preceding article.

ARTICLE 3. The president of the branch may, as necessity arises, invite a judge from the tribunal in Sussak to sit on the court for the trial of cases which have been transferred to the court according to Article 1.

ARTICLE 4. The present proclamation shall be published in the *Gazzetta ufficiale* of the Kingdom.

In addition it shall be made public, in the areas occupied by the Italian armed forces, in the record books of the respective communities of the former Kingdom of Yugoslavia, the provinces of Fiume and Ljubljana.

Headquarters of the Armed Forces, June 2, 1941–XIX.

MUSSOLINI

Royal Decree-Law No. 454, concerning Maintenance in Effect in the Province of Ljubljana of the Regulations Issued by the Italian Occupation Authorities, June 7, 1941 [17]

[EXCERPT]

ARTICLE 1. Until further order, the regulations referred to in the first paragraph of Article 6 of Royal Decree-Law No. 452, of May 18, 1941–XIX,[18] shall be in effect in the Province of Ljubljana.

[16] *Gazzetta ufficiale*, 1941, No. 155, p. 2626. [17] *Ibid.*, No. 133, p. 2241.
[18] For the decree-law referred to, see under Dalmatia, below, p. 587. —ED.

The High Commissioner for the province shall exercise the functions which formerly belonged to civil commissioners under the aforementioned regulations.

ARTICLE 2. The present decree shall go into effect from the date of its publication in the *Gazzetta ufficiale* of the Kingdom and shall be presented to the Legislative Assembly for conversion into law.

The Duce of Fascism, Head of the Government, shall be authorized to submit the draft of the corresponding law.

. . . . . .

Given in Rome, June 7, 1941–XIX.

VICTOR EMMANUEL

MUSSOLINI

Seen: Keeper of the Seal, GRANDI.

IV. DALMATIA

(Italian Occupation)

Royal Decree-Law No. 452, concerning Organization of the Territories Which Have Become an Integral Part of the Kingdom of Italy, May 18, 1941[19]

[EXCERPT]

ARTICLE 1. The territories whose boundaries are defined on the attached map,[20] drawn up at our order by the Duce of Fascism, Head of the Government, are an integral part of the Kingdom of Italy.

ARTICLE 2. Of the territories referred to in Article 1, those contiguous to the Province of Fiume, the islands of Veglia and Arbe and the smaller islands belonging to their district, shall be attached to the Province of Fiume.

ARTICLE 3. The other territories and the other islands of Dalmatia mentioned in Article 1 shall constitute, together with the present Province of Zara, the governorship (*Governatorato*) of Dalmatia, which shall include the provinces of Zara, Spalato, and Cattaro. The boundaries of the Dalmatian provinces shall be determined by royal decree, which shall define also the jurisdiction of the governor and his relationship to the prefects of these provinces. The governor shall reside at Zara and be directly responsible to the Duce, Head of the Government.

ARTICLE 4. The communes of Spalato and Curzola shall be given a special administrative organization.

The regulations relating thereto shall be issued by royal decree on recom-

[19] *Gazzetta ufficiale*, 1941, No. 133, p. 2240.
[20] The map is not printed in this publication.—ED.

mendation of the Duce of Fascism, Head of the Government and Minister of the Interior, in agreement with the other ministers involved.

ARTICLE 5. The King's Government is authorized to promulgate in the territories mentioned in Article 1 the statute and other laws of the Kingdom and to issue the necessary regulations for the coordination of the legislation there in force, in particular with respect to the enactments which shall be issued for the communities of Spalato and Curzola as set forth in Article 4.

ARTICLE 6. Until further notice, in the territories mentioned in Article 1 the regulations issued by the Italian authorities of occupation shall remain in force unless exceptions are dictated by military necessity.

The Governor of Dalmatia and the Prefect of the Province of Fiume shall exercise, in the territories defined in Article 1, the functions already assigned to the civil commissioners by the above-mentioned regulations.

. . . . . .

Rome, May 18, 1941–XIX.

VICTOR EMMANUEL
MUSSOLINI

Seen: Keeper of the Seal, GRANDI.

Royal Decree No. 453 concerning Territorial Boundaries of the Provinces of Zara, Spalato, and Cattaro, and Functions of the Governor of Dalmatia, June 7, 1941 [21]

[EXCERPTS]

ARTICLE 1. The territorial boundaries of the provinces of Zara, Spalato, and Cattaro are defined in accordance with the documents attached to the present decree, corroborated upon our order by the Duce of Fascism, Head of the Government.

ARTICLE 2. The Governor of Dalmatia, under the direct authority of the Duce of Fascism, Head of the Government, shall carry out the general directives of the government for the administrative, economic, and social ordering of the territories of the three provinces.

ARTICLE 3. The Governor:

a) Shall exercise in the territory of Dalmatia all the functions of the central government in all matters pertaining to civil government and local services.

b) Shall ensure the unity of political direction and coordination of action of the prefects and of the other authorities of the three provinces.

c) Shall refer to the Duce, Head of the Government, suggestions for the gradual extension of the statute and of other laws of the Kingdom to the territory of Dalmatia, under the terms of Article 5 of Royal Decree-Law No. 452, of May 18, 1941–XIX.

[21] *Gazzetta ufficiale*, 1941, No. 133, p. 2240.

d) Shall provide, by his own decrees, for matters concerning which the laws of the Kingdom have not yet gone into effect in the territory of Dalmatia.

e) Shall correspond with the ministers and with the other authorities of the Kingdom relative to affairs concerning Dalmatia.

ARTICLE 4. The prefects shall exercise their functions in conformity with existing laws and regulations.

ARTICLE 5. The Governor shall be assisted by a secretary general, chosen from among state officials of a rank not inferior to the fourth and appointed by royal decree, on suggestion of the Duce.

. . . . .

ARTICLE 6. The Governor shall use personnel listed in the register of the state administration and personnel actually employed in accordance with the rules and regulations established by Royal Decree-Law No. 100, of February 4, 1937–XV.

The number of personnel already employed and still to be employed shall be determined by the president of the Council of Ministers on proposal of the Governor, after consultation with the Minister of Finance.

ARTICLE 7. Regarding the functions defined in paragraph *a* of Article 3, special allowances shall be made through legislation in the expense balances of the various ministers.

The regulations in force as to salaries shall not be changed.

. . . . .

Given at Rome, June 7, 1941–XIX.

VICTOR EMMANUEL

MUSSOLINI–DI REVEL

Seen: Keeper of the Seal, GRANDI.

V. MONTENEGRO

(Italian Occupation)

Proclamation of the Duce of Fascism, First Marshal of the Empire, Commander of the Armed Forces Operating on All Fronts, on Regulations concerning the Authority of the High Commissioner for the Territory of Montenegro, June 19, 1941 [22]

[EXCERPT]

ARTICLE 1. The High Commissioner for the territory of Montenegro occupied by the Italian armed forces may exercise all the powers which are vested in an occupant under the laws of war; in regard to the exercise of civil

[22] *Gazzetta ufficiale*, 1941, No. 147, p. 2509.

authority he shall communicate directly with the Italian Minister of Foreign Affairs.

ARTICLE 2. The present order shall take effect as of the date of its publication in the *Gazzetta ufficiale* of the Kingdom. It shall be posted also outside the headquarters of the High Commissioner in Cetinje.

From the Chief Headquarters of the Armed Forces, June 19, 1941–XIX.

MUSSOLINI

Proclamation of the Duce of Fascism, First Marshal of the Empire, Commander of the Troops Operating on All Fronts, concerning the Establishment of a Governorship of Montenegro, October, 3, 1941 [23]

[EXCERPT]

ARTICLE 1. For the territory of Montenegro, previously a part of the former Kingdom of Yugoslavia and now occupied by the Italian armed forces, a governorship shall be established.

The appointment of the Governor, and when necessary the appointment of a substitute, shall be made by order of the Supreme Command.

ARTICLE 2. The Governor of Montenegro shall have under his orders the armed forces stationed in the territory of Montenegro. He shall communicate with the Ministry of Foreign Affairs in matters of a political, civil, and administrative nature, and with the Supreme Command as to military matters.

ARTICLE 3. The Governor shall establish and organize by order the services necessary for the exercise of the civil and military powers which are vested in him.

ARTICLE 4. As far as political, civil, and administrative matters are concerned, the Governor shall provide by order for the establishment of a civil commissariat, as well as for a civil commissioner, who shall be its head.

ARTICLE 5. The Governor of Montenegro shall have his headquarters in Cetinje.

ARTICLE 6. In case of absence, or in the event of inability of the Governor to act, his functions shall be exercised by the official highest in grade, or, if the grades are equal, by the senior among the military commanders under him.

ARTICLE 7. The present proclamation shall be promulgated by insertion in the *Gazzetta ufficiale* of the Kingdom and shall take effect as of the day of its promulgation. In addition it shall be posted in the headquarters of the commands of the larger units stationed in the territory of Montenegro.

From the Chief Headquarters of the Armed Forces, October 3, 1941–XIX.

MUSSOLINI

[23] *Gazzetta ufficiale*, 1941, No. 282, p. 4697.

VI. SERBIA

(German Occupation)

1. ADMINISTRATION

Proclamation to the Occupied Yugoslav Territory, April, 1941 [24]

By virtue of the authority vested in me by the Führer and Supreme Commander of the Armed Forces, I hereby order:

I. The German armed forces guarantee the inhabitants full safety of person and property. Whoever behaves quietly and peacefully has nothing to fear.

II. Acts of violence and sabotage shall be punishable by the most severe penalties. Among other acts, injury to, or conversion of, crops, supplies, and installations of every description essential to the conduct of the war, and the tearing down and damaging of official posters will be considered as sabotage. The following are placed under the special protection of the German armed forces: gas, water and electric power works, railways, sluices, and art treasures.

III. All radio transmitters, including those operated by amateurs, and all mobile power generators used or usable for operating such transmitters, as well as batteries and accumulators shall be surrendered immediately to the nearest German field or local commander.

The surrender of guns and other implements of war has been ordered by special proclamation.

The mayors shall be held responsible for the exact execution of this order.

IV. Acts punishable according to military law are:

1. Violations of the order for the surrender of radio transmitters, guns, and other implements of war.
2. Any aid given to non-German soldiers in the occupied territory.
3. Aiding civilians to escape into non-occupied territory.
4. Transmitting of any news to persons or authorities outside the occupied territory if such transmittal is prejudicial to the interests of the German armed forces and the Reich.
5. Communicating with prisoners of war.
6. Insulting the German Army and its commanders.
7. Street meetings, distribution of leaflets, arrangement of public assemblies and demonstrations without previous approval by a German commander, as well as any other manifestation of hostility towards Germany.
8. Inducing work stoppages, malicious stoppage of work, strikes, and lock-outs.

V. The state and municipal agencies, police forces, and schools shall be required to continue operations. They serve thereby their own population.

[24] *Verordnungsblatt für das besetzte jugoslawische Gebiet*, No. 1, 1941, p. 2. Proclamation issued at the front.

The heads of the several agencies and institutions shall be held responsible for loyal conduct toward the occupying power. Persons employed in public service shall receive the same remuneration as heretofore.

VI. All shops, plants, stores, banks, etc., shall remain open in the interests of the population. Any closing without sufficient reason shall be punishable.

VII. In the interests of an orderly and equitable distribution of supplies among the population, any hoarding of goods of everyday need (any undue accumulation of supplies) is forbidden. Hoarding may be considered as sabotage.

Traffic necessary for supplying the daily needs of the civilian population, including especially market traffic, shall not be suspended unless military considerations require such suspension.

VIII. Any increases in prices, remunerations of any kind and wages above the level of the day of occupation shall be prohibited unless expressly permitted.

IX. Every person shall be required to accept German currency as well as that of his own country. The rate of exchange is 100 dinars to 5 Reichsmarks. The use of any other rate of exchange shall be punishable.

In addition to the Yugoslav money the bills and coins of the German Reich Credit Institutes shall be legal tender. German coins of the denominations of 1 and 2 pfennigs, and of 1, 2, 5, and 10 Reichspfennigs or Rentenpfennigs may legally be circulated. Bills of the Reichsbank and Rentenbank and coins of the denomination of 50 Reichspfennigs, constituting legal tender in the territory of the German Reich, shall not be legal tender in the occupied territory. They may therefore neither be put in nor accepted for circulation.

X. The German soldiers and German citizens shall pay in cash for their purchases and for services received. The Army shall issue receipts in lieu of cash payments.

April, 1941.

THE COMMANDER IN CHIEF OF THE ARMY

Order Establishing the Duty of Registration for Printing and Multigraphing Apparatus, May 9, 1941 [25]

By virtue of the authority vested in me by the Commander in Chief of the Army, I hereby order as follows:

SECTION 1. Persons in the possession of rotary presses, speed presses, stereotype presses, typesetting machines of all systems, hand-setting ap-

[25] *Verordnungsblatt des Militärbefehlshabers in Serbien*, No. 4, 1941, p. 41.

paratus, and multigraphs of every description shall, within five days of the publication of this order, register the possession of the above-mentioned apparatus with the district commanders.

SECTION 2. The transfer and acquisition of apparatus mentioned in Section 1 shall be subject to the permission of the district commanders.

SECTION 3. Violation of these orders shall be punished by death, and in less serious cases by forced labor or imprisonment.

Belgrade, May 9, 1941.

THE MILITARY COMMANDER IN SERBIA

Order concerning the Press in the Serbian Territories, May 20, 1941[2]

[EXCERPTS]

By virtue of the authority vested in me by the Commander in Chief of the Army, I hereby order as follows:

SECTION 1. The determination of materials to be published by word or picture in periodicals appearing in the occupied Serbian territory is a public function. Persons fulfilling this function are called editors. Nobody may claim to be an editor unless he has been admitted to the profession of editor by virtue of this order.

SECTION 2. A person shall be admitted to the profession of editor only if the applicant:

1. Is not a Jew or gypsy, nor married to a Jewess or gypsy.
2. Is more than twenty-one years of age.
3. Has full legal capacity.
4. Has had professional training.
5. By his personality warrants the assumption that he will be able to fulfill the duties of an editor.

SECTION 3. A person has had professional training if he has acquired, through at least one year's training period in the editorial office of a periodical, the technical knowledge of an editor and can produce documentary evidence of such training.

SECTION 4. A person shall be admitted to the profession of editor by being entered, upon his application, in the Professional Roll of Editors.

The Professional Roll shall be kept by the Serbian Journalists' Association.

The Director of the Journalists' Association shall pass on the application. The applicant shall receive a written answer to his application.

From a denial of registration by the Director of the Journalists' Association an appeal shall lie to me.

[26] *Verordnungsblatt des Militärbefehlshabers*, No. 5, 1941, p. 47.

Registration in the Roll of Editors shall also take place upon my order.

SECTION 5. The Director of the Serbian Journalists' Association will be appointed by me.

The Director of the Journalists' Association shall, immediately after his appointment, submit to me for confirmation, a draft of the by-laws of the association. Upon my confirmation the by-laws shall be published by the Director of the Association.

SECTION 6. The editors shall be required to present truthfully matters which they treat in word or picture, and to judge them according to their best knowledge and their conscience. They shall be under the obligation to practice their profession conscientiously and by their conduct to show themselves worthy of the respect due to the profession.

SECTION 7. If an editor no longer meets the requirements established by this order his name shall be stricken from the Professional Roll of Editors. The Director of the Serbian Journalists' Association shall issue an order to this effect.

An appeal lies to me from such an order of the Director of the Journalists' Association. An editor shall also be stricken from the rolls upon my personal order.

SECTION 8. The publisher of a periodical shall appoint an editor in chief. The editor in chief's name shall be communicated in writing to the Director of the Journalists' Association.

The editor in chief shall be required, in accordance with the contract of employment and supplementary instructions of the publisher, to establish in writing a plan for the division of editorial work. It shall be evident from the plan which part of the editorial work shall be done by the individual editor, and to what extent an editor is authorized to give orders to other editors.

SECTION 9. Every editor of a periodical shall incur both civil and criminal liability for its contents where he cooperated in determining its contents or ordered the insertion of a contribution or picture.

The civil and criminal responsibility of other persons shall not be affected by this provision.

The editor in chief of a periodical shall be responsible for the general attitude of the text section of the periodical.

The editor in chief shall be required to see to it:

1. That only those contributions are inserted in a periodical which have been written by an editor or the insertion of which has been ordered by an editor.
2. That in each issue of a periodical shall be stated the first and family names and residences of the editor in chief, his assistant, and of any editor entrusted with the editing of a definite section of the periodical.

. . . . . .

SECTION 11. Publication of periodicals shall be subject to my approval. Application for such approval shall be filed with the Director of the Journalists' Association.

The application shall contain:

1. Title and place of issue of the periodical.
2. An indication of the periods at which the periodical appears.
3. Names and residences of the editor in chief and the editors.
4. Name and residence of the publisher.
5. Full description of the printing establishment in which the periodical is produced.

SECTION 12. A person can be a publisher only if he can meet the requirements provided in Section 2.

SECTION 13. Publication of a periodical shall take place only if it is not, in whole or in part, financed by Jewish capital.

SECTION 14. Written declarations concerning the qualifications imposed by Sections 12 and 13 shall be submitted with the application for approval of the publication.

SECTION 15. The contents of periodicals shall be subject to censorship by officials to be appointed by me. The publication of a periodical shall take place only after its contents have been approved by these officials.

SECTION 16. Any person violating the provisions of this order or making false declarations shall be punishable by imprisonment or fine or both, and in especially serious cases by hard labor.

Belgrade, May 20, 1941.

THE MILITARY COMMANDER IN SERBIA

Order concerning the Operation of Theaters, May 20, 1941 [27]

[EXCERPTS]

By virtue of the authority vested in me by the Commander in Chief of the Army, I hereby order as follows:

SECTION 1. Theaters, including opera and ballet, shall be operated only with permission of the Military Commander in Serbia.

SECTION 2. Such permission will be granted only if:

1. There is a public need.
2. There are no objections against the manager of the enterprise and the persons acting on his behalf.
3. The local provisions for protection against fire hazards and for public safety have been complied with.

[27] *Verordnungsblatt des Militärbefehlshabers*, No. 5, 1941, p. 51.

The decision shall be left to the unrestricted discretion of the Military Commander. The permission may be granted for a period of time only and is subject to revocation without notice.

Jews and gypsies or persons married to Jews or gypsies shall not be admitted to the operation of enterprises mentioned in Section 1.

. . . . . .

SECTION 4. Performances and presentations in enterprises described in Section 1 shall not be permitted unless the permission of the Military Commander in Serbia shall have been given.

Works of Jewish authors and composers may not be presented.

SECTION 5. The employment of the entire artistic and technical personnel shall be subject to the permission of the Military Commander in Serbia.

Jews and gypsies and persons married to Jews or gypsies shall not be employed or occupied in enterprises described in Section 1.

. . . . . .

Belgrade, May 20, 1941.

THE MILITARY COMMANDER IN SERBIA

Order concerning the Operation of Cabarets and Vaudeville Houses May 21, 1941[28]

[EXCERPTS]

By virtue of the authority vested in me by the Commander in Chief of the Army, I order as follows:

SECTION 1. Cabarets, vaudeville houses, and similar places of entertainment shall not be operated unless permission of the Military Commander in Serbia shall have been obtained.

SECTION 2. Such permission shall only be granted if:

1. There is a public need.
2. There are no objections against the manager of the enterprise and the persons acting on his behalf.
3. The local provisions for protection against fire hazards and for public safety have been complied with.

The decision shall be left to the unrestricted discretion of the Military Commander. The permission may be granted for a period of time only and shall be subject to revocation without notice.

Jews and gypsies or persons married to Jews or gypsies shall not be admitted to the operation of enterprises mentioned in Section 1.

SECTION 3. Applications for permits shall be submitted in the German language in triplicate to the Military Commander in Serbia through the district commanders.

[28] *Verordnungsblatt des Militärbefehlshabers*, No. 5, 1941, p. 56.

The applications shall contain the following data:

1. First and family name, date and place of birth, and residence of the applicant.
2. A written affirmation by the applicant that neither he nor his wife is a Jew or a gypsy.
3. Place of business.
4. . . . .
5. The name of the person owning or in possession of the enterprise; in the case of a lease, the name of the lessor and the amount of the stipulated rentals.
6. The kind and amount of the capital invested in the enterprise, separated according to owned and borrowed capital, as well as data concerning the participation of Jewish capital.
7. First and family names, dates, and places of birth, racial origins, and residences of agents.
8. Written affirmation of the applicant that neither the agents nor their wives are Jews or gypsies.

SECTION 4. The performances and presentations in cabarets and vaudeville houses shall not be permitted unless a permit has been obtained from the Military Commander in Serbia.

Works of Jewish authors and composers shall not be presented.

The appearance of any master of ceremonies shall not be permitted.

SECTION 5. The employment of the entire artistic and technical personnel in cabarets and vaudeville houses shall be subject to permission by the Military Commander in Serbia.

Jews and gypsies and persons married to Jews or gypsies may not be employed or occupied in cabarets or vaudeville houses.

. . . . .

Belgrade, May 21, 1941.

THE MILITARY COMMANDER IN SERBIA

2. LAW AND COURTS

Order concerning the Application of German Criminal Law and Criminal Statutes in the Occupied Yugoslav Territories [29]

By virtue of the authority vested in me by the Führer and the Supreme Commander of the Armed Forces, I hereby order as follows:

SECTION 1. Any person who commits an act punishable according to German law and is brought to trial before courts of the armed forces shall be subject to German criminal law.

[29] *Verordnungsblatt für das besetzte jugoslawische Gebiet*, No. 1, 1941, p. 4. Undated order issued at the front.

The courts of the armed forces shall also have jurisdiction to try crimes committed before the occupation by the German forces.

Prosecution of such crimes shall be at the discretion of the prosecuting authorities.

In the trial of juveniles the German courts may pass the sentence provided by statutes regardless of the age of the defendant whenever the latter in his development is equal to a person more than eighteen years old.

SECTION 2. Any person who undertakes to commit any acts of violence or sabotage against the German armed forces, its members, or installations, shall be punished by death.

SECTION 3. A person who stops work with the intention of injuring thereby the interests of the German occupation, or who locks out workers or employees or incites others to stoppage of work or lock-outs, shall be punished.

SECTION 4. Street meetings, production and distribution of leaflets, arrangement of public assemblies and demonstrations, and participation therein shall be forbidden and punishable.

SECTION 5. Manifestations of hostility of every description towards Germans, especially utterances of hatred or insults, shall be forbidden and punishable.

SECTION 6. Whoever publishes in newspapers or periodicals news which may be harmful to the German Reich, or the publication of which has been forbidden by the German Army of Occupation, shall be punished.

SECTION 7. Any person who listens in public or in conjunction with others to non-German radio programs or who makes such listening possible shall be punished.

Non-German transmitters which have been approved by public proclamation of the Army of Occupation shall be exempt from the provisions of the preceding paragraph.

SECTION 8. Any person who communicates to others radio broadcasts hostile to Germany or Germans, or other news hostile to Germany or Germans, shall be punished.

SECTION 9. Any unauthorized communication with prisoners of war or civil prisoners in the custody of the German armed forces, or of the German authorities or officials, shall be punished.

THE COMMANDER IN CHIEF OF THE ARMY

Order concerning the Confiscation of Property for Activities Hostile to the State, December 22, 1941[30]

By virtue of the authority vested in me by the Commander of the German Army, I hereby order as follows:

[30] *Verordnungsblatt des Befehlshabers Serbien*, No. 27, 1941, p. 19

SECTION 1. (1) Any person who undertakes to resist the orders of the German armed forces and the officials appointed thereby or of the Serbian Government approved by the German armed forces, (*a*) by force of arms, (*b*) by sabotage, or (*c*) by any other illegal act, may be punished, in addition to any other penalties incurred, by confiscation of his personal or real property.

(2) The same penalty may be imposed on persons attempting, or aiding in the commission of, acts described in subsection 1.

SECTION 2. The order of confiscation shall be executed against the defendant and the members of his family.

SECTION 3. The Chief of the Administrative Staff of the Commander in Serbia shall decide, by order without formal judicial procedure, (*a*) on the penalty of confiscation, (*b*) on the use to be made of the property thus confiscated.

SECTION 4. Orders issued in accordance with Section 3 cannot be appealed from and shall not be subject to judicial review.

SECTION 5. Rules and regulations for the implementation of this order, if deemed necessary, shall be issued by the Chief of the Administrative Staff of the Commander in Serbia.

Belgrade, December 22, 1941.

THE COMMANDER IN SERBIA

3. ECONOMY AND FINANCE

Order concerning the Resumption of Production, May 12, 1941 [31]

[EXCERPTS]

By virtue of the authority vested in me by the Commander in Chief of the Army, I hereby order as follows:

SECTION 1. Enterprises in which no more than twenty persons were employed before the outbreak of war shall resume operations at once.

A special permit for the resumption of operations shall not be required.

SECTION 2. Enterprises other than those mentioned in Section 1 shall require my permission for the resumption or continuation of operation.

Applications to that effect shall be submitted to the Plenipotentiary for Economic Affairs through the chambers of industry, commerce, or trades or the Central Office of Industrial Corporations or the Association of Iron and Metal Industries.

My approval shall be required even if officers of the German armed forces have permitted or ordered the resumption of operations. In these instances my approval shall be obtained in the manner described above, this section. Pending my decision on the applications, operations shall be continued.

[31] *Verordnungsblatt des Militärbefehlshabers*, No. 5, 1941, p. 41.

SECTION 3. The processing and transfer of raw materials enumerated in the Appendix are forbidden. The stocks on hand of these raw materials shall be registered and a list filed with the Plenipotentiary for Economic Affairs not later than ten days after the publication of this order. The list shall be filed with the district commanders. The transfer of these raw materials shall be subject to my approval. Applications shall be filed with the Plenipotentiary for Economic Affairs through the district commanders.

. . . .

Belgrade, May 12, 1941.

THE MILITARY COMMANDER IN SERBIA

APPENDIX TO SECTION 3 OF THE ORDER CONCERNING RESUMPTION OF WORK

[General classification of "frozen" materials.]

1. Iron.
2. Refining ores and metals: molybdenum, wolfram, including ores, ferrochrome.
3. Non-ferrous metals: zinc, nickel, cobalt, alloys of the aforementioned metals, ores, and raw materials containing the aforementioned metals, quicksilver.
4. Precious metals: platinum, iridium, rhodium, palladium, gold, silver.
5. Precious stones and crystals.
6. Industrial oils, fats, and resins.
7. Rubber and crude rubber.
8. Textile raw materials.
9. Leather, furs, skins.

Decree concerning Central Banking in Serbia, May 29, 1941 [32]

By virtue of the special powers which have been granted me by the Commander in Chief of the Army, I hereby promulgate the following decree:

SECTION 1. The National Bank of the Kingdom of Yugoslavia shall be liquidated.

SECTION 2. The Serbian National Bank shall be established as the new bank of issue.

SECTION 3. The Plenipotentiary for Economic Affairs in Serbia shall issue regulations for the execution of this decree.

Belgrade, May 29, 1941.

THE MILITARY COMMANDER IN SERBIA

[32] *Verordnungsblatt des Militärbefehlshabers*, No. 7, 1941, p. 69.

Order concerning the Reich Credit Institutes [33]

By virtue of the authority vested in me by the Commander in Chief of the Army, it is hereby ordered as follows:

SECTION 1. The order concerning Reich Credit Institutes of May 3, 1940, as published by the Reich Minister of Finance on May 15, 1940, as well as the order concerning the establishment and the scope of business of Reich Credit Institutes in the occupied territories, of May 15, 1940, shall be applicable in the Yugoslav territories occupied by the German armies.[34]

THE MILITARY COMMANDER IN SERBIA

4. GENOCIDE LEGISLATION

Order concerning the Sheltering of Jews, December 22, 1941 [35]

By virtue of the authority vested in me by the Commander in Chief of the Army, I hereby order as follows:

SECTION 1. Any person who (*a*) shelters or hides Jews; (*b*) accepts for safekeeping objects of value of any description, including furniture and money, or acquires them by way of purchase, barter, or any other transaction, shall be punished by death.

SECTION 2. Objects of value, including furniture and money, accepted from Jews for safekeeping shall be registered with the unit of the Security Police and of the S.D. (special service) in Belgrade, or, outside of Belgrade, with the field or district commanders of that area.

Any contracts of purchase, barter, or similar agreements entered into with Jews since April 6, 1941, shall be subject to the same duty of registration.

Any person failing to register as directed in the two preceding paragraphs shall be punishable in accordance with Section 1.

SECTION 3. Rules and regulations for the enforcement of this order, if deemed necessary, shall be issued by the Chief of the Administrative Staff of the Commander in Serbia.

Belgrade, December 22, 1941.

THE COMMANDER IN SERBIA

[33] *Verordnungsblatt für das besetzte jugoslawische Gebiet*, No. 3, 1941, p. 23. Undated order issued at the front.
[34] For the text of these orders, see Belgium, above, pp. 329–32. —ED.
[35] *Verordnungsblatt des Befehlshabers Serbien*, No. 27, 1941, p. 196.

5. ANTI-GUERRILLA LEGISLATION

Order concerning the Harvesting of the Corn Crop, October 9, 1941 [36]

By virtue of the authority vested in me by the Commander in Chief of the Army, I hereby order as follows:

SECTION 1. In view of the fact that the cornfields serve as hiding places for bands of Communists, the harvesting and cutting of the cornstalks shall be begun at once.

The harvesting of the crop and the collection of the stalks shall be completed not later than October 25, 1941.

The person in possession as well as the owner shall be liable for the harvesting of the crop and the collection of the stalks. Where no person in possession or owner can be found, or where either one of them delays the harvesting of the crop and the collection of the stalks, the mayors shall be responsible for the harvesting of the crop and the collection of the stalks as well as for their custody for the benefit of the community.

SECTION 2. A person violating the provisions of the preceding section shall be liable to the death penalty or, in the case of extenuating circumstances, to hard labor.

SECTION 3. The village mayors shall be personally responsible for the fulfillment of the duties imposed by Section 1.

In the case of failure to fulfill these duties in the several villages, their mayors shall be punished in accordance with Section 2. Moreover, a collective fine shall be imposed on the communities; its amount shall be determined by the Chief of the Administrative Staff of the Commander in Serbia in each individual case.

SECTION 4. This order shall take effect immediately.

Belgrade, October 9, 1941.

THE COMMANDER IN SERBIA

VII. THE BANAT

(German Occupation)

Ordinance concerning the Internal Administration of the Banat [37]

By virtue of Article 1 of the ordinance concerning the alteration of existing legal provisions and the issue of new ones, M.S. Zhl. 1118, of September 16, 1939, the council of the commissarial directors issues the following Ordinance concerning the Internal Administration of the Banat:

[36] *Verordnungsblatt des Befehlshabers Serbien*, No. 20, 1941, p. 147.

[37] *Amtsblatt der serbischen Ministerien*, June 11–July 4, 1941, No. 79–86, p. 16.

SECTION 1. (1) For the territory of the Banat, comprising the administrative districts of Pančevo, Vršac, Bela Crkva, Kovin, Jaša Tomić, Veliki Bečkerek, Velika Kikinda, Novi Becej, Nova Kanjiža, Kovačica, Alibunar, as well as the city of Pančevo, there shall be created in the area of the Danube Province (*Donaubanschaft*) a separate administrative authority with the title "Office of the Vice Governor (*Vize-Banus*) of the Danube Province for the Banat."

(2) The seat of this office shall be located in Petrovgrad. At the head of the office shall be the assistant to the Governor of the Danube Province (the Vice Governor), a German who shall be appointed by the Commissarial Director of the Ministry of the Interior in consultation with the leader of the German group in the Banat.

SECTION 2. (1) The office of the Vice Governor of the Danube Province for the Banat shall consist of eight sections, at the head of which shall be four section chiefs. The section chiefs shall be appointed by the Commissarial Director of the Ministry of the Interior on recommendation of the Vice Governor.

(2) The officials of the separate sections of the office of Vice Governor of the Danube Province for the Banat shall be appointed by the commissarial director of the appropriate ministry on recommendation of the Vice Governor.

(3) The district chiefs and their deputies, the mayors of the free cities and chiefs of the city police, as well as all state officials within the jurisdiction of this office shall be appointed by the Commissarial Director of the Ministry of the Interior in consultation with the Vice Governor of the Danube Province for the Banat.

(4) Assistant recorders and recording officials of Groups X, IX, and VIII shall be appointed in this territory by the Vice Governor of the Danube Province for the Banat.

(5) The Vice Governor of the Danube Province for the Banat shall appoint and dismiss the community notaries and other community employees in the territory of the Banat.

SECTION 3. (1) Contrary to the provisions of Sections 58 and 59 of the Civil Service Code, Germans may be immediately appointed as officials in the state service from grades X to II in the territory of the Banat if they meet the other requirements of the Civil Service Code.

(2) The provisions of this article shall be effective in all departments of state administration.

(3) This exception shall remain in force until June 30.

SECTION 4. (1) The Court of Appeals in Novi Sad shall be moved to Petrovgrad.

(2) The presiding judge of the Court of Appeals in Petrovgrad, who shall be a German, shall be appointed by the Commissarial Director of the Min-

istry of Justice in consultation with the leader of the German group in the Banat.

(3) The judges of German origin in the territory of the Banat shall be appointed by the Commissarial Director of the Ministry of Justice on the recommendation of the presiding judge of the Court of Appeals in Petrovgrad.

(4) Persons who have passed the examination for judge or attorney may be appointed as judges of German origin in the territory of the Banat.

(5) Any graduate jurist of German origin may be appointed as a provisional judge in the territory of the Banat on condition that he pass the examination for judge within one year. This exception shall remain in force until June 30, 1942.

SECTION 5. The Board of Attorneys in Novi Sad shall be moved to Petrovgrad.

SECTION 6. (1) The presiding judge of the Court of Appeals in Petrovgrad shall appoint the members of the commission for examinations of candidates for the offices of judge and attorney.

(2) The examinations for judges and attorneys may be taken at the Court of Appeals in Petrovgrad by all candidates from the territory of the former Court of Appeals in Novi Sad.

SECTION 7. (1) The notaries public of German origin in the territory of the Banat shall be appointed by the Commissarial Director of the Ministry of Justice in consultation with the presiding judge of the Court of Appeals in Petrovgrad.

(2) Contrary to the provisions of the law concerning notaries public, those persons of German origin who have passed the examination for judge or attorney may be appointed as notaries public. This exception shall remain in force until June 30, 1942.

SECTION 8. (1) The territory of the Danube Finance Authority in the province of the military commander in Serbia shall be under the Finance Authority in Belgrade. In Petrovgrad an Inspector's Office of the Belgrade Finance Authority for the Banat shall be established.

(2) At the head of the Inspector's Office of the Finance Authority shall be an Inspector, who shall be appointed by the Commissarial Director of the Ministry of Finance on the recommendation of the Vice Governor of the Danube Province for the Banat. The appointment of the other officials shall be made in like manner.

(3) The Inspector's Office shall be the secondary supervising authority of all finance (tax) administration in the territory of the Banat. In those cases in which, in accordance with the prevailing regulations, decisions must be made by the Ministry of Finance or the Finance Authority as primary authority, such decision shall be reached in collaboration with the Inspector of the Danube Finance Authority for the Banat.

(4) The Finance Section of the Office of the Vice Governor of the Danube Province for the Banat shall be incorporated into the Inspector's Office of the Finance Authority.

(5) Contrary to the provisions of the Civil Service Code, the Inspector at the Inspector's Office of the Finance Authority shall be classified in Group III, Grade 2.

(6) German state officials who in accordance with legal provisions are appointed by the Minister of Finance, shall be appointed on the recommendation of the Inspector's Office of the Danube Finance Authority for the Banat. Other appointments shall be made by the Inspector himself. The provision of Section 2, subsection 4, of this ordinance shall also be valid in this connection.

SECTION 9. (1) All revenues from state taxes and duties in the territory of the Banat shall go to the central state treasury; and the state will regularly determine the taxes for the Banat on the basis of such revenues.

(2) The revenues from provincial taxes and duties in the territory of the Banat shall be used exclusively for the needs of provincial administration. These revenues shall go to the Finance Section of the Office of the Vice Governor of the Danube Province for the Banat. They shall be controlled by the Vice Governor of the Danube Province for the Banat.

SECTION 10. (1) In Petrovgrad there shall be an Office for the Management of Mail, Telegraph, and Telephone Service, with the exception of technical units, which shall be under the immediate direction of the Mail, Telegraph, and Telephone Service in Belgrade.

(2) The Office for the Management of Mail, Telegraph, and Telephone Service in the Banat shall be directed by a Vice Director who shall be appointed by the Commissarial Director of the Ministry of Mail, Telegraph, and Telephone on the recommendation of the Vice Governor of the Danube Province for the Banat. Other officials shall be appointed on the recommendation of the Vice Director. The provision of Section 2, subsection 4, of this ordinance shall also be valid in this connection.

(3) The Office for the Management of Mail, Telegraph, and Telephone Service in the Banat shall work under the supervision and in accordance with the directives of the Mail, Telegraph, and Telephone Service in Belgrade. Detailed regulations concerning the field of activity of the office will be prescribed by the Commissarial Director of the Ministry of Mail, Telegraph, and Telephone.

SECTION 11. (1) For the supervision of railroads in the Banat, a delegate with seat in Petrovgrad will be appointed on the recommendation of the Vice Governor of the Danube Province for the Banat. The delegate shall be an official of the Belgrade-North Management in Group III, Grade 2.

(2) The field of activity of the delegate for the supervision of railroads shall be defined by the General Management of the Serbian State Railways,

in consultation with the Etra-Southeast Management in Belgrade and with the Vice Governor of the Danube Province for the Banat.

SECTION 12. Besides Serbian, German shall also be an official language.

SECTION 13. (1) As of the effective date of this ordinance, all legal provisions which may be in contradiction to its provisions shall become invalid.

(2) This ordinance shall come into force on the day of its publication in the *Amtsblatt*.

ACIMOVIĆ MILAN, m.p.
Commissarial Director of the Ministry of the Interior
[Other Officials]

VIII. CROATIA

1. ESTABLISHMENT OF THE STATE AND ITS ADMINISTRATION

Order, April 11, 1941 [38]

I order that until the establishment of the government of the State of Croatia all its administrative affairs shall be discharged by the divisional offices of the Provincial Government of Croatia.

Office of the Deputy Chief, Zagreb, April 11, 1941.

KVATERNIK, *Deputy Chief*

Decree concerning the Appointment of the First Croatian National Government, April 16, 1941 [39]

[EXCERPTS]

I. The Chief of the Independent State of Croatia hereby appoints the first Croatian National Government:

1. I shall personally preside over the government and over foreign affairs.

2. I appoint Osman Kulenović from Bihac, Vice President of the government.

3. I appoint General Slavko Kvaternik Commander of the Armed Forces and Minister of Croatian Defense, which shall comprise the land, air- and sea-borne forces, gendarmes, and all traffic police. I likewise appoint him

[38] *Zbornik zakona i naredaba*, No. 1, June 25, 1941, Text 6, p. 6.
[39] *Zbornik*, No. 1, June 25, 1941, Text 12, p. 8.

as my deputy, to serve in all cases when I am unable to perform the duties of chief of state.

4. I appoint Dr. Mirko Puk of Glina Minister of Justice.
5. I appoint Dr. Andrija Artuković of Ljubisko Minister of the Interior.
6. I appoint Dr. Ivan Petrić of Šolta Minister of Public Health.
7. I appoint Dr. Lovro Sušić of Mrkoplje Minister of National Economy
8. I appoint Dr. Milo Budak of St. Rok Minister of Religion and Education.
9. I appoint Ing. Ivica Frković of Ličko Novo Minister of Forestry and Mines.
10. I appoint Dr. Josip Dumandžić of Klobuk Minister of Corporations.
11. I appoint Dr. Milovan Žanić of Senje President of the Legislative Committee.

. . . . .

Office of the Chief, Zagreb, April 16, 1941.

Dr. ANTE PAVELIĆ, *Chief of the State*

Law concerning the Eastern Frontier of the Independent State of Croatia, June 7, 1941 [40]

SECTION 1. On the basis of Croatian sovereign rights and the principle of continuity of Croatian national territory, I determine by this law the eastern frontier of the Independent State of Croatia, which shall run:

1. From the place where the River Save empties into the Danube up the said River Save to the mouth of the River Drina at Save.
2. From the mouth of the River Drina upstream along its most eastern branch, so that all islands on the Drina shall belong to Croatia, to the place where the creek Brusnica empties into the Drina to the east of the village Zemlice.
3. From the place where the creek Brusnica empties into the Drina the boundary of the Independent State of Croatia shall run by land to the east from the Drina along the old boundary line between Bosnia and Serbia as it was before 1908.

SECTION 2. To this law shall be appended a geographical map in the scale 1:2,000,000, on which the boundary line of the Independent State of Croatia shall be drawn by a red line. This geographical map shall be a component part of this law.[41]

SECTION 3. I entrust the execution of this law to the Minister of Croatian National Defense and the Minister of the Interior, who shall at once occupy

[40] *Zbornik*, No. 3, August 1, 1941, Text 222, p. 165.
[41] The map is not included in this publication.—ED.

the above-mentioned boundary with the units of Croatian militia and Ustaše troops and place on the spot distinct landmarks, except for the area of Zemun and vicinity which, although it forms a component part of the Independent State of Croatia, shall by agreement with the Greater German Reich remain for the duration of the war under military occupation by friendly German troops.

This law shall take effect as of this day.

Zagreb, June 7, 1941.

Dr. ANTE PAVELIĆ, *Chief of the State;* Gen. SLAVKO KVATERNIK, *Minister of Croatian National Defense;* Dr. MILOVAN ŽANIĆ, *President of the Legislative Committee attached to the Chief;* Dr. MIRKO PUK, *Minister of Justice;* Dr. MILO BUDAK, *Minister of Religion and Education;* Dr. ANDRIJA ARTUKOVIĆ, *Minister of the Interior;* Dr. IVICA FRKOVIĆ, *Minister of Forestry and Mines;* Dr. LOVRO SUŠIĆ, *Minister of National Economy;* IVAN PETRIĆ; *Minister of Public Health;* Dr. JOSIP DUMANDŽIĆ, *Minister of Corporations.*

Decree concerning the Establishment of a Council of State, January 24, 1942 [42]

SECTION 1. On the basis of Croatian historical constitutional law, I hereby order the organization and composition of a Croatian Council of State.

SECTION 2. Until a new composition of the Council of State is ordered, it shall consist of the following persons:

1. Surviving representatives—Croats—of the last Croatian Diet of 1918.
2. Surviving representatives—Croats—of the Skupština elected in 1938, and the founders and life members of the Central Committee of the former Croatian Agrarian Party.
3. Surviving members of the council of the former Party for the Acquisition of Rights for the Croats, elected in 1919.
4. Chairman, their deputies, and commissioners in the national headquarters of the Ustaše liberation movement.
5. Representatives of the German national minority.

SECTION 3. The list of members of the Croatian Council of State shall be prepared and published in the Official Gazette (*Narodne Novine*), and their credentials shall be issued by the President of the Supreme Court. Any of the persons enumerated in paragraphs 1 to 5 of Section 2, who have betrayed the cause of the Independent State of Croatia or have acted against the honor and reputation of the Croatian people shall be denied membership in the Council.

[42] *Zbornik,* No. 3, February 1, 1942, Text 92, p. 93.

SECTION 4. The Croatian Council of State convoked by the present law shall be established for a period terminating at the end of 1942, after which time a new law concerning the organization and sessions of the Croatian Council of State shall be promulgated.

SECTION 5. The members of the Croatian Council of State shall enjoy rights of immunity from the date when the oath has been administered to them up to the date of the termination of their duties.

SECTION 6. After the convocation of the Council of State, its members shall, until new rules are issued, elect their officers and discharge their duties in accordance with the rules which were applied in the Croatian Diet in 1918.

SECTION 7. The Chief of State shall convoke the Croatian Council of State by a written order.

This decree shall take effect on the date of its promulgation in the Official Gazette (*Narodne Novine*), and the President of the Supreme Court shall be charged with its execution.

Zagreb, January 24, 1942.

DR. ANTE PAVELIĆ, *Chief of the State*
DR. MIRKO PUK, *Minister of Justice and Cults*

Law concerning Chambers and Professional Associations, April 18, 1942 [43]

SECTION 1. In order to promote harmony in the national life and to develop national resources, as well as to protect and promote handicraft, industry and commerce, banking, and insurance, chambers shall be established for the equitable and just settlement of differences between persons active in these fields to the end of solidly building up, maintaining, and strengthening the nation and the state.

The chambers shall have jurisdiction over all activities in handicrafts, industry, commerce, banking, and insurance. The term "commerce" covers also the hotel business and transportation facilities, and the term "industry" includes shipbuilding, mining, and foundry.

SECTION 2. The following chambers shall be established:

1. Chamber of Industry.
2. Chamber of Handicrafts.
3. Chamber of Commerce.
4. Chamber of Banking and Insurance.

All chambers shall have their seats in Zagreb and they shall exercise their activities over the entire territory of the state. The regional branches in Zagreb, Osiek, Sarajevo, and Dubrovnik, and provincial branches in the capitals of the provinces, shall serve as local organs.

[43] *Zbornik*, No. 12, May 1, 1942, Item 410, p. 425.

The chambers shall establish regional and provincial branches or appoint special commissioners as need for them may arise.

SECTION 3. The chambers shall be under the supervision of the Minister of Handicrafts, Industry, and Commerce. Detailed regulations shall be issued in the form of administrative orders concerning the legal status, objectives, and organization of the chambers and their branches, sections and subsections, offices, trade courts, institutions for insurance, provisions concerning admittance to and cessation of membership, duties and rights of members and employees of the chambers, disciplinary measures for members, collection of contributions and maintenance of the chambers, and governmental supervision of and relationship between the chambers and the authorities of the state and local government. Likewise regulations shall be issued concerning liquidation of hitherto existing chambers, distribution of their properties and liabilities, their establishments, businesses, foundations and enterprises, and personnel, as well as liquidation and membership of professional organizations and compulsory unions, and the transfer of their properties and liabilities to chambers established under the present law.

SECTION 4. All persons and legal entities carrying on any economic activities by virtue of trade licenses must be members of the respective chambers.

SECTION 5. Governmental enterprises and establishments, as well as those of the local self-government, in so far as they are engaged in economic activities, must belong to a trade chamber regardless of whether their activities are subject to the provisions of the Industrial Code. The same shall apply to all savings banks founded on the basis of a decree concerning community savings banks of November 24, 1938.

As an exception to paragraph 1, Section 53, of the law concerning productive cooperatives of September 24, 1937, all economic cooperatives shall belong to the chambers.

All licensed engineers who are engaged independently in the field of building construction, as enumerated in subsection 4, Section 16, of the law concerning licensing of engineers of August 30, 1937, as well as those who are engaged in any work subjecting them to the provisions of the Industrial Code, shall be members.

SECTION 6. On application of the newly established chambers, the Land Title Record Office shall execute, free of taxes and dues, the transfer of titles provided for by this law.

SECTION 7. In order to decide on professional and economic matters, professional associations possessing their own headquarters shall be established. The Minister of Handicrafts, Industry, and Commerce shall promulgate by administrative order detailed rules concerning the organization and jurisdiction of such professional associations and their headquarters.

SECTION 8. The chambers of handicrafts, industry, commerce, and banking and insurance shall organize a regular association under the name

"Representatives of the Croatian Trade Chambers" as a consultative body to the government. The Minister of Handicrafts, Industry, and Commerce shall issue an administrative order containing detailed regulations concerning the organization and jurisdiction of the "Representatives of the Croatian Trade Chambers."

SECTION 9. Professional organizations and compulsory unions which fall within the provisions of the third part of the Industrial Code of November 5, 1931, shall be abolished, and the matters within their jurisdiction shall be transferred to the chambers or their branches.

SECTION 10. The Minister of Handicrafts, Industry, and Commerce and the Minister of Finance shall be charged with the execution of this law.

The Minister of Handicrafts, Industry, and Commerce shall be authorized to amend, change, correct, abolish, and interpret all orders, rules, regulations, and instructions issued on the basis of this law, as well as to issue new regulations.

SECTION 11. This law shall take effect upon the day of promulgation in *Narodne Novine*, on which day all provisions to the contrary shall cease to be in effect.

Zagreb, April 18, 1942.

DR. ANTE PAVELIĆ, *Chief of the State*
DR. DRAGUTIN TOTH, *Minister of Handicrafts, Industry, and Commerce*
DR. VLADIMIR KOŠAK, *State Treasurer*
DR. MIRKO PUK, *Minister of Justice and Cults*

2. MONOPARTY

Regulations concerning the Objectives, Organization, Work and Direction of "Ustase," the Croatian Liberation Movement, August 11, 1942[44]

[EXCERPTS]

On the basis of Section 13 of the Constitution of the Ustaše—Croatian Liberation Movement—by order of the Chief of the State, I issue hereby the following Regulations concerning the Objectives, Organization, Work, and Direction of "Ustaše"—the Croatian Liberation Movement:

I. OBJECTIVES, CHARACTERISTICS, ORGANIZATION, AND MATERIAL MEANS FOR THE ACTIVITIES OF THE USTAŠE

SECTION 1. *Objectives of the Ustaše.* (1) The objectives of the Croatian liberation movement "Ustaše" are indicated in Sections 1 and 2 of the Constitution of the "Ustaše."

[44] *Zbornik*, No. 24, September 1, 1942, Text 950, p. 1028.

(2) The first objective of the movement, which was indicated in Section 1 of the Constitution—the struggle for liberation of Croatia from a foreign yoke and for the establishment of an Independent State of Croatia—has been accomplished.

(3) The other objectives of the Ustaše, the principles of the Ustaše, and the actual needs of the Croatian nation, are as follows:

a) To protect by all means the political independence of Croatia.
b) To safeguard by all means the national characteristics of the Croatian people so as never to permit that the Croatian nation shall be considered as a part of any other nation.
c) To work for the principle that the Croatian people alone will always rule in Croatia.
d) To work for the principle that the Croatian people will be completely and forever masters of their material and spiritual resources in their own land.
e) To work for the goal that the Independent State of Croatia may be organized along the line of progress and justice in the spirit of Ustaše.
f) To treat labor as a basis for any reward and any right and to consider accomplishment of duty as the source of right.
g) To imbue Croatian men with the Ustaše principles of honor, honesty, justice, and love.
h) To implant in the heart of each Croatian man and each Croatian woman the virtues of ancient heroism and courage according to the traditions of fathers and grandfathers, heroes, and knights.
i) To awaken, develop, and strengthen joy of life in working and fighting.
j) To educate the members and sympathizers, as well as the people at large, in devotion, obedience, and loyalty to the chief of the state (*Poglavnik*) and to lead them to have confidence in him.

. . . . .

SECTION 12. *Organization of the "Ustaše."* (1) The chief of the state is, in accordance with the Ustaše Constitution, the supreme head and commander of the Ustaše liberation movement.

(2) In a broad sense the Ustaše movement embraces:

a) Members and sympathizers.
b) Ustaše youth.
c) Ustaše troops, which consist of 1) active service units; 2) bodyguards of the chief of the state; 3) transport line guards; 4) Croatian guards; 5) police; 6) detective service; 7) Ustaše schools; 8) Ustaše reserve; 9) disciplinary and penal court and military organizations as the need may arise (Section 13 of the Constitution).
d) The union of professional and other organizations in accordance with the law of May 6, 1942.

(3) Members and sympathizers are organized, and must act, in accordance with the provisions of the present regulations, whereas with reference to activities of the Ustaše troops and professional and other unions special laws and regulations shall apply.

(4) Ustaše troops constitute a part of the armed forces of the Independent State of Croatia.

(5) In a strict sense the Ustaše movement, apart from troops and professional organizations, consists of:

a) Male members—ustaš.
b) Female members—ustaškinja—female lodges of the Croatian Ustaše movement.
c) Male and female sympathizers of the movement.
d) Ustaše youth, male and female.

The organization and activities of the Ustaše youth shall be determined by separate regulations approved by the chief of the state.

. . . . . .

SECTION 88. *Final Provision.* These regulations shall take effect on the day of their promulgation in *Narodne Novine.*

Given at the Ustaše Headquarters, August 11, 1942.

By order of the Chief of the State:

DR. LJUDEVIT SOLC, *Minister*
Organizational Assistant

3. LAW AND COURTS

Law-Decree on Protection of the Nation and the State, April 17, 1941[45]

SECTION 1. Whoever in any way does or has done harm to the honor and vital interests of the Croatian nation or who endangers in any way the existence of the Independent State of Croatia or its government authorities, shall be considered guilty of high treason, even if his act was but a mere attempt.

SECTION 2. Whoever is guilty of high treason under Section 1 shall be punished by the death penalty.

SECTION 3. Under this law the Minister of Justice shall establish for the trial of cases as need may arise, extraordinary People's Courts consisting of three persons, who shall judge in a summary procedure in accordance with the rules of the former Croatian penal procedure concerning summary courts.

SECTION 4. The judges shall be appointed by the Minister of Justice.

SECTION 5. This law shall take effect immediately.

Zagreb, April 17, 1941.

DR. ANTE PAVELIĆ, *Chief of the State*

[45] *Zbornik*, No. 1, June 25, 1941, Text 13, p. 8.

Law concerning the Establishment of a Supreme Court and of the Offices of Attorney General in Bania Luca and State Attorneys in Zagreb and Sarajevo; and concerning the Abolition of the Bench of Seven (Supreme Court) and of the Office of Attorney General in Zagreb, and of the Supreme Court and Attorney General in Sarajevo, January 7, 1942 [46]

[EXCERPTS]

I. SUPREME COURT

SECTION 1. For the entire territory of the state a Supreme Court shall be established, with its seat in Bania Luca.

SECTION 2. The Supreme Court in Bania Luca shall have final jurisdiction in civil and in criminal cases and also in non-trial cases.

SECTION 3. The Supreme Court shall have one president, one vice president, and an appropriate number of judges and law clerks, as well as other clerical and auxiliary personnel.

. . . . .

SECTION 7. The president or the vice president may suspend any decision of individual benches in civil cases, if such decision is in contradiction to previous important or basic decisions of the Supreme Court, or if it is in obvious contradiction to the contents of the record in the case, or if it is in obvious violation of the law. Whenever the president exercises this right, the case must be brought before the plenary session of the Supreme Court.

The president shall adopt the same procedure if the one legal issue was decided by different branches in different ways.

. . . . .

SECTION 22. The office of a national Attorney General shall be established, with its seat at Bania Luca.

. . . . .

This law shall take effect on the date of its publication in *Narodne Novine*, and on the same date all enactments hitherto in force dealing with the subject-matter of this law shall cease to be in effect unless otherwise herein provided.

Zagreb, January 7, 1942.

DR. ANTE PAVELIĆ, *Chief of the State*
DR. MIRKO PUK, *Minister of Justice and Cults*

[46] *Zbornik*, No. 2, January 21, 1942, Text 23, p. 33.

Law concerning Suppression of Violent Crimes Against the State, Individuals, and Property, July 20, 1942[47]

[EXCERPTS]

I. Confinement in Concentration Camps

SECTION 1. Individual members of the family of persons who alone or as members of armed bands violate public order and safety or threaten the peace and quiet of the Croatian people, or who undertake some violent crime against the state, individuals, or property, as well as members of the family of persons who have fled from their homes, may be confined in concentration camps. The Ministry of the Interior (Administration of Public Order and Safety) shall establish such camps in various places in the Independent State of Croatia.

All those shall be considered members of the family of persons mentioned in the preceding paragraph, who live in one household with such persons according to the law of May 9, 1889, concerning family households (*zadruga*), that is, wife, parents, children, sisters, and brothers of such persons.

SECTION 2. The Ministry of the Interior (Administration of Public Order and Safety) shall decide as to the confinement of individual members of the family of persons mentioned in paragraph 1, Section 1, in concentration camps, and shall determine the length of their stay.

All administrative authorities and those of the local self-government, as well as institutions of the "Ustaše" movement, must report to the Ministry of the Interior (Administration of Public Order and Safety) through their provincial police offices, as to persons mentioned in paragraph 1, Section 1, and members of their families who live with them in one household as defined in the law of May 9, 1889, concerning family households, that is, wives, parents, children, brothers, and sisters thus dwelling with the persons mentioned in paragraph 1, Section 1; and their real and personal properties must be reported as well.

SECTION 3. Before the decision as to confinement of persons specified in Section 1 is made, proceedings shall take place as provided in the law concerning administrative penal procedure.

These proceedings shall be carried out by the Ministry or by the authorities assigned by it for that purpose.

SECTION 4. The period of stay in a concentration camp shall be not less than three months and not more than three years.

[The Ministry may according to its discretion discontinue the confinement or reduce its term.] [48]

SECTION 5. [Time spent under arrest by the police authorities before

[47] *Zbornik*, No. 22, 1942, Text 857, p. 924.
[48] Bracketed sections summarized by the translator.

confinement is decided upon shall be counted in the assigned term of confinement.]

SECTION 6. [The Ministry shall issue special regulations concerning concentration camps and their régime.]

II. SEIZURE OF PROPERTY

SECTION 7. All real and personal properties of individual members of families of persons mentioned in Section 1, paragraph 1, may be seized and forfeited to the Independent State of Croatia.

The Ministry of the Interior (Administration of Public Order and Safety) shall decide as to the forfeiture of such property.

SECTION 8. [Such decision shall be communicated to the Treasury Division for management of property taken away from persons who violate the public order (Law of December 27, 1941). Such decision creates title under the law on execution and attachment of 1930.]

SECTION 9. [The Ministry may at any time set aside the decision as to forfeiture *in toto* or in part.]

SECTION 10. Provisions of Sections 1–9 shall not be applied to members of families of persons who have fled from their homes but who return to them within fourteen days after the promulgation of this law.

. . . . .

SECTION 15. This law shall take effect on the day of its promulgation in *Narodne Novine*.

Zagreb, July 20, 1942.

DR. ANTE PAVELIĆ, *Chief of the State*
DR. ANDRIJA ARTUKOVIĆ, *Minister of the Interior*
DR. VLADIMIR KOŠAK, *State Treasurer*
DR. MIRKO PUK, *Minister of Justice and Cults*

Law concerning Loss of Citizenship and State Nationality by Persons who Emigrated from or Left the Independent State of Croatia, August 10, 1942 [49]

SECTION 1. Persons who have emigrated from the territory of the Independent State of Croatia or who have left this territory for racial or politico-national reasons shall lose their citizenship and the state nationality of the Independent State of Croatia.

SECTION 2. The Minister of the Interior may declare by executive order that the wives and minor children of persons mentioned in Section 1 of this

[49] *Zbornik*, No. 24, September 1, 1942, Text 940, p. 1013.

law, even if they stay on the territory of the Independent State of Croatia, shall lose their citizenship or state nationality.

SECTION 3. This law shall take effect on the day of promulgation in *Narodne Novine*, and the Minister of the Interior shall be charged with its execution.

Zagreb, August 10, 1942.

DR. ANTE PAVELIĆ, *Chief of the State*
DR. ANDRIJA ARTUKOVIĆ, *Minister of the Interior*
DR. MIRKO PUK, *Minister of Justice and Cults*

4. CHURCH

Law concerning the Croatian Eastern Orthodox Church, April 3, 1942 [50]

SECTION 1. In the territory of the Independent State of Croatia there shall be established the Croatian Eastern Orthodox Church, which shall be autocephalous.

SECTION 2. The organization and jurisdiction of the Croatian Eastern Orthodox Church shall be determined by a statute approved by the chief of the state.

SECTION 3. The Minister of Justice and Cults shall be charged with the execution of this law.

SECTION 4. This law shall take effect as of today.

Zagreb, April 3, 1942.

DR. ANTE PAVELIĆ, *Chief of the State*
DR. MIRKO PUK, *Minister of Justice and Cults*

Statute concerning the Croatian Eastern Orthodox Church, June 5, 1942 [51]

[EXCERPTS]

In accordance with the law concerning the foundation of the Eastern Orthodox Church of April 3, 1942, No. XC-800-Z. 1942, I hereby approve the following statute concerning the Croatian Eastern Orthodox Church:

. . .

SECTION 1. The Croatian Eastern Orthodox Church is indivisible in its unity and is autocephalous. It shall be guided dogmatically and canonically by the principles of the Holy Eastern Orthodox Church.

[50] *Zbornik*, No. 11, April 21, 1942, Item 360, p. 390.
[51] *Ibid.*, No. 18, 1942, Item No. 659, p. 689.

SECTION 2. The Croatian Eastern Orthodox Church shall have the status of a patriarchy, with its seat at Zagreb.

SECTION 3. Every ecclesiastical Orthodox authority shall possess a seal bearing the coat of arms of the church and the inscription "Independent State of Croatia," as well as the name of the said authority.

SECTION 4. The official language, as well as official lettering, of the Croatian Eastern Orthodox Church shall be Croatian.

The flag of the Croatian Eastern Orthodox Church shall have three colors: red, white, and blue, with a simple golden cross on a white field.

SECTION 5. The Croatian Eastern Orthodox Patriarchy shall enjoy the rights of a legal entity. The bishoprics and parishes shall also have the status of legal entities.

SECTION 6. The Croatian Eastern Orthodox Church shall be ruled dogmatically and canonically by:

a) Holy Scripture and holy tradition, according to the doctrine of the Eastern Orthodox Church.
b) The canons of the Ecumenical Councils.

and with regard to administration it shall be ruled by:

a) The law concerning the foundation of the Croatian Eastern Orthodox Church.
b) The statute of the Croatian Eastern Orthodox Church.
c) The orders and decisions of authorities established by the present statute.

SECTION 7. The organization of the Croatian Eastern Orthodox Church is based upon ecclesiastical hierarchy and autonomy.

SECTION 8. The following ecclesiastical, hierarchical, and autonomous authorities and autonomous administrative organs shall be established within the Croatian Eastern Orthodox Church:

a) The Patriarch, the Holy Council of Bishops, the Supreme Ecclesiastical Court.
b) The Bishop, the diocese, the Ecclesiastical Court of the diocese.
c) The Vicar.
d) The Rector of the parish.
e) The Parochial Board of Trustees.

SECTION 9. The Croatian Eastern Orthodox Church shall be headed by the Patriarch, who at the same time shall serve as Metropolitan of the Metropoly of Zagreb. The title of the Patriarch shall be "Patriarch of the Croatian Eastern Orthodox Church and Metropolitan of Zagreb."

. . . . . .

SECTION 23. The Croatian Eastern Orthodox Church shall receive a continuing subsidy from the state budget, the amount of which shall be determined by an order of the Minister of Justice and Cults.

SECTION 24. The religious officers of the Croatian Eastern Orthodox Church shall be paid by the state as government officials are paid, in accordance with the law on government officials. The Minister of Justice and Cults, in agreement with the Supreme Head of the Croatian Eastern Orthodox Church, shall determine who shall be considered religious officers and what shall be their civil service rating. The Patriarch shall determine, in agreement with individual bishops and with the Minister of Justice and Cults and the State Treasurer, what contribution shall be collected from each parishioner of the Croatian Eastern Orthodox Church for the purpose of maintaining the churches and for other religious purposes. These contributions shall be collected by the local tax authorities in order to be transferred later to the parochial Board of Trustees.

. . . . .

SECTION 33. The Patriarch shall be elected from among the bishops of the Croatian Eastern Orthodox Church who are citizens of the Independent State of Croatia.

SECTION 34. The election shall take place in the following way: The Council of Electors shall nominate from among the bishops three candidates. The names of these nominees shall be communicated to the Minister of Justice and Cults with the minutes of the session of the council, signed by the chairman and the secretary. The chief of the state shall appoint the Patriarch of the Croatian Eastern Orthodox Church from among the three above-mentioned nominees, upon the recommendation of the Minister of Justice and Cults.

SECTION 35. The Council of Electors shall consist of:

a) All bishops of the Croatian Eastern Orthodox Church.
b) The Chief of the Eastern Orthodox Division of the Ministry of Justice and Cults.
c) The Dean of the Eastern Orthodox Faculty of the University of Zagreb.
d) Five members of the Eastern Orthodox Church appointed for each election by the chief of the state, upon recommendation of the Ministry of Justice and Cults.

. . . . .

SECTION 50. [Bishops shall be appointed by the chief of the state, upon recommendation of the Minister of Justice and Cults, from among three candidates presented by the Synod of Bishops.] [52]

SECTION 51. The Holy Synod of Bishops shall consist of an assembly of all bishops presided over by the Patriarch.

. . . . .

SECTION 116. The chief of the state shall appoint the Patriarch and the first bishops.

. . . . .

[52] Summary by the translator.

SECTION 123. This statute shall be valid upon approval by the chief of the Independent State of Croatia and shall take effect on the date of its promulgation in *Narodne Novine.*

Zagreb, June 5, 1942.

The Chief of the State, Dr. ANTE PAVELIĆ
For the Minister of Justice and Cults:
Dr. JOZO DUMANDŽIĆ, *Minister of Agriculture*

5. PROPERTY

Decree-Law concerning the Transfer and Mortgaging of Real Estate, April 18, 1941 [53]

On the proposal of the Minister of Justice I enact and promulgate the following decree-law concerning the transfer and mortgaging of real estate:

1. Transfer and mortgaging of real property by any legal transaction *inter vivos* and by voluntary or compulsory action may take place only with the permission of the Minister of Justice.

2. The Minister of Justice shall be entrusted with the execution of this law.

3. This law shall take effect on the day of promulgation in *Narodne Novine.*

Zagreb, April 18, 1941.

Dr. ANTE PAVELIĆ, *Chief of the State*
Dr. MILOVAN ŽANIĆ, *President of the Legislative Committee*

Law concerning Expropriation of Productive Establishments, August 2, 1941 [54]

[EXCERPTS]

SECTION 1. Any productive establishment of a person or a legal entity may be expropriated, with all its accessories and rights, to the benefit of the Independent State of Croatia whenever necessary for the needs of the state and nation.

. . . . .

This law shall take effect on the day of its promulgation in *Narodne Novine.*

August 2, 1941.

Dr. ANTE PAVELIĆ, *Chief of the State*
Dr. MIRKO PUK, *Minister of Justice*
MILOVAN ŽANIĆ, *President of the Legislative Committee*

[53] *Zbornik,* No. 1, April 25, 1941, Text 19, p. 11.
[54] *Ibid.,* No. 7, October 1, 1941, Text 641, p. 529.

Law concerning Investigation of the Origin of Property and concerning the Forfeiture of Property Illegally Acquired, August 30, 1941 [55]

[EXCERPTS]

SECTION 1. All persons who, during the period from December 1, 1918, to April 10, 1941, were ministers, representatives, or senators must submit to the National Committee for Investigation of the Origin of Property, within one month after this law shall take effect, a declaration concerning the status and origin of their property and of that of their wives and children.

SECTION 2. The committee for the investigation of the origin of property gained in an illegal way is authorized to ask any Croatian national or citizen to submit within one month a statement regarding the status and origin of his property and of that of his wife and children.

[Ustaše companies must report all suspected cases of property illegally gained.] [56]

. . . . .

SECTION 6. . . . (2) It shall be assumed that property was gained in an illegal way if it is in obvious and considerable disproportion to the plausible income of the suspected person, his wife and children, and to their expenses; or if he acquired the property, through the use of political or family influence, by intermediation with the national or local authorities.

. . . . .

SECTION 8. . . . If the person fails to prove that his property was not acquired illegally, the bench of the committee shall pass sentence stating that the indicted person, his wife, or children have, or formerly had, property acquired illegally after December 1, 1918, and shall condemn the indicted person, his wife, or children, to transfer all their property, or a specific part thereof, to the state or local treasury or to any person or body injured by such illegal acquisition.

. . . . .

SECTION 9. There shall be no appeal from the sentences and decisions of the committee.

. . . . .

SECTION 17. This law shall take effect on the day of its promulgation in *Narodne Novine.*

Zagreb, August 30, 1941.

ANTE PAVELIĆ, *Chief of the State*
DR. MIRKO PUK, *Minister of Justice and Cults*
DR. MILOVAN ŽANIĆ, *President of the Legislative Committee*

[55] *Zbornik*, No. 8, October 15, 1941, Text 785, p. 658.
[56] Summary by the translator.

6. FINANCE

Decree-Law concerning the Establishment of the Croatian State Bank, May 10, 1941[57]

[EXCERPTS]

On recommendation of the Minister of National Economy, I hereby enact and promulgate the following decree-law concerning the establishment of the Croatian State Bank:

SECTION 1. The Croatian State Bank is hereby established in Zagreb as the bank of issue under the sovereignty of the Independent State of Croatia.

SECTION 2. The organization and sphere of activity of the Croatian State Bank shall be set forth by further enactment.

. . . . .

This law shall take effect on the day of its promulgation in *Narodne Novine.*

Zagreb, May 10, 1941.

Dr. ANTE PAVELIĆ, *Chief of the State*
Dr. LOVRO SUŠIĆ, *Minister of National Economy*

Decree-Law concerning Currency of the Independent State of Croatia, July 7, 1941

[EXCERPTS]

SECTION 1. In the Independent State of Croatia the monetary unit shall be the kuna (kn.). The kuna contains 100 (one hundred) banica (b.).

SECTION 2. The value of the kuna shall be 17,921 milligrams (0.017921 grammes) of fine gold.

SECTION 3. In the territory of the Independent State of Croatia, the Croatian State Bank shall have the exclusive right to issue bank notes, under regulations hereafter to be issued.

SECTION 4. Pending the publication of the new decree-law (referred to in the decree-law of May 10, 1941, No. LXXXI-142-Z, p. 1941) regarding the organization and sphere of activity of the Croatian State Bank, the Croatian State Bank is authorized to exchange notes of the former National Bank of the Kingdom of Yugoslavia for new bank notes issued by the Bank of the Independent State of Croatia and bearing the signature of the Minister of National Economy, Dr. Lovro Sušić, under date of May 26, 1941.

SECTION 5. The Independent State of Croatia shall exchange old dinar notes for new (kuna) bank notes in denominations of kn. 1,000, 500, 100 and 50. . . .

[57] *Zbornik,* No. 2, July 5, 1941, Text 122, p. 82.

SECTION 6. The Croatian State Bank shall exchange dinar notes for new state currency of the same nominal value, without any deduction. The beginning and the duration of the exchange period and the time-limit for the validity of the various dinar notes shall be fixed and published by the Croatian State Bank after approval by the Minister of Finance. From the time when the new state notes are placed in circulation by the Croatian State Bank, they shall be legal tender throughout the Independent State of Croatia.

SECTION 7. Divisional currency in the form of coins is likewise to be exchanged for new coins of the Independent State of Croatia. A special decree-law will be issued regarding the number and value of the subsidiary coins. In the meantime subsidiary coins of the former Kingdom of Yugoslavia shall continue to be legal tender.

SECTION 8. The Minister of Finance shall be entrusted with the execution of the present decree-law.

SECTION 9. This decree-law shall come into force on the date of its publication in *Narodne Novine*.

Zagreb, July 7, 1941.

DR. ANTE PAVELIĆ, *Chief of the State*
DR. KOŠAK, *Minister of Finance*

7. LABOR

Statute of the Croatian Union of Workers, January 23, 1942 [58]

[EXCERPTS]

GENERAL PROVISIONS

SECTION 1. In accordance with the decree of the Chief of the State of December 25, 1941, there shall be established as a professional organization of workers united within the Croatian liberation movement "Ustaše" a Croatian Union of Workers, with headquarters in Zagreb and jurisdiction over the entire territory of the Independent State of Croatia.

SECTION 2. The Croatian Union of Workers shall have the status of a legal entity both in private and public law.

. . . . . .

THE PURPOSE OF THE UNION

SECTION 8. The purpose of the union is to secure for the Independent State of Croatia, by uniting all workers, faithful collaborators in the work initiated for the improvement of their status in accordance with the princi-

[58] *Zbornik*, No. 3, February 1, 1942, Text 82, p. 77.

ples of the Croatian Ustaše movement and the ideals of the Croatian people and to further such improvement in all respects, that is, from the social, economic, technical, educational and, in general, professional point of view.

[It is stated further in Section 8 of the decree that the union shall realize its aims in close collaboration with the Croatian Ustaše liberation movement; that the union shall represent workers in matters of their employment relations; and that all trade unions shall be united under the auspices of the Croatian Union of Workers.] [60]

. . . . .

SECTION 10. The Union of Croatian Workers shall embrace compulsorily as its members all workers and their societies, trade unions, and social institutions established for any purpose whatsoever. All employees shall be considered workers who do not belong to the group of clerical employees but who are obliged to take out sickness insurance under the law of labor insurance and who in their main or secondary occupation are obliged to be members of any other trade organizations beside that for private clerical employees.

. . . . .

OFFICERS OF THE UNION

SECTION 17. The highest office of the union is that of the leader, who shall be appointed by the governmental Leader of the Unions.

. . . . .

SECTION 37. The governmental Leader of the Unions shall be entrusted with the execution of this statute, which shall take effect at once and shall be binding on all governmental, administrative, and judicial authorities and all workers in accordance with Section 10 of the statute.

Given in the Ustaše headquarters, January 23, 1942.

DR. ANTE PAVELIĆ, *Chief of the State*

Law Regulating Labor Relations, April 30, 1942 [61]

[EXCERPTS]

I. GENERAL PRINCIPLES

SECTION 1. It is the right and duty of every citizen to work, and work alone should be the basis of his existence and the measure of his usefulness. Work is permitted only if it does not bring harm to the state and the nation but serves their progress and welfare.

SECTION 2. The state shall supervise the nature, purpose, and methods of any work and the amount of profit and remuneration for the work accom-

[60] Summary by the translator. [61] *Zbornik*, No. 13, May 11, 1942, Text 468, p. 479.

plished, and it shall also inflict penalties for failure of accomplishment or for making the work impossible or difficult.

SECTION 3. Entrepreneurs and employers of all kinds who make use in their work of executives, technical managers, equipment, and organizations, as well as their coworkers who participate in their work with physical and mental activities, must settle their mutual relations primarily upon the principle of the welfare of the nation and the state as a whole, and only secondarily with regard to individual profit.

SECTION 4. For the purpose of development of social relations along the lines stated above, all the employers and employees must obey this law as participants in a common cause.

II. COLLECTIVE BARGAINING

SECTION 5. Labor relations shall be determined by collective bargaining. . .

. . . . .

SECTION 23. This law shall take effect on the day of its promulgation in *Narodne Novine*, and on that day all provisions contrary to this law shall cease to be in effect.

Zagreb, April 30, 1942.

DR. ANTE PAVELIĆ, *Chief of the State*
DR. LOVRO SUŠIĆ, *Minister of Corporations*
DR. DRAGUTIN TOTH, *Minister for Handicrafts, Industry, and Commerce*
DR. MIRKO PUK, *Minister of Justice and Cults*

8. GENOCIDE LEGISLATION

Decree-Law concerning the Preservation of Croatian National Property, April 14, 1941 [62]

[EXCERPTS]

On the proposal of the Minister of Justice I enact and promulgate the following decree-law concerning the preservation of Croatian national property.

1. Any legal transaction between the Jews among themselves and between Jews and third parties made within two months before the independence of the State of Croatia was proclaimed, shall be declared null and void if its value exceeds 100,000 dinars, unless the transaction was subsequently ap-

[62] *Zbornik*, No. 1, June 25, 1941, Text 17, p. 10.

proved by the Minister of Justice, to whom all such transactions must be submitted for approval within ten days after the promulgation of this law.[63]

2. County courts must at once enter the nullity of such transactions in the Land Title Record on which the transferred properties are described.

. . . . .

4. This decree-law shall take effect on the day of promulgation in *Narodne Novine.*

Zagreb, April 14, 1941.

Dr. Ante Pavelić, *Chief of the State*
Dr. Milovan Žanić, *President of the Legislative Committee*

Law concerning Prohibition of the Cyrillic Alphabet, April 25, 1941 [64]

Section 1. The use of the Cyrillic alphabet in the territory of the Independent State of Croatia shall be prohibited.

Section 2. This law shall take effect on the day of promulgation in *Narodne Novine*, and the Minister of the Interior shall be entrusted with its execution.

Zagreb, April 25, 1941.

Dr. Ante Pavelić, *Chief of the State*
Dr. Milovan Žanić, *President of the Legislative Committee*

Law concerning Nationality, April 30, 1941 [65]

On the proposal of the Minister of Justice I enact and promulgate the following law concerning nationality.

Section 1. A national is a person who is under the protection of the Independent State of Croatia.

Nationality shall be acquired in accordance with the law concerning nationality.

Section 2. A citizen is a national of Aryan origin who has proven by his conduct that he did not engage in activities against the liberation efforts of

[63] By order of April 18, 1941, the provisions of Section 1 were made applicable to legal transactions entered into after the independence of Croatia was proclaimed. *Zbornik*, No. 1, June 25, 1941, Text 35, p. 18.

[64] *Zbornik*, No. 1, June 25, 1941, Text 48, p. 26. [65] *Ibid.*, Text 75, p. 42

the Croatian people and who is ready and willing to serve faithfully the Croatian nation and the Independent State of Croatia.

SECTION 3. A citizen enjoys political rights in accordance with the law.

Zagreb, April 30, 1941.

Dr. ANTE PAVELIĆ, *Chief of the State*
Dr. MILOVAN ŽANIĆ, *President of the Legislative Committee*

IX. KOSSOVO, DIBRANO, AND STRUGA

(Albanian Occupation)

Proclamation of the Duce of Fascism, First Marshal of the Empire, Commander of the Armed Forces Operating on All Fronts, concerning the Exercise of Civil Authority in Kossovo, Dibrano, and Struga, June 29, 1941 [66]

[EXCERPT]

ARTICLE 1. In the territories of Kossovo, Dibrano, and Struga, previously belonging to the former Kingdom of Yugoslavia and now occupied by the Italian armed forces, all civil powers which are vested in the occupying military authorities under the laws of war are hereby transferred to the Albanian Government.

ARTICLE 2. The present proclamation shall take effect as of the date of its publication, such publication to consist of posting the proclamation in places accessible to the public, near the headquarters of the High Commissioner for Kossovo, Dibrano, and Struga.

The present proclamation shall be also promulgated in the official gazettes of the Kingdom of Italy and of the Kingdom of Albania.

From the Chief Headquarters of the Armed Forces, June 29, 1941–XIX.

MUSSOLINI

Vicegerent's Decree No. 317 concerning the Extension of Laws and Decrees to the Secondary Schools Annexed to the Kingdom of Albania, November 12, 1941 [67]

[EXCERPTS]

ARTICLE 1. The law of May 6, 1938, on the reform of secondary schools and subsequent modifications, Decree-Law No. 514 of October 25, 1940–

[66] *Gazzetta ufficiale*, 1941, No. 155, p. 2626.
[67] *Gazzetta ufficiale del Regno d'Albania*, November 25, 1941, No. 177.

XVIII, the programs, and every other circular or instruction in effect on the functioning of secondary schools shall be extended to the annexed territories and shall be observed therein with the modifications mentioned in the following articles:

ARTICLE 2. To the secondary schools (*Scuole Medie*) existing in the Kingdom shall be added:

1. A Normal School at Prishtina.
2. A High School (*liceo*) at Prizrend.
3. A High School (*liceo*) at Tetova.
4. A Boys' Agrarian Technical Institute at Peja.
5. A Boys' Commercial Technical Institute at Gjakova.
6. A Professional School at Tetova.
7. A Professional School at Kërçova.
8. A Professional School at Dibra.
9. A Professional School at Gjilani.
10. A Professional School at Ferzoviç.
11. A Professional School at Struga.
12. A Professional School at Govistar.
13. A Professional School at Dulcigno.
14. A Girls' Professional School at Prizrend.

. . . . .

ARTICLE 8. Pupils of Albanian nationality of the discontinued Yugoslav secondary schools and those coming from abroad may also enter themselves for the secondary schools of the Kingdom of Albania existing in the territories included within the old boundaries according to the rules established by the aforesaid law on the reforms of secondary schools and subsequent modifications, provided that by suitable documents they prove that they have attended courses corresponding to those in which they intend to enroll. The Minister shall decide controversial cases after having heard the opinion of the Administrative Council of the Ministry of Education.

. . . . .

ARTICLE 12. All secondary schools of every degree and order, including civic schools, existing in the annexed territories which by virtue of the decree of August 12, 1941–XIX, No. 264, have come to form an integral part of the Kingdom of Albania, shall be closed. Exception shall be made of the secondary schools operated by religious bodies, which will be provided for separately.

The Minister of Education is detailed to take possession of the respective buildings, archives, equipment, educational and scientific endowments, and whatever else is directly or indirectly related to the aforementioned secondary schools.

. . . . .

FRANCESCO JACOMINI

E. KOLIGI—K. VRIONI

Vicegerent's Decree No. 165 concerning the Institution of Public Works Offices in Redeemed Territories, July 22, 1942 [68]

[EXCERPTS]

ARTICLE 1. As of January 1, 1942–XX, there shall be established Public Works Offices at Prishtina, Peja, Dibrano, and Tetova, regions forming part of the redeemed territories.

ARTICLE 2. The present decree shall go into effect from the day of its publication in the *Gazzetta ufficiale* of the Kingdom and shall be presented to the Fascist Upper Corporative Council for its conversion into law.

. . . . .

Tirana, July 22, 1942–XX.

FRANCESCO JACOMINI

S. GURAKUGI—I. AGUSHI—E. VLORA

Law No. 264 concerning Conversion into Law of Decree-Law No. 264 (1941), September 12, 1942 [69]

Victor Emmanuel III by grace of God and by the will of the People King of Italy and of Albania, Emperor of Ethiopia.

The Fascist Upper Corporative Council has approved;

We have approved and we promulgate as follows:

Royal Decree-Law under date of August 12, 1941–XIX, No. 264,[70] relative to the delimitation of boundaries of the new territories forming an integral part of the Kingdom of Albania, is converted into law.

We order that the present law be inserted in the *Gazzetta ufficiale* of the Kingdom, and direct whomsoever it may concern to obey it and to cause it to be obeyed.

S. Rossore, September 12, 1942–XX.

VICTOR EMMANUEL

M. KRUJA

[68] *Gazzetta ufficiale del Regno d'Albania*, 1942, No. 93, p. 14. [69] *Ibid.*, No. 128, p. 12.

[70] Royal Decree-Law No. 264 of August 12, 1941, authorized the Royal Government to extend the application of Albanian laws to the redeemed territories.—ED.

Vicegerent's Decree No. 282 concerning Extension of the Law of August 29, 1930, to the Redeemed Territories, October 2, 1942 [71]

[EXCERPTS]

We, Vicegerent of His Majesty Victor Emmanuel III, by the grace of God and the will of the People King of Italy and Albania, Emperor of Ethiopia,

By virtue of the authority vested in us;

. . . . .

Pursuant to Article 2 of Royal Decree No. 264, issued under date of 12–8–1941–XIX, which authorizes the Royal Government to extend the application of Albanian laws to the redeemed territories;

Having held that the maintenance of public order calls for the absolute and urgent necessity of extending to the redeemed territories the law on internment of families, the sequestration of property, and setting fire to the houses of criminals in hiding;

Having heard the Council of Ministers;

On recommendation of the Minister of State for the Interior;

Have decreed and decree:

ARTICLE 1. There shall be extended to the territories of the former Yugoslav Kingdom annexed to the Kingdom of Albania by Royal Decree No. 264, under date of August 12, 1941–XIX, the law of August 29, 1930, on the internment of families, sequestration of property, and setting fire to the houses of criminals in hiding, published in *Gazzetta ufficiale* No. 66, under date of September 10, 1930.

ARTICLE 2. The present decree shall take effect fifteen days after its publication in the *Gazzetta ufficiale* of the Kingdom, and shall be presented through the offices of the proposing minister to the Upper Fascist Corporative Council for its conversion into law.

. . . . .

Tirana, October 2, 1942–XXI.

FRANCESCO JACOMINI

M. KRUJA

[71] *Gazzetta ufficiale del Regno d'Albania*, 1942, No. 133, p. 15.

X. BARANJA, BAČKA, PREKOMURJE, AND MEDŽUMURJE

(Hungarian Occupation)

Law XX, 1941, concerning the Reincorporation of the Recovered Southern Territories into the Hungarian Holy Crown and their Unification with the Country, December 27, 1941 [72]

I hereby give notice to all whom it may concern that the Lower and Upper Houses of the Parliament of Hungary have by mutual consent enacted the following law:

SECTION 1. The Hungarian nation embraces with brotherly love and takes again under its protection its southern sons who after twenty-three long years of trial have been strengthened in their loyalty toward their fatherland; and it expresses its grateful admiration to the Hungarian Army for the self-sacrificing, enthusiastic way in which it has fulfilled its duty.

The Parliament takes cognizance of and confirms those measures taken by the Hungarian Royal Government concerning the incorporation of the recovered Southern Territories.

The territories that have been occupied are reincorporated by the Parliament into the territory of the Hungarian State.

SECTION 2. For the period during which citizens' electors of these territories are not able to choose representatives in Parliament by normal procedure, those persons who, on motion of the Prime Minister, have been nominated by Parliament, both houses concurring, from among the population of the Southern Territories, shall be considered, by virtue of this law, as members of the Parliament in session since June 10, 1939.

In accordance with Section 23 of Law XXII, 1926, Section 3 of Law XXXIV, 1938, Section 3 of Law VI, 1939, Section 2 of Law XXVI, 1940, the Regent of Hungary may designate, besides the above members to be appointed to the Upper House, four more Upper House members, after they have been proposed by the Cabinet.

SECTION 3. The Cabinet may take all those measures for the reincorporation of the Southern Territories which are necessary for the integration of their particular legal system into the legal system of the country, as well as for dealing with matters relating to administration, legislation, and economy. The Cabinet may take such measures even when they would otherwise belong to the jurisdiction of the Parliament.

SECTION 4. From among the inhabitants of the reincorporated Southern Territories those persons will recover their Hungarian citizenship as from April 11, 1941, who were beyond question Hungarian citizens on July 26, 1921, under Hungarian law, and became citizens of the Kingdom of the

[72] *Évi Országos Törvénytár*, 1941, p. 187.

Serbs, Croats, and Slovenes by virtue of the Treaty of Trianon (Law XXXIII, 1921), and who, during the period from June 1, 1931, to June 1, 1941, lived continuously in the reincorporated Southern Territories.

Under the preceding paragraph, Hungarian citizenship shall be accorded also to the wife of the person who has become a Hungarian citizen and to his children who have not yet completed their twenty-fourth year of age. The child born outside of wedlock shall follow his mother's citizenship, if he has not yet completed his twenty-fourth year of age.

A full orphan or fatherless orphan born a Yugoslav citizen after July 26, 1921, shall acquire Hungarian citizenship by law, effective April 11, 1941, if his father—or in case he was born later, his grandfather—was a Hungarian citizen on July 26, 1921, in accordance with the Hungarian laws in force at that time, and became a citizen of the Kingdom of the Serbs, Croats, and Slovenes in consequence of the Treaty of Trianon, forming part of Law XXXIII of 1921. A child born outside of wedlock shall follow the citizenship of his mother or that of his grandfather.

According to the preceding paragraph, Hungarian citizenship is extended to the wife and child of such person who acquired Hungarian citizenship and to the child of the woman born outside of wedlock who has become a Hungarian citizen.

The preceding paragraph does not apply to the person, or to his predecessor, who obtained foreign citizenship under Article 64 of the Treaty of Trianon, included in Law XXXIII, 1921.

Hungarian citizenship reacquired or acquired under the present section may be recalled retroactively, as of April 11, 1941, by the Minister of the Interior within five years from the effective date of the present law, in the case of any person who during the period of separation from Hungary has seriously injured the interests of the Hungarian nation by a hostile attitude.

SECTION 5. The Cabinet may enter into agreement with the interested countries for the settlement of international questions of a legal, financial, and economic character arising out of the reincorporation of the Southern Territories, and may enforce such agreements by decree.

SECTION 6. The Cabinet shall be authorized to cover—if necessary through special credits—expenses incurred in connection with the reincorporation of the Southern Territories and with their administration.

SECTION 7. The Cabinet may by decree, without Parliamentary action, settle the question of ownership of real estate and chattels which have become the property of, and still belong to, the independent legal person called "Compensation Funds of the Autonomous Bodies" (*Önkormányzati Testületek Kárpótlási Vagyona*), under paragraph 1 of Law IV, 1929, and which before the effective date of the Treaty of Trianon belonged to the autonomous organizations situated in the reincorporated Southern Territories.

SECTION 8. Within six months from their promulgation those decrees which, under the authorization of the present law, contain provisions falling within the jurisdiction of the Parliament shall be presented to the Parliament.

SECTION 9. Those decrees and measures of the Cabinet and individual ministers which relate to the Southern Territories reincorporated by the present law, and which have been put into effect before the date of its entrance into force, must be confirmed.

SECTION 10. So long as the Parliament or Cabinet does not decide otherwise by authority of the present law, those laws shall remain in force which were in effect on the day when the present law became effective, with the exception of the laws which by virtue of their subject-matter cannot be applied because of the change of sovereignty, and also those laws which have ceased to be in force because of various regulations of the Cabinet, or of individual ministers, which have been confirmed by the Parliament, as provided for in the preceding paragraph.

SECTION 11. This law shall become effective on the day of its publication. Its execution shall lie with the Hungarian Royal Cabinet.

I hereby order the publication of this law; I accept it as the will of the nation and will cause its observance by others.

Given in Budapest, December 27, 1941.

NICHOLAS HORTHY, *Regent of Hungary*
LÁSZLO BÁRDOSSY, *Hungarian Royal Prime Minister*

XI. MACEDONIA, MORAVA, SKOPLJE, AND BITOLIA REGIONS

(Bulgarian Occupation)

Decision of the Council of Ministers, No. 2012, May 26, 1941 [73]

XLII—Decision of the Council of Ministers, taken in its session of May 26, 1941, Protocol No. 97.

The following is approved:

1. All private persons and firms with domicile and residence in the regions occupied by Bulgarian troops, heretofore under the dominion of the former Yugoslavia, namely: Macedonia, the Western Regions, and Morava, are ordered to declare and deposit, from June 6 to June 19, 1941, inclusive, in the branch or agency of the Bulgarian National Bank in the respective district centers, bank notes of 100 dinars and higher denominations. If there is no office, branch, or agency of the Bulgarian National Bank in the district center, this declaration and deposit of dinar bank notes shall take place at

[73] *Durjaven Vestnik*, No. 118, 1941, p. 2.

the branch of the Bulgarian Agricultural and Cooperative Bank in the district center.

No declaration of dinar bank notes shall be required for denominations of less than 100 dinars.

2. The Bulgarian National Bank shall be entrusted with the collection in leva or dinars of the claims of the Yugoslavian National Bank from private persons and firms in the above-mentioned regions of former Yugoslavia, and these collections shall be entered in a temporary account.

3. All private persons and firms with domicile and residence in the regions occupied by the Bulgarian authorities, heretofore under the dominion of Greece, namely: Western Thrace and Eastern Macedonia, are also ordered to declare and deposit, from June 6 to June 19, 1941, inclusive, in the branch or agency of the Bulgarian National Bank in the respective district center, or, if there is no branch or agency of this bank in this center, in the branch of the Bulgarian Agricultural and Cooperative Bank, all drachmae in their possession in bank notes of 100 drachmae and higher denominations.

The declaration of drachma bank notes of less than 100 drachmae denomination is not required.

4. The Bulgarian National Bank shall be entrusted with the collection in leva or drachmae of the claims of the Greek Bank (Banque de Grèce), and the Greek National Bank against private persons and firms in the above-mentioned regions, heretofore under the dominion of Greece. Such collections shall be entered in a temporary special account.

5. The procedure outlined in points "1" and "3" shall be followed also by the private persons and firms with domicile and residence in the original boundaries of Bulgaria, who have acquired dinars and drachmae in bank notes of 100 drachmae and higher denominations from transactions allowed by the law of trade with foreign exchange or from transactions approved by the Bulgarian National Bank.

6. On accounts opened by private persons and firms for the dinar and drachma bank notes declared and deposited by them, the Bulgarian National Bank or the Bulgarian Agricultural and Cooperative Bank, payment in cash for the time being and until further notice shall not be permitted, but "virements" in the exchange medium in which accounts have been opened shall be allowed.

7. Dinars and drachma bank notes of 100 or higher denominations which have not been declared and deposited in the Bulgarian National Bank or in the Bulgarian Agricultural and Cooperative Bank within the time prescribed above, shall become invalid after June 19, 1941, within the original boundaries of Bulgaria and in the regions occupied by the Bulgarian authorities, enumerated in this decision and shall not have the force of means of payment in these regions.

8. The present rules shall be made known to the population in the Bul-

garian and Greek languages, depending on the regions concerned, by the administrative authorities, by the branches and agencies of the Bulgarian and Cooperative Bank and the Bulgarian National Bank, and also by means of radio and the newspapers.

The present decision shall be published thrice in the government gazette.

Sofia, May 28, 1941.

G. K. SERAFIMOFF
General Secretary of the Council of Ministers

Decision of the Council of Ministers, No. 3121, August 1, 1941 [74]

LXXVI—Decision of the Council of Ministers, taken in its session of August 1, 1941, Protocol No. 130.

By the oral report of the Minister of Finance, Mr. D. Bojiloff, and after an exchange of views, the Council of Ministers decided:

All accounts existing at the time of the occupation of the territories freed during the year 1941, and all amounts to be collected by the former National Bank of Yugoslavia, the Mortgage Bank of Yugoslavia, the Savings Bank of Yugoslavia, the National Bank of Greece, the Bank of Greece, and the Agricultural Bank of Greece shall be centralized in the central account of the Ministry of Finance with the Sofia branch of the Bulgarian National Bank. By debiting this account, payment to depositors of the above-mentioned institutions who are of Bulgarian nationality and who had not emigrated from these regions during the year 1941 shall be made beginning in August of the present year, as follows: for amounts up to 2,000 leva, immediate payment in full; for amounts above 2,000 leva 2,000 leva monthly.

The technical rules for organizing this service as well as the determination of offices which will pay the obligations, etc., shall be elaborated in two days by the Central Administrations of the Bulgarian National Bank, the Postal Savings Bank, and the Bulgarian Agricultural and Cooperative Bank, and approved by the Ministers of Finance and Posts, Telegraphs, and Telephones.

For the General Secretary of the Council of Ministers:
M. STEFANOFF

[Technical rules follow.]

[74] *Durjaven Vestnik*, No. 173, 1941, p. 2.

APPENDIX

CONVENTION RESPECTING THE LAWS AND CUSTOMS OF WAR ON LAND[1]

Signed at The Hague, October 18, 1907

His Majesty the German Emperor, King of Prussia; [etc.][2]

Seeing that, while seeking means to preserve peace and prevent armed conflicts between nations, it is likewise necessary to bear in mind the case where the appeal to arms has been brought about by events which their care was unable to avert;

Animated by the desire to serve, even in this extreme case, the interests of humanity and the ever progressive needs of civilization;

Thinking it important, with this object, to revise the general laws and customs of war, either with a view to defining them with greater precision or to confining them within such limits as would mitigate their severity as far as possible;

Have deemed it necessary to complete and explain in certain particulars the work of the First Peace Conference, which, following on the Brussels Conference of 1874, and inspired by the ideas dictated by a wise and generous forethought, adopted provisions intended to define and govern the usages of war on land.

According to the views of the High Contracting Parties, these provisions, the wording of which has been inspired by the desire to diminish the evils of war, as far as military requirements permit, are intended to serve as a general rule of conduct for the belligerents in their mutual relations and in their relations with the inhabitants.

It has not, however, been found possible at present to concert Regulations covering all the circumstances which arise in practice;

On the other hand, the High Contracting Parties clearly do not intend that unforeseen cases should, in the absence of a written undertaking, be left to the arbitrary judgment of military commanders.

Until a more complete code of the laws of war has been issued, the High Contracting Parties deem it expedient to declare that, in cases not included in the Regulations adopted by them, the inhabitants and the belligerents remain under the protection and the rule of the principles of the law of nations, as they result from the usages established among civilized peoples, from the laws of humanity, and the dictates of the public conscience.

. . . . .

[1] United States Statutes at Large, Vol. 36, Pt. 2, p. 2277.

[2] The 1907 Convention respecting the Laws and Customs of War on Land was concluded and signed by forty-one countries. The present status of this convention with respect to the Axis Powers is as follows: Germany, Hungary, Japan, and Rumania are parties to the convention, Germany and Japan having ratified the convention with reservation of Article 44. Italy and Bulgaria are not parties to the convention. The two latter countries are, however, parties to the 1899 Convention on the Laws and Customs of War on Land.

ANNEX TO THE CONVENTION

Regulations respecting the Laws and Customs of War on Land

Section III.—Military Authority over the Territory of the Hostile State

Article 42

Territory is considered occupied when it is actually placed under the authority of the hostile army.

The occupation extends only to the territory where such authority has been established and can be exercised.

Article 43

The authority of the legitimate power having in fact passed into the hands of the occupant, the latter shall take all the measures in his power to restore, and ensure, as far as possible, public order and safety, while respecting, unless absolutely prevented, the laws in force in the country.

Article 44

A belligerent is forbidden to force the inhabitants of territory occupied by it to furnish information about the army of the other belligerent, or about its means of defence.

Article 45

It is forbidden to compel the inhabitants of occupied territory to swear allegiance to the hostile Power.

Article 46

Family honour and rights, the lives of persons, and private property, as well as religious convictions and practice, must be respected.

Private property cannot be confiscated.

Article 47

Pillage is formally forbidden.

Article 48

If, in the territory occupied, the occupant collects the taxes, dues, and tolls imposed for the benefit of the State, he shall do so, as far as is possible, in accordance with the rules of assessment and incidence in force, and shall in consequence be bound to defray the expenses of the administration of the occupied territory to the same extent as the legitimate Government was so bound.

Article 49

If, in addition to the taxes mentioned in the above Article, the occupant levies other money contributions in the occupied territory, this shall only be for the needs of the army or of the administration of the territory in question.

Article 50

No general penalty, pecuniary or otherwise, shall be inflicted upon the population on account of the acts of individuals for which they cannot be regarded as jointly and severally responsible.

Article 51

No contribution shall be collected except under a written order, and on the responsibility of a Commander-in-chief.

The collection of the said contribution shall only be effected as far as possible in accordance with the rules of assessment and incidence of the taxes in force.

For every contribution a receipt shall be given to the contributors.

Article 52

Requisitions in kind and services shall not be demanded from municipalities or inhabitants except for the needs of the army of occupation. They shall be in proportion to the resources of the country, and of such a nature as not to involve the inhabitants in the obligation of taking part in military operations against their own country.

Such requisitions and services shall only be demanded on the authority of the commander in the locality occupied.

Contributions in kind shall as far as possible be paid for in cash; if not, a receipt shall be given and the payment of the amount due shall be made as soon as possible.

Article 53

An army of occupation can only take possession of cash, funds, and realizable securities which are strictly the property of the State, depôts of arms, means of transport, stores and supplies, and, generally, all movable property belonging to the State which may be used for military operations.

All appliances, whether on land, at sea, or in the air, adapted for the transmission of news, or for the transport of persons or things, exclusive of cases governed by naval law, depôts of arms, and, generally, all kinds of ammunition of war, may be seized, even if they belong to private individuals, but must be restored and compensation fixed when peace is made.

Article 54

Submarine cables connecting an occupied territory with a neutral territory shall not be seized or destroyed except in the case of absolute necessity. They must likewise be restored and compensation fixed when peace is made.

Article 55

The occupying State shall be regarded only as administrator and usufructuary of public buildings, real estate, forests, and agricultural estates belonging to the hostile State, and situated in the occupied country. It must safeguard the capital of these properties, and administer them in accordance with the rules of usufruct.

ARTICLE 56

The property of municipalities, that of institutions dedicated to religion, charity and education, the arts and sciences, even when State property, shall be treated as private property.

All seizure of, destruction or wilful damage done to institutions of this character, historic monuments, works of art and science, is forbidden, and should be made the subject of legal proceedings.

LIST OF WORKS CITED

I. GENERAL[1]

ADAMI, FRIEDRICH WILHELM. "Die Gesetzgebungsarbeit im Generalgouvernement," Deutsches Recht, Vol. 16 (1940), p. 605.

ADAMIC, LOUIS. My Native Land. New York: Harper & Brothers, 1943.

Affaires danubiennes. Revue de l'Europe Centrale et du Sud-Est. Bucharest, 1938—.

Allen, Henry T. (Maj. Gen., U. S. A.). The Rhineland Occupation. Indianapolis: The Bobbs-Merrill Company, 1927.

American Bar Association Journal. Chicago, 1915—.

American Journal of International Law. Washington, 1907—.

Annuaire Officiel. Luxemburg.

ARDENNE, R. German Exploitation of Belgium. Washington: The Brookings Institution, 1942.

Bank for International Settlements. Tenth Annual Report, 1st April 1939–31st March 1940. Basle, 1940.

—— Eleventh Annual Report, 1st April 1940–31st March 1941. Basle, 1941.

——— Twelfth Annual Report, 1st April 1941–31st March 1942. Basle, 1942.

BARTSCH, GEORG. *See* Scheer and Bartsch.

Belgium. New York, 1941—.

BENTWICH, NORMAN. "The Legal Administration of Palestine under the British Military Occupation," British Year Book of International Law, 1920–1921, p. 139.

Bismarck: Die gesammelten Werke. Vol. XIII, edited by W. Schüssler. Berlin, 1930.

BISSCHOP, W. R. "London International Law Conference 1943," London Quarterly of World Affairs, Vol. IX (1943), p. 73.

Black Book of Poland (The). New York: G. P. Putnam's Sons, 1942.

BRIGGS, HERBERT W. Editorial comment in American Journal of International Law, Vol. 35 (1941), p. 512.

British Year Book of International Law, 1920–21. London: Hodder and Stoughton, 1920.

BRÜEL, ERIK. "Den Dansk-Tyske Ikke-Angrebspagt," Nordisk Tidsskrift for International Ret, Vol. 10 (1939), Fasc. I, p. 50; English text, Fasc. 4, p. 157.

Bulletin of International News (The). London: The Royal Institute of International Affairs, 1925—.

CANSACCHI, GIORGIO. "L'Unione dell' Albania con Italia," Rivista di diritto internazionale, Vol. XIX (1940), p. 113.

CATALUCCIO. "L'Unione personale fra Italia e Albania," Civiltà Fascista, 1939, p. 285.

Codes.—Edmond Picard en concordance avec *Les Pandectes Belges*. Les XV Codes par MM. Charles Leurquin, Conseiller à la Cour de cassation; Léon Hennebicq, Bâtonnier de l'Ordre des Avocats près la Cour d'appel de Bruxelles, etc. Préface de M. le Bâtonnier Léon Hennebicq. Deuxième édition revue, corrigée et augmentée. Bruxelles, 1928.

COHN, ERNST J. "The Problem of War Crimes To-day," Transactions of the Grotius Society, Vol. XXVI (1941), p. 125.

Concise Statistical Year-Book of Poland, September, 1939–June, 1941. Glasgow: Polish Ministry of Information, 1941.

CONDLIFFE, J. B. The Reconstruction of World Trade. International Studies Conference, Economic Policies in Relation to World Peace. XII Session of the Conference, Bergen.

[1] In addition to works and articles cited, this list includes periodicals and newspapers referred to in the volume.

New York: W. W. Norton & Company, Inc., 1940. Issued under the auspices of the International Institute of Intellectual Co-operation.

Convention and Transitory Provision concerning Memel, signed at Paris, May 8th, 1924. Extract No. 28 from League of Nations Official Journal. Geneva, 1924.

Current History. New York, 1914—.

Current News on the Lithuanian Situation (mimeographed). Compiled by the Lithuanian Legation, Washington. June, 1943, Vol. II, 6 (30).

CURTIS, MONICA, ed. *See* Documents on International Affairs.

Czechoslovakia Fights Back. A Document of the Czechoslovak Ministry of Foreign Affairs. Introduction by Jan Masaryk. Washington: American Council on Public Affairs, 1943.

Danubian Review. Budapest, 1934—.

Der Deutsche Volkswirt. Berlin, 1926—.

Deutsche Allgemeine Zeitung. Berlin.

Deutsche Arbeit. Berlin.

Deutsche Zeitung im Osten. Riga.

Deutsches Recht. Berlin, 1931—.

Deuxième Congrès International de Droit Comparé. *See* Voeux et résolutions, etc.

Die Nation. Bern.

DLUGOSII, JOANNIS, canonici Cracoviensis. Historiae Polonicae, Libri XII. Cracoviae, 1876, III.

Documents Diplomatiques, 1938–1939. *See* France.

Documents on International Affairs, 1938. Monica Curtis, ed. London, etc.: Oxford University Press, 1943. Issued under the auspices of the Royal Institute of International Affairs.

Documents on International Affairs. Norway and the War, September 1939–December 1940. Monica Curtis, ed. London, etc.: Oxford University Press, 1941. Issued under the auspices of the Royal Institute of International Affairs.

Dziennik Ustaw (Official Gazette of Polish Government-in-Exile). Paris, Angers, London.

"Ein Jahr Generalgouvernement," Deutsches Recht, 1940.

ELLIS, HOWARD S. Exchange Control in Central Europe. Cambridge: Harvard University Press, 1941.

ERDELY, EUGENE V. Germany's First European Protectorate. London: Robert Hale, Limited, 1942.

FEDERSPIEL, HOLGER. Kongeriget Danmarks Love. Copenhagen, 1910.

FEILCHENFELD, ERNST. The International Economic Law of Belligerent Occupation. Washington: Carnegie Endowment for International Peace, 1942.

FEROCI. "L'Unione all'Italia del Regno d'Albania," Il Tribunale, November 30, 1939.

FINCH, GEORGE A. "Superior Orders and War Crimes," American Journal of International Law, Vol. 15 (1921), p. 440.

——— "Retribution for War Crimes," American Journal of International Law, Vol. 37 (1943), p. 81.

——— "Trial of War Criminals Discussed as Military Proceeding," The Evening Star (Washington), August 26, 1943.

FRANCE. MINISTÈRE DES AFFAIRES ETRANGÈRES. Documents diplomatiques, 1938–1939. Pièces relatives aux événements et aux négociations qu'ont précédé l'ouverture des hostilités entre l'Allemagne d'une part, la Pologne, la Grande-Bretagne et la France d'autre part. Paris: Imprimerie Nationale, 1939.

Frankfurter Zeitung. Frankfort.

Free Europe. Central and East European Affairs. London, 1939—.

Free Europe Pamphlets. London, 1940—.
FURLAN, BORIS. Fighting Jugoslavia. New York: Yugoslav Information Center [1943].

GARNER, JAMES W. International Law and the World War. New York: Longmans, Green and Co., 1920. Vol. II.
——— "Questions of State Succession Raised by the German Annexation of Austria," American Journal of International Law, Vol. 32 (1938), p. 421.
German Organization of Distribution in Poland. "Documents relating to the Administration of Occupied Countries in Eastern Europe," No. 3. New York: Polish Information Center [1941].
GLUECK, SHELDON. "By What Tribunal Shall War Offenders Be Tried?", Harvard Law Review, Vol. LVI (1943), p. 1059.
——— "Trial and Punishment of the Axis War Criminals," Free World, Vol. IV (1942), p. 138.
Governments of Continental Europe. James T. Shotwell, ed. New York: The Macmillan Company, 1940.
GREAT BRITAIN. British and Foreign State Papers. London: His Majesty's Stationery Office.
——— FOREIGN OFFICE, Misc. No. 8 (1938), Cmd. 5848. Munich Agreement of September 29, 1938, and Annex.
——— ——— Secret German Documents, Seized during the Raid on the Lofoten Islands on the 4th March, 1941, Norway No. 1 (1941).
——— Treaty Series, No. 3 (1942). "Exchange of Notes between His Majesty's Government in the United Kingdom and the Government of the Czechoslovak Republic concerning the Policy of His Majesty's Government in the United Kingdom in regard to Czechoslovakia."
——— War Office. Manual of Military Law. London: H. M. Stationery Office, 1914.

HAILER, DR. "Die Militärverwaltung in Belgien und Nordfrankreich," Deutsches Recht, Vol. 45/46 (1940).
HALL, JEROME. "Nulla poena sine lege," Yale Law Journal, Vol. 47 (1937), p. 165.
HARRIMAN, FLORENCE J. Mission to the North. Philadelphia, New York: J. B. Lippincott Company, 1941.
HEDIGER, ERNEST S. "Nazi Exploitation of Occupied Europe," Foreign Policy Reports, June 1, 1942. New York: Foreign Policy Association, Incorporated. Vol. XVIII, No. 6.
History of Nations (The). Henry Cabot Lodge, Editor-in-Chief. New York: P. F. Collier & Son Company, 1928. Vol. XVII.
HITLER, ADOLF. Mein Kampf. New York: Reynal & Hitchcock, 1939.
Hitler's Ten-Year War on the Jews. New York: Institute of Jewish Affairs of the American Jewish Congress, World Jewish Congress, 1943.
HRONEK, GEORGE. "Subcarpathian Russia—a Forgotten Country," Central European Observer, Vol. XVIII (1941), p. 263.
HUDSON, MANLEY O. World Court Reports. A Collection of the Judgments, Orders and Opinions of the Permanent Court of International Justice. Washington: Carnegie Endowment for International Peace, 1938. Vol. III, 1932–1935.
HYDE, CHARLES C. International Law. Boston: Little, Brown, and Company, 1922. Vol. II.

Il Giornale d'Italia. Rome.
Inter-Allied Review (The). New York: Inter-Allied Information Center, 1941–1942.
International Chamber of Commerce. Clearing and Payments Agreements (Loose-leaf edition). Basel: Verlag für Recht und Gesellschaft AG.

International Conferences of American States. First Supplement, 1933–1940. Washington: Carnegie Endowment for International Peace, 1940.

International Congress of Comparative Law. *See* Voeux et résolutions, etc.

International Labour Review. Montreal: International Labour Office, October, 1940—.

Italy's Aggression against Greece. Athens: Royal Ministry for Foreign Affairs, 1940.

JACOB, PAUL. Les lois de l'occupation en France. New York, 1942.

JAROSLAVSKIJ, E. Vielikaja otjetshestviennaja vojna sovjetskavo naroda protiv hitlerovskoj Germanii. Moskwa, 1942.

JOESTEN, JOACHIM. "Denmark Under the Jackboot," The Fortnightly (London), Vol. 148, New Series (1940), p. 565.

JOHNSON, SVEINBJORN. "Iceland and the Americas," American Bar Association Journal, Vol. 26 (1940), p. 506.

Journal officiel de la République française.

Journal officiel de l'Etat français. January 4, 1941—.

Juristische Wochenschrift. Berlin.

KALMER, JOSEPH. "Slovenes and Slovenia," Free Europe, Vol. 5 (1942), p. 202.

KOHT, HALVDAN. Norway—Neutral and Invaded. New York: The Macmillan Company, 1941.

KOSÁRY, DOMINIC G. A History of Hungary. Cleveland and New York: The Benjamin Franklin Bibliophile Society, 1941.

KOSSUTITCH, AUGUST. "The Croatian Problem," International Affairs, Vol. XII (1933), p. 79.

Krakauer Zeitung. Krakau.

KULISCHER, EUGENE M. The Displacement of Population in Europe. Montreal: International Labour Office, 1943.

LA TORRE. "L'Unione dell'Italia con l'Albania i suoi riflessi politici e giuridici," Echi e Comenti, 1939, p. 388.

Latvia under German Occupation, 1941–1943. With a Preface by Dr. Alfred Bīlmanis, Minister of Latvia to the United States. Washington: Press Bureau of the Latvian Legation, 1943.

LAUTERPACHT, H. *See* Oppenheim, International Law.

LEAGUE OF NATIONS. Monthly Bulletin of Statistics. London, 1919–20; Geneva, 1921—.

——— Official Journal. London, 1920; Geneva, 1921—.

——— World Economic Survey. Geneva, 1932—.

Législation de la Guerre de 1914–1918, Lois, décrets, arrêtés ministériels et circulaires ministérielles. Paris: L. Tenin [1915–19]. Vol. 8.

LEISTIKOW, GUNNAR. "Denmark under the Nazi Heel," Foreign Affairs, Vol. 21 (1943), p. 340.

LEMKIN, RAPHAËL. "Akte der Barbarei und des Vandalismus als *delicta iuris gentium*," Internationales Anwaltsblatt (Vienna, November, 1933).

———La Règlementation des paiements internationaux. Préface de M. van Zeeland. Paris: A. Pedone, 1939.

——— "Law and Lawyers in the European Subjugated Countries," Address before the North Carolina Bar Association. Proceedings of the Forty-fourth Annual Session of the North Carolina Bar Association, May, 1942 (Durham, N. C. [1942]), p. 107.

——— "Terrorisme. Rapport et projet de textes." Actes de la Ve Conférence Internationale pour l'Unification du Droit Pénal, p. 48. Paris: Editions A. Pedone, 1935.

——— "The Legal Framework of Totalitarian Control over Foreign Economies." Paper (mimeographed) read before the Section of International and Comparative Law of the American Bar Association, Indianapolis, 1941.

——— Valutareglering och Clearing. Stockholm University lectures. Stockholm: P. A. Norstedt & Söner, 1941.

Les XV Codes. *See* Codes Edmond Picard.

LINGELBACH, WILLIAM E. Austria Hungary, *in* "The History of Nations," Henry Cabot Lodge, Editor-in-Chief. New York: P. F. Collier & Son Company [1928]. Vol. XVII.

Lites ac res gestae inter Polonos Ordinemque Cruciferorum. I. Posnaniae, 1890.

LODGE, HENRY CABOT. *See* History of Nations.

LOEWENSTEIN, KARL. "Government and Politics in Germany," Governments of Continental Europe, James T. Shotwell, ed., pp. 281–569. New York: The Macmillan Company, 1940.

LUDENDORFF, GENERAL [ERICH]. The General Staff and its Problems. The History of the Relations between the High Command and the German Imperial Government as Revealed by Official Documents. Translated by F. A. Holt. London: Hutchinson & Co. [1920]. Vol. I.

Luxembourg and the German Invasion Before and After. Based upon Official Documents, with a Preface by M. Joseph Bech, Foreign Minister of the Grand-Duchy of Luxembourg. Published by authority of the Government of Luxembourg. London: Hutchinson & Co., Ltd. [1942]. The Luxembourg Grey Book.

MCINNIS, EDGAR. The Oxford Periodical History of the War. Toronto: Oxford University Press, Canadian Branch, March 12, 1940.

Manchester Guardian (The). Manchester.

MARCHITTO, NICOLA. "L'Albania nell'aggregato imperiale Italiano," Lo Stato, 1939, p. 555.

MARETT, R. R. "The Channel Islands," The British Isles, *in* "The Oxford Survey of the British Empire," pp. 469–98. Oxford: Clarendon Press, 1914.

Martyrdom of the Serbs. Prepared and Issued by the Serbian Eastern Orthodox Diocese for the United States of America and Canada. Chicago, 1943.

Memel, The Question of. *See* Question of Memel.

MOLOTOV, V. M. *See* Note of the People's Commissar, etc.

Moniteur Belge. London, 1941.

MORROW, IAN F. D. "The International Status of the Free City of Danzig," British Year Book of International Law, Vol. XVIII (1937), pp. 114–26.

MOSELY, PHILIP E. "Iceland and Greenland: An American Problem," Foreign Affairs, Vol. 18 (1940), p. 742.

New York Times.

NOLDE, BORIS. "La monnaie en droit international public," Académie de Droit International, Recueil des Cours. Paris: Librairie Hachette. Vol. 27 (1930), pp. 247–396.

Nordisk Tidsskrift for International Ret. Copenhagen, Oslo, 1930—.

Norsk Tidend. London, 1940—.

"Note of the People's Commissar of Foreign Affairs of the USSR, V. M. Molotov, to the ambassadors and envoys of all countries with which the USSR has diplomatic relations," April 27, 1942. Information Bulletin, Embassy of the Union of Soviet Socialist Republics. Washington, 1942.

Notes on Denmark: Before and After the German Invasion. New York: American Friends of Danish Freedom and Democracy, 1941.

Nowy Kurjer Warszawski. Warsaw.

"Occupied U.S.S.R.," Free Europe, Vol. 5 (1942), p. 124.

OPPENHEIM, L. International Law; a Treatise. 5th edition, edited by H. Lauterpacht. London: Longmans, Green and Co., 1935, 1937. Vol. II. Disputes, War and Neutrality (1935).

——— 6th edition, edited by H. Lauterpacht. London: Longmans, Green and Co., 1940. Vol. II. Disputes, War and Neutrality.

Pan American Union. Status of Pan American Treaties and Conventions. Revised to January 1, 1943, by the Juridical Division of the Pan American Union.

Pavičić, Marko. "Italian Barbarities in Dalmatia and Croatia," The Central European Observer, Vol. XIX (1942), p. 283.

Permanent Court of International Justice. Publications, Series A/B, No. 65

Poland and Danzig. Edited by the Polish Research Centre. London: The Cornwall Press, Ltd., 1941.

Poland Fights. New York: Polish Labor Group, May 16, 1942.

Polish Fortnightly Review. London, 1940—.

Polish Ministry of Information. *See* Concise Statistical Year-Book of Poland.

Polish White Book. *See* Republic of Poland, Ministry of Foreign Affairs.

Pour la Victoire. New York, 1942—.

Question of Memel (The). Diplomatic and Other Documents from the Versailles Peace Conference till the Reference of the Question by the Conference of Ambassadors to the Council of the League of Nations (1919–1923). Including Historical Sketches of the Memel Region, and other Introductory Statements. London: Lithuanian Information Bureau, Eyre and Spottiswoode, Ltd., 1924.

Rauschning, Hermann. The Voice of Destruction. New York: G. P. Putnam's Sons, 1940.

Republic of Poland, Ministry of Foreign Affairs. German Occupation of Poland. Extract of Note Addressed to the Allied and Neutral Powers. New York: The Greystone Press [1942]. Polish White Book.

Research in International Law (Under the Auspices of the Faculty of Harvard Law School). Part II. "Jurisdiction with Respect to Crimes" (Edwin D. Dickinson, Reporter), American Journal of International Law, Supp., Vol. 29 (1935).

Reveille, Thomas. The Spoil of Europe. New York: W. W. Norton & Company, Inc., 1941.

Revue internationale de droit pénal. Paris, 1924—.

Ripka, Hubert. The Repudiation of Munich. London: Czechoslovak Ministry of Foreign Affairs Information Service, 1943.

Rivista di diritto internazionale. Rome, 1906—.

Rizzo, G. B. "L'Unione dell'Albania con l'Italia e lo Statuto del Regno di Albania," Rivista di diritto pubblico, 1939, p. 18.

Robinson, Jacob. Kommentar der Konvention über das Memelgebiet vom 8. Mai. 1924. Kaunas: Verlag "Spaudos Fondas," 1934. 2 vols.

Rosenberg, Alfred. Der Mythus des 20. Jahrhunderts. München: Hoheneichenverlag, 1935.

Royal Institute of International Affairs. *See* Documents on International Affairs.

Rozycki, Harry v. "Ueber den Geltungsbereich des Reichsrechts im Grossdeutschen Reich," Deutsche Verwaltung, 1941.

Rupp, H. G. *See* Uhlman and Rupp.

Scheer (Bernhard) and Bartsch (Georg). Das Polizeiverwaltungsgesetz. Berlin, 1939.

Schäfer, Karl. Polizeiverwaltungsgesetz. Berlin, 1939.

Schwarzenberger, Georg. International Law and Totalitarian Lawlessness. London: Jonathan Cape, Ltd., 1943.

Scroggs, William O. *See* Shepardson and Scroggs.

Sereni, Angelo Piero. "The Status of Croatia under International Law," American Political Science Review, Vol. XXXV (1941), p. 1147.

Seznam obci a okresů Republiky Československé. Prague, 1938.
SHEPARDSON (WHITNEY H.) and SCROGGS (WILLIAM O.). "The Occupation of Austria," The United States in World Affairs, an Account of American Foreign Relations, 1938, pp. 25–49. New York: Council on Foreign Relations, Inc., 1939.
SHOTWELL, JAMES T. *See* Governments of Continental Europe.
Službene Novine (Official Gazette of Yugoslavia).
SMOGORZEWSKI, CASIMIR. Poland's Access to the Sea. London: Allen & Unwin, Ltd., 1934.
Staatsblad (Netherlands Law Collection).
Starvation over Europe (Made in Germany). A Documented Record, 1943. New York: [Institute of Jewish Affairs], 1943.
Strassburger Neueste Nachrichten. Strassburg.
Südost Echo. Vienna.
SUPER, PAUL. The Polish Tradition. London: George Allen & Unwin, Ltd., 1939.
SZEKFÜ, GYULA. "The Doctrine of the Holy Crown," Danubian Review, Vol. IX, No. 2 (July, 1941), p. 1.

TÁBORSKÝ, EDVARD. "'Munich,' the Vienna Arbitration and International Law," Czechoslovak Yearbook of International Law, pp. 21–38. London: International Law Association, 1942.
Thorner Freiheit. Thorn.
Times (The). London.
TOYNBEE, ARNOLD J. Survey of International Affairs, 1938. London: Oxford University Press, 1941. Issued under the auspices of the Royal Institute of International Affairs. Vol. I.

UHLMAN, R. E., and RUPP, H. G. "The German System of Administrative Courts," Illinois Law Review, Vol. 31 (1937).
United Nations Review (The). New York: United Nations Information Office, 1941—.
UNITED STATES. DEPARTMENT OF AGRICULTURE. Foreign Agriculture. Washington: Office of Foreign Agricultural Relations.
——— DEPARTMENT OF STATE. Bulletin.
——— ——— Diplomatic Correspondence with Belligerent Governments relating to Neutral Rights and Duties, "European War, No. 4," Washington, 1918.
——— ——— Executive Agreement Series 204, Defense of Greenland. Department of State Publication 1602, 1941.
——— H. R. Doc. 307, 77th Cong., 1st Sess.
——— WAR DEPARTMENT. Basic Field Manual—Rules of Land Warfare. Prepared under the direction of the Judge Advocate General. Washington, 1940.
——— White House Press Releases.

VARANINI, VARO. "L'Albania," Gerarchia, 1939, p. 299.
Violation of the Laws and Customs of War: Reports of Majority and Dissenting Reports of American and Japanese Members of the Commission of Responsibilities, Conference of Paris, 1919. Carnegie Endowment for International Peace, Division of International Law, Pamphlet No. 32. Oxford: Clarendon Press, 1919. Vol. I.
Voeux et résolutions du Deuxième Congrès International de Droit Comparé, La Haye, 4–11 Août 1937. Publié par les soins de M. Elemér Balogh. Académie Internationale de Droit Comparé.
VOLIN, LAZAR. "The 'New Agrarian Order' in Nazi-Invaded Russia," Foreign Agriculture (Washington: Department of Agriculture, April, 1943), p. 75.
Völkerbund. Zeitschrift für Internationale Politik. Geneva.

WATTEVILLE, H. DE. "The Military Administration of Occupied Territory in Time of War," Transactions of the Grotius Society, Vol. VII (1922), p. 133.

WINCH, MICHAEL. Republic for a Day: An Eye-Witness Account of the Carpatho-Ukraine Incident. London: Robt. Hale & Co., Ltd., 1939.

WRIGHT, QUINCY. "The Munich Settlement and International Law," American Journal of International Law, Vol. 33 (1939), p. 12.

XYDIS, STEPHEN G. The Economy and Finances of Greece under Axis Occupation. Pittsburgh, Pa., 1943.

Zeitschrift der Akademie für Deutsches Recht. Berlin, Munich, 1934—.

Zeitschrift für ausländisches öffentliches Recht und Völkerrecht. Berlin, 1929—.

II. DOCUMENTARY SOURCES

ALBANIA

Fletorja Zyrtare. (Law Collection of Albania.)

Gazzetta ufficiale del Regno d'Albania.

Gazzetta ufficiale del Regno d'Italia.

Leggi e Decreti.

AUSTRIA

Dokumente der deutschen Politik.

Reichsgesetzblatt.

BALTIC STATES

Amtsblatt des Generalkommissars in Reval.

Verkündungsblatt des Reichskommissars für das Ostland. (Official Gazette issued by the Reichskommissar für das Ostland at Riga.) Title subsequently changed, as indicated immediately below.

Verordnungsblatt des Reichskommissars für das Ostland, Riga.

Verordnungsblatt des Reichsministers für die besetzten Ostgebiete, Berlin.

BELGIUM

Reichsgesetzblatt.

Heeresgruppen-Verordnungsblatt für die besetzten Gebiete. (Official Gazette issued by the German Military Commander for Belgium and Northern France.) Title subsequently changed, as indicated immediately below.

Verordnungsblatt des Militärbefehlshabers in Belgien und Nordfrankreich für die besetzten Gebiete Belgiens, Luxemburgs und Nordfrankreichs. Title subsequently changed, as indicated immediately below.

Verordnungsblatt des Militärbefehlshabers in Belgien und Nordfrankreich für die besetzten Gebiete Belgiens und Nordfrankreichs.

Moniteur Belge des arrêtés ministériels. Belgisch Staatsblad der ministerieële besluiten. (Official Gazette published in French and Flemish by the Belgian central administration. Since December 1, 1941, a German translation of key laws has also been added to every issue.) Title subsequently changed, as indicated immediately below.

Moniteur Belge des arrêtés ministériels et autres des Secrétaires généraux. Belgisch Staatsblad der ministerieële besluiten en andere besluiten der Secretarissen-General.

CZECHOSLOVAKIA

Reichsgesetzblatt.

Protectorate of Bohemia and Moravia:

Amtsblatt des Protektorats Böhmen und Mähren. In German and Czech.

Landesverordnungsblatt für Mähren und Schlesien. In German and Czech.
Sammlung der Gesetze und Verordnungen des Protektorats Böhmen und Mähren.
Verordnungsblatt für Böhmen und Mähren. In German and Czech. Title subsequently changed, as indicated immediately below.
Verordnungsblatt des Reichsprotektors in Böhmen und Mähren.

Sudetenland:

Verordnungsblatt für die sudeten-deutschen Gebiete. Title subsequently changed, as indicated immediately below.
Verordnungsblatt für den Reichsgau Sudetenland.

Slovakia:

Slovenský zákonník. (Slovak Law Collection.)

Highland Territories and Subcarpathia:

Belügyi Közlöny.
Évi Országos Törvénytár. (Hungarian Law Collection.)

DANZIG

Reichsgesetzblatt.
Verordnungsblatt für die Zivilverwaltung in den dem Gauleiter Förster als Chef der Zivilverwaltung unterstellten besetzten Gebieten.
Verordnungsblatt des Militärbefehlshabers Danzig-Westpreussen. Title subsequently changed, as indicated immediately below.
Verordnungsblatt des Reichsstatthalters Reichsgau Danzig. Title subsequently changed, as indicated immediately below.
Verordnungsblatt des Reichsstatthalters Reichgau Danzig-Westpreussen. Title subsequently changed, as indicated immediately below.
Verordnungsblatt des Reichsstatthalters in Danzig-Westpreussen.

DENMARK

Lovtidenden-A.
Lovtidenden-C.

ENGLISH CHANNEL ISLANDS

Verordnungsblatt für die besetzten französischen Gebiete.

FRANCE

Alsace-Lorraine:

Verordnungsblatt des Chefs der Zivilverwaltung im Elsass. (Issued by the Chef der Zivilverwaltung im Elsass.)
Verordnungsblatt für Lothringen. (Issued by the Chef der Zivilverwaltung in Lothringen.)

Occupied France:

Verordnungsblatt für das besetzte Gebiet der französischen Departements Seine, Seine-et-Oise und Seine-et-Marne. In German and French. Title subsequently changed, as indicated immediately below.
Verordnungsblatt für die besetzten französischen Gebiete. Journal officiel contenant les ordonnances arrêtées par le Gouverneur militaire pour les territoires français occupés. Title subsequently changed, as indicated immediately below.
Verordnungsblatt des Militärbefehlshabers in Frankreich. Journal officiel contenant les ordonnances arrêtées par le Militärbefehlshaber in Frankreich.

Italian Zone:

Leggi e Decreti.
Gazzetta ufficiale del Regno d'Italia.

Vichy France:
Journal officiel de la République Française.
Journal officiel de l'Etat Français.

GREECE
Italian Occupation:
Fletorja Zyrtare.
Gazzetta ufficiale del Regno d'Italia.
Bulgarian Occupation:
Durjaven Vestnik. (Official Gazette of Bulgaria.)

LUXEMBURG
Verordnungsblatt des Militärbefehlshabers in Belgien und Nordfrankreich für die besetzten Gebiete Belgiens, Luxemburgs und Nordfrankreichs.
Verordnungsblatt für Luxemburg. (Issued by the Chef der Zivilverwaltung in Luxemburg.)

MEMEL
Reichsgesetzblatt.

NETHERLANDS
Reichsgesetzblatt.
Staatsblad. (Published by the Dutch Secretaries General in continuation of the Staatsblad formerly published in The Hague.)
Verordnungsblatt für die besetzten niederländischen Gebiete. Veordeningenblad voor het bezette Nederlandsche gebied. (Issued by the Reichskommissar für die besetzten niederländischen Gebiete in Den Haag.)

NORWAY
Norsk Lovtidend. (Published by the puppet government in Oslo.)
Reichsgesetzblatt.
Verordnungsblatt für die besetzten norwegischen Gebiete. Forordningstidend for de besatte norske områder. (Issued by the Reichskommissar für die besetzten norwegischen Gebiete, Oslo.)

POLAND
Incorporated Territories:
Reichsgesetzblatt.
Verordnungsblatt des Chefs der Zivilverwaltung beim Militärbefehlshaber von Posen; and Verordnungsblatt des Reichsstatthalters im Reichsgau Posen (Polish text in part). Title subsequently changed, as indicated immediately below.
Verordnungsblatt des Reichsstatthalters im Reichsgau Wartheland. Title subsequently changed, as indicated immediately below.
Verordnungsblatt des Reichsstatthalters im Warthegau.
Verordnungsblatt für die besetzten Gebiete in Polen.
Government General:
Amtlicher Anzeiger für das Generalgouvernement. Dziennik Urzędowy dla Generalnego Gubernatorstwa.
Verordnungsblatt des Generalgouverneurs für die besetzten polnischen Gebiete. Dziennik rozporządzeń Generalnego Gubernatora dla okupowanych polskich obszarów. Title subsequently changed, as indicated immediately below.
Verordnungsblatt für das Generalgouvernement. Dziennik rozporządzeń dla Generalnego Gubernatorstwa.
Verordnungsblatt für die besetzten Gebiete in Polen.

UNION OF SOVIET SOCIALIST REPUBLICS

Amtsblatt des Generalkommissars für Weissruthenien. In German and White-Russian. Issued by the Generalkommissar für Weissruthenien.

Reichsgesetzblatt.

Verkündungsblatt für das Ostland. Title subsequently changed, as indicated immediately below.

Verordnungsblatt des Reichskommissars für das Ostland.

Verordnungsblatt des Reichsministers für die besetzten Ostgebiete.

Bessarabia, Bukovina and Transnistria:

Monitorul oficial. (Official Gazette of Rumania.)

YUGOSLAVIA

Italian occupation before division:

Gazzetta ufficiale del Regno d'Italia.

Lower Styria, Carinthia, and Carniola:

Verordnungs-und Amtsblatt für den Reichsgau Kärnten.

Verordnungsblatt für den Amtsbereich des Landeshauptmanns für Steiermark. Title changed, as indicated immediately below.

Verordnungs-und Amtsblatt für den Reichsgau Steiermark.

Verordnungsblatt des Chefs der Zivilverwaltung in den besetzten Gebieten von Kärnten und Carniola.

Ljubljana, Dalmatia and Montenegro:

Gazzetta ufficiale del Regno d'Italia.

Serbia:

Verordnungsblatt für das besetzte jugoslawische Gebiet. In German and Serbian. Title subsequently changed, as indicated immediately below.

Verordnungsblatt des Militärbefehlshabers in Serbien. In German and Serbian. Title subsequently changed, as indicated immediately below.

Verordnungsblatt des Befehlshabers Serbien. In German and Serbian.

The Banat:

Amtsblatt der serbischen Ministerien.

Croatia:

Zbornik zakona i naredaba. (Croatian Law Collection.)

Kossovo, Dibrano, and Struga:

Gazzetta ufficiale del Regno d'Albania.

Gazzetta ufficiale del Regno d'Italia.

Baranja, Bačka, Prekomurje, and Medžumurje:

Évi Országos Törvénytár. (Hungarian Law Collection.)

Macedonia, Morava, Skoplje, and Bitolia Regions:

Durjaven Vestnik.

INDEX